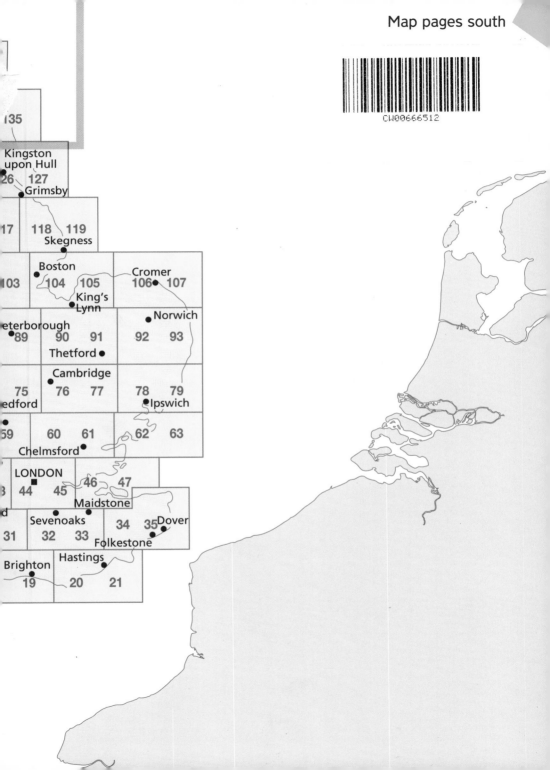

CW00666512

135

Kingston
upon Hull
26  127
Grimsby

17  118  119
Skegness

Boston
103  104  105    Cromer
                 106  107
King's
Lynn
                 Norwich
eterborough
89   90   91     92   93
Thetford

Cambridge
75   76   77     78   79
edford           Ipswich

59   60   61     62   63
Chelmsford

LONDON
44   45     46   47
Maidstone
d    Sevenoaks   34   35 Dover
31   32   33  Folkestone

Brighton  Hastings
19   20   21

# Mileage chart

The mileage chart shows distances in miles between two towns along AA-recommended routes. Using motorways and other main roads this is normally the fastest route, though not necessarily the shortest.

The journey times are shown in hours and minutes. These times should be used as a guide only and do not allow for unforeseen traffic delays, rest breaks or fuel stops.

For example, the 377 miles (607 km) journey between Glasgow and Norwich should take approximately 7 hours 18 minutes.

Journey times

Distances in miles (one mile equals 1.6093 km)

# 2022

# Driver's Atlas

# BRITAIN

Scale 1:250,000
or 3.95 miles to 1 inch

19th edition June 2021 © AA Media Limited 2021

All cartography in this atlas edited, designed and produced by the Mapping Services Department of AA Media Limited (A05785).

This atlas contains Ordnance Survey data © Crown copyright and database right 2021. Contains public sector information licensed under the Open Government Licence v3.0. Ireland mapping and Mileage chart and journey times contains data available from openstreetmap.org © under the Open Database License found at opendatacommons.org

Published by AA Media Limited, whose registered office is Grove House, Lutyens Close, Basingstoke, Hampshire RG24 8AG, UK. Registered number 06112600

ISBN: 978 0 7495 8265 4 (flexibound)

A CIP catalogue record for this book is available from The British Library.

Disclaimer: The contents of this atlas are believed to be correct at the time of the latest revision, it will not contain any subsequent amended, new or temporary information including diversions and traffic control or enforcement systems. The publishers cannot be held responsible or liable for any loss or damage occasioned to any person acting or refraining from action as a result of any use or reliance on material in this atlas, nor for any errors, omissions or changes in such material. This does not affect your statutory rights.

The publishers would welcome information to correct any errors or omissions and to keep this atlas up to date. Please write to the Atlas Editor, AA Media Limited, Grove House, Lutyens Close, Basingstoke, Hampshire, RG24 8AG, UK. E-mail: roadatlasfeedback@aamediagroup.co.uk

Acknowledgements: AA Media Limited would like to thank the following for information used in the creation of this atlas: Cadw, English Heritage, Forestry Commission, Historic Scotland, National Trust and National Trust for Scotland, RSPB, The Wildlife Trust, Scottish Natural Heritage, Natural England, The Countryside Council for Wales. Award winning beaches from 'Blue Flag' and 'Keep Scotland Beautiful' (summer 2019 data): for latest information visit www.blueflag.org and www.keepscotlandbeautiful.org Ireland mapping: Republic of Ireland census 2016 © Central Statistics Office and Northern Ireland census 2016 © NISRA (population data); Logainm.ie (placenames); Roads Service and Transport Infrastructure Ireland
Printed by Oriental Press, Dubai.

## Contents

| | |
|---|---|
| Map pages south | inside front cover |
| Mileage chart and journey times | endpaper |
| Route planner | II–VII |
| Motorways | VIII–X |
|    Restricted junctions | VIII–IX |
|    Smart motorways | X |
| Atlas symbols | 1 |
| Road maps 1:250,000 scale | 2–237 |
|    Channel Islands 1:150,000 scale | 236 |
|    Isle of Man 1:317,000 scale | 237 |
|    Orkney Islands 1:636,000 scale | 234 |
|    Shetland Islands 1:636,000 scale | 235 |
|    Western Isles 1:700,000 scale | 232–233 |
| Index to place names | 238–318 |
|    County, administrative area map | 238–239 |
|    Place name index | 240–318 |
| Ireland | endpaper |
| Map pages north | inside back cover |

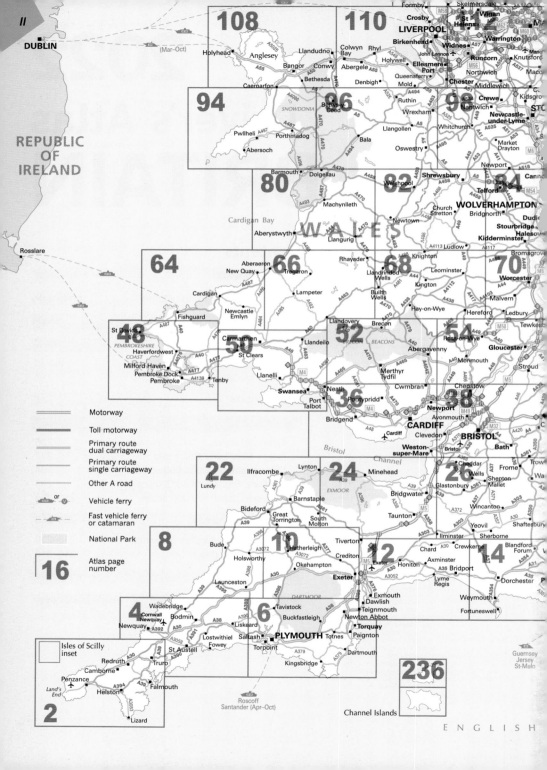

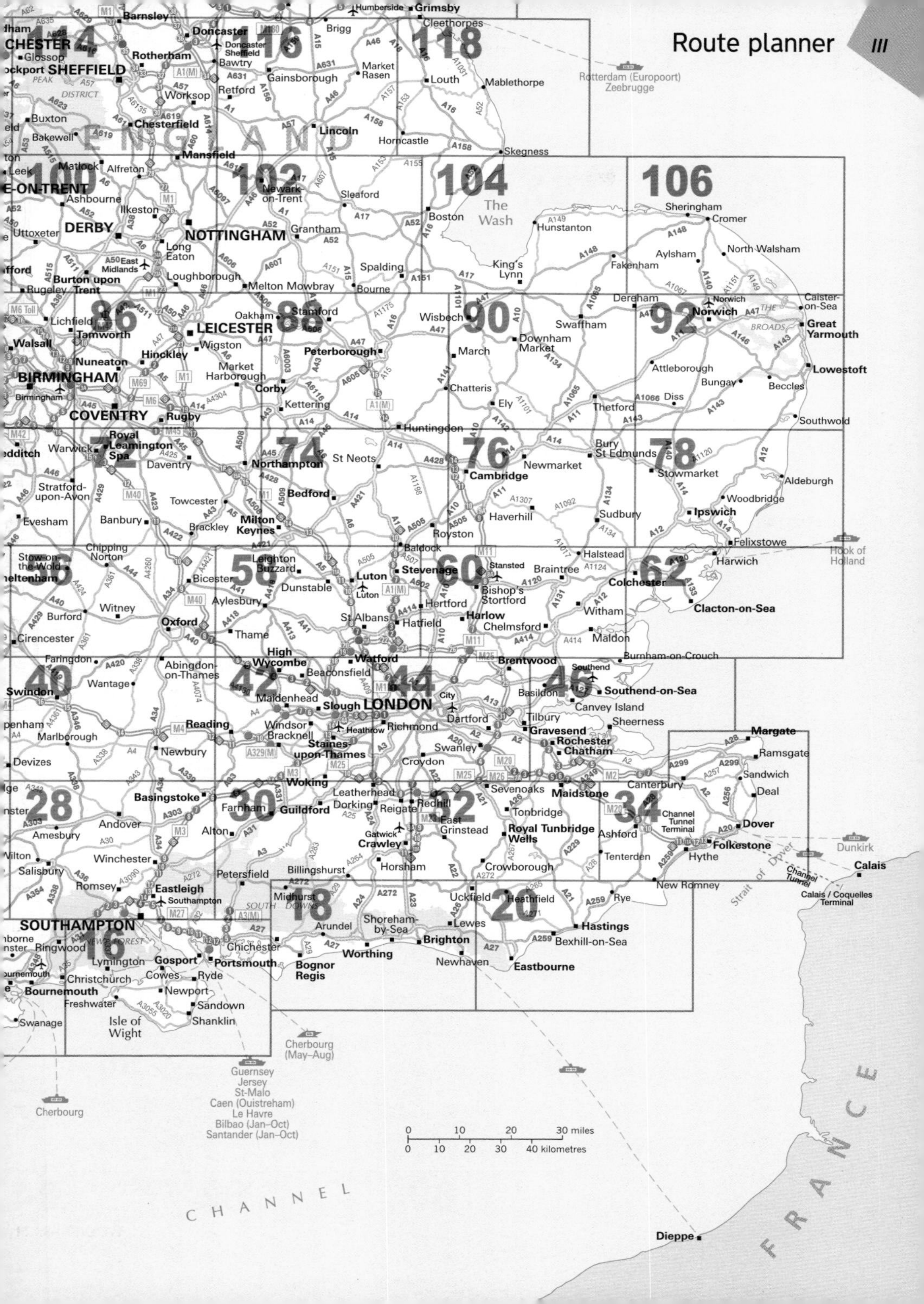
114
116
118
100
102
104
106
86
88
90
92
72
74
76
78
56
58
60
62
40
42
44
46
28
30
32
34
16
18
20
Barnsley
Grimsby
Humberside
Cleethorpes
Doncaster
Doncaster Sheffield
Brigg
CHESTER
Glossop
Rotherham
SHEFFIELD
Bawtry
Market Rasen
Louth
Mablethorpe
Rotterdam (Europoort)
Zeebrugge
PEAK DISTRICT
Gainsborough
Worksop
Retford
Buxton
Chesterfield
Lincoln
Bakewell
Horncastle
ENGLAND
Mansfield
Skegness
Leek
Matlock
Alfreton
Newark-on-Trent
Sleaford
Boston
The Wash
Hunstanton
Sheringham
Cromer
Ashbourne
Ilkeston
DERBY
NOTTINGHAM
Grantham
Uttoxeter
Long Eaton
East Midlands
Aylsham
North Walsham
Fakenham
Spalding
King's Lynn
Burton upon Trent
Loughborough
Melton Mowbray
Bourne
Dereham
Norwich
Caister-on-Sea
Great Yarmouth
THE BROADS
Rugeley
Lichfield
Oakham
Stamford
Wisbech
Swaffham
Tamworth
LEICESTER
Walsall
Wigston
Peterborough
Downham Market
March
Nuneaton
Hinckley
Market Harborough
Attleborough
Lowestoft
BIRMINGHAM
Corby
Chatteris
Bungay
Beccles
Birmingham
Diss
COVENTRY
Rugby
Kettering
Ely
Thetford
Southwold
Huntingdon
Redditch
Warwick
Royal Leamington Spa
Daventry
Northampton
St Neots
Cambridge
Newmarket
Bury St Edmunds
Stowmarket
Aldeburgh
Stratford-upon-Avon
Towcester
Bedford
Woodbridge
Haverhill
Sudbury
Ipswich
Evesham
Banbury
Brackley
Milton Keynes
Royston
Felixstowe
Baldock
Hook of Holland
Stow-on-the-Wold
Chipping Norton
Cheltenham
Leighton Buzzard
Stevenage
Stansted
Halstead
Braintree
Harwich
Bicester
Dunstable
Luton
Bishop's Stortford
Colchester
Witney
Aylesbury
Hertford
Clacton-on-Sea
Burford
Oxford
St Albans
Hatfield
Harlow
Witham
Thame
Chelmsford
Maldon
Cirencester
High Wycombe
Watford
Burnham-on-Crouch
Faringdon
Abingdon-on-Thames
Beaconsfield
Brentwood
Southend
Swindon
Wantage
Basildon
Southend-on-Sea
Maidenhead
City
Canvey Island
Slough
LONDON
Dartford
Tilbury
Chippenham
Reading
Windsor
Heathrow
Richmond
Sheerness
Marlborough
Bracknell
Gravesend
Margate
Staines-upon-Thames
Swanley
Rochester
Newbury
Chatham
Ramsgate
Devizes
Croydon
Sandwich
Woking
Canterbury
Basingstoke
Leatherhead
Sevenoaks
Maidstone
Deal
Farnham
Guildford
Dorking
Reigate
Redhill
Tonbridge
Channel Tunnel Terminal
Andover
East Grinstead
Royal Tunbridge Wells
Dover
Amesbury
Alton
Gatwick
Crawley
Ashford
Folkestone
Dunkirk
Winchester
Tenterden
Hythe
Salisbury
Horsham
Calais
Billingshurst
Crowborough
Petersfield
Romsey
Eastleigh
Southampton
New Romney
Strait of Dover
Channel Tunnel
Calais / Coquelles Terminal
Midhurst
Uckfield
Heathfield
Rye
SOUTH DOWNS
SOUTHAMPTON
Arundel
Shoreham-by-Sea
Lewes
Hastings
NEW FOREST
Ringwood
Chichester
Worthing
Brighton
Bexhill-on-Sea
Lymington
Gosport
Portsmouth
Bognor Regis
Newhaven
Eastbourne
Christchurch
Cowes
Ryde
Bournemouth
Newport
Freshwater
Sandown
Swanage
Isle of Wight
Shanklin
Cherbourg (May–Aug)
Guernsey
Jersey
St-Malo
Caen (Ouistreham)
Le Havre
Bilbao (Jan–Oct)
Santander (Jan–Oct)
Cherbourg
0 10 20 30 miles
0 10 20 30 40 kilometres
CHANNEL
FRANCE
Dieppe

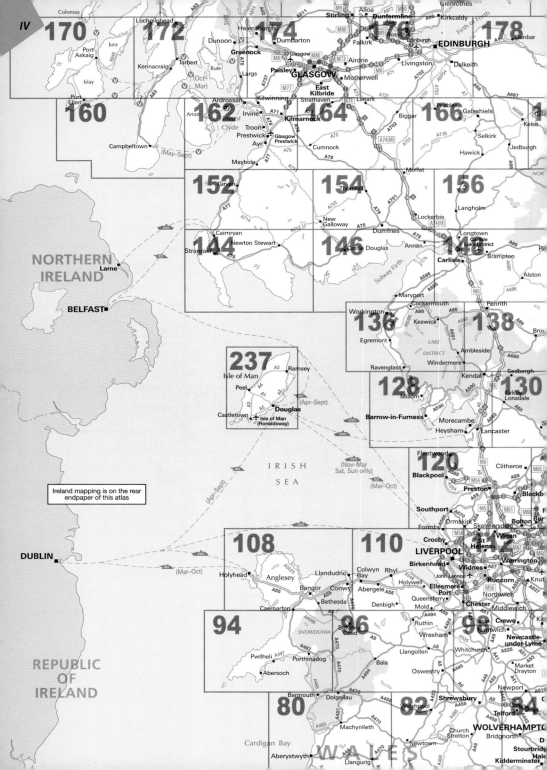

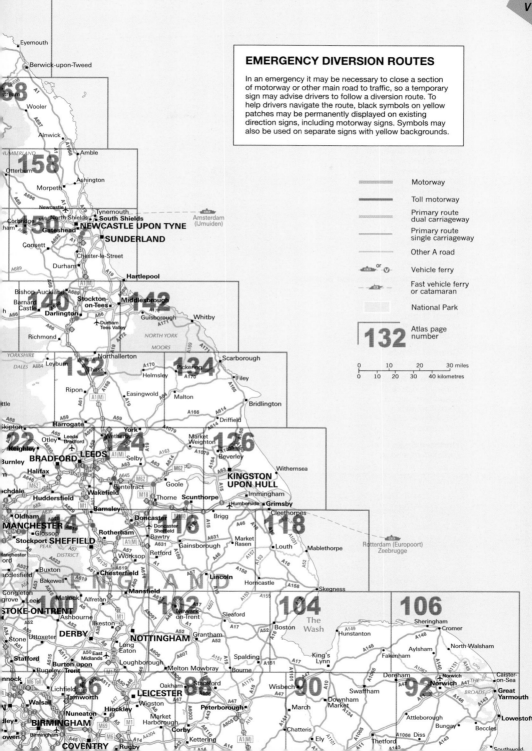

## FERRY OPERATORS

### Hebrides and west coast Scotland
calmac.co.uk
skyeferry.co.uk
western-ferries.co.uk

### Orkney and Shetland
northlinkferries.co.uk
pentlandferries.co.uk
orkneyferries.co.uk
shetland.gov.uk/ferries

### Isle of Man
steam-packet.com

### Ireland
irishferries.com
poferries.com
stenaline.co.uk

### North Sea (Scandinavia and Benelux)
dfdsseaways.co.uk
poferries.com

### Isle of Wight
wightlink.co.uk
redfunnel.co.uk

### Channel Islands
condorferries.co.uk

### France and Belgium
brittany-ferries.co.uk
condorferries.co.uk
eurotunnel.com
dfdsseaways.co.uk
poferries.com

### Northern Spain
brittany-ferries.co.uk

| | |
|---|---|
| ═══════ | Motorway |
| ━━━━━━━ | Toll motorway |
| ═══════ | Primary route dual carriageway |
| ─────── | Primary route single carriageway |
| ─────── | Other A road |
| 🚢 or ⓥ | Vehicle ferry |
| 🚤 | Fast vehicle ferry or catamaran |
| ▭ | National Park |
| **192** | Atlas page number |

0   10   20   30 miles
0  10  20  30  40 kilometres

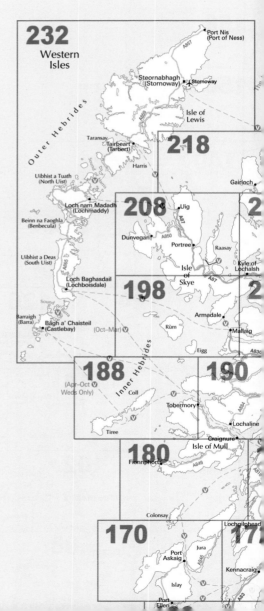

**232** Western Isles

Port Nis (Port of Ness)

Steornabhagh (Stornoway) • Stornoway

Isle of Lewis

Outer Hebrides

Taransay
Tairbeart (Tarbert)

Harris

**218**

Uibhist a Tuath (North Uist)

Gairloch

Loch nam Madadh (Lochmaddy)

**208** Uig

Dunvegan

Portree

Raasay

Beinn na Faoghla (Benbecula)

Uibhist a Deas (South Uist)

Isle of Skye

Kyle of Lochalsh

Loch Baghasdail (Lochboisdale)

**198**

Armadale

Barraigh (Barra)

Bàgh a' Chaisteil (Castlebay)

(Oct–Mar) ⓥ

Rùm

Mallaig

Eigg

**188**

(Apr–Oct ⓥ Weds Only)

Inner Hebrides

Coll

**190**

Tobermory

Lochaline

Tiree

Craignure

Isle of Mull

**180**

Fionnphort

Colonsay

Lochgilphead

**170**

Jura

**171**

Port Askaig

Kennacraig

Islay

Port Ellen

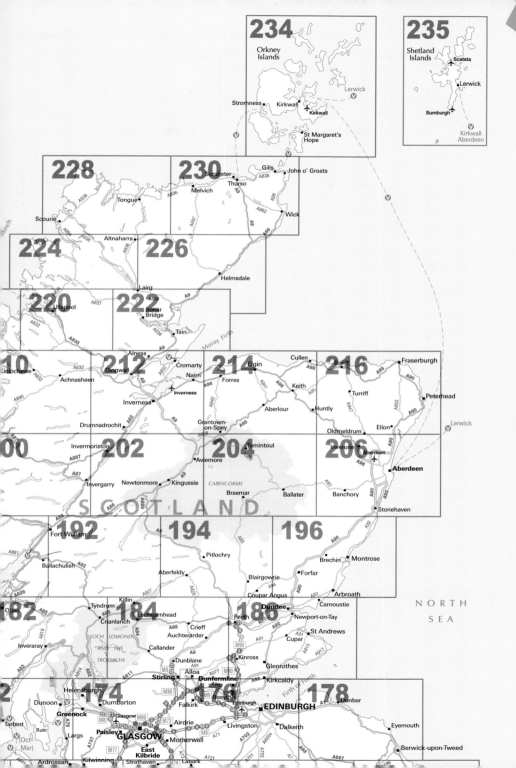

# Restricted junctions

Motorway and primary route junctions which have access or exit restrictions are shown on the map pages thus:

## M1 London - Leeds

| Junction | Northbound | Southbound |
|---|---|---|
| 2 | Access only from A1 (northbound) | Exit only to A1 (southbound) |
| 4 | Access only from A41 (northbound) | Exit only to A41 (southbound) |
| 6A | Access only from M25 (no link from A405) | Exit only to M25 (no link from A405) |
| 7 | Access only from A414 | Exit only to A414 |
| 17 | Exit only to M45 | Access only from M45 |
| 19 | Exit only to M6 (northbound) | Exit only to A14 (southbound) |
| 21A | Exit only, no access | Access only, no exit |
| 24A | Access only, no exit | Access only from A50 (eastbound) |
| 35A | Access only, no exit | Access only, no exit |
| 43 | Exit only to M621 | Access only from M621 |
| 48 | Exit only to A1(M) (northbound) | Access only from A1(M) (southbound) |

## M2 Rochester - Faversham

| Junction | Westbound | Eastbound |
|---|---|---|
| 1 | No exit to A2 (eastbound) | No access from A2 (westbound) |

## M3 Sunbury - Southampton

| Junction | Northeastbound | Southwestbound |
|---|---|---|
| 8 | Access only from A303, no exit | Exit only to A303, no access |
| 10 | Exit only, no access | Access only, no exit |
| 14 | Access from M27 only, no exit | No access to M27 (westbound) |

## M4 London - South Wales

| Junction | Westbound | Eastbound |
|---|---|---|
| 1 | Access only from A4 (westbound) | Exit only to A4 (eastbound) |
| 2 | Access only from A4 (westbound) | Access only from A4 (eastbound) |
| 21 | Exit only to M48 | Access only from M48 |
| 23 | Access only from M48 | Exit only to M48 |
| 25 | Exit only, no access | Access only, no exit |
| 25A | Exit only, no access | Access only, no exit |
| 29 | Exit only to A48(M) | Access only from A48(M) |
| 38 | Exit only, no access | No restriction |
| 39 | Access only, no exit | No access or exit |
| 42 | Exit only to A483 | Access only from A483 |

## M5 Birmingham - Exeter

| Junction | Northeastbound | Southwestbound |
|---|---|---|
| 10 | Access only, no exit | Exit only, no access |
| 11A | Access only from A417 (eastbound) | Exit only to A417 (eastbound) |
| 18A | Exit only to M49 | Access only from M49 |
| 18 | Exit only, no access | Access only, no exit |

## M6 Toll Motorway

| Junction | Northwestbound | Southeastbound |
|---|---|---|
| T1 | Access only, no exit | No access or exit |
| T2 | No access or exit | Exit only, no access |
| T5 | Access only, no exit | Exit only to A5148 (northbound), no access |
| T7 | Exit only, no access | Access only, no exit |
| T8 | Exit only, no access | Access only, no exit |

## M6 Rugby - Carlisle

| Junction | Northbound | Southbound |
|---|---|---|
| 3A | Exit only to M6 Toll | Access only from M6 Toll |
| 4 | Exit only to M42 (southbound) & A446 | Exit only to A446 |
| 4A | Access only from M42 (southbound) | Exit only to M42 |
| 5 | Exit only, no access | Access only, no exit |
| 10A | Exit only to M54 | Access only from M54 |
| 11A | Access only from M6 Toll | Exit only to M6 Toll |
| with M56 (jct 20A) | No restriction | Access only from M56 (eastbound) |
| 20 | Exit only to M56 (westbound) | Access only from M56 (eastbound) |
| 24 | Access only, no exit | Exit only, no access |
| 25 | Exit only, no access | Access only, no exit |
| 30 | Access only from M61 | Exit only to M61 |
| 31A | Exit only, no access | Access only, no exit |
| 45 | Exit only, no access | Access only, no exit |

## M8 Edinburgh - Bishopton

| Junction | Westbound | Eastbound |
|---|---|---|
| 6 | Exit only, no access | Access only, no exit |
| 6A | Access only, no exit | Exit only, no access |
| 7 | Access only, no exit | Exit only, no access |
| 7A | Exit only, no access | Access only from A725 (northbound), no exit |
| 8 | No access from M73 (southbound) or from A8 (eastbound) & A89 | No exit to M73 (northbound) or to A8 (westbound) & A89 |
| 9 | Access only, no exit | Exit only, no access |
| 13 | Access only from M80 (southbound) | Exit only to M80 (northbound) |
| 14 | Access only, no exit | Exit only, no access |
| 16 | Exit only to A804 | Access only from A879 |
| 17 | Exit only to A82 | No restriction |
| 18 | Access only from A82 (eastbound) | Exit only to A814 |
| 19 | No access from A814 (westbound) | Exit only to A814 (westbound) |
| 20 | Exit only, no access | Access only, no exit |
| 21 | Access only, no exit | Exit only to A8 |
| 22 | Exit only to M77 (southbound) | Access only from M77 (northbound) |
| 23 | Exit only to B768 | Access only from B768 |
| 25 | No access or exit from or to A8 | No access or exit from or to A8 |
| 25A | Exit only, no access | Access only, no exit |
| 28 | Exit only, no access | Access only, no exit |
| 28A | Exit only to A737 | Access only from A737 |
| 29A | Exit only to A8 | Access only, no exit |

## M9 Edinburgh - Dunblane

| Junction | Northwestbound | Southeastbound |
|---|---|---|
| 2 | Access only, no exit | Exit only, no access |
| 3 | Exit only, no access | Access only, no exit |
| 6 | Access only, no exit | Exit only to A905 |
| 8 | Exit only to M876 (southwestbound) | Access only from M876 (northeastbound) |

## M11 London - Cambridge

| Junction | Northbound | Southbound |
|---|---|---|
| 4 | Access only from A406 (eastbound) | Exit only to A406 |
| 5 | Access only, no exit | Exit only, no access |
| 8A | Exit only, no access | No direct access, use jct 8 |
| 9 | Exit only to A11 | Access only from A11 |
| 13 | Exit only, no access | Access only, no exit |
| 14 | Exit only, no access | Access only, no exit |

## M20 Swanley - Folkestone

| Junction | Northwestbound | Southeastbound |
|---|---|---|
| 2 | Staggered junction; follow signs - access only | Staggered junction; follow signs - exit only |
| 3 | Exit only to M26 (westbound) | Access only from M26 (eastbound) |
| 5 | Access only from A20 | For access follow signs - exit only to A20 |
| 6 | No restriction | For exit follow signs |
| 11A | Access only, no exit | Exit only, no access |

## M23 Hooley - Crawley

| Junction | Northbound | Southbound |
|---|---|---|
| 7 | Exit only to A23 (northbound) | Access only from A23 (southbound) |
| 10A | Access only, no exit | Exit only, no access |

## M25 London Orbital Motorway

| Junction | Clockwise | Anticlockwise |
|---|---|---|
| 1B | No direct access, use slip road to jct 2 Exit only | Access only, no exit |
| 5 | No exit to M26 (eastbound) | No access from M26 |
| 19 | Exit only, no access | Access only, no exit |
| 21 | Access only from M1 (southbound) Exit only to M1 (northbound) | Access only from M1 (southbound) Exit only to M1 (northbound) |
| 31 | No exit (use slip road via jct 30), access only | No access (use slip road via jct 30), exit only |

## M26 Sevenoaks - Wrotham

| Junction | Westbound | Eastbound |
|---|---|---|
| with M25 (jct 5) | Exit only to clockwise M25 (westbound) | Access only from anticlockwise M25 (eastbound) |
| with M20 (jct 3) | Access only from M20 (northwestbound) | Exit only to M20 (southeastbound) |

## M27 Cadnam - Portsmouth

| Junction | Westbound | Eastbound |
|---|---|---|
| 4 | Staggered junction; follow signs - access only from M3 (southbound). Exit only to M3 (northbound) | Staggered junction; follow signs - access only from M3 (southbound). Exit only to M3 (northbound) |
| 10 | Exit only, no access | Access only, no exit |
| 12 | Staggered junction; follow signs - exit only to M275 (southbound) | Staggered junction; follow signs - access only from M275 (northbound) |

## M40 London - Birmingham

| Junction | Northwestbound | Southeastbound |
|---|---|---|
| 3 | Exit only, no access | Access only, no exit |
| 7 | Exit only, no access | Access only, no exit |
| 8 | Exit only to M40/A40 | Access only from M40/A40 |
| 13 | Exit only, no access | Access only, no exit |
| 14 | Access only, no exit | Exit only, no access |
| 16 | Access only, no exit | Exit only, no access |

## M42 Bromsgrove - Measham

| Junction | Northeastbound | Southwestbound |
|---|---|---|
| 1 | Access only, no exit | Exit only, no access |
| 7 | Exit only to M6 (northwestbound) | Access only from M6 (northwestbound) |
| 7A | Exit only to M6 (southeastbound) | No access or exit |
| 8 | Access only from M6 (southeastbound) | Exit only to M6 (northwestbound) |

## M45 Coventry - M1

| Junction | Westbound | Eastbound |
|---|---|---|
| Dunchurch (unnumbered) | Access only from A45 | Exit only, no access |
| with M1 (jct 17) | Access only from M1 (northbound) | Exit only to M1 (southbound) |

## M48 Chepstow

| Junction | Westbound | Eastbound |
|---|---|---|
| 21 | Access only from M4 (westbound) | Exit only to M4 (eastbound) |
| 23 | No exit to M4 (eastbound) | No Access from M4 (westbound) |

## M53 Mersey Tunnel - Chester

| Junction | Northbound | Southbound |
|---|---|---|
| 11 | Access only from M56 (westbound) Exit only to M56 (eastbound) | Access only from M56 (westbound) Exit only to M56 (eastbound) |

## M54 Telford - Birmingham

| Junction | Westbound | Eastbound |
|---|---|---|
| with M6 (jct 10A) | Access only from M6 (northbound) | Exit only to M6 (southbound) |

## M56 Chester - Manchester

| Junction | Westbound | Eastbound |
|---|---|---|
| 1 | Access only from M60 (westbound) | Exit only to M60 (eastbound) & A34 (northbound) |
| 2 | Exit only, no access | Access only, no exit |
| 3 | Access only, no exit | Exit only, no access |
| 4 | Exit only, no access | Access only, no exit |
| 7 | Exit only, no access | No restriction |
| 8 | Access only, no exit | No access or exit |
| 9 | No exit to M6 (southbound) | No access from M6 (northbound) |
| 15 | Exit only to M53 | Access only from M53 |
| 16 | No access or exit | No restriction |

## M57 Liverpool Outer Ring Road

| Junction | Northwestbound | Southeastbound |
|---|---|---|
| 3 | Access only, no exit | Exit only, no access |
| 5 | Access only from A580 (westbound) | Exit only, no access |

## M60 Manchester Orbital

| Junction | Clockwise | Anticlockwise |
|---|---|---|
| 2 | Access only, no exit | Exit only, no access |
| 3 | No access from M56 | Access only from A34 (northbound) |
| 4 | Access only from A34 (northbound). Exit only to M56 | Access only from M56 (eastbound). Exit only to A34 (southbound) |
| 5 | Access and exit only from and to A5103 (northbound) | Access and exit only from and to A5103 (southbound) |
| 7 | No direct access, use slip road to jct 8. Exit only to A56 | Access only from A56. No exit, use jct 8 |
| 14 | Access from A580 (eastbound) | Exit only to A580 (westbound) |
| 16 | Access only, no exit | Exit only, no access |
| 20 | Exit only, no access | Access only, no exit |
| 22 | No restriction | Exit only, no access |
| 25 | Access only, no exit | No restriction |
| 26 | No restriction | Exit only, no access |
| 27 | Exit only, no access | Exit only, no access |

## M61 Manchester - Preston

| Junction | Northwestbound | Southeastbound |
|---|---|---|
| 3 | No access or exit | Exit only, no access |
| with M6 (jct 30) | Exit only to M6 (northbound) | Access only from M6 (southbound) |

## M62 Liverpool - Kingston upon Hull

| Junction | Westbound | Eastbound |
|---|---|---|
| 23 | Access only, no exit | Exit only, no access |
| 32A | No access to A1(M) (southbound) | No restriction |

## M65 Preston - Colne

| Junction | Northeastbound | Southwestbound |
|---|---|---|
| 9 | Exit only, no access | Access only, no exit |
| 11 | Access only, no exit | Exit only, no access |

## M66 Bury

| Junction | Northbound | Southbound |
|---|---|---|
| with A56 | Exit only to A56 (northbound) | Access only from A56 (southbound) |
| 1 | Exit only, no access | Access only, no exit |

## M67 Hyde Bypass

| Junction | Westbound | Eastbound |
|---|---|---|
| 1A | Access only, no exit | Exit only, no access |
| 2 | Exit only, no access | Access only, no exit |

## M69 Coventry - Leicester

| Junction | Northbound | Southbound |
|---|---|---|
| 2 | Access only, no exit | Exit only, no access |

## M73 East of Glasgow

| Junction | Northbound | Southbound |
|---|---|---|
| 1 | No exit to A74 & A721 | No exit to A74 & A721 |
| 2 | No access from or exit to A89. No access from M8 (eastbound) | No access from or exit to A89. No exit to M8 (westbound) |

## M74 and A74(M) Glasgow - Gretna

| Junction | Northbound | Southbound |
|---|---|---|
| 3 | Exit only, no access | Access only, no exit |
| 3A | Access only, no exit | Exit only, no access |
| 4 | No access from A74 & A721 | Access only, no exit to A74 & A721 |
| 7 | Access only, no exit | Exit only, no access |
| 9 | No access or exit | Exit only, no access |
| 10 | No restriction | Access only, no exit |
| 11 | Access only, no exit | Access only, no exit |
| 12 | Exit only, no access | Access only, no exit |
| 18 | Exit only, no access | Access only, no exit |

## M77 Glasgow - Kilmarnock

| Junction | Northbound | Southbound |
|---|---|---|
| with M8 (jct 22) | No exit to M8 (westbound) | No access from M8 (eastbound) |
| 4 | Access only, no exit | Exit only, no access |
| 6 | Access only, no exit | Exit only, no access |
| 7 | Access only, no exit | No restriction |
| 8 | Exit only, no access | Exit only, no access |

## M80 Glasgow - Stirling

| Junction | Northbound | Southbound |
|---|---|---|
| 4A | Exit only, no access | Access only, no exit |
| 6A | Access only, no exit | Access only, no exit |
| 8 | Exit only to M876 (northeastbound) | Access only from M876 (southwestbound) |

## M90 Edinburgh - Perth

| Junction | Northbound | Southbound |
|---|---|---|
| 1 | No exit, access only | Exit only to A90 (eastbound) |
| 2A | Exit only to A92 (eastbound) | Access only from A92 (westbound) |
| 7 | Access only, no exit | Exit only, no access |
| 8 | Access only, no exit | Access only, no exit |
| 10 | No access from A912. No exit to A912 (southbound) | No access from A912 (northbound). No exit to A912 |

## M180 Doncaster - Grimsby

| Junction | Westbound | Eastbound |
|---|---|---|
| 1 | Access only, no exit | Exit only, no access |

## M606 Bradford Spur

| Junction | Northbound | Southbound |
|---|---|---|
| 2 | Exit only, no access | No restriction |

## M621 Leeds - M1

| Junction | Clockwise | Anticlockwise |
|---|---|---|
| 2A | Access only, no exit | Exit only, no access |
| 4 | No exit or access | No restriction |
| 5 | Access only, no exit | Exit only, no access |
| 6 | Exit only, no access | Access only, no exit |
| with M1 (jct 43) | Exit only to M1 (southbound) | Access only from M1 (northbound) |

## M876 Bonnybridge - Kincardine Bridge

| Junction | Northeastbound | Southwestbound |
|---|---|---|
| with M80 (jct 5) | Access only from M80 (northeastbound) | Exit only to M80 (southwestbound) |
| with M9 (jct 8) | Exit only to M9 (eastbound) | Access only from M9 (westbound) |

## A1(M) South Mimms - Baldock

| Junction | Northbound | Southbound |
|---|---|---|
| 2 | Exit only, no access | Access only, no exit |
| 3 | No restriction | Exit only, no access |
| 5 | Access only, no exit | No access or exit |

## A1(M) Pontefract - Bedale

| Junction | Northbound | Southbound |
|---|---|---|
| 41 | No access to M62 (eastbound) | No restriction |
| 43 | Access only from M1 (northbound) | Exit only to M1 (southbound) |

## A1(M) Scotch Corner - Newcastle upon Tyne

| Junction | Northbound | Southbound |
|---|---|---|
| 57 | Exit only to A66(M) (eastbound) | Access only from A66(M) (westbound) |
| 65 | No access | No exit |
| | Exit only to A194(M) & A1 (northbound) | Access only from A194(M) & A1 (southbound) |

## A3(M) Horndean - Havant

| Junction | Northbound | Southbound |
|---|---|---|
| 1 | Access only from A3 | Exit only to A3 |
| 4 | Exit only, no access | Access only, no exit |

## A38(M) Birmingham, Victoria Road (Park Circus)

| Junction | Northbound | Southbound |
|---|---|---|
| with B4132 | No exit | No access |

## A48(M) Cardiff Spur

| Junction | Westbound | Eastbound |
|---|---|---|
| 29 | Access only from M4 (westbound) | Exit only to M4 (westbound) |
| 29A | Exit only to A48 (westbound) | Access only from A48 (eastbound) |

## A57(M) Manchester, Brook Street (A34)

| Junction | Northbound | Eastbound |
|---|---|---|
| with A34 | No exit | No access |

## A58(M) Leeds, Park Lane and Westgate

| Junction | Northbound | Southbound |
|---|---|---|
| with A58 | No restriction | No access |

## A64(M) Leeds, Clay Pit Lane (A58)

| Junction | Westbound | Eastbound |
|---|---|---|
| with A58 | No exit (to Clay Pit Lane) | No access (from Clay Pit Lane) |

## A66(M) Darlington Spur

| Junction | Westbound | Eastbound |
|---|---|---|
| with A1(M) (jct 57) | Exit only to A1(M) (northbound) | Access only from A1(M) (northbound) |

## A74(M) Gretna - Abington

| Junction | Northbound | Southbound |
|---|---|---|
| 18 | Exit only, no access | Access only, no exit |

## A194(M) Newcastle upon Tyne

| Junction | Northbound | Southbound |
|---|---|---|
| with A1(M) (jct 65) | Access only from A1(M) (northbound) | Exit only to A1(M) (southbound) |

## A12 M25 - Ipswich

| Junction | Northeastbound | Southwestbound |
|---|---|---|
| 13 | Access only, no exit | No restriction |
| 14 | Exit only, no access | Access only, no exit |
| 20A | Access only, no exit | Access only, no exit |
| 20B | Access only, no exit | Exit only, no access |
| 21 | No restriction | Access only, no exit |
| 23 | Exit only, no access | Access only, no exit |
| 24 | Access only, no exit | Exit only, no access |
| 27 | Exit only, no access | Access only, no exit |
| Dedham & Stratford St Mary (unnumbered) | Exit only | Access only |

## A14 M1 - Felixstowe

| Junction | Westbound | Eastbound |
|---|---|---|
| with M1/M6 (jct 19) | Exit only to M6 and M1 (northbound) | Access only from M6 and M1 (southbound) |
| 4 | Access only, no exit | Access only, no exit |
| 21 | Access only, no exit | Exit only, no access |
| 22 | Exit only, no access | Access only from A1 (southbound) |
| 23 | Access only, no exit | Exit only, no access |
| 26 | No restriction | Access only, no exit |
| 34 | Access only, no exit | Exit only, no access |
| 36 | Exit only to A11, access only from A1303 | Access only from A11 |
| 38 | Access only from A11 | Exit only to A11 |
| 39 | Access only, no exit | Access only, no exit |
| 61 | Access only, no exit | Exit only, no access |

## A55 Holyhead - Chester

| Junction | Westbound | Eastbound |
|---|---|---|
| 8A | Exit only, no access | Access only, no exit |
| 23A | Access only, no exit | Exit only, no access |
| 24A | Exit only, no access | No access or exit |
| 27A | No restriction | No access or exit |
| 33A | Access only, no exit | No access or exit |
| 33B | Exit only, no access | Access only, no exit |
| 36A | Exit only to A5104 | Access only from A5104 |

# Smart motorways

Since Britain's first motorway (the Preston Bypass) opened in 1958, motorways have changed significantly. A vast increase in car journeys over the last 62 years has meant that motorways quickly filled to capacity. To combat this, the recent development of **smart motorways** uses technology to monitor and actively manage traffic flow and congestion.

## Various active traffic management methods are used:
- Traffic flow is monitored using CCTV
- Speed limits are changed to smooth traffic flow and reduce stop-start driving
- Capacity of the motorway can be increased by either temporarily or permanently opening the hard shoulder to traffic
- Warning signs and messages alert drivers to hazards and traffic jams ahead
- Lanes can be closed in the case of an accident or emergency by displaying a red X sign
- Emergency refuge areas are located regularly along the motorway where there is no hard shoulder available

**Smart motorways can be classified into three different types as shown below. The table lists smart motorways operating by 2021 and the colour-coded text indicates the type of smart motorway.**

| CONTROLLED MOTORWAY | Variable speed limits without hard shoulder (the hard shoulder is used in emergencies only) |
|---|---|
| HARD SHOULDER RUNNING | Variable speed limits with part-time hard shoulder (the hard shoulder is open to traffic at busy times when signs permit) |
| ALL LANE RUNNING | Variable speed limits with hard shoulder as permanent running lane (there is no hard shoulder); this is standard for all new smart motorway schemes since 2013 |

| SMART MOTORWAY SECTIONS | |
|---|---|
| M1 | J6A–10, J10–13, J16–19, J23A–25, J25–28, J28–31, J31–32, J32–35A, J39–42 |
| M3 | J2–4A |
| M4 | J19–20, J24–28 |
| M5 | J4A–6, J15–17 |
| M6 | J2–4, J4–10A, J10A–13, J16–19 |
| M9 | J1–1A |
| M20 | J3–5, J4–7 |
| M23 | J8–10 |
| M25 | J2–3, J5–6, J6–23, J23–27, J27–30 |
| M42 | J3A–7, J7–9 |
| M56 | J6–8 |
| M60 | J8–18 |
| M62 | J10–12, J18–20, J25–26, J26–28, J28–29, J29–30 |
| M90 | M9 J1A–M90 J3 |

## Quick tips

- Never drive in a lane closed by a red X
- Keep to the speed limit shown on the gantries
- A solid white line indicates the hard shoulder – do not drive in it unless directed

- A broken white line indicates a normal running lane
- Exit the smart motorway where possible if your vehicle is in difficulty. In an emergency, move onto the hard shoulder where there is one, or the nearest emergency refuge area
- Put on your hazard lights if you break down

| Symbol | Description |
|---|---|
| M4 | Motorway with number |
| Toll | Toll motorway with toll station |
| 5 | Restricted motorway junctions |
| Fleet S R Todhills | Motorway service area, rest area |
| | Motorway and junction under construction |
| A3 | Primary route single/dual carriageway |
| | Primary route junction with and without number |
| 3 | Restricted primary route junctions |
| S | Primary route service area |
| BATH | Primary route destination |
| A1123 | Other A road single/dual carriageway |
| B2070 | B road single/dual carriageway |
| | Minor road more than 4 metres wide, less than 4 metres wide |
| | Roundabout |
| | Interchange/junction |
| | Narrow primary/other A/B road with passing places (Scotland) |
| | Road under construction |
| | Road tunnel |
| Toll | Road toll, steep gradient (arrows point downhill) |
| 5 | Distance in miles between symbols |
| | Railway line, in tunnel |
| | Railway station, tram stop, level crossing |
| | Preserved or tourist railway |
| 628 637 Lecht Summit | Height in metres, mountain pass |
| | Snow gates (on main routes) |
| or V V | Vehicle ferry (all year, seasonal) |
| | Fast vehicle ferry or catamaran |
| or P P | Passenger ferry (all year, seasonal) |
| | Airport (major/minor), heliport |

| Symbol | Description |
|---|---|
| F | International freight terminal |
| H | 24-hour Accident & Emergency hospital |
| C | Crematorium |
| P+R | Park and Ride (at least 6 days per week) |
| | City, town, village or other built-up area |
| | National boundary, county or administrative boundary |
| | Scenic route |
| i | Tourist Information Centre (all year, seasonal) |
| V | Visitor or heritage centre |
| | Caravan site (AA inspected) |
| | Camping site (AA inspected) |
| | Caravan & camping site (AA inspected) |
| | Abbey, cathedral or priory |
| | Ruined abbey, cathedral or priory |
| | Castle, historic house or building |
| | Museum or art gallery, industrial interest |
| | Aqueduct or viaduct |
| | Garden, arboretum |
| | Vineyard, brewery or distillery |
| | Country park, theme park |
| | Showground |
| | Farm or animal centre |
| | Zoological or wildlife collection |
| | Bird collection, aquarium |
| | RSPB site |
| | National Nature Reserve (England, Scotland, Wales) |
| | Local nature reserve, Wildlife Trust reserve |
| | Forest drive |
| | National trail |

| Symbol | Description |
|---|---|
| | Picnic site |
| | Waterfall |
| | Viewpoint |
| | Hill-fort |
| | Prehistoric monument, Roman antiquity |
| 1066 | Battle site with year |
| | Preserved or tourist railway |
| | Cave or cavern |
| | Windmill, monument or memorial |
| | Beach (award winning) |
| | Lighthouse |
| | Golf course |
| | Football stadium |
| | County cricket ground |
| | Rugby Union national stadium |
| | International athletics stadium |
| | Horse racing, show jumping |
| | Air show venue, motor-racing circuit |
| | Ski slope (natural, artificial) |
| | National Trust site (England & Wales, Scotland) |
| | English Heritage site |
| | Historic Scotland site |
| | Cadw (Welsh heritage) site |
| | Major shopping centre, other place of interest |
| | Attraction within urban area |
| | World Heritage Site (UNESCO) |
| | National Park and National Scenic Area (Scotland) |
| | Forest Park |
| | Heritage coast |

**2**

## Isles of Scilly

White Island
St Helen's
King Charles's
Castle
St Martin's Head
Cromwell's Castle
BRYHER
Old
Grimsby
Old Blockhouse
ST.MARTIN'S
Higher
Town
New
Grimsby
Great Ganilly
Eastern Isles
Isles of Scilly
Heritage Coast
Tresco Abbey
TRESCO
Innisidgen
Tombs
Crow Bay
Crow Sound
Samson
Bant's Carn
Burial
ST MARY'S
Higher & Lower Moors
Harry's Walls
A3
Deep Point
Hugh Town
Porth-Hellick-Down-Tomb
Garrison Walls
Isles of Scilly (St Mary's)
Old Town
Peninnis Head
North West Passage
Middle
Town
Penzance
(Mar-Oct)
Annet
Gugh
St Mary's Sound
Broad Sound
ST.AGNES
Horse Point
Smith Sound
Western Rocks

0    1    2    3 miles
0   1   2   3   4   5 kilometres

**a**                    **b**

Carn Naun
Point
Porthmeor
The Island or
St Ives Head
St Ives Bay
St Ives
Godrev
Zennor
Head
Gurnards
Head.
Zennor
Halsetown
Towednack
Carbis
Bay
Hay
South West Coast-Path
Lelant
Penwith Heritage Coast
Pendeen
Watch
B3306 Carn Galver
Mine
Chysauster
Ancient
Village
Bakers
Pit
R Hayle
Men-
An-Tol
Mulfra
Quoit
Canonstown
A30
Morvah
Pendeen
New Mill
Ludgvan
St Erth
Crowlas
Geevor Tin Mine
Levant Mine &
Beam Engine
Lanyon
Quoit
Relubb
P+R
Botallack
St Just
Mining District
A3071
Trengwainton
Garden
Madron
P+R
Gulval
Longrock
St Hilary
Marazion
Goldsithne
Cape Cornwall
St Just
Newbridge
7
Heamoor
Polgoon
Chyandour
St Michael's
Mount
Perranuthnoe
Ballowall Barrow
Trereife
Penzance
Carn Euny
Ancient
Village
Sancreed
Penlee House
Kelynack
Drift
14
Newlyn
Whitesand
Bay
Land's
End
Cudden
Point
10
Paul
Crows-
an-Wra
St Buryan
Mousehole
MOUNT'S BAY
Sennen
Cove
LAND'S END
Sennen
The Merry
Maidens
Lamorna
Trevescan
B3315
Tretheway
Lamorna
Cove
Treen
B3315
Porthcurno
Merthen
Point
Telegraph
Cribba Head
Porthgwarra
Mipact
Open Air Theatre
Isles of Scilly
(Mar-Oct)
Gwennap
Head
St
Levan

0    1    2    3    4 miles
0   1   2   3   4   5 kilometres

**8**

A  B  C  D  E  F

1
2
3
4
5
6
7
8

Higher Sharp

Lower Sharp

Bude
Bay

Dizzard Point
St Gennys
Crackington Haven  Coxfor
Cambeak
Sweets  Wainh
Corn
I 5  B3263  A39
Witchcraft  Marshga
& Magic
Pentire Point - Widemouth  Tresparrett  O
Heritage Coast
Boscastle
Trevalga
Castle  Trethevey  Lesnewth
TINTAGEL HEAD  Tintagel
Old Post Office  Bossiney  B3266
Penhallic Point  Davidstow
Treknow  Trewarmett
Arthurian
Centre  Tremail
B3314
B3266
South West Coast Path  Delabole  Pengelly
Westdowns  Camelford
Rumps  Kellan  Varley  Lanteglos  Crowdy
Point  Head  Head  Port Isaac  Trewalder  Helstone  Reservoir
Port Quin  Bay  Bay  Port-Gaverne
Pentire Point  Bay  Port  Port  B3314  419
Padstow Bay  Quin  Isaac  St Teath  BROWN
Hayle Bay  Long  Treveighan  WILLY
Cross  Trelights  Pendoggett
Stepper Point  Polzeath  Michaelstow  BOD
A  Mothe  4  C  B3314  D elill  A39  F
Ivey's  St Minver  St Endelli  Trequite  E  Churchtown  Jamaica Inn
Trevose  Bay  Trevigian
Heritage Coast  Churchtown  St  St Breward
TREVOSE HEAD  St Kew  Tudy
Dinas  St Kew
Head  Highway
Constantine  Trevone

4

0  1  2  3  4 miles
0  1  2  3  4  5 kilometres

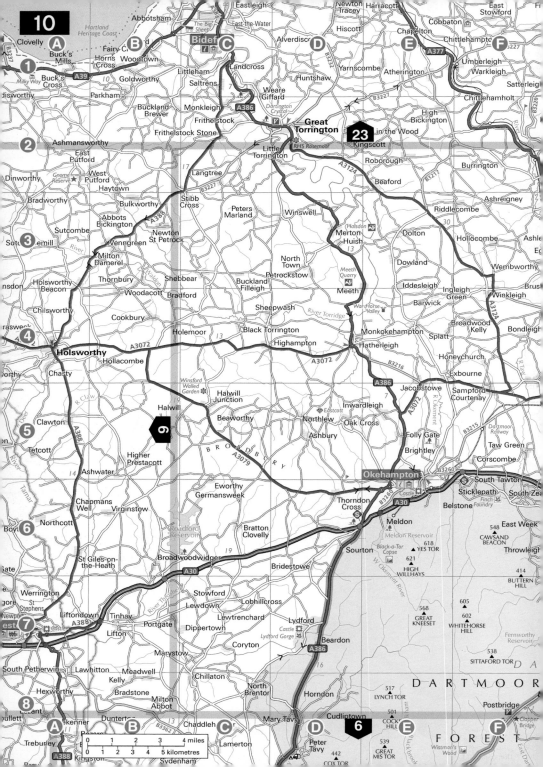

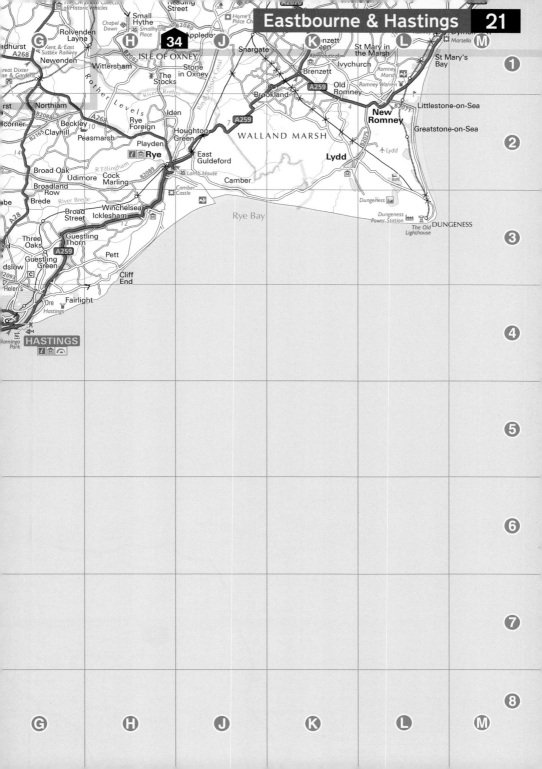

**22**

1

2

North West
Point

Lundy
Heritage Coast    LUNDY

3    ▲142    Ⓟ Bideford (Apr-Oct)
Marine                    Ilfracombe (Apr-Oct)
Reserve
Shutter Point        Surf Point

Baggy
Point

Croyde B.

4

BARNSTAPLE

5    OR

BIDEFORD BAY    **Westward**

Shipload
Bay
HARTLAND POINT                                        Abbotsham

Titchberry                                    Hartland
Damehole                Hartland Abbey                Heritage Coast
Point            & Gardens
Stoke            Ⓥ    Clovelly    Ford
6    Hartland Quay                    B3248        Fairy Cross
Speke's Mill            Hartland        4    Buck's    Horns    Woodtown
Mouth    Milford                            Mills    Cross
Docton            Milky Way    Buck's    A39    10    Goldworthy
Mill    Philham                    Cross
Woolfardisworthy            Parkham
Hardisworthy                                            Buckland
Brewer

Welcombe                                        Ashmansworthy    Frithe
7    Darracott    Meddon        **9**    East
Putford
Gooseham                            Dinworthy    Gnome    ★ West    Haytown
Morwenstow                                    Reserve    Putford
Higher Sharpnose Point                        Bradworthy            Bulkworthy
Shop
South West    Woodford    A39                            Abbots
Coast Path                                        Bickington    Newt
Lower Sharpnose Point                    Tamar        Sutcombe    A388    St Petr
8    Lakes
Steeple Point    Ⓒbb        Sutcom    Ⓔll    Venr    on
Milton
A        B        Ⓒ        Ⓓ        Ⓔ    Damerel    Ⓕ

0    1    2    3    4 miles
0  1  2  3  4  5 kilometres

Northcott        Poughill        Dunsdon    Holsworthy    Thornbury    SI

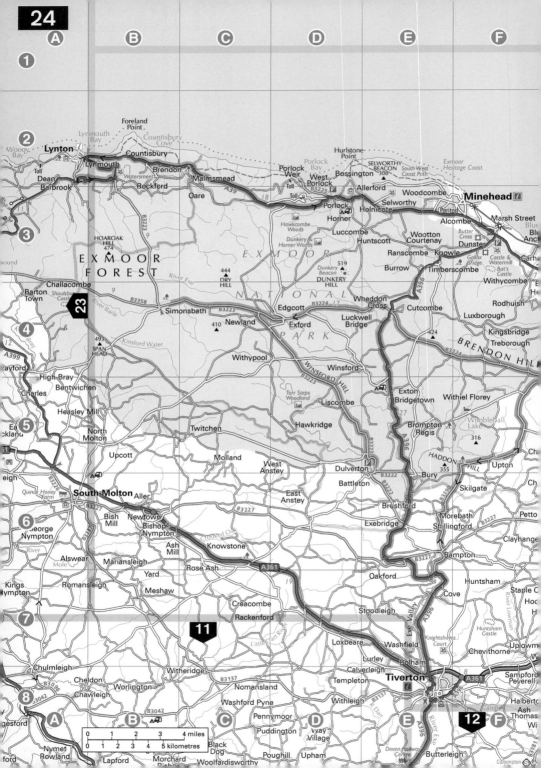

G  H  J  **37**  K  L  M

①
②
③
**26**
④
⑤
⑥
⑦
⑧

**Burnham-on-Sea**

**Highbridge**

BRIDGWATER
BAY

**Watchet**

Old
Cleeve
Washford
Williton
Sampford
Brett
Woolston
Lower
Roadwater
Roadwater
Monksilver

West
Quantoxhead
Weacombe
Holford
Doniford
Kilve
East
Quantoxhead
Lilstock
Knighton
Burton
Stogursey
Shurton
Stolford
Steart
Otterhampton
Combwich
Pawlett
Dunball
Puriton
Woolavington
Cossington
Bawdrip
Chilton
Polden

West Somerset
Railway
St
Audrie's
Bay

Hinkley Point
Power Station
Bridgwater
Bay

Stockland
Bristol
West Huntspill
Stretcholt
Huntspill
Bason Bridge
East Huntspill

Secret World
Wildlife
Rescue

Chedzoy
Sutton
Mallet

**Bridgwater**

Cannington
Chilton
Trinity
Horsey
Wembdon

Stringston
Dodington
Fiddington
Nether
Stowey
Charlinch
Spaxton
Four
Forks
Enmore
Lexworthy
Durleigh
Huntworth
Westonzoyland
Middlezoy
Burrow
Bridge
Burrow
Mump
⑤

Bicknoller
Kingswood
Stogumber
Preston
Lawford
Crowcombe
Over
Stowey
Aley
Adscombe
Lower
Aisholt
Goathurst
Huntstile
North
Petherton
North
Newton
St Michael
Church
Lyng
Athelney
Stathe
Willett
Flaxpool
Triscombe
Aisholt
Lower
Merridge
Courtway
Broomfield
Shearston
Kingston
St Mary
Thurloxton
Adsborough
West
Newton
Hedging
West Lyng
Combe
Sydenham
Elworthy
Brompton
Ralph
Rooks
Nest
Tolland
West Leigh
West Bagborough
Toulton
Gotton
Cheddon
Fitzpaine
West
Monkton
Durston
Woodhill
Oath
Stoke
St Gregory
Meare
Green
Huntham
Heale
Willows &
Wetlands
Clatworthy
Reservoir
Clatworthy
Whitefield
Pyleigh
Lydeard St Lawrence
Combe
Florey
Bishops
Lydeard
Ash
Priors
Pickney
Fulford
Monkton
Heathfield
Creech
Heathfield
Langaller
Charlton
Creech
St Michael
Knapp
North Curry
Swell
Wood
Langley Marsh
Maundown
Langley
Wiveliscombe
Chapel Leigh
Fitzhead
Halse
Nailsbourne
Hestercombe
Bathpool
Greenway
⑥ lltown
Milverton
Vale of Taunton Deane
Preston
Bowyer
Heathfield
Cotford
St Luke
Norton
Fitzwarren
Staplegrove
P+R
Bishop's
Hull
Comeytrowe
Trull
Ruishton
Henlade
Ham
Thornfalcon
Fivehead
Isle
Abbotts
Isle
Brewers
⑦
Waterrow
Bathealton
Langford
Budville
Nynehead
Hillfarrance
Oake
Bradford-
on-Tone
**Taunton**
Shoreditch
Staplehay
Stoke
St Mary
Orchard
Portman
West Hatch
Meare
Green
Curry
Mallet
Beercrocombe
Westport
Stawley
Kittisford
Appley
Thorne St
Margaret
Tonedale
West
Buckland
Dipford
Duddlestone
Heale
Thurlbear
Beercrocombe
Stewley
Ashill
Ilton
Puckington
Ilford
Appley
**Wellington**
Ford
Street
Lowton
Corfe
Pitminster
Blagdon
Staple
Fitzpaine
Slough
Green
Kenny
Windmill
Hill
Greenham
White Ball
Sampford Arundel
Sampford Moor
Red Ball
Wrangway
Wellington
Blagdon
Hill
Curland
Barrington
Hill
Blackwater
Broadway
Horton
Donyatt
**Ilminster**
Kingstone
Burlescombe
Ayshford
Appledore
Nicholashayne
Woodgate
Culm
Davy
Rosemary
Lane
Clayhidon
Burnworthy
Buckland
St Mary
Whitelackington
BLACKDOWN HILLS
Prescott
Culmstock
Hemyock
Stapley
Birch
Wood
Bishopswood
Knowle
St Giles
Wake
Cudworth
Uffculme
Craddock
Bolham
Water
Churchinford
Newtown
Beetham
Combe
St Nicholas
Chardleigh
Green
Chaffcombe
Cricket
St Thomas
Ashill
Blackborough
Bradfield
Kentisbeare
Sheldon
Smeatharpe
Churchstanton
Howley
Higher
Wambrook
Whitestaunton

G  H  **12**  J  **13**  K  L

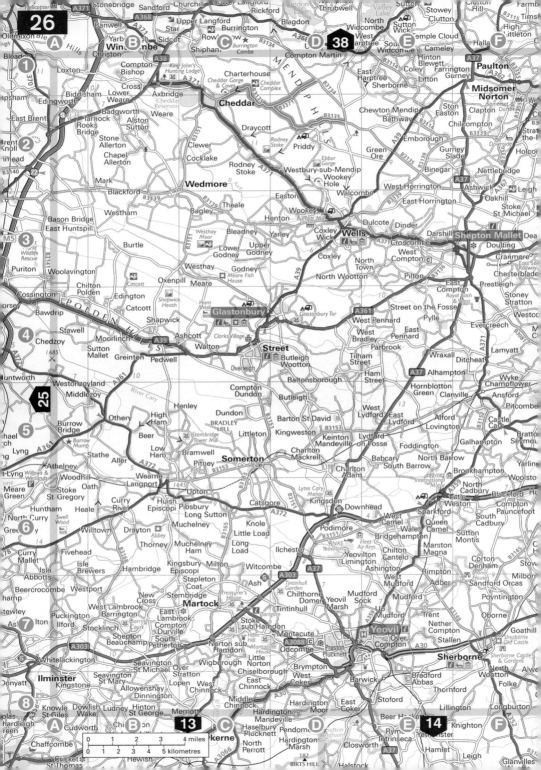

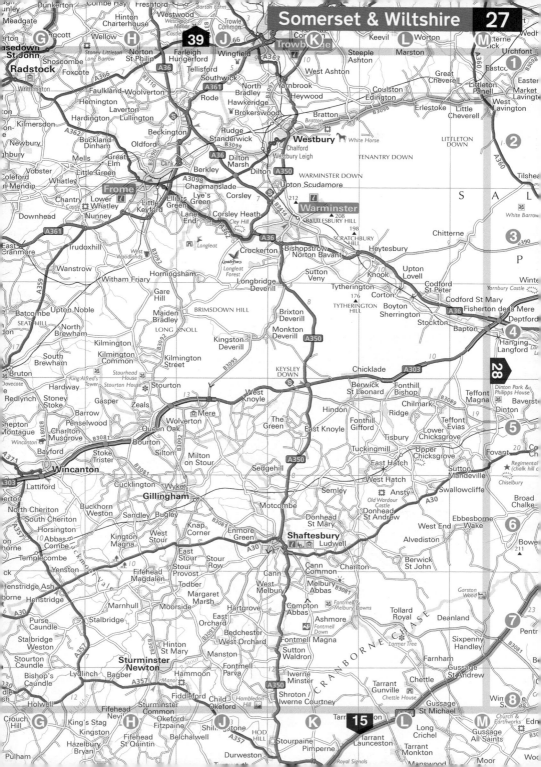

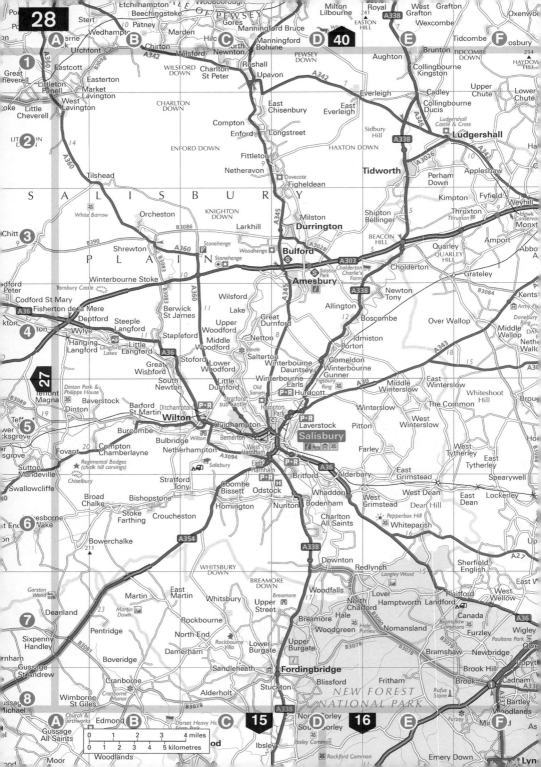

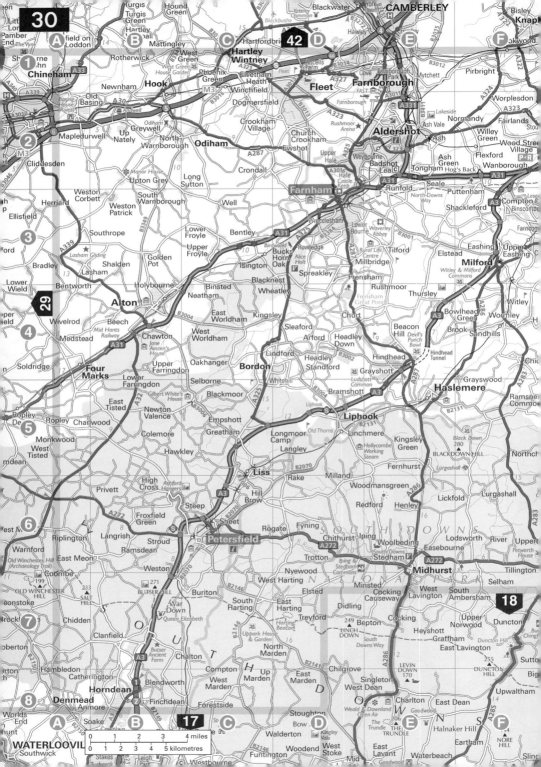

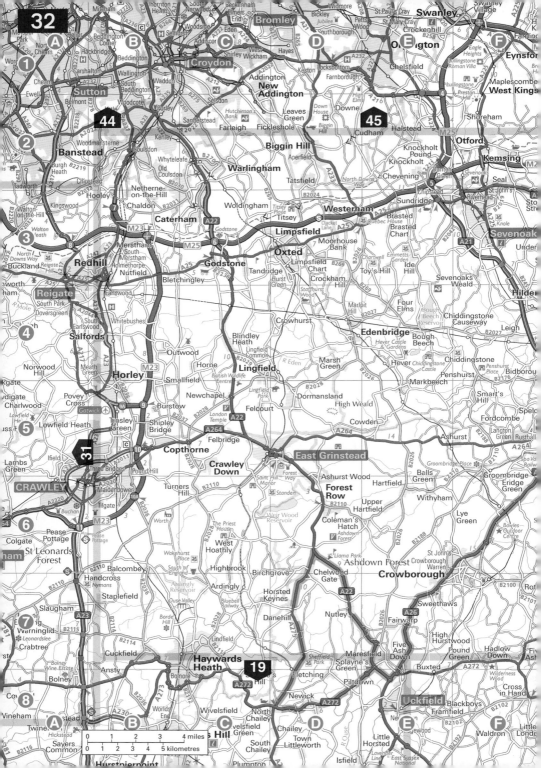

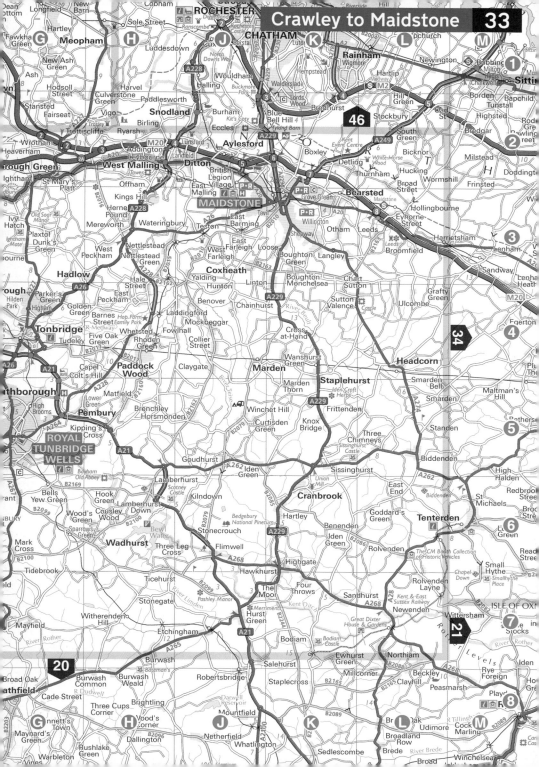

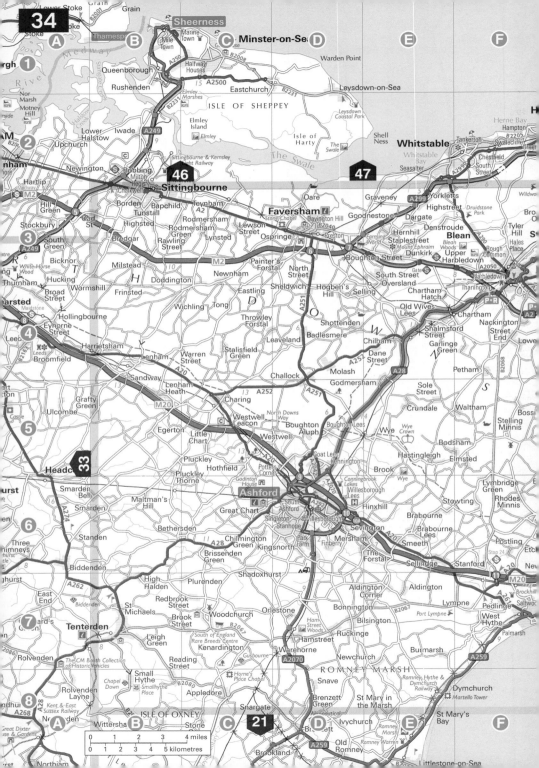

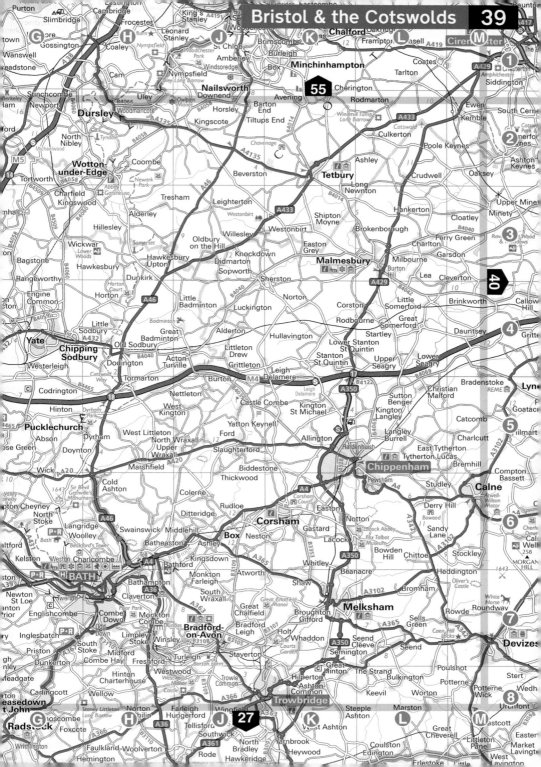

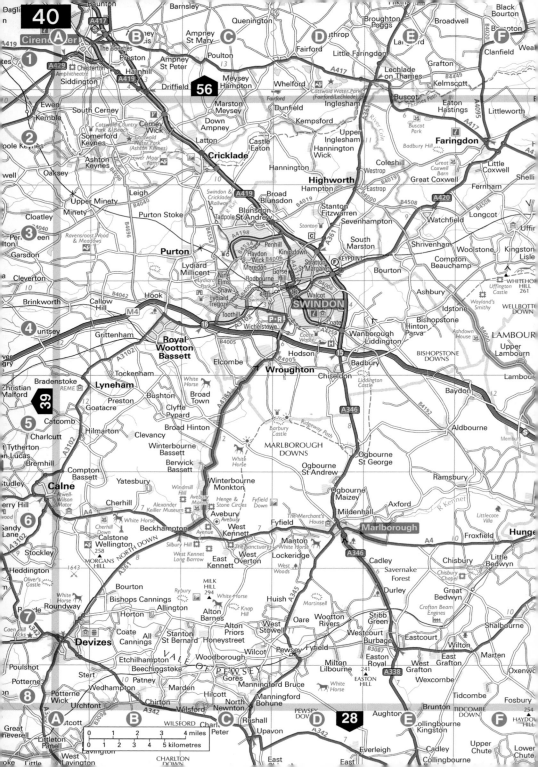

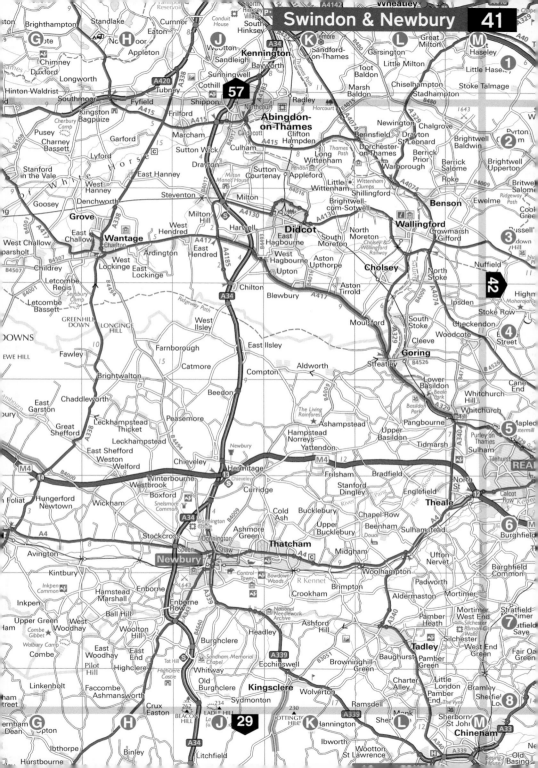

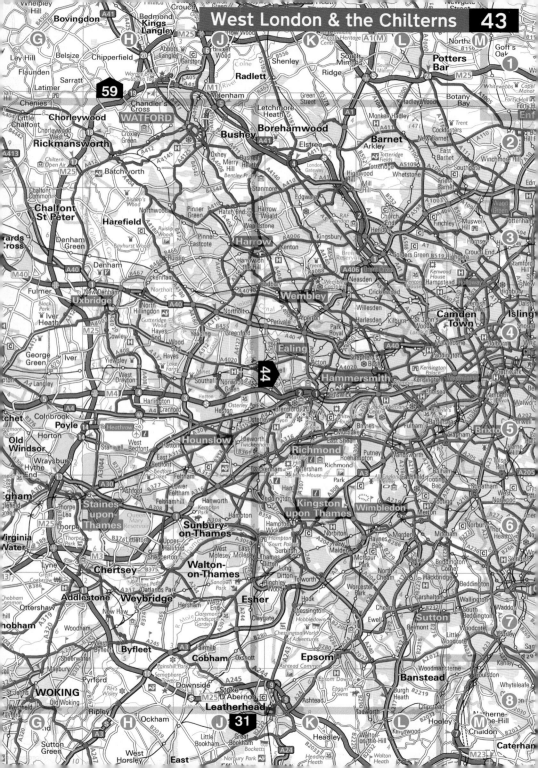

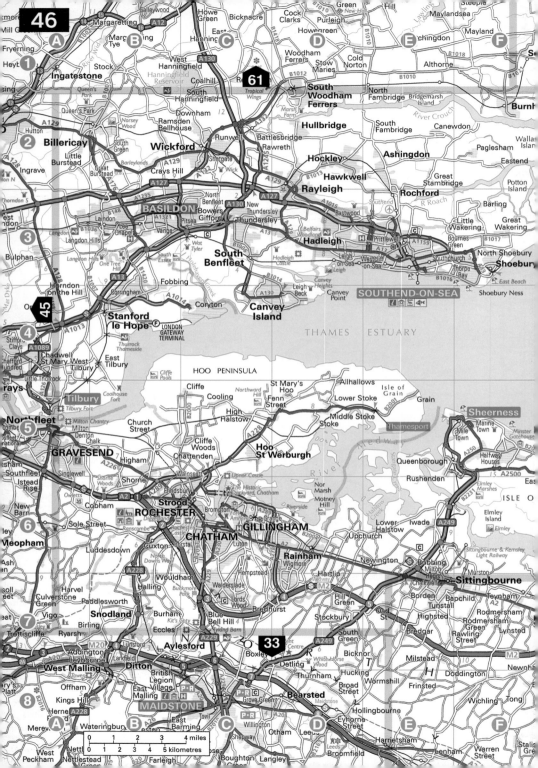

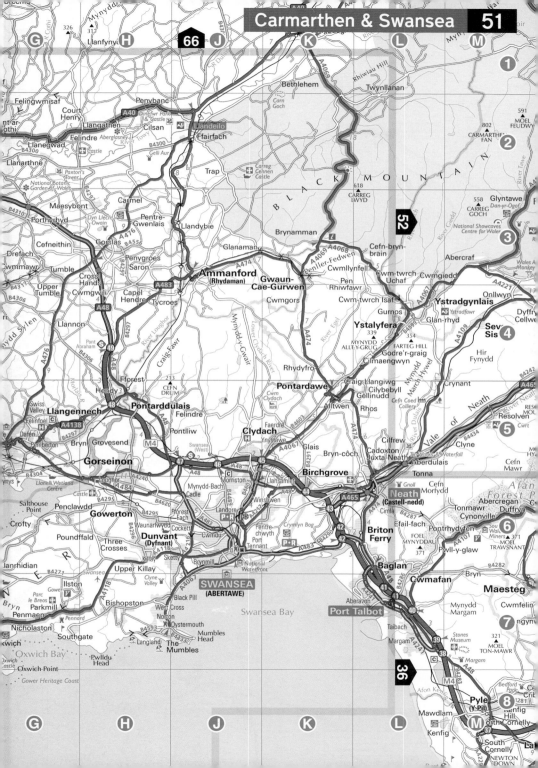

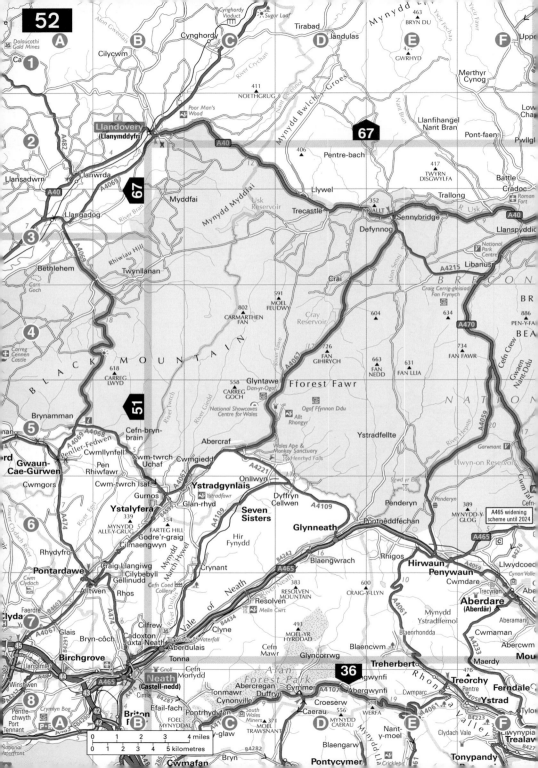

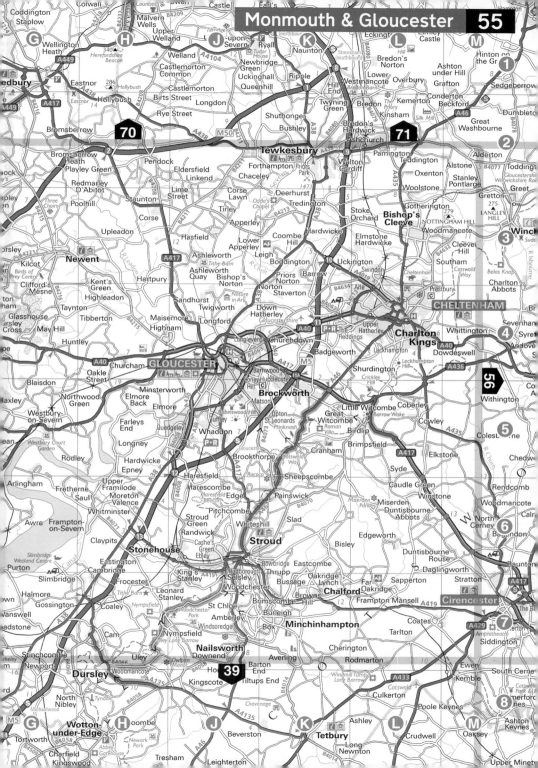

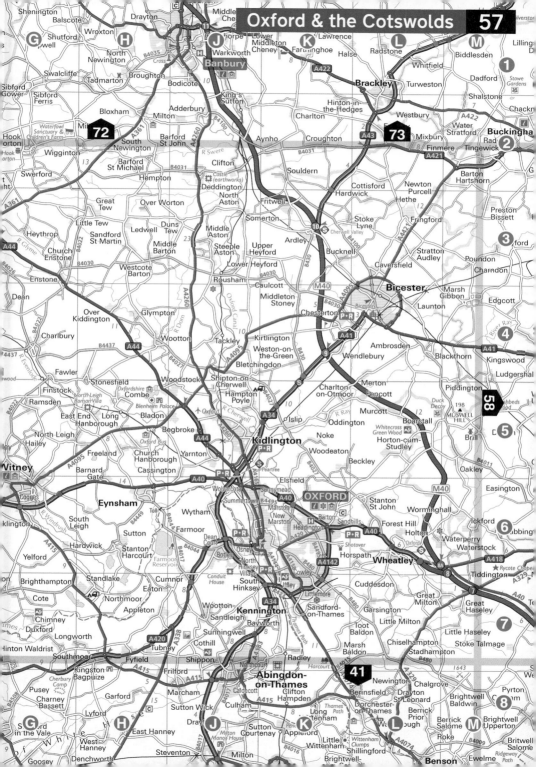

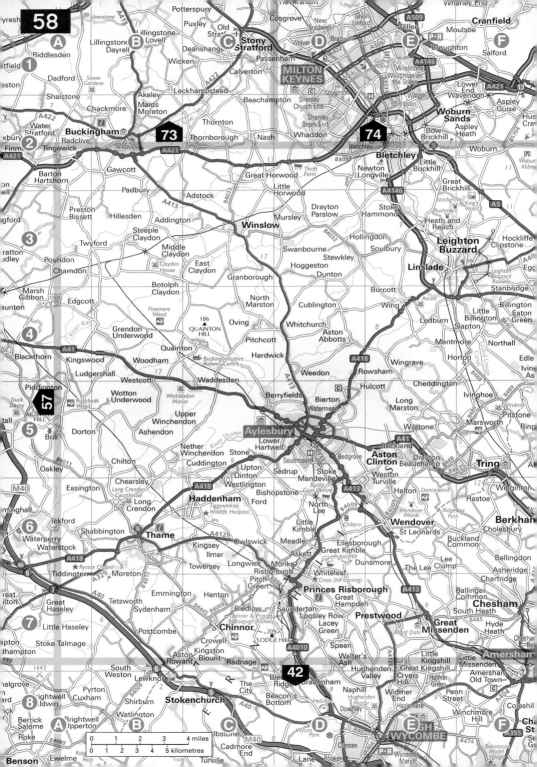

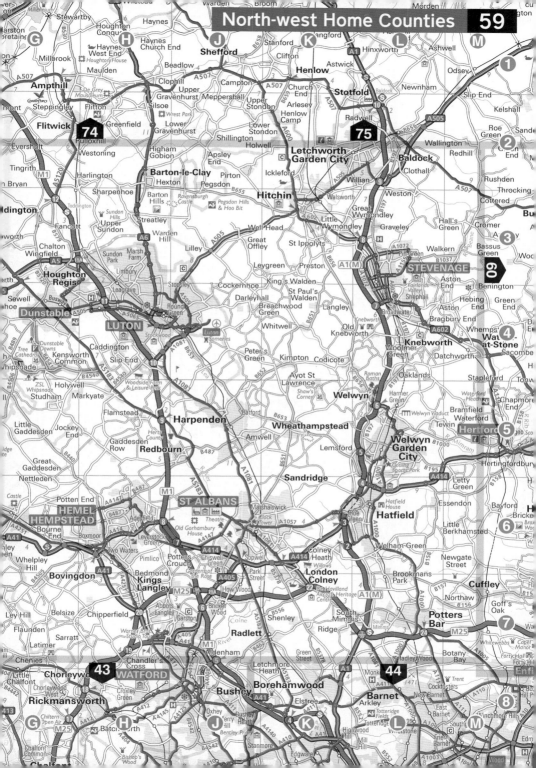

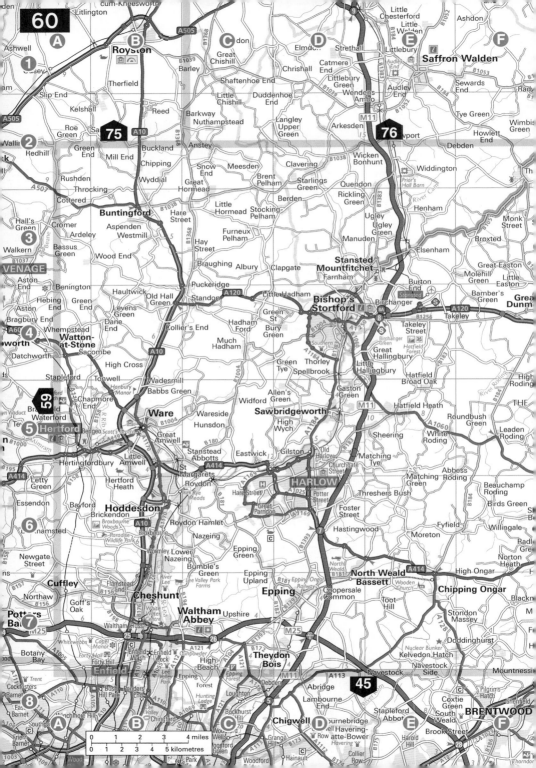

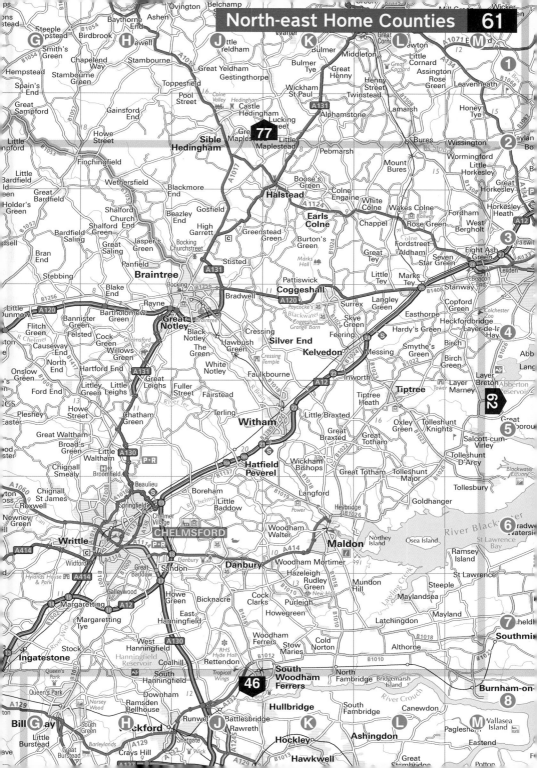

Hollesley Bay

G   H   J   K   L   M

❶

Bourne
Hemley
Alderton
River D
Bawdsey
Falkenham

Trimley
St Mary
Old
Felixstowe
alton

79

Felixstowe   ❷

Landguard Fort

Landguard
Point

Hook of Holland   ❸

e
on-
ze   ❹

a

❺

❻

❼

❽

G   H   J   K   L   M

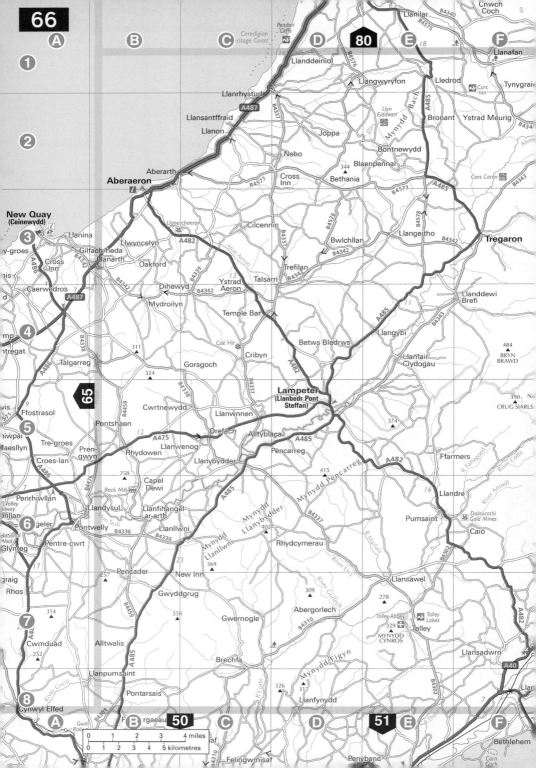

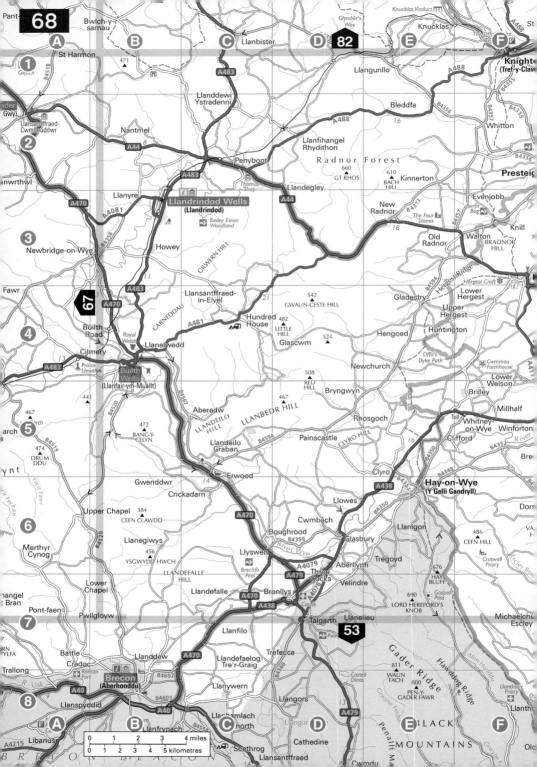

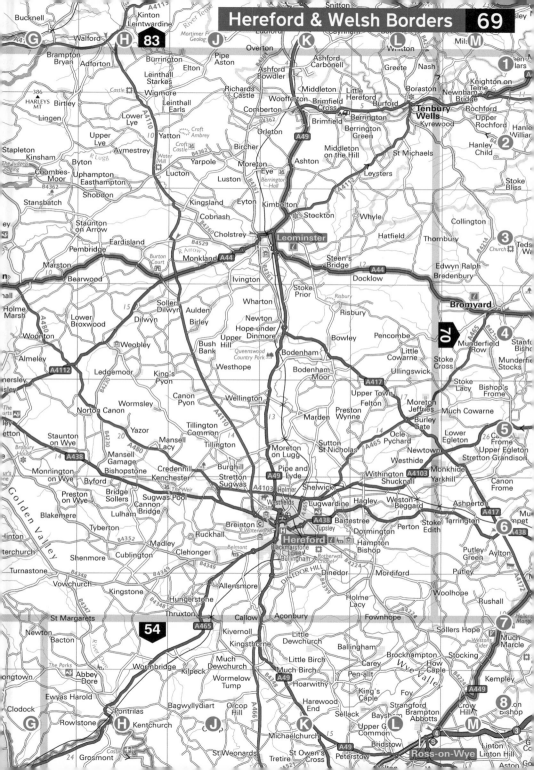

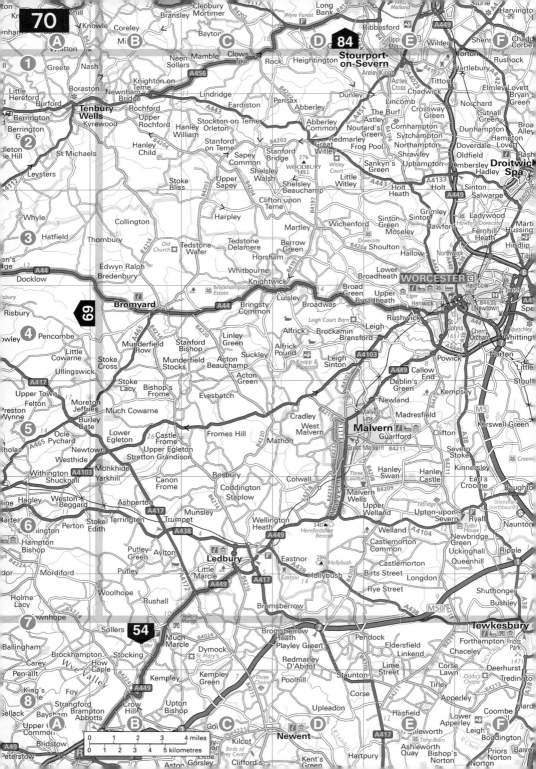

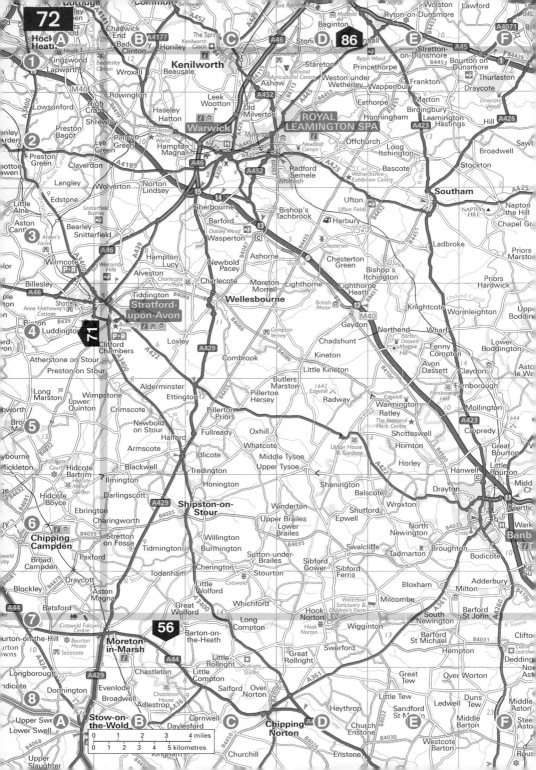

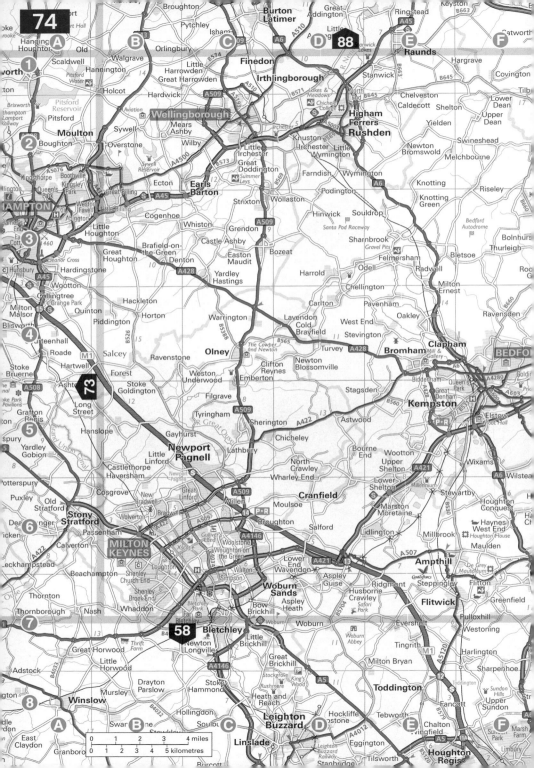

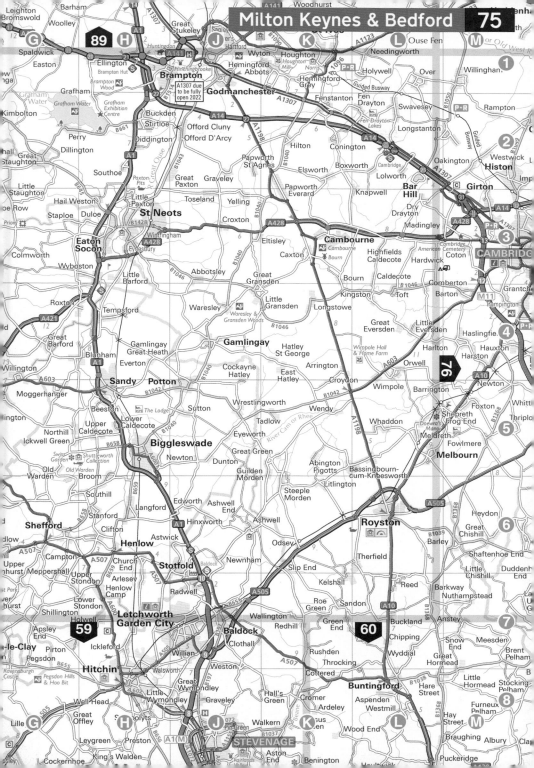

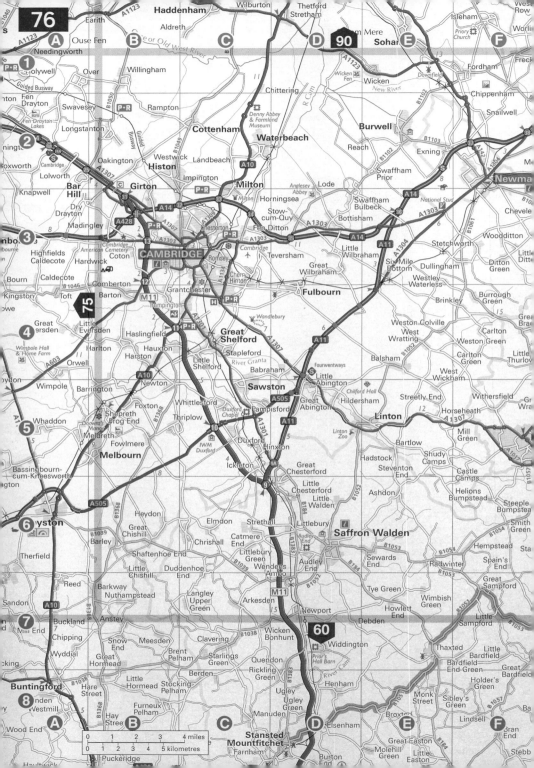

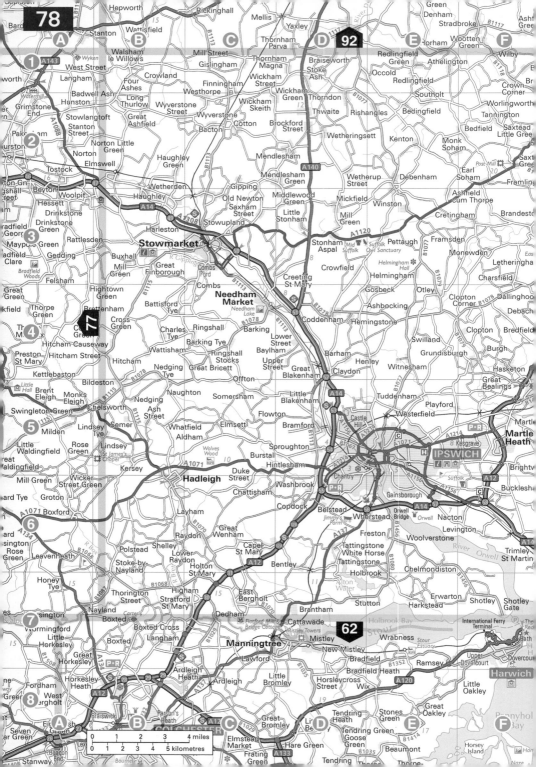

Cratfield
Huntingfield
Blackheath
Blythburgh
Walpole
Thorington
Walberswick
Bramfield
A144
J 93
K
L
M

G
H
Lamfield
Hevenington
Suffolk Coast
1

Ubbeston
Green
Darsham
Dunwich Forest
Westleton Heath
Dunwich
Street

Peasenhall
Sibton
Westleton
Badingham
Yoxford
Middleton
Minsmere
Dunwich Heath

Bruisyard
Middleton Moor
Eastbridge
2
nnington
Bruisyard
Theberton
Street

nawsgate
Cransford
Rendham
Carlton Meres
Kelsale
Leiston Abbey
Power Station
North Green
Swefling
Saxmundham
Carlton
Knodishall
Leiston
3
Great
Glemham
Benhall
Street
Benhall
Green
Sternfield
Aldringham
Thorpe Ness
Parham
Stratford
St Andrew
Friday Street
Friston
Knodishall Common
Thorpeness
rgh
Hacheston
Farnham
Snape
North Warren
Easton
Marlesford
Little Glemham
Snape Street
A1094
3
Aldeburgh
 m
Blaxhall
Snape Maltings
Campsea Ash
Snape
River Alde
Aldeburgh Bay
4
tistree
Tunstall

10
Rendlesham
Chillesford
Sudbourne
Ufford

Eyke
Butley
Bromeswell
Castle
Orford
dbridge
Sutton Hoo
Sutton Heath
Capel St Andrew
Orford Ness
bridge Mill
Sutton
Boyton
Orford Ness
5
aldringfield
Shottisham
Hollesley
Orfordness-Havergate
Suffolk Heritage Coast

bourne
Hemley
North Weir Point
Hollesley Bay
Alderton

Falkenham
Bawdsey
6

Trimley
St Mary
Old Felixstowe
walton

Felixstowe
7
Landguard Fort
Landguard Point

Hook of Holland
8
G
H
J
K
L
M

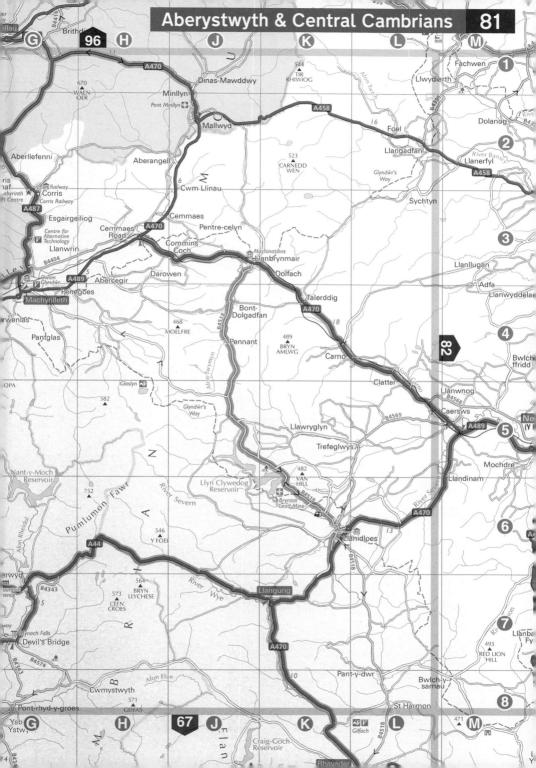

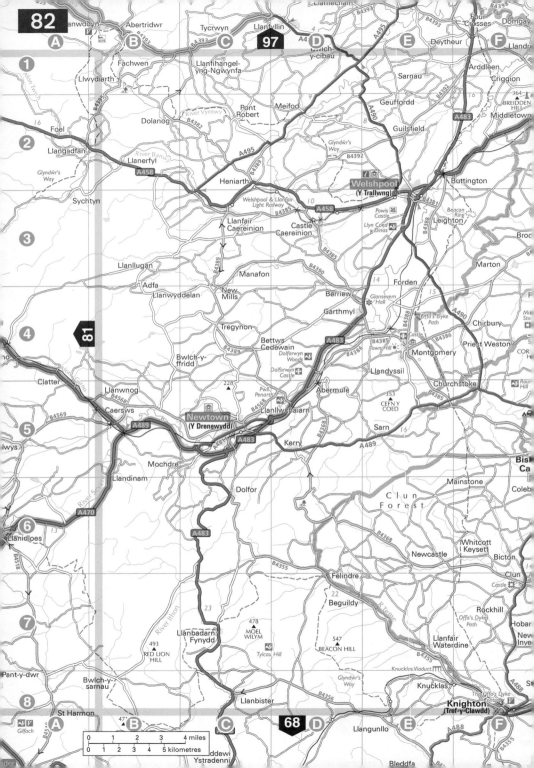

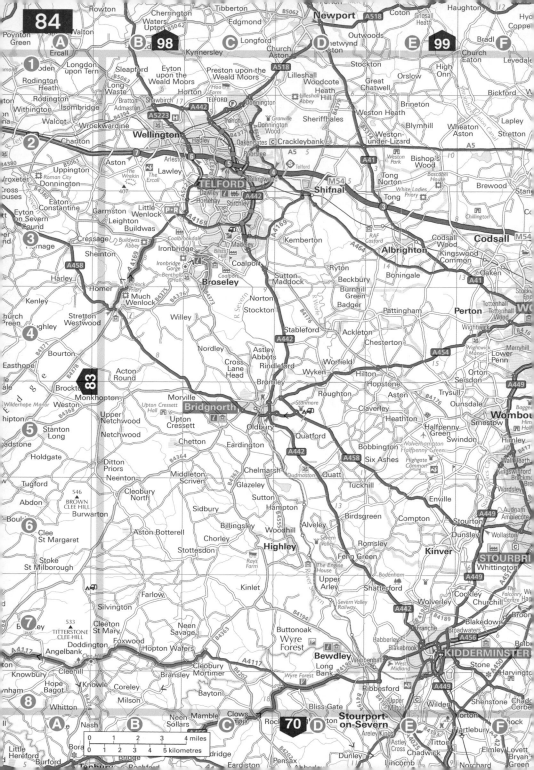

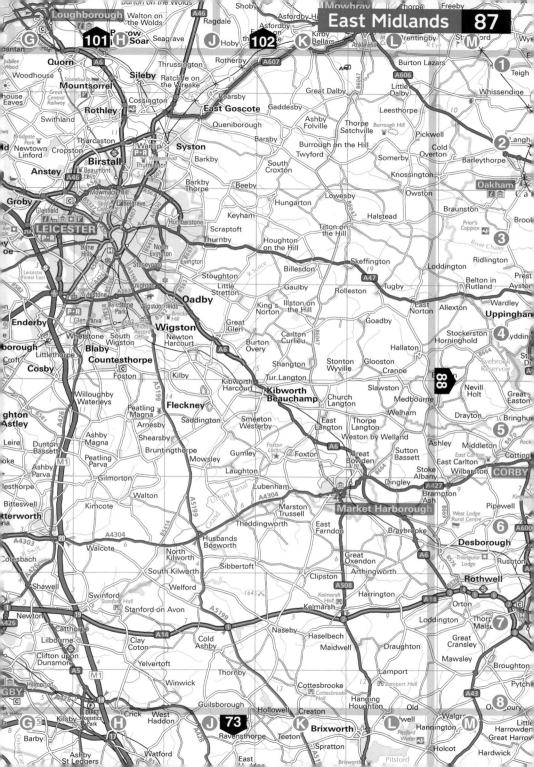

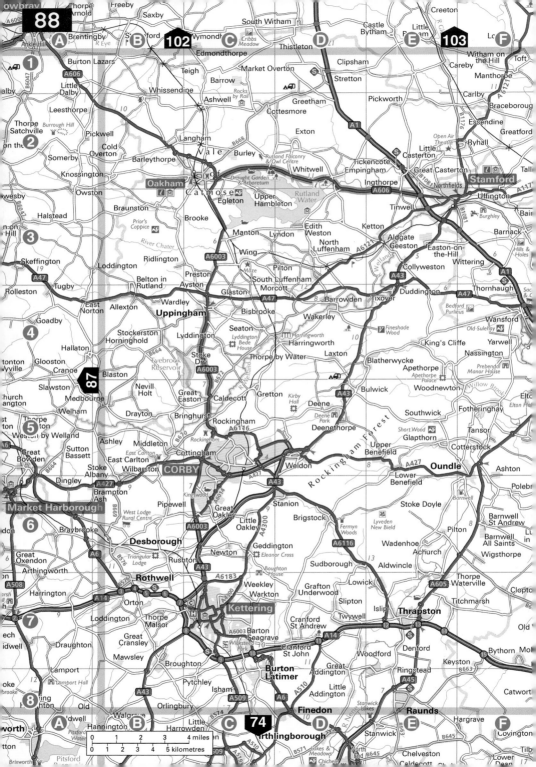

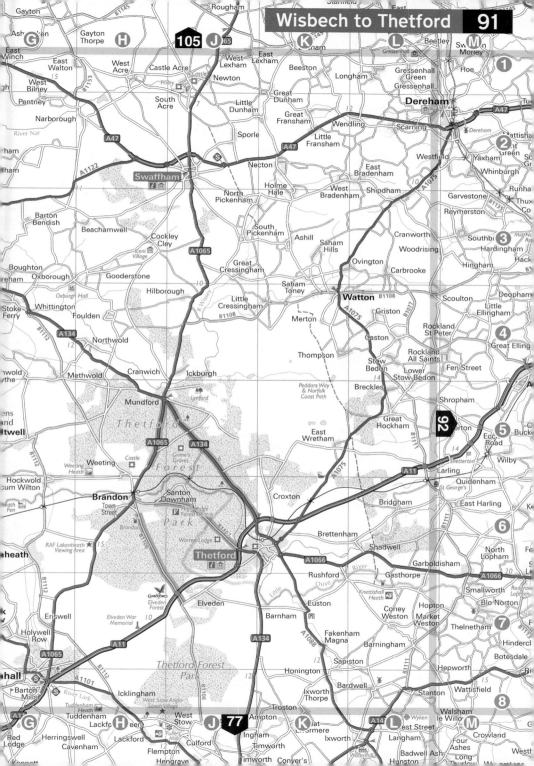

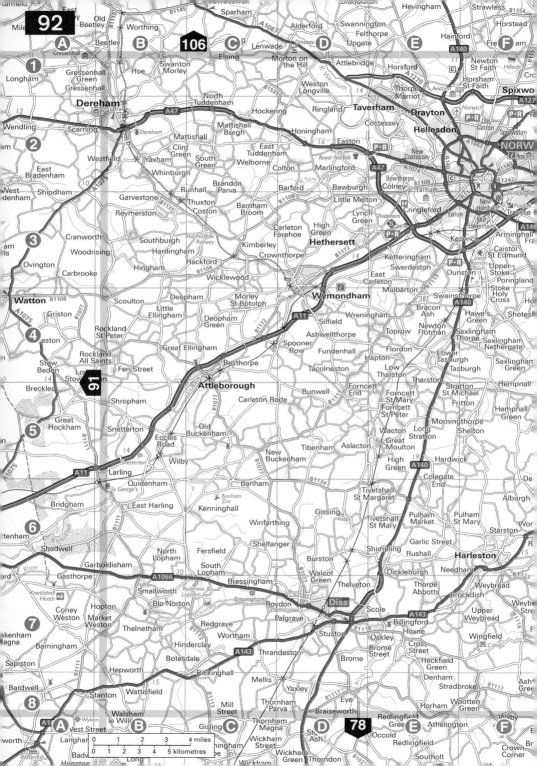

**94**

1

2

3

4

5

6

7

8

C A E R N A R F O N

B A Y

Aberffraw Bay
Heritage Coast

Mallt

Llanddw

Lleyn Heritage
Coast

Tre

Trwyn y
Grolech

56
YR EI

Llith

Carreg Ddu

Porth
Nefyn

Morfa
Nefyn

Pistyll

**Nefyn**

Edern

Boduan

Llan

Porth Ysgaden

Tudweiliog

Dinas

371
Carn Fadrun

L L E Y N

Efailne

B4415

Rhyd-y-clafdy

A497

7

A499

Porth
Colmon

Llaniestyn

Penrhos

Pen-y-graig

14

B4417

Sarn
Mellteyrn

Bryn
mawr

Llanbedrog

7

Llangwnnadl

Botwnnog

Trwyn Llanbed

Porth Oer

Bryncroes

B4413

17

B4413

St Tudwal's
Road

Rhoshirwaun

Plas yn
Rhiw

Llangian

**Abersoch**

Y Rhiw

B4413

Llanengan

Aberdaron

Llanfaelrhys

Porth Neigwl
or
Hell's Mouth

Bwlchtocyn

Machroes

St Tudwal's
Island East

Aberdaron
Bay

Porth
Ysgo

St Tudwal's
Island West

Porth
Ceiriad

Bardsey Sound

Lleyn Heritage
Coast

St Mary's

Ynys
Enlli

BARDSEY ISLAND

0    1    2    3    4 miles
0  1  2  3  4  5 kilometres

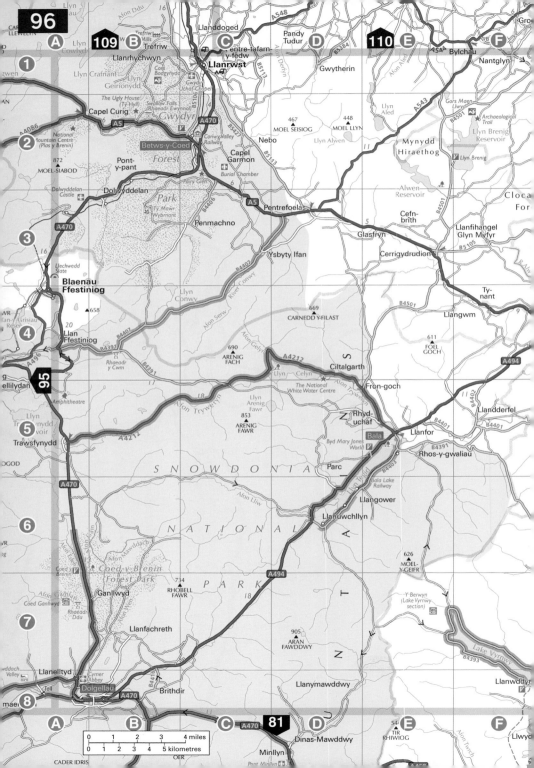

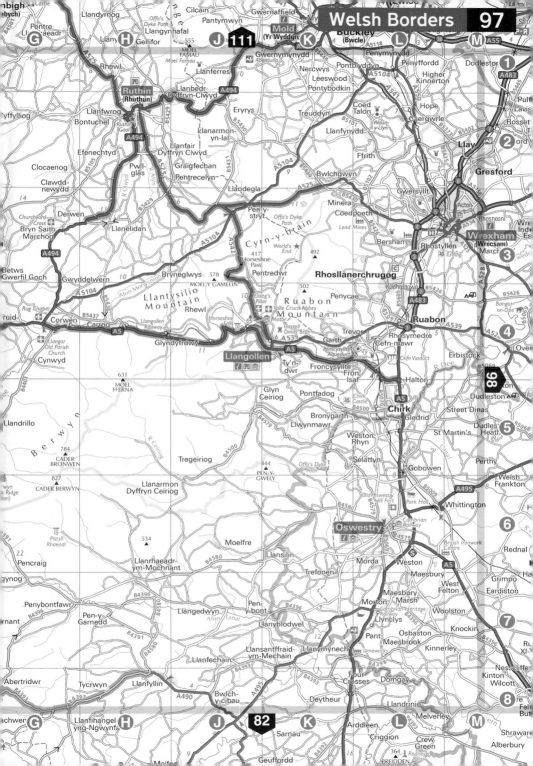

G H J K L M

1
2
3
4
5
6
7
8

ningham
Mundesley
Stow Mill
Paston
Knapton
B1159
Edingthorpe
Bacton
Walcott
Edingthorpe
Green
Witton
Ridlington
Happisburgh
Whimpwell Green
Meeting
House Hill
Happisburgh
Common
Hempstead
Honing
Lessingham
Ingham
Corner
Sea Palling
Briggate
East
Ruston
Ingham
Waxham
Worstead
Calthorpe
Street
Dilham
Stalham
Hickling
Smallburgh
Barton
Turf
Sutton
Hickling Green
Horsey
Wood
Street
Tunstead
Sutton
Fen
Hickling
Broad
Horsey Windpump
Neatishead
Barton
Broad
Catfield
Irstead
Martham
Broad
Wrexham
Boads
RAF Radar
Potter
Heigham
Hoveton
BeWILDerwood
Ludham
Martham
Winterton-on-Sea
Upper
Street
Bastwick
Hemsby
Hemsby
Hole
am
Horning
Repps
Woodbastwick
Bure
Marshes
r Street
Thurne
Ormesby
Bro
Scratby
Broads Wildlife
Centre
Fleggburgh/
Burgh St Margaret
Ormesby
St Michael
California
Salhouse
Ranworth
Ranworth Broad
Pilson
Green
Clippesby
Billockby
Ormesby
St Margaret
**Caister-on-**
B1140
Fairhouse

**93**

G H J K L M

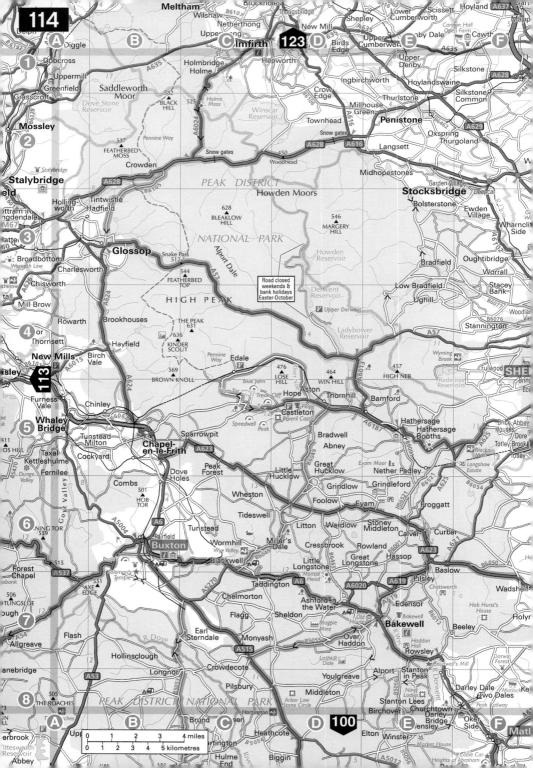

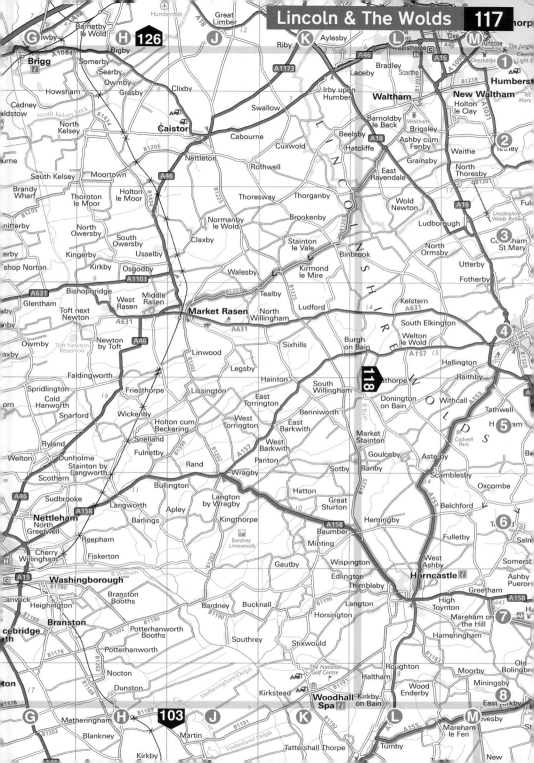

G  H  J  K  L  M

1
2
3
4
5
6
7
8

etby ~
llethorpe Dunes

oy
s
heddlethorpe
t Helen

Seal Sanctuary &
Wildlife Centre

**Mablethorpe**

Trusthorpe

by
arsh  Sutton on Sea

Sandilands

Markby

Huttoft
Isby
Thurlby

Anderby
arlesthorpe  On Your Marques
berworth  **Mumby**

Chapel Point

lloughby  Hogsthorpe

Sloothby  **Chapel
St Leonards**

Habertoft  Addlethorpe
elton
Marsh  **Ingoldmells**

Fantasy Island

Ingoldmells
Point

Orby  Lincolnshire Coast
Light Railway

**Burgh le Marsh**

A158
toft  Natureland Seal
Sanctuary

y in the Marsh  Village Church
Farm  **Skegness**

G  **104**  H  J  K  L  M

Croft

horpe St Peter  Wainfleet
Haven

Wainfleet

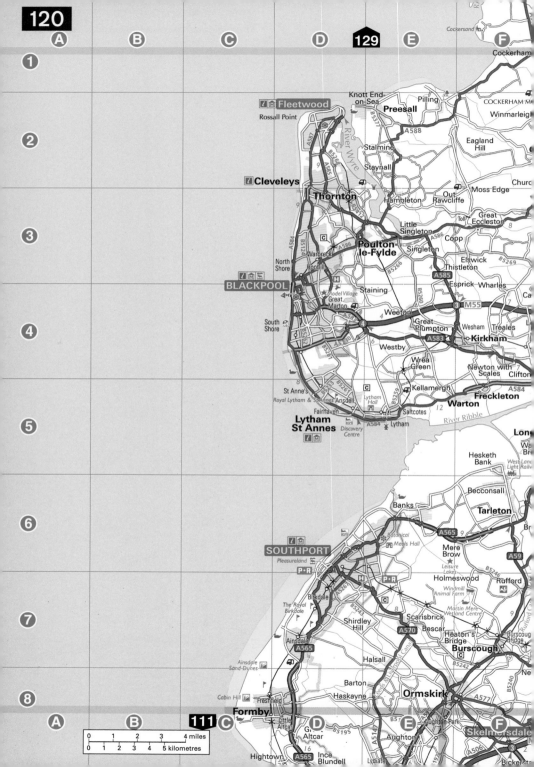

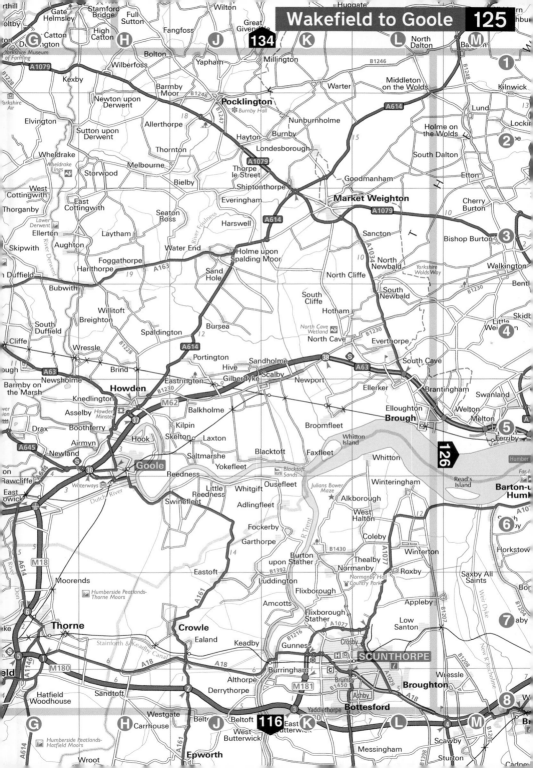

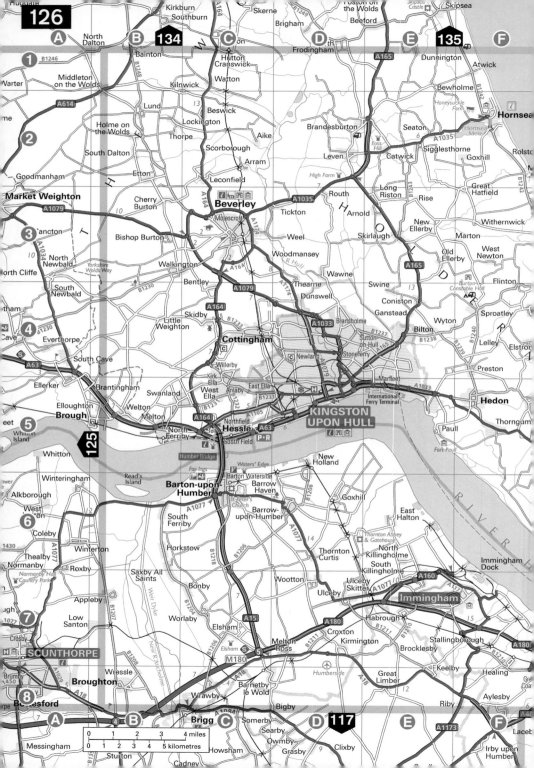

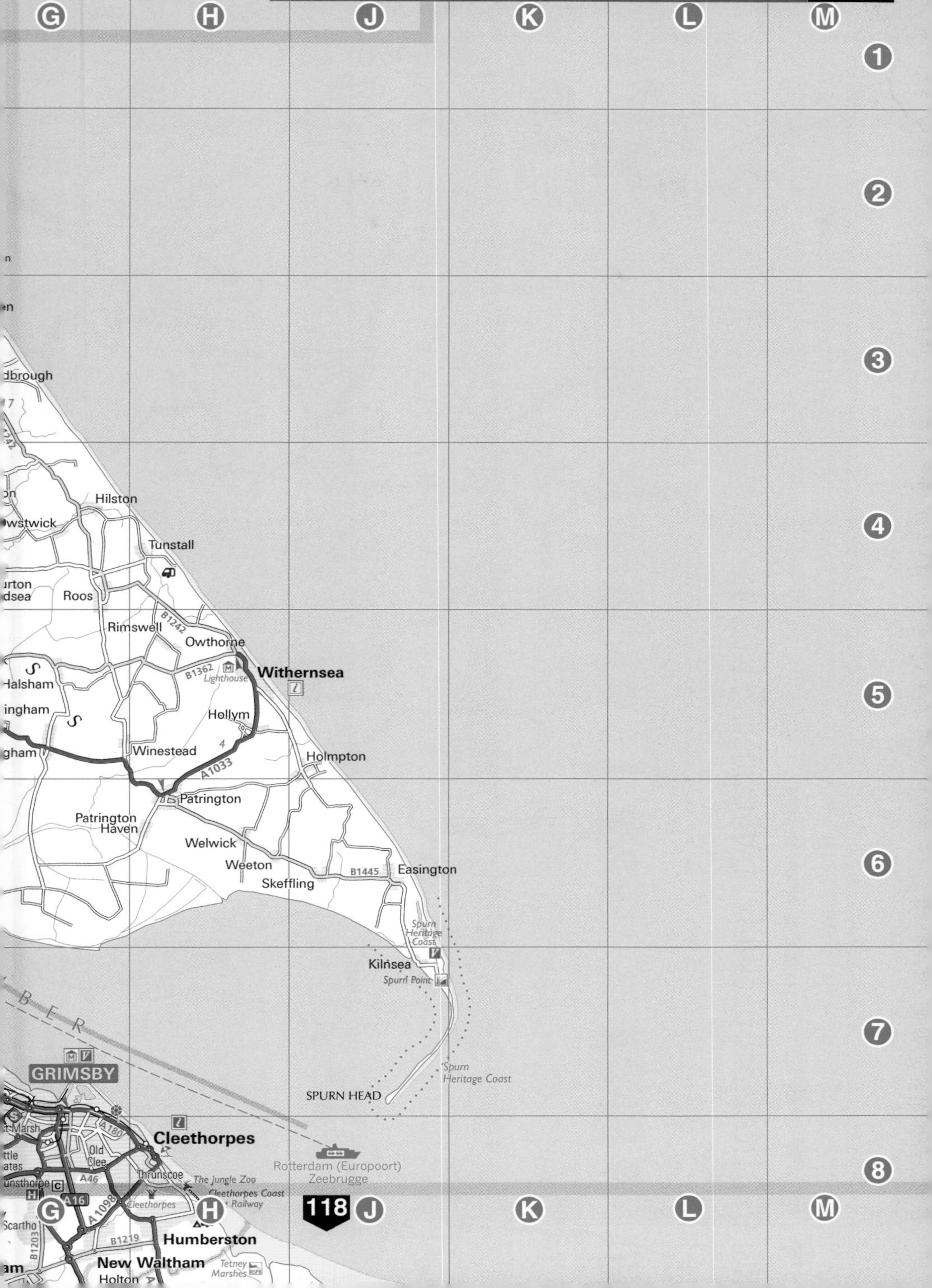

G    H    J    K    L    M

1
2
3

dbrough

Hilston

wstwick

Tunstall

urton
dsea    Roos

Rimswell

Owthorne

Halsham

ingham

Hollym

Winestead

Patrington

Patrington
Haven

Welwick

Weeton

Skeffling

B1362
Lighthouse    **Withernsea**

Holmpton

A1033

B1445    Easington

Spurn
Heritage
Coast

Kilnsea
Spurn Point

SPURN HEAD

Spurn
Heritage Coast

4
5
6
7

BER

GRIMSBY

**Cleethorpes**

Old
Slee    A46

unsthorpe

Cleethorpes

Thrunscoe

The Jungle Zoo

Cleethorpes Coast
Railway

Rotterdam (Europoort)
Zeebrugge

8

G    H    **118**    J    K    L    M

**Humberston**

Scartho

B1219

**New Waltham**
Holton

Tetney
Marshes

am

A16

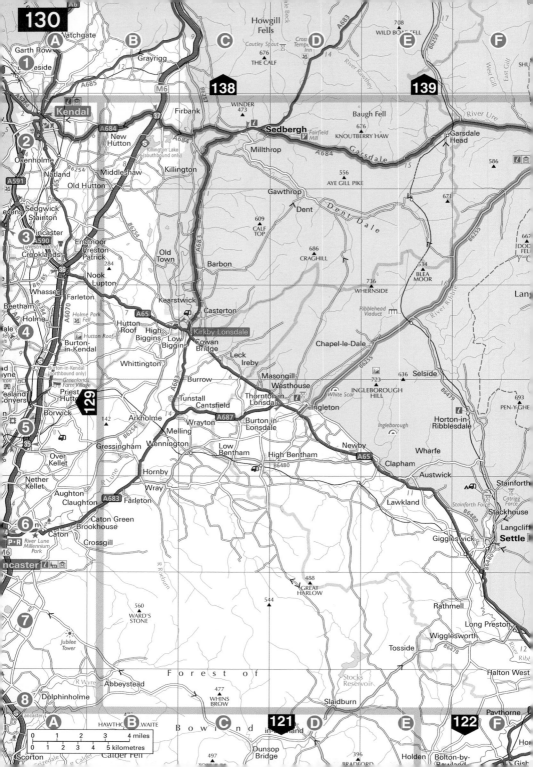

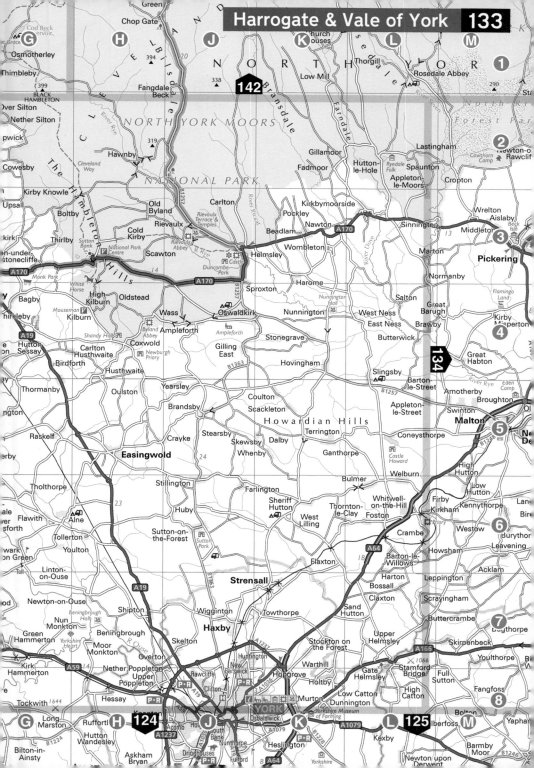

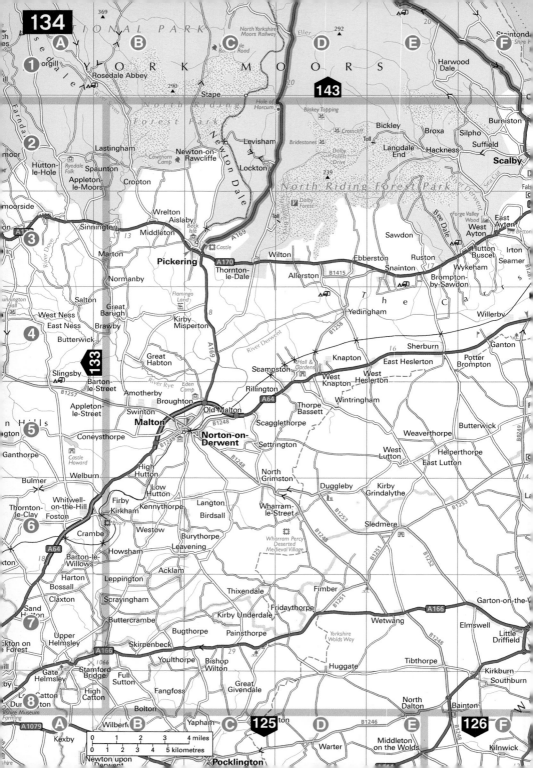

G H J K L M

1

2

...ner Point

...land Way

North Bay
...a Railway

Castle

3

**Scarborough**

Oliver's Mount

A165

P·R  Osgodby  Cayton
Bay

B1261

...tes  7  Cayton

Lebberston  The
Wyke

A1039

Gristhorpe

R. Hertford  Filey Brigg

Folkton  Muston  **Filey**

...xton  7  A1039

Filey Bay

**Hunmanby**

Fordon  Reighton

Flamborough Head
Heritage Coast

Wold  Speeton
Newton  B1229  Bempton
Cliffs  Thornwick
Burton  Bay
Fleming  Buckton  North
Bempton  Landing

Grindale  A165  B1229  Flamborough Cliffs
Flamborough  Selwicks Bay

...ving  B1255  **FLAMBOROUGH
HEAD**
B1250

Sewerby
Hall &
Gardens

B1253  Boynton  Bondville
Miniature Village

Rudston  Monolith  Bessingby  **Bridlington**

Carnaby  Hilderthorpe  BRIDLINGTON
BAY

Haisthorpe  A1038
Thornholme

Kilham  Bridlington

Burton Agnes  A165  Norman
Manor
House

...on Parva  12  Harpham

A614  Lowthorpe  Fraisthorpe

Nafferton  Gransmoor

Great Kelk  Lissett  Barmston

...d  B1242  15

Gembling

Wansford  16  Ulrome

Foston on  Skipsea
the Wolds  Castle  Skipsea

...Skerne  B1249

Brigham  Beeford

North
Frodingham

G  **H**  A165  **126**  **J**  Atwick  **K**  **L**  **M**

Dunning...

Bewholme

B1242

Honeysuckle...

4

5

6

7

8

A    B    C    D    E    F

1

147

2

3

4

5

6

7

128

8

A    B    C    D    E    F

Greysouceronby
Crosby
Gil
Senhouse
River Ellen
Maryport
Dearham
Taller
Flimby
Broughton Moor
Brideki
Standingstone
Dovenby
Great Broughton
Papcastle
Camerton
Brigham
Seaton
Great Clifton
Greysouthen
Stainburn
Little Clifton
Eaglesfield
Workington
Mossbay
Deanscales
Westfield
High Harrington
Salterbeck
Branthwaite
Dean
Harrington
Pardshaw
Ullock
Distington
Mockerkin
Common End
Gilgarran
Lowswate
Lowca
Howgate
Lamplugh
Parton
Low Moresby
Asby
Arlecdon
Whitehaven
Harras
Rowrah
Kirkland
Kells
Hensingham
High Leys
Saltom Bay
Frizington
Ennerdale Bridge
Ennerd Wate
Sandwith
Mirehouse
Cleator Moor
Rottington
Cleator
LANK RIGG
St Bees Head
Bigrigg
Egremont
LAK
St Bees Head Heritage Coast
St Bees
Worm Gill
Thornhill
Haile
River Bleng
Nethertown
Beckermet
Calder Bridge
Wellington
Sellafield Station
Gosforth
Sante
Seascale
Halsenna Moor
Drigg
Holmrook
Ravenglass
Roman Bath House
Muncaster C & Owl Centr
Wabert
Hycemoor
Selker Bay
Bootle

0 1 2 3 4 miles
0 1 2 3 4 5 kilometres

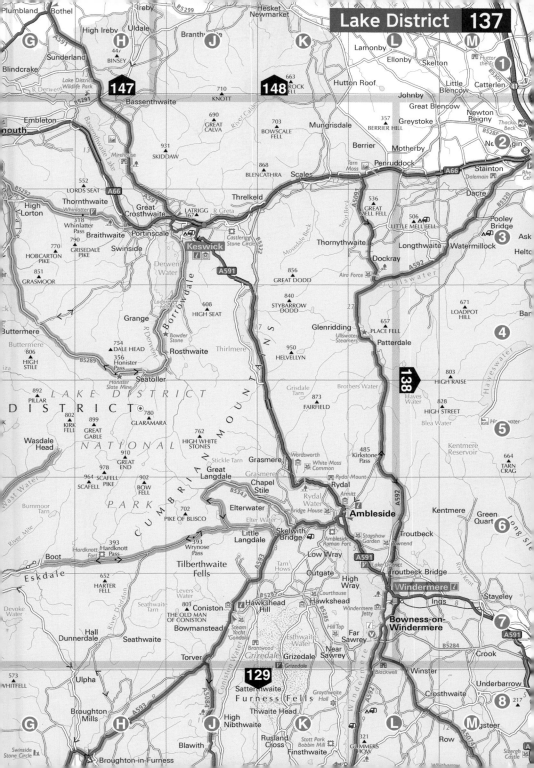

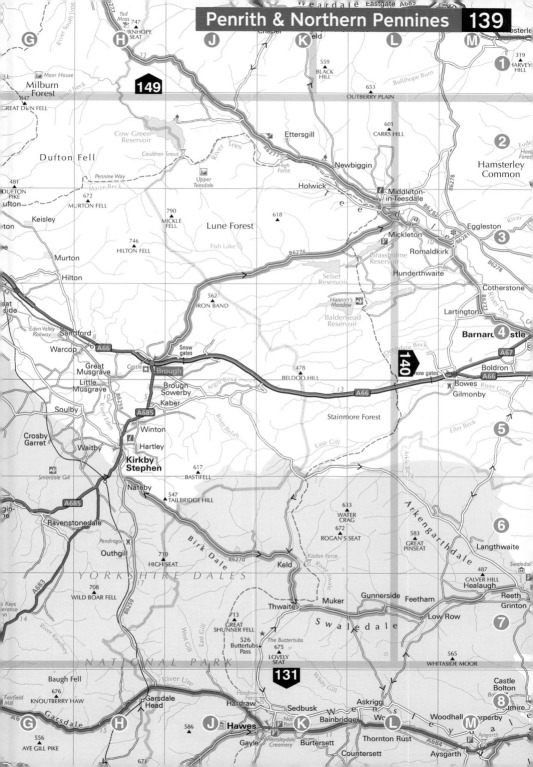

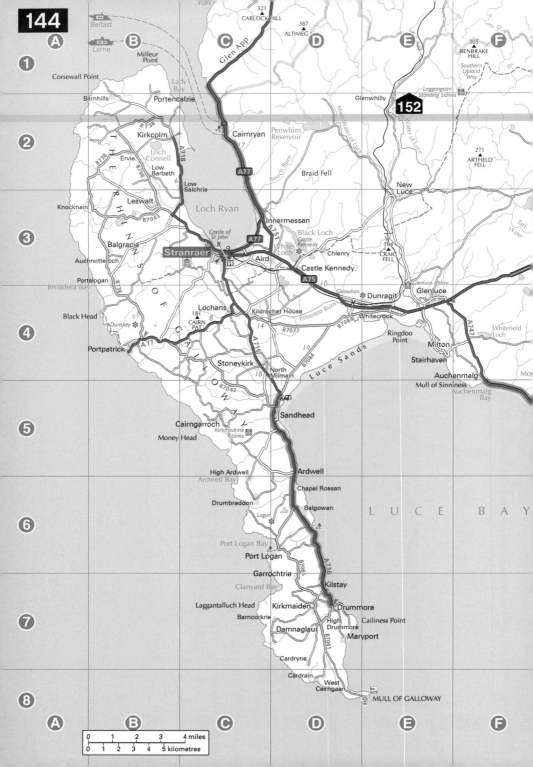

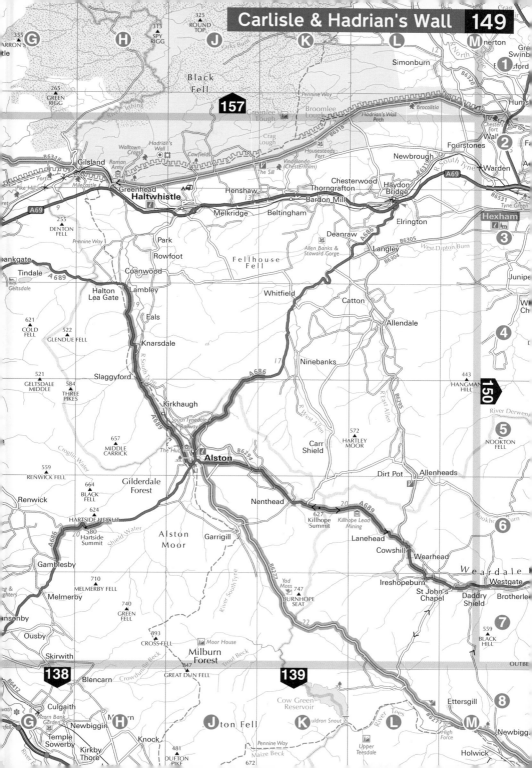

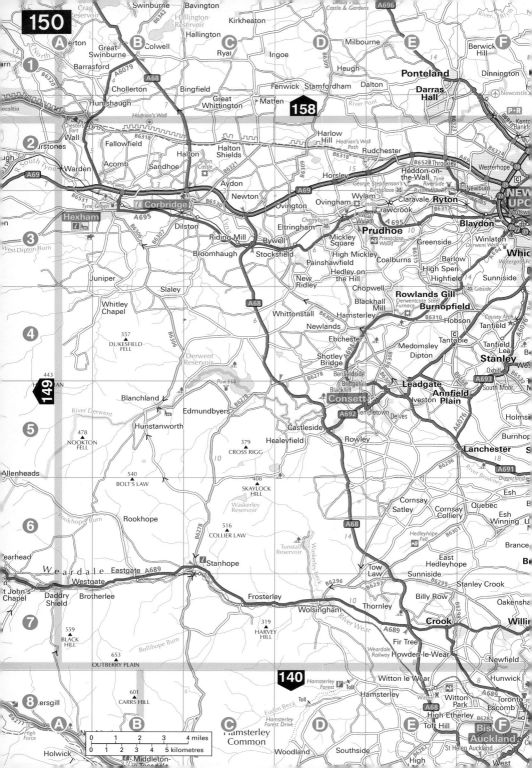

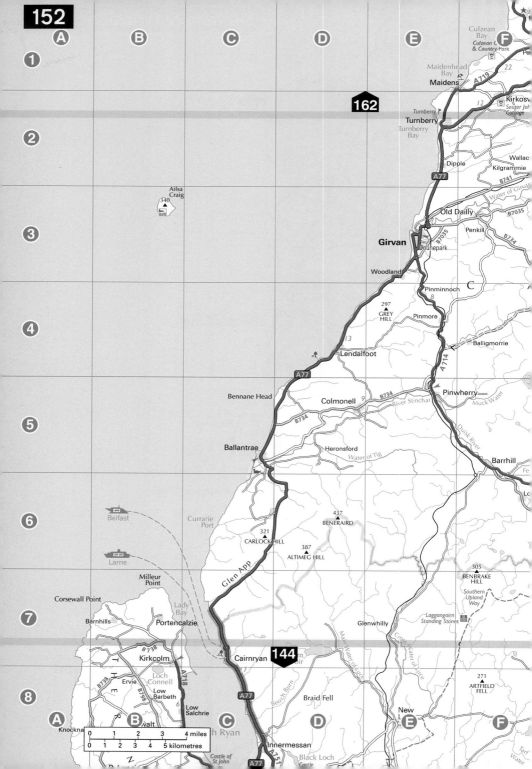

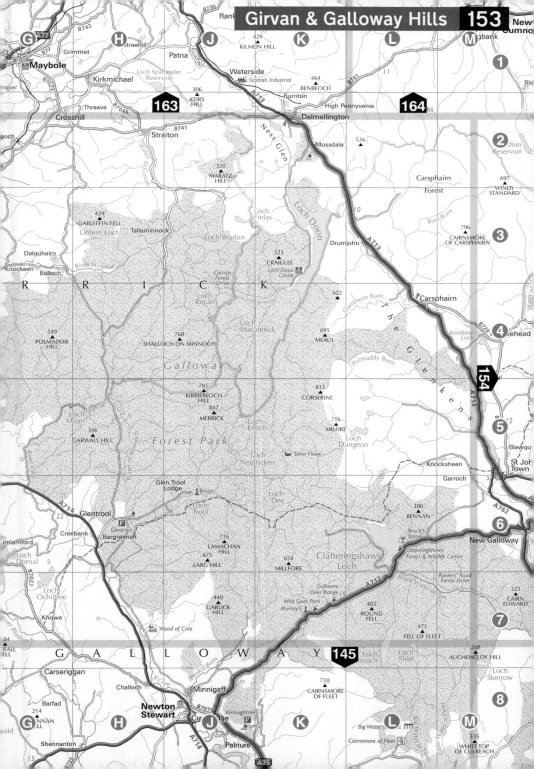

New Cumno

**G** 477

**H** treehill

Grimmet

B742

B730

Rank

**J**

Patna

B741

**K**

429
KILMEIN HILL

**L**

**M** gbank

**1**

Maybole

Kirkmichael

Loch Spallander Reservoir

Waterside

Scottish Industrial

464
BENBEOCH

Bl

163

306
KEIRS HILL

Burnton

High Pennyvenie

164

LL

Threave

B7045

Crosshill

Straiton

B741

Loch Doon

536

Mossdale

2 fton Reservoir

Dalmellington

A713

Carsphairn Forest

697
WINDY STANDARD

320
MARATZ HILL

Loch Finlas

Loch Doon

Bow Burn

796
CAIRNSMORE OF CARSPHAIRN

3

429
GARLEFFIN FELL

Linfern Loch

Tallaminnock

Loch Bradan

523
CRAIGLEE

Loch Doon Castle

Drumjohn

Garryhorn Burn

Carsphairn

The

B729

Kendoon Loch

gehead

4

Dalquhairn

Knockeen

Balloch

River Stinchar

549
POLMADDIE HILL

768
SHALLOCH ON MINNOCH

Loch Recar

622

695
MEAUL

Polmaddy Burn

Glenkens

154

A713

9

B

5

12

**R   R   I   C   K**

Galloway

Loch Macaterick

781
KIRRIEREOCH HILL

842
MERRICK

813
CORSERINE

716
MILFIRE

Blawqu

St Joh Town

346
GARWALL HILL

Loch Moan

Forest Park

Loch Enoch

Loch Neldricken

Loch Dungeon

Silver Flowe

Knocksheen

Garroch

5

6

Glen Trool Lodge

Bruce

Loch Trool

Loch Dee

380
BENNAN

Bruce's Stone

A762

Glentrool

Creebank

A714

22

Glentrool
Bargrennan

716
LAMACHAN HILL

Clatteringshaws Loch

Clatteringshaws Forest & Wildlife Centre

New Galloway

6

lamford

Loch Dornal

675
LARG HILL

654
MILLFORE

Raiders' Road Forest Drive

325
CAIRN EDWARD

B7027

Loch Ochiltree

Knowe

440
GARLICK HILL

Galloway Deer Range

Wild Goat Park

Murray's

Black Water of Dee

402
ROUND FELL

471
FELL OF FLEET

7

84
RALL ELL

Wood of Cree

A712

Loch innoch

Loch Fleet

208
AUCHENCLOY HILL

Loch Skerrow

**G   A   L   L   O   W   O   Y**

145

Carseriggan

Challoch

R Cree

Minnigaff

710
CAIRNSMORE OF FLEET

8

214
NNAN LL

**G**

Barfad

Newton Stewart

**H**

B7079

Cre

**J** ge

Kirroughtree

Big Water o

**K**

Cairnsmore of Fleet

**L**

**M**

335
WHITE TOP OF CULREACH

Shennanton

A714

Palnure

A75

15

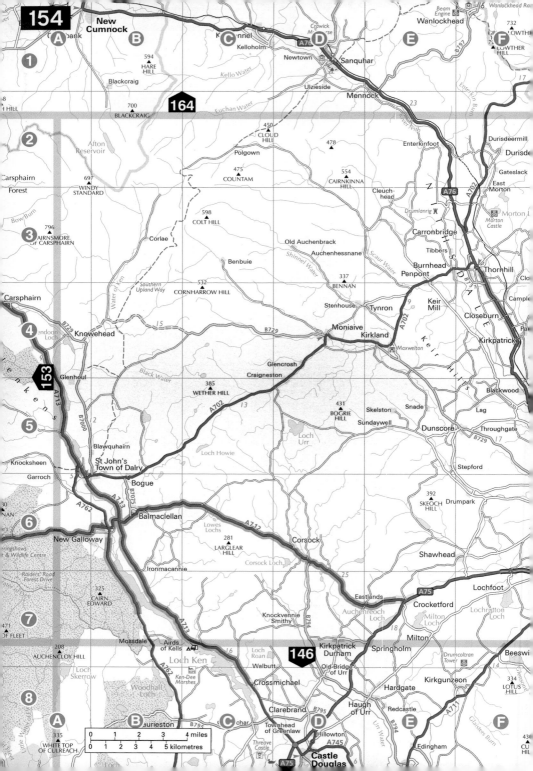

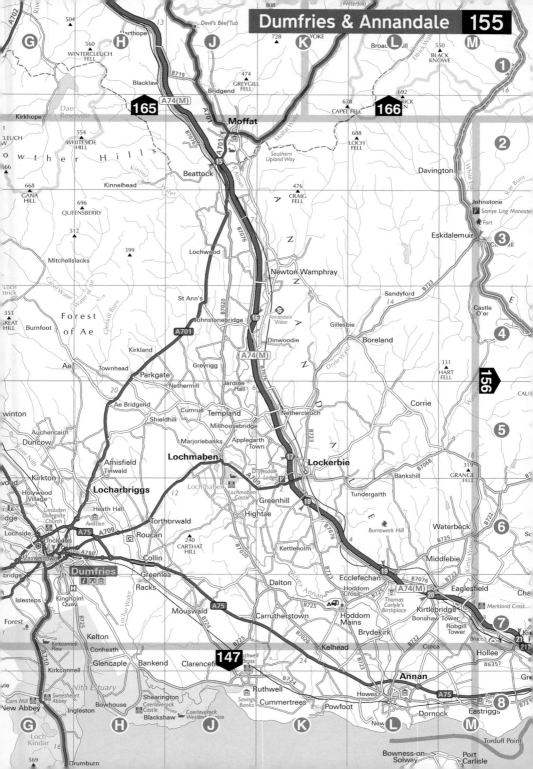

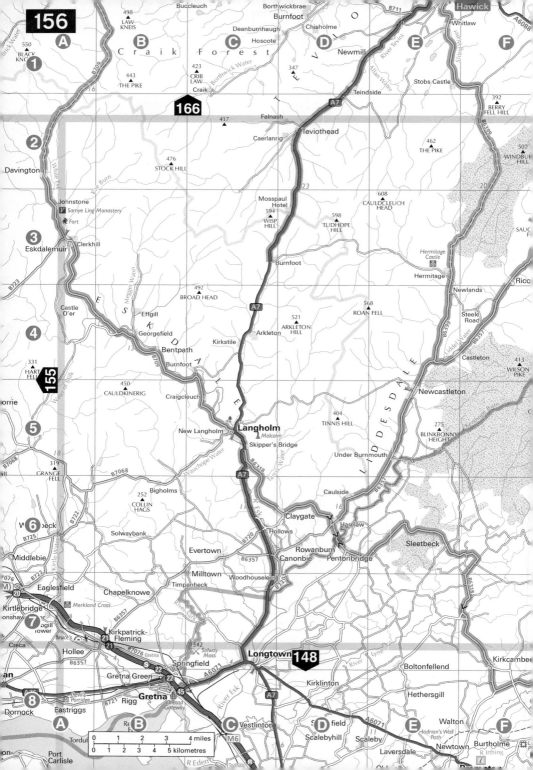

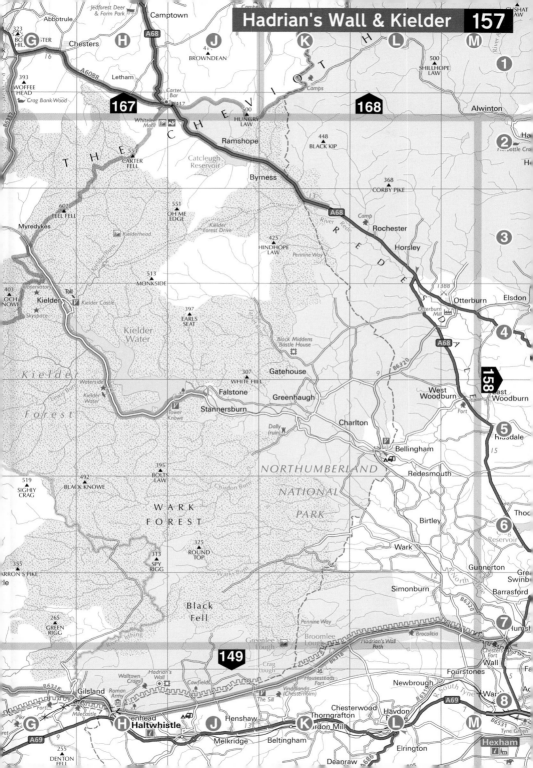

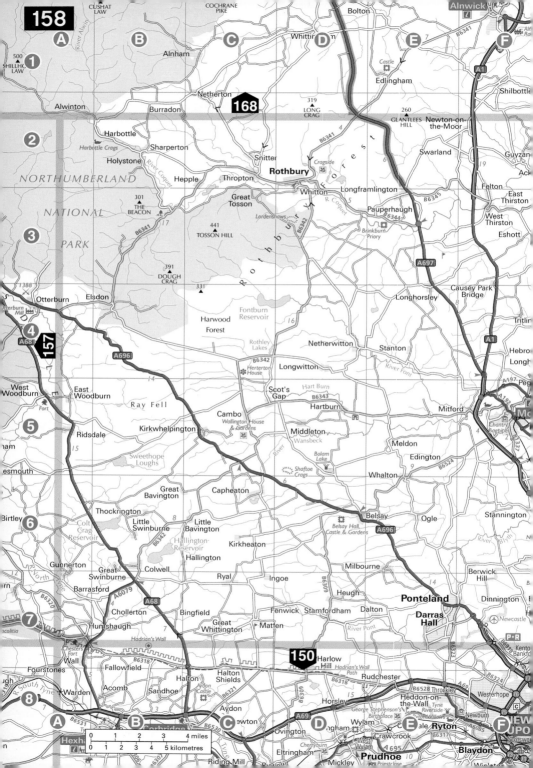

Rubha Mòr

BEINN SHOLUM

Eilean
a' Chùirn

Port Ellen - Kennacraig

165
MAOL BUIDHE

T H E   O A

Port
Ellen

A846

Ardbeg

Rubha na
Gainmhich

Lagavulin

Laphroaig

Texa

I S L A Y

Lower
Killeyan

Risabus

Kinnabus
American

Loch
Kinnabus

MULL
OF OA

Ballycastle
(Apr-Sept)

Rubha nan Leacan

Earad

M
KIN

0   1   2   3   4 miles
0   1   2   3   4   5 kilometres

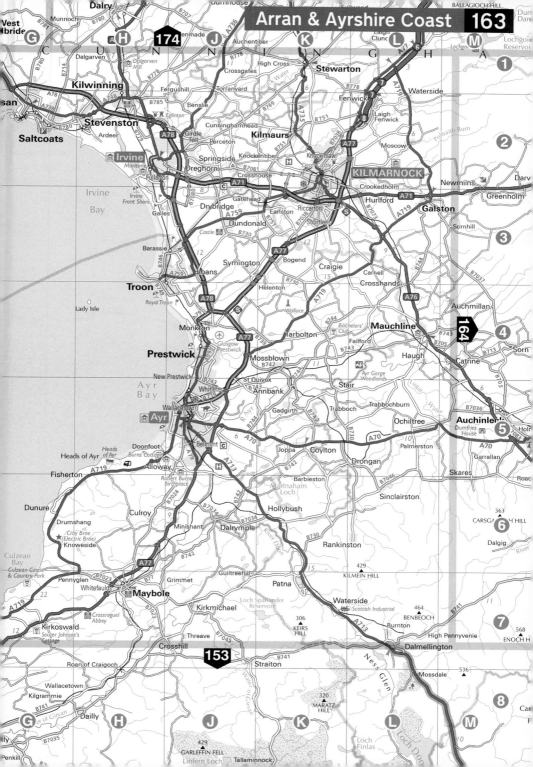

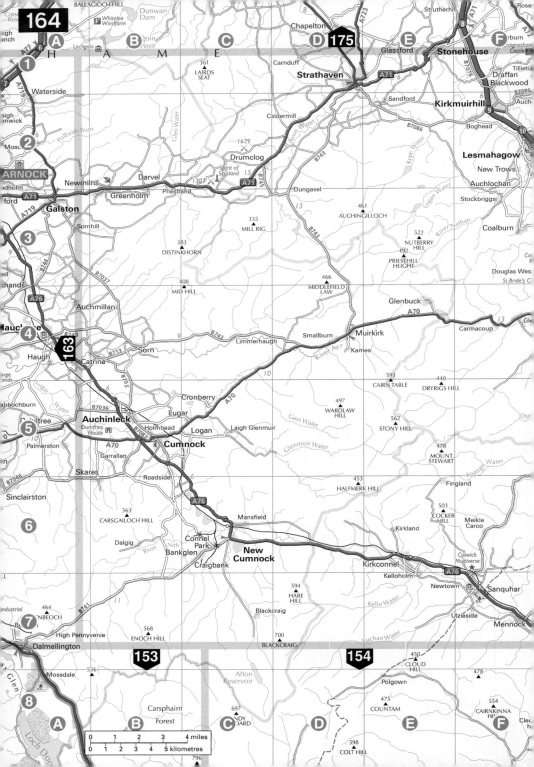

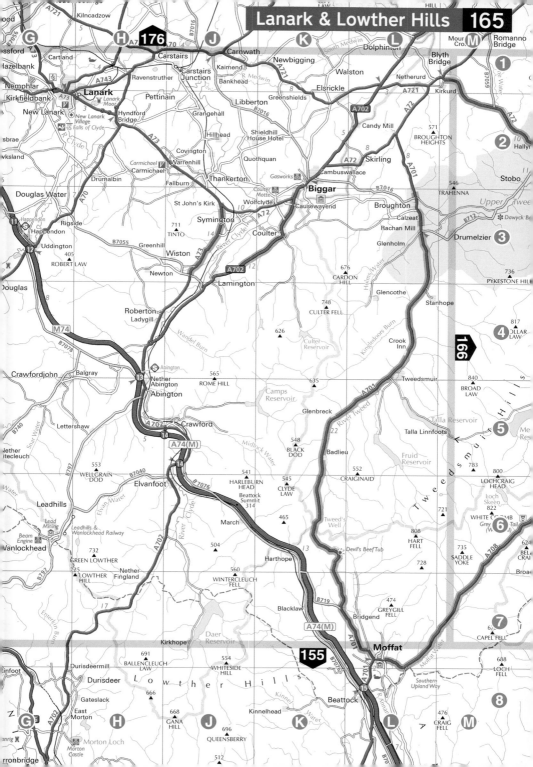

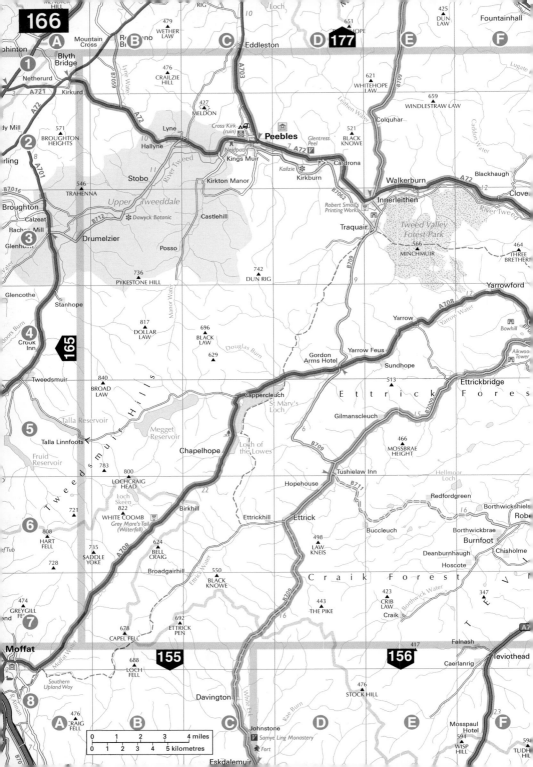

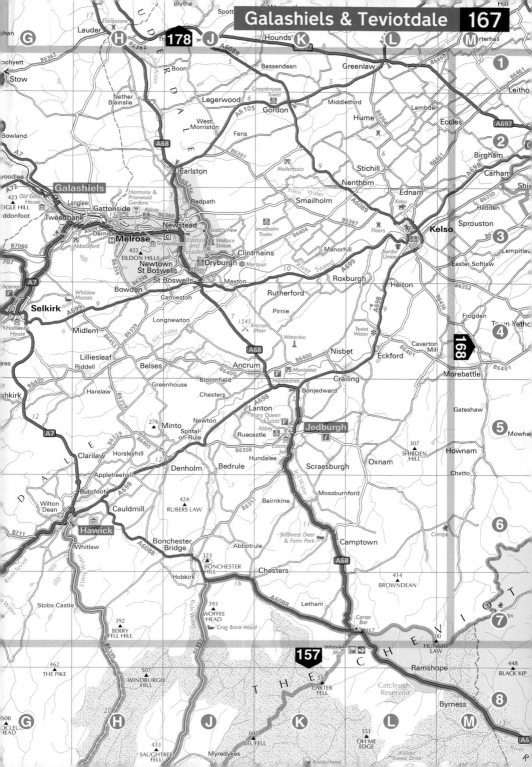

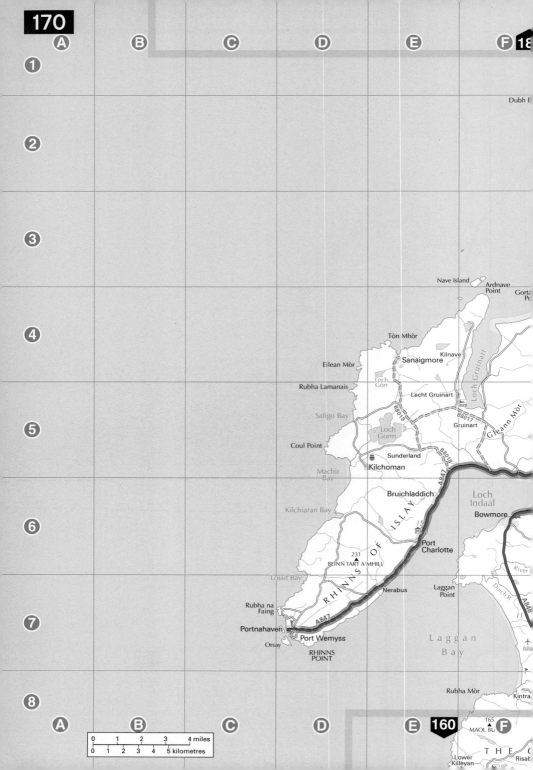

1

2

3

Dubh E

Nave Island    Ardnave
                Point
              Gorta
                Po

4    Tòn Mhòr          Kilnave
                    Sanaigmore

Eilean Mòr        Loch
                  Gorr

Rubha Lamanais        Lecht Gruinart

Saligo Bay                    B8017    Gruinart

5                Loch
                 Gorm

Coul Point                B8018

Machir              Sunderland
Bay                 Kilchoman

            Bruichladdich        Loch
                                 Indaal
Kilchiaran Bay                   Bowmore

6                                A847
                         Port
                         Charlotte

        231                           River
7  BEINN TART A'MHILL
                        Nerabus       Duich R.    A846

Lossit Bay                      Laggan
                                Point
Rubha na
Faing

Portnahaven                           Laggan
            Port Wemyss              Bay
Orsay
      RHINNS
      POINT

8
                                 Rubha Mòr        Kintra

165
MAOL BU    F

0   1   2   3   4 miles
0  1  2  3  4  5 kilometres

THE
Lower
Killeyan       Risat

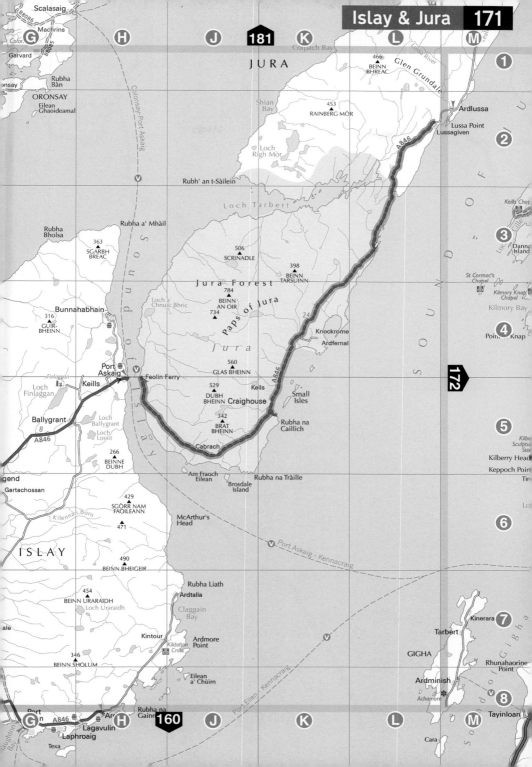

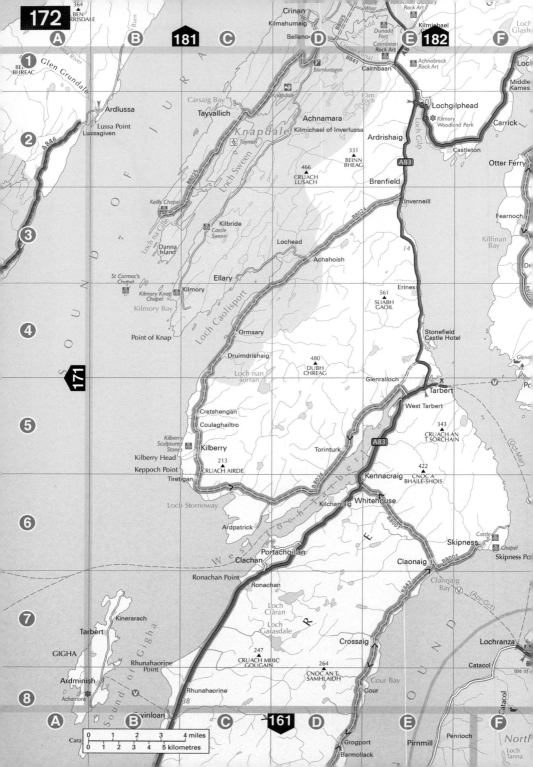

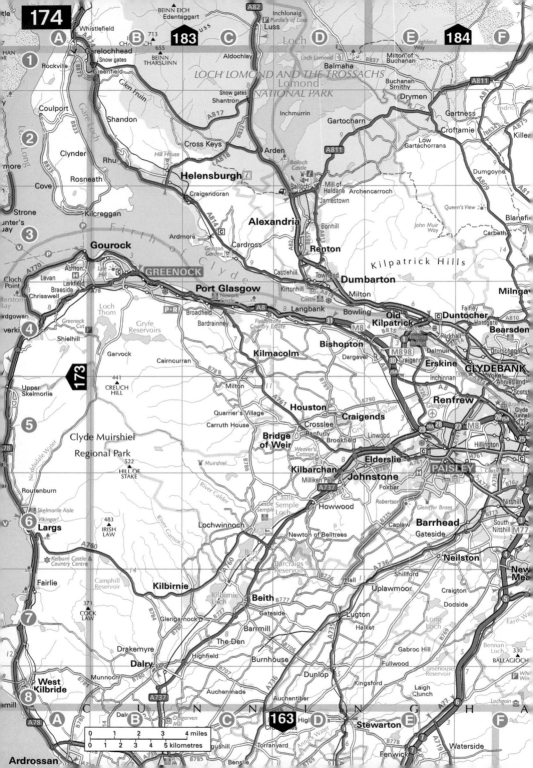

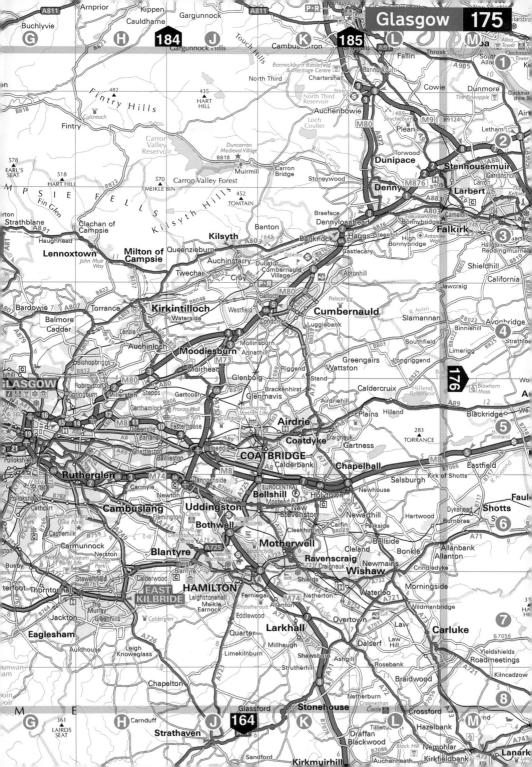

G  H  J  K  L  M

1

2

3

4

Reed
Point
Cove      Pease      Siccar
          Bay        Point        Fast Castle Head
spath

A1      A1107                                    ST ABB'S HEAD
     Pease Dean                196
                            BROWN
                            RIG      Coldingham
                                     Loch
Southern                                           St Abbs
Upland Way
Butterdean      Grantshouse    Coldingham         Coldingham
                                                   Bay

Water                          Houndwood                        Eyemouth
                        21                    A1107
kwood                          Heugh          22
                               Head    Cairncross
           262
roch    14   HORSELEY HILL              A1      B6355
                               Reston              Burnmouth
                B6438          Ayton

           Marygold                              Lamberton
A6112      Lintlaw
           Preston                    B6355                  Marshall Meadows Bay
           B6355                                   North Northumberland
ill    Cumledge    B6355    Chirnside    Foulden        Heritage Coast
B6365  Edrom Church                                 1333
       Edrom      15    Chirnsidebridge    Foulden  X
    Manderston                    Edington  Whiteadder Water  Tithe Barn
Duns            Broadhaugh               Hutton    A6105    Berwick-upon-Tweed
                         Allanton                          Barracks &
           Blackadder    B6437           Paxton    Castle   Main Guard
A6105                                              Town
           Whitsome    B6460    Hilton    B6461    Ramparts
Nisbet                                             Tweedmouth  Spital
Hill       Sinclair's                  Paxton                  Huds
           Hill                                                Head
A6112      6    B6437    Horndean    Horncliffe           Scremerston
                         Ladykirk           Murton
    Swinton    B6470    Norham    A698  Thornton    A1    Cheswick
rterhall                              B6394
G      Upsettlington    **168**          Haggerston
       Simprim              J         K    Ancroft    L    M
Leitholm                                              Causeway
                                                      flooded at
                                                      high tide

5

6

7

8

Bac Mòr or Dutchman's Cap

eag

Little Colonsay

Staffa

Fingal's

*Loch na Keal*
*Isle of Mull*

Inch Kenneth
Inchkenneth Chapel
(ruin)

491
CREACH BHEINN

Fossil Tree

Burg

LOC

Rubha nan Cearc

Iona Abbey
& Nunnery

IONA

Baile Mòr

MacLean's Cross

P Fionnphort

Kintra

Aridhglas

St Columba
Exhibition
Centre

Loch na
Lathaich

A849

Bunessan

Loch Assapol

CRU

ROSS OF MULL

Soa Island

Erraid

Ardchiavaig

Uisken

'Rubh'
Ardalanish

Rubh
Brài

Torran Rocks

Eilean
Dubh

Kiloran Bay

Rubh'

143
CARNAN
EOIN

COLONSAY

Kiloran

Kilchattan

Scalasaig

B8086

B8085

Machrins

Colonsay

Garh

Oronsay

Rubha
Bàn

Dubh Eilean

0　1　2　3　4 miles
0　1　2　3　4　5 kilometres

ISLE

OF

MULL

G
H
190
J
K
L
M
1

Eorsa

Mausoleum

NAN LUS

Loch Na Keal

BEINN A'GRAIG

BB035

BEINN MHEADHO.

766
DUN DA
GHAOITHE

Craignure

Duart
Bay
Duart
Point
Duart
Torosay

2

966
BEN
MORE

704
CRUACHAN
DEARG

A849

17

Lochdonhead
Lochdon

Gorsten

Loch Don

Grass Point

KERRER

Strathcoil

Aird of
Kinloch

A849

Glen More

Loch
Fuaran

698
BEN CREACH

247
CARN
BAN

Gylen

3

Tiroran

Pennycross

Pennyghael

717
BEN
BUIE

Loch Spelve

Croggan

Rubha Seanach

idain

14

Leidle Water

503
BEINN NA
CROISE

Lochbuie

Loch
Uisg

337
MAOL
BAN

376
BEINN
CHREAGACH

Carsaig

Loch Buie

Rubha
Dubh

377
DRUIM
FADA

Malcolm's
Point

FIRTH

OF

LORNE

Insh
Island

Clachan

B844

Clachan Seil
SEIL

4

Ellenabeich

Easdale

Balvicar

Ardmaddy

Folk

Colonsay–Oban

Cuan

Seil Sound

182

Garbh Eileach

Eilean
Dubh Mòr

LUING

Cullipool

Torsa

Degnish

Loch Melfo

5

Arduaine
Garden

Arduaine

GARVELLACHS
Monastery &
Beehive Cells

Eileach
an Naoimh

LUNGA

Toberonochy

Sound of Luing

SHUNA

Shuna Sound

Craobh
Haven

Craigdh

Scarba–Lunga
and the
Garvellachs

Shuna
Point

SCARBA

448
CRUACH SCARBA

Ardfe

6

Kin

En Mh

En R

Gulf of Corryvreckan

Aird

Craignish Point

Island
Macaskin

lockavull
wood
cles

7

Glengarrisdale
Bay

295
CRUACH NA
SEILCHEIG

Ri Cruin
Poltallo

Glendebadel Bay

Loch Crinan

JURA

364
BEN
GARRISDALE

Leidi Burn

Crinan

Kilmahumaig

Bellanoch

8

Corpach Bay

Fessa River

B841

Barnluasgan

G
H
171
J
len Grundale
466
BEINN
BHREAC
K
L
172
M

Shian

453

Carsaig Bay

Knapdale

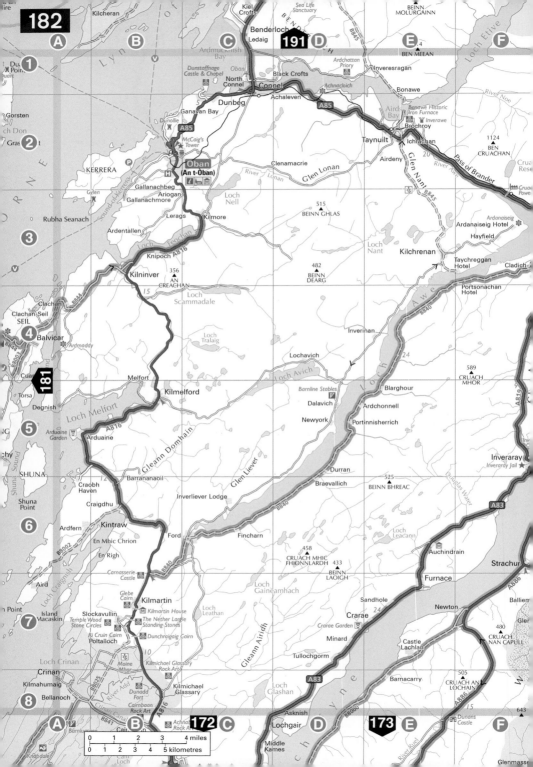

A  B  C  D  E  F

1

2

3

4

Arnat
Grishipoll
Clabhach
Hogh Bay  Ballyhaugh
Totronald
Coll
Bàgh a' Chaisteil
(Castlebay)  Feall  Arileod  Acha
5  Bay
Uig

Calgary Point  Crossapol
Bay  Rubha
Fasachd
Gunna

Rubha Port  Caoles  Rubha Dubh
Bhiosd  Clachan  B8069
Mor  Balephetrish  Ruaig
Loch  Bay  B8069
6  Hough  Bhasapoll
Bay  Ballevullin  Cornoigmore  Kenovay  Gott
Kilkenneth  Tiree  Bay
Moss  Scarinish
Middleton  Heylipoll  B8065
B8065  Crossapol  TIREE
Barrapoll  B8065
Loch a'  Hynish Bay
Phuill  B8067  Balemartine
Rinn  Mannal
Thorbhais  Balephuil
7  Bay  Hynish

8

A  B  C  D  E  F

0  1  2  3  4 miles
0  1  2  3  4  5 kilometres

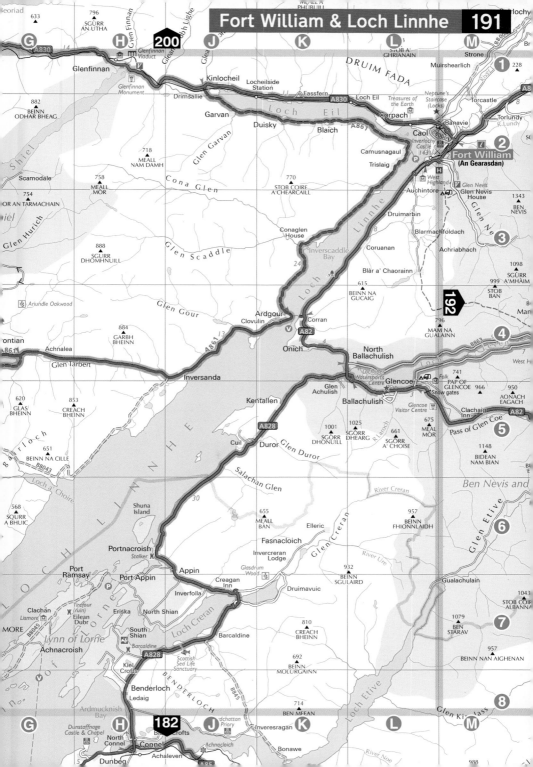

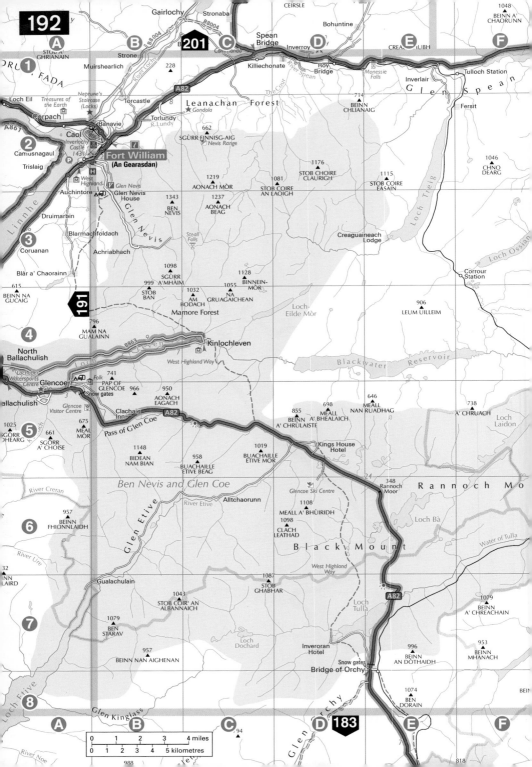

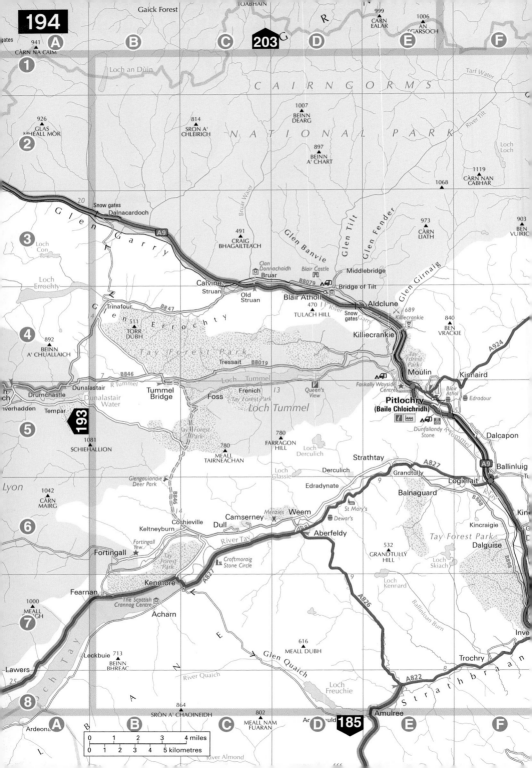

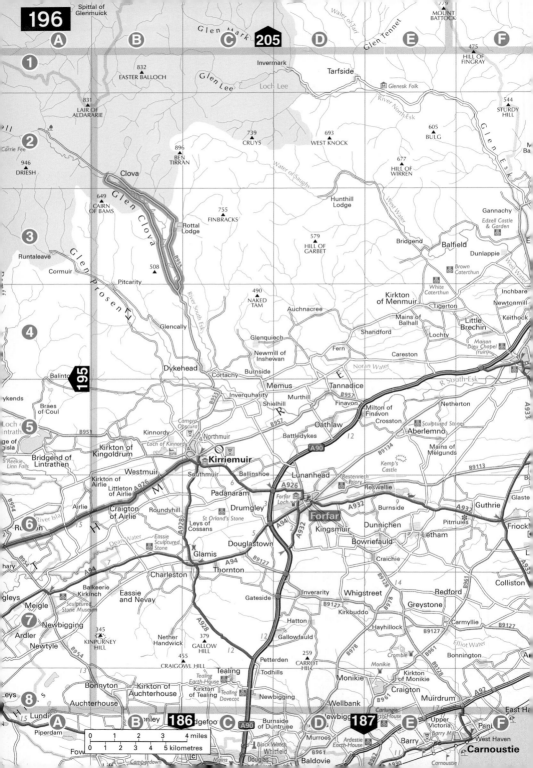

**A** **B** **C** **D** **E** **F**

1

2

3

4

5

6

7

8

Bay    Talisker
Minginish
en Eynort
Gru
Brittle
Forest
147
BEINN
BHREAC
Loch Eynort
434
AN CRUACHIN
Glenbrittle
Bualintur
Loch Brittle
CEA
Rubha an Dùnain

Loch Baghasdail
(Lochboisdale)
CU

CANNA
210
CÀRN A' GHAILL
A'Chill
Garrisdale Point
Canna
Harbour
Kilmory
Bay
Rubha
Shamhnan
Insir
Sanday
Sound of Canna
302
MULLACH
MÒR
570
ORVAL
A' Bhrideanach
Kinloch
Loch
Oigh-sgeir
RÙM
810
ASKIVAL
Harris
Bay
763
SGÙRR NAN
GILLEAN
The Small Isles
Rubha nam
Meirleach
Sound o
S

Eilean
nan Each
ML

**A** **B** **C** **D** **E** **F**

Port M

0   1   2   3   4 miles
0  1  2  3  4  5 kilometres

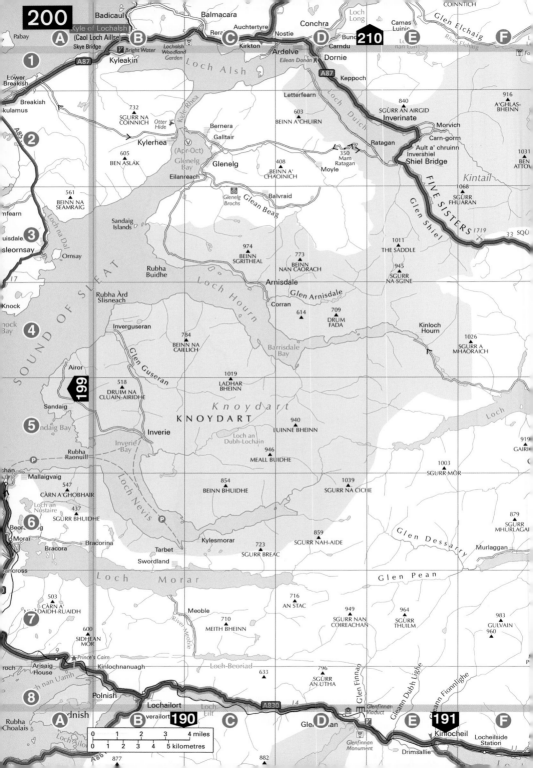

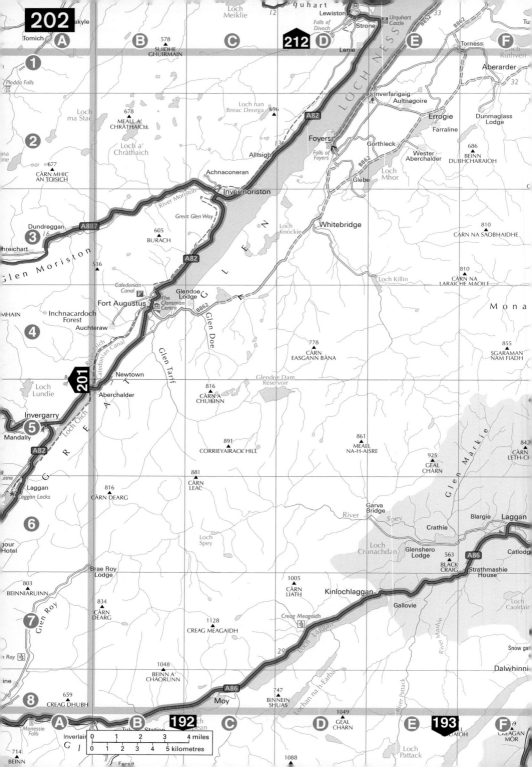

G H 213 J K L M

CARN GLAC 603
AN FICH
Croact

707
CÀRN NA
SAOBHAIDH

805
BEINN
BHREAC MHÒR

Coignafearn

Strathdearn

BEN
BHLEAC

Garbole

Clune

Tomatin
Tomatin
Lodge

Findhorn Viaduct

405
Slochd
Summit

A9

River Findhorn

Dalnahaitnach

617
CÀRN PHRÌS
MHÒIR

750
CARN DUH'
IC AN-DEÒIR

River Dulnain

790
CÀRN COIRE
NA H-EASGAINN

745
CNOC
FRAING

813
CALPA
MÒR

729
CAIRN
DULNAN

824
GEAL-CHÀRN MÒR

878
CÀRN AN
FHREICEADAIN

928
A CHAILLEACH

Raitts Burn

Highland
Wildlife Park

Kincraig

Loch
Alvie

A9

B9152

Loch an
Eilean

Kingussie
Pitmain
Ruthven
Newtonmore
(Baile Ur an t-Sleibh)

Farr
Lynchat
Insh
Inveruglass
Drumguish

Insh Marshes
Ruthven
Barracks

Highland
Folk

Ralia

A9

A86

Glentruim

Etteridge

593
GARBH-
MHEALL MÒR

768
MEALLACH
MHÒR

627
MEALL
BUIDHE

857
CÀRN
DEARG MÒR

CAIRNGORMS

NATIONAL PARK

Loch na
Cuaich

A9

898
BAGHA-
CLOICHE

Loch an
t-Seilich

910
LEATHAD AN
TOABHAIN

Gaick Forest

River Tromie

Glen Feshie

River Feshie

Glenfeshie Forest

Auchlean

1108
SGÒR AN
DUBH MÒR

1049
CÀRN
BAN MÒR

Loch
Einich

1017
MULLACH CLACH
A BHLÀIR

River Eidart

999
CÀRN
EALAR

1006
AN
SGARSOCH

941
CÀRN NA CAIM

G H an Dùin J 194 K L M

Duthil
Skye
of Curr

A938

Carrbridge
Bogroy
Auchterblair

Landmark Forest
Adventure Park

Drumuillie

Kinveachy

B9153

Boat of
Garten

Loch
Garten

Osprey
Centre

Strathspey
Railway

Cairngorm

Aviemore

Craigellachie

Inverdruie

Rothiemurchus

Coylumbridge

River Spey

B970

Glenmore
Forest Park

MEALL A' BHUACH
809

Glenmore
Loch
Morlich

Reindeer
Centre

Glenmore Lodge

Cairngorm
Ski Area

Rothiemurchus
Lodge

Glen More

Loch an
Eilean

Feshiebridge
Lagganlia

Invereshie &
Inshriach

204

CAIRNGORM

1295
BRAERIACH

1309
BEN
MACDHUI

1293
CAIRN
TOUL

1157
BEINN
BHROTAIN

Lairig Ghru

River Dee

Glen Dee

GRAMPIAN

Nethy
Bridge

A95

Straanruie

B970

712 Aviemore

1 2 3 4 5 6 7 8

Achnahanne

13

Loch
an

1007

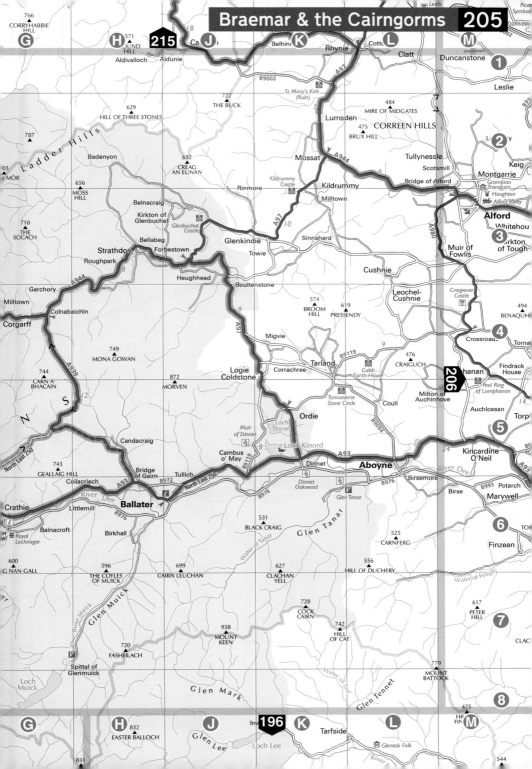

**G** 766 CORRYHABBIE HILL

**H** UND HILL 571

**215**

Ca J

**J**

Aldivalloch   Aldunie

Belhini

**K**

Rhynie   Cott

**L**

Clatt   Clatt

Duncanstone

**M**

**1**

B9002

Leslie

A97

722 THE BUCK

St. Mary's Kirk (Ruin)

484 MIRE OF MIDGATES

L y

**2**

629 HILL OF THREE STONES

787

Lumsden

CORREEN HILLS

475 BRUX HILL

Keig

Montgarrie

*Ladder Hills*

Badenyon

Mossat

A944   6

Tullynessle

Scotsmill

Grampian Transport

03 MÒR

656 MOSS HILL

632 CREAG AN EUNAN

Rinmore

Kildrummy Castle

A97

Kildrummy

Milltown

Bridge of Alford

Haughton

Alford Valley

**3**

718 THE SOCACH

Belnacraig

Kirkton of Glenbuchat

Glenbuchat Castle

Glenkindie

Towie

Sinnahard

Cushnie

**Alford**

Whitehou

A980

Muir of Fowlis

irkton of Tough

Strathdon

Bellabeg   Forbestown

Roughpark

Heughhead

10

A97

Boultenstone

Garchory

A944

8

Leochel-Cushnie

Craigievar Castle

494 BENAQUH

Milltown

Colnabaichin

9

574 BROOM HILL

619 PRESSENDY

Crossroad

hanan

Torna

**4**

Corgarff

A939

749 MONA GOWAN

Migvie

476 CRAIGUCH

B9119

9

Findrack House

N

744 CARN A' BHACAIN

S

872 MORVEN

Logie Coldstone

Corrachree

Tarland

Culsh Earth-House

Tomnaverie Stone Circle

Milton of Auchinhove

Peel Ring of Lumphanan

**206**

Auchlossan

Torp

14

**5**

12

Candacraig

Muir of Dinnet

Loch Davan

Ordie

Coull

B9094

Kincardine O'Neil

743 GEALLAIG HILL

Cambus o' May

Loch Kinord

A93

24

Coilacriech

Bridge of Gairn

Tullich

Dinnet

**Aboyne**

*River Dee*

**North East 250**

A93

B972

B9119

Birsemore

B976

B993 Potarch

Crathie

*River Dee*

Littlelmill

**Ballater**

**North East 250**

Dinnet Oakwood

Glen Tanar

Birse

Marywell

**6**

TO

al Royal Lochnagar

Balnacroft

Birkhall

B976

531 BLACK CRAIG

Glen Tanar

525 CARNFERG

Finzean

600 G NAN GALL

596 THE COYLES OF MUICK

Glen Muick

699 CAIRN LEUCHAN

627 CLACHAN YELL

556 HILL OF DUCHERY

*Water of Feugh*

617 PETER HILL

CLAC

**7**

*River Muick*

*Glen Muick*

728 COCK CAIRN

742 HILL OF CAT

Water of Tanar

720 FASHEILACH

938 MOUNT KEEN

779 MOUNT BATTOCK

**8**

Spittal of Glenmuick

Loch Muick

Glen Mark

Glen Tennet

475 HI FIN

**M**

Water of Aa

**G**

832 EASTER BALLOCH

**H**

**196**

Inv

**J**

Glen Lee

Loch Lee

Tarfside

**K**

Glenesk Folk

**L**

544

831

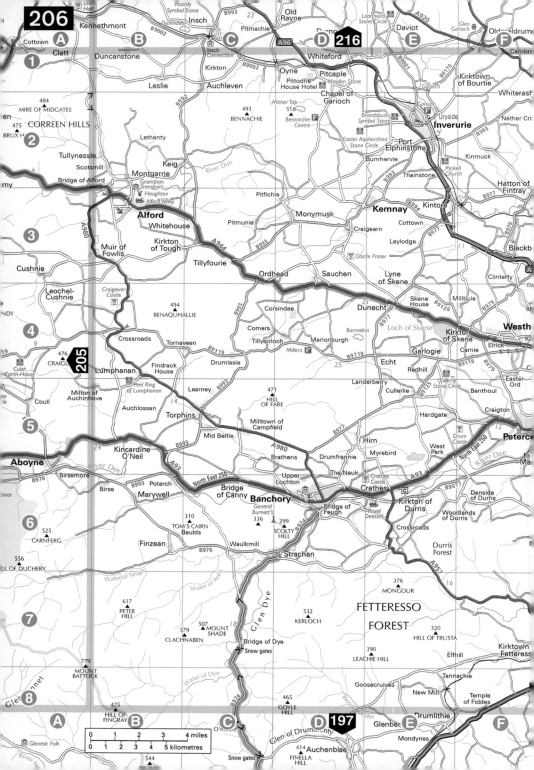

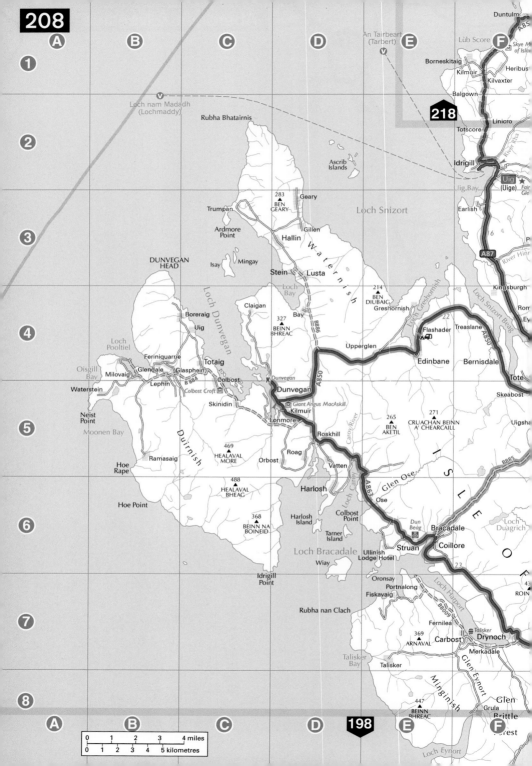

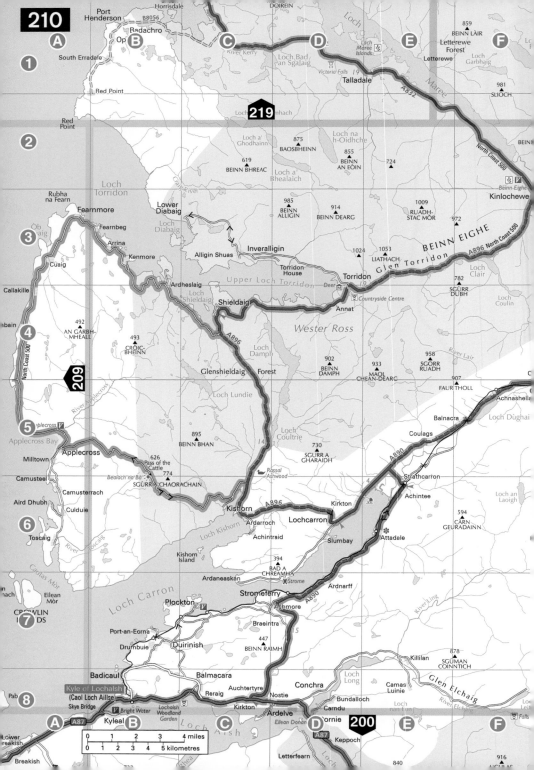

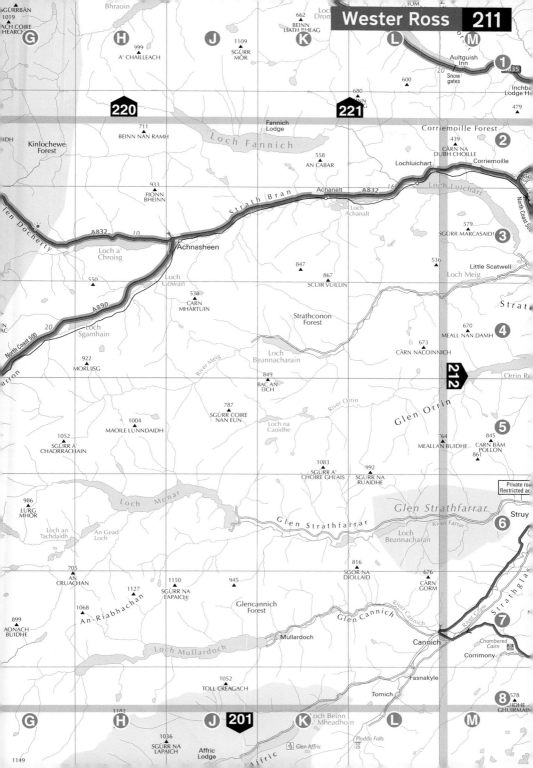

**220**

**221**

**212**

**201**

**G** | **H** | **J** | **K** | **L** | **M**

SGÙRRBÀN
1019
ACH COIRE
HEARCH

Bhraoin

IÓM

Loch
Drom

BEINN
LIATH BHEAG

662

INN
NG

680

Aultguish
Inn

Snow
gates

A' CHAILLEACH
999

SGÙRR
MÒR
1109

600

20

835

Inchba
Lodge H

479

Loch Fannich

Fannich
Lodge

Corriemoille Forest

CÀRN NA
DUBH CHOILLE
439

Corriemoille

Kinlochewe
Forest

IDH

BEINN NAN RAMH
711

AN CABAR
558

Lochluichart

Loch Luichart

North Coast 50

Strath Bran

Achanalt

A832

16

SGÙRR MARCASAID
579

FIONN
BHEINN
933

Loch
Achanalt

Ten Docherty

A832

1.0

Loch a'
Chroisg

Achnasheen

Loch
Gowan

536

Little Scatwell

Loch Meig

550

847

867
SCUIR VUILLIN

Stra

A890

CARN
MHÀRTUIN
538

Strathconon
Forest

MEALL NAN DAMH
670

North Coast 500

20

Loch
Sgamhain

Loch
Beannacharain

CÀRN NACOINNICH
673

MORUISG
922

River Meig

BAC AN
EICH
849

River Orrin

Glen Orrin

**212**

Orrin Re

arron

SGÙRR COIRE
NAN EUN
787

Loch na
Caoidhe

MAOILE LÙNNDAIDH
1004

MEALLAN BUIDHE
764

CÀRN BÀN
POLLON
845
861

SGÙRR A'
CHAORRACHAIN
1052

SGÙRR A'
CHOIRE GHLAIS
1083

SGÙRR NA
RUAIDHE
992

Private roa
Restricted ac

LURG
MHOR
986

Loch Monar

Glen Strathfarrar

Glen Strathfarrar

Loch an
Tachdaidh

An Gead
Loch

Loch
Beannacharan

River Farrar

Struy

**6**

AN
CRUACHAN
705

SGÙRR NA
LAPAICH
1150

945

SGOR NA
DIOLLAID
816

CÀRN
GORM
676

Strathglas

An-Riabhachan
1127

An-Riabhachan

AONACH
BUIDHE
899

1068

Glencannich
Forest

Glen Cannich

River Cannich

River Glass

Corrimony

**7**

Chambered
Cairn

Loch Mullardoch

Mullardoch

Cannich

Fasnakyle

TOLL CREAGACH
1052

Tomich

JIDHE
GHUIRMAIN
578

**8**

**G** | **H** | **J** | **K** | **L** | **M**

1182

**201**

1036
SGÙRR NA
LAPAICH

Affric
Lodge

Loch Beinn
a' Mheadhoin

Glen Affric

Plodda
Falls

1149

Affric

1 | 2 | 3 | 4 | 5 | 6 | 7 | 8

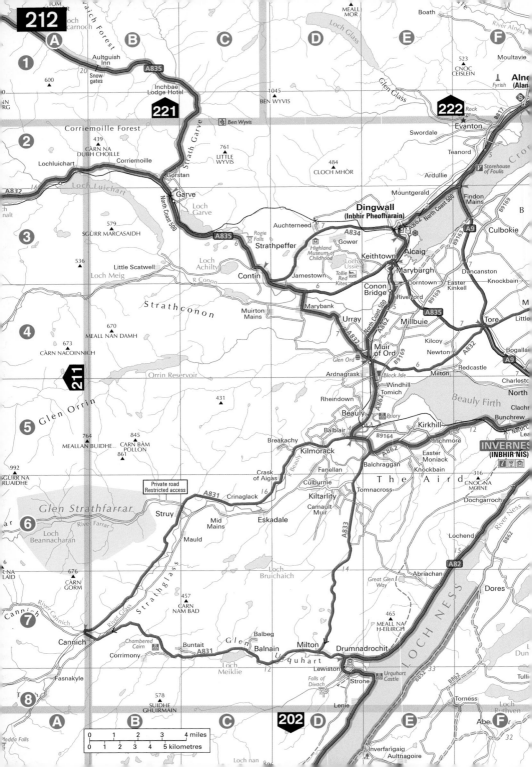

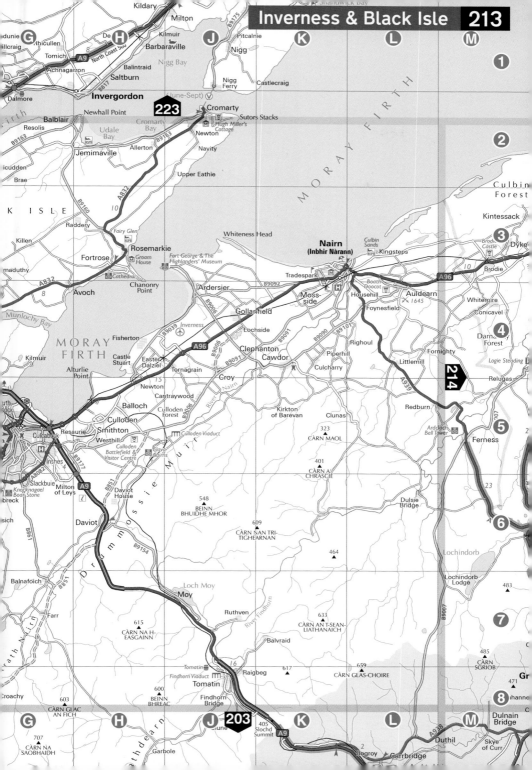

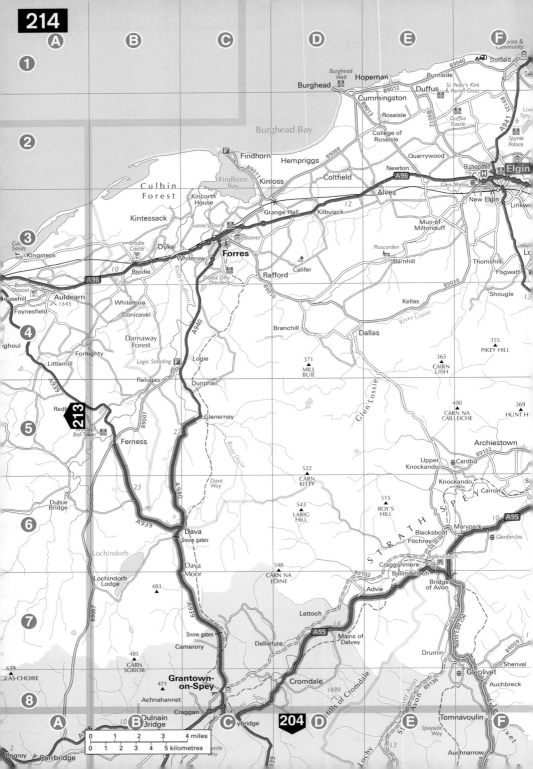

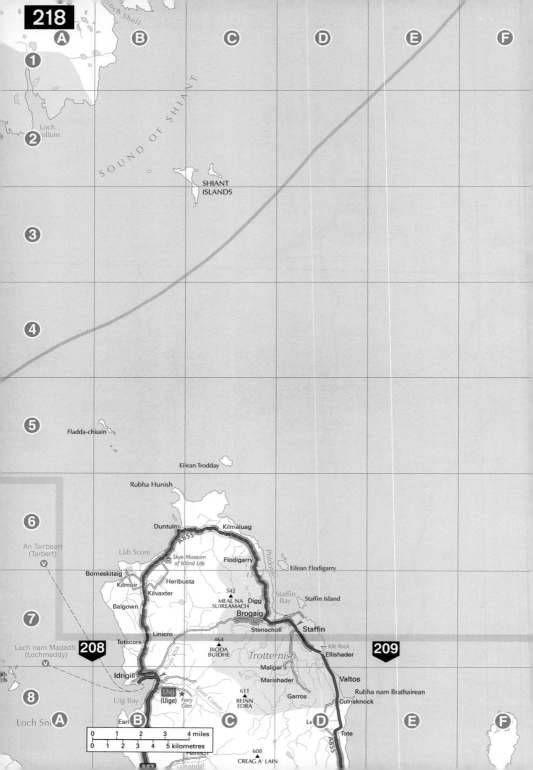

A B C D E F

1

2

Loch ollum

SOUND OF SHIANT

3

4

5

6

7

8

Loch Shell

SHIANT ISLANDS

Fladda-chùain

Eilean Trodday

Rubha Hunish

Duntulm    Kilmaluag

A855

Lùb Score

Skye Museum of Island Life

Flodigarry

Eilean Flodigarry

Borneskitaig

Heribusta

Kilmuir

Kilvaxter

Balgown

542
MEAL NA
SUIREAMACH

Digg

Staffin
Bay

Staffin Island

Brogaig

An Tairbeart
(Tarbert)

Loch nam Madadh
(Lochmaddy)

Linicro

Totscore

Stenscholl

Staffin

464
BIODA
BUIDHE

Trotternish

Kilt Rock

Ellishader

Idrigill

Uig Bay

River Rha

River Conon

Fairy Glen

Maligar

611
BEINN
EDRA

Marishader

Garros

Valtos

Rubha nam Brathairean

Culnaknock

Uig
(Ùige)

Earl

Le

Tote

Loch Sni

A

B

C

D

E

F

608
CREAG A' LAIN

Pennin

A87

**208**    **209**

0  1  2  3       4 miles
0  1  2  3  4    5 kilometres

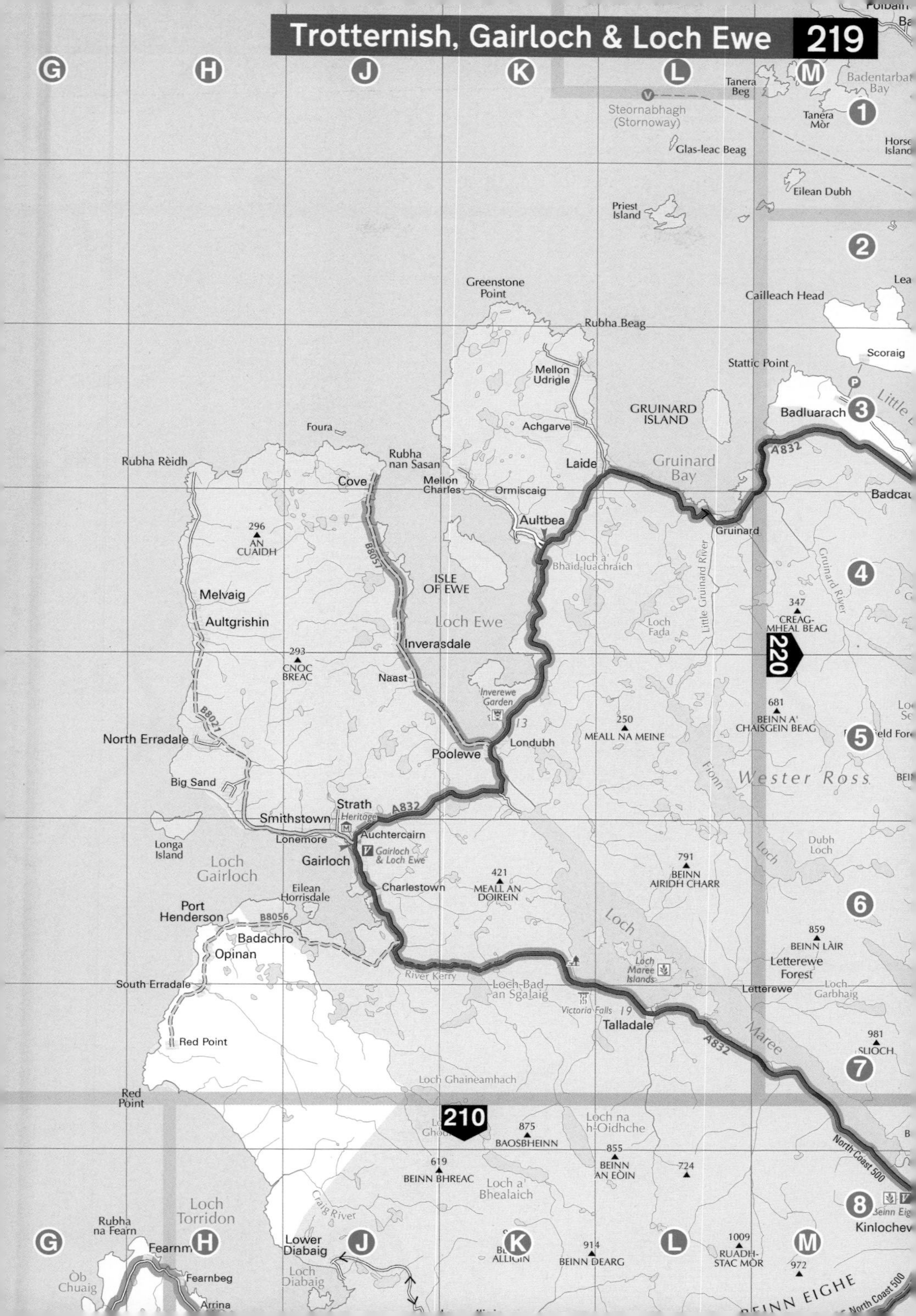
G
H
J
K
L
M
1
2
3
4
5
6
7
8
Tanera Beg
Tanera Mòr
Badentarbat Bay
Steornabhagh (Stornoway)
Horse Island
Glas-leac Beag
Eilean Dubh
Priest Island
Greenstone Point
Cailleach Head
Scoraig
Rubha Beag
Mellon Udrigle
Stattic Point
GRUINARD ISLAND
Badluarach
Achgarve
Foura
Rubha Rèidh
Rubha nan Sasan
Cove
Laide
Gruinard Bay
A832
Mellon Charles
Ormiscaig
Badcaul
Aultbea
Gruinard
296 AN CUAIDH
B8057
Loch a' Bhaid-luachraich
Gruinard River
Little Gruinard River
ISLE OF EWE
Melvaig
Aultgrishin
Loch Ewe
Loch Fada
347 CREAG-MHEAL BEAG
220
Inverasdale
293 CNOC BREAC
Naast
Inverewe Garden
B8021
681 BEINN A' CHAISGEIN BEAG
250 MEALL NA MEINE
North Erradale
Poolewe
Londubh
Fionn
Wester Ross
Big Sand
Strath
Heritage
Smithstown
Auchtercairn
Longa Island
Lonemore
Gairloch & Loch Ewe
Dubh Loch
Loch Gairloch
Gairloch
421 MEALL AN DOIREIN
791 BEINN AIRIDH CHARR
Charlestown
Eilean Horrisdale
Port Henderson
B8056
Badachro
Opinan
859 BEINN LÀIR
Loch
Loch Maree Islands
Letterewe Forest
River Kerry
Loch Bad an Sgalaig
South Erradale
Letterewe
Loch Garbhaig
Victoria Falls
Talladale
Red Point
Maree
981 SLIOCH
Loch Ghaineamhach
Red Point
210
Loch na h-Oidhche
875 BAOSBHEINN
855 BEINN AN EÒIN
619 BEINN BHREAC
724
North Coast 500
Loch a' Bhealaich
Loch Torridon
Craig River
Beinn Eighe
Kinlochewe
Rubha na Fearn
Lower Diabaig
914 BEINN DEARG
1009 RUADH-STAC MÒR
972
Òb Chuaig
Fearnbeg
Loch Diabaig
ALLIGIN
BEINN EIGHE
Arrina

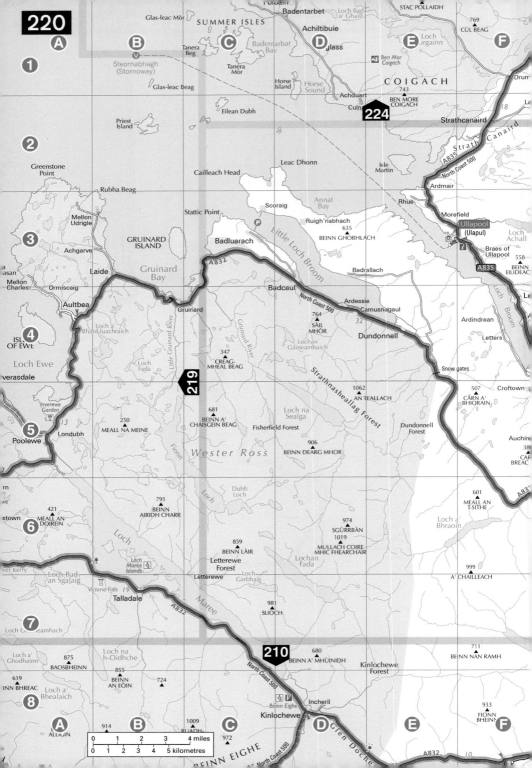

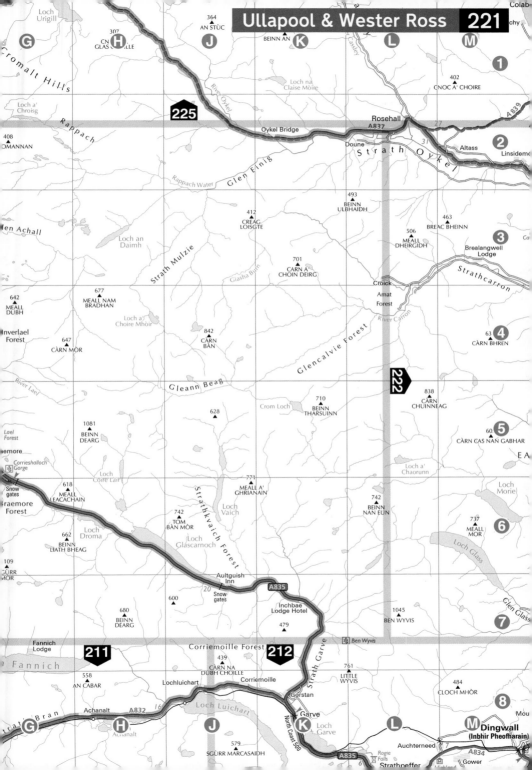

G H J K L M

1

2

3

4

5

6

7

8

Loch Urigill

Cromalt Hills

307 CN GLAS...LLE

364 AN STÙC

BEINN AN

402 CNOC A' CHOIRE

A839

225

River Oykel

Loch na Claise Mòire

Rappach

Rosehall
A837

Oykel Bridge

Doune

Strath Oykel

27

31

Altass

Linsidemo

408 ...OMANNAN

Glen Achall

Rappach Water

Glen Einig

Strath Mulzie

Loch an Daimh

412 CREAG LOISGTE

493 BEINN ULBHAIDH

506 MEALL DHEIRGIDH

463 BREAC BHEINN

Brealangwell Lodge

3

Giasha Burn

701 CARN A' CHOIN DEIRG

Croick

Amat Forest

Strathcarron

River Carron

677 MEALL NAM BRADHAN

642 MEALL DUBH

Loch a' Choire Mhòir

842 CARN BÀN

Glencalvie Forest

63 CÀRN BHREN

4

Inverlael Forest

647 CÀRN MÒR

River Lael

Gleann Beag

628

Crom Loch

710 BEINN THARSUINN

222

838 CÀRN CHUINNEAG

Lael Forest

1081 BEINN DEARG

Loch a' Chaorunn

60. CÀRN CAS NAN GABHAR

5

E A

Corrieshalloch Gorge

Loch Coire Lair

771 MEALL A' GHRIANAIN

742 BEINN NAN EUN

Loch Morie

Snow gates

618 MEALL LEACACHAIN

Strathvaich Forest

Loch Vaich

737 MEALL MÒR

6

raemore Forest

662 BEINN LIATH BHEAG

Loch Droma

742 TOM BÀN MÒR

Loch Glascarnoch

Loch Glass

Glen Glass

109 GÙRR MÓR

Aultguish Inn

A835

Inchbae Lodge Hotel

1045 BEN WYVIS

7

20

Snow gates

600

680 BEINN DEARG

479

Ben Wyvis

Fannich Lodge

211

Corriemoille Forest

212

Strath Garve

761 LITTLE WYVIS

484 CLOCH MHÒR

8

Fannich

558 AN CABAR

439 CÀRN NA DUBH CHOILLE

Corriemoille

Gorstan

Achanalt

A832

Lochluichart

Loch Luichart

Garve

North Coast 500

Dingwall (Inbhir Pheofharain)

...th Bran

G H J K L M

Achanalt

579 SGÙRR MARCASAIDH

Loch Garve

Auchterneed

7

A834

A835

Rogie Falls

Strathpeffer

Gower

Mou

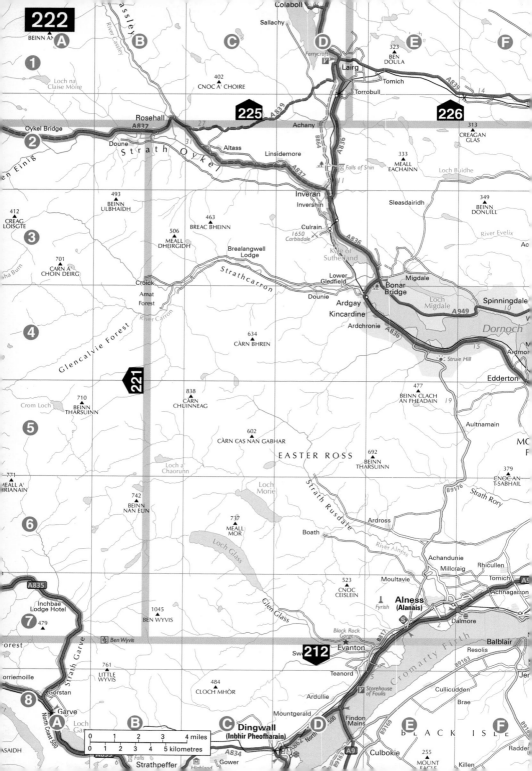

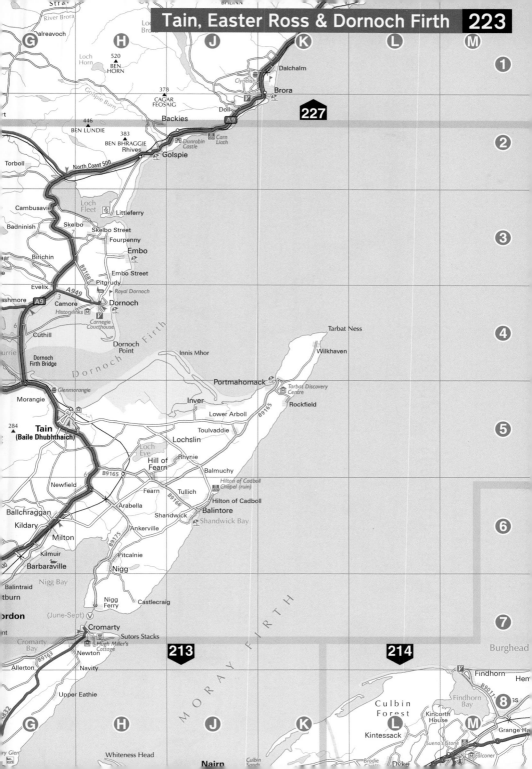

**G**  **H**  **J**  **K**  **L**  **M**

**1**
**2**
**3**
**4**
**5**
**6**
**7**
**8**

Stra
River Brora
Dalreavoch
Loch Horn
520 ▲ BEN HORN
Golspie Burn
378 ▲ CAGAR FEOSAIG
Dalchalm
Clynelish
Brora
Doll
Backies
A9
**227**
446 ▲ BEN LUNDIE
383 ▲ BEN BHRAGGIE
Rhives
Dunrobin Castle
Carn Liath
North Coast 500
Golspie
Torboll
Loch Fleet
Cambusavie
Littleferry
Badninish
Skelbo
Skelbo Street
Fourpenny
Birichin
Embo
B9168
Embo Street
Pitgrudy
Evelix
Royal Dornoch
shmore
A9
A949
Camore
Dornoch
Cuthill
Historylinks
Carnegie Courthouse
Dornoch Point
Tarbat Ness
urrie
Dornoch Firth Bridge
Innis Mhor
Wilkhaven
Dornoch Firth
Glenmorangie
Morangie
Portmahomack
Tarbat Discovery Centre
284 ▲
Inver
Rockfield
Tain (Baile Dhubhthaich)
Lower Arboll
B9165
Toulvaddie
Newfield
B9165
Lochslin
Hill of Fearn
Rhynie
Loch Eye
Balmuchy
Hilton of Cadboll Chapel (ruin)
Ballchraggan
Fearn
Tullich
Kildary
Arabella
Shandwick
Hilton of Cadboll
Balintore
Milton
Ankerville
B9175
Shandwick Bay
Kilmuir
Pitcalnie
Barbaraville
Nigg
Balintraid
tburn
Nigg Bay
Nigg Ferry
Castlecraig
ordon
(June-Sept)
Cromarty
Sutors Stacks
**213**
**214**
Burghead
Cromarty Bay
Hugh Miller's Cottage
B9163
Newton
Navity
Allerton
Findhorn
Hem
Culbin Forest
Findhorn Bay
Upper Eathie
Kincorth House
Kintessack
Sueno's Stone
Grange Ha
B832
n Glen
Whiteness Head
**Nairn**
Culbin Sands
Brodie
Dyke
Falconer
MORAY FIRTH

**G**  **H**  **J**  **K**  **L**  **M**

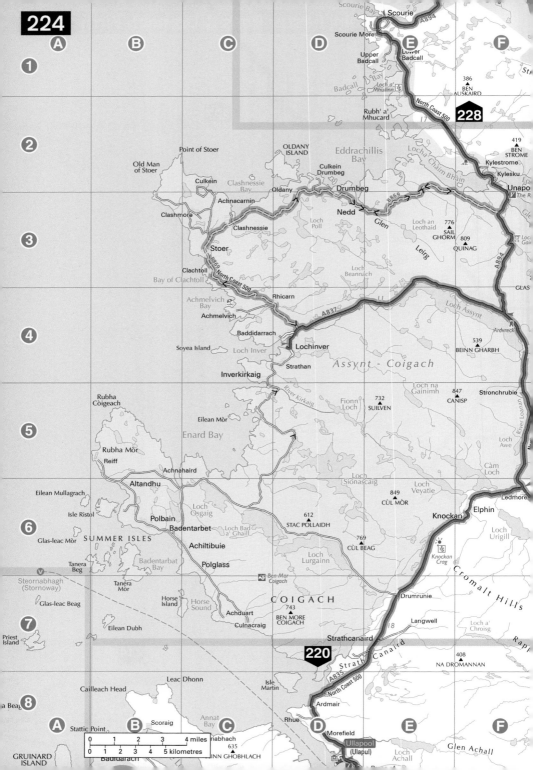

A  B  C  D  E  F

1

2

Scourie Bay
Scourie
A894
Scourie More
Upper Badcall
Lower Badcall
Badcall
Badcall Bay
Loch a' Mhuilinn
Rubh' a' Mhucard
North Coast 500

386
BEN AUSKAIRD

**228**

419
BEN STROME
Kylestrome
Kylesku
Unapo
The R

Point of Stoer
OLDANY ISLAND
Eddrachillis Bay
Locha Chàirn Bhàin

Old Man of Stoer
Culkein
Culkein Drumbeg
Clashnessie Bay
Oldany
Drumbeg
Achnacarnin
Clashmore
Nedd
Glen
Clashnessie
Loch Poll
Leirg
776 SAIL GHORM
809 QUINAG
B869

Loch an Leothaid

Loc Gain

3

Stoer
Clachtoll
Bay of Clachtoll
B869
North Coast 500
Rhicarn
Loch Beannach
A894
GLAS

Achmelvich Bay
Achmelvich
Baddidarrach
A837
Loch Assynt
Ardvreck

4

Soyea Island
Loch Inver
Lochinver
Strathan
Assynt - Coigach
539 BEINN GHARBH

Inverkirkaig
River Kirkaig
Fionn Loch
732 SUILVEN
Loch na Gainimh
847 CANISP
Stronchrubie

Rubha Còigeach
Eilean Mòr
Enard Bay
Loch Lourra
River Loanan

5

Rubha Mòr
Reiff
Achnahaird
Loch Sionascaig
Loch Veyatie
849 CÙL MÒR
Loch Awe
Càm Loch

Eilean Mullagrach
Isle Ristol
Altandhu
Loch Osgaig
612 STAC POLLAIDH
Knockan
Elphin
Ledmore

6

Glas-leac Mòr
SUMMER ISLES
Polbain
Badentarbet
Loch Bad a' Ghaill
Loch Lurgainn
769 CÙL BEAG
Knockan Crag
Loch Urigill

Steornabhagh (Stornoway)
Badentarbat Bay
Achiltibuie
Ben-Mòr Coigach
Glas-leac Beag
Tanera Beg
Tanera Mòr
Polglass

7

Priest Island
Horse Island
Horse Sound
Achduart
Culnacraig
COIGACH
743 BEN MORE COIGACH
635
Drumrunie
Langwell
Loch a' Chroisg
408 NA DROMANNAN
Rapl

Eilean Dubh
Strathcanaird
Strath Canaird
18

**220**
North Coast 500

8

Caileach Head
Leac Dhonn
Scoraig
Annat Bay
Isle Martin
Ardmair
Rhue
Morefield
Ullapool (Ulapul)
Loch Achall
Glen Achall

a Beag
Stattic Point
iabhach
INN GHOBHLACH
D
E
F

GRUINARD ISLAND
Baddarach

0  1  2  3  4 miles
0  1  2  3  4  5 kilometres

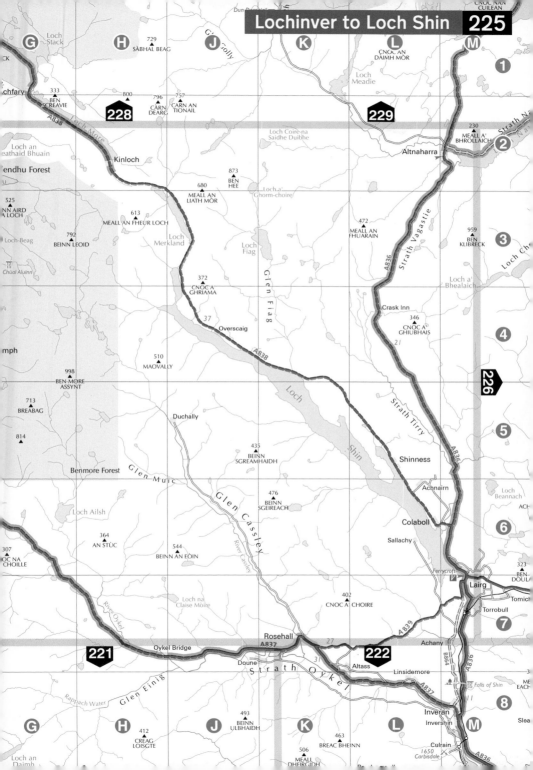

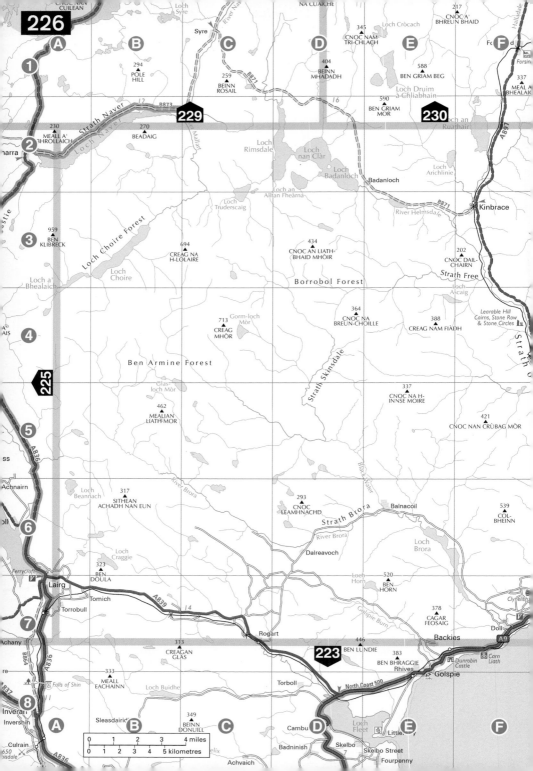

CNOC
NAN GALL
Achavanich
Loch
inster
Grey
of Cam

Loch an
Thulachan
Loch
Sand
Loch
Rangag
STEMSTER HILL
248

**1**

Rumsdale Water
Strathmore W.
Dalnawillan Lodge

226
COIRE
NA BEINNE
287
BEN-A-
CHIELT
**231**
Upper
Lybster

**230**
348
BEN
ALISKY
Glutt Lodge
264
CNOCAN
CONACHREAG
Houstry

**2**
Swiney
Invershore
Forse
Lybster
Lybster
Harbour
Oc
M

KNOCKFIN
HEIGHTS
40
Land-
hallow
Smerral
Latheronwheel
Clan
Gunn
Latheron
Lybster
Bay

317
CNOC LOCH
MHADADH
Dunbeath Water
Janetstown

437
NOC COIRE
NA FEARNA
Berriedale Water
Braemore
484
MAIDEN
PAP
A9
Laidhay Croft

**3**
705
MORVEN
Knockally
Snow
gates
Dunbeath
Heritage
Dunbeath
Bay

518
CNOC AN
EIREANNAICH
arn
626
SCARABEN
Ramscraigs

Langwell Forest
Newport
Borgue
20

**4**
554
CREAG
SCALABSDALE
Langwell
House
Berriedale
Lodge
401
CNOC NA
MAOILE
North Coast 500

416
BEINN
DUBHAIN
nan
A897
Torrish
A9
Badbea
Historic Village

**5**
24
NN
RAIN
591
BEINN
MHEALAICH
404
CREAG
THORARAIDH
Ord of Caithness
River Helmsdale
Navidale
Timespan
Snow gates
West
Helmsdale
Gartymore
East Helmsdale
Portgower
Helmsdale

Glen Loth
Lothmore

**6**
Lothbeg
2

halm

**7**

**8**

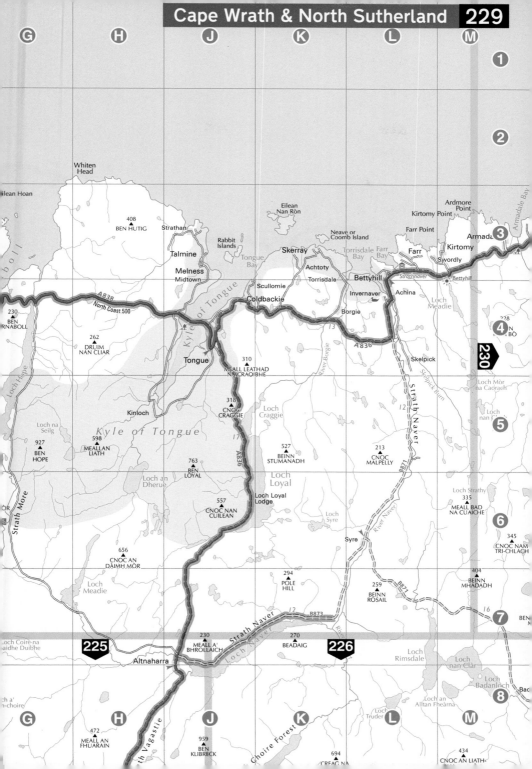

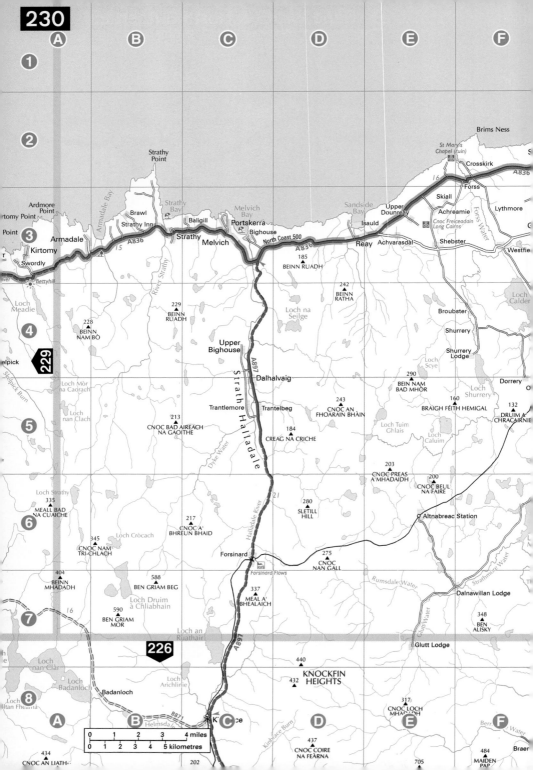

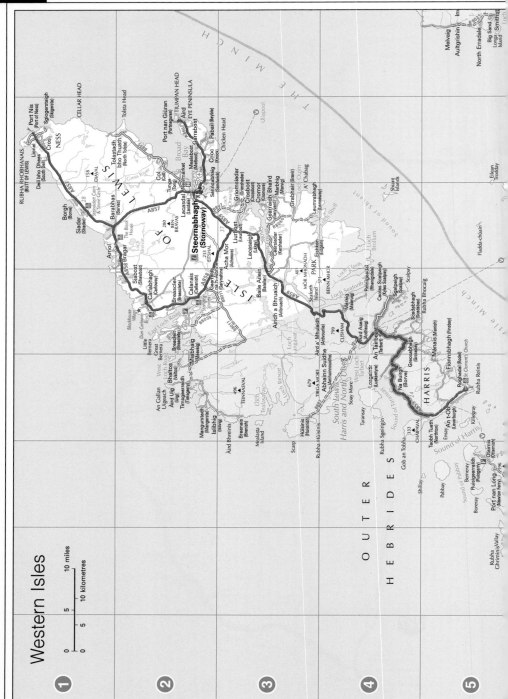

# Western Isles

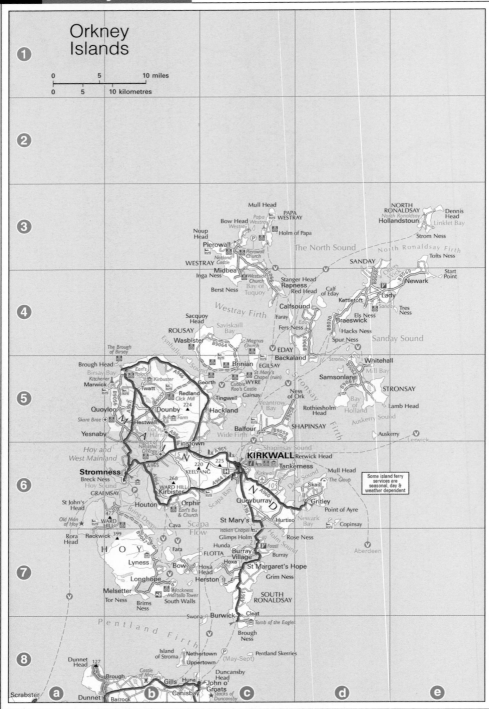

# Orkney Islands

0    5        10 miles
0  5     10 kilometres

Mull Head
PAPA
WESTRAY
Bow Head
Westray
Noup
Head
Holm of Papa
NORTH
RONALDSAY
North Ronaldsay
Hollandstoun
Dennis
Head
Linklet Bay
Pierowall
Netland
Castle
Pierowall
Church
The North Sound
North Ronaldsay Firth
Strom Ness
WESTRAY
Midbea
Westside
Church
Stanger Head
SANDAY
Tofts Ness
Start
Point
Inga Ness
Bay of
Tuquoy
Red Head
Berst Ness
Rapness
Calf
of Eday
Newark
Kettletoft
Lady
Westray Firth
Calfsound
Faray
Els Ness
Tres
Ness
Sacquoy
Head
Saviskaill
Bay
St Magnus
Church
Fers Ness
Braeswick
Sanday Sound
ROUSAY
Wasbister
B9064
EDAY
Hacks Ness
The Brough
of Birsay
Brinian
Backaland
Spur Ness
Stronsay
Whitehall
Brough Head
Birsay Bay
Earl's
Palace
EGILSAY
St Mary's
Chapel (ruin)
Samsonlane
Mill Bay
Kitchener
Marwick
Twatt
Kirbuster
Georth
Cubbie
Roo's Castle
WYRE
STRONSAY
Redland
Click Mill
224
Gairsay
Ness
of Ork
Bay
of
Holland
Quoyloo
Tingwell
Dounby
Skara Brae
Hestwall
Hackland
Rothiesholm
Head
Lamb Head
Yesnaby
Loch of
Harray
Ness of
Mainland
Orkney
Bay of
Firth
SHAPINSAY
Auskerry
Finstown
Balfour
Wide Firth
Lerwick
Hoy and
West Mainland
220
B9055
Shapinsay Sound
B965
225
MAINLAND
KIRKWALL
Rerwick Head
Stromness
KEELYANG
Tankerness
Mull Head
Breck Ness
268
Kirkwall
Skaill
The Gloup
Some island ferry
services are
seasonal, day &
weather dependent
Hoy Sound
WARD HILL
Kirbister
Dyer Sound
GRAEMSAY
Houton
Orphir
Earl's Bu
& Church
Queyburray
Gritley
Point of Ayre
St John's
Head
Cava
Scapa
Flow
St Mary's
Hurtiso
Newark
Bay
Copinsay
Old Man
of Hoy
WARD
HILL
477
Rackwick
399
Bring Deeps
Italian Chapel
Glimps Holm
Rose Ness
Rora
Head
HOY
Fara
Hunda
Aberdeen
Lyness
FLOTTA
Burray
Village
Hoxa
Burray
Bow
Hoxa
Head
St Margaret's Hope
Longhope
Herston
Grim Ness
Melsetter
Hackness
Martello Tower
South Walls
SOUTH
RONALDSAY
Tor Ness
Brims
Ness
Swona
Burwick
Cleat
Tomb of the Eagles
Pentland Firth
Brough
Ness
Dunnet
Head
127
Island
of Stroma
Netherton
Uppertown
Pentland Skerries
(May-Sept)
Brough
Castle
of Mey
Gills
Huna
Duncansby
Head
Scrabster
Dunnet
Barrock
Canisby
John o'
Groats
Stacks of
Duncansby

a    b    c    d    e

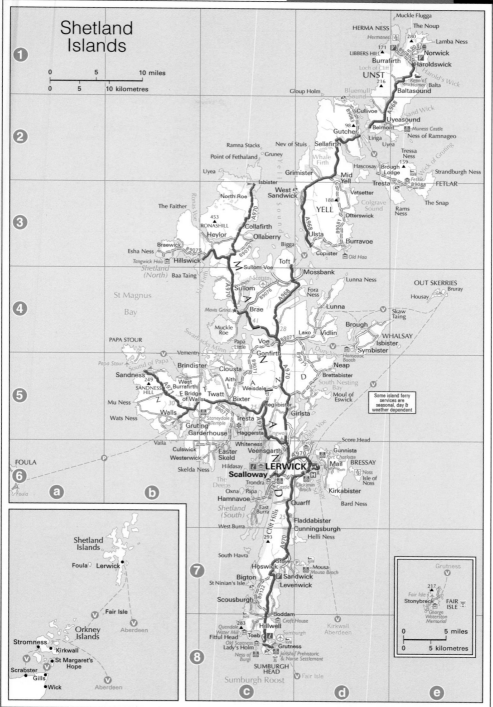

# Shetland Islands

0   5   10 miles
0   5   10 kilometres

**HERMA NESS**
Muckle Flugga
The Noup
Hermaness
280
Lamba Ness
LIBBERS HILL
171
Norwick
Burrafirth
Haroldswick
**UNST**
Harold's Wick
216
Baltasound
Gloup Holm
Balta
Bluemull Sound
Cullivoe
Uyeasound
98
Uyea Sound
Gutcher
Belmont
Muness Castle
Linga
Ness of Ramnageo
Ramna Stacks
Nev of Stuis
Sellafirth
Uyea
Tressa Ness
Point of Fethaland
Gruney
Whale Firth
Brough Lodge
159
Fetlar
Uyea
Grimister
Hascosay
Strandburgh Ness
**FETLAR**
West
Mid
Tresta
Isbister
Sandwick
Yell
Vatsetter
The Snap
North Roe
188
Colgrave Sound
453
**YELL**
RONASHILL
Collafirth
Otterswick
Rams Ness
Heylor
Ollaberry
Bigga
Ulsta
Burravoe
Braewick
Copister
Old Haa
Esha Ness
Hillswick
Tangwick Haa
Shetland (North)
Baa Taing
Sullom Voe
Toft
Mossbank
Lunna Ness
OUT SKERRIES
Housay
Bruray
Sullom
Skaw Taing
St Magnus
Bay
Mavis Grind
Brae
Muckle Roe
Papa Little
Laxo
Vidlin
Brough
WHALSAY
Isbister
PAPA STOUR
Vementry
Voe
Gonfirth
Neap
Symbister
Hanseatic Booth
Papa Stour
Sound of Papa
Brindister
Clousta
Brettabister
South Nesting Bay
Sandness
249
Aith
Weisdale
Moul of Eswick
SANDNESS HILL
West Burrafirth
Twatt
Bixter
Heglibister
Girlsta
Mu Ness
E Bridge of Walls
Some island ferry services are seasonal, day & weather dependent
Wats Ness
Walls
30
Gruting
Tresta
Score Head
Garderhouse
Haggersta
Gunnista
Vaila
Culswick
Whiteness
Veensgarth
Fort Charlotte
Mail
BRESSAY
Westerwick
Easter Skeld
Hildasay
**LERWICK**
Noss
Isle of Noss
FOULA
Skelda Ness
**Scalloway**
Trondra
Clickimin Broch
Kirkabister
Foula
The Deeps
Oxna
Papa
Castle
Bard Ness
Hamnavoe
Quarff
East Burra
Shetland (South)
Fladdabister
West Burra
293
Cunningsburgh
Helli Ness
South Havra
Clift Hills
Hoswick
Stove
Mousa
Mousa Broch
Bigton
Sandwick
St Ninian's Isle
Levenwick
Scousburgh
Boddam
Kirkwall
Aberdeen
Quendale
283
Croft House
Water Mill
Hillwell
Fitful Head
Toab
Sumburgh
Lady's Holm
Grutness
Old Scatness
Jarlshof Prehistoric & Norse Settlement
Ness of Burgi
Fair Isle
SUMBURGH HEAD
Sumburgh Roost

## Inset (bottom left)

Shetland Islands
Foula
Lerwick
Fair Isle
Aberdeen
Orkney Islands
Stromness
Kirkwall
St Margaret's Hope
Scrabster
Gills
Wick
Aberdeen

## Inset (bottom right)

Grutness
217
Fair Isle
Stonybreck
FAIR ISLE
George Waterston Memorial
0   5 miles
0   5 kilometres

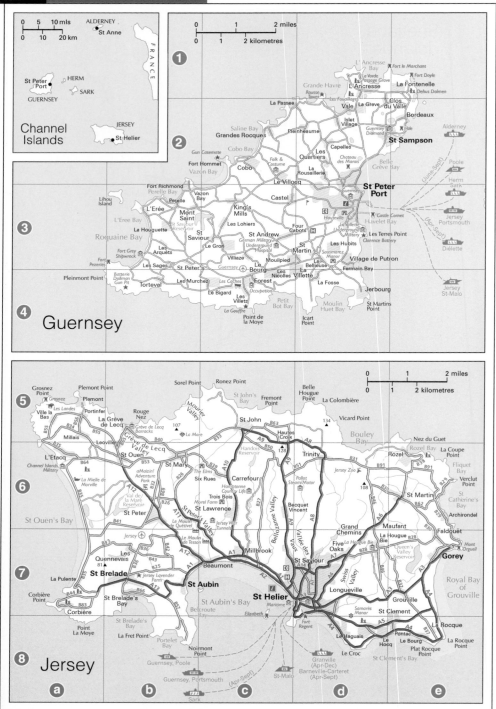

## Channel Islands

ALDERNEY
St Anne

FRANCE

St Peter Port
HERM
SARK
GUERNSEY

JERSEY
St Helier

## Guernsey

① ② ③ ④

L'Ancresse Bay
Fort le Marchant
Fort Doyle
La Varde Passage Grave
L'Ancresse Fort Doyle
Delus Dolmen
La Fontenelle
Grande Havre
Rousse Tower
Les Fouaillages
Vale
Islet Village
La Greve
Clos du Valle
Bordeaux
St Sampson
Saline Bay
Grandes Rocques
Pleinheaume
Capelles
Les Quartiers
Chateau des Marais
Guernsey Diamond
Belle Greve Bay
Alderney

Cobo Bay
Folk & Costume
La Rousaillerie
St Peter Port
Gun Casemate
Fort Hommet
Cobo
Vazon Bay
Le Villocq
Castel
Herm Sark

Fort Richmond
Perelle Bay
Vazon Bay
King's Mills
Guernsey
Jersey Portsmouth

Lihou Island
L'Erée
Mont Saint
Perelle
Les Lohiers
Four Cabots
Houguerville
Underground Military
Les Terres Point
Clonnce Battery
Diélette

L'Eree Bay
St Saviour Reservoir
La Houguette
St Saviour
St Andrew
German Military Underground Hospital
St Martin
Les Hubits
Sausmarez Manor
Village de Putron

Roquaine Bay
Les Arquéts
Le Gron
Villaze
Mouilpied
La Bellieuse
Fermain Bay

Fort Grey Shipwreck
Les Sages
St Peter's
Le Bourg
Les Nicolles
La Villette
La Fosse

Fort Pezeries
Les Murchez
Les Caches
Forest Occupation
Jerbourg
Jersey St-Malo

Pleinmont Point
Batterie Dollman Gun Pit
Torteval
Le Bigard
Les Villets
Petit Bot Bay
Icart Point
St Martins Point

La Gouffre
Point de la Moye
Moulin Huet Bay

## Jersey

⑤ ⑥ ⑦ ⑧

Grosnez Point
Gronez
Plemont Point
Sorel Point
Ronez Point
St John's Bay
Fremont Point
Belle Hougue Point
La Colombière

Ville la Bas
Les Landes
Plemont
Portinfer
Rouge Nez
Mourier Valley
107
La Mare
St John
Hautes Croix
128
Vicard Point
134
Bouley Bay
Nez du Guet

Millais
La Grève de Lecq
Grève de Lecq Barracks
B63
Trinity
Rozel Bay
La Coupe Point

L'Etacq
Leoville
St Ouen
St Mary
Handois Reservoir
Carrefour
Pallot Steam/Motor
Jersey Zoo
108
Rozel
Fliquet Bay
Verclut Point

Channel Islands Military
La Mielle de Morville
aMaizin! Adventure Park
The Elms
Six Rues
Hamptonne Country Life
Trois Bois
Morel Farm
Becquet Vincent
St Martin
St Catherine's Bay
Archirondel

Val de la Mare Reservoir
St Peter
St Lawrence
Jersey War Tunnels
Grand Chemins
Maufant
La Hougue Bie
Faldouet
Mont Orgueil

St Ouen's Bay
Le Moulin de Quétivel
Le Moulin de Tesson
Millbrook
St Saviour
Five Oaks
Queen's Valley Reservoir
Gorey

Les Quennevais
Jersey Lavender Farm
Beaumont
Longueville
Grouville
Royal Bay of Grouville

St Brelade
St Aubin
St Helier
Maritime
Swiss Valley
St Clement

Corbière Point
St Brelade's Bay
St Aubin's Bay
Fort Regent
Samarès Manor
La Rocque

Corbière
Belcroute
Elizabeth
La Haguais
Pontac
La Rocque Point

Point La Moye
St Brelade's Bay
Portelet Bay
Noirmont Point
Le Hocq
Le Bourg
Plat Rocque Point

La Fret Point
Guernsey, Poole
Guernsey, Portsmouth
Sark
St-Malo
Le Croc
Granville (Apr-Dec)
Barneville-Carteret (Apr-Sept)
St Clement's Bay

ⓐ ⓑ ⓒ ⓓ ⓔ

0 5 10 mls
0 10 20 km

0 1 2 miles
0 1 2 kilometres

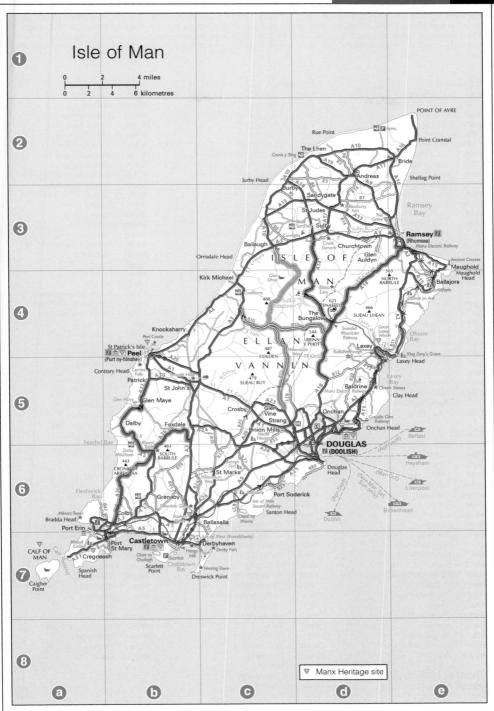

Isle of Man

0  2  4 miles
0  2  4  6 kilometres

POINT OF AYRE

Rue Point
The Lhen
Point Cranstal

Cronk y Bing
A10
Bride

Jurby Head
Jurby
A19
Shellag Point

Sandygate
Andreas
A9

St Judes
Ramsey
Bay

Ballaugh
Sulby
Ballachurry
Fort
The Grove

Orrisdale Head
Curraghs
Sulby Glen
Ramsey
(Rhumsaa)
Manx Electric Railway

Kirk Michael
Cronk
Sumark
Churchtown
Glen
Auldyn

ISLE OF

Glen
Dhoo
MAN
Black
Eary
NORTH
BARRULE
Maughold
Maughold
Head

Cooildarry
Sulby
Reservoir
488
621
SNAEFELL
SLIEAU LHEAN
466
Ballajora

Knocksharry
Peel Castle
The
Bungalow
Great
Laxey
Wheel
Gob ny Rona

St Patrick's Isle
Peel
(Purt ny-hInshey)
ELLAN
COLDEN
544
BEINN
Y PHOTT
Snaefell
Mountain
Railway
Laxey
Dhoon
Bay
King Orry's Grave

Contrary Head
A20
487
Millennium
TT Circuit
Laxey Head

Patrick
A1
VANNIN
479
SLIEAU RUY
Cloven Stones

St John's
Crosby
Glen
Vine
Baldrine
Laxey
Bay

Glen Maye
Glen Maye
Strang
Onchan
Clay Head

Dalby
Foxdale
Union Mills
Onchan Head
Belfast

Dalby
Mountain
483
SOUTH
BARRULE
DOUGLAS
(DOOLISH)

Niarbyl Bay
443
CRONK-NY-
ARREY LAA
St Marks
Douglas
Head
Heysham

Fleshwick
Bay
Grenaby
Port Soderick
Liverpool

Colby
Ballasalla
Isle of Man
Steam Railway
Santon Head
Birkenhead

Milner's Tower
Bradda Head
Port Erin
A5
Dublin

CALF OF
MAN
Port
St Mary
Castletown
Derbyhaven
Derby Fort

Cregneash
Scarlett
Point
Hango
Hill
Castletown
Bay
Herring Tower

Caigher
Point
Spanish
Head
Dreswick Point

⊽ Manx Heritage site

ⓐ  ⓑ  ⓒ  ⓓ  ⓔ

This index lists places appearing in the main map section of the atlas in alphabetical order. The reference following each name gives the atlas page number and grid reference of the square in which the place appears. The map shows counties, unitary authorities and administrative areas, together with a list of the abbreviated name forms used in the index. The top 100 places of tourist interest are indexed in **red**, World Heritage sites in **green**, motorway service areas in **blue**, airports in blue *italic* and National Parks in green *italic*.

## Scotland

| | |
|---|---|
| **Abers** | Aberdeenshire |
| **Ag & B** | Argyll and Bute |
| **Angus** | Angus |
| **Border** | Scottish Borders |
| **C Aber** | City of Aberdeen |
| **C Dund** | City of Dundee |
| **C Edin** | City of Edinburgh |
| **C Glas** | City of Glasgow |
| **Clacks** | Clackmannanshire (1) |
| **D & G** | Dumfries & Galloway |
| **E Ayrs** | East Ayrshire |
| **E Duns** | East Dunbartonshire (2) |
| **E Loth** | East Lothian |
| **E Rens** | East Renfrewshire (3) |
| **Falk** | Falkirk |
| **Fife** | Fife |
| **Highld** | Highland |
| **Inver** | Inverclyde (4) |
| **Mdloth** | Midlothian (5) |
| **Moray** | Moray |
| **N Ayrs** | North Ayrshire |
| **N Lans** | North Lanarkshire (6) |
| **Ork** | Orkney Islands |
| **P & K** | Perth & Kinross |
| **Rens** | Renfrewshire (7) |
| **S Ayrs** | South Ayrshire |
| **S Lans** | South Lanarkshire |
| **Shet** | Shetland Islands |
| **Stirlg** | Stirling |
| **W Duns** | West Dunbartonshire (8) |
| **W Isls** | Western Isles |
| | (Na h-Eileanan an Iar) |
| **W Loth** | West Lothian |

## Wales

| | |
|---|---|
| **Blae G** | Blaenau Gwent (9) |
| **Brdgnd** | Bridgend (10) |
| **Caerph** | Caerphilly (11) |
| **Cardif** | Cardiff |
| **Carmth** | Carmarthenshire |
| **Cerdgn** | Ceredigion |
| **Conwy** | Conwy |
| **Denbgs** | Denbighshire |
| **Flints** | Flintshire |
| **Gwynd** | Gwynedd |
| **IoA** | Isle of Anglesey |
| **Mons** | Monmouthshire |
| **Myr Td** | Merthyr Tydfil (12) |
| **Neath** | Neath Port Talbot (13) |
| **Newpt** | Newport (14) |
| **Pembks** | Pembrokeshire |
| **Powys** | Powys |
| **Rhondd** | Rhondda Cynon Taf (15) |
| **Swans** | Swansea |
| **Torfn** | Torfaen (16) |
| **V Glam** | Vale of Glamorgan (17) |
| **Wrexhm** | Wrexham |

## Channel Islands & Isle of Man

| | |
|---|---|
| **Guern** | Guernsey |
| **Jersey** | Jersey |
| **IoM** | Isle of Man |

## England

| | |
|---|---|
| **BaNES** | Bath & N E Somerset (18) |
| **Barns** | Barnsley (19) |
| **BCP** | Bournemouth, Christchurch and Poole (20) |
| **Bed** | Bedford |
| **Birm** | Birmingham |
| **Bl w D** | Blackburn with Darwen (21) |
| **Bolton** | Bolton (22) |
| **Bpool** | Blackpool |
| **Br & H** | Brighton & Hove (23) |
| **Br For** | Bracknell Forest (24) |
| **Bristl** | City of Bristol |
| **Bucks** | Buckinghamshire |
| **Bury** | Bury (25) |
| **C Beds** | Central Bedfordshire |
| **C Brad** | City of Bradford |
| **C Derb** | City of Derby |
| **C KuH** | City of Kingston upon Hull |
| **C Leic** | City of Leicester |
| **C Nott** | City of Nottingham |
| **C Pete** | City of Peterborough |
| **C Plym** | City of Plymouth |
| **C Port** | City of Portsmouth |
| **C Sotn** | City of Southampton |
| **C Stke** | City of Stoke-on-Trent |
| **C York** | City of York |
| **Calder** | Calderdale (26) |
| **Cambs** | Cambridgeshire |
| **Ches E** | Cheshire East |
| **Ches W** | Cheshire West and Chester |
| **Cnwll** | Cornwall |
| **Covtry** | Coventry |
| **Cumb** | Cumbria |
| **Darltn** | Darlington (27) |
| **Derbys** | Derbyshire |
| **Devon** | Devon |
| **Donc** | Doncaster (28) |
| **Dorset** | Dorset |
| **Dudley** | Dudley (29) |
| **Dur** | Durham |
| **E R Yk** | East Riding of Yorkshire |
| **E Susx** | East Sussex |
| **Essex** | Essex |
| **Gatesd** | Gateshead (30) |
| **Gloucs** | Gloucestershire |
| **Gt Lon** | Greater London |
| **Halton** | Halton (31) |
| **Hants** | Hampshire |
| **Hartpl** | Hartlepool (32) |
| **Herefs** | Herefordshire |
| **Herts** | Hertfordshire |
| **IoS** | Isles of Scilly |
| **IoW** | Isle of Wight |
| **Kent** | Kent |
| **Kirk** | Kirklees (33) |
| **Knows** | Knowsley (34) |
| **Lancs** | Lancashire |
| **Leeds** | Leeds |
| **Leics** | Leicestershire |
| **Lincs** | Lincolnshire |
| **Lpool** | Liverpool |
| **Luton** | Luton |
| **M Keyn** | Milton Keynes |

| | |
|---|---|
| **Manch** | Manchester |
| **Medway** | Medway |
| **Middsb** | Middlesbrough |
| **N Linc** | North Lincolnshire |
| **N Som** | North Somerset |
| **N Tyne** | North Tyneside (35) |
| **N u Ty** | Newcastle upon Tyne |
| **N York** | North Yorkshire |
| **NE Lin** | North East Lincolnshire |
| **Nhants** | Northamptonshire |
| **Norfk** | Norfolk |
| **Notts** | Nottinghamshire |
| **Nthumb** | Northumberland |
| **Oldham** | Oldham (36) |
| **Oxon** | Oxfordshire |
| **R & Cl** | Redcar & Cleveland |
| **Readg** | Reading |
| **Rochdl** | Rochdale (37) |
| **Rothm** | Rotherham (38) |
| **Rutlnd** | Rutland |
| **S Glos** | South Gloucestershire (39) |
| **S on T** | Stockton-on-Tees (40) |
| **S Tyne** | South Tyneside (41) |
| **Salfd** | Salford (42) |
| **Sandw** | Sandwell (43) |
| **Sefton** | Sefton (44) |
| **Sheff** | Sheffield |
| **Shrops** | Shropshire |
| **Slough** | Slough (45) |
| **Solhll** | Solihull (46) |
| **Somset** | Somerset |
| **St Hel** | St Helens (47) |
| **Staffs** | Staffordshire |
| **Sthend** | Southend-on-Sea |
| **Stockp** | Stockport (48) |
| **Suffk** | Suffolk |
| **Sundld** | Sunderland |
| **Surrey** | Surrey |
| **Swindn** | Swindon |
| **Tamesd** | Tameside (49) |
| **Thurr** | Thurrock (50) |
| **Torbay** | Torbay |
| **Traffd** | Trafford (51) |
| **W & M** | Windsor & Maidenhead (52) |
| **W Berk** | West Berkshire |
| **W Susx** | West Sussex |
| **Wakefd** | Wakefield (53) |
| **Warrtn** | Warrington (54) |
| **Warwks** | Warwickshire |
| **Wigan** | Wigan (55) |
| **Wilts** | Wiltshire |
| **Wirral** | Wirral (56) |
| **Wokham** | Wokingham (57) |
| **Wolves** | Wolverhampton (58) |
| **Worcs** | Worcestershire |
| **Wrekin** | Telford & Wrekin (59) |
| **Wsall** | Walsall (60) |

## A

**Abbas Combe**
Somset..................27 G6
**Abberley** Worcs......70 D2
**Abberley Common**
Worcs..................70 D2
**Abberton** Essex......62 B4
**Abberton** Worcs......71 H4
**Abbess Roding**
Essex..................60 F5
**Abbeydale** Sheff......114 F6
**Abbey Dore** Herefs....54 B3
**Abbey Green** Staffs....99 L2
**Abbey St Bathans**
Border..................178 F6
**Abbeystead** Lancs....130 B8
**Abbeytown** Cumb......147 L5
**Abbey Village** Lancs...121 J6
**Abbey Wood** Gt Lon...45 J4
**Abbotrule** Border......167 J6
**Abbots Bickington**
Devon..................9 K3
**Abbots Bromley**
Staffs..................100 B7
**Abbotsbury** Dorset....14 B5
**Abbots Deuglie**
P & K..................186 B5
**Abbotsham** Devon.....22 F6
**Abbotskerswell**
Devon..................7 K3
**Abbots Langley**
Herts..................59 H7
**Abbots Leigh** N Som...38 D5
**Abbotsley** Cambs......75 J3
**Abbots Morton**
Worcs..................71 H4
**Abbots Ripton**
Cambs..................89 J7
**Abbot's Salford**
Warwks..................71 J4
**Abbots Worthy** Hants...29 J5
**Abbotts Ann** Hants....29 G3
**Abbott Street** Dorset...15 J3
**Abdon** Shrops..........83 L6
**Aberaeron** Cerdgn......66 B3
**Aberaman** Rhondd......52 F7
**Aberangell** Gwynd......81 J2
**Aberarder** Highld......202 F1
**Aberargie** P & K.......186 B4
**Aberarth** Cerdgn.......66 B2
**Aberavon** Neath.......51 L7
**Abercanaid** Myr Td....53 G7
**Abercarn** Caerph.......37 K2
**Abercastle** Pembks....64 B7
**Abercegir** Powys.......81 H3
**Aberchalder** Highld....202 B5
**Aberchirder** Abers....216 C4
**Abercorn** W Loth.......176 E3
**Abercraf** Powys........52 C5
**Abercregan** Neath......36 D2
**Abercwmboi** Rhondd...52 F7
**Abercych** Pembks......65 H6
**Abercynon** Rhondd.....37 G2
**Aberdalgie** P & K......185 M4
**Aberdare** Rhondd......52 F7
**Aberdaron** Gwynd......94 C7
**Aberdeen** C Aber......207 H4
*Aberdeen Airport*
*C Aber..................207 G3*
**Aberdour** Fife..........177 G2
**Aberdulais** Neath......52 B7
**Aberdyfi** Gwynd........80 E4
**Aberedw** Powys.........68 C5
**Abereiddy** Pembks.....48 D2
**Abererch** Gwynd........95 G5
**Aberfan** Myr Td........53 G7
**Aberfeldy** P & K.......194 D6
**Aberffraw** IoA..........108 D7
**Aberford** Leeds........124 C3
**Aberfoyle** Stirlg......184 C7
**Abergavenny** Mons.....53 L5
**Abergele** Conwy.......110 C6
**Abergorlech** Carmth....66 D1
**Abergwesyn** Powys.....67 J4
**Abergwili** Carmth......50 F2
**Abergwynfi** Neath......36 D2

**Abergwyngregyn**
Gwynd..................109 J6
**Abergynolwyn** Gwynd...80 F1
**Aberkenfig** Brdgnd.....36 D4
**Aberlady** E Loth.......178 B3
**Aberlemno** Angus......196 E5
**Aberllefenni** Gwynd....81 G2
**Aberllynfi** Powys.......68 D6
**Aberlour,**
**Charlestown of**
Moray..................215 G5
**Abermule** Powys.......82 D5
**Abernant** Carmth......50 D2
**Abernant** Rhondd......52 F7
**Abernethy** P & K.......186 C4
**Abernyte** P & K........186 D2
**Aberporth** Cerdgn......65 J4
**Abersoch** Gwynd.......94 E6
**Abersychan** Torfn......53 K7
**Aberthin** V Glam.......36 F5
**Abertillery** Blae G.....53 K7
**Abertridwr** Caerph.....37 H3
**Abertridwr** Powys......97 G8
**Aberuthven** P & K......185 K4
**Aberystwyth** Cerdgn...80 D6
**Abingdon-on-**
**Thames** Oxon..........41 J2
**Abinger Common**
Surrey..................31 J3
**Abinger Hammer**
Surrey..................31 H2
**Abington** Nhants.......73 L3
**Abington** S Lans.......165 H5
**Abington Pigotts**
Cambs..................75 K5
*Abington Services*
*S Lans..................165 H4*
**Abingworth** W Susx....18 F3
**Ab Kettleby** Leics.....102 B7
**Ablington** Gloucs......56 C6
**Abney** Derbys..........114 D5
**Aboyne** Abers..........205 L5
**Abhainn Suidhe**
W Isls..................232 d4
**Abram** Wigan...........112 E2
**Abriachan** Highld......212 E7
**Abridge** Essex.........45 J2
**Abronhill** N Lans.......175 K3
**Abson** S Glos..........39 G5
**Abthorpe** Nhants.......73 J5
**Aby** Lincs.............118 F5
**Acaster Malbis**
C York..................124 E2
**Acaster Selby**
N York..................124 E2
**Accrington** Lancs......121 L5
**Acha** Ag & B...........188 F5
**Achahoish** Ag & B......172 D3
**Achalader** P & K.......195 H7
**Achaleven** Ag & B......182 D1
**Acha Mor** W Isls.......232 f3
**Achanalt** Highld.......211 K3
**Achandunie** Highld.....222 E6
**Achany** Highld.........222 D2
**Acharacle** Highld......190 D3
**Acharn** Highld.........190 E6
**Acharn** P & K..........194 B7
**Achavanich** Highld.....231 H6
**Achduart** Highld.......224 C7
**Achfary** Highld........228 D7
**Achgarve** Highld.......219 K3
**A'Chill** Highld.........198 D4
**Achiltibuie** Highld.....224 C6
**Achina** Highld..........229 L4
**Achinhoan** Ag & B......161 J6
**Achintee** Highld.......210 E6
**Achintraid** Highld......210 C6
**Achlyness** Highld......228 C5
**Achmelvich** Highld.....224 C4
**Achmore** Highld.......210 D7
**Achmore** W Isls.......232 f3
**Achnacarnin** Highld....224 C3
**Achnacarry** Highld.....201 J7
**Achnacloich** Highld....199 J4
**Achnaconeran**
Highld..................202 C2
**Achnacroish** Ag & B....191 G7
**Achnadrish** Ag & B.....189 L6

**Achnafauld** P & K......185 J1
**Achnagarron** Highld....222 F7
**Achnaha** Highld........189 L3
**Achnahaird** Highld.....224 B5
**Achnahannet** Highld....214 B8
**Achnairn** Highld.......225 L6
**Achnalea** Highld.......191 G4
**Achnamara** Ag & B.....172 D2
**Achnasheen** Highld.....211 J3
**Achnashellach**
Highld..................210 F5
**Achnastank** Moray......215 G7
**Achosnich** Highld......189 K3
**Achranich** Highld......190 E6
**Achreamie** Highld......230 E3
**Achriabhach** Highld....192 B3
**Achriesgill** Highld.....228 C5
**Achtoty** Highld........229 K3
**Achurch** Nhants.......88 E6
**Achvaich** Highld.......222 F3
**Achvarasdal** Highld....230 E3
**Ackergill** Highld.......231 L5
**Acklam** Middsb........141 L4
**Acklam** N York........134 B7
**Ackleton** Shrops......84 D4
**Acklington** Nthumb....159 G2
**Ackton** Wakefd.......124 C6
**Ackworth Moor Top**
Wakefd..................124 C7
**Acle** Norfk............93 J2
**Acock's Green** Birm...85 K6
**Acol** Kent.............35 J2
**Acomb** C York.........124 E1
**Acomb** Nthumb........150 B2
**Aconbury** Herefs......54 D2
**Acton** Ches E.........98 F2
**Acton** Gt Lon.........44 D4
**Acton** Staffs.........99 J4
**Acton** Suffk..........77 K5
**Acton** Wrexhm........97 M3
**Acton Beauchamp**
Herefs..................70 C4
**Acton Bridge**
Ches W..................112 E6
**Acton Burnell** Shrops...83 K3
**Acton Green** Herefs....70 C4
**Acton Round** Shrops...84 B4
**Acton Scott** Shrops....83 J5
**Acton Trussell** Staffs...99 L8
**Acton Turville** S Glos..39 J4
**Adbaston** Staffs.......99 H6
**Adber** Dorset..........26 E7
**Adbolton** Notts.......101 L5
**Adderbury** Oxon.......72 F7
**Adderley** Shrops......98 F4
**Addiewell** W Loth......176 D5
**Addingham** C Brad.....123 G1
**Addington** Bucks.......58 C3
**Addington** Gt Lon......45 G7
**Addington** Kent........33 H2
**Addiscombe** Gt Lon....45 G6
**Addlestone** Surrey.....43 H7
**Addlethorpe** Lincs.....119 H7
**Adeyfield** Herts.......59 H6
**Adfa** Powys............82 B4
**Adforton** Herefs.......69 H1
**Adisham** Kent.........35 G4
**Adlestrop** Gloucs......56 E3
**Adlingfleet** E R Yk....125 K6
**Adlington** Lancs......121 J7
**Admaston** Staffs......100 B7
**Admaston** Wrekin......84 B2
**Adpar** Cerdgn.........65 J6
**Adsborough** Somset...25 L5
**Adscombe** Somset.....25 J4
**Adstock** Bucks........58 C3
**Adstone** Nhants.......73 H4
**Adversane** W Susx.....31 H6
**Advie** Highld..........214 D7
**Adwick le Street**
Donc..................124 E8
**Adwick upon**
**Dearne** Donc.........115 J2
**Ae** D & G.............155 H4
**Ae Bridgend** D & G....155 H5
**Afan Forest Park**
Neath..................36 D2
**Affleck** Abers.........216 B6

**Affpuddle** Dorset......14 F4
**Affric Lodge** Highld....201 J2
**Afon-wen** Flints.......110 F6
**Afton** IoW.............16 D5
**Agglethorpe** N York...131 K3
**Aigburth** Lpool........111 L4
**Aike** E R Yk...........126 C2
**Aiketgate** Cumb.......148 E5
**Aikton** Cumb..........148 B4
**Ailsworth** C Pete......89 G4
**Ainderby Quernhow**
N York..................132 E4
**Ainderby Steeple**
N York..................132 E2
**Aingers Green** Essex..62 D4
**Ainsdale** Sefton......120 D7
**Ainstable** Cumb.......148 F5
**Ainsworth** Bury.......121 L8
**Ainthorpe** N York......142 E5
**Aintree** Sefton........111 L2
**Ainville** W Loth.......176 F5
**Aird** Ag & B...........181 M7
**Aird** D & G............144 D3
**Aird** Highld...........199 J5
**Aird** W Isls...........232 g2
**Àird a' Mhulaidh**
W Isls..................232 e3
**Aird Asaig** W Isls......232 e4
**Aird Dhubh** Highld....209 L6
**Airdeny** Ag & B.......182 E2
**Airdrie** N Lans........175 K5
**Airdriehill** N Lans.....175 K5
**Airds of Kells** D & G...154 B7
**Àird Uig** W Isls.......232 d2
**Airidh a bhruaich**
W Isls..................232 e3
**Airieland** D & G.......146 D4
**Airlie** Angus..........195 L6
**Airmyn** E R Yk........125 H5
**Airntully** P & K........186 A1
**Airor** Highld..........199 L4
**Airth** Falk............176 B2
**Airton** N York.........131 G7
**Aisby** Lincs...........103 G5
**Aisby** Lincs...........116 E3
**Aish** Devon...........7 G4
**Aish** Devon...........7 J4
**Aisholt** Somset.......25 J4
**Aiskew** N York........132 D2
**Aislaby** N York.......134 B3
**Aislaby** N York.......143 H5
**Aislaby** S on T.......141 J5
**Aisthorpe** Lincs.......116 F5
**Aith** Shet............235 c5
**Akeld** Nthumb........168 E4
**Akeley** Bucks.........73 K6
**Albaston** Cnwll........6 B2
**Alberbury** Shrops......83 G1
**Albourne** W Susx......19 H3
**Albrighton** Shrops.....84 E3
**Albrighton** Shrops.....98 C8
**Alburgh** Norfk........92 F6
**Albury** Herts..........60 C3
**Albury** Surrey.........31 H2
**Albury Heath** Surrey...31 H3
**Alcaig** Highld.........212 E3
**Alcaston** Shrops......83 J6
**Alcester** Warwks......71 K3
**Alciston** E Susx.......20 B5
**Alcombe** Somset......24 F3
**Alconbury** Cambs......89 H7
**Alconbury Weald**
Cambs..................89 H7
**Alconbury Weston**
Cambs..................89 H7
**Aldborough** N York....132 F6
**Aldborough** Norfk.....106 E5
**Aldbourne** Wilts.......40 E5
**Aldbrough** E R Yk.....127 G3
**Aldbrough St John**
N York..................140 F5
**Aldbury** Herts.........58 F5
**Aldcliffe** Lancs.......129 K7
**Aldclune** P & K.......194 E4
**Aldeburgh** Suffk......79 K3
**Aldeby** Norfk.........93 J5
**Aldenham** Herts.......43 J2
**Alderbury** Wilts.......28 D5

Alderford Norfk............106 D8
Alderholt Dorset............28 C8
Alderley Gloucs............39 H3
Alderley Edge
  Ches E............113 J5
Aldermans Green
  Covtry............86 D6
Aldermaston W Berk............41 L7
Alderminster Warwks......72 B5
Aldershot Hants............30 E2
Alderton Gloucs............55 M2
Alderton Nhants............73 K5
Alderton Suffk............79 H6
Alderton Wilts............39 J4
Aldfield N York............132 D5
Aldford Ches W............98 B2
Aldgate Rutlnd............88 E3
Aldham Essex............61 L3
Aldham Suffk............78 C5
Aldingbourne W Susx......18 C5
Aldingham Cumb............129 G5
Aldington Kent............34 E7
Aldington Worcs............71 J5
Aldington Corner
  Kent............34 E7
Aldivalloch Moray......205 H1
Aldochlay Ag & B......174 C1
Aldreth Cambs............90 C8
Aldridge Wsall............85 J4
Aldringham Suffk............79 J3
Aldsworth Gloucs............56 D6
Aldunie Moray............215 H8
Aldwark Derbys............100 E2
Aldwark N York............133 G6
Aldwick W Susx............18 C6
Aldwincle Nhants............88 E6
Aldworth W Berk............41 K4
Alexandria W Duns......174 D3
Aley Somset............25 J4
Alfington Devon............12 E3
Alfold Surrey............31 H5
Alfold Crossways
  Surrey............31 H4
Alford Abers............206 B3
Alford Lincs............118 F6
Alford Somset............26 E5
Alfreton Derbys............101 H2
Alfrick Worcs............70 D4
Alfrick Pound Worcs......70 D4
Alfriston E Susx............20 B5
Algarkirk Lincs............103 M5
Alhampton Somset............26 E4
Alkborough N Linc......125 K6
Alkham Kent............35 H6
Alkmonton Derbys......100 D5
Allaleigh Devon............7 J3
Allanaquoich Abers......204 D6
Allanbank N Lans......175 L6
Allanton Border............179 H7
Allanton N Lans............175 L4
Allanton S Lans............175 K7
Allaston Gloucs............54 F6
Allbrook Hants............29 J7
All Cannings Wilts............40 B7
Allendale Nthumb......149 L4
Allen End Warwks......85 L4
Allenheads Nthumb......149 L6
Allen's Green Herts......60 D5
Allensmore Herefs......69 J7
Allenton C Derb............101 G6
Aller Devon............24 B6
Aller Somset............26 B5
Allerby Cumb............147 J6
Allercombe Devon............12 D4
Allerford Somset............24 D3
Allerston N York............134 D3
Allerthorpe E R Yk......125 J2
Allerton C Brad............123 G4
Allerton Highld............213 H2
Allerton Lpool............111 L4
Allerton Bywater
  Leeds............124 C5
Allerton Mauleverer
  N York............132 F7
Allesley Covtry............86 C7
Allestree C Derb............101 G5
Allexton Leics............88 B4
Allgreave Ches E............113 L7

Allhallows Medway............46 D4
Alligin Shuas
  Highld............210 C3
Allington Dorset............13 L4
Allington Lincs............102 E4
Allington Wilts............28 D4
Allington Wilts............39 K5
Allington Wilts............40 B7
Allithwaite Cumb............129 J4
Alloa Clacks............185 J8
Allonby Cumb............147 J6
Alloway S Ayrs............163 J5
Allowenshay Somset......26 B8
All Stretton Shrops......83 J4
Alltchaorunn Highld......192 C6
Alltsigh Highld............202 C2
Alltwalis Carmth............66 B7
Alltwen Neath............51 K5
Alltyblaca Cerdgn......66 C5
Almeley Herefs............69 G4
Almington Staffs............99 G5
Almondbank P & K......185 M3
Almondbury Kirk............123 H7
Almondsbury S Glos......38 E4
Alne N York............133 G6
Alness Highld............222 E7
Alnham Nthumb............168 E7
Alnmouth Nthumb......169 J7
Alnwick Nthumb............169 J6
Alperton Gt Lon............44 D4
Alphamstone Essex......77 K7
Alpheton Suffk............77 K4
Alphington Devon............11 L6
Alport Derbys............114 E8
Alpraham Ches E............98 E1
Alresford Essex............62 C4
Alrewas Staffs............85 L1
Alsager Ches E............99 H2
Alsop en le Dale
  Derbys............100 D2
Alston Cumb............149 J5
Alston Devon............13 H2
Alstone Gloucs............55 M2
Alstonefield Staffs......100 C2
Alston Sutton Somset......26 B2
Alswear Devon............23 L6
Altandhu Highld............224 B6
Altarnun Cnwll............9 G8
Altass Highld............222 C2
Altcreich Ag & B......190 D8
Altgaltraig Ag & B......173 H4
Althorne Essex............61 L7
Althorpe N Linc............125 K8
Altnabreac Station
  Highld............230 E6
Altnaharra Highld......225 M2
Altofts Wakefd............124 B5
Alton Derbys............115 G8
Alton Hants............30 B4
Alton Staffs............100 B4
Alton Barnes Wilts......40 C7
Alton Pancras Dorset......14 D3
Alton Priors Wilts......40 C7
Alton Towers Staffs......100 B4
Altrincham Traffd......113 H4
Altskeith Hotel
  Stirlg............184 B6
Alva Clacks............185 J7
Alvanley Ches W............112 D6
Alvaston C Derb............101 H5
Alvechurch Worcs......85 J8
Alvecote Warwks......86 B3
Alvediston Wilts............27 L6
Alveley Shrops............84 D6
Alverdiscott Devon......23 H6
Alverstoke Hants............17 H3
Alverstone IoW............17 H5
Alverthorpe Wakefd......123 L6
Alverton Notts............102 C4
Alves Moray............214 E3
Alvescot Oxon............56 F6
Alveston S Glos............38 F3
Alveston Warwks............72 B3
Alvingham Lincs............118 E4
Alvington Gloucs............54 E7
Alwalton C Pete............89 G4
Alweston Dorset............26 F8
Alwinton Nthumb......168 D7

Alwoodley Leeds............123 K3
Alyth P & K............195 K6
Am Bàgh a Tuath
  W Isls............233 b9
Ambergate Derbys......101 G3
Amberley Gloucs............55 J7
Amberley W Susx............18 D3
Amble Nthumb............159 G2
Amblecote Dudley......84 F6
Ambler Thorn
  C Brad............123 G5
Ambleside Cumb............137 K6
Ambleston Pembks......49 G3
Ambrosden Oxon............57 L4
Amcotts N Linc............125 K7
Amersham Bucks............42 F2
Amersham
  Common Bucks......42 F2
Amersham Old
  Town Bucks......42 F2
Amersham on the
  Hill Bucks............58 F7
Amesbury Wilts............28 D3
Amhuinnsuidhe
  W Isls............232 d4
Amington Staffs............86 B3
Amisfield D & G............155 H5
Amlwch IoA............108 F3
Ammanford Carmth......51 J3
Amotherby N York......134 B5
Ampfield Hants............29 H6
Ampleforth N York......133 J4
Ampney Crucis
  Gloucs............56 B7
Ampney St Mary
  Gloucs............56 C7
Ampney St Peter
  Gloucs............56 B7
Amport Hants............28 F3
Ampthill C Beds............74 F6
Ampton Suffk............77 J1
Amroth Pembks............49 K6
Amulree P & K............185 J1
Amwell Herts............59 K5
Anaheilt Highld............191 G4
Ancaster Lincs............103 G4
Ancells Farm Hants......30 D1
Ancroft Nthumb............168 E1
Ancrum Border............167 K4
Ancton W Susx............18 D5
Anderby Lincs............119 G6
Andover Hants............29 G3
Andoversford Gloucs......56 A4
Andreas IoM............237 d2
Anerley Gt Lon............45 G6
Anfield Lpool............111 K3
Angarrack Cnwll............3 G4
Angelbank Shrops......83 L7
Angle Pembks............48 E6
Anglesey IoA............108 E5
Anglesey Abbey
  Cambs............76 D3
Angmering W Susx......18 E5
Angram N York............124 D2
Ankerville Highld......223 H6
Ankle Hill Leics............102 C8
Anlaby E R Yk............126 C5
Anmer Norfk............105 H6
Anmore Hants............17 J1
Annan D & G............147 L2
Annandale Water
  Services D & G......155 K4
Annat Highld............210 D4
Annathill N Lans............175 J4
Anna Valley Hants......29 G3
Annbank S Ayrs............163 K5
Anne Hathaway's
  Cottage Warwks......71 L4
Annfield Plain Dur......150 F5
Anniesland C Glas......174 F5
Ansdell Lancs............120 D5
Ansford Somset............26 F5
Ansley Warwks............86 C5
Anslow Staffs............100 E7
Anslow Gate Staffs......100 D7
Anstey Herts............60 C2
Anstey Leics............87 G2
Anstruther Fife............187 J6

Ansty W Susx............19 J2
Ansty Warwks............86 E6
Ansty Wilts............27 L6
An Tairbeart W Isls......232 e4
Anthorn Cumb............147 L4
Antingham Norfk......106 F5
An t-Ob W Isls............232 d5
Antonine Wall............175 L3
Anton's Gowt Lincs......103 M3
Antony Cnwll............6 B5
Antrobus Ches W......112 F5
Anwick Lincs............103 J3
Anwoth D & G............145 M4
Aperfield Gt Lon............32 D2
Apethorpe Nhants......88 E4
Apley Lincs............117 J6
Apperknowle Derbys......115 G5
Apperley Gloucs............55 K3
Appin Ag & B............191 J6
Appleby N Linc............126 B7
Appleby-in-
  Westmorland
  Cumb............139 G3
Appleby Magna Leics......86 C2
Appleby Parva Leics......86 C2
Applecross Highld......209 L5
Appledore Devon............23 G5
Appledore Devon............25 G8
Appledore Kent............34 C8
Appleford Oxon............41 K2
Applegarth Town
  D & G............155 J5
Appleshaw Hants............28 F2
Appleton Halton......112 D4
Appleton Oxon............57 H7
Appleton Warrtn......112 F5
Appleton-le-Moors
  N York............133 L3
Appleton-le-Street
  N York............134 B5
Appleton Roebuck
  N York............124 E3
Appleton Thorn
  Warrtn............112 F5
Appleton Wiske
  N York............141 J6
Appletreehall Border......167 H6
Appletreewick
  N York............131 K7
Appley Somset............25 G6
Apse Heath IoW............17 G5
Apsley End C Beds......59 J2
Apuldram W Susx......18 A5
Arabella Highld............223 H6
Arbirlot Angus............196 F7
Arborfield Wokham......42 C6
Arborfield Cross
  Wokham............42 C6
Arbourthorne Sheff......115 G4
Arbroath Angus............197 G7
Arbuthnott Abers......197 K2
Archddu Carmth............50 F5
Archdeacon Newton
  Darltn............141 G4
Archencarroch
  W Duns............174 D3
Archiestown Moray......214 F5
Archirondel Jersey......236 e6
Arclid Ches E............99 H1
Ardallie Abers............217 J6
Ardanaiseig Hotel
  Ag & B............182 F3
Ardaneaskan Highld......210 C7
Ardarroch Highld......210 C6
Ardbeg Ag & B............160 D1
Ardbeg Ag & B............173 J5
Ardbeg Ag & B............173 K2
Ardcharnich Highld......220 F4
Ardchiavaig Ag & B......180 E4
Ardchonnel Ag & B......182 D5
Ardchronie Highld......222 E4
Ardchullarie More
  Stirlg............184 D5
Arddarroch Ag & B......183 J7
Arddleen Powys............82 F1
Ard Dorch Highld......209 J8
Ardechive Highld......201 H7
Ardeer N Ayrs............163 H2

Ardeley Herts...60 A3
Ardelve Highld...210 D8
Arden Ag & B...174 C2
Ardens Grafton
  Warwks...71 K4
Ardentallen Ag & B...182 B3
Ardentinny Ag & B...173 L2
Ardentraive Ag & B...173 H4
Ardeonaig Stirlg...184 E1
Ardersier Highld...213 J4
Ardessie Highld...220 D4
Ardfern Ag & B...182 A6
Ardfernal Ag & B...171 K4
Ardgartan Ag & B...183 J6
Ardgay Highld...222 D4
Ardgour Highld...191 K4
Ardgowan Inver...173 L4
Ardhallow Ag & B...173 K4
Ardhasig W Isls...232 e4
Ardheslaig Highld...210 B3
Ardindrean Highld...220 F4
Ardingly W Susx...32 C7
Ardington Oxon...41 H3
Ardlamont Ag & B...173 G5
Ardleigh Essex...62 C3
Ardleigh Heath
  Essex...62 C2
Ardler P & K...195 L7
Ardley Oxon...57 K3
Ardlui Ag & B...183 K4
Ardlussa Ag & B...172 B2
Ardmair Highld...220 E2
Ardmaleish Ag & B...173 J5
Ardminish Ag & B...172 B8
Ardmolich Highld...190 E3
Ardmore Ag & B...174 C3
Ardmore Highld...222 F4
Ardnadam Ag & B...173 K3
Ardnagrask Highld...212 E4
Ardnamurchan
  Highld...190 B3
Ardnarff Highld...210 D7
Ardnastang Highld...190 F4
Ardpatrick Ag & B...172 C6
Ardrishaig Ag & B...172 E2
Ardross Highld...222 E6
Ardrossan N Ayrs...163 G2
Ardslignish Highld...190 B4
Ardtalla Ag & B...171 J7
Ardtoe Highld...190 C3
Arduaine Ag & B...182 A5
Ardullie Highld...212 E2
Ardvasar Highld...199 K5
Ardvorlich P & K...184 D3
Ardvourlie W Isls...232 e3
Ardwell D & G...144 D5
Ardwick Manch...113 J3
Areley Kings Worcs...70 E1
Arevegaig Highld...190 D3
Arford Hants...30 D4
Argoed Caerph...53 J7
Argyll Forest Park
  Ag & B...183 J6
Aribruach W Isls...232 e3
Aridhglas Ag & B...180 D3
Arileod Ag & B...188 F5
Arinagour Ag & B...189 G5
Ariogan Ag & B...182 C3
Arisaig Highld...199 K7
Arisaig House
  Highld...199 L7
Arkendale N York...132 F7
Arkesden Essex...76 C2
Arkholme Lancs...130 B5
Arkleton D & G...156 C4
Arkley Gt Lon...44 E2
Arksey Donc...115 L1
Arkwright Town
  Derbys...115 H7
Arle Gloucs...55 L4
Arlecdon Cumb...136 E4
Arlesey C Beds...75 H7
Arleston Wrekin...84 B2
Arley Ches E...112 F5
Arlingham Gloucs...55 G6
Arlington Devon...23 K4
Arlington E Susx...20 B4
Armadale Highld...199 K5

Armadale Highld...230 A3
Armadale W Loth...176 C5
Armathwaite Cumb...148 E5
Arminghall Norfk...92 F3
Armitage Staffs...85 J1
Armley Leeds...123 K4
Armscote Warwks...72 B5
Armthorpe Donc...115 L1
Arnabost Ag & B...188 F4
Arncliffe N York...131 H5
Arncroach Fife...187 H6
Arndilly House
  Moray...215 G5
Arne Dorset...15 H5
Arnesby Leics...87 H5
Arngask P & K...186 B5
Arnisdale Highld...200 C3
Arnish Highld...209 J5
Arniston Mdloth...177 K6
Arnol W Isls...232 f1
Arnold E R Yk...126 E3
Arnold Notts...101 L4
Arnprior Stirlg...184 D7
Arnside Cumb...129 K4
Aros Ag & B...190 B7
Arrad Foot Cumb...129 G4
Arram E R Yk...126 C2
Arran N Ayrs...162 B3
Arrathorne N York...132 C2
Arreton IoW...17 G5
Arrina Highld...210 B3
Arrington Cambs...75 K4
Arrochar Ag & B...183 K6
Arrow Warwks...71 J4
Arscott Shrops...83 J2
Artafallie Highld...212 F4
Arthington Leeds...123 K2
Arthingworth Nhants...87 L7
Arthrath Abers...217 H6
Artrochie Abers...217 J7
Arundel W Susx...18 D4
Asby Cumb...136 E3
Ascog Ag & B...173 J5
Ascot W & M...42 F6
Ascott-under-
  Wychwood Oxon...56 F4
Asenby N York...132 F4
Asfordby Leics...102 B8
Asfordby Hill Leics...102 B8
Asgarby Lincs...103 J4
Ash Kent...35 H3
Ash Kent...45 L6
Ash Somset...26 C7
Ash Surrey...30 E2
Ashampstead W Berk...41 K5
Ashbocking Suffk...78 E4
Ashbourne Derbys...100 D3
Ashbrittle Somset...25 G6
Ashburton Devon...7 H2
Ashbury Devon...10 D5
Ashbury Oxon...40 E4
Ashby N Linc...125 L8
Ashby by Partney
  Lincs...118 F7
Ashby cum Fenby
  NE Lin...118 C2
Ashby de la Launde
  Lincs...103 H2
Ashby-de-la-Zouch
  Leics...86 D1
Ashby Folville Leics...87 K2
Ashby Magna Leics...87 H5
Ashby Parva Leics...87 G5
Ashby Puerorum
  Lincs...118 D7
Ashby St Ledgers
  Nhants...73 H2
Ashby St Mary Norfk...93 G3
Ashchurch Gloucs...55 L2
Ashcombe Devon...11 L8
Ashcombe N Som...37 M7
Ashcott Somset...26 C4
Ashdon Essex...76 E6
Ashdown Forest
  E Susx...32 E6
Ashe Hants...29 K2
Asheldham Essex...62 A7
Ashen Essex...77 H6

Ashendon Bucks...58 B5
Asheridge Bucks...58 F6
Ashfield Herefs...54 E4
Ashfield Stirlg...185 G6
Ashfield cum
  Thorpe Suffk...78 E3
Ashfield Green Suffk...92 F8
Ashford Devon...7 G6
Ashford Devon...23 H4
Ashford Kent...34 D6
Ashford Surrey...43 H6
Ashford Bowdler
  Shrops...69 K1
Ashford Carbonell
  Shrops...69 K1
Ashford Hill Hants...41 K7
Ashford in the
  Water Derbys...114 D7
Ashgill S Lans...175 K7
Ash Green Surrey...30 E2
Ash Green Warwks...86 D6
Ashill Devon...12 E1
Ashill Norfk...91 K3
Ashill Somset...25 L7
Ashingdon Essex...46 E2
Ashington Nthumb...159 G5
Ashington Somset...26 E6
Ashington W Susx...18 F3
Ashkirk Border...167 G5
Ashleworth Gloucs...55 J3
Ashleworth Quay
  Gloucs...55 J3
Ashley Cambs...77 G3
Ashley Ches E...113 H5
Ashley Devon...10 F3
Ashley Gloucs...39 L2
Ashley Hants...16 B4
Ashley Hants...29 G5
Ashley Kent...35 J5
Ashley Nhants...87 L5
Ashley Staffs...99 H5
Ashley Wilts...39 J6
Ashley Green Bucks...58 F6
Ash Magna Shrops...98 E4
Ashmansworth Hants...41 H8
Ashmansworthy
  Devon...22 E7
Ash Mill Devon...24 C6
Ashmore Dorset...27 K7
Ashmore Green
  W Berk...41 J6
Ashorne Warwks...72 C3
Ashover Derbys...115 G8
Ashow Warwks...72 C1
Asherton Herefs...70 B6
Ashprington Devon...7 J4
Ash Priors Somset...25 J5
Ashreigney Devon...10 F3
Ash Street Suffk...78 B5
Ashtead Surrey...44 D8
Ash Thomas Devon...12 C1
Ashton Cnwll...3 G5
Ashton Devon...11 K7
Ashton Herefs...69 K2
Ashton Inver...173 L3
Ashton Nhants...73 L5
Ashton Nhants...88 F5
Ashton Common
  Wilts...39 K8
Ashton Hayes
  Ches W...112 D7
Ashton-in-
  Makerfield
  Wigan...112 E2
Ashton Keynes Wilts...40 B2
Ashton under Hill
  Worcs...71 H6
Ashton-under-Lyne
  Tamesd...113 L2
Ashton Vale Bristl...38 E6
Ashurst Hants...16 D1
Ashurst Kent...32 F5
Ashurst Lancs...121 G8
Ashurst W Susx...19 G3
Ashurst Wood
  W Susx...32 D5
Ash Vale Surrey...30 E2
Ashwater Devon...9 K5

Ashwell Herts...75 J4
Ashwell Rutlnd...88 C2
Ashwell End Herts...75 J6
Ashwellthorpe Norfk...92 D4
Ashwick Somset...26 F2
Ashwicken Norfk...105 H8
Askam in Furness
  Cumb...128 F4
Askern Donc...124 E7
Askerswell Dorset...14 A4
Askett Bucks...58 D6
Askham Cumb...138 D3
Askham Notts...116 C6
Askham Bryan
  C York...124 E2
Askham Richard
  C York...124 E2
Asknish Ag & B...172 F1
Askrigg N York...131 H2
Askwith N York...123 H2
Aslackby Lincs...103 H6
Aslacton Norfk...92 D5
Aslockton Notts...102 C4
Aspatria Cumb...147 K6
Aspenden Herts...60 B3
Aspley Guise C Beds...74 D7
Aspley Heath C Beds...74 D7
Aspull Wigan...121 J8
Asselby E R Yk...125 H5
Assington Suffk...77 L6
Assington Green
  Suffk...77 H4
Astbury Ches E...99 J1
Astcote Nhants...73 J4
Asterby Lincs...118 C5
Asterley Shrops...83 H3
Asterton Shrops...83 H5
Asthall Oxon...56 F5
Asthall Leigh Oxon...56 F5
Astle Highld...223 G3
Astley Shrops...98 D8
Astley Warwks...86 C5
Astley Wigan...113 G2
Astley Worcs...70 D2
Astley Abbots
  Shrops...84 C4
Astley Bridge
  Bolton...121 K7
Astley Cross Worcs...70 E1
Aston Birm...85 J5
Aston Ches E...98 E3
Aston Ches W...112 E5
Aston Derbys...114 D5
Aston Flints...111 J7
Aston Herts...59 L4
Aston Oxon...57 G7
Aston Rothm...115 J4
Aston Shrops...84 E5
Aston Shrops...98 D6
Aston Staffs...99 H4
Aston Staffs...99 K7
Aston Wokham...42 C4
Aston Wrekin...84 B2
Aston Abbotts Bucks...58 D4
Aston Botterell
  Shrops...84 B6
Aston-by-Stone
  Staffs...99 K6
Aston Cantlow
  Warwks...71 K3
Aston Clinton Bucks...58 E5
Aston Crews Herefs...54 F4
Aston End Herts...59 L3
Aston Fields Worcs...71 G1
Aston Flamville Leics...86 F5
Aston Ingham Herefs...55 G4
Aston le Walls
  Nhants...72 F4
Aston Magna Gloucs...71 L7
Aston Munslow
  Shrops...83 K6
Aston on Clun
  Shrops...83 H6
Aston Pigott Shrops...83 G3
Aston Rogers Shrops...83 G3
Aston Rowant Oxon...58 B7
Aston Somerville
  Worcs...71 J6

Aston-sub-Edge
  Gloucs .............................**71** K6
Aston Tirrold Oxon .......**41** K3
Aston-upon-Trent
  Derbys ............................**101** H6
Aston Upthorpe
  Oxon ..................................**41** K3
Astwick C Beds ...............**75** J6
Astwood M Keyn ...........**74** D5
Astwood Worcs ...............**71** G2
Astwood Bank Worcs ....**71** J3
Aswarby Lincs ...............**103** H4
Aswardby Lincs .............**118** E7
Atcham Shrops ................**83** K2
Athelhampton Dorset ...**14** E4
Athelington Suffk .........**78** E1
Athelney Somset ............**25** M5
Athelstaneford
  E Loth ...........................**178** C3
Atherington Devon ........**23** J6
Atherstone Warwks ........**86** C4
Atherstone on Stour
  Warwks ............................**72** B4
Atherton Wigan .............**113** G2
Atlow Derbys ..................**100** E3
Attadale Highld ............**210** E6
Atterby Lincs .................**117** G3
Attercliffe Sheff ...........**115** G4
Atterton Leics .................**86** D4
Attingham Park
  Shrops .............................**83** K2
Attleborough Norfk .......**92** C4
Attleborough
  Warwks ............................**86** D5
Attlebridge Norfk ..........**92** D1
Attleton Green Suffk .....**77** G4
Atwick E R Yk ................**126** F1
Atworth Wilts ..................**39** J7
Auborn Lincs .................**116** F8
Auchbreck Moray .........**214** F8
Auchedly Abers .............**217** G7
Auchenblae Abers ........**197** H1
Auchenbowie Stirlg .....**175** L2
Auchencairn D & G ......**146** D5
Auchencairn D & G ......**155** G5
Auchencairn N Ayrs ....**162** D4
Auchencrow Border .....**179** H6
Auchendinny Mdloth ...**177** H6
Auchengray S Lans .....**176** D7
Auchenhalrig Moray ....**215** J3
Auchenheath S Lans ...**164** F2
Auchenhessnane
  D & G ............................**154** E3
Auchenlochan
  Ag & B ...........................**173** G4
Auchenmade N Ayrs ...**174** C8
Auchenmalg D & G ......**144** E4
Auchentiber N Ayrs .....**174** C8
Auchindrain Ag & B .....**182** E6
Auchindrean Highld ....**221** G5
Auchininna Abers .........**216** C5
Auchinleck E Ayrs ........**164** B5
Auchinloch S Lans .......**175** H4
Auchinstarry N Lans ...**175** J3
Auchintore Highld .......**191** L2
Auchiries Abers ............**217** K6
Auchlean Highld ..........**203** K5
Auchlee Abers ..............**207** G6
Auchleven Abers ..........**206** C1
Auchlochan S Lans .......**164** F3
Auchlossan Abers .........**206** B5
Auchlyne Stirlg ............**184** B2
Auchmillan E Ayrs ......**164** A4
Auchmithie Angus .......**197** G7
Auchmuirbridge
  Fife .................................**186** C6
Auchnacree Angus ......**196** D4
Auchnagatt Abers ........**217** H6
Auchnarrow Moray ......**204** F2
Auchnotteroch
  D & G ............................**144** B3
Auchroisk Moray ..........**215** H4
Auchterarder P & K .....**185** K5
Auchteraw Highld .......**202** B4
Auchterblair Highld ....**203** L2
Auchtercairn Highld ...**219** J6
Auchterderran Fife......**186** C7
Auchterhouse Angus ...**196** B8

Auchterless Abers ........**216** D6
Auchtermuchty Fife .....**186** D5
Auchterneed Highld....**212** D3
Auchtertool Fife ..........**177** H1
Auchtertyre Highld .....**210** C8
Auchtubh Stirlg ...........**184** C4
Auckengill Highld .......**231** L3
Auckley Donc ...............**115** M2
Audenshaw Tamesd .....**113** K3
Audlem Ches E ...............**98** F4
Audley Staffs ..................**99** J3
Audley End Essex .........**76** D6
Audley End House
  & Gardens Essex ........**76** D6
Audnam Dudley .............**84** F6
Aughton E R Yk ............**125** G3
Aughton Lancs .............**111** L1
Aughton Lancs .............**129** L6
Aughton Rothm ...........**115** J4
Aughton Wilts ...............**28** E1
Aughton Park
  Lancs .............................**112** B1
Auldearn Highld ..........**213** L4
Aulden Herefs .................**69** J4
Auldgirth D & G ...........**154** F5
Auldhouse S Lans ........**175** H7
Ault a' chruinn
  Highld ...........................**200** E2
Aultbea Highld .............**219** K4
Aultgrishin Highld .......**219** H4
Aultguish Inn
  Highld ...........................**221** J7
Ault Hucknall
  Derbys ............................**115** J7
Aultmore Moray ...........**215** J4
Aultnagoire Highld......**202** E2
Aultnamain Highld.......**222** F5
Aunsby Lincs .................**103** H5
Aust S Glos ......................**38** E3
Austerfield Donc ..........**116** A3
Austrey Warwks ..............**86** C4
Austwick N York ...........**130** E5
Authorpe Lincs ..............**118** E5
Avebury Wilts ..................**40** C6
Avebury Wilts ..................**40** C6
Aveley Thurr ....................**45** L4
Avening Gloucs ...............**39** K2
Averham Notts ..............**102** C2
Aveton Gifford Devon .....**7** G4
Aviemore Highld ..........**203** L3
Avington W Berk ............**41** G6
Avoch Highld ................**213** G4
Avon Hants .......................**15** L3
Avonbridge Falk ...........**176** B4
Avon Dassett Warwks ...**72** E4
Avonmouth Bristl ..........**38** D5
Avonwick Devon ...............**7** G4
Awbridge Hants ..............**28** F6
Awliscombe Devon .........**12** E3
Awre Gloucs .....................**55** G6
Awsworth Notts ............**101** J4
Axbridge Somset ............**26** B1
Axford Hants ...................**29** L3
Axford Wilts .....................**40** E6
Axminster Devon .............**13** H3
Axmouth Devon ..............**13** G4
Aycliffe Dur ..................**141** B4
Aydon Nthumb ..............**150** C2
Aylburton Gloucs ...........**54** E7
Aylesbeare Devon ..........**12** D4
Aylesbury Bucks ............**58** D5
Aylesby NE Lin .............**126** F8
Aylesford Kent ...............**33** J2
Aylesham Kent ...............**35** H4
Aylestone C Leic .............**87** H4
Aylestone Park
  C Leic ...............................**87** H4
Aylmerton Norfk ...........**106** E5
Aylsham Norfk ...............**106** E6
Aylton Herefs ..................**70** B6
Aylworth Gloucs .............**56** C4
Aymestrey Herefs ...........**69** H2
Aynho Nhants ..................**57** K2
Ayot St Lawrence
  Herts ................................**59** K5
Ayr S Ayrs .....................**163** J5
Aysgarth N York ...........**131** J2
Ayshford Devon ..............**25** G7

Ayside Cumb .................**129** J3
Ayston Rutlnd ..................**88** C4
Ayton Border .................**179** J6
Azerley N York ..............**132** C5

# B

Babbacombe Torbay .........**7** L3
Babbs Green Herts .........**60** C5
Babcary Somset ..............**26** E5
Babraham Cambs ...........**76** D4
Babworth Notts .............**116** B5
Backaland Ork ..............**234** d4
Backfolds Abers .............**217** J4
Backford Ches W ............**111** L6
Backies Highld ..............**223** H2
Back of Keppoch
  Highld ...........................**199** K7
Backwell N Som ..............**38** C6
Baconsthorpe Norfk ....**106** D5
Bacton Herefs ..................**54** A2
Bacton Norfk .................**107** H5
Bacton Suffk ....................**78** C2
Bacup Lancs ..................**122** C6
Badachro Highld ..........**219** J6
Badanloch Highld .........**226** E2
Badbury Swindn .............**40** D4
Badby Nhants ..................**73** H3
Badcall Highld ..............**228** C4
Badcaul Highld .............**220** D3
Baddeley Edge
  C Stke ..............................**99** K3
Baddeley Green
  C Stke ..............................**99** K3
Baddesley Clinton
  Warwks ............................**86** B8
Baddesley Ensor
  Warwks ............................**86** C4
Baddidarrach Highld ...**224** D4
Baddinsgill Border .......**176** F7
Badenscoth Abers .........**216** D6
Badentarbet Highld......**224** B6
Badenyon Abers ...........**205** H2
Badger Shrops .................**84** D4
Badgeworth Gloucs ........**55** K4
Badgworth Somset .........**26** B2
Badical Highld ..............**210** B8
Badingham Suffk ...........**79** G2
Badlesmere Kent ............**34** D4
Badlieu Border ..............**165** K5
Badlipster Highld .........**231** J5
Badluarach Highld........**220** C3
Badninish Highld..........**223** G3
Badrallach Highld .........**220** D3
Badsey Worcs ...................**71** J5
Badshot Lea Surrey ........**30** E2
Badsworth Wakefd .......**124** C7
Badwell Ash Suffk .........**78** B2
Bagber Dorset .................**27** H8
Bagby N York .................**133** G4
Bag Enderby Lincs ........**118** E6
Bagendon Gloucs ...........**56** A6
Bàgh a' Chaisteil
  W Isls ...........................**233** b9
Bagillt Flints .................**111** H6
Baginton Warwks ...........**86** D8
Baglan Neath ..................**51** L6
Bagley Shrops .................**98** B6
Bagley Somset ................**26** C3
Bagnall Staffs .................**99** L3
Bagshot Surrey ...............**42** E7
Bagstone S Glos ..............**39** G3
Bagworth Leics ...............**86** F2
Bagwyllydiart Herefs......**54** C3
Baildon C Brad .............**123** H3
Baildon Green
  C Brad ..........................**123** H3
Baile Ailein W Isls ......**232** f3
Baile a' Mhanaich
  W Isls ...........................**233** b6
Baile Mòr Ag & B .........**180** D3
Baillieston C Glas .......**175** J5
Bainbridge N York ......**131** H2
Bainshole Abers ...........**216** B7
Bainton C Pete ...............**89** G3
Bainton E R Yk .............**126** B1

Baintown Fife ...............**186** F6
Bairnkine Border .........**167** K6
Bakewell Derbys ...........**114** E7
Bala Gwynd ......................**96** E5
Balallan W Isls .............**232** f3
Balbeg Highld ...............**212** C7
Balbeggie P & K ...........**186** C2
Balblair Highld .............**212** D5
Balblair Highld .............**213** G2
Balby Donc ...................**115** K2
Balcary D & G ...............**146** E5
Balchraggan Highld .....**212** E5
Balchrick Highld ..........**228** B4
Balcombe W Susx ...........**32** B6
Balcomie Links Fife .....**187** K5
Baldersby N York ..........**132** C5
Baldersby St James
  N York ...........................**132** E4
Balderstone Lancs ........**121** J4
Balderton Notts ............**102** D3
Baldinnie Fife ...............**187** G5
Baldinnies P & K ..........**185** L4
Baldock Herts ................**75** J7
Baldock Services
  Herts ................................**75** J6
Baldovie C Dund ...........**187** G2
Baldrine IoM .................**237** d5
Baldslow E Susx .............**20** F3
Bale Norfk ....................**106** B5
Baledgarno P & K .........**186** D2
Balemartine Ag & B .....**188** C7
Balerno C Edin ..............**177** G5
Balfarg Fife ...................**186** D6
Balfield Angus ...............**196** E3
Balfour Ork ...................**234** c5
Balfron Stirlg ................**174** F1
Balgaveny Abers ...........**216** C6
Balgonar Fife ................**185** L8
Balgowan D & G ...........**144** D6
Balgowan Highld ..........**202** F6
Balgown Highld ............**218** B7
Balgracie D & G ...........**144** B3
Balgray S Lans ..............**165** H5
Balham Gt Lon ................**44** F5
Balhary P & K ...............**195** L6
Balholmie P & K ...........**186** B1
Baligill Highld ..............**230** C3
Balintore Angus ............**195** L5
Balintore Highld ...........**223** J6
Balintraid Highld ..........**223** G7
Balivanich W Isls .........**233** b6
Balkeerie Angus ............**196** B7
Balkholme E R Yk .........**125** J5
Ballachulish Highld .....**191** L5
Ballajora IoM ................**237** e4
Ballantrae S Ayrs .........**152** C5
Ballasalla IoM ...............**237** b6
Ballater Abers ...............**205** J6
Ballaugh IoM .................**237** c3
Ballchraggan Highld ...**223** G6
Ballencrieff E Loth ......**178** B3
Ballevullin Ag & B ........**188** B6
Ball Green C Stke ...........**99** K3
Ball Haye Green
  Staffs ................................**99** M2
Ball Hill Hants ................**41** H7
Ballianlay Ag & B .........**173** H6
Ballidon Derbys ............**100** D2
Balliekine N Ayrs ..........**161** L2
Balliemore Ag & B ........**182** F7
Balligmorrie S Ayrs ......**152** F4
Ballimore Stirlg ............**184** C4
Ballindalloch Moray ....**214** E7
Ballindean P & K ..........**186** D2
Ballinger Common
  Bucks ...............................**58** E7
Ballingham Herefs .........**54** E2
Ballingry Fife ................**186** C7
Ballinluig P & K ...........**194** F5
Ballinshoe Angus ..........**196** C5
Ballintuim P & K ..........**195** H5
Balloch Highld ..............**213** H5
Balloch N Lans ..............**175** K4
Balloch P & K ...............**185** H4
Balloch S Ayrs ..............**153** G3
Balloch W Duns ............**174** D3
Balls Cross W Susx .........**31** G6
Balls Green E Susx .........**32** E6

Ballygown Ag & B ........ 189 K7
Ballygrant Ag & B ....... 171 G5
Ballyhaugh Ag & B....... 188 F5
Balmacara Highld ......... 210 C8
Balmaclellan D & G ..... 154 B6
Balmae D & G ............... 146 C6
Balmaha Stirlg ............ 174 D1
Balmalcolm Fife .......... 186 E5
Balmangan Ag & B ....... 146 B5
Balmedie Abers ........... 207 H2
Balmerino Fife ............ 186 F3
Balmichael N Ayrs ....... 162 B3
Balmore E Duns ........... 175 G4
Balmuchy Highld........... 223 J5
Balmule Fife ............... 177 G2
Balmullo Fife .............. 187 G4
Balnacoil Highld .......... 226 E6
Balnacra Highld .......... 210 F5
Balnacroft Abers ......... 205 G6
Balnafoich Highld ........ 213 G7
Balnaguard P & K ....... 194 E6
Balnahard Ag & B ........ 180 F1
Balnain Highld ............. 212 C2
Balnakeil Highld .......... 228 F2
Balne N York ............... 124 F6
Balquharn P & K .......... 185 L1
Balquhidder Stirlg ...... 184 C3
**Balsall Common**
 Solhll .........................86 B7
Balsall Heath Birm ......85 J6
Balscote Oxon ...............72 E6
Balsham Cambs .............76 E4
Baltasound Shet ......... 235 e1
Baltersan D & G ........... 145 J3
Balthangie Abers ........ 216 F4
**Baltonsborough**
 Somset .......................26 D4
Balvicar Ag & B........... 181 M4
Balvraid Highld ........... 200 C3
Balvraid Highld ........... 213 K7
**Bamber Bridge**
 Lancs ........................ 121 H5
**Bamber's Green**
 Essex .........................60 F4
Bamburgh Nthumb ...... 169 H3
**Bamburgh Castle**
 Nthumb ..................... 169 H3
Bamford Derbys .......... 114 E5
Bampton Cumb ........... 138 D4
Bampton Devon .............24 E6
Bampton Oxon ..............56 F7
**Bampton Grange**
 Cumb ........................ 138 D4
Banavie Highld............ 191 L2
Banbury Oxon ...............72 F6
**Bancffosfelen**
 Carmth .......................50 F3
Banchory Abers .......... 206 D6
**Banchory-Devenick**
 Abers ....................... 207 G5
Bancycapel Carmth .......50 E3
Bancyfelin Carmth.........50 D2
Bandirran P & K .......... 186 C2
Banff Abers ................ 216 D2
Bangor Gwynd ............ 109 H6
**Bangor-on-Dee**
 Wrexhm .......................98 B4
Bangors Cnwll ................9 G5
Banham Norfk ...............92 C6
Bank Hants ...................16 C2
Bankend D & G ........... 147 H2
Bankfoot P & K ........... 185 M1
Bankglen E Ayrs .......... 164 C6
Bankhead C Aber ........ 207 G4
Bankhead S Lans ........ 165 J1
Banknock Falk ............ 175 K3
Banks Lancs ............... 120 E6
Bankshill D & G ........... 155 L5
Banningham Norfk ...... 106 F6
**Bannister Green**
 Essex .........................61 H4
Bannockburn Stirlg .... 175 L1
Banstead Surrey ...........44 E7
Bantham Devon ..............6 F6
Banton N Lans ............ 175 K3
Banwell N Som ..............38 B8
Bapchild Kent ...............34 C3
Bapton Wilts .................27 M4

Barabhas W Isls ........ 232 f1
Barassie S Ayrs .......... 163 J3
Barbaraville Highld .... 223 G6
Barbieston S Ayrs ....... 163 K5
Barbon Cumb .............. 130 C3
Barbrook Devon ............23 L2
Barby Nhants ................73 G1
Barcaldine Ag & B ...... 191 J7
Barcombe E Susx ..........19 L3
**Barcombe Cross**
 E Susx .......................19 L3
Barden Park Kent..........33 G4
**Bardfield End Green**
 Essex .........................61 G2
**Bardfield Saling**
 Essex .........................61 G3
Bardney Lincs ............. 117 J7
Bardon Leics ................86 F2
Bardon Mill Nthumb .... 149 K3
Bardowie E Duns ........ 175 G4
Bardrainney Inver ...... 174 C4
Bardsea Cumb ............ 129 G5
Bardsey Leeds ............ 124 B2
**Bardsey Island**
 Gwynd .......................94 B7
Bardwell Suffk ..............91 L8
Bare Lancs .................. 129 K6
Barfad D & G ............... 145 G2
Barford Norfk ...............92 D3
Barford Warwks ...........72 C3
**Barford St John**
 Oxon ..........................57 H2
**Barford St Martin**
 Wilts ..........................28 B5
**Barford St Michael**
 Oxon ..........................57 H2
Barfrestone Kent ..........35 H5
Bargeddie N Lans ....... 175 J5
Bargoed Caerph ...........53 J7
Bargrennan D & G ...... 153 H6
Barham Cambs ..............89 G7
Barham Kent .................35 G5
Barham Suffk ................78 D4
**Bar Hill** Cambs ..........75 L2
Barholm Lincs ..............88 F2
Barkby Leics .................87 J2
Barkby Thorpe Leics ....87 J2
**Barkestone-le-Vale**
 Leics ........................ 102 C5
Barkham Wokham .........42 C6
Barking Gt Lon .............45 H3
Barking Suffk ...............78 C4
Barkingside Gt Lon .......45 H3
Barking Tye Suffk .........78 C4
Barkisland Calder ....... 122 F6
Barkla Shop Cnwll ..........3 J2
Barkston Lincs ........... 102 F4
Barkston Ash N York ... 124 D4
Barkway Herts ..............75 L7
Barlanark C Glas ........ 175 H5
Barlaston Staffs ...........99 K5
Barlavington W Susx ....18 C3
Barlborough Derbys .... 115 J6
Barlby N York .............. 124 F4
Barlestone Leics ...........86 E3
Barley Herts .................76 B6
Barley Lancs ............... 122 B3
Barleythorpe Rutlnd.....88 B2
Barling Essex ...............46 F3
Barlings Lincs ............. 117 H6
Barlochan D & G ......... 146 E4
Barlow Derbys ............ 115 G6
Barlow Gatesd ............ 150 E3
Barlow N York ............. 124 F5
**Barmby Moor**
 E R Yk ...................... 125 J2
**Barmby on the**
 **Marsh** E R Yk ......... 125 J2
Barmollack Ag & B ...... 161 K1
Barmouth Gwynd ..........80 E1
Barmpton Darltn ........ 141 H4
Barmston E R Yk ......... 135 J7
Barnacarry Ag & B ...... 182 E8
Barnack C Pete ..............88 F3
Barnard Castle Dur .... 140 D4
Barnard Gate Oxon .......57 H6
Barnardiston Suffk.......77 G5
Barnbarroch D & G ..... 146 E4

Barnburgh Donc ......... 115 J2
Barnby Suffk .................93 K5
Barnby Dun Donc ....... 124 F8
**Barnby in the**
 **Willows** Notts........ 102 E3
Barnby Moor Notts ..... 116 A5
Barncorkrie D & G ...... 144 D7
Barnes Gt Lon ...............44 E5
Barnes Street Kent .......33 H4
Barnet Gt Lon ...............44 E2
**Barnetby le Wold**
 N Linc ...................... 126 C8
Barney Norfk .............. 106 B6
Barnham Suffk .............91 K7
Barnham W Susx ..........18 C5
**Barnham Broom**
 Norfk .........................92 C3
Barnhead Angus ......... 197 G5
Barnhill C Dund .......... 187 H2
Barnhill Moray ........... 214 E3
Barnhills D & G .......... 152 B7
Barningham Dur ......... 140 D5
Barningham Suffk .........91 L7
**Barnoldby le Beck**
 NE Lin ...................... 118 C2
Barnoldswick Lancs .... 122 C2
Barns Green W Susx .....31 J6
Barnsley Barns ........... 115 G1
Barnsley Gloucs ...........56 B6
Barnstaple Devon .........23 J5
Barnston Essex .............61 G4
Barnston Wirral .......... 111 J5
Barnstone Notts ......... 102 B5
Barnt Green Worcs .......85 H8
Barnton C Edin ........... 177 G4
Barnton Ches W .......... 112 F6
**Barnwell All Saints**
 Nhants .......................88 F6
**Barnwell St Andrew**
 Nhants .......................88 F6
Barnwood Gloucs .........55 K4
Barr S Ayrs ................. 153 G4
Barra W Isls ............... 233 b9
**Barra Airport** W Isls .. 233 b9
Barrachan D & G ........ 145 H5
Barraigh W Isls .......... 233 b9
Barrananaoil Ag & B ... 182 B6
Barrapoll Ag & B ........ 188 B7
Barrasford Nthumb .... 158 A7
Barregarrow IoM
Barrhead E Rens ........ 174 F6
Barrhill S Ayrs ........... 152 F5
Barrington Cambs .........76 B5
Barrington Somset .......26 B7
Barripper Cnwll ..............3 H4
Barrmill N Ayrs .......... 174 C7
Barrock Highld ........... 231 J2
Barrow Gloucs ..............55 K3
Barrow Lancs .............. 121 L3
Barrow Rutlnd ..............88 C1
Barrow Somset .............27 G5
Barrow Suffk .................77 H2
Barrowby Lincs .......... 102 E5
Barrowden Rutlnd .........88 D4
Barrowford Lancs ....... 122 C3
**Barrow Gurney**
 N Som .......................38 D6
Barrow Haven N Linc .. 126 D6
**Barrow-in-Furness**
 Cumb ....................... 128 E5
Barrow Island Cumb ... 128 E5
**Barrow-upon-**
 **Humber** N Linc ...... 126 D6
**Barrow upon Soar**
 Leics ........................ 101 L8
**Barrow upon Trent**
 Derbys ...................... 101 G6
Barry Angus ............... 187 J1
Barry V Glam ................37 H6
Barry Island V Glam .....37 H6
Barsby Leics .................87 K2
Barsham Suffk ..............93 H5
Barston Solhll ...............86 B7
Bartestree Herefs .........69 L6
**Barthol Chapel**
 Abers ....................... 216 F7
**Bartholomew Green**
 Essex .........................61 H4
Barthomley Ches E .......99 H3

Bartley Hants ...............28 F8
Bartley Green Birm ......85 H6
Bartlow Cambs ..............76 E5
Barton Cambs ...............76 B4
Barton Ches W ..............98 C2
Barton Gloucs ...............56 C3
Barton Lancs ............... 120 E8
Barton Lancs ............... 121 G3
Barton N York ............. 141 G5
Barton Oxon .................57 K6
Barton Torbay ..................7 K3
**Barton Bendish**
 Norfk .........................91 G3
**Barton End** Gloucs......39 J2
**Barton Hartshorn**
 Bucks .........................57 M2
**Barton in Fabis**
 Notts ........................ 101 K6
**Barton in the Beans**
 Leics ..........................86 E3
**Barton-le-Clay**
 C Beds ........................59 H2
**Barton-le-Street**
 N York ...................... 133 L5
**Barton-le-Willows**
 N York ...................... 133 L6
**Barton Mills** Suffk .....91 G8
**Barton-on-Sea**
 Hants .........................16 B4
**Barton-on-the-**
 **Heath** Warwks ..........56 E2
**Barton Park**
 Services N York......... 140 F5
**Barton St David**
 Somset .......................26 D5
**Barton Seagrave**
 Nhants .......................88 C7
Barton Stacey Hants .....29 H3
Barton Town Devon .......23 L4
Barton Turf Norfk ....... 107 H7
**Barton-under-**
 **Needwood** Staffs .... 100 D8
**Barton-upon-**
 **Humber** N Linc ....... 126 C6
**Barton Waterside**
 N Linc ...................... 126 C6
Barvas W Isls ............. 232 f1
Barway Cambs ..............90 D7
Barwell Leics ................86 F4
Barwick Devon ..............10 E4
Barwick Somset ...........26 E8
**Barwick in Elmet**
 Leeds ....................... 124 B3
Baschurch Shrops ........98 B7
Bascote Warwks ...........72 E2
Bashall Eaves Lancs ... 121 K2
Basildon Essex .............46 B3
Basingstoke Hants ...... 29 M2
Baslow Derbys ............ 114 E6
Bason Bridge Somset ...25 M3
Bassaleg Newpt ............37 L3
Bassendean Border..... 167 K1
Bassenthwaite Cumb .. 137 H2
Bassett C Sotn ..............29 H7
**Bassingbourn-cum-**
 **Kneesworth**
 Cambs .......................75 L5
Bassingham Lincs ...... 102 E1
Bassingthorpe Lincs .. 102 F6
Bassus Green Herts ......60 B3
Baston Lincs .................89 G2
Bastwick Norfk .......... 107 J8
Batchworth Herts .........43 H2
Batcombe Dorset ..........14 C2
Batcombe Somset .........27 G4
Batford Herts ................59 J5
Bath BaNES ...................39 H7
**Bath** BaNES .................39 H7
Bathampton BaNES.......39 H7
Bathealton Somset .......25 G6
Batheaston BaNES ........39 H6
Bathford BaNES.............39 H7
Bathgate W Loth ......... 176 D5
Bathley Notts .............. 102 C2
Bathpool Cnwll ...............5 L2
Bathpool Somset ..........25 K6
**Bath Side** Essex ..........62 F2
Bathville W Loth ......... 176 C5

Bathway Somset............26 E2
Batley Kirk..................123 J5
Batsford Gloucs............71 L7
Battersby N York..........142 D5
Battersea Gt Lon..........44 F5
Battisford Tye Suffk....78 B4
Battle E Susx..............20 F3
Battle Powys..............52 F2
Battledykes Angus....196 D5
Battlefield Shrops........83 K1
Battlesbridge Essex....46 C2
Battleton Somset........24 E6
Baughton Worcs..........70 F6
Baughurst Hants..........41 L7
Baulds Abers..............206 B6
Baulking Oxon............40 F3
Baumber Lincs............117 L6
Baunton Gloucs..........56 A6
Baverstock Wilts..........28 B5
Bawburgh Norfk..........92 D2
Bawdeswell Norfk....106 C7
Bawdrip Somset..........25 M4
Bawdsey Suffk............79 H6
Bawtry Donc..............115 M3
Baxenden Lancs........122 B5
Baxterley Warwks......86 C4
Bay Highld..................208 D4
Bayble W Isls..............232 g2
Baybridge Hants..........29 K6
Baycliff Cumb............129 G5
Baydon Wilts..............40 F5
Bayford Herts............60 A6
Bayford Somset..........27 G5
Bayhead W Isls..........233 b6
Baylham Suffk............78 D4
Baysham Herefs..........54 E3
Bayston Hill Shrops....83 J2
Baythorne End Essex..77 G6
Bayton Worcs..............84 C8
Bayworth Oxon............57 J7
Beachampton Bucks....73 L6
Beachamwell Norfk....91 H3
Beachy Head E Susx....20 C6
Beacon Devon..............12 F2
Beacon End Essex......62 A3
Beacon Hill Notts......102 D2
Beacon Hill Surrey......30 E4
Beacon's Bottom
    Bucks......................42 C2
Beaconsfield Bucks......42 F3
Beaconsfield
    Services Bucks........42 F3
Beadlam N York........133 K3
Beadlow C Beds..........75 G6
Beadnell Nthumb......169 J4
Beaford Devon............10 E2
Beal N York................124 E5
Beal Nthumb............169 G2
Bealsmill Cnwll............6 A1
Beaminster Dorset......13 L3
Beamish Dur..............151 G4
Beamish Open Air
    Museum Dur..........150 F4
Beamsley N York........131 K8
Beanacre Wilts............39 K7
Beanley Nthumb........169 G5
Beardon Devon............10 D7
Beare Green Surrey......31 K3
Bearley Warwks..........71 L3
Bearpark Dur............151 G6
Bearsden E Duns......174 F4
Bearsted Kent............33 K3
Bearstone Shrops........99 G5
Bearwood BCP............15 K3
Bearwood Birm..........85 H6
Bearwood Herefs........69 H4
Beattock D & G..........155 J2
Beauchamp Roding
    Essex....................60 F6
Beauchief Sheff........115 G5
Beaufort Blae G..........53 J5
Beaulieu Hants............16 E3
Beaulieu Hants............16 E3
Beauly Highld............212 G1
Beaumaris IoA..........109 H6
Beaumaris Castle
    IoA......................109 J6
Beaumont Cumb......148 C3

Beaumont Essex..........62 E3
Beaumont Jersey......236 c7
Beaumont Leys
    C Leic....................87 H2
Beausale Warwks........72 B1
Beauworth Hants........29 L6
Beaworthy Devon........10 C5
Beazley End Essex......61 H3
Bebington Wirral......111 K5
Beccles Suffk..............93 J5
Becconsall Lancs......120 F6
Beckbury Shrops........84 D3
Beckenham Gt Lon....45 G6
Beckermet Cumb......136 E6
Beckfoot Cumb..........147 J5
Beckford Worcs..........71 H7
Beckhampton Wilts....40 C6
Beckingham Lincs....102 E2
Beckingham Notts....116 C4
Beckington Somset....27 J2
Beckjay Shrops..........83 H7
Beckley E Susx............21 G2
Beckley Oxon..............57 K5
Beck Row Suffk..........91 G7
Beck Side Cumb........128 F3
Beckton Gt Lon..........45 H4
Beckwithshaw
    N York..................132 D8
Becontree Gt Lon......45 J3
Becquet Vincent
    Jersey..................236 c6
Bedale N York..........132 D2
Bedchester Dorset......27 J7
Beddau Rhondd..........37 G4
Beddgelert Gwynd......95 K3
Beddingham E Susx....19 L4
Beddington Gt Lon....44 F6
Beddington Corner
    Gt Lon..................44 F6
Bedfield Suffk............78 F2
Bedford Bed..............74 F5
Bedgrove Bucks..........58 D5
Bedhampton Hants....17 K2
Bedingfield Suffk........78 E2
Bedlam N York..........132 D7
Bedlington Nthumb..159 G5
Bedlinog Myr Td........53 H7
Bedminster Bristl......38 E4
Bedminster Down
    Bristl....................38 E6
Bedmond Herts..........59 J7
Bednall Staffs..............99 L8
Bedrule Border..........167 J5
Bedstone Shrops........83 G7
Bedwas Caerph..........37 J3
Bedwellty Caerph......53 J7
Bedworth Warwks......86 D6
Beeby Leics................87 J2
Beech Hants................30 B4
Beech Staffs................99 J5
Beech Hill W Berk......42 B7
Beechingstoke Wilts..40 C8
Beedon W Berk..........41 J5
Beeford E R Yk..........135 H8
Beeley Derbys............114 E7
Beelsby NE Lin..........117 K2
Beenham W Berk........41 L6
Beer Devon................13 G5
Beer Somset................26 B5
Beercrocombe
    Somset..................25 L7
Beer Hackett Dorset..14 B1
Beesands Devon............7 J7
Beesby Lincs............118 F5
Beeson Devon..............7 J7
Beeston C Beds..........75 H5
Beeston Ches W..........98 D2
Beeston Leeds..........123 K4
Beeston Norfk............91 K1
Beeston Notts..........101 K5
Beeston Regis Norfk..106 E4
Beeswing D & G........146 F2
Beetham Cumb........129 K4
Beetham Somset........25 L8
Beetley Norfk............106 A8
Begbroke Oxon..........57 J5
Begelly Pembks..........49 J6
Beguildy Powys..........82 D7

Beighton Norfk............93 H2
Beighton Sheff..........115 H5
Beinn Na Faoghla
    W Isls..................233 c7
Beith N Ayrs..............174 C7
Bekesbourne Kent......35 G4
Belaugh Norfk..........107 G8
Belbroughton Worcs..85 G7
Belchalwell Dorset......14 E1
Belchamp Otten
    Essex....................77 J6
Belchamp St Paul
    Essex....................77 H6
Belchamp Walter
    Essex....................77 J6
Belchford Lincs........118 D6
Belford Nthumb........169 G3
Belgrave C Leic..........87 H3
Belhaven E Loth......178 E3
Belhelvie Abers........207 H2
Belhinnie Abers........215 K8
Bellabeg Abers..........205 H3
Bellanoch Ag & B......182 A8
Bellaty Angus............195 K4
Bell Busk N York......131 G7
Belleau Lincs............118 E5
Bell End Worcs............85 G7
Bellerby N York........131 L2
Belle Vue Cumb........148 C4
Belle Vue Wakefd....123 L6
Bellfield S Lans........164 F3
Bellfields Surrey..........31 G2
Bellingdon Bucks........58 F6
Bellingham Nthumb..157 L5
Belloch Ag & B..........161 H2
Bellochantuy Ag & B..161 H3
Bell o' th' Hill Ches W..98 D4
Bellshill N Lans........175 J6
Bellside N Lans........175 L6
Bellsquarry W Loth..176 E5
Bells Yew Green
    E Susx....................33 G6
Belluton BaNES..........38 E7
Belmaduthy Highld..213 G3
Belmont Bl w D........121 K7
Belmont Gt Lon..........44 E7
Belmont S Ayrs..........163 J5
Belmont Shet............235 d2
Belnacraig Abers......205 J3
Belper Derbys..........101 G3
Belsay Nthumb........158 D6
Belses Border............167 J4
Belsford Devon............7 H4
Belsize Herts..............59 G7
Belstead Suffk............78 D6
Belstone Devon..........10 F6
Belthorn Bl w D........121 L5
Beltinge Kent..............47 K6
Beltingham Nthumb..149 K3
Beltoft N Linc............116 D1
Belton Leics..............101 H7
Belton Lincs..............102 F4
Belton N Linc............116 C1
Belton Norfk................93 K3
Belton House Lincs..102 F5
Belton in Rutland
    Rutlnd....................88 B3
Belvedere Gt Lon......45 J4
Belvoir Leics............102 D5
Bembridge IoW..........17 J3
Bemerton Wilts..........28 C5
Bempton E R Yk......135 J5
Benacre Suffk..............93 K6
Benbecula W Isls....233 c7
Benbecula Airport
    W Isls..................233 c6
Benbuie D & G........154 C3
Benderloch Ag & B..191 H8
Benenden Kent..........33 K6
Benfieldside Dur......150 D4
Bengeo Herts..............60 A5
Bengeworth Worcs....71 J5
Benhall Green Suffk..79 H3
Benhall Street Suffk..79 H3
Benholm Abers........197 K3
Beningbrough
    N York..................133 H7
Benington Herts..........59 M4

Benington Lincs........104 C3
Benllech IoA............109 G5
Benmore Ag & B......173 K2
Bennan N Ayrs..........162 C5
Ben Nevis Highld......192 B3
Benniworth Lincs......117 K5
Benover Kent..............33 J4
Ben Rhydding
    C Brad..................123 H2
Benslie N Ayrs..........163 J2
Benson Oxon..............41 L3
Benthoul C Aber......206 F5
Bentley Donc............115 K1
Bentley E R Yk..........126 C4
Bentley Hants............30 C3
Bentley Suffk..............78 D6
Bentley Warwks..........86 C4
Bentpath D & G........156 B4
Bentworth Devon........24 B5
Bentworth Hants........30 A4
Benvie Angus..........186 E2
Benville Dorset..........14 A2
Benwick Cambs..........89 L5
Beoley Worcs..............71 J1
Beoraidbeg Highld..199 L6
Bepton W Susx............18 B3
Berden Essex..............60 D3
Berea Pembks............48 D2
Bere Alston Devon........6 C3
Bere Ferrers Devon......6 C3
Bere Regis Dorset......14 F4
Bergh Apton Norfk....93 G4
Berinsfield Oxon........41 L2
Berkeley Gloucs..........55 G7
Berkhamsted Herts....59 G6
Berkley Somset..........27 J2
Berkswell Solhll..........86 B7
Bermondsey Gt Lon....45 G4
Bernera Highld........200 C2
Bernisdale Highld....208 F4
Berrick Prior Oxon....41 L2
Berrick Salome Oxon..41 L2
Berriedale Highld....227 K4
Berrier Cumb............137 L2
Berriew Powys............82 D4
Berrington Shrops......83 K3
Berrington Worcs......69 L2
Berrington Green
    Worcs....................69 L2
Berrow Somset..........25 L2
Berrow Green Worcs..70 D3
Berryfields Bucks........58 C5
Berryhillock Moray....215 L3
Berryhillock Moray....215 L4
Berrynarbor Devon......23 J3
Berry Pomeroy
    Devon......................7 J4
Bersham Wrexhm......97 L3
Bersted W Susx..........18 C5
Berwick E Susx..........20 B5
Berwick Bassett
    Wilts......................40 C5
Berwick Hill Nthumb..158 F6
Berwick St James
    Wilts......................28 B4
Berwick St John
    Wilts......................27 L6
Berwick St Leonard
    Wilts......................27 L5
Berwick-upon-
    Tweed Nthumb......179 K7
Bescar Lancs............120 E7
Besford Worcs............71 G5
Bessacarr Donc........115 L2
Bessingby E R Yk....135 J6
Bessingham Norfk....106 E5
Besthorpe Norfk........92 C4
Besthorpe Notts......116 D8
Bestwood Village
    Notts....................101 K3
Beswick E R Yk........126 C2
Betchworth Surrey....31 K2
Bethania Cerdgn........66 D2
Bethel Gwynd..........109 G7
Bethel IoA..............108 E7
Bethersden Kent........34 C6
Bethesda Gwynd......109 J7
Bethesda Pembks......49 J4

Bethlehem Carmth .........51 K1
Bethnal Green Gt Lon...45 G4
Betley Staffs..............99 H3
Betsham Kent.............45 L5
Betteshanger Kent.......35 J4
Bettiscombe Dorset.....13 K3
Bettisfield Wrexhm......98 C5
Bettws Brdgnd............36 D3
Bettws Newpt.............37 L3
Bettws Cedewain
　Powys..................82 C4
Bettws Ifan Cerdgn.....65 J5
Bettws-Newydd
　Mons...................54 A6
Bettyhill Highld.........229 L3
Betws Bledrws
　Cerdgn.................66 D4
Betws Gwerfil Goch
　Denbgs.................97 G3
Betws-y-Coed
　Conwy..................96 C2
Betws-yn-Rhos
　Conwy.................110 C6
Beulah Cerdgn...........65 J5
Beulah Powys............67 K4
Bevercotes Notts.......116 B6
Beverley E R Yk.........126 C3
Beverston Gloucs........39 K2
Bewcastle Cumb........156 F7
Bewdley Worcs...........84 D7
Bewerley N York........132 B6
Bewholme E R Yk.......126 E1
Bexhill-on-Sea
　E Susx..................20 E4
Bexley Gt Lon............45 J5
Bexleyheath Gt Lon....45 J5
Bexwell Norfk............90 F3
Beyton Suffk.............77 L2
Beyton Green Suffk.....77 L2
Bhaltos W Isls..........232 d2
Bhatarsaigh W Isls....233 b10
Bibury Gloucs............56 C6
Bicester Oxon............57 L4
Bickenhill Solhll.........85 L6
Bicker Lincs.............103 L5
Bickerstaffe Lancs.....112 C2
Bickerton N York.......124 C1
Bickford Staffs..........84 F2
Bickington Devon......... 7 J2
Bickington Devon........23 H5
Bickleigh Devon........... 6 D4
Bickleigh Devon..........12 B2
Bickley Ches W..........98 D3
Bickley Gt Lon............45 H6
Bickley N York..........134 E2
Bicknacre Essex.........61 J7
Bicknoller Somset......25 H4
Bicknor Kent.............33 L2
Bicton Shrops............82 F6
Bicton Shrops............83 J1
Bidborough Kent........32 F5
Biddenden Kent..........33 L5
Biddenham Bed..........74 E4
Biddestone Wilts........39 K5
Biddisham Somset......26 B3
Biddlesden Bucks.......73 J6
Biddulph Staffs..........99 K2
Biddulph Moor Staffs...99 K2
Bideford Devon..........23 G6
Bidford-on-Avon
　Warwks.................71 K4
Bielby E R Yk...........125 J2
Bieldside C Aber.......207 G5
Bierley IoW...............17 G6
Bierton Bucks............58 D5
Big Balcraig D & G....145 H6
Bigbury Devon............ 6 F6
Bigbury-on-Sea
　Devon................... 6 F6
Bigby Lincs.............117 H1
Biggar S Lans..........165 K2
Biggin Derbys..........100 D2
Biggin Hill Gt Lon......32 D2
Biggleswade C Beds....75 H5
Bigholms D & G........156 B6
Bighouse Highld.......230 C3
Bighton Hants...........29 L4
Biglands Cumb.........148 A4

Bignor W Susx..........18 D3
Bigrigg Cumb...........136 D5
Big Sand Highld.......219 H5
Bigton Shet............235 c7
Bilborough C Nott....101 K4
Bilbrook Somset........25 G3
Bilbrough N York......124 E2
Bilbster Highld........231 K5
Bildershaw Dur........140 F3
Bildeston Suffk.........78 B5
Billericay Essex........46 B2
Billesdon Leics.........87 K3
Billesley Warwks.......71 K3
Billingborough Lincs...103 J5
Billinge St Hel.........112 D2
Billingford Norfk........92 E7
Billingford Norfk......106 B7
Billingham S on T......141 K3
Billinghay Lincs.......103 J2
Billingley Barns.......115 H1
Billingshurst W Susx...31 H6
Billingsley Shrops......84 C6
Billington C Beds.......58 F4
Billington Lancs........121 L4
Billockby Norfk..........93 J2
Billy Row Dur..........150 E7
Bilsborrow Lancs......121 G3
Bilsby Lincs............119 G6
Bilsham W Susx.........18 D5
Bilsington Kent.........34 D7
Bilsthorpe Notts......101 M1
Bilston Mdloth........177 H5
Bilston Wolves..........85 G4
Bilstone Leics...........86 D3
Bilton E R Yk..........126 E4
Bilton N York..........132 D7
Bilton Warwks..........86 F8
Bilton-in-Ainsty
　N York................124 D1
Binbrook Lincs........117 K3
Bincombe Dorset........14 D5
Binegar Somset.........26 E2
Binfield Br For..........42 D6
Binfield Heath Oxon...42 C5
Bingfield Nthumb.....158 B7
Bingham Notts.........102 B4
Bingley C Brad........123 G3
Binham Norfk..........106 B5
Binley Covtry............86 E7
Binley Hants............29 H2
Binley Woods
　Warwks................86 E7
Binnegar Dorset........15 G5
Binniehill Falk.........176 B4
Binscombe Surrey......30 F3
Binstead IoW............17 H4
Binsted Hants..........30 C3
Binsted W Susx.........18 D4
Binton Warwks..........71 K4
Bintree Norfk..........106 B7
Birch Essex..............61 M4
Birchall Staffs..........99 M2
Bircham Newton
　Norfk..................105 J5
Bircham Tofts Norfk...105 J6
Birchanger Essex.......60 E4
Birchanger Green
　Services Essex........60 E4
Birch Cross Staffs....100 C6
Bircher Herefs..........69 J2
Birchfield Birm.........85 J5
Birch Green Essex......61 M4
Birchgrove Cardif......37 J4
Birchgrove Swans......51 K5
Birchgrove W Susx.....32 D7
Birchington Kent.......35 J2
Birchley Heath
　Warwks................86 C5
Birchover Derbys.....100 E1
Birch Services
　Rochdl................122 C8
Birch Vale Derbys....114 A4
Birchwood Lincs......116 F7
Birch Wood Somset....25 K8
Birchwood Warrtn....112 F4
Bircotes Notts........115 M3
Birdbrook Essex........77 G6
Birdforth N York......133 G4

Birdham W Susx........17 M3
Birdingbury Warwks...72 E2
Birdlip Gloucs...........55 L5
Birdsall N York.......134 C6
Birds Edge Kirk.......123 J8
Birds Green Essex......60 F6
Birdsgreen Shrops......84 D6
Birdsmoorgate
　Dorset..................13 K3
Birdwell Barns.........115 G2
Birgham Border.......168 B2
Birichin Highld........223 G3
Birkby N York..........141 H6
Birkdale Sefton.......120 D7
Birkenbog Abers......215 L2
Birkenhead Wirral....111 K4
Birkenhead
　(Queensway)
　Tunnel Lpool........111 K4
Birkenhills Abers......216 E5
Birkenshaw Kirk......123 J5
Birkhall Abers.........205 H6
Birkhill Angus.........186 F1
Birkhill D & G.........166 B6
Birkin N York..........124 E5
Birley Herefs............69 J4
Birley Carr Sheff......115 G3
Birling Kent.............46 B7
Birlingham Worcs......71 G5
Birmingham Birm......85 J6
Birmingham Airport
　Solhll.....................85 L6
Birnam P & K..........195 G7
Birness Abers.........217 J7
Birse Abers............206 B6
Birsemore Abers......205 L5
Birstall Kirk...........123 J5
Birstall Leics...........87 H2
Birstwith N York......132 C7
Birtley Gatesd........151 G4
Birtley Herefs..........69 G2
Birtley Nthumb.......157 L6
Birts Street Worcs.....70 D7
Bisbrooke RutInd......88 C4
Biscathorpe Lincs....118 C5
Bisham W & M..........42 D4
Bishampton Worcs.....71 H4
Bish Mill Devon.........24 B6
Bishop Auckland
　Dur....................140 F2
Bishopbridge Lincs...117 G4
Bishopbriggs E Duns...175 G4
Bishop Burton
　E R Yk.................126 B3
Bishop Middleham
　Dur....................141 H2
Bishopmill Moray.....214 F2
Bishop Monkton
　N York................132 E6
Bishop Norton Lincs...117 G3
Bishopsbourne Kent...35 G4
Bishops Cannings
　Wilts....................40 B7
Bishop's Castle
　Shrops..................83 G5
Bishop's Caundle
　Dorset..................27 G8
Bishop's Cleeve
　Gloucs..................55 L3
Bishop's Frome
　Herefs..................70 B5
Bishop's Green Essex...60 F4
Bishop's Hull Somset...25 J6
Bishop's Itchington
　Warwks................72 E3
Bishops Lydeard
　Somset..................25 J5
Bishop's Norton
　Gloucs..................55 J3
Bishop's Nympton
　Devon..................24 B6
Bishop's Offley Staffs...99 H6
Bishop's Stortford
　Herts....................60 D4
Bishop's Sutton
　Hants....................29 L5
Bishop's Tachbrook
　Warwks................72 C3

Bishop's Tawton
　Devon..................23 J5
Bishopsteignton
　Devon.................... 7 K2
Bishopstoke Hants.....29 J7
Bishopston Swans......51 H7
Bishopstone Bucks.....58 D6
Bishopstone E Susx....19 M5
Bishopstone Herefs....69 H5
Bishopstone Kent......47 K6
Bishopstone Swindn...40 E4
Bishopstone Wilts......28 B6
Bishopstrow Wilts......27 K3
Bishop Sutton BaNES...38 E7
Bishop's Waltham
　Hants....................29 K7
Bishopswood Somset...25 K8
Bishop's Wood Staffs...84 G2
Bishopsworth Bristl...38 E6
Bishop Thornton
　N York................132 D6
Bishopthorpe C York...124 F2
Bishopton Darltn.....141 J3
Bishopton Rens.......174 E4
Bishop Wilton E R Yk...134 C7
Bishton Newpt..........38 B3
Bishton Staffs.........100 A7
Bisley Gloucs............55 K6
Bisley Surrey............42 F8
Bissoe Cnwll.............. 3 K3
Bisterne Hants..........15 L3
Bitchfield Lincs.......103 G6
Bittadon Devon.........23 J3
Bittaford Devon.......... 6 F4
Bitterley Shrops........83 L7
Bitterne C Sotn.........29 J8
Bitteswell Leics........87 G6
Bitton S Glos............39 G6
Bix Oxon.................42 B4
Bixter Shet............235 c5
Blaby Leics.............87 H4
Blackadder Border....179 H7
Blackawton Devon...... 7 J5
Blackborough Devon...12 E1
Blackborough End
　Norfk....................90 F1
Black Bourton Oxon...56 F6
Blackboys E Susx......20 B2
Blackbrook Derbys....101 G3
Blackbrook St Hel....112 D3
Blackbrook Staffs......99 H5
Blackburn Abers......206 F3
Blackburn Bl w D.....121 K5
Blackburn W Loth....176 D5
Blackburn with
　Darwen Services
　Bl w D................121 K5
Blackcraig E Ayrs.....164 C7
Black Crofts Ag & B...182 D1
Blackdog Abers.......207 H3
Black Dog Devon........11 J3
Blackdown Dorset......13 K2
Blacker Hill Barns....115 G2
Blackfen Gt Lon........45 J5
Blackfield Hants........16 E3
Blackford P & K.......185 J5
Blackford Somset......26 B2
Blackford Somset......26 F6
Blackfordby Leics.....101 G8
Blackhall C Edin......177 H4
Blackhall Colliery
　Dur....................151 K6
Blackhall Mill
　Gatesd.................150 E4
Blackhaugh Border...166 F2
Blackheath Gt Lon.....45 G5
Blackheath Sandw.....85 H6
Blackheath Suffk.......93 J8
Blackheath Surrey......31 G3
Blackhill Abers........217 K3
Blackhill Abers........217 K5
Blackhill Dur..........150 D7
Blackhill of
　Clackriach Abers...217 H5
Blackhorse Devon......12 C4
Blacklaw D & G.......165 K7
Blackley Manch.......113 J2
Blacklunans P & K....195 J4

**Blackmarstone**
Herefs .......................69 K6
**Blackmill** Brdgnd .........36 E3
**Blackmoor** Hants..........30 C5
**Blackmoor** N Som..........38 C7
**Blackmoorfoot** Kirk... 123 G7
**Blackmore** Essex............60 F7
**Blackmore End**
Essex.............................61 H2
**Black Mountains** ........53 K3
**Blackness** Falk .......... 176 E3
**Blacknest** Hants...........30 D3
**Black Notley** Essex .....61 J4
**Blacko** Lancs............. 122 C3
**Black Pill** Swans ..........51 J7
**Blackpool** Bpool......... 120 D4
**Blackpool** Devon ............ 7 K6
**Blackpool Zoo** Bpool .... 120 D4
**Blackridge** W Loth... 176 B5
**Blackrod** Bolton ......... 121 J7
**Blacksboat** Moray...... 214 E6
**Blackshaw** D & G ....... 147 J2
**Blackshaw Head**
Calder ...................... 122 E5
**Blackstone** W Susx ......19 H3
**Black Street** Suffk ......93 K6
**Blackthorn** Oxon..........57 L4
**Blackthorpe** Suffk .......77 K2
**Blacktoft** E R Yk.........125 J5
**Blacktop** C Aber ........ 207 G4
**Black Torrington**
Devon ..........................10 C4
**Blackwall** Derbys .... 100 E3
**Blackwall Tunnel**
Gt Lon.......................45 H4
**Blackwater** Cnwll........... 3 J3
**Blackwater** Hants..........42 D7
**Blackwater** IoW ...........17 G5
**Blackwater** Somset ......25 K7
**Blackwaterfoot**
N Ayrs....................... 162 A4
**Blackwell** Cumb ....... 148 D4
**Blackwell** Derbys..... 101 H2
**Blackwell** Derbys ..... 114 C6
**Blackwell** Warwks.......72 B5
**Blackwell** Worcs ..........71 H1
**Blackwood** Caerph ......37 J2
**Blackwood** D & G ...... 154 F5
**Blackwood** S Lans .... 164 F1
**Blacon** Ches W ........ 111 L7
**Bladnoch** D & G........ 145 J4
**Bladon** Oxon ...............57 J5
**Blaenannerch** Cerdgn...65 H5
**Blaenau Ffestiniog**
Gwynd ........................96 A4
**Blaenavon** Torfn..........53 K6
**Blaenavon**
Industrial
Landscape Torfn........53 K6
**Blaencwm** Rhondd.......52 E7
**Blaenffos** Pembks ........65 H6
**Blaengarw** Brdgnd.......36 D2
**Blaengwrach** Neath......52 D6
**Blaengwynfi** Neath.......36 D2
**Blaenpennal** Cerdgn......66 E2
**Blaenplwyf** Cerdgn.......80 D7
**Blaenporth** Cerdgn.......65 J5
**Blaenrhondda**
Rhondd......................52 E7
**Blaenwaun** Carmth......50 B1
**Blaen-y-coed**
Carmth.......................50 D1
**Blagdon** N Som............38 D8
**Blagdon** Somset ...........25 K7
**Blagdon** Torbay.............. 7 K4
**Blagdon Hill** Somset .....25 K7
**Blaich** Highld ............. 191 K2
**Blain** Highld .............. 190 D3
**Blaina** Blae G................53 J6
**Blair Atholl** P & K ..... 194 D4
**Blair Drummond**
Stirlg ....................... 184 F7
**Blairgowrie** P & K...... 195 J7
**Blairhall** Fife ............. 176 D2
**Blairingone** P & K....... 185 K7
**Blairlogie** Stirlg......... 185 H7
**Blairmore** Ag & B...... 173 L2
**Blairmore** Highld...... 228 C4

**Blair's Ferry** Ag & B...... 173 G4
**Blaisdon** Gloucs..............55 G5
**Blakebrook** Worcs........84 E7
**Blakedown** Worcs..........84 F7
**Blake End** Essex............61 H4
**Blakemere** Ches W .... 112 D7
**Blakemere** Herefs..........69 G6
**Blakenall Heath**
Wsall.........................85 H3
**Blakeney** Gloucs..........54 F6
**Blakeney** Norfk........ 106 B4
**Blakenhall** Ches E.........99 G3
**Blakenhall** Wolves........85 G4
**Blakesley** Nhants..........73 J4
**Blanchland** Nthumb... 150 B5
**Blandford Forum**
Dorset .......................15 G2
**Blandford St Mary**
Dorset .......................15 G2
**Blanefield** Stirlg....... 174 F3
**Blankney** Lincs......... 103 H1
**Blantyre** S Lans......... 175 J6
**Blàr a' Chaorainn**
Highld...................... 191 L3
**Blarghour** Ag & B...... 182 E5
**Blargie** Highld .......... 202 F6
**Blarmachfoldach**
Highld...................... 191 L3
**Blaston** Leics...............88 B4
**Blatherwycke** Nhants .....88 D4
**Blawith** Cumb ........... 129 G2
**Blawquhairn** D & G ..... 154 B5
**Blaxhall** Suffk...............79 H3
**Blaxton** Donc ........... 116 A2
**Blaydon** Gatesd......... 150 F3
**Bleadney** Somset .........26 C3
**Bleadon** N Som ...........25 M1
**Blean** Kent....................34 F3
**Bleasby** Notts .......... 102 B3
**Blebocraigs** Fife....... 187 G4
**Bleddfa** Powys..............68 E2
**Bledington** Gloucs........56 E4
**Bledlow** Bucks............58 C7
**Bledlow Ridge** Bucks .....42 D2
**Blegbie** E Loth........... 178 B6
**Blencarn** Cumb ......... 138 F2
**Blencogo** Cumb ........ 147 L5
**Blendworth** Hants ........30 B8
**Blenheim Palace**
Oxon..........................57 H5
**Blennerhasset** Cumb .. 147 L6
**Bletchingdon** Oxon........57 J4
**Bletchingley** Surrey......32 B3
**Bletchley** M Keyn ........58 E2
**Bletchley** Shrops...........98 F5
**Bletchley Park**
Museum M Keyn........74 C7
**Bletherston** Pembks .....49 H4
**Bletsoe** Bed.................74 E3
**Blewbury** Oxon.............41 K4
**Blickling** Norfk.......... 106 E6
**Blidworth** Notts ........ 101 L2
**Blidworth Bottoms**
Notts...................... 101 L2
**Blindcrake** Cumb ...... 147 K7
**Blindley Heath**
Surrey .......................32 C4
**Blisland** Cnwll............... 5 H2
**Blissford** Hants............28 D8
**Bliss Gate** Worcs..........84 D8
**Blisworth** Nhants..........73 K4
**Blithbury** Staffs......... 100 B8
**Blockley** Gloucs...........71 L7
**Blofield** Norfk...............93 G2
**Blofield Heath** Norfk....93 G2
**Blo Norton** Norfk..........92 B7
**Bloomfield** Border..... 167 J4
**Blore** Staffs................ 100 C3
**Bloxham** Oxon..............72 E7
**Bloxholm** Lincs......... 103 H2
**Bloxwich** Wsall............85 H3
**Bloxworth** Dorset.........15 G4
**Blubberhouses**
N York..................... 132 B7
**Blue Anchor** Somset .....24 F3
**Blue Bell Hill** Kent........46 C7
**Blue John Cavern**
Derbys..................... 114 C5

**Blundellsands**
Sefton...................... 111 J2
**Blundeston** Suffk..........93 L4
**Blunham** C Beds...........75 H4
**Blunsdon St**
Andrew Swindn ........40 C3
**Bluntington** Worcs........84 F8
**Bluntisham** Cambs.........89 L8
**Blurton** C Stke ..............99 K4
**Blyborough** Lincs...... 116 F3
**Blyford** Suffk................93 J7
**Blymhill** Staffs..............84 E2
**Blyth** Notts................ 115 L4
**Blyth** Nthumb............ 159 H5
**Blyth Bridge** Border.. 165 M1
**Blythburgh** Suffk..........93 J7
**Blythe** Border............ 178 D7
**Blythe Bridge** Staffs .....99 L4
**Blyth Services** Notts.... 115 L4
**Blyton** Lincs.............. 116 D3
**Boarhills** Fife ............ 187 J5
**Boarhunt** Hants............17 H2
**Boarstall** Bucks............57 L5
**Boath** Highld............. 222 D6
**Boat of Garten**
Highld...................... 203 L2
**Bobbing** Kent................46 E6
**Bobbington** Staffs.........84 E5
**Bocking** Essex ..............61 J4
**Bocking**
Churchstreet
Essex.........................61 J3
**Boddam** Abers........... 217 L6
**Boddam** Shet............. 235 c7
**Boddington** Gloucs.......55 K3
**Bodedern** IoA............ 108 D5
**Bodelwyddan**
Denbgs..................... 110 D6
**Bodenham** Herefs.........69 K4
**Bodenham** Wilts...........28 D6
**Bodenham Moor**
Herefs........................69 K4
**Bodewryd** IoA........... 108 E4
**Bodfari** Denbgs.......... 110 F7
**Bodffordd** IoA............ 108 F6
**Bodham** Norfk........... 106 D4
**Bodiam** E Susx..............33 K7
**Bodicote** Oxon..............72 F6
**Bodinnick** Cnwll............ 5 H5
**Bodle Street Green**
E Susx ......................20 D3
**Bodmin** Cnwll................ 5 G3
**Bodmin Moor** Cnwll....... 5 J1
**Bodsham** Kent...............34 E5
**Boduan** Gwynd.............94 F5
**Bodwen** Cnwll................ 5 G4
**Bogallan** Highld........ 212 F4
**Bogbrae** Abers.......... 217 J7
**Bogend** S Ayrs........... 163 K3
**Boggs Holdings**
E Loth..................... 177 L4
**Boghall** Mdloth......... 177 H5
**Boghall** W Loth......... 176 D5
**Boghead** S Lans........ 164 F2
**Bogmoor** Moray........ 215 H2
**Bogmuir** Abers.......... 197 G3
**Bogniebrae** Abers...... 216 B5
**Bognor Regis** W Susx...18 C6
**Bogroy** Highld........... 203 L2
**Bogue** D & G.............. 154 B6
**Bohortha** Cnwll............. 3 L5
**Bohuntine** Highld...... 201 L8
**Bolam** Dur................. 140 F3
**Bolberry** Devon.............. 7 G7
**Boldmere** Birm............85 K5
**Boldre** Hants................16 C3
**Boldron** Dur............... 140 C4
**Bole** Notts................. 116 C4
**Bolehill** Derbys......... 100 F2
**Bolham** Devon..............24 E7
**Bolham Water** Devon....25 J8
**Bolingey** Cnwll.............. 3 K1
**Bollington** Ches E...... 113 L6
**Bolney** W Susx..............31 L6
**Bolnhurst** Bed.............74 F3
**Bolnore** W Susx............19 J2
**Bolshan** Angus........... 197 G6
**Bolsover** Derbys........ 115 J7

**Bolsterstone** Sheff...... 114 F3
**Boltby** N York............ 133 G3
**Bolton** Bolton............ 121 L8
**Bolton** Cumb.............. 138 F3
**Bolton** E Loth............ 178 B4
**Bolton** E R Yk............ 125 J1
**Bolton** Nthumb.......... 169 G6
**Bolton Abbey** N York.. 131 K8
**Bolton-by-Bowland**
Lancs....................... 122 B1
**Boltonfellend** Cumb.... 148 E2
**Boltongate** Cumb...... 147 M6
**Bolton-le-Sands**
Lancs....................... 129 K6
**Bolton Low Houses**
Cumb....................... 147 M6
**Bolton-on-Swale**
N York..................... 141 G7
**Bolton Percy** N York... 124 E3
**Bolton upon Dearne**
Barns....................... 115 J2
**Bolventor** Cnwll............. 5 J1
**Bomere Heath**
Shrops.......................98 C8
**Bonar Bridge** Highld.. 222 E3
**Bonawe** Ag & B.......... 182 E2
**Bonby** N Linc............. 126 C7
**Boncath** Pembks...........65 H6
**Bonchester Bridge**
Border...................... 167 J6
**Bondleigh** Devon..........10 F4
**Bonds** Lancs............... 121 G2
**Bo'ness** Falk.............. 176 D3
**Boney Hay** Staffs..........85 J2
**Bonhill** W Duns.......... 174 D3
**Boningale** Shrops.........84 E3
**Bonjedward** Border... 167 K5
**Bonkle** N Lans............ 175 L6
**Bonnington** Angus..... 196 F7
**Bonnington** Kent..........34 E7
**Bonnybank** Fife......... 186 F6
**Bonnybridge** Falk...... 175 L3
**Bonnykelly** Abers....... 217 G4
**Bonnyrigg** Mdloth...... 177 J5
**Bonnyton** Angus........ 196 B8
**Bonsall** Derbys.......... 100 F2
**Bonshaw Tower**
D & G....................... 155 M7
**Bont-Dolgadfan**
Powys........................81 J4
**Bont-goch** Cerdgn.......80 F6
**Bontnewydd** Cerdgn....66 E2
**Bontnewydd** Gwynd....95 H1
**Bontuchel** Denbgs........97 G2
**Bonvilston** V Glam........37 G5
**Boode** Devon................23 H4
**Booker** Bucks...............42 D3
**Boon** Border.............. 167 J1
**Boosbeck** R & Cl........ 142 E4
**Boose's Green** Essex....61 K2
**Boot** Cumb................ 137 G6
**Booth** Calder............. 122 F5
**Boothby Graffoe**
Lincs....................... 103 G2
**Boothby Pagnell**
Lincs....................... 102 F6
**Boothferry** E R Yk...... 125 H5
**Boothstown** Salfd...... 113 G2
**Boothtown** Calder..... 123 G5
**Boothville** Nhants........73 L2
**Bootle** Cumb.............. 128 D2
**Bootle** Sefton............ 111 K3
**Boraston** Shrops...........70 B1
**Bordeaux** Guern........ 236 e2
**Borden** Kent.................34 B3
**Bordon** Hants..............30 D4
**Boreham** Essex............61 J4
**Boreham Street**
E Susx ......................20 D4
**Borehamwood** Herts....44 D2
**Boreland** D & G......... 155 L4
**Boreraig** Highld......... 208 C4
**Borgh** W Isls.............. 232 f1
**Borgh** W Isls.............. 233 b9
**Borgie** Highld............ 229 K4
**Borgue** D & G............. 146 B5
**Borgue** Highld........... 227 K4
**Borley** Essex................77 J6

**Borneskitaig** Highld ..... 218  B7
**Borness** D & G ................ 146  A5
**Boroughbridge**
    N York ........................... 132  F6
**Borough Green** Kent......33  G2
**Borrowash** Derbys........101  H5
**Borrowby** N York.............132  F2
**Borrowdale** Cumb .......137  J4
**Borrowstoun** Falk .......176  D3
**Borstal** Medway.............46  B6
**Borth** Cerdgn...................80  E5
**Borthwick** Mdloth .......177  K6
**Borthwickbrae**
    Border .......................... 166  F6
**Borthwickshiels**
    Border .......................... 166  F6
**Borth-y-Gest** Gwynd ....95  K5
**Borve** Highld..................209  G5
**Borve** W Isls..................232  d4
**Borve** W Isls..................232  f1
**Borve** W Isls..................233  b9
**Borwick** Lancs...............129  L5
**Bosbury** Herefs ..............70  C5
**Boscastle** Cnwll................8  E6
**Boscombe** BCP..................15  L4
**Boscombe** Wilts..............28  D4
**Bosham** W Susx................17  L2
**Bosherston** Pembks ......49  G8
**Bosley** Ches E. ..............113  K7
**Bossall** N York...............133  L7
**Bossiney** Cnwll..................8  E6
**Bossingham** Kent...........34  F5
**Bossington** Somset ......24  D2
**Bostock Green**
    Ches W..........................112  F7
**Boston** Lincs...................104  B4
**Boston Spa** Leeds.........124  C2
**Boswinger** Cnwll...............4  F7
**Botallack** Cnwll..................2  C5
**Botany Bay** Gt Lon .......59  M7
**Botesdale** Suffk.............92  C7
**Bothal** Nthumb .............159  G5
**Bothamsall** Notts..........116  A6
**Bothel** Cumb .................147  L6
**Bothenhampton**
    Dorset .............................13  L4
**Bothwell** S Lans ...........175  J6
**Bothwell Services**
    **(southbound)**
    S Lans ...........................175  J6
**Botley** Bucks...................59  G7
**Botley** Hants...................29  K8
**Botley** Oxon ....................57  J6
**Botolph Claydon**
    Bucks...............................58  B3
**Botolphs** W Susx ...........19  G4
**Bottesford** Leics..........102  D5
**Bottesford** N Linc.........125  L8
**Bottisham** Cambs..........76  D3
**Bottomcraig** Fife..........186  F3
**Bottoms** Calder ...........122  D6
**Botusfleming** Cnwll.........6  B4
**Botwnnog** Gwynd............94  E4
**Bough Beech** Kent.........32  E4
**Boughrood** Powys..........68  C6
**Boughton** Nhants...........73  L2
**Boughton** Norfk .............91  G3
**Boughton** Notts.............116  B7
**Boughton Aluph**
    Kent..................................34  D5
**Boughton Green**
    Kent..................................33  K3
**Boughton Lees** Kent......34  D5
**Boughton**
    **Monchelsea** Kent.......33  K3
**Boughton Street**
    Kent..................................34  E3
**Bouldon** Shrops..............83  K6
**Boulmer** Nthumb ..........169  K6
**Boultenstone** Abers.....205  J3
**Boultham** Lincs..............116  F7
**Bourn** Cambs...................75  K3
**Bournbrook** Birm............85  J6
**Bourne** Lincs...................103  H7
**Bournebridge** Essex.....45  J2
**Bourne End** Bucks..........42  E3
**Bourne End** C Beds.......74  D5
**Bourne End** Herts..........59  G6

**Bournemouth** BCP..........15  K4
**Bournemouth**
    Airport BCP....................15  L3
**Bournes Green**
    Sthend.............................46  E3
**Bournheath** Worcs........85  G8
**Bournmoor** Dur..............151  H5
**Bournville** Birm..............85  J7
**Bourton** Dorset...............27  H5
**Bourton** Oxon.................40  E3
**Bourton** Shrops...............83  L4
**Bourton** Wilts.................40  B7
**Bourton on**
    **Dunsmore**
    Warwks............................72  E1
**Bourton-on-the-**
    **Hill** Gloucs..................56  D2
**Bourton-on-the-**
    **Water** Gloucs.............56  D4
**Bousd** Ag & B ...............189  G4
**Bouth** Cumb....................129  H3
**Bouthwaite** N York......131  L5
**Boveridge** Dorset...........28  B7
**Bovey Tracey** Devon........7  J1
**Bovingdon** Herts............59  G7
**Bow** Devon.......................11  G4
**Bow** Gt Lon......................45  G4
**Bow** Ork...........................234  b7
**Bow Brickhill** M Keyn....74  C7
**Bowbridge** Gloucs.........55  J6
**Bowburn** Dur..................151  H7
**Bowcombe** IoW...............16  F5
**Bowd** Devon.....................12  E4
**Bowden** Border..............167  H4
**Bowden Hill** Wilts..........39  L6
**Bowdon** Traffd...............113  H4
**Bower** Highld..................231  J3
**Bowerchalke** Wilts.........28  A6
**Bowermadden**
    Highld.............................231  J3
**Bowers** Staffs..................99  J5
**Bowers Gifford**
    Essex................................46  C3
**Bowershall** Fife.............176  F1
**Bower's Row** Leeds......124  B5
**Bowes** Dur......................140  C4
**Bowgreave** Lancs..........121  G2
**Bowhouse** D & G...........147  H2
**Bowland** Border.............167  G2
**Bowley** Herefs................69  K4
**Bowlhead Green**
    Surrey..............................30  E4
**Bowling** C Brad.............123  H4
**Bowling** W Duns............174  E4
**Bowmanstead** Cumb....137  J7
**Bowmore** Ag & B..........170  F6
**Bowness-on-**
    **Solway** Cumb..............147  L3
**Bowness-on-**
    **Windermere**
    Cumb...............................137  L7
**Bow of Fife** Fife...........186  E5
**Bowriefauld** Angus......196  E6
**Bowsden** Nthumb.........168  E2
**Bow Street** Cerdgn........80  E6
**Bowthorpe** Norfk...........92  E2
**Box** Gloucs.......................55  K7
**Box** Wilts..........................39  J6
**Boxford** Suffk.................77  L6
**Boxford** W Berk..............41  H6
**Boxgrove** W Susx ...........18  B4
**Boxley** Kent.....................33  K2
**Boxmoor** Herts................59  H6
**Boxted** Essex...................62  B2
**Boxted** Essex...................62  B2
**Boxted** Suffk...................77  J4
**Boxted Cross** Essex.......62  B2
**Boxworth** Cambs............75  L2
**Boyden Gate** Kent.........47  L6
**Boylestone** Derbys......100  D5
**Boyndie** Abers...............216  C2
**Boyndlie** Abers..............217  G2
**Boynton** E R Yk.............135  H6
**Boysack** Angus..............197  G6
**Boythorpe** Derbys.........115  G7
**Boyton** Cnwll.....................9  J6
**Boyton** Suffk...................79  H5
**Boyton** Wilts...................27  L4

**Boyton Cross** Essex......61  G6
**Boyton End** Suffk...........77  G5
**Bozeat** Nhants.................74  C3
**Brabourne** Kent..............34  E6
**Brabourne Lees** Kent....34  E6
**Brabstermire**
    Highld.............................231  K2
**Bracadale** Highld...........208  E6
**Braceborough** Lincs......88  F2
**Bracebridge Heath**
    Lincs...............................117  G7
**Bracebridge Low**
    **Fields** Lincs.................116  F7
**Braceby** Lincs.................103  G5
**Bracewell** Lancs............122  C2
**Brackenfield** Derbys....101  G2
**Brackenhirst** N Lans....175  K5
**Brackla** Brdgnd................36  E4
**Bracklesham** W Susx.....17  L3
**Brackletter** Highld........201  J8
**Brackley** Nhants.............73  H6
**Bracknell** Br For.............42  E6
**Braco** P & K...................185  H5
**Bracobrae** Moray...........215  L4
**Bracon Ash** Norfk...........92  E4
**Bracora** Highld...............199  L6
**Bracorina** Highld...........199  L6
**Bradbourne** Derbys......100  D3
**Bradbury** Dur.................141  H2
**Bradden** Nhants..............73  J5
**Bradeley** C Stke...............99  K3
**Bradenham** Bucks...........42  D3
**Bradenstoke** Wilts.........39  M4
**Bradfield** Devon..............12  D1
**Bradfield** Essex...............62  D2
**Bradfield** Norfk.............106  F5
**Bradfield** Sheff.............114  F3
**Bradfield** W Berk............41  L6
**Bradfield Combust**
    Suffk................................77  K3
**Bradfield Green**
    Ches E...............................99  G2
**Bradfield Heath**
    Essex................................62  D3
**Bradfield St Clare**
    Suffk................................77  K3
**Bradfield St George**
    Suffk................................77  K3
**Bradford** C Brad.............123  H4
**Bradford** Devon.................9  L4
**Bradford Abbas**
    Dorset...............................26  E8
**Bradford Leigh** Wilts.....39  J7
**Bradford-on-Avon**
    Wilts.................................39  J7
**Bradford-on-Tone**
    Somset.............................25  J6
**Bradford Peverell**
    Dorset...............................14  C4
**Bradiford** Devon..............23  J5
**Brading** IoW.....................17  H5
**Bradley** Derbys...............100  E4
**Bradley** Hants..................29  M3
**Bradley** NE Lin...............118  C1
**Bradley** Staffs..................99  K8
**Bradley** Wolves...............85  G4
**Bradley** Worcs.................71  H3
**Bradley Green** Worcs ...71  H3
**Bradley in the**
    **Moors** Staffs...............100  B4
**Bradley Stoke** S Glos...38  E4
**Bradmore** Notts.............101  L6
**Bradninch** Devon............12  C2
**Bradnop** Staffs..............100  A2
**Bradpole** Dorset.............13  L4
**Bradshaw** Calder...........123  G4
**Bradstone** Devon..............9  K8
**Bradwall Green**
    Ches E.............................113  H8
**Bradwell** Derbys............114  D5
**Bradwell** Essex...............61  J4
**Bradwell** M Keyn.............74  B6
**Bradwell** Norfk................93  K3
**Bradwell-on-Sea**
    Essex................................62  B6
**Bradwell Waterside**
    Essex................................62  B6
**Bradworthy** Devon............9  J3

**Brae** Highld....................213  G2
**Brae** Shet........................235  c4
**Braeface** Falk.................175  K3
**Braehead** Angus............197  H5
**Braehead** D & G..............145  J4
**Braehead** S Lans...........176  C7
**Braeintra** Highld............210  D7
**Braemar** Abers................204  E6
**Braemore** Highld............221  G5
**Braemore** Highld............227  J3
**Brae Roy Lodge**
    Highld.............................201  L6
**Braeside** Inver...............173  L4
**Braes of Coul** Angus....195  L5
**Braes of Enzie**
    Moray..............................215  J3
**Braes of Ullapool**
    Highld.............................220  F3
**Braeswick** Ork...............234  d4
**Braevallich** Ag & B........182  D6
**Braewick** Shet................235  b3
**Brafferton** Darltn..........141  H3
**Brafferton** N York..........132  F5
**Brafield-on-the-**
    **Green** Nhants..............74  B3
**Bragar** W Isls.................232  f2
**Bragbury End** Herts.......59  L4
**Braidwood** S Lans.........175  L8
**Brailsford** Derbys..........100  E4
**Braintree** Essex...............61  J4
**Braiseworth** Suffk..........78  D1
**Braishfield** Hants............29  G6
**Braiswick** Essex...............62  B3
**Braithwaite** Cumb..........137  H3
**Braithwell** Donc.............115  K3
**Bramber** W Susx..............19  G4
**Bramcote** Warwks...........86  E5
**Bramdean** Hants..............29  L5
**Bramerton** Norfk.............93  G3
**Bramfield** Herts...............59  M5
**Bramfield** Suffk...............93  H8
**Bramford** Suffk................78  D5
**Bramhall** Stockp............113  K5
**Bramham** Leeds..............124  C2
**Bramhope** Leeds............123  K2
**Bramley** Hants.................41  M8
**Bramley** Leeds................123  K4
**Bramley** Rothm..............115  J3
**Bramley** Surrey................31  G3
**Bramling** Kent.................35  G4
**Brampford Speke**
    Devon...............................11  L5
**Brampton** Cambs............75  J1
**Brampton** Cumb.............138  F3
**Brampton** Cumb.............148  F3
**Brampton** Lincs..............116  D5
**Brampton** Norfk.............106  F7
**Brampton** Rothm............115  H2
**Brampton** Suffk...............93  J6
**Brampton Abbotts**
    Herefs...............................54  E3
**Brampton Ash**
    Nhants..............................87  L6
**Brampton Bryan**
    Herefs...............................83  G8
**Brampton-en-le-**
    **Morthen** Rothm...........115  J4
**Bramshall** Staffs...........100  B6
**Bramshaw** Hants..............28  F7
**Bramshott** Hants.............30  D5
**Bramwell** Somset............26  B5
**Branault** Highld..............190  B3
**Brancaster** Norfk...........105  J4
**Brancaster Staithe**
    Norfk...............................105  J4
**Brancepeth** Dur.............150  F7
**Branchill** Moray.............214  D4
**Branderburgh** Moray.....214  F1
**Brandesburton**
    E R Yk............................126  E2
**Brandeston** Suffk............78  F3
**Brandiston** Norfk...........106  D7
**Brandon** Dur...................151  G6
**Brandon** Lincs................102  E3
**Brandon** Suffk.................91  H6
**Brandon** Warwks.............86  E7
**Brandon Parva**
    Norfk................................92  C2

Brandsby N York............133 J5
Brandy Wharf Lincs....117 G3
Bran End Essex............61 G3
Branksome BCP.............15 K4
Branksome Park
  BCP.............................15 K4
Bransbury Hants...........29 H3
Bransby Lincs...............116 E5
Branscombe Devon........12 F5
Bransford Worcs...........70 E4
Bransgore Hants...........16 A3
Bransholme C KuH......126 D4
Bransley Shrops............84 B7
Branston Leics.............102 D6
Branston Lincs.............117 G7
Branston Staffs............100 E7
Branston Booths
  Lincs..........................117 H7
Branstone IoW..............17 G5
Brant Broughton
  Lincs..........................102 E2
Brantham Suffk............78 D7
Branthwaite Cumb......136 E3
Branthwaite Cumb......148 B7
Brantingham E R Yk....125 L5
Branton Donc...............115 M2
Branton Nthumb..........168 F6
Branton Green
  N York........................132 F6
Branxton Nthumb........168 D2
Brassington Derbys.....100 E2
Brasted Kent.................32 E3
Brasted Chart Kent.......32 E3
Brathens Abers............206 D5
Bratoft Lincs................119 G8
Brattleby Lincs.............116 F5
Bratton Wilts................27 K2
Bratton Wrekin..............84 B2
Bratton Clovelly
  Devon..........................10 C6
Bratton Fleming
  Devon..........................23 K4
Bratton Seymour
  Somset.........................26 F5
Braughing Herts............60 C3
Braunston Nhants.........73 G2
Braunston Rutlnd..........88 B3
Braunton Devon............23 H4
Brawby N York............134 B4
Brawl Highld...............230 B3
Bray W & M..................42 E4
Braybrooke Nhants.......87 L6
Brayford Devon.............23 L4
Bray Shop Cnwll............5 M2
Brayton N York............124 F4
Braywick W & M............42 E4
Breachwood Green
  Herts...........................59 J4
Breacleit W Isls..........232 e2
Breaclete W Isls..........232 e2
Breadsall Derbys.........101 G5
Breadstone Gloucs........55 G7
Breage Cnwll...................3 G5
Breakachy Highld.......212 D5
Breakish Highld..........199 L2
Brealangwell Lodge
  Highld........................222 C3
Bream Gloucs................54 C3
Breamore Hants............28 D7
Brean Somset...............25 L1
Breanais W Isls..........232 d3
Brearton N York..........132 E7
Breascleit W Isls.......232 e2
Breasclete W Isls.......232 e2
Breaston Derbys.........101 J5
Brechfa Carmth............66 C7
Brechin Angus............196 F4
Breckles Norfk..............91 L5
Brecon Powys................53 G3
Brecon Beacons
  National Park.............52 F3
Bredbury Stockp.........113 L3
Brede E Susx................21 G3
Bredenbury Herefs.......69 L3
Bredfield Suffk..............78 F4
Bredgar Kent.................34 B3
Bredhurst Kent.............46 D7
Bredon Worcs................71 G6

Bredon's Hardwick
  Worcs..........................71 G7
Bredon's Norton
  Worcs..........................71 G6
Bredwardine Herefs......69 G5
Breedon on the Hill
  Leics.........................101 H7
Breich W Loth..............176 C6
Breightmet Bolton......121 L8
Breighton E R Yk........125 G4
Breinton Herefs............69 J6
Bremhill Wilts...............39 L5
Brenchley Kent.............33 H5
Brendon Devon..............24 B2
Brenfield Ag & B.........172 E2
Brenish W Isls............232 d3
Brent Cross Gt Lon......44 E3
Brent Eleigh Suffk........77 L5
Brentford Gt Lon.........44 D5
Brentingby Leics.........102 C8
Brent Knoll Somset......25 M2
Brent Mill Devon............7 G4
Brent Pelham Herts......60 C2
Brentwood Essex..........45 L2
Brenzett Kent...............21 K1
Brenzett Green Kent.....34 D8
Brereton Staffs.............85 J1
Brereton Green
  Ches E........................113 H8
Bressay Shet...............235 d6
Bressingham Norfk.......92 C7
Bretby Derbys.............100 F7
Bretford Warwks..........86 E7
Bretforton Worcs..........71 K5
Bretherton Lancs........121 G6
Brettabister Shet........235 d5
Brettenham Norfk........91 L6
Brettenham Suffk.........77 L4
Bretton C Pete..............89 H4
Bretton Flints..............111 K8
Brewood Staffs.............84 F2
Briantspuddle Dorset....14 F4
Brickendon Herts..........60 A6
Bricket Wood Herts......59 J7
Brick Houses Sheff.....114 F5
Bricklehampton
  Worcs..........................71 H6
Bride IoM....................237 e2
Bridekirk Cumb...........147 K7
Bridestowe Devon........10 D6
Brideswell Abers........216 B6
Bridford Devon.............11 J7
Bridge Kent..................35 G4
Bridgefoot Angus.......186 F1
Bridgehampton
  Somset.........................26 E6
Bridge Hewick
  N York........................132 E5
Bridgehill Dur.............150 D5
Bridgemary Hants.........17 H2
Bridgend Abers...........215 L7
Bridgend Ag & B.........161 K2
Bridgend Ag & B.........171 G6
Bridgend Angus..........196 E3
Bridgend Brdgnd..........36 E4
Bridgend Cerdgn..........65 G5
Bridgend D & G...........165 L7
Bridgend Devon..............6 E6
Bridgend Fife..............186 F5
Bridgend Moray..........215 J7
Bridgend P & K..........186 B3
Bridgend W Loth........176 E3
Bridgend of
  Lintrathen Angus......195 L5
Bridge of Alford
  Abers........................206 B2
Bridge of Allan
  Stirlg.........................185 G7
Bridge of Avon
  Moray........................204 E2
Bridge of Avon
  Moray........................214 E7
Bridge of Balgie
  P & K.........................193 J6
Bridge of
  Brewlands Angus......195 J4
Bridge of Brown
  Highld........................204 D2

Bridge of Cally
  P & K.........................195 J6
Bridge of Canny
  Abers........................206 C6
Bridge of Craigisla
  Angus........................195 K5
Bridge of Dee D & G...146 C3
Bridge of Don
  C Aber........................207 H4
Bridge of Dun Angus...197 G5
Bridge of Dye Abers....206 C7
Bridge of Earn P & K...186 B4
Bridge of Ericht
  P & K.........................193 H5
Bridge of Feugh
  Abers........................206 D6
Bridge of Gairn
  Abers........................205 H6
Bridge of Gaur
  P & K.........................193 H5
Bridge of Marnoch
  Abers........................216 B4
Bridge of Muchalls
  Abers........................207 G6
Bridge of Orchy
  Ag & B.......................192 E7
Bridge of Tilt P & K....194 D4
Bridge of Tynet
  Moray........................215 J3
Bridge of Walls Shet...235 b5
Bridge of Weir Rens...174 D5
Bridgerule Devon...........9 H4
Bridge Sollers
  Herefs.........................69 H6
Bridge Street Suffk......77 K6
Bridgetown Somset......24 E5
Bridge Trafford
  Ches W.......................112 C7
Bridgham Norfk............91 L6
Bridgnorth Shrops........84 C5
Bridgwater Somset......25 L4
Bridgwater Services
  Somset.........................25 L4
Bridlington E R Yk......135 J6
Bridport Dorset............13 L4
Bridstow Herefs............54 E3
Brierfield Lancs..........122 C3
Brierley Barns............124 C7
Brierley Gloucs............54 F5
Brierley Hill Dudley......85 G6
Brigg N Linc...............117 G1
Briggate Norfk............107 G6
Briggswath N York.....143 H5
Brigham Cumb............136 F2
Brigham E R Yk..........135 G8
Brighouse Calder........123 H6
Brighstone IoW............16 E5
Brighthampton Oxon....57 G7
Brightley Devon............10 E5
Brightling E Susx.........20 D2
Brightlingsea Essex.....62 C5
Brighton Br & H............19 J5
Brighton City
  Airport W Susx..........19 G5
Brighton le Sands
  Sefton.......................111 J2
Brightons Falk.............176 C3
Brightwalton W Berk....41 H5
Brightwell Suffk...........78 F5
Brightwell Baldwin
  Oxon...........................41 M2
Brightwell-cum-
  Sotwell Oxon..............41 L3
Brightwell
  Upperton Oxon...........42 A2
Brignall Dur................140 D5
Brig o'Turk Stirlg........184 C6
Brigsley NE Lin...........118 C2
Brigsteer Cumb...........129 K2
Brigstock Nhants..........88 D6
Brill Bucks....................58 A5
Brill Cnwll......................3 J5
Brilley Herefs................68 F5
Brimfield Herefs...........69 K2
Brimfield Cross
  Herefs.........................69 K2
Brimington Derbys.....115 H6
Brimley Devon................7 J1

Brimpsfield Gloucs.......55 L5
Brimpton W Berk..........41 K7
Brimscombe Gloucs......55 K7
Brimstage Wirral........111 J5
Brincliffe Sheff...........115 F4
Brind E R Yk...............125 H4
Brindister Shet...........235 c5
Brindle Lancs..............121 J5
Brineton Staffs.............84 E2
Bringhurst Leics...........88 B5
Bringsty Common
  Herefs.........................70 C4
Brington Cambs............88 F7
Brinian Ork.................234 c5
Briningham Norfk.......106 C5
Brinkhill Lincs.............118 E6
Brinkley Cambs............76 F4
Brinklow Warwks.........86 E7
Brinkworth Wilts...........40 A4
Brinscall Lancs...........121 J6
Brinsley Notts............101 J3
Brinsworth Rothm......115 H4
Brinton Norfk..............106 C5
Brisley Norfk...............105 M7
Brislington Bristl..........38 F6
Brissenden Green
  Kent............................34 C6
Bristol Bristl.................38 E5
*Bristol Airport* N Som...38 D7
Bristol Zoo Gardens
  Bristl..........................38 E5
Briston Norfk..............106 C6
Britannia Lancs..........122 D6
Britford Wilts................28 D5
Brithdir Caerph............53 J7
Brithdir Gwynd.............96 B8
British Legion
  Village Kent...............33 J2
Briton Ferry Neath.......51 L6
Britwell Salome
  Oxon...........................42 A2
Brixham Torbay..............7 L5
Brixton Devon................6 E5
Brixton Gt Lon..............44 F5
Brixton Deverill Wilts...27 K4
Brixworth Nhants..........73 L1
Brize Norton Oxon.......56 F6
*Brize Norton*
  *Airport* Oxon.............56 F6
Broad Alley Worcs........70 F2
Broad Blunsdon
  Swindn........................40 D3
Broadbottom
  Tamesd.....................113 M3
Broadbridge W Susx....17 M2
Broadbridge Heath
  W Susx.......................31 J5
Broad Campden
  Gloucs........................71 L6
Broad Carr Calder.....123 G6
Broad Chalke Wilts......28 B6
Broadclyst Devon.........12 C3
Broadfield Inver.........174 C4
Broadford Highld.......199 K2
Broadford Bridge
  W Susx.......................31 H6
Broadgairhill Border...166 C7
Broad Green Worcs......70 D4
Broadhaugh Border....179 H7
Broad Haven Pembks....48 E5
Broadheath Traffd.....113 H4
Broadhembury
  Devon..........................12 E2
Broadhempston
  Devon............................7 J3
Broad Hinton Wilts.......40 C5
Broadland Row
  E Susx.........................21 G2
Broadley Moray..........215 J3
Broad Marston
  Worcs..........................71 K5
Broadmayne Dorset.....14 D5
Broad Meadow
  Staffs..........................99 J3
Broadmoor Pembks......49 J6
Broadoak Dorset..........13 K3
Broad Oak E Susx........20 C2
Broad Oak E Susx........21 G2

Broad Oak Herefs............54 C4
Broad Oak Kent............35 G3
Broad Oak St Hel............112 D3
Broadsands Torbay............7 K4
Broad's Green Essex....61 H5
Broadstairs Kent............35 K2
Broadstone BCP............15 J4
Broadstone Shrops....83 K5
Broad Street E Susx....21 H3
Broad Street Kent....33 L2
Broad Town Wilts............40 C5
Broadwas Worcs............70 D4
Broadwater Herts............59 L4
Broadwater W Susx....18 F5
Broadwaters Worcs....84 E2
Broadway Pembks....48 E5
Broadway Somset............25 L7
Broadway Worcs............71 K6
Broadwell Gloucs............54 E5
Broadwell Gloucs............56 D3
Broadwell Oxon............56 E6
Broadwell Warwks....72 F2
Broadwindsor Dorset....13 K2
Broadwood Kelly
  Devon..........................10 F4
Broadwoodwidger
  Devon..........................9 K6
Brochel Highld............209 J3
Brochroy Ag & B....182 E2
Brockamin Worcs....70 D4
Brockbridge Hants....29 L7
Brockdish Norfk....92 E7
Brockenhurst Hants....16 C3
Brocketsbrae S Lans....164 F2
Brockford Street
  Suffk..........................78 D2
Brockhall Nhants....73 J2
Brockhall Village
  Lancs........................121 K3
Brockham Surrey....31 K2
Brockhampton
  Gloucs........................56 B4
Brockhampton Hants....17 K2
Brockhampton
  Herefs........................54 E2
Brockholes Kirk....123 H7
Brocklesby Lincs....126 E7
Brockley N Som....38 C6
Brockley Suffk....77 J1
Brockley Green Suffk....77 G5
Brockley Green Suffk....77 J4
Brockmoor Dudley....84 F5
Brockton Shrops....83 G3
Brockton Shrops....83 G6
Brockton Shrops....83 L5
Brockweir Gloucs....54 D7
Brockworth Gloucs....55 K5
Brocton Staffs....99 L8
Brodick N Ayrs....162 C3
Brodie Moray....214 B3
Brodsworth Donc....115 J1
Brogaig Highld....218 C7
Brokenborough Wilts....39 K3
Broken Cross Ches E....113 K6
Brokerswood Wilts....27 J2
Bromborough Wirral....111 K5
Brome Suffk....92 D7
Brome Street Suffk....92 D7
Bromeswell Suffk....79 G4
Bromfield Cumb....147 L5
Bromfield Shrops....83 J7
Bromham Bed....74 E4
Bromham Wilts....39 L7
Bromley Dudley....85 G6
Bromley Gt Lon....45 H6
Bromley Shrops....84 D4
Bromley Cross
  Bolton......................121 L7
Brompton Medway....46 C6
Brompton N York....141 J7
Brompton-by-
  Sawdon N York....134 E3
Brompton-on-
  Swale N York....140 F7
Brompton Ralph
  Somset........................25 G5
Brompton Regis
  Somset........................24 E5

Bromsberrow Gloucs....70 D7
Bromsberrow Heath
  Gloucs........................55 G2
Bromsgrove Worcs....71 G1
Bromyard Herefs....70 B4
Bronant Cerdgn....66 E2
Brongest Cerdgn....65 K5
Bronington Wrexhm....98 C4
Bronllys Powys....68 D7
Bronwydd Carmth....50 E2
Bronygarth Shrops....97 K5
Brook Hants....28 F8
Brook IoW....16 E5
Brook Kent....34 E6
Brook Surrey....30 F4
Brooke Norfk....93 G4
Brooke Rutlnd....88 B3
Brookenby Lincs....117 K3
Brookfield Rens....174 D5
Brookhampton
  Somset........................26 F5
Brook Hill Hants....28 F8
Brookhouse Lancs....129 L6
Brookhouse
  Rothm........................115 K4
Brookhouse Green
  Ches E........................99 J1
Brookhouses Derbys....114 B4
Brookland Kent....21 K1
Brooklands Traffd....113 H4
Brookmans Park
  Herts..........................59 L7
Brook Street Essex....45 L2
Brook Street Kent....34 C7
Brookthorpe Gloucs....55 J5
Brookwood Surrey....42 F8
Broom C Beds....75 H6
Broom Rothm....115 H3
Broom Warwks....71 K4
Broome Norfk....93 H5
Broome Shrops....83 H7
Broome Worcs....84 F7
Broomedge Warrtn....113 G4
Broomfield Essex....61 H5
Broomfield Kent....33 L3
Broomfield Kent....47 K6
Broomfield Somset....25 K5
Broomfleet E R Yk....125 K5
Broomhaugh
  Nthumb......................150 C3
Broom Hill Barns....115 H2
Broom Hill Notts....101 K3
Broomhill Nthumb....159 G3
Broompark Dur....151 G6
Brora Highld....226 F7
Broseley Shrops....84 C3
Brotherlee Dur....150 A7
Brotherton N York....124 D5
Brotton R & Cl....142 E4
Broubster Highld....230 F4
Brough Cumb....139 H4
Brough E R Yk....125 L5
Brough Highld....231 J2
Brough Notts....102 D2
Brough Shet....235 d4
Broughall Shrops....98 E4
Brough Lodge Shet....235 d2
Brough Sowerby
  Cumb........................139 H5
Broughton Border....165 L3
Broughton Cambs....89 K7
Broughton Flints....111 H8
Broughton Hants....28 F5
Broughton Lancs....121 G4
Broughton M Keyn....74 C6
Broughton N Linc....126 B8
Broughton N York....122 D1
Broughton N York....134 D5
Broughton Nhants....88 B7
Broughton Oxon....72 E6
Broughton Salfd....113 J2
Broughton V Glam....36 E6
Broughton Astley
  Leics..........................87 G5
Broughton Gifford
  Wilts..........................39 K7
Broughton Green
  Worcs........................71 G3

Broughton Hackett
  Worcs........................71 G4
Broughton-in-
  Furness Cumb....128 F3
Broughton Mains
  D & G........................145 J6
Broughton Mills
  Cumb........................128 F2
Broughton Moor
  Cumb........................147 J7
Broughton Poggs
  Oxon..........................56 E7
Broughty Ferry
  C Dund......................187 H2
Brown Candover
  Hants..........................29 L4
Brown Edge Staffs....99 K2
Brownhill Abers....217 G6
Brownhills Fife....187 H4
Brownhills Wsall....85 J3
Browninghill Green
  Hants..........................41 L7
Brown Lees Staffs....99 K2
Brownsea Island
  Dorset........................15 J5
Brown's Green Birm....85 J5
Browns Hill Gloucs....55 K7
Brownston Devon....7 G5
Broxa N York....134 E2
Broxbourne Herts....60 B6
Broxburn E Loth....178 E3
Broxburn W Loth....176 E4
Broxted Essex....60 F3
Bruan Highld....231 K7
Bruar P & K....194 C3
Bruchag Ag & B....173 J6
Bruichladdich
  Ag & B......................170 E6
Bruisyard Suffk....79 G2
Bruisyard Street
  Suffk..........................79 G2
Brumby N Linc....125 K8
Brund Staffs....100 C1
Brundall Norfk....93 G2
Brundish Suffk....78 F1
Brundish Street
  Suffk..........................78 F1
Brunery Highld....190 E3
Brunswick Village
  N u Ty......................159 G7
Brunthwaite C Brad....122 F2
Bruntingthorpe
  Leics..........................87 H5
Brunton Fife....186 E3
Brunton Wilts....28 E1
Brushford Devon....11 G4
Brushford Somset....24 E6
Bruton Somset....27 G4
Bryan's Green Worcs....70 F2
Bryanston Dorset....15 G2
Brydekirk D & G....155 L7
Bryher IoS....2 a1
Brympton Somset....26 D7
Bryn Carmth....51 G5
Bryn Neath....36 C3
Bryn Wigan....112 E2
Brynamman Carmth....51 K3
Brynberian Pembks....64 F7
Bryncir Gwynd....95 H4
Bryn-côch Neath....51 L5
Bryncroes Gwynd....94 D6
Bryncrug Gwynd....80 E3
Bryneglwys Denbgs....97 H3
Brynford Flints....111 G6
Bryn Gates Wigan....112 E2
Bryngwran IoA....108 D6
Bryngwyn Mons....54 B6
Bryngwyn Powys....68 D5
Bryn-Henllan
  Pembks........................64 E6
Brynhoffnant Cerdgn....65 K4
Brynmawr Blae G....53 J3
Bryn-mawr Gwynd....94 D5
Brynmenyn Brdgnd....36 D4
Brynmill Swans....51 J6
Brynna Rhondd....36 F4
Brynrefail Gwynd....109 H8
Brynsadler Rhondd....37 G4

Bryn Saith Marchog
  Denbgs........................97 G3
Brynsiencyn IoA....108 F7
Brynteg IoA....109 G5
Bryn-y-Maen Conwy....110 B6
Bualintur Highld....198 F2
Bubbenhall Warwks....86 D8
Bubwith E R Yk....125 H4
Buccleuch Border....166 E6
Buchanan Smithy
  Stirlg........................174 E1
Buchanhaven Abers....217 L5
Buchanty P & K....185 J2
Buchany Stirlg....184 F6
Buchlyvie Stirlg....184 C8
Buckabank Cumb....148 C5
Buckden Cambs....75 H2
Buckden N York....131 H4
Buckenham Norfk....93 H3
Buckerell Devon....12 E3
Buckfast Devon....7 H3
Buckfastleigh Devon....7 H3
Buckhaven Fife....186 F7
Buckholt Mons....54 D5
Buckhorn Weston
  Dorset........................27 H6
Buckhurst Hill Essex....45 H2
Buckie Moray....215 J2
Buckingham Bucks....73 K7
Buckland Bucks....58 E5
Buckland Devon....7 G6
Buckland Gloucs....71 J7
Buckland Herts....75 L7
Buckland Kent....35 J6
Buckland Oxon....41 G2
Buckland Surrey....31 K2
Buckland Brewer
  Devon........................22 F7
Buckland Common
  Bucks..........................58 F6
Buckland Dinham
  Somset........................27 H2
Buckland Filleigh
  Devon........................10 C3
Buckland in the
  Moor Devon....7 G2
Buckland
  Monachorum
  Devon........................6 D3
Buckland Newton
  Dorset........................14 D2
Buckland Ripers
  Dorset........................14 C6
Buckland St Mary
  Somset........................25 L8
Buckland-Tout-
  Saints Devon....7 H6
Bucklebury W Berk....41 K6
Bucklers Hard Hants....16 E3
Bucklesham Suffk....78 F6
Buckley Flints....111 J8
Bucklow Hill Ches E....113 G5
Buckminster Leics....102 F7
Bucknall C Stke....99 K3
Bucknall Lincs....117 K7
Bucknell Oxon....57 K3
Bucknell Shrops....83 G8
Buckpool Moray....215 J2
Bucksburn C Aber....207 G4
Buck's Cross Devon....22 E6
Bucks Green W Susx....31 H5
Buckshaw Village
  Lancs........................121 H6
Bucks Horn Oak
  Hants..........................30 D7
Buck's Mills Devon....22 E6
Buckton E R Yk....135 J5
Buckton Nthumb....169 G2
Buckworth Cambs....89 G7
Budby Notts....115 L7
Bude Cnwll....9 G4
Budge's Shop Cnwll....5 M4
Budleigh Salterton
  Devon........................12 D6
Budock Water Cnwll....3 K5
Buerton Ches E....99 G4
Bugbrooke Nhants....73 J3
Bugle Cnwll....4 F4

**Bugley** Dorset ..................**27** H6
**Bugthorpe** E R Yk...**134** B7
**Buildwas** Shrops...........**84** B3
**Builth Road** Powys...**68** B4
**Builth Wells** Powys....**68** B4
**Bulbridge** Wilts............**28** C5
**Bulford** Wilts.................**28** D3
**Bulkeley** Ches E.............**98** D2
**Bulkington** Warwks...**86** E6
**Bulkington** Wilts..........**39** L8
**Bulkworthy** Devon....... **9** K3
**Bullbrook** Br For ...........**42** E6
**Bullington** Hants..........**29** J3
**Bullington** Lincs...........**117** H6
**Bulmer** Essex.................**77** J6
**Bulmer** N York...............**133** L6
**Bulmer Tye** Essex..........**77** J6
**Bulphan** Thurr.............**45** M3
**Bulwark** Abers.............**217** H5
**Bulwell** C Nott.............**101** K4
**Bulwick** Nhants ............**88** D5
**Bumble's Green**
   Essex.........................**60** C6
**Bunacaimb** Highld....**199** K7
**Bunarkaig** Highld......**201** J7
**Bunbury** Ches E..............**98** E2
**Bunchrew** Highld......**212** F5
**Bundalloch** Highld....**210** D8
**Bunessan** Ag & B........**180** E3
**Bungay** Suffk................**93** G5
**Bunnahabhain**
   Ag & B......................**171** H4
**Bunny** Notts.................**101** L6
**Buntait** Highld...........**212** C7
**Buntingford** Herts........**60** B3
**Bunwell** Norfk...............**92** D5
**Burbage** Leics...............**86** F5
**Burbage** Wilts...............**40** E7
**Burchett's Green**
   W & M........................**42** D4
**Burcombe** Wilts............**28** B5
**Burcott** Bucks...............**58** E4
**Bures** Essex....................**77** K7
**Burford** Oxon................**56** E5
**Burford** Shrops..............**69** L2
**Burg** Ag & B.................**189** J7
**Burgess Hill** W Susx......**19** J2
**Burgh** Suffk...................**78** F4
**Burgh by Sands**
   Cumb.......................**148** B3
**Burgh Castle** Norfk.....**93** K3
**Burghclere** Hants..........**41** J7
**Burghead** Moray.........**214** D1
**Burghfield** W Berk.........**42** A6
**Burghfield Common**
   W Berk.......................**42** A6
**Burgh Heath** Surrey......**44** E7
**Burghill** Herefs..............**69** J5
**Burgh Island** Devon...... **6** F6
**Burgh le Marsh**
   Lincs.......................**119** G7
**Burgh next Aylsham**
   Norfk.......................**106** F7
**Burgh on Bain** Lincs....**117** L4
**Burgh St Margaret**
   Norfk.........................**93** J2
**Burgh St Peter** Norfk....**93** K5
**Burghwallis** Donc.......**124** E7
**Burham** Kent.................**46** B7
**Buriton** Hants...............**30** C7
**Burland** Ches E...............**98** E2
**Burlawn** Cnwll............... **4** F2
**Burleigh** Gloucs.............**55** K7
**Burlescombe** Devon......**25** G7
**Burleston** Dorset...........**14** E4
**Burley** Hants..................**16** B2
**Burley** Rutlnd................**88** C2
**Burleydam** Ches E..........**98** E4
**Burley Gate** Herefs......**69** L5
**Burley in**
   **Wharfedale**
   C Brad......................**123** H2
**Burley Street** Hants......**16** B2
**Burley Wood Head**
   C Brad......................**123** H2
**Burlton** Shrops..............**98** C7
**Burmarsh** Kent.............**34** E7
**Burmington** Warwks...**72** C6

**Burn** N York.................**124** F5
**Burnage** Manch...........**113** K3
**Burnaston** Derbys.......**100** F6
**Burnbrae** N Lans........**176** B6
**Burnby** E R Yk...............**125** K2
**Burneside** Cumb.........**138** D7
**Burneston** N York.......**132** D3
**Burnett** BaNES..............**38** F7
**Burnfoot** Border..........**166** F6
**Burnfoot** Border..........**167** H6
**Burnfoot** D & G............**155** G4
**Burnfoot** D & G............**156** C3
**Burnfoot** D & G............**156** C4
**Burnfoot** P & K.............**185** K6
**Burnham** Bucks............**42** F4
**Burnham Deepdale**
   Norfk.......................**105** J4
**Burnham Market**
   Norfk.......................**105** K4
**Burnham Norton**
   Norfk.......................**105** K4
**Burnham-on-**
   **Crouch** Essex............**46** F2
**Burnham-on-Sea**
   Somset.......................**25** L2
**Burnham Overy**
   Norfk.......................**105** K4
**Burnham Overy**
   **Staithe** Norfk...........**105** K4
**Burnham Thorpe**
   Norfk.......................**105** K4
**Burnhead** D & G...........**154** E3
**Burnhervie** Abers........**206** D2
**Burnhill Green** Staffs....**84** E4
**Burnhope** Dur..............**150** F5
**Burnhouse** N Ayrs.......**174** D7
**Burniston** N York.........**134** F2
**Burnley** Lancs...............**122** C4
**Burnmouth** Border......**179** K6
**Burn of Cambus**
   Stirlg........................**184** F6
**Burnopfield** Dur.........**150** F4
**Burnsall** N York............**131** J7
**Burnside** Angus...........**196** C4
**Burnside** Angus...........**196** E6
**Burnside** Fife...............**186** B5
**Burnside** Moray...........**214** E1
**Burnside** W Loth.........**176** E3
**Burnside of**
   **Duntrune** Angus.....**187** G1
**Burntisland** Fife...........**177** H2
**Burnton** E Ayrs............**163** L7
**Burntwood** Staffs..........**85** J2
**Burntwood Green**
   Staffs.........................**85** J2
**Burnt Yates** N York......**132** C7
**Burnworthy** Somset......**25** J7
**Burpham** Surrey............**31** G2
**Burpham** W Susx...........**18** E4
**Burradon** Nthumb......**168** E7
**Burrafirth** Shet............**235** e1
**Burravoe** Shet.............**235** d3
**Burray Village** Ork......**234** c7
**Burrells** Cumb.............**138** F4
**Burrelton** P & K..........**195** K8
**Burridge** Devon.............**13** H2
**Burridge** Hants.............**17** G1
**Burrill** N York..............**132** C3
**Burringham** N Linc......**125** K8
**Burrington** Devon.........**10** F2
**Burrington** Herefs.........**69** J1
**Burrington** N Som.........**38** C8
**Burrough Green**
   Cambs.......................**76** F4
**Burrough on the**
   **Hill** Leics.................**87** L2
**Burrow** Lancs..............**130** C4
**Burrow** Somset.............**24** E3
**Burrow Bridge**
   Somset.......................**26** A5
**Burrowhill** Surrey.........**42** F7
**Burry Green** Swans.......**50** F7
**Burry Port** Carmth.......**50** F5
**Burscough** Lancs.........**120** F7
**Burscough Bridge**
   Lancs.......................**120** F7
**Bursea** E R Yk...............**125** J4
**Bursledon** Hants...........**16** F1

**Burstall** Suffk................**78** D5
**Burstock** Dorset............**13** K2
**Burston** Norfk................**92** D6
**Burstow** Surrey..............**32** B5
**Burstwick** E R Yk..........**126** F5
**Burtersett** N York........**131** G2
**Burtholme** Cumb........**148** F3
**Burthorpe Green**
   Suffk..........................**77** H2
**Burtle** Somset................**26** B3
**Burtoft** Lincs...............**103** L5
**Burton** BCP....................**15** M4
**Burton** Ches W.............**111** K6
**Burton** Ches W.............**112** D8
**Burton** Pembks.............**49** G6
**Burton** Somset...............**25** J3
**Burton** Wilts..................**39** J4
**Burton Agnes** E R Yk...**135** H6
**Burton Bradstock**
   Dorset........................**13** L4
**Burton-by-Lincoln**
   Lincs.......................**116** F6
**Burton Coggles** Lincs...**103** G7
**Burton End** Essex..........**60** E4
**Burton Fleming**
   E R Yk.......................**135** G5
**Burton Hastings**
   Warwks......................**86** E5
**Burton Hill** Wilts..........**39** L3
**Burton-in-Kendal**
   Cumb.......................**129** L4
**Burton-in-Kendal**
   **Services** Cumb.........**129** L4
**Burton in Lonsdale**
   N York......................**130** C5
**Burton Joyce** Notts.....**101** M4
**Burton Latimer**
   Nhants........................**88** C8
**Burton Lazars** Leics.....**87** L1
**Burton Leonard**
   N York......................**132** E6
**Burton on the**
   **Wolds** Leics.............**101** L7
**Burton Overy** Leics .....**87** J4
**Burton Pedwardine**
   Lincs.......................**103** J4
**Burton Pidsea**
   E R Yk.......................**127** G4
**Burton Salmon**
   N York......................**124** D5
**Burton's Green** Essex....**61** K3
**Burton upon**
   **Stather** N Linc.........**125** K6
**Burton upon Trent**
   Staffs.......................**100** E7
**Burton Waters** Lincs....**116** F6
**Burtonwood** Warrtn....**112** E3
**Burtonwood**
   **Services** Warrtn......**112** E4
**Burwardsley** Ches W......**98** D2
**Burwarton** Shrops.........**84** B6
**Burwash** E Susx............**33** H7
**Burwash Common**
   E Susx........................**20** D2
**Burwash Weald**
   E Susx........................**20** D2
**Burwell** Cambs...............**76** E2
**Burwell** Lincs...............**118** E5
**Burwen** IoA..................**108** E3
**Burwick** Ork................**234** c8
**Bury** Bury....................**122** B7
**Bury** Cambs...................**89** K6
**Bury** Somset..................**24** E6
**Bury** W Susx..................**18** D3
**Bury Green** Herts...........**60** D4
**Bury St Edmunds**
   Suffk..........................**77** J2
**Burythorpe** N York......**134** C6
**Busby** E Rens...............**175** G6
**Buscot** Oxon..................**40** F2
**Bush** Abers...................**197** J4
**Bush Bank** Herefs..........**69** J4
**Bushbury** Wolves...........**85** G3
**Bushey** Herts.................**43** J2
**Bushey Heath** Herts......**43** J2
**Bush Hill Park** Gt Lon....**45** G2
**Bushley** Worcs...............**70** F7
**Bushmoor** Shrops..........**83** J6

**Bushton** Wilts................**40** B5
**Bussage** Gloucs..............**55** K7
**Butcombe** N Som...........**38** D7
**Bute** Ag & B.................**173** H4
**Butleigh** Somset............**26** D5
**Butleigh Wootton**
   Somset.......................**26** D4
**Butlers Marston**
   Warwks......................**72** D4
**Butley** Suffk...................**79** H4
**Buttercrambe** N York...**133** L7
**Butterdean** Border......**179** G5
**Butterknowle** Dur.......**140** E3
**Butterleigh** Devon.........**12** C2
**Buttermere** Cumb........**137** G4
**Buttershaw** C Brad.......**123** H5
**Butterstone** P & K.......**195** G7
**Butterton** Staffs.............**99** J4
**Butterton** Staffs...........**100** B2
**Butterwick** Lincs..........**104** C4
**Butterwick** N York.......**133** L4
**Butterwick** N York.......**134** F5
**Buttington** Powys..........**82** E2
**Buttonoak** Shrops.........**84** D7
**Buxhall** Suffk.................**78** B3
**Buxted** E Susx................**20** A2
**Buxton** Derbys.............**114** B6
**Buxton** Norfk...............**106** F7
**Buxton Heath** Norfk....**106** E7
**Bwlch** Powys..................**53** J4
**Bwlchgwyn** Wrexhm......**97** K2
**Bwlchllan** Cerdgn..........**66** D3
**Bwlchtocyn** Gwynd.......**94** E7
**Bwlch-y-cibau**
   Powys........................**97** J8
**Bwlch-y-ffridd**
   Powys........................**82** B4
**Bwlch-y-groes**
   Pembks......................**65** H7
**Bwlch-y-sarnau**
   Powys........................**82** B8
**Byers Green** Dur..........**150** F7
**Byfield** Nhants...............**73** G4
**Byfleet** Surrey................**43** H7
**Byford** Herefs................**69** H6
**Byker** N u Ty................**151** G3
**Bylchau** Conwy...........**110** D8
**Byley** Ches W................**113** G7
**Byram** N York...............**124** D5
**Byrness** Nthumb..........**157** K2
**Bystock** Devon...............**12** D5
**Bythorn** Cambs.............**88** F7
**Byton** Herefs..................**69** G2
**Bywell** Nthumb............**150** D3
**Byworth** W Susx.............**31** G7

## C

**Cabourne** Lincs............**117** J2
**Cabrach** Ag & B...........**171** J5
**Cabrach** Moray............**215** J8
**Cabus** Lancs................**121** G2
**Cadbury** Devon..............**11** L4
**Cadbury World** Birm......**85** J7
**Cadder** E Duns.............**175** G4
**Caddington** C Beds........**59** H4
**Caddonfoot** Border......**167** G3
**Cadeby** Donc................**115** K2
**Cadeby** Leics.................**86** E3
**Cadeleigh** Devon...........**11** L4
**Cade Street** E Susx........**20** C2
**Cadgwith** Cnwll.............. **3** J7
**Cadham** Fife................**186** D6
**Cadishead** Salfd..........**113** G3
**Cadle** Swans..................**51** J6
**Cadley** Lancs................**121** G4
**Cadley** Wilts..................**28** E2
**Cadley** Wilts..................**40** E6
**Cadmore End** Bucks......**42** C3
**Cadnam** Hants...............**28** F8
**Cadney** N Linc..............**117** G2
**Cadoxton** V Glam..........**37** H6
**Cadoxton Juxta-**
   **Neath** Neath.............**51** L5
**Caeathro** Gwynd...........**95** J1
**Caenby** Lincs...............**117** G4

Caerau Brdgnd.................36 D2
Caerau Cardif..................37 H5
Caer Farchell
   Pembks ......................48 D3
Caergeiliog IoA ..........108 D5
Caergwrle Flints ..........97 L2
Caerlanrig Border........156 D2
Caerleon Newpt ...........37 M3
Caernarfon Gwynd ....108 F8
Caernarfon Castle
   Gwynd ....................108 F8
Caerphilly Caerph.........37 J3
Caersws Powys ............82 B5
Caerwedros Cerdgn .....65 L4
Caerwent Mons..............38 C3
Caerwys Flints ...........110 F6
Caio Carmth...................66 F6
Cairinis W Isls ...........233 c6
Cairnbaan Ag & B ......172 E1
Cairnbulg Abers..........217 J2
Cairncross Border .......179 J5
Cairncurran Inver ......174 C4
Cairndow Ag & B........183 H5
Cairneyhill Fife ..........176 E2
Cairngarroch D & G ...144 C5
Cairngorms
   National Park .......204 C5
Cairnie Abers ..............215 K5
Cairnorrie Abers..........217 G6
Cairnryan D & G .........144 C2
Cairnty Moray .............215 H4
Caister-on-Sea
   Norfk..........................93 L2
Caistor Lincs ..............117 J2
Caistor St Edmund
   Norfk..........................92 F3
Calanais W Isls..........232 e2
Calbourne IoW ............16 E5
Calcoed Flints ............111 G6
Calcot Gloucs ...............56 C6
Calcot Row W Berk .....42 A6
Calcots Moray.............215 G2
Caldbeck Cumb ...........148 B6
Caldecote Cambs.........75 L3
Caldecote Cambs.........89 G5
Caldecott Nhants..........74 E2
Caldecott Oxon ...........41 J2
Caldecott Rutlnd...........88 C5
Calderbank N Lans......175 K5
Calder Bridge Cumb ...136 E6
Caldercruix N Lans......175 L5
Calder Grove Wakefd...123 L6
Caldermill S Lans ........164 D2
Calder Vale Lancs .......121 G2
Calderwood S Lans .....175 H7
Caldey Island
   Pembks ......................49 K7
Caldicot Mons...............38 C3
Caldmore Wsall...........85 H4
Caldwell N York..........140 E5
Calf of Man IoM .........237 a7
Calfsound Ork ............234 d4
Calgary Ag & B..........189 J6
Califer Moray .............214 D3
California Falk.............176 B3
California Norfk............93 K1
Calke Derbys ..............101 G7
*Calke Abbey Derbys....101 G7*
Callakille Highld .........209 L4
Callander Stirlg............184 D5
Callanish W Isls..........232 e2
Callestick Cnwll..............3 K2
Calligarry Highld ........199 K5
Callington Cnwll ............6 A3
Callow Herefs ...............69 J7
Callow End Worcs .......70 E4
Calmore Hants .............29 G2
Calmsden Gloucs .........56 B6
Calne Wilts ...................39 M6
Calshot Hants ..............16 F3
Calstock Cnwll ...............6 C3
Calstone Wellington
   Wilts..........................40 B6
Calthorpe Norfk .........106 E6
Calthorpe Street
   Norfk........................107 J7
Calthwaite Cumb ........148 E6

Calton Staffs ..............100 C3
Calveley Ches E ...........98 E2
Calver Derbys .............114 E6
Calverhall Shrops ........98 E5
Calverleigh Devon .......11 L3
Calverley Leeds ..........123 J3
Calverton M Keyn........73 L6
Calverton Notts..........101 L3
Calvine P & K .............194 C3
Calzeat Border............165 L3
Cam Gloucs..................55 H7
Camasachoirce
   Highld......................190 F4
Camasine Highld........190 F4
Camas Luinie Highld..210 E8
Camastianavaig
   Highld......................209 H6
Camault Muir Highld ..212 D6
Camber E Susx ............21 J2
Camberley Surrey.........42 E7
Camberwell Gt Lon ......44 F5
Camblesforth N York ..124 F5
Cambo Nthumb ...........158 C5
Camborne Cnwll.............3 H4
Camborne &
   Redruth Mining
   District Cnwll...............3 H4
Cambourne Cambs.......75 K3
Cambridge Cambs........76 C3
Cambridge Gloucs........55 H7
*Cambridge Airport*
   *Cambs* .......................76 C3
Cambrose Cnwll..............3 H3
Cambus Clacks ...........185 H8
Cambusavie Highld ....223 G3
Cambusbarron
   Stirlg.......................185 G8
Cambuskenneth
   Stirlg.......................185 G8
Cambuslang S Lans ....175 H6
Cambus o' May
   Abers.......................205 J5
Cambuswallace
   S Lans ....................165 K2
Camden Town Gt Lon...44 F4
Cameley BaNES............38 E8
Camelford Cnwll ............8 E7
Camelon Falk..............176 B3
Camerory Highld ........214 C7
Camerton BaNES..........39 G8
Camerton Cumb..........136 E2
Camghouran P & K.....193 J5
Camieston Border ......167 J4
Cammachmore
   Abers.......................207 G6
Cammeringham
   Lincs........................116 F5
Camore Highld...........223 G4
Campbeltown
   Ag & B ....................161 J5
*Campbeltown*
   *Airport Ag & B*.......161 H5
Cample D & G .............154 F4
Campmuir P & K........195 K8
Camps W Loth ...........176 E5
Campsall Donc ...........124 E7
Campsea Ash Suffk.....79 G4
Campton C Beds ...........75 G6
Camptown Border ......167 K6
Camrose Pembks .........48 F4
Camserney P & K .......194 C6
Camusnagaul Highld ..191 L2
Camusnagaul Highld ..220 D4
Camusteel Highld .......209 L6
Camusterrach
   Highld......................209 L6
Canada Hants ..............28 F7
Candacraig Abers.......205 H5
Candlesby Lincs ..........118 F7
Candy Mill Border ......165 L2
Cane End Oxon.............42 B4
Canewdon Essex ..........46 E2
Canford Cliffs BCP........15 K5
Canford Heath BCP......15 J4
Canisbay Highld ..........231 L2
Canley Covtry..............86 C7
Cann Dorset..................27 K7
Canna Highld ..............198 C4

Cann Common
   Dorset.......................27 K7
Cannich Highld ...........211 L7
Cannington Somset.......25 K4
Canning Town Gt Lon...45 H4
Cannock Staffs .............85 H2
Cannock Chase
   Staffs.........................99 M8
Cannon Bridge
   Herefs .......................69 H6
Canonbie D & G .........156 C6
Canon Frome Herefs....70 B5
Canon Pyon Herefs......69 J5
Canons Ashby
   Nhants.......................73 H4
Canonstown Cnwll.........2 F4
Canterbury Kent ..........34 F3
Canterbury
   Cathedral Kent ........34 F3
Cantley Norfk...............93 H3
Canton Cardif...............37 J5
Cantraywood Highld ...213 J5
Cantsfield Lancs .........130 C5
Canvey Island Essex ....46 D4
Canwick Lincs.............117 G7
Canworthy Water
   Cnwll...........................9 G6
Caol Highld ................191 L2
Caolas Scalpaigh
   W Isls.....................232 e4
Caoles Ag & B ...........188 D6
Caonich Highld ..........201 G6
Capel Kent ...................33 H4
Capel Surrey.................31 K4
Capel Bangor Cerdgn ...80 E7
Capel Coch IoA ..........108 F5
Capel Curig Conwy......96 A2
Capel Dewi Carmth......50 F2
Capel Dewi Cerdgn......66 B6
Capel-Dewi Cerdgn......80 E6
Capel Garmon Conwy...96 C2
Capel Hendre Carmth...51 H4
Capel Iwan Carmth......65 J7
Capel-le-Ferne Kent ....35 H6
Capelles Guern ..........236 d2
Capel Parc IoA ...........108 F4
Capel St Andrew
   Suffk.........................79 H5
Capel St Mary Suffk....78 C6
Capel Seion Cerdgn.....80 E7
Capelulo Conwy .........109 L6
Capenhurst Ches W ....111 K6
Cape Wrath Highld.....228 D1
Capheaton Nthumb.....158 C6
Caplaw E Rens ...........174 E6
Cappercleuch Border...166 C5
Capton Devon.................7 J5
Caputh P & K..............195 H7
Caradon Mining
   District Cnwll..............5 L2
Carbeth Stirlg.............174 F3
Carbis Bay Cnwll...........2 F4
Carbost Highld ...........208 F5
Carbost Highld ...........208 F7
Carbrook Sheff...........115 G4
Carbrooke Norfk..........91 L3
Car Colston Notts.......102 B4
Carcroft Donc.............124 E8
Cardenden Fife...........186 C2
Cardhu Moray .............214 F5
Cardiff Cardif...............37 J5
*Cardiff Airport*
   *V Glam*......................37 G6
Cardiff Gate
   Services Cardif..........37 K4
Cardiff West
   Services Cardif..........37 H4
Cardigan Cerdgn .........65 G5
Cardington Bed............74 F5
Cardington Shrops.......83 K4
Cardinham Cnwll ...........5 H3
Cardrain D & G ...........144 D8
Cardrona Border ........166 D2
Cardross Ag & B .........174 C3
Cardryne D & G ..........144 D7
Cardurnock Cumb ......147 L3
Careby Lincs.................88 E1
Careston Angus...........196 E4

Carew Pembks .............49 H6
Carew Cheriton
   Pembks ......................49 H6
Carew Newton
   Pembks ......................49 H6
Carey Herefs ................54 E2
Carfin N Lans .............175 K6
Carfraemill Border .....178 B2
Cargate Green Norfk...93 H2
Cargenbridge D & G ...155 G7
Cargill P & K..............195 J8
Cargo Cumb...............148 C3
Cargreen Cnwll..............6 C4
Carham Nthumb .........168 B2
Carhampton Somset....24 F3
Carharrack Cnwll...........3 J3
Carie P & K ................193 K5
Carinish W Isls ...........233 c6
Carisbrooke IoW .........16 F5
Cark Cumb .................129 H4
Carkeel Cnwll.................6 B4
Càrlabhagh W Isls......232 e2
Carlbury Darltn...........140 F4
Carlby Lincs..................88 F2
Carleen Cnwll.................3 G5
Carleton Forehoe
   Norfk..........................92 C3
Carleton-in-Craven
   N York......................122 E1
Carleton Rode Norfk...92 D5
Carleton St Peter
   Norfk..........................93 H3
Carlincraig Abers .......216 D5
Carlingcott BaNES.......38 G8
Carlisle Cumb .............148 D4
*Carlisle Lake*
   *District Airport*
   *Cumb*......................148 E3
Carlops Border ...........177 G6
Carloway W Isls ..........232 e2
Carlton Barns ............124 B7
Carlton Bed..................74 D4
Carlton Cambs.............76 F4
Carlton Leeds ............123 L5
Carlton Leics................86 E3
Carlton N York............124 F5
Carlton N York............131 K3
Carlton N York............133 J3
Carlton Notts..............101 L4
Carlton S on T............141 J3
Carlton Suffk................79 H2
Carlton Colville Suffk...93 K5
Carlton Curlieu Leics...87 K4
Carlton Green Cambs...76 F4
Carlton Husthwaite
   N York......................133 G4
Carlton-in-
   Cleveland N York.....142 B6
Carlton in Lindrick
   Notts........................115 L5
Carlton-le-
   Moorland Lincs........102 E2
Carlton Miniott
   N York......................132 F4
Carlton-on-Trent
   Notts........................116 D8
Carlton Scroop
   Lincs........................102 F4
Carluke S Lans ...........175 L7
Carmacoup S Lans .....164 F4
Carmarthen Carmth.....50 E2
Carmel Carmth .............51 H3
Carmel Flints ..............111 G6
Carmel Gwynd .............95 H2
Carmichael S Lans ......165 H2
Carmunnock C Glas ....175 G6
Carmyle C Glas...........175 H6
Carmyllie Angus.........196 E7
Carnaby E R Yk ..........135 H6
Carnbee Fife ..............187 J6
Carnbo P & K .............185 L6
Carn Brea Cnwll ............3 H3
Carnbrogie Abers .......216 F8
Candu Highld .............210 D8
Carnduff S Lans..........164 E2
Carnell E Ayrs .............163 L3
Carnforth Lancs .........129 K5
Carn-gorm Highld ......200 E1

Carnhell Green Cnwll....... 3 G4
Carnie Abers.................. 206 F4
Carnkie Cnwll ................... 3 H4
Carnkie Cnwll ................... 3 J4
Carno Powys...................81 K4
Carnock Fife ................. 176 E1
Carnon Downs Cnwll....... 4 C7
Carnousie Abers ......... 216 C4
Carnoustie Angus ........ 187 J1
Carnwath S Lans ......... 165 J1
Carol Green Solhll..........86 C7
Carperby N York ........... 131 J2
Carradale Ag & B ......... 161 K2
Carradale Village
   Ag & B........................ 161 K2
Carrbridge Highld........ 203 L2
Carrefour Jersey......... 236 c6
Carreglefn IoA ............. 108 E4
Carr Gate Wakefd........ 123 L5
Carrhouse N Linc ........ 116 C1
Carrick Ag & B .............. 172 F2
Carrick Castle Ag & B.. 183 H8
Carriden Falk ............... 176 D3
Carrington Mdloth ...... 177 J6
Carrington Traffd ........ 113 H3
Carrog Denbgs...............97 H4
Carron Falk .................. 176 B2
Carron Moray............... 214 F6
Carronbridge D & G...... 154 F3
Carron Bridge Stirlg... 175 K2
Carronshore Falk ........ 176 B2
Carr Shield Nthumb..... 149 K5
Carrutherstown
   D & G.......................... 155 J7
Carruth House Inver ... 174 C5
Carrville Dur ............... 151 H6
Carsaig Ag & B ............ 181 H3
Carseriggan D & G ...... 145 G2
Carsethorn D & G ........ 147 H3
Carshalton Gt Lon........44 F6
Carsington Derbys .... 100 E2
Carskey Ag & B ........... 161 H7
Carsluith D & G ........... 145 K4
Carsphairn D & G ....... 153 L4
Carstairs S Lans ......... 165 H1
Carstairs Junction
   S Lans........................ 165 J1
Carterton Oxon ............56 F6
Carthew Cnwll ................. 4 F5
Carthorpe N York......... 132 D3
Cartland S Lans ........... 165 G1
Cartmel Cumb............... 129 H4
Carway Carmth ..............50 F4
Cashe's Green Gloucs....55 J6
Cassington Oxon ...........57 J5
Cassop Dur.................... 151 J7
Castel Guern ................ 236 c3
Casterton Cumb .......... 130 C4
Castle Acre Norfk..........91 J1
Castle Ashby Nhants....74 C3
Castlebay W Isls .......... 233 b9
Castle Bolton N York ... 131 J2
Castle Bromwich
   Solhll...........................85 K5
Castle Bytham Lincs .. 103 G8
Castlebythe Pembks....49 H2
Castle Caereinion
   Powys..........................82 D3
Castle Camps Cambs....76 F6
Castle Carrock
   Cumb ......................... 148 F4
Castlecary Falk ........... 175 K3
Castle Cary Somset .....26 F5
Castle Combe Wilts ......39 J5
Castlecraig Highld...... 223 H7
Castle Donington
   Leics .......................... 101 H6
Castle Douglas
   D & G.......................... 146 D3
Castle Eaton Swindn....40 C2
Castle Eden Dur .......... 151 K7
Castleford Wakefd..... 124 C5
Castle Frome Herefs....70 C5
Castle Gresley
   Derbys ...................... 100 F8
Castle Hedingham
   Essex...........................77 H7
Castlehill Border.......... 166 C3

Castlehill Highld............ 231 H2
Castle Hill Suffk.............78 D5
Castlehill W Duns......... 174 D3
Castle Howard
   N York ..................... 133 L5
Castle Kennedy
   D & G......................... 144 D3
Castle Lachlan
   Ag & B....................... 182 E7
Castlemartin Pembks...48 F7
Castlemilk C Glas ........ 175 G6
Castlemorton Worcs....70 E6
Castlemorton
   Common Worcs .......70 E6
Castle O'er D & G......... 156 A4
Castle Rising Norfk..... 105 G7
Castleside Dur ............. 150 D5
Castle Stuart Highld.... 213 H4
Castlethorpe M Keyn....74 B5
Castleton Ag & B.......... 172 E2
Castleton Border......... 156 E4
Castleton Derbys ........ 114 D5
Castleton N York ......... 142 E5
Castleton Newpt ..........37 K4
Castleton Rochdl......... 122 D7
Castletown Highld...... 231 H3
Castletown IoM ........... 237 b7
Castletown Sundld..... 151 J4
Castley N York .............. 123 K2
Caston Norfk..................91 L4
Castor C Pete.................89 G4
Catacol N Ayrs ............. 172 F7
Catcliffe Rothm ........... 115 H4
Catcomb Wilts...............40 A5
Catcott Somset .............26 B4
Caterham Surrey...........32 C3
Catfield Norfk .............. 107 H7
Catford Gt Lon ..............45 G5
Catforth Lancs ............ 121 G4
Cathcart C Glas ........... 175 G6
Cathedine Powys ..........53 H3
Catherington Hants ....30 B8
Catherston
   Leweston Dorset ....13 J4
Catisfield Hants ...........17 G2
Catlodge Highld .......... 202 F6
Catmere End Essex......76 C6
Catmore W Berk ...........41 J4
Caton Lancs................. 129 L6
Caton Green Lancs..... 129 L6
Catrine E Ayrs.............. 164 B4
Catsfield E Susx............20 E3
Catsgore Somset ..........26 D6
Catshill Worcs...............85 G8
Cattadale Ag & B ........ 161 H7
Cattal N York ............... 133 G8
Cattawade Suffk ...........62 D2
Catterall Lancs ........... 121 G3
Catterick N York .......... 141 G7
Catterick Bridge
   N York ....................... 141 G7
Catterlen Cumb ........... 148 E7
Catterline Abers ......... 197 L2
Catterton N York ........ 124 D2
Catteshall Surrey.........31 G3
Catthorpe Leics............87 G7
Cattistock Dorset........14 B3
Catton N York .............. 132 E4
Catton Nthumb............ 149 L4
Catwick E R Yk............. 126 E2
Catworth Cambs ..........88 F8
Caudle Green Gloucs....55 L6
Caulcott Oxon ...............57 K3
Cauldcots Angus......... 197 G6
Cauldhame Stirlg........ 184 E8
Cauldmill Border......... 167 H6
Cauldon Staffs........... 100 B3
Cauldwell Derbys.........86 B1
Caulkerbush D & G...... 147 G4
Caulside D & G ............ 156 D6
Caundle Marsh
   Dorset ........................27 G8
Caunton Notts ............ 102 C1
Causeway End D & G... 145 J3
Causeway End Essex....61 G4
Causewayend S Lans.. 165 K3
Causewayhead Stirlg.. 185 G7
Causeyend Abers......... 207 H2

Causey Park Bridge
   Nthumb...................... 158 F3
Cavendish Suffk............77 J5
Cavenham Suffk............77 H1
Caversfield Oxon ..........57 L3
Caversham Readg ........42 B5
Caverswall Staffs..........99 L4
Caverton Mill Border... 167 M4
Cawdor Highld ............ 213 K4
Cawood N York ............ 124 E3
Cawsand Cnwll ............... 6 C5
Cawston Norfk............. 106 D7
Cawthorne Barns ....... 123 K8
Caxton Cambs...............75 K3
Caynham Shrops...........83 K8
Caythorpe Lincs ......... 102 F3
Caythorpe Notts ......... 102 B4
Cayton N York ............. 135 G3
Ceannabeinne
   Highld....................... 228 F3
Ceann a Bhaigh
   W Isls ....................... 233 b6
Ceannacroc Lodge
   Highld....................... 201 K3
Cearsiadar W Isls ....... 232 f3
Cefn Newpt ....................37 L3
Cefn-brith Conwy ..........96 E3
Cefn-bryn-brain
   Carmth........................51 L3
Cefn-coed-y-
   cymmer Myr Td.........53 G6
Cefn Cribwr Brdgnd......36 D4
Cefneithin Carmth........51 G3
Cefngorwydd Powys.....67 J5
Cefn-mawr Wrexhm......97 L4
Cefn-y-pant Carmth.....49 K3
Cellardyke Fife............. 187 J6
Cellarhead Staffs..........99 L3
Cemaes IoA ................ 108 E3
Cemmaes Powys...........81 H3
Cemmaes Road
   Powys..........................81 H3
Cenarth Cerdgn ...........65 J6
Ceres Fife .................... 186 F5
Cerne Abbas Dorset ....14 C3
Cerney Wick Gloucs.....40 B2
Cerrigydrudion
   Conwy ........................96 E3
Ceunant Gwynd ...........95 J1
Chaceley Gloucs...........55 J2
Chacewater Cnwll ......... 3 K3
Chackmore Bucks........73 K7
Chacombe Nhants........72 F5
Chadbury Worcs...........71 H5
Chadderton Oldham.... 113 K1
Chaddesden C Derb... 101 G5
Chaddesley Corbett
   Worcs..........................84 F8
Chaddlehanger
   Devon .......................... 6 C1
Chaddleworth
   W Berk........................41 H5
Chadlington Oxon ........57 G4
Chadshunt Warwks......72 D4
Chadwell Leics ........... 102 C7
Chadwell Heath
   Gt Lon .........................45 J3
Chadwell St Mary
   Thurr ..........................45 M4
Chadwick Worcs ...........70 E2
Chadwick End Solhll......86 B8
Chaffcombe Somset ....13 J1
Chafford Hundred
   Thurr ..........................45 L4
Chagford Devon ........... 11 G7
Chailey E Susx...............19 K2
Chainhurst Kent...........33 J4
Chaldon Surrey ............32 B3
Chaldon Herring
   Dorset ........................14 E5
Chale IoW ..................... 16 F6
Chale Green IoW .......... 16 F6
Chalfont Common
   Bucks..........................43 G3
Chalfont St Giles
   Bucks..........................43 G2
Chalfont St Peter
   Bucks..........................43 G3

Chalford Gloucs............55 K7
Chalford Wilts...............27 K2
Chalgrove Oxon ...........41 M2
Chalk Kent ....................46 A5
Chalkwell Kent..............34 B2
Challacombe Devon......23 L3
Challoch D & G ............ 145 H2
Challock Kent................34 D5
Chalton C Beds..............59 G3
Chalton Hants...............30 B7
Chalvey Slough.............42 F4
Chalvington E Susx.......20 B4
Chandler's Cross
   Herts ..........................43 H2
Chandler's Ford
   Hants..........................29 H7
Channel Tunnel
   Terminal Kent ..........35 G6
Chantry Somset ...........27 G3
Chantry Suffk................78 D5
Chapel Fife ................. 186 D8
Chapel Allerton
   Leeds........................ 123 L3
Chapel Allerton
   Somset .......................26 B2
Chapel Amble Cnwll....... 4 F2
Chapel Brampton
   Nhants........................73 K2
Chapel Chorlton
   Staffs..........................99 J5
Chapelend Way
   Essex...........................77 G6
Chapel-en-le-Frith
   Derbys ...................... 114 B5
Chapel Green
   Warwks.......................72 F3
Chapel Haddlesey
   N York ....................... 124 E5
Chapelhall N Lans ...... 175 K5
Chapel Hill Abers ....... 217 K7
Chapel Hill Lincs......... 103 K2
Chapel Hill N York ...... 123 L2
Chapelhope Border..... 166 C5
Chapelknowe D & G.... 156 B7
Chapel Lawn Shrops....82 F7
Chapel-le-Dale
   N York ....................... 130 E4
Chapel Leigh Somset....25 H5
Chapel of Garioch
   Abers........................ 206 D1
Chapel Rossan D & G.. 144 D6
Chapel Row W Berk .....41 L6
Chapel St Leonards
   Lincs ........................ 119 H6
Chapel Stile Cumb ..... 137 K6
Chapelton Abers ........ 207 G6
Chapelton Angus ....... 197 G6
Chapelton Devon ........23 J6
Chapelton S Lans ....... 175 J8
Chapeltown Bl w D...... 121 L7
Chapeltown Moray..... 204 F2
Chapeltown Sheff...... 115 G3
Chapmanslade Wilts....27 J2
Chapmans Well
   Devon .......................... 9 J6
Chapmore End Herts....60 B5
Chappel Essex..............61 L3
Chard Somset ............. 13 H2
Chard Junction
   Somset ...................... 13 J2
Chardleigh Green
   Somset ...................... 13 H1
Chardstock Devon ...... 13 H2
Charfield S Glos ..........39 G3
Charing Kent.................34 C5
Charingworth Gloucs....71 L6
Charlbury Oxon ............57 G4
Charlcombe BaNES......39 H6
Charlcutt Wilts.............39 M5
Charlecote Warwks......72 C3
Charlemont Sandw ......85 H5
Charles Devon ..............23 L5
Charleston Angus ...... 196 C7
Charlestown Abers ..... 207 H5
Charlestown C Brad... 123 H3
Charlestown Calder.. 122 E5
Charlestown Cnwll......... 5 G5
Charlestown Cnwll......... 5 G5

**Charlestown** Fife......... 176 E2
**Charlestown** Highld .... 213 G5
**Charlestown** Highld .... 219 J6
**Charlestown** Salfd........ 113 J2
**Charlestown of**
**Aberlour** Moray ...... 215 G5
**Charles Tye** Suffk...........78 B4
**Charlesworth** Derbys... 114 A3
**Charlinch** Somset........25 K4
**Charlottetown** Fife...... 186 E5
**Charlton** Gt Lon..............45 H4
**Charlton** Nhants.............73 G7
**Charlton** Nthumb........ 157 K5
**Charlton** Oxon................41 H3
**Charlton** Somset............25 L6
**Charlton** Somset............27 G2
**Charlton** W Susx............18 B3
**Charlton** Wilts................27 K6
**Charlton** Wilts................39 L3
**Charlton** Worcs..............71 H5
**Charlton** Wrekin............83 L2
**Charlton Abbots**
Gloucs .......................56 B3
**Charlton Adam**
Somset......................26 D5
**Charlton All Saints**
Wilts...........................28 D6
**Charlton Down**
Dorset.......................14 D4
**Charlton**
**Horethorne**
Somset......................26 F6
**Charlton Kings**
Gloucs .......................55 L4
**Charlton Mackrell**
Somset......................26 D5
**Charlton Marshall**
Dorset.......................15 G2
**Charlton Musgrove**
Somset......................27 G5
**Charlton-on-**
**Otmoor** Oxon.........57 K5
**Charlton on the Hill**
Dorset.......................15 G2
**Charlton St Peter**
Wilts...........................28 C1
**Charlwood** Hants...........30 A5
**Charlwood** Surrey..........31 L3
**Charminster** Dorset......14 D4
**Charmouth** Dorset.........13 J4
**Charndon** Bucks.............58 A3
**Charney Bassett**
Oxon...........................41 G2
**Charnock Richard**
Lancs ...................... 121 H7
**Charnock Richard**
**Services** Lancs ... 121 H7
**Charsfield** Suffk...............78 F3
**Charter Alley** Hants.......41 L8
**Charterhall** Border....... 179 G8
**Charterhouse** Somset...26 D1
**Chartershall** Stirlg...... 175 K1
**Chartham** Kent................34 E4
**Chartham Hatch**
Kent............................34 E4
**Chartridge** Bucks...........58 F7
**Chart Sutton** Kent..........33 K4
**Charvil** Wokham..............42 C5
**Charwelton** Nhants.........73 G4
**Chase Terrace** Staffs....85 J2
**Chasetown** Staffs..........85 J2
**Chastleton** Oxon............56 E3
**Chasty** Devon...................9 J4
**Chatburn** Lancs............ 121 L2
**Chatcull** Staffs................99 H5
**Chatham** Medway...........46 C6
**Chatham Green**
Essex..........................61 H5
**Chathill** Nthumb........... 169 J4
**Chatsworth House**
Derbys..................... 114 E7
**Chattenden** Medway.....46 C5
**Chatteris** Cambs............90 B6
**Chatterton** Lancs........ 122 B6
**Chattisham** Suffk...........78 C6
**Chatto** Border.............. 168 B5
**Chatton** Nthumb......... 168 F4
**Chawleigh** Devon...........11 G3

**Chawton** Hants...............30 B4
**Cheadle** Staffs.............. 100 A4
**Cheadle** Stockp............ 113 K4
**Cheadle Hulme**
Stockp..................... 113 K4
**Cheam** Gt Lon..................44 E7
**Chearsley** Bucks............58 B6
**Chebsey** Staffs................99 J6
**Checkendon** Oxon.........42 A4
**Checkley** Ches E.............99 G4
**Checkley** Staffs............ 100 B5
**Chedburgh** Suffk............77 H3
**Cheddar** Somset............26 C2
**Cheddington** Bucks.......58 F4
**Cheddleton** Staffs..........99 L3
**Cheddon Fitzpaine**
Somset......................25 K6
**Chedgrave** Norfk...........93 H4
**Chedington** Dorset........13 L2
**Chediston** Suffk..............93 H7
**Chedworth** Gloucs.........56 B5
**Chedzoy** Somset............25 M4
**Cheetham Hill**
Manch...................... 113 J2
**Cheldon** Devon...............11 H3
**Chelford** Ches E.......... 113 J6
**Chellaston** C Derb....... 101 G6
**Chellington** Bed............74 D4
**Chelmarsh** Shrops.........84 C5
**Chelmer Village**
Essex..........................61 H6
**Chelmondiston** Suffk....78 E6
**Chelmorton** Derbys..... 114 C7
**Chelmsford** Essex.........61 H6
**Chelmsley Wood**
Solhll..........................85 L6
**Chelsea** Gt Lon...............44 F4
**Chelsfield** Gt Lon...........45 J7
**Chelsworth** Suffk...........77 L5
**Cheltenham** Gloucs......55 L4
**Chelveston** Nhants........74 E1
**Chelvey** N Som...............38 C6
**Chelwood** BaNES..........38 F7
**Chelwood Gate**
E Susx........................32 D6
**Cheney Longville**
Shrops.......................83 H6
**Chenies** Bucks................43 G2
**Chepstow** Mons.............38 D2
**Cherhill** Wilts.................40 B6
**Cherington** Gloucs.........55 K7
**Cherington** Warwks.......72 C6
**Cheriton** Hants...............29 L5
**Cheriton** Kent.................35 G7
**Cheriton** Pembks...........49 G7
**Cheriton** Swans.............50 F6
**Cheriton Bishop**
Devon.........................11 H6
**Cheriton Fitzpaine**
Devon.........................11 K4
**Cherrington** Wrekin.......98 F8
**Cherry Burton**
E R Yk...................... 126 B3
**Cherry Hinton** Cambs...76 C3
**Cherry Orchard**
Worcs.........................70 F4
**Cherry Willingham**
Lincs........................ 117 G6
**Chertsey** Surrey.............43 H6
**Cherwell Valley**
**Services** Oxon.......57 K3
**Cheselbourne** Dorset...14 E3
**Chesham** Bucks..............58 F7
**Chesham** Bury.............. 122 B7
**Chesham Bois** Bucks.....58 F7
**Cheshunt** Herts.............60 B7
**Chesil Beach** Dorset.....14 B6
**Cheslyn Hay** Staffs........85 H3
**Chessetts Wood**
Warwks......................85 L8
**Chessington** Gt Lon......44 D7
**Chessington World**
**of Adventures**
Gt Lon........................44 D7
**Chester** Ches W.......... 112 B7
**Chesterblade** Somset...26 F3
**Chesterfield** Derbys..... 115 G7
**Chesterfield** Staffs........85 K3

**Chesterhill** Mdloth...... 177 K5
**Chester-le-Street**
Dur.......................... 151 G5
**Chester Moor** Dur....... 151 G5
**Chesters** Border.......... 167 J5
**Chesters** Border.......... 167 K7
**Chester Services**
Ches W.................... 112 C1
**Chesterton** Cambs........76 C3
**Chesterton** Cambs........89 G4
**Chesterton** Gloucs........56 A7
**Chesterton** Oxon...........57 K4
**Chesterton** Shrops........84 D4
**Chesterton** Staffs..........99 J3
**Chesterton Green**
Warwks......................72 D3
**Chesterwood** Nthumb.. 149 L2
**Chester Zoo** Ches W... 112 B7
**Chestfield** Kent..............47 J6
**Cheston** Devon.................7 G4
**Cheswardine** Shrops.....99 G6
**Cheswick** Nthumb....... 168 F1
**Chetnole** Dorset............14 B2
**Chettisham** Cambs........90 D6
**Chettle** Dorset................27 L8
**Chetton** Shrops..............84 B5
**Chetwynd** Wrekin..........99 G7
**Chetwynd Aston**
Wrekin........................99 H8
**Cheveley** Cambs............76 F3
**Chevening** Kent..............32 E2
**Chevington** Suffk...........77 H3
**Cheviot Hills** ................ 168 A7
**Chevithorne** Devon.......24 F7
**Chew Magna** BaNES.....38 E7
**Chew Stoke** BaNES.......38 E7
**Chewton Keynsham**
BaNES........................38 F6
**Chewton Mendip**
Somset......................26 E2
**Chicheley** M Keyn..........74 C5
**Chichester** W Susx........18 B5
**Chickerell** Dorset...........14 C6
**Chicklade** Wilts..............27 K4
**Chidden** Hants................30 A7
**Chiddingfold** Surrey......30 F4
**Chiddingly** E Susx..........20 B3
**Chiddingstone** Kent......32 E4
**Chiddingstone**
**Causeway** Kent........32 F4
**Chideock** Dorset............13 K4
**Chidham** W Susx............17 L2
**Chidswell** Kirk.............. 123 K6
**Chieveley** W Berk..........41 J5
**Chieveley Services**
W Berk........................41 J6
**Chignall St James**
Essex..........................61 G6
**Chignall Smealy**
Essex..........................61 G5
**Chigwell** Essex...............45 H2
**Chigwell Row** Essex......45 J2
**Chilbolton** Hants...........29 H4
**Chilcomb** Hants..............29 J5
**Chilcombe** Dorset.........13 M4
**Chilcompton** Somset....26 F2
**Chilcote** Leics................86 C2
**Childer Thornton**
Ches W...................... 111 K6
**Child Okeford** Dorset...27 J8
**Childrey** Oxon.................41 G3
**Child's Ercall** Shrops.....98 F7
**Childswickham**
Worcs.........................71 J6
**Childwall** Lpool............ 112 B4
**Chilfrome** Dorset..........14 B3
**Chilgrove** W Susx..........18 A3
**Chilham** Kent..................34 E4
**Chillaton** Devon.............10 C8
**Chillenden** Kent.............35 H4
**Chillerton** IoW...............16 F5
**Chillesford** Suffk............79 H4
**Chillington** Devon............7 J7
**Chillington** Somset........13 K1
**Chilmark** Wilts................27 L5
**Chilmington Green**
Kent............................34 C6
**Chilson** Oxon..................56 F4

**Chilsworthy** Cnwll...........6 B2
**Chilsworthy** Devon..........9 J4
**Chiltern Hills** ...............42 C2
**Chilthorne Domer**
Somset......................26 D7
**Chilton** Bucks.................58 B5
**Chilton** Dur.................. 141 H2
**Chilton** Oxon..................41 J4
**Chilton Candover**
Hants.........................29 L4
**Chilton Cantelo**
Somset......................26 E6
**Chilton Foliat** Wilts.......40 F6
**Chilton Polden**
Somset......................26 B4
**Chilton Street** Suffk......77 H5
**Chilton Trinity**
Somset......................25 L4
**Chilwell** Notts.............. 101 K5
**Chilworth** Hants.............29 H7
**Chilworth** Surrey...........31 G3
**Chimney** Oxon................57 G7
**Chineham** Hants.............30 A1
**Chingford** Gt Lon...........45 G2
**Chinley** Derbys............ 114 B5
**Chinnor** Oxon.................58 C7
**Chipnall** Shrops.............99 G6
**Chippenham** Cambs......76 F1
**Chippenham** Wilts.........39 L5
**Chipperfield** Herts........59 H7
**Chipping** Herts...............60 B2
**Chipping** Lancs............ 121 J2
**Chipping Campden**
Gloucs .......................71 L6
**Chipping Norton**
Oxon...........................56 F3
**Chipping Ongar**
Essex..........................60 E7
**Chipping Sodbury**
S Glos.........................39 G4
**Chipping Warden**
Nhants.......................72 F5
**Chipstable** Somset........25 G6
**Chipstead** Kent..............32 E3
**Chipstead** Surrey...........32 B2
**Chirbury** Shrops.............82 F4
**Chirk** Wrexhm.................97 L5
**Chirnside** Border......... 179 H6
**Chirnsidebridge**
Border...................... 179 H7
**Chirton** Wilts..................40 B8
**Chisbury** Wilts................40 F6
**Chiselborough**
Somset......................26 C8
**Chiseldon** Swindn.........40 D4
**Chiselhampton** Oxon....57 L7
**Chiserley** Calder.......... 122 F5
**Chisholme** Border....... 166 F6
**Chislehurst** Gt Lon........45 H6
**Chislet** Kent....................47 L6
**Chiswell Green** Herts....59 J6
**Chiswick** Gt Lon.............44 E4
**Chisworth** Derbys........ 113 M3
**Chithurst** W Susx...........30 D6
**Chittering** Cambs..........76 C1
**Chitterne** Wilts...............27 M3
**Chittlehamholt**
Devon.........................23 K7
**Chittlehampton**
Devon.........................23 K6
**Chittoe** Wilts..................40 A6
**Chivelstone** Devon..........7 H7
**Chivenor** Devon.............23 H4
**Chlenry** D & G.............. 144 D3
**Chobham** Surrey............42 F7
**Cholderton** Wilts...........28 E3
**Cholesbury** Bucks.........58 F6
**Chollerton** Nthumb..... 158 B7
**Cholsey** Oxon.................41 L3
**Cholstrey** Herefs...........69 J3
**Chop Gate** N York....... 142 C7
**Choppington**
Nthumb.................... 159 G5
**Chopwell** Gatesd........ 150 E4
**Chorley** Ches E...............98 D3
**Chorley** Lancs.............. 121 H6
**Chorley** Shrops..............84 C6
**Chorleywood** Herts.......43 H2

**Chorleywood West**
Herts ............................43 G2
**Chorlton** Ches E ...........99 G3
**Chorlton-cum-**
**Hardy** Manch.........113 J3
**Chorlton Lane**
Ches W........................98 C3
**Choulton** Shrops .........83 H5
**Chrishall** Essex............76 C6
**Chrisswell** Inver ......173 L4
**Christchurch** BCP........15 M4
**Christchurch** Cambs....90 C4
**Christchurch** Newpt....37 M3
**Christian Malford**
Wilts............................39 L5
**Christon** N Som ...........38 B8
**Christon Bank**
Nthumb ....................169 J5
**Christow** Devon ..........11 J7
**Chudleigh** Devon .......11 K8
**Chudleigh Knighton**
Devon ..........................7 J1
**Chulmleigh** Devon.......11 G3
**Church** Lancs ............121 L5
**Churcham** Gloucs ........55 H4
**Church Aston** Wrekin...99 H8
**Church Brampton**
Nhants........................73 K2
**Church Broughton**
Derbys ......................100 D5
**Church Cove** Cnwll........3 J8
**Church Crookham**
Hants..........................30 D2
**Churchdown** Gloucs....55 K4
**Church Eaton** Staffs .....99 J8
**Churchend** Essex.........47 G2
**Church End** C Beds......75 H6
**Churchend** Essex.........61 H3
**Church End** Gt Lon......44 E3
**Church Enstone**
Oxon..........................57 G3
**Church Fenton**
N York ......................124 D3
**Churchfield** Sandw......85 H5
**Churchgate Street**
Essex..........................60 D5
**Church Green** Devon ..12 F3
**Church Hanborough**
Oxon..........................57 H5
**Church Houses**
N York ......................142 E7
**Churchill** Devon ..........13 H3
**Churchill** N Som ..........38 C7
**Churchill** Oxon ............56 F3
**Churchill** Worcs...........71 G4
**Churchill** Worcs...........84 F7
**Churchinford** Somset ...25 K8
**Church Knowle**
Dorset ........................15 H6
**Church Langton**
Leics ..........................87 K5
**Church Lawford**
Warwks........................86 F7
**Church Leigh** Staffs ..100 A5
**Church Lench** Worcs ...71 H4
**Church Mayfield**
Staffs ........................100 D4
**Church Minshull**
Ches E ........................98 F1
**Church Norton**
W Susx ........................18 B6
**Churchover** Warwks.....87 G7
**Church Preen** Shrops ...83 K4
**Church Pulverbatch**
Shrops ........................83 H3
**Churchstanton**
Somset ........................25 J8
**Churchstoke** Powys ...82 F5
**Churchstow** Devon .......7 G6
**Church Stowe**
Nhants........................73 J3
**Church Street** Kent......46 B5
**Church Stretton**
Shrops ........................83 J5
**Churchtown** Cnwll.........5 H1
**Churchtown** Derbys ...114 E8
**Churchtown** IoM ........237 d3
**Churchtown** Lancs .....121 G2

**Church Village**
Rhondd........................37 H3
**Church Warsop**
Notts ........................115 K7
**Churston Ferrers**
Torbay ..........................7 K5
**Churt** Surrey................30 D4
**Churton** Ches W ..........98 B2
**Churwell** Leeds .........123 K5
**Chwilog** Gwynd...........95 G5
**Chyandour** Cnwll ..........2 E5
**Cilcain** Flints .............111 G7
**Cilcennin** Cerdgn ........66 C3
**Cilfrew** Neath..............52 B7
**Cilfynydd** Rhondd ........37 G3
**Cilgerran** Pembks ........65 H6
**Cilmaengwyn** Neath ....51 L4
**Cilmery** Powys..............67 L4
**Cilsan** Carmth..............51 H2
**Ciltalgarth** Gwynd.......96 D4
**Cilycwm** Carmth..........67 G6
**Cimla** Neath ................36 B2
**Cinderford** Gloucs ......54 F5
**Cinder Hill** Wolves........85 G5
**Cippenham** Slough ......42 F4
**Cirencester** Gloucs......56 A7
**City** Gt Lon..................45 G4
*City Airport* Gt Lon........45 H4
**Clabhach** Ag & B .......188 F5
**Clachaig** Ag & B .......173 J3
**Clachaig Inn** Highld....192 B5
**Clachan** Ag & B .........172 C6
**Clachan** Ag & B .........182 A4
**Clachan** Ag & B .........182 F6
**Clachan** Ag & B .........191 G7
**Clachan** Highld ..........209 H6
**Clachan-a-Luib**
W Isls........................233 c6
**Clachan Mor** Ag & B ..188 C6
**Clachan na Luib**
W Isls........................233 c6
**Clachan of Campsie**
E Duns......................175 G3
**Clachan-Seil** Ag & B ..181 M4
**Clachnaharry** Highld...213 G5
**Clachtoll** Highld .........224 C3
**Clacket Lane**
Services Surrey...........32 D3
**Clackmannan** Clacks ..185 J8
**Clackmannanshire**
**Bridge** Fife..............176 C2
**Clackmarras** Moray ...214 F2
**Clacton-on-Sea**
Essex..........................62 E5
**Cladich** Ag & B ..........182 F3
**Cladswell** Worcs ..........71 J3
**Claggan** Highld ..........190 E6
**Claigan** Highld ..........208 C4
**Clanfield** Hants............30 B7
**Clanfield** Oxon.............56 F7
**Clanville** Hants ............28 F2
**Clanville** Somset .........26 F5
**Claonaig** Ag & B .........172 E6
**Clapgate** Herts ............60 C3
**Clapham** Bed...............74 F4
**Clapham** Gt Lon ..........44 F4
**Clapham** N York .........130 E5
**Clapham** W Susx .........18 F4
**Clapton** Somset ..........13 K2
**Clapton** Somset ..........26 F2
**Clapton-in-**
**Gordano** N Som.........38 C5
**Clapton-on-the-**
**Hill** Gloucs ...............56 D4
**Claravale** Gatesd........150 E3
**Clarbeston** Pembks ......49 H3
**Clarbeston Road**
Pembks ......................49 H4
**Clarborough** Notts .....116 B5
**Clare** Suffk...................77 H5
**Clarebrand** D & G .......146 D2
**Clarencefield** D & G ...147 J2
**Clarilaw** Border ..........167 H5
**Clarkston** E Rens........175 G6
**Clashmore** Highld ......223 G4
**Clashmore** Highld ......224 C3
**Clashnessie** Highld.....224 C3
**Clashnoir** Moray ........204 F2

**Clathy** P & K...............185 K4
**Clathymore** P & K.......185 L3
**Clatt** Abers.................205 L1
**Clatter** Powys...............81 L5
**Clatworthy** Somset......25 G5
**Claughton** Lancs ........121 G3
**Claughton** Lancs ........130 B6
**Claughton** Wirral .......111 J4
**Claverdon** Warwks.......71 L2
**Claverham** N Som........38 C6
**Clavering** Essex ...........60 D2
**Claverley** Shrops ..........84 E5
**Claverton** BaNES..........39 H7
**Clawdd-coch** V Glam...37 G5
**Clawdd-newydd**
Denbgs........................97 G3
**Clawton** Devon ..............9 J5
**Claxby** Lincs ...............117 J3
**Claxton** N York ...........133 L1
**Claxton** Norfk...............93 H3
**Claybrooke Magna**
Leics ..........................86 F5
**Clay Coton** Nhants.......87 H7
**Clay Cross** Derbys ......115 H8
**Claydon** Oxon ..............72 F4
**Claydon** Suffk ..............78 D5
**Claygate** D & G ..........156 D6
**Claygate** Kent...............33 J4
**Claygate** Surrey............44 D7
**Clayhall** Gt Lon ............45 J3
**Clayhanger** Devon .......24 F6
**Clayhidon** Devon..........25 J7
**Clayhill** E Susx .............21 G2
**Clayock** Highld............231 H4
**Claypits** Gloucs ...........55 H6
**Claypole** Lincs ...........102 D3
**Clayton** C Brad...........123 G4
**Clayton** Donc ..............124 C8
**Clayton** W Susx ............19 J3
**Clayton-le-Moors**
Lancs ........................121 L4
**Clayton-le-Woods**
Lancs ........................121 H6
**Clayton West** Kirk .....123 K7
**Clayworth** Notts .........116 B4
**Cleadale** Highld ..........199 G7
**Cleadon** S Tyne ..........151 J3
**Cleadon Park** S Tyne ..151 J3
**Clearbrook** Devon ..........6 D3
**Clearwell** Gloucs ..........54 E6
**Cleasby** N York ...........141 G5
**Cleat** Ork...................234 c8
**Cleatlam** Dur ..............140 E4
**Cleator** Cumb .............136 D4
**Cleator Moor** Cumb ...136 E4
**Cleckheaton** Kirk .......123 J5
**Cleehill** Shrops ............83 L7
**Cleekhimin** N Lans .....175 K6
**Clee St Margaret**
Shrops ........................83 L6
**Cleethorpes** NE Lin ...127 H8
**Cleeton St Mary**
Shrops ........................84 B7
**Cleeve** N Som...............38 C7
**Cleeve** Oxon.................41 L4
**Cleeve Hill** Gloucs ......55 M3
**Cleeve Prior** Worcs ......71 J5
**Cleghornie** E Loth........178 D2
**Clehonger** Herefs.........69 J6
**Cleish** P & K................186 A7
**Cleland** N Lans ...........175 L6
**Clenamacrie** Ag & B....182 C2
**Clenchwarton** Norfk....104 F7
**Clenerty** Abers ...........216 E3
**Clent** Worcs..................85 G7
**Cleobury Mortimer**
Shrops ........................84 C7
**Cleobury North**
Shrops ........................84 B6
**Cleongart** Ag & B .......161 H3
**Clephanton** Highld......213 J4
**Clerkhill** D & G ...........156 A3
**Cleuch-head** D & G .....154 E3
**Clevancy** Wilts .............40 B5
**Clevedon** N Som...........38 B6
**Cleveleys** Lancs ..........120 D2
**Cleverton** Wilts ............39 L4
**Clewer** Somset .............26 C2

**Cley next the Sea**
Norfk ........................106 C4
**Cliburn** Cumb .............138 E3
**Cliddesden** Hants........29 M2
**Cliffe** Medway ..............46 C5
**Cliffe** N York ...............125 G4
**Cliff End** E Susx............21 H3
**Cliffe Woods** Medway....46 C5
**Clifford** Herefs..............68 E5
**Clifford** Leeds .............124 C2
**Clifford Chambers**
Warwks........................71 L4
**Clifford's Mesne**
Gloucs ........................55 G4
**Clifton** Bristl................38 E5
**Clifton** C Beds..............75 H6
**Clifton** C Nott .............101 K5
**Clifton** C York .............133 J8
**Clifton** Calder .............123 H6
**Clifton** Cumb ..............138 D2
**Clifton** Derbys ............100 D4
**Clifton** Devon ..............23 J3
**Clifton** Donc ...............115 K3
**Clifton** Lancs ..............120 F4
**Clifton** N York .............123 J2
**Clifton** Oxon.................57 J2
**Clifton** Worcs...............70 F5
**Clifton Campville**
Staffs ..........................86 B2
**Clifton Hampden**
Oxon..........................41 K2
**Clifton Reynes**
M Keyn .......................74 C4
**Clifton upon**
**Dunsmore**
Warwks........................87 G7
**Clifton upon Teme**
Worcs..........................70 C3
**Cliftonville** Kent...........35 K1
**Climping** W Susx..........18 D5
**Clink** Somset ................27 H2
**Clint** N York ...............132 D7
**Clinterty** C Aber .........206 F3
**Clint Green** Norfk........92 B2
**Clintmains** Border ......167 J3
**Clippesby** Norfk..........93 J2
**Clipsham** Rutlnd ..........88 D1
**Clipston** Nhants...........87 K7
**Clipston** Notts ...........101 M5
**Clipstone** C Beds..........58 F3
**Clipstone** Notts .........115 L8
**Clitheroe** Lancs ..........121 L3
**Clive** Shrops ................98 D7
**Cliveden** Bucks............42 E4
**Clixby** Lincs ...............117 J2
**Cloatley** Wilts...............39 M3
**Clocaenog** Denbgs .......97 G2
**Clochan** Moray ...........215 J3
**Clodock** Herefs ............53 L3
**Clola** Abers .................217 J5
**Clophill** C Beds ............74 F6
**Clopton** Nhants............88 F7
**Clopton** Suffk...............78 F4
**Clopton Corner** Suffk...78 F4
**Clos du Valle** Guern.....236 d2
**Closeburn** D & G ........154 F4
**Closeburnmill** D & G ...154 F3
**Closworth** Somset .......14 B1
**Clothall** Herts ..............59 L2
**Clotton** Ches W ..........112 D8
**Clough Foot** Calder ....122 D5
**Clough Head** Calder ...123 G6
**Cloughton** N York .......143 K7
**Clousta** Shet ...............235 c5
**Clova** Angus...............196 B2
**Clovelly** Devon ............22 E6
**Clovenfords** Border.....167 G3
**Clovulin** Highld ..........191 K4
**Clowne** Derbys ...........115 J6
**Clows Top** Worcs .........70 C1
**Cluanie Inn** Highld.....201 G3
**Cluanie Lodge**
Highld .......................201 G3
**Clugston** D & G ..........145 H4
**Clun** Shrops ................82 F7
**Clunas** Highld .............213 K5
**Clunbury** Shrops ..........83 G7
**Clunderwen** Carmth ....49 J4

**Clune** Highld..............203 J1
**Clunes** Highld..............201 J7
**Clungunford** Shrops....83 H7
**Clunie** P & K..............195 H7
**Cluny** Fife..............186 D7
**Clutton** BaNES..............38 F8
**Clutton** Ches W..............98 C2
**Clutton Hill** BaNES..............38 F8
**Clydach** Mons..............53 K5
**Clydach** Swans..............51 K5
**Clydach Vale** Rhondd....36 F2
**Clydebank** W Duns....174 F4
**Clyffe Pypard** Wilts....40 B5
**Clynder** Ag & B..............174 A2
**Clyne** Neath..............52 C7
**Clynnog Fawr** Gwynd....95 G3
**Clyro** Powys..............68 E5
**Clyst Honiton** Devon....12 C4
**Clyst Hydon** Devon....12 D3
**Clyst St George**
Devon..............12 C5
**Clyst St Lawrence**
Devon..............12 D3
**Clyst St Mary** Devon....12 C4
**Cnoc** W Isls..............232 g2
**Cnwch Coch** Cerdgn....80 F8
**Coad's Green** Cnwll..............5 L1
**Coalburn** S Lans..............164 F3
**Coalburns** Gatesd..............150 E3
**Coaley** Gloucs..............55 H7
**Coalhill** Essex..............61 J7
**Coalpit Heath** S Glos....38 F4
**Coal Pool** Wsall..............85 H4
**Coalport** Wrekin..............84 C3
**Coalsnaughton**
Clacks..............185 J7
**Coaltown of**
Balgonie Fife..............186 E7
**Coaltown of**
Wemyss Fife..............186 E7
**Coalville** Leics..............86 E2
**Coanwood** Nthumb....149 H3
**Coat** Somset..............26 C7
**Coatbridge** N Lans....175 J5
**Coatdyke** N Lans..............175 K5
**Coate** Swindn..............40 D4
**Coate** Wilts..............40 B7
**Coates** Cambs..............89 K4
**Coates** Gloucs..............55 L7
**Coates** Lincs..............116 E5
**Coates** W Susx..............18 D3
**Cobbaton** Devon..............23 K6
**Coberley** Gloucs..............55 L5
**Cobham** Kent..............46 A6
**Cobham** Surrey..............43 J7
**Cobham Services**
Surrey..............43 J8
**Cobnash** Herefs..............69 J3
**Cobo** Guern..............236 c2
**Cobridge** C Stke..............99 K3
**Coburby** Abers..............217 H2
**Cockayne Hatley**
C Beds..............75 J5
**Cock Bridge** Abers....205 G4
**Cockburnspath**
Border..............179 G4
**Cock Clarks** Essex....61 K7
**Cockenzie and Port**
Seton E Loth..............177 L4
**Cockerham** Lancs....120 F1
**Cockermouth** Cumb....136 F2
**Cockernhoe** Herts..............59 J4
**Cockett** Swans..............51 J6
**Cockfield** Dur..............140 E3
**Cockfield** Suffk..............77 K4
**Cockfosters** Gt Lon....44 F2
**Cock Green** Essex....61 H4
**Cocking** W Susx..............18 B3
**Cocking Causeway**
W Susx..............18 B2
**Cockington** Torbay..............7 K3
**Cocklake** Somset..............26 C2
**Cockley Cley** Norfk....91 H3
**Cock Marling** E Susx....21 H2
**Cockpole Green**
Wokham..............42 D4
**Cockshutt** Shrops....98 B6

**Cockthorpe** Norfk....106 B4
**Cockwood** Devon..............12 C6
**Cockyard** Derbys..............114 B5
**Coddenham** Suffk..............78 D4
**Coddington** Herefs....70 C6
**Coddington** Notts....102 D2
**Codford St Mary**
Wilts..............27 L4
**Codford St Peter**
Wilts..............27 L4
**Codicote** Herts..............59 K4
**Codmore Hill** W Susx....31 H7
**Codnor** Derbys..............101 H3
**Codrington** S Glos....39 G5
**Codsall** Staffs..............84 F3
**Codsall Wood** Staffs....84 F3
**Coedpoeth** Wrexhm....97 L3
**Coed Talon** Flints..............97 L2
**Coed-y-paen** Mons....53 M7
**Coed-yr-ynys** Powys....53 J4
**Coffinswell** Devon..............7 K3
**Cofton** Devon..............12 C6
**Cofton Hackett**
Worcs..............85 H7
**Cogan** V Glam..............37 J6
**Cogenhoe** Nhants..............74 B3
**Cogges** Oxon..............57 G6
**Coggeshall** Essex....61 K4
**Coignafearn** Highld....203 H2
**Coilacriech** Abers....205 H6
**Coilantogle** Stirlg....184 D6
**Coillore** Highld..............208 E6
**Coity** Brdgnd..............36 E4
**Col** W Isls..............232 g2
**Colaboll** Highld..............225 L6
**Colan** Cnwll..............4 D4
**Colaton Raleigh**
Devon..............12 D5
**Colbost** Highld..............208 C5
**Colburn** N York..............140 F7
**Colby** Cumb..............138 F3
**Colby** IoM..............237 b6
**Colchester** Essex....62 B3
**Colchester Zoo**
Essex..............62 A4
**Cold Ash** W Berk....41 K6
**Cold Ashby** Nhants....87 J7
**Cold Ashton** S Glos....39 H6
**Cold Aston** Gloucs....56 C4
**Coldbackie** Highld....229 J4
**Cold Brayfield**
M Keyn..............74 D4
**Coldean** Br & H..............19 J4
**Coldeast** Devon..............7 J2
**Colden** Calder..............122 E5
**Colden Common**
Hants..............29 J6
**Cold Hanworth** Lincs....117 G5
**Coldharbour** Surrey....31 J3
**Cold Higham** Nhants....73 J4
**Coldingham** Border....179 J5
**Cold Kirby** N York....133 H3
**Coldmeece** Staffs....99 J6
**Cold Norton** Essex....61 K7
**Cold Overton** Leics....88 B2
**Coldred** Kent..............35 H5
**Coldridge** Devon..............11 G4
**Coldstream** Border....168 C2
**Coldwaltham** W Susx....18 D3
**Coldwells** Abers..............217 H6
**Cole** Somset..............26 F5
**Colebatch** Shrops....83 G6
**Colebrook** Devon..............12 C2
**Colebrooke** Devon....11 H5
**Coleby** Lincs..............102 F1
**Coleby** N Linc..............125 L6
**Coleford** Devon..............11 H5
**Coleford** Gloucs..............54 E6
**Coleford** Somset..............27 G2
**Colegate End** Norfk....92 E6
**Colehill** Dorset..............15 J3
**Coleman's Hatch**
E Susx..............32 D6
**Colemere** Shrops..............98 B6
**Colemore** Hants..............30 B5
**Colenden** P & K..............186 B2
**Colerne** Wilts..............39 J6
**Colesbourne** Gloucs....56 A5

**Coleshill** Bucks..............42 F2
**Coleshill** Oxon..............40 E2
**Coleshill** Warwks....85 L5
**Coley** BaNES..............26 E1
**Colgate** W Susx..............31 L5
**Colinsburgh** Fife....187 H6
**Colinton** C Edin..............177 H5
**Colintraive** Ag & B....173 H4
**Colkirk** Norfk..............105 L7
**Coll** Ag & B..............189 G5
**Coll** W Isls..............232 g2
**Collace** P & K..............186 C2
**Collafirth** Shet..............235 c3
**Coll Airport** Ag & B....188 F5
**Collaton** Devon..............7 G7
**Collaton St Mary**
Torbay..............7 K4
**College of Roseisle**
Moray..............214 E2
**College Town** Br For....42 D7
**Collessie** Fife..............186 E5
**Collier Row** Gt Lon....45 J2
**Collier's End** Herts....60 B4
**Collier Street** Kent....33 J4
**Colliston** Abers..............217 K8
**Collin** D & G..............155 H6
**Collingbourne**
Ducis Wilts..............28 E2
**Collingbourne**
Kingston Wilts..............28 E1
**Collingham** Leeds....124 B2
**Collingham** Notts....102 D1
**Collington** Herefs....70 B3
**Collingtree** Nhants....73 L4
**Collins Green** Warrtn....112 E3
**Colliston** Angus..............196 F7
**Colliton** Devon..............12 E2
**Collyweston** Nhants....88 E3
**Colmonell** S Ayrs....152 D5
**Colmworth** Bed..............75 G3
**Colnabaichin** Abers....205 G4
**Colnbrook** Slough....43 G5
**Colne** Cambs..............89 L7
**Colne** Lancs..............122 D3
**Colne Engaine** Essex....61 K3
**Colney** Norfk..............92 E3
**Colney Heath** Herts....59 K6
**Coln Rogers** Gloucs....56 B6
**Coln St Aldwyns**
Gloucs..............56 C6
**Coln St Dennis**
Gloucs..............56 B5
**Colonsay** Ag & B....180 E7
**Colonsay Airport**
Ag & B..............180 E8
**Colpy** Abers..............216 C7
**Colquhar** Border....166 E2
**Colsterworth** Lincs....102 F7
**Colston Bassett**
Notts..............102 B5
**Coltfield** Moray..............214 D2
**Coltishall** Norfk..............106 F8
**Colton** Cumb..............129 G3
**Colton** Leeds..............124 B4
**Colton** N York..............124 C3
**Colton** Norfk..............92 D2
**Colton** Staffs..............100 B7
**Colt's Hill** Kent..............33 H4
**Colvend** D & G..............146 F4
**Colwall** Herefs..............70 D6
**Colwell** Nthumb..............158 B6
**Colwich** Staffs..............100 A7
**Colwinston** V Glam....36 E5
**Colworth** W Susx..............18 C5
**Colwyn Bay** Conwy....110 B5
**Colyford** Devon..............13 G4
**Colyton** Devon..............13 G4
**Combe** Oxon..............57 H5
**Combe** W Berk..............41 G7
**Combe Down** BaNES....39 H7
**Combe Fishacre**
Devon..............7 J3
**Combe Florey**
Somset..............25 J5
**Combe Hay** BaNES....39 G7
**Combeinteignhead**
Devon..............7 K2
**Combe Martin** Devon....23 J3

**Combe Raleigh**
Devon..............12 F3
**Comberbach** Ches W....112 F6
**Comberford** Staffs....85 L3
**Comberton** Cambs....75 L4
**Comberton** Herefs....69 K2
**Combe St Nicholas**
Somset..............13 H1
**Combrook** Warwks....72 C4
**Combs** Derbys..............114 B6
**Combs** Suffk..............78 C3
**Combs Ford** Suffk....78 C3
**Combwich** Somset....25 K3
**Comers** Abers..............206 D4
**Comeytrowe** Somset....25 J6
**Comhampton** Worcs....70 E2
**Commins Coch**
Powys..............81 J3
**Commondale** N York....142 E5
**Common End** Cumb....136 D3
**Common Moor** Cnwll....5 K2
**Compstall** Stockp....113 L4
**Compstonend** D & G....146 B4
**Compton** Devon..............7 K3
**Compton** Hants..............29 J6
**Compton** Staffs..............84 E6
**Compton** Surrey..............30 F3
**Compton** W Berk..............41 K4
**Compton** W Susx..............30 C7
**Compton** Wilts..............28 C2
**Compton Abbas**
Dorset..............27 K7
**Compton Abdale**
Gloucs..............56 B5
**Compton Bassett**
Wilts..............40 B6
**Compton
Beauchamp** Oxon....40 F3
**Compton Bishop**
Somset..............26 B1
**Compton
Chamberlayne**
Wilts..............28 B5
**Compton Dando**
BaNES..............38 F7
**Compton Dundon**
Somset..............26 C5
**Compton Durville**
Somset..............26 B7
**Compton Greenfield**
S Glos..............38 E4
**Compton Martin**
BaNES..............38 D8
**Compton
Pauncefoot**
Somset..............26 F6
**Compton Valence**
Dorset..............14 B4
**Comrie** Fife..............176 D1
**Comrie** P & K..............185 G3
**Conaglen House**
Highld..............191 K3
**Conchra** Highld..............210 D8
**Concraigie** P & K....195 H7
**Conderton** Worcs....71 G6
**Condicote** Gloucs....56 D3
**Condorrat** N Lans....175 K4
**Condover** Shrops..............83 J3
**Coney Hill** Gloucs....55 J4
**Coneyhurst** W Susx....31 J6
**Coneysthorpe** N York....133 L5
**Coney Weston** Suffk....91 L7
**Congerstone** Leics....86 D3
**Congham** Norfk..............105 H7
**Congleton** Ches E....113 J8
**Congresbury** N Som....38 C7
**Conheath** D & G....147 H2
**Conicavel** Moray..............214 B4
**Coningsby** Lincs....103 L2
**Conington** Cambs....75 K2
**Conington** Cambs....89 H6
**Conisbrough** Donc....115 K2
**Conisholme** Lincs....118 E3
**Coniston** Cumb..............137 J7
**Coniston** E R Yk....126 E4
**Coniston Cold** N York....131 G8
**Conistone** N York....131 J6
**Connah's Quay** Flints....111 J7

Connel Ag & B.............182 C1
Connel Park E Ayrs......164 C6
Connor Downs Cnwll.......3 G4
Conon Bridge Highld..212 E4
Cononley N York.........122 E2
Consall Staffs..............99 M3
Consett Dur ...............150 E5
Constable Burton
  N York ...................132 B2
Constable Lee Lancs ...122 B5
Constantine Cnwll.........3 J5
Constantine Bay
  Cnwll .........................4 D2
Contin Highld ............212 C3
Conwy Conwy.............109 L6
Conwy Castle Conwy ...109 L6
Conyer's Green Suffk....77 K2
Cooden E Susx.............20 E4
Cookbury Devon............9 K4
Cookham W & M..........42 E4
Cookham Dean
  W & M......................42 E4
Cookham Rise
  W & M......................42 E4
Cookhill Worcs.............71 J3
Cookley Suffk...............93 H7
Cookley Worcs..............84 E7
Cookley Green Oxon.....42 B3
Cookney Abers............207 G6
Cook's Green Essex.......62 E4
Cooks Green Suffk........77 L4
Cooksmill Green
  Essex........................61 G6
Coolham W Susx...........31 J6
Cooling Medway............46 C5
Coombe Cnwll................4 E5
Coombe Devon...............7 L2
Coombe Devon..............12 E4
Coombe Hants...............30 A7
Coombe Bissett
  Wilts.........................28 C6
Coombe Cellars
  Devon.........................7 K2
Coombe Hill Gloucs......55 K3
Coombe Keynes
  Dorset.......................14 F5
Coombe Pafford
  Torbay........................7 L3
Coombes W Susx...........19 G4
Coombes-Moor
  Herefs........................69 G2
Coombeswood
  Dudley.......................85 H6
Coopersale
  Common Essex...........60 D7
Copdock Suffk...............78 D6
Copford Green Essex....61 L4
Copgrove N York.........132 E6
Copister Shet..............235 d3
Cople Bed....................75 G5
Copley Dur .................140 D3
Copmanthorpe
  C York......................124 E2
Compere End Staffs......99 J6
Copp Lancs.................120 F3
Coppenhall Staffs..........99 K8
Copperhouse Cnwll........2 F4
Coppingford Cambs......89 H7
Copplestone Devon.......11 H4
Coppull Lancs.............121 H7
Copsale W Susx.............31 K6
Copster Green Lancs...121 K4
Copston Magna
  Warwks.....................86 F5
Cop Street Kent............35 J3
Copt Hewick N York....132 E2
Copthorne W Susx........32 B5
Copt Oak Leics.............86 F2
Copythorne Hants........28 F8
Corbets Tey Gt Lon......45 K3
Corbière Jersey..........236 a7
Corbridge Nthumb......150 C3
Corby Nhants...............88 C5
Corby Glen Lincs........103 G7
Cordon N Ayrs...........162 D4
Coreley Shrops............84 B8
Corfe Somset...............25 K7

Corfe Castle Dorset .....15 H6
Corfe Mullen Dorset....15 J3
Corfton Shrops............83 J6
Corgarff Abers............205 G4
Corhampton Hants.......29 L7
Corlae D & G..............154 B3
Corley Warwks.............86 C6
Corley Services
  Warwks....................86 C6
Cormuir Angus...........195 L3
Cornard Tye Suffk........77 K6
Cornforth Dur ............151 H7
Cornhill Abers.............216 B3
Cornhill-on-Tweed
  Nthumb....................168 C2
Cornholme Calder .....122 D5
Cornoigmore Ag & B ...188 C6
Cornsay
  Dur..........................150 E6
Cornsay Colliery Dur ..150 F6
Corntown Highld........212 E3
Corntown V Glam........36 E5
Cornwall Airport
  Newquay Cnwll ...........4 D3
Cornwell Oxon.............56 F3
Cornwood Devon...........6 E4
Cornworthy Devon.........7 J5
Corpach Highld...........191 L2
Corpusty Norfk..........106 D6
Corrachree Abers........205 K4
Corran Highld.............191 K4
Corran Highld.............200 C4
Corrie N Ayrs.............155 L5
Corrie N Ayrs.............162 C2
Corriecravie N Ayrs....162 B5
Corriegills N Ayrs......162 D3
Corriegour Lodge
  Hotel Highld............201 K6
Corriemoille Highld ....212 B2
Corrimony Highld .......212 B7
Corringham Lincs........116 E4
Corringham Thurr........46 B4
Corris Gwynd...............81 G2
Corris Uchaf Gwynd....81 G2
Corrow Ag & B............183 H7
Corry Highld...............199 K1
Corscombe Devon.........10 F5
Corscombe Dorset........13 M2
Corse Highld...............55 H3
Corse Lawn Gloucs......55 J2
Corsham Wilts.............39 K6
Corsindae Abers........206 D4
Corsley Wilts...............27 J3
Corsley Heath Wilts.....27 J3
Corsock D & G...........154 D6
Corston BaNES.............39 G7
Corston Wilts...............39 L4
Corstorphine C Edin....177 G4
Cortachy Angus..........196 C4
Corton Suffk................93 L4
Corton Wilts................27 L4
Corton Denham
  Somset......................26 F6
Coruanan Highld.........191 L3
Corwen Denbgs...........97 G4
Coryton Devon.............10 C7
Coryton Thurr.............46 C4
Cosby Leics.................87 G4
Coseley Dudley............85 G5
Cosgrove Nhants..........73 L6
Cosham C Port.............17 J2
Cosheston Pembks.......49 G6
Coshieville P & K .......194 C6
Cossall Notts..............101 J4
Cossington Leics..........87 H2
Cossington Somset.......26 A4
Costessey Norfk...........92 E2
Costock Notts.............101 L7
Coston Leics...............102 D7
Coston Norfk...............92 C3
Cote Oxon...................57 G7
Cotebrook Ches W .....112 E7
Cotehill Cumb.............148 E5
Cotes Leics.................101 K7
Cotesbach Leics...........87 G6
Cotford St Luke
  Somset......................25 J6
Cotgrave Notts...........101 M5

Cothal Abers..............207 G3
Cotham Notts.............102 C3
Cotherstone Dur ........140 C4
Cothill Oxon................57 J7
Cotleigh Devon.............13 G3
Cotmanhay Derbys......101 J4
Coton Cambs...............76 B3
Coton Nhants..............73 J1
Coton Staffs.................99 J7
Coton Clanford
  Staffs........................99 K7
Coton Hill Shrops.........83 J2
Coton in the Elms
  Derbys......................86 B1
Cotswold Airport
  Wilts.........................39 L2
Cotswolds .................55 M6
Cotswold Wildlife
  Park & Gardens
  Oxon.........................56 E6
Cott Devon....................7 H4
Cottam Lancs.............121 G4
Cottam Notts..............116 D5
Cottenham Cambs........76 C2
Cottered Herts.............60 A3
Cotteridge Birm...........85 J7
Cotterstock Nhants......88 F5
Cottesbrooke Nhants....87 K8
Cottesmore Rutlnd......88 C2
Cottingham E R Yk......126 C4
Cottingham Nhants......88 B5
Cottingley C Brad........123 G3
Cottisford Oxon............57 L2
Cotton Suffk................78 C2
Cottown Abers............206 E3
Cottown Abers............215 L8
Cottown of Gight
  Abers........................216 F6
Cotts Devon...................6 C3
Coughton Warwks........71 J3
Coulaghailtro Ag & B...172 C5
Coulags Highld ..........210 E5
Coulby Newham
  Middsb.....................142 B4
Coull Abers................205 L5
Coulport Ag & B.........173 L2
Coulsdon Gt Lon..........32 B2
Coulston Wilts.............27 L2
Coulter S Lans............165 K3
Coulton N York...........133 K5
Coultra Fife................186 F3
Cound Shrops...............83 L3
Coundon Dur..............141 G2
Countersett N York.....131 H2
Countess Wear
  Devon.......................12 B4
Countesswells
  C Aber......................207 G4
Countesthorpe Leics....87 H4
Countisbury Devon......24 B2
Coupar Angus P & K....195 K7
Coupland Nthumb......168 D3
Cour Ag & B...............172 D8
Courteachan Highld....199 L6
Courteenhall Nhants....73 L4
Court Henry Carmth....51 H2
Courtsend Essex..........47 G2
Courtway Somset.........25 J5
Cousland Mdloth........177 K5
Cousley Wood E Susx...33 H6
Cove Ag & B...............173 L2
Cove Border................179 G4
Cove Devon.................24 E7
Cove Hants..................30 E1
Cove Highld................219 J3
Cove Bay C Aber........207 H5
Covehithe Suffk...........93 L6
Coven Staffs................85 G3
Coveney Cambs...........90 C6
Covenham St
  Bartholomew
  Lincs.......................118 D3
Covenham St Mary
  Lincs.......................118 D3
Coventry Covtry..........86 D7
Coverack Cnwll.............3 K7
Coverack Bridges
  Cnwll ........................3 H5

Coverham N York .......131 L3
Covington Cambs.........74 F1
Covington S Lans........165 J2
Cowan Bridge Lancs...130 C4
Cowbeech E Susx........20 C3
Cowbit Lincs...............103 L8
Cowbridge V Glam.......36 F5
Cowden Kent...............32 E5
Cowdenbeath Fife......177 G1
Cowers Lane Derbys...100 F3
Cowes IoW....................16 F3
Cowesby N York.........133 G2
Cowfold W Susx...........31 K6
Cowhill S Glos.............38 E3
Cowie Stirlg................175 L1
Cowley Devon..............11 K5
Cowley Gloucs.............55 L5
Cowley Gt Lon.............43 H4
Cowley Oxon................57 K7
Cowling Lancs............121 H6
Cowling N York...........122 E2
Cowling N York...........132 C3
Cowlinge Suffk.............77 G4
Cowpen Nthumb.........159 H5
Cowplain Hants............17 K1
Cowshill Dur..............149 L6
Cowslip Green
  N Som.......................38 C7
Cowthorne N York......132 F8
Coxbank Ches E...........98 F4
Coxbench Derbys........101 G4
Coxford Cnwll................8 F5
Coxford Norfk............105 K6
Coxheath Kent.............33 J3
Coxhoe Dur................151 H7
Coxley Somset.............26 D3
Coxley Wick Somset....26 D3
Coxtie Green Essex......45 K2
Coxwold N York.........133 H4
Coychurch Brdgnd.......36 E4
Coylton S Ayrs............163 K5
Coylumbridge Highld..203 L3
Coytrahen Brdgnd........36 D4
Crabbs Cross Worcs.....71 J2
Crabtree W Susx..........31 K6
Crackenthorpe Cumb...138 F3
Crackington Haven
  Cnwll ..........................8 F5
Crackley Staffs.............99 J3
Crackleybank Shrops....84 D2
Cracoe N York............131 J7
Craddock Devon...........25 G8
Cradley Dudley............85 G6
Cradley Herefs.............70 D5
Cradley Heath Sandw...85 G6
Cradoc Powys..............52 F2
Crafthole Cnwll............6 B5
Craggan Highld...........204 C1
Cragganmore Moray ...214 G6
Craghead Dur.............150 F5
Cragside House &
  Garden Nthumb......158 D2
Crai Powys..................52 D3
Craibstone Moray.......215 L3
Craichie Angus...........196 E6
Craig Angus...............197 H5
Craig Highld..............211 G4
Craigbank E Ayrs........164 C6
Craigburn Border.......177 H7
Craigdhu Ag & B........182 B6
Craigdam Abers..........216 F7
Craigearn Abers.........206 D3
Craigellachie Moray....215 G5
Craigend P & K..........186 B4
Craigend Rens............174 E4
Craigendoran
  Ag & B.....................174 C3
Craigends Rens..........174 D5
Craighlaw D & G.........145 G3
Craighouse Ag & B......171 K5
Craigie P & K.............195 H7
Craigie S Ayrs............163 K3
Craigiefold Abers........217 H2
Craigley D & G...........146 D4
Craig Llangiwg
  Neath........................51 K4
Craiglockhart C Edin...177 H4

**Craigmillar** C Edin ...... 177 J4
**Craigneston** D & G ...... 154 D5
**Craigneuk** N Lans ...... 175 K5
**Craigneuk** N Lans ...... 175 K6
**Craignure** Ag & B ...... 190 E8
**Craigo** Angus ...... 197 H4
**Craigrothie** Fife ...... 186 F5
**Craigruie** Stirlg ...... 184 B4
**Craigton** Angus ...... 196 E8
**Craigton** C Aber ...... 206 F5
**Craigton** E Rens ...... 174 F7
**Craigton of Airlie**
  Angus ...... 196 B6
**Craik** Border ...... 166 E7
**Crail** Fife ...... 187 K5
**Crailing** Border ...... 167 L4
**Craiselound** N Linc ...... 116 C2
**Crakehall** N York ...... 132 C2
**Crambe** N York ...... 133 L6
**Cramlington** Nthumb ...... 159 G6
**Cramond** C Edin ...... 177 G3
**Cramond Bridge**
  C Edin ...... 177 G4
**Cranage** Ches E ...... 113 H7
**Cranberry** Staffs ...... 99 J5
**Cranborne** Dorset ...... 28 B8
**Cranbourne** Br For ...... 42 F5
**Cranbrook** Devon ...... 12 C4
**Cranbrook** Kent ...... 33 K6
**Cranfield** C Beds ...... 74 D6
**Cranford** Gt Lon ...... 43 J5
**Cranford St Andrew**
  Nhants ...... 88 D7
**Cranford St John**
  Nhants ...... 88 D7
**Cranham** Gloucs ...... 55 K5
**Crank** St Hel ...... 112 D2
**Cranleigh** Surrey ...... 31 H4
**Cranmore** Somset ...... 26 F3
**Cranoe** Leics ...... 87 L4
**Cransford** Suffk ...... 79 G2
**Cranshaws** Border ...... 178 E6
**Crantock** Cnwll ...... 4 C4
**Cranwell** Lincs ...... 103 G3
**Cranwich** Norfk ...... 91 H4
**Cranworth** Norfk ...... 92 B3
**Craobh Haven**
  Ag & B ...... 182 A6
**Crarae** Ag & B ...... 182 E7
**Crask Inn** Highld ...... 225 L4
**Crask of Aigas**
  Highld ...... 212 D6
**Craster** Nthumb ...... 169 K5
**Cratfield** Suffk ...... 93 G7
**Crathes** Abers ...... 206 E6
**Crathie** Abers ...... 205 G6
**Crathie** Highld ...... 202 E6
**Crathorne** N York ...... 141 K5
**Craven Arms** Shrops ...... 83 H6
**Crawcrook** Gatesd ...... 150 E3
**Crawford** S Lans ...... 165 J5
**Crawfordjohn** S Lans ...... 165 G5
**Crawley** Hants ...... 29 H4
**Crawley** Oxon ...... 57 G5
**Crawley** W Susx ...... 31 L4
**Crawley Down**
  W Susx ...... 32 C5
**Crawton** Abers ...... 197 L1
**Cray** N York ...... 131 H4
**Cray** P & K ...... 195 J4
**Crayford** Gt Lon ...... 45 K5
**Crayke** N York ...... 133 H5
**Crays Hill** Essex ...... 46 B2
**Creacombe** Devon ...... 24 C7
**Creagan** Ag & B ...... 191 J7
**Creag Ghoraidh**
  W Isls ...... 233 c7
**Creagorry** W Isls ...... 233 c7
**Creaguaineach**
  **Lodge** Highld ...... 192 E3
**Creaton** Nhants ...... 73 K1
**Creca** D & G ...... 155 M7
**Credenhill** Herefs ...... 69 J5
**Crediton** Devon ...... 11 J5
**Creebank** D & G ...... 153 H6
**Creebridge** D & G ...... 145 J2
**Creech Heathfield**
  Somset ...... 25 L6

**Creech St Michael**
  Somset ...... 25 L6
**Creed** Cnwll ...... 4 E6
**Creekmouth** Gt Lon ...... 45 J4
**Creeting St Mary**
  Suffk ...... 78 D3
**Creeton** Lincs ...... 103 G8
**Creetown** D & G ...... 145 K3
**Cregneash** IoM ...... 237 a7
**Creich** Fife ...... 186 E3
**Creigiau** Cardif ...... 37 G4
**Cremyll** Cnwll ...... 6 C5
**Cressage** Shrops ...... 83 L3
**Cressbrook** Derbys ...... 114 D6
**Cresselly** Pembks ...... 49 H6
**Cressex** Bucks ...... 42 D3
**Cressing** Essex ...... 61 J4
**Cresswell** Nthumb ...... 159 H4
**Cresswell** Pembks ...... 49 H6
**Cresswell** Staffs ...... 99 L5
**Creswell** Derbys ...... 115 K6
**Cretingham** Suffk ...... 78 F3
**Cretshengan** Ag & B ...... 172 C5
**Crewe** Ches E ...... 99 G2
**Crewe-by-Farndon**
  Ches W ...... 98 B2
**Crewe Green** Ches E ...... 99 G2
**Crew Green** Powys ...... 83 G1
**Crewkerne** Somset ...... 13 K1
**Crewton** C Derb ...... 101 G5
**Crianlarich** Stirlg ...... 183 L3
**Cribyn** Cerdgn ...... 66 C4
**Criccieth** Gwynd ...... 95 J5
**Crich** Derbys ...... 101 G2
**Crichton** Mdloth ...... 177 K6
**Crick** Nhants ...... 87 H8
**Crickadarn** Powys ...... 68 C6
**Cricket St Thomas**
  Somset ...... 13 J2
**Crickhowell** Powys ...... 53 K4
**Cricklade** Wilts ...... 40 C2
**Cricklewood** Gt Lon ...... 44 E3
**Crieff** P & K ...... 185 H3
**Criggion** Powys ...... 82 F1
**Crigglestone** Wakefd ...... 123 L7
**Crimond** Abers ...... 217 K3
**Crimplesham** Norfk ...... 90 F3
**Crimscote** Warwks ...... 72 B5
**Crinaglack** Highld ...... 212 C6
**Crinan** Ag & B ...... 182 A8
**Crindledyke** N Lans ...... 175 L6
**Cringleford** Norfk ...... 92 E3
**Crinow** Pembks ...... 49 J5
**Croachy** Highld ...... 213 G8
**Crockenhill** Kent ...... 45 J6
**Crocker End** Oxon ...... 42 B3
**Crockernwell** Devon ...... 11 H6
**Crockerton** Wilts ...... 27 K3
**Crocketford** D & G ...... 154 E7
**Crockham Hill** Kent ...... 32 D3
**Croeserw** Neath ...... 36 D2
**Croes-goch** Pembks ...... 48 D2
**Croes-lan** Cerdgn ...... 65 L5
**Croesor** Gwynd ...... 95 L4
**Croesyceiliog** Carmth ...... 50 E3
**Croesyceiliog** Torfn ...... 37 L2
**Croft** Leics ...... 87 G4
**Croft** Lincs ...... 104 E1
**Croft** Warrtn ...... 112 F3
**Croftamie** Stirlg ...... 174 E2
**Crofton** Wakefd ...... 124 B6
**Croft-on-Tees**
  N York ...... 141 H5
**Croftown** Highld ...... 220 F5
**Crofts** Moray ...... 215 G4
**Crofts Bank** Traffd ...... 113 H3
**Crofts of Dipple**
  Moray ...... 215 H3
**Crofts of Haddo**
  Abers ...... 216 F6
**Crofts of Savoch**
  Abers ...... 217 K3
**Crofty** Swans ...... 51 G6
**Croggan** Ag & B ...... 181 L3
**Croglin** Cumb ...... 148 F5
**Croick** Highld ...... 222 B3
**Cromarty** Highld ...... 223 H7
**Crombie** Fife ...... 176 E2

**Cromdale** Highld ...... 214 D8
**Cromer** Herts ...... 59 M3
**Cromer** Norfk ...... 106 F4
**Cromford** Derbys ...... 100 F2
**Cromhall** S Glos ...... 39 G3
**Cromor** W Isls ...... 232 f3
**Cromore** W Isls ...... 232 f3
**Cromwell** Notts ...... 102 C1
**Cronberry** E Ayrs ...... 164 C5
**Crondall** Hants ...... 30 C2
**Cronton** Knows ...... 112 C4
**Crook** Cumb ...... 138 C7
**Crook** Dur ...... 150 E7
**Crookedholm** E Ayrs ...... 163 L3
**Crookes** Sheff ...... 114 F4
**Crookham** Nthumb ...... 168 D2
**Crookham** W Berk ...... 41 K7
**Crookham Village**
  Hants ...... 30 C2
**Crook Inn** Border ...... 165 L4
**Crooklands** Cumb ...... 129 L3
**Crook of Devon**
  P & K ...... 185 L7
**Cropredy** Oxon ...... 72 F5
**Cropston** Leics ...... 87 G2
**Cropthorne** Worcs ...... 71 H5
**Cropton** N York ...... 134 B2
**Cropwell Bishop**
  Notts ...... 102 B5
**Cropwell Butler**
  Notts ...... 102 B5
**Cros** W Isls ...... 232 g1
**Crosbost** W Isls ...... 232 f3
**Crosby** Cumb ...... 147 J7
**Crosby** IoM ...... 237 c5
**Crosby** N Linc ...... 125 K7
**Crosby** Sefton ...... 111 J2
**Crosby Garret** Cumb ...... 139 G5
**Crosby Ravensworth**
  Cumb ...... 138 F4
**Croscombe** Somset ...... 26 E3
**Cross** Somset ...... 26 B1
**Crossaig** Ag & B ...... 172 E7
**Crossapol** Ag & B ...... 188 C7
**Cross Ash** Mons ...... 54 B4
**Cross-at-Hand** Kent ...... 33 K4
**Crossbost** W Isls ...... 232 f3
**Crosscanonby** Cumb ...... 147 J6
**Crossdale Street**
  Norfk ...... 106 F5
**Cross Flatts** C Brad ...... 123 G3
**Crossford** Fife ...... 176 E2
**Crossford** S Lans ...... 175 L8
**Crossgatehall** E Loth ...... 177 K5
**Crossgates** E Ayrs ...... 163 J1
**Crossgates** Fife ...... 176 F1
**Cross Gates** Leeds ...... 124 B4
**Crossgates** N York ...... 134 F3
**Crossgill** Lancs ...... 129 L6
**Cross Green** Leeds ...... 123 L4
**Cross Green** Suffk ...... 77 H4
**Cross Green** Suffk ...... 78 A4
**Cross Hands** Carmth ...... 51 H3
**Crosshands** E Ayrs ...... 163 L4
**Crosshill** Fife ...... 186 C7
**Crosshill** S Ayrs ...... 163 J7
**Crosshouse** E Ayrs ...... 163 K2
**Cross Houses** Shrops ...... 83 K3
**Cross in Hand** E Susx ...... 20 B2
**Cross Inn** Cerdgn ...... 65 L3
**Cross Inn** Cerdgn ...... 66 D2
**Cross Keys** Ag & B ...... 174 C2
**Crosskeys** Caerph ...... 37 K3
**Crosskirk** Highld ...... 230 F2
**Cross Lane** IoW ...... 17 G4
**Cross Lane Head**
  Shrops ...... 84 C4
**Crosslee** Rens ...... 174 D5
**Crossmichael** D & G ...... 146 C2
**Cross of Jackston**
  Abers ...... 216 E7
**Cross o' th' hands**
  Derbys ...... 100 F4
**Crossroads** Abers ...... 206 B4
**Crossroads** Abers ...... 206 E6
**Cross Street** Suffk ...... 92 E7
**Crosston** Angus ...... 196 E5
**Cross Town** Ches E ...... 113 H5

**Crossway Green**
  Worcs ...... 70 E2
**Crossways** Dorset ...... 14 E5
**Crosswell** Pembks ...... 64 F6
**Crosthwaite** Cumb ...... 129 J2
**Croston** Lancs ...... 121 G6
**Crostwick** Norfk ...... 92 F1
**Crouch End** Gt Lon ...... 44 F3
**Croucheston** Wilts ...... 28 B6
**Crouch Hill** Dorset ...... 14 D1
**Croughton** Nhants ...... 73 G7
**Crovie** Abers ...... 216 F2
**Crowan** Cnwll ...... 3 H4
**Crowborough** E Susx ...... 32 F6
**Crowborough**
  **Warren** E Susx ...... 32 E6
**Crowcombe** Somset ...... 25 H4
**Crowdecote** Derbys ...... 114 C7
**Crowden** Derbys ...... 114 C4
**Crow Edge** Barns ...... 114 D2
**Crowell** Oxon ...... 58 C7
**Crowfield** Suffk ...... 78 D3
**Crowhill** E Loth ...... 178 F4
**Crow Hill** Herefs ...... 54 F3
**Crowhurst** E Susx ...... 20 F3
**Crowhurst** Surrey ...... 32 D4
**Crowland** Lincs ...... 89 J2
**Crowland** Suffk ...... 78 B1
**Crowlas** Cnwll ...... 2 F5
**Crowle** N Linc ...... 125 J7
**Crowle** Worcs ...... 71 G4
**Crowle Green** Worcs ...... 71 G3
**Crowmarsh Gifford**
  Oxon ...... 41 L3
**Crown Corner** Suffk ...... 78 F1
**Crownhill** C Plym ...... 6 C4
**Crownpits** Surrey ...... 30 F3
**Crownthorpe** Norfk ...... 92 C3
**Crowntown** Cnwll ...... 3 H5
**Crows-an-Wra** Cnwll ...... 2 B5
**Crowthorne** Wokham ...... 42 D7
**Crowton** Ches W ...... 112 E6
**Croxdale** Dur ...... 151 G7
**Croxden** Staffs ...... 100 B5
**Croxley Green** Herts ...... 43 H2
**Croxteth** Lpool ...... 111 L3
**Croxton** Cambs ...... 75 J3
**Croxton** N Linc ...... 126 D7
**Croxton** Norfk ...... 91 K6
**Croxton** Norfk ...... 106 B6
**Croxton** Staffs ...... 99 H6
**Croxton Kerrial**
  Leics ...... 102 D6
**Croy** Highld ...... 213 J4
**Croy** N Lans ...... 175 J3
**Croyde** Devon ...... 23 G4
**Croydon** Cambs ...... 75 K5
**Croydon** Gt Lon ...... 44 F6
**Crubenmore** Highld ...... 203 G2
**Cruckmeole** Shrops ...... 83 H2
**Cruckton** Shrops ...... 83 H2
**Cruden Bay** Abers ...... 217 K6
**Crudgington** Wrekin ...... 98 F8
**Crudie** Abers ...... 216 E3
**Crudwell** Wilts ...... 39 L2
**Crumlin** Caerph ...... 37 K2
**Crumplehorn** Cnwll ...... 5 K5
**Crumpsall** Manch ...... 113 J2
**Crundale** Kent ...... 34 E5
**Crux Easton** Hants ...... 29 H1
**Crwbin** Carmth ...... 50 F3
**Cryers Hill** Bucks ...... 42 E2
**Crymych** Pembks ...... 65 G2
**Crynant** Neath ...... 52 C6
**Crystal Palace** Gt Lon ...... 45 G5
**Cuaig** Highld ...... 209 L3
**Cuan** Ag & B ...... 181 L2
**Cubbington** Warwks ...... 72 D2
**Cublington** Bucks ...... 58 D4
**Cublington** Herefs ...... 69 H6
**Cuckfield** W Susx ...... 32 B7
**Cucklington** Somset ...... 27 H6
**Cuckney** Notts ...... 115 K7
**Cuddesdon** Oxon ...... 57 L7
**Cuddington** Bucks ...... 58 C5
**Cuddington** Ches W ...... 112 E7
**Cuddington Heath**
  Ches W ...... 98 C3

**Cudham** Gt Lon...............32 D2
**Cudliptown** Devon............6 D1
**Cudnell** BCP....................15 K3
**Cudworth** Barns............124 B8
**Cudworth** Somset............13 J1
**Cuffley** Herts..................59 M7
**Cuil** Highld.....................191 J5
**Culbokie** Highld.............212 F3
**Culburnie** Highld............212 D6
**Culcabock** Highld............213 G5
**Culcharry** Highld.............213 K4
**Culcheth** Warrtn.............112 F3
**Culdrain** Abers...............215 L7
**Culduie** Highld................209 L6
**Culford** Suffk...................77 J1
**Culgaith** Cumb...............138 E2
**Culham** Oxon...................41 J2
**Culkein** Highld................224 C2
**Culkein Drumbeg**
    Highld.........................224 D2
**Culkerton** Gloucs.............39 L2
**Cullen** Moray..................215 L2
**Cullercoats** N Tyne.........159 J7
**Cullerlie** Abers...............206 E5
**Cullicudden** Highld.........213 G2
**Cullingworth** C Brad.......123 G3
**Cuillin Hills** Highld.........199 G2
**Cullipool** Ag & B.............181 L5
**Cullivoe** Shet.................235 d2
**Culloden** Highld.............213 H5
**Cullompton** Devon...........12 C2
**Cullompton
    Services** Devon..........12 D2
**Culm Davy** Devon............25 H7
**Culmington** Shrops.........83 J6
**Culmstock** Devon.............25 H8
**Culnacraig** Highld..........224 C7
**Culnaightrie** D & G.........146 D5
**Culnaknock** Highld.........209 H2
**Culrain** Highld................222 D3
**Culross** Fife....................176 D2
**Culroy** S Ayrs..................163 H6
**Culsalmond** Abers..........216 C7
**Culscadden** D & G..........145 K5
**Culshabbin** D & G...........145 G5
**Culswick** Shet.................235 b6
**Cultercullen** Abers.........207 H1
**Cults** C Aber...................207 G5
**Culverstone Green**
    Kent............................45 M7
**Culverthorpe** Lincs........103 G4
**Culworth** Nhants............73 G5
**Culzean Castle &
    Country Park**
    S Ayrs.........................163 G7
**Cumbernauld** N Lans.....175 K4
**Cumbernauld
    Village** N Lans...........175 K3
**Cumberworth** Lincs.......119 G6
**Cuminestown** Abers.......216 F4
**Cumledge** Border...........179 G6
**Cummersdale** Cumb.......148 D4
**Cummertrees** D & G.......147 K2
**Cummingston** Moray......214 E1
**Cumnock** E Ayrs.............164 B5
**Cumnor** Oxon..................57 J7
**Cumrew** Cumb.................148 F5
**Cumrue** D & G.................155 J5
**Cumwhinton** Cumb.........148 D4
**Cumwhitton** Cumb..........148 E4
**Cundall** N York...............132 F5
**Cunninghamhead**
    N Ayrs........................163 J2
**Cunningsburgh** Shet.....235 c7
**Cupar** Fife.......................186 F4
**Cupar Muir** Fife...............186 F5
**Curbar** Derbys.................114 E6
**Curbridge** Hants..............17 G1
**Curbridge** Oxon...............57 G6
**Curdridge** Hants..............29 K8
**Curdworth** Warwks..........85 L5
**Curland** Somset...............25 L7
**Curridge** W Berk...............41 J6
**Currie** C Edin..................177 G5
**Curry Mallet** Somset........25 L6
**Curry Rivel** Somset..........26 B6
**Curtisden Green**
    Kent............................33 J5

**Curtisknowle** Devon.........7 H5
**Cury** Cnwll........................3 H6
**Cushnie** Abers................205 L3
**Cusworth** Donc..............115 K2
**Cutcloy** D & G..................145 J7
**Cutcombe** Somset............24 E4
**Cuthill** Highld..................223 G4
**Cutnall Green** Worcs........70 F2
**Cutsdean** Gloucs..............56 C3
**Cutthorpe** Derbys...........115 G6
**Cuxham** Oxon...................42 A2
**Cuxton** Medway................46 B6
**Cuxwold** Lincs.................117 K2
**Cwm** Denbgs...................110 E6
**Cwmafan** Neath...............36 B3
**Cwmaman** Rhondd...........52 F7
**Cwmbach** Carmth.............50 B1
**Cwmbach** Powys...............68 D6
**Cwmbach** Rhondd.............52 F7
**Cwmbran** Torfn................37 L2
**Cwmcarn** Caerph.............37 K2
**Cwmcarvan** Mons............54 C6
**Cwm-cou** Cerdgn.............65 J6
**Cwm Crawnon**
    Powys.........................53 H4
**Cwmdare** Rhondd.............52 F7
**Cwmdu** Powys...................53 J4
**Cwmdu** Swans..................51 J6
**Cwmduad** Carmth............65 L7
**Cwmfelin** Brdgnd.............36 D3
**Cwmfelin** Myr Td..............53 H7
**Cwmfelin Boeth**
    Carmth.........................49 K4
**Cwmfelinfach** Caerph......37 J3
**Cwmffrwd** Carmth............50 E3
**Cwmgiedd** Powys.............52 C5
**Cwmgorse** Carmth............51 K4
**Cwmgwili** Carmth............51 H4
**Cwmhiraeth** Carmth.........65 K6
**Cwm Llinau** Powys...........81 J2
**Cwmllynfell** Neath............51 L3
**Cwmmawr** Carmth............51 G3
**Cwmparc** Rhondd.............36 E2
**Cwmpengraig**
    Carmth.........................65 K7
**Cwmtillery** Blae G............53 K6
**Cwm-twrch Isaf**
    Powys.........................52 B6
**Cwm-twrch Uchaf**
    Powys.........................51 L4
**Cwm-y-glo** Gwynd.........109 H8
**Cwmystwyth** Cerdgn........81 H8
**Cwrtnewydd** Cerdgn........66 C5
**Cyfarthfa Castle
    Museum** Myr Td...........53 G6
**Cyffylliog** Denbgs............97 G2
**Cylibebyll** Neath.............51 L5
**Cymmer** Neath.................36 D2
**Cymmer** Rhondd..............36 F3
**Cyncoed** Cardif................37 J4
**Cynghordy** Carmth...........67 H6
**Cynonville** Neath..............36 C2
**Cynwyd** Denbgs................97 G4
**Cynwyl Elfed** Carmth........65 L8

---

**D**

---

**Daccombe** Devon...............7 K3
**Dacre** Cumb....................138 C2
**Dacre** N York..................132 B7
**Dacre Banks** N York.......132 B6
**Daddry Shield** Dur..........149 M7
**Dadford** Bucks..................73 J6
**Dadlington** Leics..............86 E4
**Dafen** Carmth...................51 G5
**Dagenham** Gt Lon............45 J3
**Daglingworth** Gloucs........55 M6
**Dagnall** Bucks...................59 G5
**Dail bho Dheas**
    W Isls........................232 g1
**Dailly** S Ayrs...................152 F2
**Dairsie** Fife....................187 G4
**Dalabrog** W Isls..............233 b8
**Dalavich** Ag & B..............182 D5
**Dalby** IoM.......................237 b5

**Dalby** N York..................133 K5
**Dalcapon** P & K..............194 F5
**Dalchalm** Highld.............226 F7
**Dalchreichart** Highld......201 L3
**Dalchruin** P & K.............184 F4
**Dalcrue** P & K..................185 L2
**Dalditch** Devon.................12 D5
**Dale** Pembks....................48 D6
**Dale Abbey** Derbys.........101 H5
**Dalelia** Highld.................190 E3
**Dalgarven** N Ayrs............163 H1
**Dalgety Bay** Fife............177 G2
**Dalgig** E Ayrs..................164 B6
**Dalginross** P & K............185 G3
**Dalguise** P & K................194 F6
**Dalhalvaig** Highld...........230 C5
**Dalham** Suffk...................77 G3
**Daliburgh** W Isls............233 b8
**Dalkeith** Mdloth.............177 K5
**Dallas** Moray..................214 D4
**Dallinghoo** Suffk...............78 F4
**Dallington** E Susx............20 D2
**Dallington** Nhants............73 K3
**Dalmally** Ag & B..............183 H3
**Dalmary** Stirlg.................185 G3
**Dalmellington** E Ayrs......153 K2
**Dalmeny** C Edin..............176 F3
**Dalmore** Highld...............222 F7
**Dalmuir** W Duns.............174 E4
**Dalnabreck** Highld..........190 D2
**Dalnacardoch** P & K.......194 B3
**Dalnahaitnach** Highld.....203 K2
**Dalnaspidal** P & K...........193 K2
**Dalnawillan Lodge**
    Highld.........................230 F7
**Dalqueich** P & K..............185 M6
**Dalquharn** S Ayrs...........153 G3
**Dalreavoch** Highld..........226 D6
**Dalry** N Ayrs...................174 B7
**Dalrymple** E Ayrs............163 J6
**Dalserf** S Lans................175 L7
**Dalsmeran** Ag & B..........161 G6
**Dalston** Gt Lon...............148 C5
**Dalston** Cumb.................45 G3
**Dalswinton** D & G...........155 G5
**Dalton** D & G...................155 K7
**Dalton** N York.................132 F4
**Dalton** N York.................140 E5
**Dalton** Nthum.................158 E7
**Dalton-in-Furness**
    Cumb.........................128 F5
**Dalton-le-Dale** Dur........151 K5
**Dalton-on-Tees**
    N York.......................141 H5
**Dalton Piercy** Hartpl......141 L2
**Dalveich** Stirlg................184 D3
**Dalwhinnie** Highld..........202 F7
**Dalwood** Devon.................13 G3
**Damerham** Hants.............28 C7
**Damgate** Norfk.................93 J2
**Damnaglaur** D & G..........144 D7
**Danbury** Essex.................61 J6
**Danby** N York..................142 F5
**Danby Wiske** N York.......141 H7
**Dandaleith** Moray...........215 G5
**Danderhall** Mdloth..........177 J4
**Danebridge** Ches E.........113 L7
**Dane End** Herts................60 B4
**Danehill** E Susx................32 D7
**Dane Hills** C Leic..............87 H3
**Dane Street** Kent.............34 E4
**Danshillock** Abers..........216 D3
**Danskine** E Loth.............178 C5
**Darenth** Kent....................45 K5
**Daresbury** Halton...........112 E5
**Darfield** Barns.................115 H1
**Dargate** Kent....................34 E3
**Dargavel** Rens................174 D4
**Darite** Cnwll.......................5 K3
**Darlaston** Wsall................85 H4
**Darlaston Green**
    Wsall...........................85 H4
**Darley** N York..................132 C7
**Darley Abbey** C Derb......101 G5
**Darley Bridge**
    Derbys........................100 E1
**Darley Dale** Derbys.........114 F8
**Darley Green** Solhll.........85 L8

**Darleyhall** Herts................59 J4
**Darley Head** N York........132 B7
**Darlingscott** Warwks........72 B6
**Darlington** Darltn...........141 H4
**Darlton** Notts..................116 C6
**Darnick** Border................167 H3
**Darowen** Powys................81 H3
**Darra** Abers....................216 E5
**Darracott** Devon.................9 G2
**Darracott** Devon..............23 G4
**Darras Hall** Nthumb.......158 E7
**Darrington** Wakefd.........124 D6
**Darsham** Suffk.................79 J1
**Darshill** Somset...............26 E3
**Dartford** Kent...................45 K5
**Dartford Crossing**
    Kent............................45 K5
**Dartington** Devon..............7 H4
**Dartmoor National
    Park** Devon................11 G8
**Dartmouth** Devon..............7 K5
**Darton** Barns..................123 L7
**Darvel** E Ayrs..................164 B2
**Darwen** Bl w D................121 K6
**Datchet** W & M..................43 G5
**Datchworth** Herts............59 L4
**Daubhill** Bolton...............121 K8
**Daugh of
    Kinermony**
    Moray.........................214 F6
**Dauntsey** Wilts.................39 M4
**Dava** Highld....................214 C6
**Davenham** Ches W..........112 F7
**Daventry** Nhants..............73 H3
**Davidson's Mains**
    C Edin.........................177 G4
**Davidstow** Cnwll................8 F7
**Davington** D & G.............155 M2
**Davington Hill** Kent.........34 D3
**Daviot** Abers...................216 E8
**Daviot** Highld..................213 H6
**Daviot House** Highld.......213 H6
**Davoch of Grange**
    Moray.........................215 K4
**Davyhulme** Traffd..........113 H3
**Daw End** Wsall.................85 J4
**Dawesgreen** Surrey..........31 K3
**Dawley** Wrekin..................84 C2
**Dawlish** Devon..................12 B6
**Dawlish Warren**
    Devon.........................12 C6
**Daybrook** Notts...............101 L4
**Daylesford** Gloucs............56 E3
**Deal** Kent..........................35 K4
**Dean** Cumb.....................136 E3
**Dean** Devon........................7 G3
**Dean** Devon.......................23 L2
**Dean** Hants.......................29 K7
**Dean** Oxon.........................57 G4
**Dean** Somset.....................26 F3
**Dean Bottom** Kent...........45 L6
**Deanburnhaugh**
    Border.........................166 F6
**Deancombe** Devon.............7 G3
**Dean Court** Oxon..............57 J6
**Deane** Bolton..................121 K8
**Deane** Hants.....................29 K2
**Deanhead** Kirk................122 F7
**Deanland** Dorset..............27 M7
**Dean Prior** Devon...............7 H3
**Deanraw** Nthumb...........149 L3
**Deans** W Loth.................176 D5
**Deanscales** Cumb...........136 F2
**Deanshanger** Nhants........73 L6
**Deanshaugh** Moray.........215 H4
**Deanston** Stirlg...............184 F6
**Dearham** Cumb................147 J7
**Debach** Suffk....................78 F4
**Debden** Essex....................45 H2
**Debden** Essex....................60 E2
**Debenham** Suffk...............78 E2
**Deblin's Green** Worcs........70 E5
**Dechmont** W Loth...........176 D4
**Dechmont Road**
    W Loth........................176 D4
**Deddington** Oxon.............57 J2
**Dedham** Essex..................62 C2
**Dedworth** W & M..............42 F5

Deene Nhants .................88 D5
Deenethorpe Nhants ......88 D5
Deepcar Sheff................114 F3
Deeping Gate C Pete ....89 G2
Deeping St James
   Lincs..........................89 H2
Deeping St Nicholas
   Lincs...........................89 J1
Deerhurst Gloucs...........55 K3
Defford Worcs................71 G6
Defynnog Powys............52 E3
Deganwy Conwy...........109 L5
Degnish Ag & B ..........182 A5
Deighton C York .........124 F2
Deighton N York...........141 J6
Deiniolen Gwynd...........109 H8
Delabole Cnwll.................8 E7
Delamere Ches W ........112 E7
Delfrigs Abers ..............207 H2
Delliefure Highld...........214 D7
Dell Quay W Susx...........18 A5
Delnabo Moray.............204 E3
Delny Highld.................223 G6
Delph Oldham..............122 E8
Delves Dur....................150 E5
Dembleby Lincs ...........103 H5
Denaby Donc.................115 J2
Denbigh Denbgs............110 E7
Denbrae Fife.................186 F4
Denbury Devon.................7 J3
Denby Derbys................101 H4
Denby Dale Kirk ..........123 J8
Denchworth Oxon..........41 G3
Dendron Cumb .............128 F5
Denfield P & K..............185 K4
Denford Nhants..............88 E7
Dengie Essex..................62 B7
Denham Bucks................43 H3
Denham Suffk.................77 H3
Denham Suffk.................92 E8
Denham Green
   Bucks...........................43 H3
Denhead Abers .............217 J4
Denhead Fife................187 G5
Denhead of Gray
   C Dund.......................186 F2
Denholm Border ...........167 J5
Denholme C Brad .........123 G4
Denmead Hants ..............30 A8
Denmore C Aber ..........207 H3
Dennington Suffk...........79 G2
Denny Falk ...................175 L2
Dennyloanhead Falk ....175 L3
Den of Lindores Fife....186 D4
Denshaw Oldham ..........122 E7
Denside of Durris
   Abers..........................206 F6
Densole Kent..................35 G6
Denston Suffk.................77 H4
Denstone Staffs ...........100 C4
Denstroude Kent ...........34 E3
Dent Cumb ...................130 D3
Denton Cambs................89 G6
Denton Darltn...............140 F4
Denton E Susx................19 L5
Denton Kent....................35 G5
Denton Kent....................46 A5
Denton Lincs.................102 E6
Denton N York..............123 H2
Denton Nhants................74 B3
Denton Norfk..................93 G5
Denton Tamesd.............113 L3
Denver Norfk...................90 E3
Denwick Nthumb...........169 J6
Deopham Norfk...............92 C4
Deopham Green
   Norfk...........................92 C4
Depden Suffk...................77 H3
Deptford Gt Lon.............45 G4
Deptford Wilts................28 A4
Derby C Derb.................101 G5
Derby Devon...................23 J5
Derbyhaven IoM............237 b7
Derculich P & K............194 D5
Dereham Norfk................92 B2
Deri Caerph....................53 H7
Derringstone Kent..........35 G5
Derrington Staffs ...........99 K7

Derry Hill Wilts...............39 L6
Derrythorpe N Linc.......125 J8
Dersingham Norfk.........105 H6
Dervaig Ag & B ...........189 K6
Derwen Denbgs...............97 G3
Derwenlas Powys...........80 F4
Derwent Valley Mills
   Derbys........................100 F2
Derwent Water Cumb...137 J3
Desborough Nhants........88 B6
Desford Leics..................86 F3
Detling Kent...................33 K2
Devauden Mons..............54 C7
Devil's Bridge Cerdgn...81 G7
Devizes Wilts..................40 A7
Devonport C Plym............6 C5
Devonside Clacks .........185 J7
Devoran Cnwll..................4 C7
Devoran & Perran
   Cnwll............................3 K4
Dewarton Mdloth..........177 K5
Dewlish Dorset...............14 E3
Dewsbury Kirk..............123 K6
Dewsbury Moor Kirk....123 J6
Deytheur Powys..............97 K8
Dibden Hants..................16 E2
Dibden Purlieu
   Hants...........................16 E2
Dickleburgh Norfk..........92 E6
Didbrook Gloucs.............56 B2
Didcot Oxon...................41 K3
Diddington Cambs..........75 H2
Diddlebury Shrops..........83 K6
Didling W Susx...............18 A3
Didmarton Gloucs...........39 J3
Didsbury Manch............113 J3
Digby Lincs..................103 H2
Digg Highld..................218 C7
Diggle Oldham..............122 F8
Digmoor Lancs..............112 C1
Dihewyd Cerdgn.............66 C4
Dilham Norfk.................107 G7
Dilhorne Staffs...............99 L4
Dill Hall Lancs..............121 L4
Dillington Cambs...........75 G2
Dilston Nthumb.............150 B3
Dilton Wilts....................27 K2
Dilton Marsh Wilts.........27 J2
Dilwyn Herefs.................69 H4
Dinas Gwynd...................94 E5
Dinas Cross Pembks.......64 E6
Dinas-Mawddwy
   Gwynd.........................81 J1
Dinas Powys V Glam.......37 J6
Dinder Somset................26 E3
Dinedor Herefs...............69 K6
Dingestow Mons.............54 C6
Dingle Lpool.................111 K4
Dingley Nhants...............87 L6
Dingwall Highld............212 E3
Dinnet Abers.................205 K5
Dinnington N u Ty........158 F7
Dinnington Rothm........115 K4
Dinnington Somset.........26 B8
Dinorwic Gwynd.............95 K1
Dinton Bucks..................58 C5
Dinton Wilts...................28 A5
Dinwoodie D & G.........155 K4
Dinworthy Devon.............9 J2
Dipford Somset...............25 J6
Dippen Ag & B.............161 K2
Dippertown Devon.........10 C7
Dippin N Ayrs...............162 D5
Dipple Moray................215 H3
Dipple S Ayrs................152 E2
Diptford Devon.................7 G4
Dipton Dur...................150 E4
Dirleton E Loth.............178 B2
Dirt Pot Nthumb...........149 L5
Diseworth Leics............101 J7
Dishforth N York..........132 F5
Disley Ches E...............113 L5
Diss Norfk......................92 D7
Distington Cumb...........136 D3
Ditchampton Wilts.........28 C5
Ditcheat Somset............26 F4
Ditchingham Norfk..........93 G5
Ditchling E Susx.............19 J3

Ditherington Shrops........83 K2
Ditteridge Wilts..............39 J6
Dittisham Devon...............7 K5
Ditton Kent....................33 J2
Ditton Green Cambs.......76 F3
Ditton Priors Shrops.......83 L5
Dixton Mons...................54 D5
Dobcross Oldham..........113 M1
Dobwalls Cnwll.................5 K3
Doccombe Devon...........11 H7
Dochgarroch Highld......212 F6
Docking Norfk..............105 J5
Docklow Herefs..............69 L3
Dockray Cumb..............137 L3
Doddinghurst Essex........60 F7
Doddington Cambs..........90 B5
Doddington Kent............34 C4
Doddington Lincs..........116 E7
Doddington Nthumb.....168 E3
Doddington Shrops.........84 B7
Doddiscombsleigh
   Devon.........................11 K7
Dodd's Green Ches E.....98 E4
Dodford Nhants..............73 H3
Dodford Worcs...............85 G8
Dodington S Glos...........39 H4
Dodington Somset..........25 J4
Dodleston Ches W..........98 A1
Dodside E Rens.............174 F7
Dod's Leigh Staffs........100 A5
Dodworth Barns...........114 F1
Doe Bank Birm..............85 K4
Dogdyke Lincs..............103 K2
Dogmersfield Hants........30 C2
Dogsthorpe C Pete.........89 H4
Dolanog Powys...............82 B2
Dolbenmaen Gwynd.......95 J4
Dolfach Powys................81 K3
Dolfor Powys..................82 C6
Dolgarrog Conwy..........109 L7
Dolgellau Gwynd............96 B8
Doll Highld...................226 F7
Dollar Clacks................185 K7
Dollarfield Clacks..........185 K7
Dolphin Flints...............111 H6
Dolphinholme Lancs......129 L8
Dolphinton S Lans........176 F8
Dolton Devon.................10 E3
Dolwen Conwy..............110 B6
Dolwyddelan Conwy......96 B3
Domgay Powys...............97 L8
Doncaster Donc............115 L2
Doncaster North
   Services Donc............125 G7
Doncaster Sheffield
   Airport Donc.............115 M2
Donhead St Andrew
   Wilts...........................27 K6
Donhead St Mary
   Wilts...........................27 K6
Donibristle Fife............177 G2
Doniford Somset............25 G3
Donington Lincs...........103 K5
Donington on Bain
   Lincs.........................118 C5
Donington Park
   Services Leics............101 J7
Donisthorpe Leics..........86 C2
Donnington Gloucs.........56 D3
Donnington Shrops.........83 L2
Donnington W Berk........41 J6
Donnington W Susx........18 B5
Donnington Wrekin........84 C2
Donnington Wood
   Wrekin........................84 C2
Donyatt Somset..............25 M8
Doonfoot S Ayrs...........163 H5
Dorback Lodge
   Highld.......................204 D3
Dorchester Dorset..........14 D4
Dorchester-on-
   Thames Oxon............41 L2
Dordon Warwks.............86 C4
Dore Sheff....................114 F5
Dores Highld................212 F7
Dorking Surrey...............31 K2
Dormansland Surrey.......32 D5
Dormington Herefs.........69 L6

Dormston Worcs.............71 H3
Dorney Bucks.................42 F5
Dornie Highld...............200 D1
Dornoch Highld.............223 H4
Dornock D & G.............147 M2
Dorrery Highld..............230 F5
Dorridge Solhll..............85 L8
Dorrington Lincs...........103 H2
Dorrington Shrops..........83 J3
Dorrington Shrops..........99 G4
Dorsington Warwks........71 K4
Dorstone Herefs.............69 G6
Dorton Bucks..................58 B5
Douglas IoM.................237 d6
Douglas S Lans.............165 G4
Douglas and Angus
   C Dund.......................187 G2
Douglas Pier Ag & B....183 H7
Douglastown Angus......196 C6
Douglas Water
   S Lans........................165 G3
Douglas West S Lans....164 F3
Doulting Somset.............26 F3
Dounby Ork...................234 b5
Doune Highld................221 L2
Doune Stirlg.................184 F6
Dounepark S Ayrs.........152 E3
Dounie Highld...............222 D4
Dousland Devon...............6 D3
Dove Dale Derbys.........100 D3
Dove Holes Derbys.......114 B6
Dovenby Cumb.............147 J7
Dover Kent.....................35 J6
Dover Castle Kent..........35 J6
Dovercourt Essex...........62 F2
Doverdale Worcs............70 F2
Doveridge Derbys.........100 C5
Doversgreen Surrey........31 L2
Dowally P & K..............194 F6
Dowdeswell Gloucs........55 M4
Dowlais Myr Td..............53 G6
Dowland Devon..............10 E3
Dowlish Wake
   Somset........................26 A8
Down Ampney
   Gloucs........................40 C2
Downderry Cnwll.............5 L5
Downe Gt Lon.................45 H7
Downend Gloucs.............55 J7
Downend S Glos............38 F5
Downfield C Dund.........186 F1
Downgate Cnwll...............6 A2
Downham Essex.............46 B2
Downham Gt Lon...........45 H5
Downham Lancs............122 B2
Downham Market
   Norfk...........................90 E3
Down Hatherley
   Gloucs........................55 K4
Downhead Somset..........26 E6
Downhead Somset..........27 G3
Downhill P & K..............186 A2
Downholme N York........140 E7
Downies Abers..............207 H6
Downley Bucks...............42 D2
Down St Mary Devon.....11 H4
Downside Surrey............43 J8
Down Thomas Devon.......6 D6
Downton Wilts................28 D6
Dowsby Lincs................103 J6
Doynton S Glos..............39 G5
Draethen Caerph............37 K3
Draffan S Lans..............164 F1
Drakeholes Notts..........116 B4
Drakemyre N Ayrs.........174 B7
Drakes Broughton
   Worcs..........................71 G5
Draughton N York.........131 K8
Draughton Nhants..........87 L7
Drax N York..................125 G5
Draycote Warwks...........72 F1
Draycott Derbys............101 H6
Draycott Gloucs.............71 L7
Draycott Somset.............26 C2
Draycott in the Clay
   Staffs.........................100 D6
Draycott in the
   Moors Staffs..............99 M4

Drayton C Port..............17 J2
Drayton Leics..............88 B5
Drayton Norfk..............92 E2
Drayton Oxon..............41 J2
Drayton Oxon..............72 E6
Drayton Somset..............26 B6
Drayton Worcs..............85 G7
Drayton Bassett
    Staffs..............85 L4
Drayton Beauchamp
    Bucks..............58 E5
Drayton Manor Park
    Staffs..............85 L4
Drayton Parslow
    Bucks..............58 D3
Drayton St Leonard
    Oxon..............41 L2
Dreen Hill Pembks..............48 F5
Drefach Carmth..............51 G3
Drefach Carmth..............65 K6
Drefach Cerdgn..............66 C5
Dreghorn N Ayrs..............163 J2
Drellingore Kent..............35 H6
Drem E Loth..............178 B3
Dresden C Stke..............99 K4
Drewsteignton
    Devon..............11 H6
Driffield E R Yk..............134 F7
Driffield Gloucs..............56 B7
Drift Cnwll..............2 D5
Drigg Cumb..............136 E7
Drighlington Leeds..............123 J5
Drimnin Highld..............190 B5
Drimpton Dorset..............13 K2
Drimsallie Highld..............191 J1
Dringhouses C York..............124 E2
Drinkstone Suffk..............77 L3
Drinkstone Green
    Suffk..............77 L3
Drointon Staffs..............100 A6
Droitwich Spa Worcs..............70 F2
Dron P & K..............186 B4
Dronfield Derbys..............115 G5
Drongan E Ayrs..............163 K5
Dronley Angus..............186 E1
Droop Dorset..............14 E2
Droxford Hants..............29 L7
Droylsden Tamesd..............113 K2
Druid Denbgs..............97 G4
Druidston Pembks..............48 E4
Druimarbin Highld..............191 L3
Druimavuic Ag & B..............191 K7
Druimdrishaig
    Ag & B..............172 C4
Druimindarroch
    Highld..............199 L7
Drum Ag & B..............172 F3
Drum P & K..............185 L7
Drumalbin S Lans..............165 H2
Drumbeg Highld..............224 D3
Drumblade Abers..............216 B6
Drumbreddon
    D & G..............144 C6
Drumbuie Highld..............210 B7
Drumburgh Cumb..............148 A3
Drumburn D & G..............146 F4
Drumburn D & G..............147 G3
Drumchapel C Glas..............174 F4
Drumchastle P & K..............193 L5
Drumclog S Lans..............164 C2
Drumeldrie Fife..............187 G6
Drumelzier Border..............165 M3
Drumfearn Highld..............199 L3
Drumfrennie Abers..............206 D5
Drumgley Angus..............196 C6
Drumguish Highld..............203 J5
Drumin Moray..............214 E7
Drumjohn D & G..............153 L3
Drumlamford S Ayrs..............153 G6
Drumlasie Abers..............206 C4
Drumleaning Cumb..............148 A5
Drumlemble Ag & B..............161 H5
Drumlithie Abers..............197 J1
Drummoddie D & G..............145 H6
Drummore D & G..............144 D7
Drummuir Moray..............215 J5
Drumnadrochit
    Highld..............212 D7

Drumnagorrach
    Moray..............215 L4
Drumpark D & G..............154 F6
Drumrunie Highld..............224 E7
Drumshang S Ayrs..............163 G6
Drumuie Highld..............209 G5
Drumuillie Highld..............204 B2
Drumvaich Stirlg..............184 E6
Drunzie P & K..............186 B5
Drybeck Cumb..............138 F4
Drybridge Moray..............215 K2
Drybridge N Ayrs..............163 J3
Drybrook Gloucs..............54 F4
Dryburgh Border..............167 J3
Dry Doddington
    Lincs..............102 D3
Dry Drayton Cambs..............75 L3
Drymen Stirlg..............174 E2
Drymuir Abers..............217 G5
Drynoch Highld..............208 F7
Dubford Abers..............216 F2
Duchally Highld..............225 J5
Ducklington Oxon..............57 G6
Duddenhoe End
    Essex..............76 C7
Duddingston C Edin..............177 J4
Duddington Nhants..............88 E4
Duddlestone Somset..............25 K7
Duddo Nthumb..............168 D2
Duddon Ches W..............112 D8
Dudleston Shrops..............97 M5
Dudleston Heath
    Shrops..............98 A5
Dudley Dudley..............85 G5
Dudley N Tyne..............159 G7
Dudley Port Sandw..............85 G5
Dudsbury Dorset..............15 K3
Duffield Derbys..............101 G4
Duffryn Neath..............36 C2
Dufftown Moray..............215 H6
Duffus Moray..............214 E2
Dufton Cumb..............139 G3
Duggleby N York..............134 D6
Duirinish Highld..............210 B7
Duisky Highld..............191 K2
Dukestown Blae G..............53 H6
Duke Street Suffk..............78 C6
Dukinfield Tamesd..............113 L2
Dulcote Somset..............26 E3
Dulford Devon..............12 D2
Dull P & K..............194 C6
Dullatur N Lans..............175 K3
Dullingham Cambs..............76 F3
Dulnain Bridge
    Highld..............204 B1
Duloe Bed..............75 H3
Duloe Cnwll..............5 K4
Dulsie Bridge
    Highld..............213 L6
Dulverton Somset..............24 E5
Dulwich Gt Lon..............45 G5
Dumbarton W Duns..............174 D4
Dumbleton Gloucs..............71 H7
Dumfries D & G..............155 G6
Dumgoyne Stirlg..............174 F2
Dummer Hants..............29 L3
Dumpton Kent..............35 K2
Dun Angus..............197 G4
Dunalastair P & K..............193 L5
Dunan Ag & B..............173 K4
Dunan Highld..............209 J8
Dunan P & K..............193 G5
Dunaverty Ag & B..............161 H7
Dunball Somset..............25 L3
Dunbar E Loth..............178 E3
Dunbeath Highld..............227 L3
Dunbeg Ag & B..............182 C2
Dunblane Stirlg..............185 G6
Dunbog Fife..............186 E4
Duncanston Highld..............212 F3
Duncanstone Abers..............216 B8
Dunchideock Devon..............11 K7
Dunchurch Warwks..............72 F1
Duncow D & G..............155 G5
Duncrievie P & K..............186 B5
Duncton W Susx..............18 C3
Dundee C Dund..............186 F2

Dundee Airport
    C Dund..............186 F2
Dundon Somset..............26 C5
Dundonald S Ayrs..............163 J3
Dundonnell Highld..............220 E4
Dundraw Cumb..............147 L5
Dundreggan Highld..............201 L3
Dundrennan D & G..............146 D5
Dundry N Som..............38 E6
Dunecht Abers..............206 E4
Dunfermline Fife..............176 F2
Dunfield Gloucs..............40 C2
Dungavel S Lans..............164 D3
Dungeness Kent..............21 L3
Dunham Massey
    Traffd..............113 H4
Dunham-on-the-
    Hill Ches W..............112 C6
Dunham-on-Trent
    Notts..............116 D6
Dunhampton Worcs..............70 F2
Dunham Town Traffd..............113 H4
Dunham
    Woodhouses
    Traffd..............113 G4
Dunholme Lincs..............117 G5
Dunino Fife..............187 J5
Dunipace Falk..............175 L2
Dunkeld P & K..............195 G7
Dunkerton BaNES..............39 G8
Dunkeswell Devon..............12 E2
Dunkeswick N York..............123 L2
Dunkirk Kent..............34 E3
Dunkirk S Glos..............39 H4
Dunk's Green Kent..............33 G3
Dunlappie Angus..............196 F3
Dunley Worcs..............70 E2
Dunlop E Ayrs..............174 D8
Dunmaglass Highld..............202 F2
Dunmore Falk..............176 B1
Dunnet Highld..............231 J2
Dunnichen Angus..............196 E6
Dunning P & K..............185 L4
Dunnington C York..............133 K8
Dunnington E R Yk..............126 E1
Dunnington Warwks..............71 J4
Dunoon Ag & B..............173 K3
Dunphail Moray..............214 C5
Dunragit D & G..............144 E4
Duns Border..............179 G7
Dunsby Lincs..............103 J6
Dunscore D & G..............154 F5
Dunscroft Donc..............124 F8
Dunsdale R & Cl..............142 D4
Dunsden Green Oxon..............42 C5
Dunsdon Devon..............9 J3
Dunsfold Surrey..............31 G4
Dunsford Devon..............11 J6
Dunshalt Fife..............186 D5
Dunshillock Abers..............217 J5
Dunsill Notts..............101 J1
Dunsley N York..............143 H5
Dunsley Staffs..............84 F6
Dunsmore Bucks..............58 E6
Dunsop Bridge
    Lancs..............121 K1
Dunstable C Beds..............59 G4
Dunstall Staffs..............100 D7
Dunstan Nthumb..............169 K5
Dunster Somset..............24 F3
Duns Tew Oxon..............57 J3
Dunston Gatesd..............151 G3
Dunston Lincs..............117 H8
Dunston Norfk..............92 F3
Dunston Staffs..............99 L8
Dunstone Devon..............6 E5
Dunstone Devon..............7 G2
Dunsville Donc..............124 F8
Dunswell E R Yk..............126 D4
Dunsyre S Lans..............176 E8
Dunterton Devon..............6 B1
Duntisbourne
    Abbots Gloucs..............55 L6
Duntisbourne
    Rouse Gloucs..............55 M6
Duntish Dorset..............14 D2
Duntocher W Duns..............174 E4
Dunton Bucks..............58 D3

Dunton C Beds..............75 J5
Dunton Norfk..............105 L6
Dunton Bassett Leics..............87 G5
Dunton Green Kent..............32 F2
Duntulm Highld..............218 C6
Dunure S Ayrs..............163 G6
Dunvant Swans..............51 H6
Dunvegan Highld..............208 D5
Dunwich Suffk..............79 K1
Durgan Cnwll..............3 K5
Durham Dur..............151 G6
Durham Cathedral
    Dur..............151 G6
Durham Services
    Dur..............151 H7
Durham Tees Valley
    Airport S on T..............141 J5
Durisdeer D & G..............154 F2
Durisdeermill D & G..............154 F2
Durleigh Somset..............25 L4
Durley Hants..............29 K7
Durley Wilts..............40 E7
Durley Street Hants..............29 K7
Durlock Kent..............35 H3
Durlock Kent..............35 J2
Durness Highld..............228 F3
Durno Abers..............216 D8
Duror Highld..............191 K5
Durran Ag & B..............182 D5
Durrington W Susx..............18 F5
Durrington Wilts..............28 D3
Dursley Gloucs..............39 H2
Dursley Cross Gloucs..............55 G4
Durston Somset..............25 L5
Durweston Dorset..............15 G2
Duston Nhants..............73 K3
Duthil Highld..............203 L1
Dutton Ches W..............112 E5
Duxford Cambs..............76 C5
Duxford Oxon..............57 G7
Duxford IWM Cambs..............76 C5
Dwygyfylchi Conwy..............109 L6
Dwyran IoA..............108 F7
Dyce C Aber..............207 G3
Dyfatty Carmth..............50 F5
Dyffryn Ardudwy
    Gwynd..............95 K7
Dyffryn Cellwen
    Neath..............52 D6
Dyke Lincs..............103 J7
Dyke Moray..............214 B3
Dykehead Angus..............195 K5
Dykehead Angus..............196 C4
Dykehead N Lans..............176 B6
Dykehead Stirlg..............184 D7
Dykelands Abers..............197 H3
Dykends Angus..............195 K5
Dykeside Abers..............216 D5
Dymchurch Kent..............34 E8
Dymock Gloucs..............55 G2
Dyrham S Glos..............39 H5
Dysart Fife..............186 E8
Dyserth Denbgs..............110 E5

## E

Eagland Hill Lancs..............120 F2
Eagle Lincs..............116 E7
Eaglesfield Cumb..............136 E3
Eaglesfield D & G..............155 M7
Eaglesham E Rens..............175 G7
Eagley Bolton..............121 L7
Eakring Notts..............102 A1
Ealand N Linc..............125 J7
Ealing Gt Lon..............44 D4
Eals Nthumb..............149 H4
Eamont Bridge Cumb..............138 D2
Earby Lancs..............122 D2
Earcroft Bl w D..............121 K5
Eardington Shrops..............84 C5
Eardisland Herefs..............69 H3
Eardisley Herefs..............68 F5
Eardiston Shrops..............98 A7
Eardiston Worcs..............70 C2
Earith Cambs..............89 L8
Earlestown St Hel..............112 E3

**Earley** Wokham......42 C6
**Earlham** Norfk......92 E2
**Earlish** Highld......208 F3
**Earls Barton** Nhants......74 C2
**Earls Colne** Essex......61 K3
**Earls Common** Worcs......71 G3
**Earl's Croome** Worcs......70 F6
**Earlsdon** Covtry......86 D7
**Earlsferry** Fife......187 H7
**Earlsfield** Gt Lon......44 E5
**Earlsford** Abers......216 F7
**Earlsheaton** Kirk......123 K6
**Earl Shilton** Leics......86 F4
**Earl Soham** Suffk......78 F2
**Earl Sterndale**
  Derbys......114 C7
**Earlston** Border......167 J2
**Earlston** E Ayrs......163 K3
**Earlswood** Surrey......32 B4
**Earlswood** Warwks......85 K8
**Earnley** W Susx......17 M3
**Earsdon** N Tyne......159 H7
**Earsham** Norfk......93 G5
**Eartham** W Susx......18 C4
**Easby** N York......142 C5
**Easdale** Ag & B......181 L4
**Easebourne** W Susx......30 E6
**Easenhall** Warwks......86 F7
**Eashing** Surrey......30 F3
**Easington** Bucks......58 B6
**Easington** Dur......151 K6
**Easington** E R Yk......127 J6
**Easington** R & Cl......142 F4
**Easington Colliery**
  Dur......151 K6
**Easington Lane**
  Sundld......151 J5
**Easingwold** N York......133 H5
**Eassie and Nevay**
  Angus......196 B7
**East Aberthaw**
  V Glam......37 G6
**East Allington** Devon......7 H6
**East Anstey** Devon......24 D6
**East Ardsley** Leeds......123 K5
**East Ashey** IoW......17 H5
**East Ashling** W Susx......17 M2
**East Ayton** N York......134 F3
**East Barkwith** Lincs......117 K5
**East Barming** Kent......33 J3
**East Barnby** N York......143 G5
**East Barnet** Gt Lon......44 F2
**East Barns** E Loth......178 F3
**East Barsham** Norfk......105 L5
**East Beckham** Norfk......106 E4
**East Bedfont** Gt Lon......43 H5
**East Bergholt** Suffk......78 C7
**East Bilney** Norfk......106 A8
**East Blatchington**
  E Susx......20 A5
**East Boldon** S Tyne......151 J3
**East Boldre** Hants......16 D3
**Eastbourne** Darltn......141 H4
**Eastbourne** E Susx......20 C5
**East Bradenham**
  Norfk......91 L2
**East Brent** Somset......25 M2
**Eastbridge** Suffk......79 J2
**East Bridgford** Notts......102 B4
**East Buckland** Devon......23 L5
**East Budleigh** Devon......12 D5
**Eastbury** C Brad......122 F2
**Eastbury** W Berk......41 G5
**East Butterwick**
  N Linc......116 D1
**Eastby** N York......131 J8
**East Calder** W Loth......176 E5
**East Carleton** Norfk......92 E3
**East Carlton** Leeds......123 J2
**East Carlton** Nhants......88 B5
**East Chaldon** Dorset......14 E5
**East Challow** Oxon......41 G3
**East Charleton**
  Devon......7 H7
**East Chelborough**
  Dorset......14 A2
**East Chiltington**
  E Susx......19 K3

**East Chinnock**
  Somset......26 C8
**East Chisenbury**
  Wilts......28 C2
**Eastchurch** Kent......47 G5
**East Clandon** Surrey......31 H2
**East Claydon** Bucks......58 C3
**East Coker** Somset......26 D8
**Eastcombe** Gloucs......55 K6
**East Compton**
  Somset......26 E3
**East Cornworthy**
  Devon......7 J5
**Eastcote** Gt Lon......43 J3
**Eastcote** Nhants......73 K4
**Eastcote** Solhll......85 L7
**Eastcott** Wilts......28 A1
**East Cottingwith**
  E R Yk......125 G3
**Eastcourt** Wilts......40 E7
**East Cowes** IoW......16 F4
**East Cowick** E R Yk......125 G6
**East Cowton** N York......141 K6
**East Cranmore**
  Somset......27 G3
**East Dean** E Susx......20 B6
**East Dean** Gloucs......54 F4
**East Dean** Hants......28 F6
**East Dean** W Susx......18 B3
**East Drayton** Notts......116 C6
**East Dulwich** Gt Lon......45 G5
**East Dundry** N Som......38 E7
**East Ella** C KuH......126 C5
**Eastend** Essex......46 F2
**East End** Hants......16 D3
**East End** Hants......41 H7
**East End** Kent......33 L6
**East End** Oxon......57 H5
**East End** Somset......26 F3
**Easter Balmoral**
  Abers......205 G6
**Easter Compton**
  S Glos......38 E4
**Easter Dalziel** Highld......213 H4
**Eastergate** W Susx......18 C5
**Easterhouse** C Glas......175 J5
**Easter Howgate**
  Mdloth......177 H5
**Easter Kinkell** Highld......212 E4
**Easter Moniack**
  Highld......212 E5
**Eastern Green** Covtry......86 C7
**Easter Ord** Abers......206 F4
**Easter Pitkierie** Fife......187 J6
**Easter Skeld** Shet......235 c6
**Easter Softlaw**
  Border......168 A3
**Easterton** Wilts......28 A1
**East Everleigh** Wilts......28 D2
**East Farleigh** Kent......33 J3
**East Farndon** Nhants......87 K6
**East Ferry** Lincs......116 D2
**Eastfield** N Lans......176 B5
**Eastfield** N York......135 G3
**East Fortune** E Loth......178 C3
**East Garston** W Berk......41 G5
**Eastgate** Dur......150 B7
**Eastgate** Lincs......103 J8
**Eastgate** Norfk......106 D7
**East Goscote** Leics......87 J2
**East Grafton** Wilts......40 E7
**East Grimstead** Wilts......28 E5
**East Grinstead**
  W Susx......32 D5
**East Guldeford**
  E Susx......21 J2
**East Haddon** Nhants......73 J2
**East Hagbourne**
  Oxon......41 K3
**East Halton** N Linc......126 E6
**East Ham** Gt Lon......45 H4
**Easthampton** Herefs......69 H2
**East Hanney** Oxon......41 H2
**East Hanningfield**
  Essex......61 J7
**East Hardwick**
  Wakefd......124 C6
**East Harling** Norfk......92 B6

**East Harlsey** N York......141 K7
**East Harnham** Wilts......28 C5
**East Harptree** BaNES......26 E1
**East Harting** W Susx......30 D7
**East Hatch** Wilts......27 L5
**East Hatley** Cambs......75 K4
**East Hauxwell** N York......132 B2
**East Haven** Angus......187 J1
**East Heckington**
  Lincs......103 K4
**East Hedleyhope** Dur......150 E6
**East Helmsdale**
  Highld......227 H5
**East Hendred** Oxon......41 J3
**East Heslerton**
  N York......134 E4
**East Hoathly** E Susx......20 B3
**East Holme** Dorset......15 G5
**Easthope** Shrops......83 L4
**East Horrington**
  Somset......26 E3
**East Horsley** Surrey......31 H2
**East Howe** BCP......15 K4
**East Huntspill**
  Somset......25 M3
**East Ilsley** W Berk......41 J4
**Eastington** Devon......11 H3
**Eastington** Gloucs......55 H6
**Eastington** Gloucs......56 C5
**East Keal** Lincs......118 E8
**East Kennett** Wilts......40 C6
**East Keswick** Leeds......124 B2
**East Kilbride** S Lans......175 H7
**East Kirkby** Lincs......118 D8
**East Knighton** Dorset......14 F5
**East Knoyle** Wilts......27 K5
**East Lambrook**
  Somset......26 B7
**Eastlands** D & G......154 E7
**East Langdon** Kent......35 J5
**East Langton** Leics......87 K5
**East Lavant** W Susx......18 B4
**East Lavington**
  W Susx......18 C3
**East Layton** N York......140 E5
**Eastleach Martin**
  Gloucs......56 D6
**Eastleach Turville**
  Gloucs......56 D6
**East Leake** Notts......101 K7
**Eastleigh** Devon......23 H5
**Eastleigh** Hants......29 J7
**East Lexham** Norfk......105 K8
**Eastling** Kent......34 C4
**East Linton** E Loth......178 D3
**East Lockinge** Oxon......41 H3
**East Lound** N Linc......116 C2
**East Lulworth** Dorset......15 G6
**East Lutton** N York......134 E5
**East Lydford** Somset......26 E5
**East Malling** Kent......33 J2
**East Marden** W Susx......30 D8
**East Markham** Notts......116 C6
**East Martin** Hants......28 B7
**East Marton** N York......122 D1
**East Meon** Hants......30 B6
**East Mersea** Essex......62 C5
*East Midlands*
  *Airport* Leics......101 J7
**East Molesey** Surrey......43 J6
**East Morden** Dorset......15 G4
**East Morton** C Brad......123 G3
**East Morton** D & G......154 F3
**East Ness** N York......133 L4
**Eastney** C Port......17 J3
**Eastnor** Herefs......70 D6
**East Norton** Leics......87 L4
**Eastoft** N Linc......125 J7
**East Ogwell** Devon......7 J2
**Easton** Cambs......75 G1
**Easton** Devon......11 G6
**Easton** Dorset......14 D7
**Easton** Hants......29 K5
**Easton** Lincs......102 F7
**Easton** Norfk......92 D2
**Easton** Somset......26 D3
**Easton** Suffk......79 G3

**Easton** Wilts......39 K6
**Easton Grey** Wilts......39 K3
**Easton-in-Gordano**
  N Som......38 D5
**Easton Maudit**
  Nhants......74 C3
**Easton-on-the-Hill**
  Nhants......88 E3
**Easton Royal** Wilts......40 D7
**East Orchard** Dorset......27 J7
**East Peckham** Kent......33 H4
**East Pennard** Somset......26 E4
**East Portlemouth**
  Devon......7 H7
**East Prawle** Devon......7 H8
**East Preston** W Susx......18 E5
**East Putford** Devon......9 K2
**East Quantoxhead**
  Somset......25 H3
**East Rainton** Sundld......151 H5
**East Ravendale**
  NE Lin......118 C2
**East Raynham** Norfk......105 L7
**Eastrea** Cambs......89 K4
**Eastriggs** D & G......147 M2
**East Rigton** Leeds......124 B2
**Eastrington** E R Yk......125 J4
**Eastrop** Swindn......40 D2
**East Rounton** N York......141 K6
**East Rudham** Norfk......105 K6
**East Runton** Norfk......106 E4
**East Ruston** Norfk......107 H6
**Eastry** Kent......35 J4
**East Saltoun** E Loth......178 B5
**East Sheen** Gt Lon......44 D5
**East Shefford** W Berk......41 H5
**East Stockwith** Lincs......116 C3
**East Stoke** Dorset......15 G5
**East Stoke** Notts......102 C3
**East Stour** Dorset......27 J6
**East Stourmouth**
  Kent......35 H3
**East Stowford** Devon......23 K6
**East Stratton** Hants......29 K4
**East Studdal** Kent......35 J5
**East Taphouse** Cnwll......5 J3
**East-the-Water**
  Devon......23 G6
**East Thirston**
  Nthumb......158 F3
**East Tilbury** Thurr......46 B4
**East Tisted** Hants......30 B5
**East Torrington** Lincs......117 J5
**East Tuddenham**
  Norfk......92 C2
**East Tytherley** Hants......28 F5
**East Tytherton** Wilts......39 L5
**East Village** Devon......11 J4
**Eastville** Bristl......38 E5
**Eastville** Lincs......104 C2
**East Walton** Norfk......91 G1
**East Week** Devon......10 F6
**Eastwell** Leics......102 C6
**East Wellow** Hants......28 F7
**East Wemyss** Fife......186 E7
**East Whitburn**
  W Loth......176 C5
**Eastwick** Herts......60 C5
**East Wickham** Gt Lon......45 J5
**East Williamston**
  Pembks......49 J6
**East Winch** Norfk......91 G1
**East Winterslow**
  Wilts......28 E5
**East Wittering**
  W Susx......17 L3
**East Witton** N York......131 L3
**Eastwood** Notts......101 J3
**Eastwood** Sthend......46 D3
**East Woodburn**
  Nthumb......158 A5
**East Woodhay** Hants......41 H7
**East Worldham**
  Hants......30 C4
**East Worthing**
  W Susx......19 G5
**East Wretham** Norfk......91 K5
**Eathorpe** Warwks......72 E2

Eaton Ches E .................. 113 K7
Eaton Ches W .................. 112 E8
Eaton Leics .................. 102 D6
Eaton Norfk .................. 92 E3
Eaton Notts .................. 116 B6
Eaton Oxon .................. 57 H7
Eaton Shrops .................. 83 K5
Eaton Bray C Beds .......... 58 F4
Eaton Constantine
   Shrops .................. 83 L3
Eaton Green C Beds ...... 58 F4
Eaton Hastings Oxon ...... 56 E7
Eaton Mascott
   Shrops .................. 83 K3
Eaton Socon Cambs ...... 75 H3
Eaton upon Tern
   Shrops .................. 98 F7
Ebberston N York .......... 134 D3
Ebbesborne Wake
   Wilts .................. 27 M6
Ebbw Vale Blae G .......... 53 J6
Ebchester Dur .............. 150 D4
Ebford Devon .............. 12 C5
Ebley Gloucs .............. 55 J6
Ebnal Ches W .............. 98 C3
Ebrington Gloucs .......... 71 L6
Ecclaw Border .............. 178 F5
Ecclefechan D & G ...... 155 L7
Eccles Border .............. 168 A2
Eccles Kent .............. 46 B7
Eccles Salfd .............. 113 H2
Ecclesall Sheff .............. 114 F5
Ecclesfield Sheff .......... 115 G3
Eccleshall Staffs .......... 99 J6
Eccleshill C Brad .......... 123 H4
Ecclesmachan
   W Loth .................. 176 E4
Eccles Road Norfk ........ 92 B5
Eccleston Ches W ........ 112 B8
Eccleston Lancs .......... 121 G6
Eccleston St Hel .......... 112 C3
Echt Abers .............. 206 E4
Eckford Border .............. 167 L4
Eckington Derbys ........ 115 H5
Eckington Worcs .......... 71 G6
Ecton Nhants .............. 74 B2
Edale Derbys .............. 114 C4
Eday Ork .................. 234 d4
Eday Airport Ork .......... 234 d4
Edburton W Susx ........ 19 H4
Edderton Highld .......... 222 F4
Eddleston Border ........ 177 H8
Eddlewood S Lans ........ 175 J7
Edenbridge Kent .......... 32 D4
Edenfield Lancs .......... 122 B6
Edenhall Cumb .......... 138 E2
Edenham Lincs .......... 103 H7
Eden Park Gt Lon .......... 45 G6
Eden Project Cnwll ...... 5 G5
Edensor Derbys .......... 114 E7
Edentaggart Ag & B ...... 183 K8
Edenthorpe Donc .......... 115 L1
Edern Gwynd .............. 94 E5
Edgbaston Birm .......... 85 J6
Edgcott Bucks .............. 58 B4
Edgcott Somset .......... 24 D4
Edge Gloucs .............. 55 J6
Edgefield Norfk .......... 106 C5
Edgefield Green
   Norfk .................. 106 D5
Edgerton Kirk .............. 123 H6
Edgeworth Gloucs ........ 55 L6
Edgmond Wrekin .......... 99 G8
Edgton Shrops .............. 83 H6
Edgware Gt Lon .......... 44 D2
Edgworth Bl w D .......... 121 L6
Edinbane Highld .......... 208 E4
Edinburgh C Edin .......... 177 H4
Edinburgh Airport
   C Edin .................. 176 F4
Edinburgh Castle
   C Edin .................. 177 H4
Edinburgh Old &
   New Town C Edin .... 177 H4
Edinburgh Royal
   Botanic Gardens
   C Edin .................. 177 H4

Edinburgh Zoo
   RZSS C Edin .......... 177 G4
Edingale Staffs .............. 86 B2
Edingham D & G .......... 146 E3
Edingley Notts .............. 102 A2
Edingthorpe Norfk ........ 107 G6
Edingthorpe Green
   Norfk .................. 107 G6
Edington Border .......... 179 J7
Edington Nthumb ........ 158 E5
Edington Somset .......... 26 B4
Edington Wilts .............. 27 L2
Edingworth Somset ...... 26 A2
Edithmead Somset ...... 25 L2
Edith Weston Rutlnd ...... 88 D3
Edlesborough Bucks ...... 58 F4
Edlingham Nthumb ...... 169 G7
Edlington Lincs .......... 118 C7
Edmondsham Dorset .... 15 K1
Edmondsley Dur .......... 151 G5
Edmondthorpe Leics .... 102 E8
Edmonton Gt Lon ........ 45 G2
Edmundbyers Dur ........ 150 C5
Ednam Border .............. 167 L2
Edradynate P & K ........ 194 D6
Edrom Border .............. 179 H7
Edstaston Shrops .......... 98 D6
Edstone Warwks .......... 71 L3
Edwalton Notts .......... 101 L5
Edwinstowe Notts ........ 115 L7
Edworth C Beds .......... 75 J6
Edwyn Ralph Herefs ...... 70 B3
Edzell Angus .............. 196 F3
Edzell Woods Abers ...... 197 G3
Efail-fach Neath .......... 36 B2
Efail Isaf Rhondd .......... 37 G4
Efailnewydd Gwynd ...... 94 F5
Efailwen Carmth .......... 49 K3
Efenechtyd Denbgs ...... 97 H2
Effgill D & G .............. 156 B4
Effingham Surrey .......... 31 J2
Egerton Bolton .......... 121 K7
Egerton Kent .............. 34 B5
Eggborough N York ...... 124 E5
Eggbuckland C Plym .... 6 D4
Eggesford Devon .......... 11 G3
Eggington C Beds ........ 58 F3
Egginton Derbys .......... 100 E6
Eggleston Dur .............. 140 C3
Egham Surrey .............. 43 G6
Egleton Rutlnd .............. 88 C3
Eglingham Nthumb ...... 169 G5
Egloshayle Cnwll .......... 4 F2
Egloskerry Cnwll .......... 9 H7
Eglwysbach Conwy ...... 109 M7
Eglwys Cross
   Wrexhm .................. 98 C4
Eglwyswrw Pembks ...... 65 G3
Egmanton Notts .......... 116 B7
Egremont Cumb .......... 136 D5
Egremont Wirral .......... 111 K3
Egton N York .............. 143 G6
Egton Bridge N York .... 143 G6
Egypt Bucks .............. 42 F3
Eigg Highld .............. 199 G7
Eight Ash Green
   Essex .................. 61 M3
Eilanreach Highld ........ 200 C2
Eilean Donan Castle
   Highld .................. 200 D1
Eisgein W Isls .............. 232 f3
Eishken W Isls .............. 232 f3
Elan Valley Powys .......... 67 J2
Elan Village Powys ........ 67 K2
Elberton S Glos .......... 38 E3
Elburton C Plym .......... 6 D5
Elcombe Swindn .......... 40 C4
Eldersfield Worcs .......... 55 H2
Elderslie Rens .............. 174 E5
Eldon Dur .................. 141 G2
Elerch Cerdgn .............. 80 F6
Elfhill Abers .............. 206 F7
Elford Staffs .............. 85 L2
Elgin Moray .............. 214 F2
Elgol Highld .............. 199 H3
Elham Kent .............. 35 G6
Elie Fife .................. 187 H7
Elim IoA .................. 108 D4

Eling Hants .............. 29 G8
Elkesley Notts .............. 116 B6
Elkstone Gloucs .......... 55 L5
Ella Abers .............. 216 C3
Ellacombe Torbay .......... 7 L3
Elland Calder .............. 123 G6
Ellary Ag & B .............. 172 C3
Ellastone Staffs .......... 100 C4
Ellel Lancs .............. 129 K7
Ellemford Border ........ 178 F6
Ellenabeich Ag & B ...... 181 L4
Ellenhall Staffs .......... 99 J7
Ellen's Green Surrey ...... 31 H4
Ellerbeck N York .......... 141 K7
Ellerby N York .............. 143 G4
Ellerdine Heath
   Wrekin .................. 98 F7
Elleric Ag & B .............. 191 K6
Ellerker E R Yk .......... 125 L5
Ellerton E R Yk .......... 125 G3
Ellerton N York .......... 141 G4
Ellesborough Bucks ...... 58 D6
Ellesmere Shrops .......... 98 B5
Ellesmere Port
   Ches W .................. 111 L6
Ellingham Norfk .......... 93 H5
Ellingham Nthumb ...... 169 H4
Ellingstring N York ...... 132 B3
Ellington Cambs .......... 75 H1
Ellington Nthumb ........ 159 G4
Elliots Green Somset .... 27 J3
Ellisfield Hants .......... 29 M3
Ellishader Highld ........ 209 H2
Ellistown Leics .......... 86 E2
Ellon Abers .............. 217 H7
Ellonby Cumb .............. 148 D7
Elloughton E R Yk ...... 125 L5
Ellwood Gloucs .......... 54 E6
Elm Cambs .............. 90 C3
Elmbridge Worcs .......... 70 F2
Elmdon Essex .............. 76 C6
Elmdon Solhll .............. 85 L6
Elmer W Susx .............. 18 D5
Elmers End Gt Lon ...... 45 G6
Elmer's Green Lancs .... 112 D1
Elmesthorpe Leics ...... 86 F4
Elmhurst Staffs .......... 85 K2
Elmley Castle Worcs .... 71 H6
Elmley Lovett Worcs .... 70 F1
Elmore Gloucs .......... 55 H5
Elmore Back Gloucs .... 55 H5
Elm Park Gt Lon .......... 45 K3
Elmsett Suffk .............. 78 C5
Elmstead Market
   Essex .................. 62 C3
Elmsted Kent .............. 34 F5
Elmstone Kent .......... 35 H3
Elmstone
   Hardwicke Gloucs .... 55 K3
Elmswell E R Yk .......... 134 F7
Elmswell Suffk .......... 78 B2
Elmton Derbys .......... 115 J6
Elphin Highld .............. 224 F6
Elphinstone E Loth ...... 177 K4
Elrick Abers .............. 206 F4
Elrig D & G .............. 145 G5
Elrington Nthumb ...... 149 L3
Elsdon Nthumb .......... 158 B4
Elsenham Essex .......... 60 E3
Elsfield Oxon .............. 57 K6
Elsham N Linc .......... 126 C7
Elsing Norfk .............. 92 C1
Elslack N York .......... 122 D2
Elson Hants .............. 17 H3
Elsrickle S Lans .......... 165 K2
Elstead Surrey .......... 30 E3
Elsted W Susx .......... 30 D7
Elsthorpe Lincs .......... 103 H7
Elston Notts .............. 102 C3
Elstow Bed .............. 74 F5
Elstree Herts .............. 44 D2
Elstronwick E R Yk ...... 126 F4
Elswick Lancs .......... 120 F3
Elswick N u Ty .......... 151 G3
Elsworth Cambs .......... 75 K2
Elterwater Cumb ........ 137 K6
Eltham Gt Lon .......... 45 H5
Eltisley Cambs .......... 75 J3

Elton Cambs .............. 88 F5
Elton Ches W .............. 112 C6
Elton Derbys .............. 100 E1
Elton Herefs .............. 69 J1
Elton S on T .............. 141 J4
Elton-on-the-Hill
   Notts .................. 102 C5
Eltringham Nthumb .... 150 D3
Elvanfoot S Lans .......... 165 J6
Elvaston Derbys .......... 101 H6
Elveden Suffk .............. 91 J7
Elvetham Heath
   Hants .................. 30 D1
Elvington E Loth .......... 178 A4
Elvington C York .......... 125 G2
Elvington Kent .......... 35 H5
Elwick Hartpl .............. 141 K2
Elworth Ches E .......... 99 H1
Elworthy Somset .......... 25 G4
Ely Cambs .............. 90 D7
Ely Cardif .............. 37 H5
Emberton M Keyn ...... 74 C5
Embleton Cumb .......... 137 G2
Embleton Nthumb ...... 169 J5
Embo Highld .............. 223 H3
Emborough Somset ...... 26 E2
Embo Street Highld ...... 223 H3
Embsay N York .......... 131 J8
Emery Down Hants .... 16 C2
Emley Kirk .............. 123 K7
Emmington Oxon ........ 58 C2
Emneth Norfk .............. 90 C3
Emneth Hungate
   Norfk .................. 90 D3
Empingham Rutlnd ...... 88 D2
Empshott Hants .......... 30 C5
Emsworth Hants .......... 17 K2
Enborne W Berk .......... 41 H7
Enborne Row W Berk .... 41 H7
Enderby Leics .............. 87 G4
Endmoor Cumb .......... 129 L3
Endon Staffs .............. 99 L2
Endon Bank Staffs ...... 99 L2
Enfield Gt Lon .............. 60 B7
Enfield Lock Gt Lon ...... 60 B7
Enfield Wash Gt Lon .... 60 B7
Enford Wilts .............. 28 C2
Engine Common
   S Glos .................. 39 G4
Englefield W Berk ........ 41 L6
Englefield Green
   Surrey .................. 43 G6
English Bicknor
   Gloucs .................. 54 E5
Englishcombe BaNES .... 39 G7
English Frankton
   Shrops .................. 98 C6
Enham Alamein
   Hants .................. 29 G2
Enmore Somset .......... 25 K4
Enmore Green
   Dorset .................. 27 J6
Ennerdale Bridge
   Cumb .................. 136 E4
Enochdhu P & K ........ 195 J2
Ensay Ag & B .............. 189 J6
Ensbury BCP .............. 15 K3
Ensdon Shrops .......... 83 H1
Enstone Oxon .......... 57 G3
Enterkinfoot D & G .... 154 E2
Enville Staffs .............. 84 E6
Eochar W Isls .............. 233 b7
Eòlaigearraidh
   W Isls .................. 233 b9
Eoligarry W Isls .......... 233 b9
Epney Gloucs .......... 55 H5
Epperstone Notts ...... 102 A3
Epping Essex .............. 60 D7
Epping Green Essex .... 60 C6
Epping Upland Essex .... 60 C6
Eppleby N York .......... 140 F5
Epsom Surrey .............. 44 E7
Epwell Oxon .............. 72 D6
Epworth N Linc .......... 116 C2
Erbistock Wrexhm ...... 97 M4
Erdington Birm .......... 85 K5
Eridge Green E Susx .... 32 F6
Erines Ag & B .............. 172 E4

Eriska Ag & B ............... 191 H7
Eriskay W Isls .............. 233 c9
Eriswell Suffk ............... 91 G7
Erith Gt Lon ................. 45 K4
Erlestoke Wilts ............. 27 L2
Ermington Devon .......... 6 F5
Erpingham Norfk ....... 106 E6
Errogie Highld ............ 202 E2
Errol P & K ................. 186 D3
Erskine Rens .............. 174 E4
Erskine Bridge Rens ... 174 E4
Ervie D & G ................ 144 B2
Erwarton Suffk ............. 78 F7
Erwood Powys ............. 68 C6
Eryholme N York ........ 141 H5
Eryrys Denbgs .............. 97 J2
Escomb Dur ............... 140 F2
Escrick N York ........... 124 F2
Esgairgeiliog Powys .... 81 G3
Esh Dur ..................... 150 F6
Esher Surrey ................ 43 J7
Eshott Nthumb ............ 158 F3
Esh Winning Dur ........ 150 F6
Eskadale Highld ......... 212 C6
Eskbank Mdloth .......... 177 J5
Eskdale Green Cumb .. 137 G6
Eskdalemuir D & G .... 155 M3
Esprick Lancs ............ 120 E3
Essendine Rutlnd ......... 88 F2
Essendon Herts ............ 59 L6
Essich Highld ............. 213 G6
Essington Staffs .......... 85 G3
Esslemont Abers ........ 217 H7
Eston R & Cl .............. 142 C4
Etal Nthumb ............... 168 D2
Etchilhampton Wilts ..... 40 B7
Etchingham E Susx ....... 33 J7
Etchinghill Kent ........... 34 F6
Etchinghill Staffs ........ 100 B8
Eton W & M ................. 42 F5
Eton Wick W & M ......... 42 F5
Etruria C Stke .............. 99 K3
Etteridge Highld ......... 203 G6
Ettersgill Dur ............. 139 K2
Ettiley Heath Ches E ..... 99 G1
Ettingshall Wolves ........ 85 G4
Ettington Warwks ......... 72 C5
Etton C Pete ................ 89 G3
Etton E R Yk .............. 126 B2
Ettrick Border ............ 166 D6
Ettrickbridge Border .. 166 F4
Ettrickhill Border ...... 166 C6
Etwall Derbys ............ 100 F6
Euston Suffk ................ 91 K7
Euxton Lancs ............. 121 H6
Evanton Highld .......... 212 F2
Evedon Lincs ............. 103 H3
Evelix Highld ............. 223 G4
Evenjobb Powys .......... 68 F3
Evenley Nhants ............ 73 H7
Evenlode Gloucs .......... 56 E3
Evenwood Dur ............ 140 E3
Evercreech Somset ...... 26 F4
Everingham E R Yk .... 125 J3
Everleigh Wilts ............ 28 D2
Eversholt C Beds .......... 59 G2
Evershot Dorset ........... 14 B2
Eversley Hants ............. 42 C7
Eversley Cross Hants .... 42 C7
Everton C Beds ............ 75 H4
Everton Hants .............. 16 C4
Everton Lpool ............ 111 K3
Everton Notts ............. 116 B4
Evertown D & G ......... 156 C6
Evesbatch Herefs ......... 70 C5
Evesham Worcs ........... 71 J5
Evington C Leic ........... 87 J3
Ewden Village Sheff ... 114 F3
Ewell Surrey ................ 44 E7
Ewell Minnis Kent ....... 35 H6
Ewelme Oxon .............. 41 M3
Ewen Gloucs ................ 40 A2
Ewenny V Glam ........... 36 D5
Ewerby Lincs ............. 103 J3
Ewhurst Surrey ............ 31 H4
Ewhurst Green
E Susx ..................... 20 F2

Ewhurst Green
Surrey ...................... 31 H4
Ewloe Flints ............... 111 J7
Ewood Bl w D ............ 121 K5
Eworthy Devon ............ 10 C6
Ewshot Hants .............. 30 D2
Ewyas Harold Herefs ... 54 B3
Exbourne Devon .......... 10 E4
Exbury Hants ............... 16 E3
Exebridge Somset ........ 24 E6
Exelby N York ............ 132 D3
Exeter Devon ............... 11 L6
Exeter Airport Devon ... 12 C4
Exeter Services
Devon ...................... 12 C4
Exford Somset ............. 24 D4
Exfordsgreen Shrops .... 83 J3
Exhall Warwks ............. 71 K4
Exhall Warwks ............. 86 D6
Exlade Street Oxon ...... 42 A4
Exminster Devon .......... 12 B5
Exmoor National
Park ......................... 24 D4
Exmouth Devon ........... 12 C6
Exning Suffk ................ 76 E2
Exton Devon ................ 12 C5
Exton Hants ................. 29 L7
Exton Rutlnd ............... 88 D2
Exton Somset .............. 24 E5
Exwick Devon .............. 11 K6
Eyam Derbys .............. 114 E6
Eydon Nhants .............. 73 G4
Eye C Pete .................. 89 J3
Eye Herefs ................... 69 J2
Eye Suffk .................... 92 D8
Eyemouth Border ...... 179 K5
Eyeworth C Beds .......... 75 J5
Eyhorne Street Kent ..... 33 L3
Eyke Suffk ................... 79 G4
Eynesbury Cambs ........ 75 H3
Eynsford Kent .............. 45 K6
Eynsham Oxon ............ 57 H6
Eype Dorset ................ 13 L4
Eyre Highld ............... 208 F4
Eythorne Kent ............. 35 H5
Eyton Herefs ............... 69 J3
Eyton Shrops .............. 98 C7
Eyton on Severn
Shrops ...................... 83 L3
Eyton upon the
Weald Moors
Wrekin ..................... 84 B1

**F**

Faccombe Hants .......... 41 H8
Faceby N York ........... 141 L6
Fachwen Powys ........... 82 B1
Faddiley Ches E ........... 98 E3
Fadmoor N York ........ 133 K2
Faerdre Swans ............. 51 K5
Faifley W Duns .......... 174 F4
Failand N Som ............. 38 D6
Failford S Ayrs ........... 163 L4
Failsworth Oldham ..... 113 K2
Fairbourne Gwynd ....... 80 E2
Fairburn N York ......... 124 D5
Fairfield Derbys ......... 114 B6
Fairfield Worcs ............ 85 G7
Fairford Gloucs ........... 56 D7
Fairgirth D & G .......... 146 F4
Fair Green Norfk .......... 90 F1
Fairhaven Lancs ......... 120 D5
Fair Isle Shet ............. 235 e7
Fair Isle Airport Shet .. 235 e7
Fairlands Surrey .......... 30 F2
Fairlie N Ayrs ............ 173 L7
Fairlight E Susx ........... 21 G4
Fairmile Devon ............ 12 E3
Fairmile Surrey ............ 43 J7
Fairmilehead C Edin ... 177 H5
Fairnilee Border ........ 167 G3
Fair Oak Hants ............ 29 J7
Fairoak Staffs .............. 99 H6
Fair Oak Green
Hants ....................... 42 A7

Fairseat Kent ............... 45 L7
Fairstead Essex ............ 61 J5
Fairstead Norfk .......... 105 G8
Fairwarp E Susx ........... 32 E7
Fairwater Cardif .......... 37 H5
Fairy Cross Devon ....... 22 F6
Fakenham Norfk ........ 105 L6
Fakenham Magna
Suffk ........................ 91 K7
Fala Mdloth ............... 177 L6
Fala Dam Mdloth ....... 177 L6
Faldingworth Lincs ..... 117 H5
Faldouët Jersey .......... 236 e7
Falfield S Glos ............. 39 G2
Falkenham Suffk .......... 79 G6
Falkirk Falk ............... 176 B3
Falkirk Wheel Falk .... 176 A3
Falkland Fife ............. 186 D6
Fallburn S Lans .......... 165 J2
Fallin Stirlg ............... 185 H8
Fallodon Nthumb ....... 169 J5
Fallowfield Manch ..... 113 J3
Fallowfield Nthumb ... 150 B2
Falmer E Susx ............. 19 K4
Falmouth Cnwll ............ 3 K5
Falnash Border .......... 156 D2
Falsgrave N York ....... 134 F2
Falstone Nthumb ....... 157 J5
Fanagmore Highld ..... 228 B5
Fancott C Beds ............ 59 G3
Fanellan Highld ......... 212 D5
Fangdale Beck
N York ..................... 142 C7
Fangfoss E R Yk ........ 134 B8
Fanmore Ag & B ........ 189 K7
Fannich Lodge
Highld ..................... 211 K2
Fans Border ............... 167 J2
Far Bletchley M Keyn ... 74 C7
Farcet Cambs .............. 89 H5
Far Cotton Nhants ....... 73 L3
Fareham Hants ............ 17 H2
Farewell Staffs ............ 85 J2
Faringdon Oxon .......... 40 F2
Farington Lancs ......... 121 H5
Farlam Cumb ............. 148 F3
Farleigh N Som ........... 38 D6
Farleigh Surrey ........... 32 C2
Farleigh
Hungerford
Somset ..................... 39 J8
Farleigh Wallop
Hants ....................... 29 L3
Farlesthorpe Lincs .... 119 G6
Farleton Cumb .......... 129 L4
Farleton Lancs .......... 130 B6
Farley Staffs .............. 100 B4
Farley Wilts ................ 28 E5
Farley Green Surrey ..... 31 H3
Farley Hill Wokham ..... 42 C7
Farleys End Gloucs ...... 55 H5
Farlington C Port ......... 17 J2
Farlington N York ...... 133 J6
Farlow Shrops ............. 84 B7
Farmborough BaNES ... 38 F7
Farmcote Gloucs .......... 56 B3
Farmington Gloucs ...... 56 C5
Farmoor Oxon ............ 57 J6
Far Moor Wigan ........ 112 D2
Farmtown Moray ....... 215 L4
Farnborough Gt Lon .... 45 H7
Farnborough Hants ...... 30 E2
Farnborough W Berk .... 41 H4
Farnborough Warwks ... 72 E5
Farnborough Park
Hants ....................... 30 E1
Farncombe Surrey ....... 31 G3
Farndish Bed .............. 74 D2
Farndon Ches W .......... 98 B2
Farndon Notts ........... 102 C3
Farne Islands
Nthumb .................. 169 J2
Farnell Angus ............ 197 G5
Farnham Dorset .......... 27 L7
Farnham Essex ............ 60 D3
Farnham N York ........ 132 E7
Farnham Suffk ............ 79 H3
Farnham Surrey ........... 30 D3

Farnham Common
Bucks ....................... 42 F4
Farnham Royal
Bucks ....................... 42 F4
Farningham Kent ......... 45 K6
Farnley Leeds ............ 123 K4
Farnley N York .......... 123 J2
Farnley Tyas Kirk ...... 123 H7
Farnsfield Notts ......... 101 M2
Farnworth Bolton ...... 113 G3
Farnworth Halton ...... 112 D4
Far Oakridge Gloucs .... 55 L7
Farr Highld ................ 203 K5
Farr Highld ................ 213 G7
Farr Highld ................ 229 L3
Farraline Highld ........ 202 E2
Farringdon Devon ....... 12 C4
Farrington Gurney
BaNES ...................... 26 F1
Far Sawrey Cumb ...... 137 K7
Farsley Leeds ............ 123 J4
Farthinghoe Nhants ..... 73 G6
Farthingstone
Nhants ..................... 73 H4
Fartown Kirk ............. 123 H6
Fasnacloich Ag & B ... 191 K6
Fasnakyle Highld ....... 211 L8
Fassfern Highld ......... 191 K2
Fatfield Sundld .......... 151 H4
Fauldhouse W Loth ... 176 C6
Faulkbourne Essex ...... 61 J5
Faulkland Somset ........ 27 H1
Fauls Shrops ............... 98 E6
Faversham Kent .......... 34 D3
Fawdington N York .... 132 F5
Fawdon N u Ty .......... 151 G2
Fawkham Green
Kent ......................... 45 L6
Fawler Oxon ............... 57 G4
Fawley Bucks ............. 42 C3
Fawley Hants .............. 16 F2
Fawley W Berk ........... 41 H4
Faxfleet E R Yk ......... 125 K5
Faygate W Susx .......... 31 K4
Fazakerley Lpool ....... 111 K3
Fazeley Staffs ............. 85 L3
Fearby N York ........... 132 B4
Fearn Highld ............. 223 H6
Fearnan P & K ........... 194 B7
Fearnbeg Highld ........ 210 B3
Fearnmore Highld ..... 209 L3
Fearnoch Ag & B ....... 172 F3
Featherstone Staffs ..... 85 G3
Featherstone
Wakefd .................... 124 C6
Feckenham Worcs ....... 71 H3
Feering Essex .............. 61 L4
Feetham N York ........ 140 C7
Felbridge Surrey ......... 32 C5
Felbrigg Norfk .......... 106 E5
Felcourt Surrey ........... 32 C5
Felindre Carmth .......... 51 G2
Felindre Carmth .......... 65 K6
Felindre Powys ........... 82 D7
Felindre Swans ........... 51 J5
Felindre Farchog
Pembks ..................... 64 F6
Felinfoel Carmth ......... 51 G5
Felingwmisaf Carmth .. 51 G2
Felingwmuchaf
Carmth ..................... 51 G1
Felixkirk N York ........ 133 G4
Felixstowe Suffk ......... 79 G7
Felling Gatesd ........... 151 G3
Felmersham Bed ......... 74 E3
Felmingham Norfk .... 106 F6
Felpham W Susx ......... 18 C5
Felsham Suffk ............. 77 L3
Felsted Essex .............. 61 G4
Feltham Gt Lon ........... 43 J5
Felthamhill Surrey ...... 43 H4
Felthorpe Norfk ........ 106 E8
Felton Herefs .............. 69 L5
Felton N Som .............. 38 D7
Felton Nthumb .......... 158 F3
Felton Butler Shrops ... 98 B8
Feltwell Norfk ............ 91 G5
Fence Lancs .............. 122 C3

Fence Rothm.................. 115 H4
Fencott Oxon..................57 L5
Fendike Corner
  Lincs.................. 104 D1
Fen Ditton Cambs..........76 C3
Fen Drayton Cambs......75 L2
Feniscliffe Bl w D...... 121 K5
Feniscowles Bl w D...... 121 J5
Feniton Devon...............12 E3
Feniton Court Devon....12 E3
Fenn Green Shrops........84 D6
Fenn Street Medway......46 D5
Fenny Bentley
  Derbys.................. 100 D3
Fenny Bridges Devon....12 E3
Fenny Compton
  Warwks.................72 E4
Fenny Drayton Leics......86 D4
Fenstanton Cambs........75 K2
Fen Street Norfk...........92 B4
Fenton Cambs...............89 K7
Fenton Cumb.............. 118 E4
Fenton Lincs.............. 102 E3
Fenton Lincs.............. 116 D6
Fenton Notts.............. 116 C5
Fenton Nthumb.......... 168 E3
Fenton Barns E Loth.... 178 B3
Fenwick Donc.............. 124 F7
Fenwick E Ayrs.......... 163 L2
Fenwick Nthumb........ 158 D7
Fenwick Nthumb........ 169 G2
Feock Cnwll.................... 4 C7
Feolin Ferry Ag & B.... 171 H4
Fergushill N Ayrs........ 163 J2
Ferinquarrie Highld.... 208 B4
Fermain Bay Guern.... 236 d3
Fern Angus.................. 196 D4
Ferndale Rhondd..........36 F2
Ferndown Dorset..........15 K3
Ferness Highld.......... 214 B5
Fernham Oxon...............40 F3
Fernhill Heath Worcs....70 F3
Fernhurst W Susx.........30 E5
Fernie Fife.................. 186 E4
Ferniegair S Lans........ 175 K7
Fernilea Highld.......... 208 F7
Fernilee Derbys.......... 114 A5
Fernwood Notts.......... 102 D3
Ferrensby N York........ 132 E7
Ferrindonald Highld.... 199 K4
Ferring W Susx.............18 F5
Ferrybridge
  Services Wakefd... 124 D6
Ferryden Angus.......... 197 H5
Ferryhill Dur.............. 141 H2
Ferryhill Station Dur... 141 H2
Ferry Point Highld...... 223 G4
Ferryside Carmth..........50 D4
Fersfield Norfk.............92 C6
Fersit Highld.............. 192 F2
Feshiebridge Highld.... 203 K4
Fetcham Surrey............31 J1
Fetlar Shet.................. 235 e2
Fetterangus Abers...... 217 J4
Fettercairn Abers...... 197 G2
Fewston N York.......... 132 B8
Ffairfach Carmth..........51 J2
Ffair Rhos Cerdgn........67 G2
Ffarmers Carmth..........66 E5
Ffestiniog Railway
  Gwynd.....................95 K5
Fforest Carmth.............51 H5
Ffostrasol Cerdgn........65 L5
Ffrith Flints.................97 L2
Ffynnongroyw Flints.. 110 F5
Fickleshole Surrey........32 C2
Fiddington Somset......25 K4
Fiddleford Dorset..........27 J8
Fiddlers Green Cnwll.....4 C5
Field Staffs................ 100 A5
Field Dalling Norfk...... 106 B5
Field Head Leics..........86 F2
Fifehead Magdalen
  Dorset.....................27 H6
Fifehead Neville
  Dorset.....................14 E1
Fifehead St Quintin
  Dorset.....................14 E1

Fife Keith Moray.......... 215 J4
Fifield Oxon..................56 E4
Fifield W & B................42 E5
Figheldean Wilts..........28 D3
Filby Norfk....................93 K2
Filey N York................ 135 H4
Filgrave M Keyn...........74 C5
Filkins Oxon..................56 E6
Filleigh Devon...............23 K5
Fillingham Lincs........ 116 F4
Fillongley Warwks........86 C6
Filton S Glos.................38 E5
Fimber E R Yk.............. 134 D7
Finavon Angus.......... 196 D5
Fincham Norfk.............91 G3
Finchampstead
  Wokham.................42 D7
Fincharn Ag & B........ 182 C6
Finchdean Hants..........30 C8
Finchingfield Essex......61 G2
Finchley Gt Lon............44 F2
Findern Derbys.......... 100 F6
Findhorn Moray........ 214 C2
Findhorn Bridge
  Highld.................. 213 J8
Findochty Moray........ 215 K2
Findo Gask P & K........ 185 L4
Findon Abers.............. 207 H6
Findon W Susx..............18 F4
Findon Mains Highld.. 212 F3
Findon Valley W Susx..18 F4
Findrack House
  Abers.................. 206 B4
Finedon Nhants.......... 88 D8
Fingask P & K.............. 186 C4
Fingest Bucks...............42 C3
Finghall N York.......... 132 B2
Fingland D & G............ 164 E6
Finglesham Kent..........35 J4
Fingringhoe Essex........62 B4
Finlarig Stirlg............ 184 C1
Finmere Oxon...............57 M2
Finnart P & K.............. 193 H5
Finningham Suffk........78 C1
Finningley Donc........ 116 A2
Finsbay W Isls............ 232 d5
Finstall Worcs...............71 H1
Finsthwaite Cumb...... 129 H2
Finstock Oxon...............57 G5
Finstown Ork.............. 234 b6
Fintry Abers.............. 216 E4
Fintry Stirlg................ 175 H2
Finzean Abers............ 206 B6
Fionnphort Ag & B.... 180 D3
Fionnsbhagh W Isls... 232 d5
Firbank Cumb............ 130 C2
Firbeck Rothm............ 115 K4
Firby N York.............. 132 D3
Firby N York.............. 134 B6
Firle E Susx..................19 M4
Firsby Lincs................ 118 F8
Fir Tree Dur................ 150 E2
Fishbourne IoW...........17 G4
Fishbourne W Susx......18 A5
Fishbourne Roman
  Palace W Susx........18 A5
Fishburn Dur.............. 141 J2
Fishcross Clacks........ 185 J7
Fisherford Abers........ 216 C2
Fisherrow E Loth........ 177 K4
Fisher's Pond Hants.....29 J7
Fisherton Highld........ 213 H4
Fisherton S Ayrs........ 163 H6
Fisherton de la
  Mere Wilts...............27 M4
Fishery W & M..............42 E4
Fishguard Pembks........64 D6
Fishnish Pier Ag & B... 190 D7
Fishponds Bristl..........38 F5
Fishtoft Lincs............ 104 B4
Fishtoft Drove Lincs.. 104 A3
Fishwick Lancs.......... 121 H4
Fiskavaig Highld........ 208 E7
Fiskerton Lincs.......... 117 H6
Fiskerton Notts.......... 102 C3
Fittleton Wilts.............28 D2

Fittleworth W Susx.......18 D2
Fitz Shrops...................98 C8
Fitzhead Somset..........25 H5
Fitzwilliam Wakefd.... 124 C7
Five Ash Down
  E Susx.....................19 M2
Five Ashes E Susx........32 F7
Fivehead Somset..........26 A4
Fivelanes Cnwll.............9 G8
Five Oak Green Kent....33 H4
Five Oaks Jersey........ 236 d7
Five Oaks W Susx..........31 H5
Five Roads Carmth........50 F4
Flackwell Heath
  Bucks.....................42 E3
Fladbury Worcs.............71 H5
Fladdabister Shet...... 235 c6
Flagg Derbys.............. 114 C7
Flamborough E R Yk... 135 K5
Flamborough Head
  E R Yk.................. 135 K5
Flamingo Land
  Theme Park
  N York.................. 134 B4
Flamstead Herts..........59 H5
Flamstead End Herts....60 B7
Flansham W Susx.........18 C5
Flanshaw Wakefd...... 123 L6
Flasby N York.............. 131 H7
Flash Staffs................ 114 A7
Flashader Highld........ 208 E4
Flaunden Herts............59 G7
Flawborough Notts.... 102 C4
Flawith N York............ 133 G6
Flax Bourton N Som.....38 D6
Flaxby N York.............. 132 F7
Flaxley Gloucs..............55 G5
Flaxpool Somset..........25 H4
Flaxton N York............ 133 K6
Fleckney Leics..............87 J5
Flecknoe Warwks.........73 G2
Fledborough Notts.... 116 D6
Fleet Dorset.................14 C6
Fleet Hants..................30 D2
Fleet Lincs................ 104 C7
Fleet Hargate Lincs... 104 C7
Fleet Services Hants....30 D1
Fleetwood Lancs........ 120 D2
Fleggburgh Norfk........93 J2
Flemingston V Glam....36 F6
Flemington S Lans...... 175 H6
Flempton Suffk............77 J1
Fletchertown Cumb... 147 L6
Fletching E Susx..........19 L2
Flexbury Cnwll...............9 G4
Flexford Surrey............30 F2
Flimby Cumb.............. 147 H7
Flimwell E Susx............33 J6
Flint Flints................ 111 H6
Flintham Notts.......... 102 C4
Flinton E R Yk............ 126 F4
Flitcham Norfk.......... 105 H6
Flitch Green Essex........61 G4
Flitton C Beds..............74 F7
Flitwick C Beds............74 F7
Flixborough N Linc.... 125 K7
Flixborough Stather
  N Linc.................. 125 K7
Flixton N York.......... 135 G4
Flixton Suffk.................93 G6
Flixton Traffd............ 113 H3
Flockton Kirk............ 123 J7
Flockton Green Kirk.. 123 K7
Flodigarry Highld...... 218 C6
Flookburgh Cumb...... 129 H4
Flordon Norfk..............92 E4
Flore Nhants................73 J3
Flowton Suffk...............78 C5
Flushing Cnwll...............3 L4
Fluxton Devon.............12 E4
Flyford Flavell Worcs...71 H4
Fobbing Thurr..............46 B4
Fochabers Moray...... 215 H3
Fochriw Caerph...........53 H6
Fockerby N Linc........ 125 K6
Foddington Somset.....26 E5
Foel Powys...................81 L2
Foggathorpe E R Yk... 125 H3

Fogo Border................ 179 G8
Fogwatt Moray.......... 214 F3
Foindle Highld.......... 228 B5
Folda Angus.............. 195 J4
Fole Staffs................ 100 B5
Foleshill Covtry...........86 D6
Folke Dorset.................26 F8
Folkestone Kent...........35 H7
Folkingham Lincs...... 103 H5
Folkington E Susx.........20 B5
Folksworth Cambs.......89 G5
Folkton N York.......... 135 G4
Folla Rule Abers........ 216 D7
Follifoot N York.......... 132 E8
Folly Gate Devon.........10 E5
Fonthill Bishop Wilts...27 L5
Fonthill Gifford Wilts...27 L5
Fontmell Magna
  Dorset.....................27 K7
Fontmell Parva
  Dorset.....................27 J8
Fontwell W Susx..........18 C4
Foolow Derbys.......... 114 D6
Forbestown Abers...... 205 H3
Forcett N York............ 140 F5
Ford Ag & B................ 182 C6
Ford Bucks...................58 C6
Ford Derbys.............. 115 H5
Ford Devon...................22 F6
Ford Gloucs..................56 C3
Ford Nthumb.............. 168 E2
Ford Somset.................25 H5
Ford Staffs................ 100 B2
Ford W Susx..................18 D5
Ford Wilts.....................39 J5
Fordcombe Kent...........32 F5
Fordell Fife................ 177 G2
Forden Powys...............82 E4
Ford End Essex............61 G5
Forder Green Devon.......7 H3
Fordham Cambs...........76 F1
Fordham Essex.............61 L3
Fordham Norfk.............90 E4
Fordingbridge Hants....28 D8
Fordon E R Yk............ 135 G4
Fordoun Abers............ 197 J2
Fordstreet Essex..........61 L3
Ford Street Somset......25 J7
Fordwich Kent..............35 G3
Fordyce Abers............ 216 B2
Forebridge Staffs.........99 L7
Forest Guern.............. 236 c4
Forest Chapel Ches E.. 113 L6
Forest Gate Gt Lon......45 H3
Forest Green Surrey....31 J3
Forest Hall N Tyne...... 151 G2
Forest Hill Gt Lon.........45 G5
Forest Hill Oxon...........57 L6
Forest Lane Head
  N York.................. 132 E7
Forest Mill Clacks...... 185 K8
Forest of Bowland
  Lancs.................. 130 C8
Forest of Dean
  Gloucs...................54 F5
Forest Row E Susx.......32 D6
Forestside W Susx........30 C8
Forest Town Notts...... 101 K1
Forfar Angus.............. 196 D6
Forgandenny P & K.... 186 A4
Forge Hammer Torfn....37 L2
Forgie Moray............ 215 J4
Forgieside Moray...... 215 J4
Forgue Abers.............. 216 B5
Formby Sefton.......... 111 J1
Forncett End Norfk......92 D5
Forncett St Mary
  Norfk.....................92 E5
Forncett St Peter
  Norfk.....................92 E5
Fornham All Saints
  Suffk.....................77 J2
Fornham St Martin
  Suffk.....................77 J2
Fornighty Highld........ 213 L4
Forres Moray............ 214 C3
Forsbrook Staffs.........99 L4
Forse Highld.............. 227 M2

Forsinard Highld ........ 230 C6
Forss Highld .................. 230 F2
Fort Augustus
Highld .......................... 202 B4
Forteviot P & K .......... 185 L4
Forth S Lans ................ 176 C7
Forthampton Gloucs ....55 K2
Fort Hommet Guern ... 236 c2
Forth Rail Bridge
C Edin .......................... 176 F3
Forth Road Bridge
Fife .............................. 176 F3
Fortingall P & K ......... 194 B6
Forton Hants .................29 H3
Forton Lancs .............. 121 G1
Forton Shrops ...............83 H1
Forton Somset ..............13 J2
Forton Staffs .................99 H7
Fort Richmond
Guern .......................... 236 b3
Fortrie Abers .............. 216 C5
Fortrose Highld ......... 213 H3
Fortuneswell Dorset .....14 D7
Fort William Highld .. 191 L2
Forty Hill Gt Lon ..........60 B7
Fosbury Wilts ...............40 F8
Foscot Oxon ..................56 E4
Fosdyke Lincs ............ 104 A5
Foss P & K ................... 194 C5
Fossebridge Gloucs .....56 B5
Foster Street Essex ......60 D6
Foston Derbys ............ 100 D6
Foston Leics .................87 H4
Foston Lincs ............... 102 E4
Foston N York ............ 133 L6
Foston on the
Wolds E R Yk ............ 135 H7
Fotherby Lincs ........... 118 D3
Fotheringhay Nhants ...88 F5
Foula Shet .................. 235 a6
*Foula Airport Shet ..... 235 a6*
Foulden Border ......... 179 J7
Foulden Norfk ..............91 H4
Foul End Warwks .........86 B4
Foulness Island
Essex .............................47 G2
Foulridge Lancs ........ 122 D3
Foulsham Norfk ........ 106 B7
Fountainhall Border .. 177 L8
Four Ashes Suffk .........78 B1
Four Cabots Guern .... 236 c3
Four Crosses Powys ....97 K8
Four Elms Kent .............32 E4
Four Forks Somset .......25 K4
Four Gotes Cambs .......90 C1
Four Lanes Cnwll .......... 3 J4
Four Marks Hants .........30 A4
Four Mile Bridge
IoA .............................. 108 C5
Four Oaks Birm ............85 K4
Four Oaks Solhll ..........86 B7
Fourpenny Highld ..... 223 H3
Four Roads Carmth .....50 F4
Fourstones Nthumb .. 149 M2
Four Throws Kent .........33 K7
Fovant Wilts .................28 A5
Foveran Abers ........... 207 H2
Fowey Cnwll ................... 5 H5
Fowlhall Kent ...............33 J4
Fowlis Angus ............. 186 E2
Fowlis Wester P & K .. 185 J3
Fowlmere Cambs .........76 B5
Fownhope Herefs .........69 L7
Foxbar Rens .............. 174 E6
Foxcote Somset ...........27 G1
Foxdale IoM ............... 237 b5
Foxearth Essex .............77 J5
Foxfield Cumb ........... 128 F3
Foxhole Cnwll ............... 4 F5
Foxholes N York ........ 134 F5
Foxley Norfk .............. 106 C7
Foxt Staffs ................. 100 B3
Foxton Cambs ..............76 B5
Foxton Leics ................87 K5
Foxton N York ........... 141 K7
Foxwood Shrops ..........84 B7
Foy Herefs ....................54 E3
Foyers Highld ............ 202 D2

Foynesfield Highld ...... 213 L4
Fraddon Cnwll ................ 4 E4
Fradley Staffs ...............85 L2
Fradswell Staffs ...........99 M6
Fraisthorpe E R Yk .... 135 J7
Framfield E Susx ..........20 A2
Framingham Earl
Norfk ............................92 F3
Framingham Pigot
Norfk ............................92 F3
Framlingham Suffk .....79 G2
Frampton Dorset .........14 C4
Frampton Lincs ......... 104 B5
Frampton Cotterell
S Glos ............................38 F4
Frampton Mansell
Gloucs ..........................55 L7
Frampton-on-
Severn Gloucs .............55 H6
Framsden Suffk ............78 E3
Framwellgate Moor
Dur ............................. 151 G6
Franche Worcs .............84 E7
Frankby Wirral ........... 111 H4
Frankley Worcs ............85 H7
Frankley Services
Worcs ............................85 H7
Frankton Warwks ........72 E1
Frant E Susx .................33 G6
Fraserburgh Abers .... 217 J2
Frating Essex ................62 C4
Frating Green Essex ....62 C4
Fratton C Port .............17 J3
Freathy Cnwll ................ 6 B5
Freckenham Suffk .......76 F1
Freckleton Lancs ...... 120 F5
Freeby Leics .............. 102 D7
Freefolk Hants .............29 J2
Freeland Oxon .............57 H5
Freethorpe Norfk ........93 J3
Freethorpe
Common Norfk .........93 J3
Freiston Lincs ........... 104 B4
Fremington Devon .......23 H5
Fremington N York ... 140 D7
Frenchay S Glos ..........38 F5
Frenich P & K ............ 194 C5
Frensham Surrey .........30 D3
Freshfield Sefton ...... 120 C8
Freshford Wilts ...........39 H7
Freshwater IoW ...........16 D5
Fressingfield Suffk ......92 F7
Freston Suffk ...............78 E6
Freswick Highld ........ 231 L3
Fretherne Gloucs .......55 G6
Frettenham Norfk ..... 106 F8
Freuchie Fife ............. 186 E6
Freystrop Pembks .......49 G5
Friar Park Sandw .........85 H4
Friday Bridge Cambs ...90 C3
Friday Street Suffk ......79 H3
Fridaythorpe E R Yk .. 134 D7
Friendly Calder .......... 122 F5
Friern Barnet Gt Lon ...44 F2
Friesthorpe Lincs ..... 117 H5
Frieston Lincs ........... 102 F3
Frieth Bucks ................42 D3
Frilford Oxon ...............41 H2
Frilsham W Berk ..........41 K5
Frimley Surrey .............42 E8
Frindsbury Medway .....46 C6
Fring Norfk ................ 105 H5
Fringford Oxon ...........57 L3
Frinsted Kent ...............34 B4
Frinton-on-Sea
Essex .............................62 F4
Friockheim Angus .... 196 F6
Frisby on the
Wreake Leics ........... 102 B8
Friskney Lincs ........... 104 D2
Friston E Susx ..............20 B6
Friston Suffk ................79 J3
Fritchley Derbys ....... 101 G3
Fritham Hants ..............28 E8
Frithelstock Devon ......23 G7
Frithelstock Stone
Devon ...........................23 G7
Frithville Lincs .......... 104 A3

Frittenden Kent ............33 K5
Frittiscombe Devon ...... 7 J6
Fritton Norfk ................92 F5
Fritton Norfk ................93 K4
Fritwell Oxon ...............57 K3
Frizinghall C Brad...... 123 H4
Frizington Cumb ....... 136 E4
Frocester Gloucs .........55 H7
Frodesley Shrops ........83 K3
Frodsham Ches W ..... 112 D6
Frogden Border ........ 168 B4
Frog End Cambs ..........76 B5
Froggatt Derbys ........ 114 E6
Froghall Staffs .......... 100 A3
Frogmore Devon .......... 7 H7
Frognall Lincs ..............89 H2
Frog Pool Worcs ..........70 E2
Frogwell Cnwll .............. 6 A3
Frolesworth Leics........87 G5
Frome Somset ..............27 H2
Frome St Quintin
Dorset ...........................14 B2
Fromes Hill Herefs......70 C5
Froncysyllte Wrexhm ...97 L4
Fron-goch Gwynd ........96 D5
Fron Isaf Wrexhm ........97 L4
Frosterley Dur ........... 150 C7
Froxfield Wilts .............40 F6
Froxfield Green
Hants ............................30 B6
Fryern Hill Hants .........29 H7
Fryerning Essex ...........61 G7
Fuinary Highld .......... 190 C6
Fulbeck Lincs ............ 102 F3
Fulbourn Cambs ..........76 D4
Fulbrook Oxon .............56 E5
Fulflood Hants .............29 J5
Fulford C York ........... 124 F2
Fulford Somset ............25 K5
Fulford Staffs ...............99 L5
Fulham Gt Lon .............44 E5
Fulking W Susx .............19 J3
Fullarton N Ayrs ........ 163 H2
Fuller Street Essex ......61 H5
Fullerton Hants ...........29 G4
Fulletby Lincs ............ 118 D6
Fullready Warwks ........72 C5
Full Sutton E R Yk ..... 134 B7
Fullwood E Ayrs ........ 174 E7
Fulmer Bucks ...............43 G4
Fulmodeston Norfk... 106 B6
Fulnetby Lincs ........... 117 H5
Fulney Lincs .............. 103 L7
Fulstow Lincs ............ 118 D3
Fulwell Sundld ........... 151 J3
Fulwood Lancs .......... 121 H4
Fulwood Sheff ........... 114 F4
Fundenhall Norfk ........92 D4
Funtington W Susx .....17 L2
Funtullich P & K ........ 184 F3
Furley Devon ...............13 H2
Furnace Ag & B .......... 182 E7
Furnace Carmth ..........51 G5
Furness Vale Derbys .. 114 A5
Furneux Pelham
Herts .............................60 C3
Furzley Hants ...............28 F7
Fyfield Essex ................60 F6
Fyfield Hants ................28 E3
Fyfield Oxon .................57 H7
Fyfield Wilts .................40 C6
Fyfield Wilts .................40 D7
Fylingthorpe N York... 143 J6
Fyning W Susx .............30 D6
Fyvie Abers ................ 216 E6

**G**

Gabroc Hill E Ayrs ..... 174 E7
Gaddesby Leics ...........87 K2
Gaddesden Row
Herts .............................59 H5
Gadgirth S Ayrs .......... 163 K5
Gaerllwyd Mons..........38 C2
Gaerwen IoA .............. 108 F7
Gailes N Ayrs ............. 163 H3

Gailey Staffs .................85 G2
Gainford Dur .............. 140 F4
Gainsborough Lincs... 116 D4
Gainsborough Suffk....78 E6
Gainsford End Essex ....77 G7
Gairloch Highld ......... 219 J6
Gairlochy Highld ....... 201 J8
Gairneybridge P & K .. 186 B7
Gaitsgill Cumb .......... 148 C5
Galashiels Border ..... 167 G3
Galgate Lancs ........... 129 K7
Galhampton Somset ...26 F5
Gallanachbeg
Ag & B ........................ 182 B2
Gallanachmore
Ag & B ........................ 182 B3
Gallatown Fife ........... 186 E8
Galleywood Essex .......61 H7
Gallovie Highld ......... 202 E7
Galloway Forest
Park ........................... 153 J5
Gallowfauld Angus.... 196 D7
Gallowhill P & K ........ 186 B1
Galltair Highld........... 200 C2
Galmisdale Highld .... 199 G8
Galmpton Devon .......... 7 G7
Galmpton Torbay .......... 7 K5
Galphay N York ......... 132 C5
Galston E Ayrs ........... 163 L3
Gamblesby Cumb ..... 149 G6
Gamlingay Cambs .......75 J4
Gamlingay Great
Heath Cambs ..............75 J4
Gamrie Abers ............ 216 F2
Gamston Notts .......... 101 L5
Gamston Notts .......... 116 B6
Ganavan Bay Ag & B .. 182 B2
Ganllwyd Gwynd .........96 B7
Gannachy Angus ....... 196 F3
Ganstead E R Yk ....... 126 E4
Ganthorpe N York .... 133 L5
Ganton N York .......... 134 F4
Garbity Moray ........... 215 H4
Garboldisham Norfk ...92 B7
Garbole Highld........... 203 H1
Garchory Abers ........ 205 G4
Gardeners Green
Wokham .......................42 D6
Gardenstown Abers... 216 F2
Garden Village Sheff.. 114 E2
Garderhouse Shet ..... 235 c5
Gare Hill Somset .........27 H4
Garelochhead
Ag & B ........................ 173 L1
Garford Oxon ..............41 H2
Garforth Leeds .......... 124 B4
Gargrave N York ....... 131 H8
Gargunnock Stirlg .... 184 F8
Garlic Street Norfk......92 E6
Garlieston D & G ....... 145 K5
Garlinge Kent ..............35 J2
Garlinge Green Kent ...34 F4
Garlogie Abers .......... 206 E4
Garmond Abers ........ 216 F4
Garmouth Moray ...... 215 H2
Garmston Shrops ........83 L3
Garndolbenmaen
Gwynd ..........................95 J4
Garrabost W Isls....... 232 g2
Garrallan E Ayrs ....... 164 B5
Garras Cnwll ................. 3 J6
Garreg Gwynd ..............95 K4
Garrigill Cumb .......... 149 J6
Garroch D & G ........... 153 M6
Garrochtrie D & G ..... 144 D7
Garrochty Ag & B ...... 173 J7
Garros Highld ............ 209 H2
Garsdale Head Cumb . 130 E2
Garsdon Wilts ..............39 L3
Garshall Green Staffs ...99 L5
Garsington Oxon..........57 L7
Garstang Lancs ......... 121 G2
Garston Herts ..............59 J7
Garston Lpool ........... 112 B5
Gartachossan Ag & B .. 171 G6
Gartcosh N Lans ....... 175 J5
Garth Powys .................67 K5
Garth Wrexhm ............97 K4

Garthamlock C Glas..... 175 H5
Garthmyl Powys.........82 E4
Garthorpe Leics ...... 102 D7
Garthorpe N Linc ..... 125 K6
Garth Row Cumb...... 138 D7
Gartly Abers ............ 215 L7
Gartmore Stirlg ....... 184 C7
Gartness N Lans ...... 175 K5
Gartness Stirlg ........ 174 F2
Gartocharn W Duns... 174 D2
Garton-on-the-
    Wolds E R Yk.... 134 F7
Gartymore Highld ...... 227 H5
Garva Bridge Highld .... 202 E6
Garvald Border ........ 176 F8
Garvald E Loth ........ 178 D4
Garvan Highld .......... 191 J2
Garvard Ag & B........ 171 G1
Garve Highld............ 212 B3
Garvellachs Ag & B ... 181 K5
Garvestone Norfk ...... 92 B3
Garvock Inver........... 174 B4
Garway Herefs.......... 54 C4
Garynahine W Isls... 232 e2
Garyvard W Isls........ 232 f3
Gasper Wilts............ 27 H5
Gastard Wilts .......... 39 K6
Gasthorpe Norfk ...... 91 L7
Gatcombe IoW ......... 16 F5
Gate Burton Lincs .... 116 D5
Gateforth N York ...... 124 E5
Gatehead E Ayrs....... 163 K3
Gate Helmsley
    N York .............. 133 L7
Gatehouse Nthumb... 157 K4
Gatehouse of Fleet
    D & G............... 146 A4
Gateley Norfk.......... 106 A7
Gatenby N York........ 132 E3
Gateshaw Border ..... 168 B5
Gateshead Gatesd..... 151 G3
Gateside Angus ....... 196 D7
Gateside E Rens ...... 174 E6
Gateside Fife .......... 186 C5
Gateside N Ayrs....... 174 C7
Gateslack D & G....... 154 F2
Gatley Stockp .......... 113 J4
Gattonside Border .... 167 H3
Gatwick Airport
    W Susx ..............32 B5
Gaulby Leics............ 87 K4
Gauldry Fife ........... 186 F3
Gauldswell P & K..... 195 K6
Gautby Lincs ........... 117 K6
Gavinton Border ...... 179 G7
Gawcott Bucks.......... 58 B2
Gawsworth Ches E ... 113 K7
Gawthrop Cumb........ 130 D3
Gawthwaite Cumb .... 129 G3
Gaydon Warwks........ 72 D4
Gayhurst M Keyn....... 74 B5
Gayle N York ............ 131 G2
Gayles N York .......... 140 E5
Gayton Nhants .......... 73 K4
Gayton Norfk........... 105 H8
Gayton Staffs ..........99 M6
Gayton le Marsh
    Lincs ................ 118 F5
Gayton Thorpe Norfk... 105 H8
Gaywood Norfk ....... 105 G7
Gazeley Suffk...........77 G2
Gearraidh Bhaird
    W Isls............... 232 f3
Gearraidh na
    h-Aibhne W Isls... 232 e2
Geary Highld............ 208 D3
Gedding Suffk...........77 L3
Geddington Nhants.... 88 C6
Gedling Notts .......... 101 L4
Gedney Lincs........... 104 C7
Gedney Broadgate
    Lincs ................ 104 C7
Gedney Drove End
    Lincs ................ 104 D6
Gedney Dyke Lincs.... 104 C7
Gedney Hill Lincs......89 L2
Geeston Rutlnd..........88 E3

Geirinis W Isls......... 233 b7
Geldeston Norfk.........93 H5
Gellideg Myr Td.........53 G6
Gellifor Denbgs........ 110 F8
Gelligaer Caerph........37 H2
Gellilydan Gwynd.......95 M4
Gellinudd Neath.........51 K5
Gellyburn P & K........ 195 H8
Gellywen Carmth........50 C2
Gelston D & G.......... 146 D3
Gelston Lincs .......... 102 E4
Gembling E R Yk ...... 135 H7
Gentleshaw Staffs......85 J2
Georgefield D & G..... 156 B4
George Green Bucks ... 43 G4
Georgeham Devon ......23 G4
Georgemas
    Junction Station
    Highld ............... 231 H4
George Nympton
    Devon ................23 L6
Geortth Ork ............ 234 b5
Gerinish W Isls........ 233 b7
Germansweek Devon ...10 C6
Gerrans Cnwll ............4 D8
Gerrards Cross
    Bucks .................43 G3
Gerrick R & Cl ........ 142 E5
Gestingthorpe Essex...77 J6
Geuffordd Powys........82 E2
Gidea Park Gt Lon......45 K3
Giffnock E Rens....... 175 G6
Gifford E Loth ........ 178 C5
Giffordtown Fife ...... 186 E5
Giggleswick N York.... 130 F6
Gigha Ag & B ........... 171 L7
Gilberdyke E R Yk ... 125 K5
Gilchriston E Loth.... 178 B5
Gilcrux Cumb .......... 147 K7
Gildersome Leeds .... 123 K5
Gildingwells Rothm... 115 K4
Gilesgate Moor Dur... 151 H6
Gileston V Glam........36 F6
Gilfach Caerph..........53 J7
Gilfach Goch Brdgnd...36 F3
Gilfachrheda Cerdgn...65 L3
Gilgarran Cumb........ 136 E3
Gillamoor N York ..... 133 K2
Gillen Highld........... 208 D3
Gillesbie D & G ....... 155 K4
Gilling East N York ... 133 J4
Gillingham Dorset.....27 J6
Gillingham Medway....46 C6
Gillingham Norfk.......93 J5
Gilling West N York ... 140 F6
Gillock Highld.......... 231 J4
Gills Highld............. 231 K2
Gilmanscleuch
    Border .............. 166 E5
Gilmerton C Edin...... 177 J5
Gilmerton P & K....... 185 J3
Gilmonby Dur.......... 140 C5
Gilmorton Leics........87 H6
Gilsland Nthumb...... 149 G2
Gilston Border ........ 177 L6
Gilston Herts............60 D5
Gilwern Mons ..........53 K5
Gimingham Norfk..... 107 G5
Gipping Suffk...........78 C2
Gipsey Bridge Lincs... 103 M3
Girdle Toll N Ayrs .... 163 J2
Girlsta Shet ............ 235 c5
Girsby N York .......... 141 J5
Girthon D & G......... 146 A4
Girton Cambs ...........76 B3
Girton Notts ........... 116 D7
Girvan S Ayrs.......... 152 E3
Gisburn Lancs ......... 122 C2
Gislehan Suffk..........93 K5
Gislingham Suffk.......78 C1
Gissing Norfk ...........92 D6
Gittisham Devon .......12 E3
Gladestry Powys........68 G4
Gladsmuir E Loth ... 177 M4
Glais Swans ............51 K5
Glaisdale N York ..... 143 G6
Glamis Angus .......... 196 C6
Glanaman Carmth......51 J3

Glandford Norfk....... 106 C4
Glandwr Pembks........49 K2
Glandyfi Cerdgn........80 F4
Glanllynfi Brdgnd......36 D3
Glan-rhyd Powys........52 B6
Glanton Nthumb ...... 169 G6
Glanvilles Wootton
    Dorset ................14 D2
Glan-y-don Flints..... 111 G5
Glapthorn Nhants......88 E5
Glapwell Derbys....... 115 J7
Glasbury Powys.........68 D6
Glascote Staffs.........86 B3
Glascwm Powys.........68 D4
Glasfryn Conwy.........96 E3
Glasgow C Glas ....... 175 G5
Glasgow Airport
    Rens .................. 174 E5
Glasgow Prestwick
    Airport S Ayrs...... 163 J4
Glasgow Science
    Centre C Glas..... 175 G5
Glasinfryn Gwynd..... 109 H7
Glasnacardoch Bay
    Highld ............... 199 L6
Glasnakille Highld.... 199 H3
Glasphein Highld..... 208 B4
Glassford S Lans ..... 175 J8
Glasshouse Gloucs .....55 G4
Glasshouses N York... 132 B6
Glasslaw Abers........ 216 F3
Glasson Cumb ......... 148 A3
Glasson Lancs ......... 129 K7
Glassonby Cumb ..... 149 G7
Glasterlaw Angus .... 196 F6
Glaston Rutlnd..........88 C4
Glastonbury Somset...26 D4
Glatton Cambs..........89 H6
Glazebrook Warrtn... 113 G3
Glazebury Warrtn.... 112 F3
Glazeley Shrops........84 C5
Gleaston Cumb ....... 128 F5
Glebe Highld........... 202 D2
Gledhow Leeds........ 123 L3
Gledpark D & G ...... 146 B5
Gledrid Shrops..........97 L5
Glemsford Suffk........77 J5
Glen Achulish
    Highld ............... 191 K5
Glenallachie Moray... 215 G6
Glenancross Highld... 199 K6
Glenaros House
    Ag & B ............... 190 B7
Glen Auldyn IoM ..... 237 d3
Glenbarr Ag & B ..... 161 H3
Glenbarry Abers...... 216 B4
Glenbeg Highld........ 190 C4
Glenbervie Abers..... 197 J1
Glenboig N Lans...... 175 J5
Glenborrodale
    Highld ............... 190 C4
Glenbranter Ag & B... 183 G7
Glenbreck Border .... 165 K5
Glenbrittle Highld.... 198 F2
Glenbuck E Ayrs ..... 164 E4
Glencally Angus ...... 196 B4
Glencaple D & G ..... 147 H2
Glencarse P & K....... 186 C3
Glencoe Highld........ 191 L5
Glencothe Border .... 165 L4
Glencraig Fife ......... 186 C6
Glencrosh D & G..... 154 D4
Glendale Highld....... 208 B4
Glendaruel Ag & B... 173 G2
Glendevon P & K...... 185 K6
Glendoe Lodge
    Highld ............... 202 C4
Glendoick P & K....... 186 C3
Glenduckie Fife ...... 186 D4
Glenegedale Ag & B... 170 F7
Glenelg Highld......... 200 C2
Glenernery Moray.... 214 C5
Glenfarg P & K........ 186 B5
Glenfield Leics.........87 G3
Glenfinnan Highld.... 191 H1
Glenfintaig Lodge
    Highld ............... 201 K7
Glenfoot P & K........ 186 C4

Glenfyne Lodge
    Ag & B............... 183 H4
Glengarnock N Ayrs... 174 C7
Glengolly Highld...... 231 G3
Glengorm Castle
    Ag & B............... 189 K5
Glengrasco Highld... 209 G5
Glenholm Border .... 165 L3
Glenhoul D & G ...... 154 A5
Glenkin Ag & B ....... 173 K3
Glenkindie Abers..... 205 K3
Glenlivet Moray....... 214 F8
Glenlochar D & G .... 146 C3
Glenlomond P & K.... 186 C6
Glenluce D & G ....... 144 E4
Glenmassen Ag & B... 173 J2
Glenmavis N Lans.... 175 K5
Glen Maye IoM ....... 237 b5
Glenmore Highld..... 209 G6
Glenmore Lodge
    Highld ............... 204 B4
Glen Nevis House
    Highld ............... 192 B3
Glenochil Clacks ..... 185 H7
Glen Parva Leics ......87 H4
Glenquiech Angus ... 196 C4
Glenralloch Ag & B... 172 E5
Glenridding Cumb ... 137 L4
Glenrothes Fife....... 186 D7
Glenshero Lodge
    Highld ............... 202 E6
Glenstriven Ag & B... 173 J3
Glentham Lincs ...... 117 G4
Glentrool D & G...... 153 H6
Glen Trool Lodge
    D & G............... 153 J6
Glentruim Highld .... 203 G6
Glentworth Lincs .... 116 F4
Glenuig Highld........ 190 D2
Glenvarragill Highld... 209 G6
Glen Vine IoM ........ 237 c5
Glenwhilly D & G .... 152 E7
Glespin S Lans ....... 164 F4
Glewstone Herefs..... 54 E4
Glinton C Pete..........89 H3
Glooston Leics..........87 L4
Glossop Derbys....... 114 B3
Gloster Hill Nthumb ... 159 G2
Gloucester Gloucs .....55 J4
Gloucester Services
    Gloucs ...............55 J5
Gloucestershire
    Airport Gloucs......55 K4
Glusburn N York ..... 122 F2
Glutt Lodge Highld... 227 H2
Glympton Oxon ........57 H4
Glynarthen Cerdgn ...65 K5
Glyn Ceiriog Wrexhm...97 J5
Glyncoch Rhondd......37 G3
Glyncorrwg Neath.....52 D7
Glynde E Susx ..........19 L4
Glyndyfrdwy Denbgs... 97 J4
Glynneath Neath.......52 D6
Glyntawe Powys........52 D5
Glynteg Carmth........65 K6
Gnosall Staffs..........99 J7
Gnosall Heath Staffs...99 J7
Goadby Leics...........87 L4
Goadby Marwood
    Leics ................ 102 C7
Goatacre Wilts..........40 A5
Goathill Dorset .........26 F7
Goathland N York .... 143 H6
Goathurst Somset.....25 K5
Goat Lees Kent.........34 D5
Gobowen Shrops.......97 L5
Godalming Surrey ......30 F3
Goddard's Green
    Kent..................33 L6
Godmanchester
    Cambs ...............75 J1
Godmanstone Dorset...14 C3
Godmersham Kent.....34 E5
Godney Somset.........26 C3
Godolphin Cross
    Cnwll ...................3 G5
Godre'r-graig Neath...51 L4
Godshill IoW ...........17 G6

Godstone Surrey ............. 32 C3
Goetre Mons ..................... 53 L6
Goff's Oak Herts ............... 60 B7
Gogar C Edin .................. 177 G4
Goginan Cerdgn ............... 80 F7
Golan Gwynd ................... 95 J4
Golant Cnwll ....................... 5 H5
Golberdon Cnwll .................. 5 M2
Golborne Wigan ............ 112 E3
Golcar Kirk ..................... 123 G7
Goldcliff Newpt ................ 38 A4
Golden Green Kent ......... 33 H4
Goldenhill C Stke ............. 99 J2
Golden Pot Hants ............. 30 B3
Golders Green Gt Lon .... 44 E3
Goldhanger Essex .......... 61 L6
Goldington Bed ................ 74 F4
Goldsborough N York .. 132 F7
Goldsborough N York .. 143 H4
Golds Green Sandw ........ 85 H5
Goldsithney Cnwll .............. 2 F5
Goldthorpe Barns .......... 115 J2
Goldworthy Devon ............ 22 F6
Gollanfield Highld ........... 213 J4
Golspie Highld ................ 223 H2
Gomeldon Wilts ............... 28 D4
Gomshall Surrey .............. 31 H2
Gonalston Notts .............. 102 B3
Gonerby Hill Foot
  Lincs .............................. 102 E5
Gonfirth Shet .................. 235 c4
Good Easter Essex .......... 60 F5
Gooderstone Norfk ......... 91 H3
Goodleigh Devon ............. 23 J5
Goodmanham E R Yk .. 125 K2
Goodmayes Gt Lon ......... 45 J3
Goodnestone Kent .......... 34 D3
Goodnestone Kent .......... 35 H4
Goodrich Herefs .............. 54 E4
Goodrington Torbay .......... 7 K4
Goodshaw Lancs ............ 122 B5
Goodwick Pembks ........... 64 C6
Goodworth Clatford
  Hants .............................. 29 G3
Goole E R Yk .................. 125 H5
Goom's Hill Worcs ........... 71 H4
Goonbell Cnwll ................... 3 J2
Goonhavern Cnwll .............. 3 K1
Goonvrea Cnwll .................. 3 J2
Goosecruives Abers .... 206 E8
Gooseford Devon ............. 11 G6
Goose Green Essex ........ 62 D3
Goose Green S Glos ....... 38 F5
Gooseham Cnwll ................ 9 G2
Goosey Oxon .................... 41 G3
Goosnargh Lancs ........... 121 H3
Goostrey Ches E ............. 113 H7
Gordano Services
  N Som ............................. 38 D5
Gordon Border ............... 167 K2
Gordon Arms Hotel
  Border ........................... 166 D4
Gordonstoun Abers ...... 216 B3
Gordonstown Abers ...... 216 D6
Gorebridge Mdloth ........ 177 K6
Gorefield Cambs ............. 90 B2
Gores Wilts ...................... 40 C8
Gorey Jersey .................. 236 e7
Goring Oxon ..................... 41 L4
Goring-by-Sea
  W Susx .......................... 18 F5
Gorleston-on-Sea
  Norfk .............................. 93 L3
Gorrachie Abers ........... 216 E3
Gorran Churchtown
  Cnwll ................................ 4 F7
Gorran Haven Cnwll ......... 4 F7
Gorsedd Flints .............. 111 G6
Gorse Hill Swindn .......... 40 D3
Gorseinon Swans ............ 51 H5
Gorsgoch Cerdgn ............ 66 C4
Gorslas Carmth ............... 51 H3
Gorsley Gloucs ................ 55 G3
Gorsley Common
  Herefs ............................. 54 F3
Gorstan Highld ............... 212 B2
Gorsten Ag & B ............. 181 L2
Gorsty Hill Staffs ......... 100 C6

Gorthleck Highld .......... 202 E2
Gorton Manch ................ 113 K3
Gosbeck Suffk .................. 78 D4
Gosberton Lincs ............ 103 L6
Gosfield Essex ................. 61 J3
Gosforth Cumb ............. 136 E6
Gosforth N u Ty ............. 151 G2
Gosport Hants .................. 17 H3
Gossington Gloucs ......... 55 H7
Gotham Notts ................ 101 K6
Gotherington Gloucs ...... 55 L3
Gotton Somset ................ 25 K5
Goudhurst Kent ............... 33 J5
Goulceby Lincs .............. 118 C5
Gourdas Abers ............... 216 E6
Gourdie C Dund ............. 186 F2
Gourdon Abers ............... 197 K3
Gourock Inver ................ 173 L3
Govan C Glas ................. 174 F5
Goveton Devon .................. 7 H6
Govilon Mons ................... 53 K5
Gowdall E R Yk .............. 124 F6
Gower Highld .................. 212 D3
Gower Swans .................... 51 G7
Gowerton Swans .............. 51 H6
Gowkhall Fife ................. 176 E1
Goxhill E R Yk ................ 126 F2
Goxhill N Linc ................ 126 D6
Grabhair W Isls ............. 232 f3
Graffham W Susx ............ 18 C3
Grafham Cambs ............... 75 H2
Grafham Surrey ................ 31 G3
Grafton N York ............... 132 F6
Grafton Oxon .................... 56 F7
Grafton Shrops ................ 98 B8
Grafton Worcs .................. 71 H6
Grafton Flyford
  Worcs ............................. 71 G4
Grafton Regis Nhants ... 73 L5
Grafton Underwood
  Nhants ............................ 88 D7
Grafty Green Kent ........... 34 B5
Graig Conwy ................... 109 M6
Graigfechan Denbgs ....... 97 J2
Grain Medway .................. 46 E5
Grainsby Lincs ............... 118 C2
Grainthorpe Lincs .......... 118 E3
Grampound Cnwll .............. 4 E6
Grampound Road
  Cnwll ................................ 4 E5
Gramsdal W Isls ............ 233 d7
Gramsdale W Isls .......... 233 c6
Granborough Bucks ........ 58 C3
Granby Notts .................. 102 C5
Grandborough
  Warwks .......................... 72 F2
Grand Chemins
  Jersey ............................ 236 d7
Grandes Rocques
  Guern ............................. 236 c2
Grandtully P & K ........... 194 E5
Grange Cumb .................. 137 H4
Grange Medway ............... 46 D6
Grange P & K ................. 186 D3
Grange Crossroads
  Moray ............................. 215 K4
Grange Hall Moray ....... 214 C3
Grangehall S Lans ......... 165 J2
Grange Hill Essex ............ 45 H2
Grangemill Derbys ........ 100 E2
Grange Moor Kirk .......... 123 J7
Grangemouth Falk ......... 176 C3
Grange of Lindores
  Fife ................................ 186 D4
Grange-over-Sands
  Cumb .............................. 129 J4
Grangepans Falk ........... 176 D3
Grange Park Nhants ....... 73 L4
Grangetown R & Cl ....... 142 C3
Grangetown Sundld ...... 151 K4
Grange Villa Dur ........... 151 G4
Gransmoor E R Yk ........ 135 H7
Granston Pembks ............ 64 C7
Grantchester Cambs ....... 76 B4
Grantham Lincs ............. 102 E5
Granton C Edin .............. 177 H3
Grantown-on-Spey
  Highld ............................ 214 C8

Grantshouse Border .... 179 G5
Grappenhall Warrtn ...... 112 F4
Grasby Lincs .................. 117 H1
Grasmere Cumb ............ 137 K5
Grasscroft Oldham ....... 113 L1
Grassendale Lpool ....... 111 L4
Grassington N York ...... 131 J6
Grassmoor Derbys ....... 115 H7
Grassthorpe Notts ....... 116 C7
Grateley Hants ............... 28 F3
Graveley Cambs .............. 75 J2
Graveley Herts ................ 59 L3
Gravelly Hill Birm .......... 85 K5
Graveney Kent ................ 34 E3
Gravesend Kent .............. 46 A5
Gravir W Isls ................. 232 f3
Grayingham Lincs ......... 116 F3
Grayrigg Cumb .............. 138 E7
Grays Thurr ..................... 45 L4
Grayshott Hants .............. 30 E4
Grayswood Surrey .......... 30 E4
Greasbrough Rothm ..... 115 H3
Greasby Wirral .............. 111 H4
Great Abington
  Cambs ............................ 76 D5
Great Addington
  Nhants ............................ 88 D7
Great Alne Warwks ......... 71 K3
Great Altcar Lancs ....... 111 K1
Great Amwell Herts ....... 60 B5
Great Asby Cumb ......... 138 F5
Great Ashfield Suffk ....... 78 B2
Great Ayton N York ...... 142 C5
Great Baddow Essex ...... 61 H6
Great Badminton
  S Glos ............................ 39 J4
Great Bardfield
  Essex ............................. 61 G2
Great Barford Bed ......... 75 G4
Great Barr Sandw .......... 85 J4
Great Barrington
  Gloucs ............................ 56 E5
Great Barrow Ches W .. 112 C7
Great Barton Suffk ......... 77 K2
Great Barugh N York .. 134 B4
Great Bavington
  Nthumb .......................... 158 C6
Great Bealings Suffk ...... 78 F5
Great Bedwyn Wilts ....... 40 F7
Great Bentley Essex ....... 62 D4
Great Billing Nhants ....... 74 B3
Great Bircham Norfk .... 105 J6
Great Blakenham
  Suffk .............................. 78 D4
Great Blencow Cumb .. 138 C2
Great Bolas Wrekin ........ 98 F7
Great Bookham
  Surrey ............................. 31 J1
Great Bourton Oxon ....... 72 F5
Great Bowden Leics ....... 87 L5
Great Bradley Suffk ....... 76 F4
Great Braxted Essex ...... 61 K5
Great Bricett Suffk ......... 78 C4
Great Brickhill Bucks ..... 58 E3
Great Bridgeford
  Staffs ............................. 99 K6
Great Brington
  Nhants ............................ 73 J2
Great Bromley Essex ...... 62 C3
Great Broughton
  Cumb .............................. 136 E2
Great Broughton
  N York ............................ 142 C6
Great Budworth
  Ches W .......................... 112 F6
Great Burdon Darltn .... 141 H4
Great Burstead
  Essex ............................. 46 B2
Great Busby N York ...... 142 B6
Great Carlton Lincs ...... 118 E4
Great Casterton
  Rutlnd ............................. 88 E2
Great Chalfield Wilts ...... 39 K7
Great Chart Kent ............ 34 C6
Great Chatwell Staffs ..... 84 E1
Great Chell C Stke .......... 99 K3
Great Chesterford
  Essex ............................. 76 D6

Great Cheverell Wilts ..... 27 M1
Great Chishill Cambs ...... 76 B6
Great Clacton Essex ....... 62 E5
Great Clifton Cumb ....... 136 E2
Great Coates NE Lin .... 126 F8
Great Comberton
  Worcs ............................. 71 G6
Great Corby Cumb ........ 148 E4
Great Cornard Suffk ....... 77 K6
Great Cowden E R Yk .. 126 F3
Great Coxwell Oxon ....... 40 F2
Great Cransley
  Nhants ............................ 88 B7
Great Cressingham
  Norfk .............................. 91 J3
Great Crosthwaite
  Cumb .............................. 137 J3
Great Cubley Derbys .... 100 D5
Great Cumbrae
  Island N Ayrs ............... 173 K6
Great Dalby Leics .......... 87 L2
Great Denham Bed ......... 74 E5
Great Doddington
  Nhants ............................ 74 C2
Great Dunham Norfk ...... 91 K1
Great Dunmow Essex .... 61 G4
Great Durnford Wilts ...... 28 C4
Great Easton Essex ........ 60 F3
Great Easton Leics ......... 88 B5
Great Eccleston
  Lancs ............................. 120 F3
Great Ellingham
  Norfk .............................. 92 B4
Great Elm Somset ........... 27 H2
Great Everdon
  Nhants ............................ 73 H3
Great Eversden
  Cambs ............................ 75 L4
Great Fencote
  N York ............................ 132 D2
Great Finborough
  Suffk .............................. 78 B3
Greatford Lincs ............... 88 F2
Great Fransham
  Norfk .............................. 91 K2
Great Gaddesden
  Herts .............................. 59 G5
Greatgate Staffs ........... 100 B4
Great Gidding Cambs .... 89 G6
Great Givendale
  E R Yk ........................... 134 C8
Great Glemham
  Suffk .............................. 79 H3
Great Glen Leics ............. 87 J4
Great Gonerby Lincs .... 102 E5
Great Gransden
  Cambs ............................ 75 J4
Great Green Cambs ....... 75 K5
Great Green Suffk .......... 77 K4
Great Habton N York .. 134 B4
Great Hale Lincs ........... 103 J4
Great Hallingbury
  Essex ............................. 60 E4
Greatham Hants .............. 30 C5
Greatham Hartpl .......... 141 L2
Greatham W Susx ........... 18 E3
Great Hampden
  Bucks ............................. 58 D7
Great Harrowden
  Nhants ............................ 74 C1
Great Harwood
  Lancs ............................. 121 L4
Great Haseley Oxon ....... 57 M7
Great Hatfield E R Yk .. 126 F3
Great Haywood
  Staffs ............................. 100 A7
Great Heck N York ....... 124 E6
Great Henny Essex ......... 77 K6
Great Hinton Wilts .......... 39 K8
Great Hockham
  Norfk .............................. 91 L5
Great Holland Essex ....... 62 E4
Great Hollands
  Br For ............................. 42 E6
Great Horkesley
  Essex ............................. 62 B2
Great Hormead
  Herts .............................. 60 C3

| Place | | Page | Grid |
|---|---|---|---|
| Great Horton C Brad | | 123 | H4 |
| Great Horwood | | | |
| Bucks | | 58 | C2 |
| Great Houghton | | | |
| Barns | | 115 | H1 |
| Great Houghton | | | |
| Nhants | | 73 | L3 |
| Great Hucklow | | | |
| Derbys | | 114 | D6 |
| Great Kelk E R Yk | | 135 | H7 |
| Great Kimble Bucks | | 58 | D6 |
| Great Kingshill Bucks | | 42 | E2 |
| Great Langdale | | | |
| Cumb | | 137 | J6 |
| Great Langton N York | | 141 | H7 |
| Great Leighs Essex | | 61 | H4 |
| Great Limber Lincs | | 126 | E8 |
| Great Linford M Keyn | | 74 | C6 |
| Great Livermere | | | |
| Suffk | | 77 | K1 |
| Great Longstone | | | |
| Derbys | | 114 | D6 |
| Great Lumley Dur | | 151 | H5 |
| Great Malvern Worcs | | 70 | D5 |
| Great Maplestead | | | |
| Essex | | 77 | J7 |
| Great Marton Bpool | | 120 | D4 |
| Great Massingham | | | |
| Norfk | | 105 | J7 |
| Great Milton Oxon | | 57 | L7 |
| Great Missenden | | | |
| Bucks | | 58 | E7 |
| Great Mitton Lancs | | 121 | K3 |
| Great Mongeham | | | |
| Kent | | 35 | K4 |
| Great Moulton Norfk | | 92 | E5 |
| Great Musgrave | | | |
| Cumb | | 139 | H4 |
| Great Ness Shrops | | 98 | B8 |
| Great Notley Essex | | 61 | H4 |
| Great Oak Mons | | 54 | B6 |
| Great Oakley Essex | | 62 | E3 |
| Great Oakley Nhants | | 88 | C6 |
| Great Offley Herts | | 59 | J3 |
| Great Ormside Cumb | | 139 | G4 |
| Great Orton Cumb | | 148 | B4 |
| Great Ouseburn | | | |
| N York | | 133 | G6 |
| Great Oxendon | | | |
| Nhants | | 87 | K6 |
| Great Park N u Ty | | 158 | F7 |
| Great Parndon Essex | | 60 | C6 |
| Great Paxton Cambs | | 75 | H2 |
| Great Plumpton | | | |
| Lancs | | 120 | E4 |
| Great Plumstead | | | |
| Norfk | | 93 | G2 |
| Great Ponton Lincs | | 102 | F6 |
| Great Preston Leeds | | 124 | B5 |
| Great Raveley Cambs | | 89 | J7 |
| Great Rissington | | | |
| Gloucs | | 56 | D5 |
| Great Rollright Oxon | | 56 | F2 |
| Great Ryburgh Norfk | | 106 | A6 |
| Great Ryton Shrops | | 83 | J3 |
| Great Saling Essex | | 61 | H3 |
| Great Salkeld Cumb | | 148 | F7 |
| Great Sampford | | | |
| Essex | | 76 | F7 |
| Great Saughall | | | |
| Ches W | | 111 | K7 |
| Great Shefford | | | |
| W Berk | | 41 | G5 |
| Great Shelford | | | |
| Cambs | | 76 | C4 |
| Great Smeaton | | | |
| N York | | 141 | H6 |
| Great Snoring Norfk | | 105 | M5 |
| Great Somerford | | | |
| Wilts | | 39 | L4 |
| Great Soudley | | | |
| Shrops | | 99 | G6 |
| Great Stainton Darltn | | 141 | H3 |
| Great Stambridge | | | |
| Essex | | 46 | E2 |
| Great Staughton | | | |
| Cambs | | 75 | G2 |
| Great Steeping Lincs | | 118 | F8 |
| Great Stoke S Glos | | 38 | F4 |
| Greatstone-on-Sea | | | |
| Kent | | 21 | L2 |
| Great Strickland | | | |
| Cumb | | 138 | D3 |
| Great Stukeley | | | |
| Cambs | | 89 | J8 |
| Great Sturton Lincs | | 117 | K6 |
| Great Swinburne | | | |
| Nthumb | | 158 | B6 |
| Great Tew Oxon | | 57 | H3 |
| Great Tey Essex | | 61 | L3 |
| Great Thurlow Suffk | | 76 | F4 |
| Great Torrington | | | |
| Devon | | 23 | H7 |
| Great Tosson Nthumb | | 158 | C3 |
| Great Totham Essex | | 61 | K5 |
| Great Totham Essex | | 61 | L5 |
| Great Urswick Cumb | | 129 | G5 |
| Great Wakering | | | |
| Essex | | 46 | F3 |
| Great Waldingfield | | | |
| Suffk | | 77 | K5 |
| Great Walsingham | | | |
| Norfk | | 105 | M5 |
| Great Waltham Essex | | 61 | H5 |
| Great Warley Essex | | 45 | L2 |
| Great Washbourne | | | |
| Gloucs | | 71 | H7 |
| Great Weeke Devon | | 11 | G7 |
| Great Wenham Suffk | | 78 | C6 |
| Great Whittington | | | |
| Nthumb | | 158 | C7 |
| Great Wigborough | | | |
| Essex | | 62 | A5 |
| Great Wilbraham | | | |
| Cambs | | 76 | D3 |
| Great Wishford Wilts | | 28 | B4 |
| Great Witcombe | | | |
| Gloucs | | 55 | K5 |
| Great Witley Worcs | | 70 | D2 |
| Great Wolford | | | |
| Warwks | | 72 | B7 |
| Greatworth Nhants | | 73 | G6 |
| Great Wratting Suffk | | 77 | G5 |
| Great Wymondley | | | |
| Herts | | 59 | K3 |
| Great Wyrley Staffs | | 85 | H3 |
| Great Yarmouth | | | |
| Norfk | | 93 | L3 |
| Great Yeldham Essex | | 77 | H6 |
| Greenburn W Loth | | 176 | C6 |
| Green End Herts | | 60 | B2 |
| Green End Herts | | 60 | B4 |
| Greenfield Ag & B | | 173 | M1 |
| Greenfield C Beds | | 74 | F7 |
| Greenfield Flints | | 111 | H6 |
| Greenfield Highld | | 201 | J5 |
| Greenfield Oldham | | 113 | M2 |
| Greenford Gt Lon | | 43 | J4 |
| Greengairs N Lans | | 175 | K4 |
| Greengates C Brad | | 123 | J3 |
| Greenham Somset | | 25 | G7 |
| Green Hammerton | | | |
| N York | | 133 | G7 |
| Greenhaugh Nthumb | | 157 | K5 |
| Greenhead Nthumb | | 149 | H3 |
| Green Heath Staffs | | 85 | H2 |
| Greenhill D & G | | 155 | J6 |
| Greenhill Falk | | 175 | L3 |
| Greenhill Kent | | 47 | K6 |
| Greenhill Leics | | 86 | F2 |
| Greenhills S Lans | | 165 | H3 |
| Greenhills S Lans | | 175 | H7 |
| Greenhithe Kent | | 45 | L5 |
| Greenholm E Ayrs | | 164 | B3 |
| Greenhouse Border | | 167 | H5 |
| Greenhow Hill | | | |
| N York | | 131 | L6 |
| Greenland Highld | | 231 | J3 |
| Greenland Sheff | | 115 | H4 |
| Greenlaw Border | | 167 | L1 |
| Greenlea D & G | | 155 | J3 |
| Greenloaning P & K | | 185 | H6 |
| Greenmount Bury | | 122 | B7 |
| Greenock Inver | | 174 | B3 |
| Greenodd Cumb | | 129 | G3 |
| Green Ore Somset | | 26 | E2 |
| Green Park Readg | | 42 | B6 |
| Green Quarter Cumb | | 138 | C6 |
| Greenshields S Lans | | 165 | K2 |
| Greenside Gatesd | | 150 | E3 |
| Greenside Kirk | | 123 | H7 |
| Greens Norton | | | |
| Nhants | | 73 | J4 |
| Greenstead Green | | | |
| Essex | | 61 | K3 |
| Green Street Herts | | 59 | K7 |
| Green Street Herts | | 60 | D4 |
| Green Tye Herts | | 60 | C4 |
| Greenway Somset | | 25 | L6 |
| Greenwich Gt Lon | | 45 | G4 |
| Greenwich | | | |
| Maritime Gt Lon | | 45 | H4 |
| Greet Gloucs | | 56 | B3 |
| Greete Shrops | | 69 | L1 |
| Greetham Lincs | | 118 | D7 |
| Greetham Rutlnd | | 88 | D2 |
| Greetland Calder | | 123 | G6 |
| Greinton Somset | | 26 | B4 |
| Grenaby IoM | | 237 | b6 |
| Grendon Nhants | | 74 | C3 |
| Grendon Warwks | | 86 | C4 |
| Grendon | | | |
| Underwood Bucks | | 58 | B4 |
| Grenoside Sheff | | 115 | G3 |
| Greosabhagh W Isls | | 232 | e4 |
| Gresford Wrexhm | | 97 | M2 |
| Gresham Norfk | | 106 | E5 |
| Greshornish Highld | | 208 | E4 |
| Gressenhall Norfk | | 91 | L1 |
| Gressenhall Green | | | |
| Norfk | | 91 | L1 |
| Gressingham Lancs | | 130 | B5 |
| Greta Bridge Dur | | 140 | D5 |
| Gretna D & G | | 148 | B2 |
| Gretna Green D & G | | 148 | B2 |
| Gretna Services | | | |
| D & G | | 148 | B2 |
| Gretton Gloucs | | 56 | A2 |
| Gretton Nhants | | 88 | C5 |
| Gretton Shrops | | 83 | K4 |
| Grewelthorpe N York | | 132 | C4 |
| Greyrigg D & G | | 155 | J4 |
| Greys Green Oxon | | 42 | B4 |
| Greysouthen Cumb | | 136 | E2 |
| Greystoke Cumb | | 138 | B2 |
| Greystone Angus | | 196 | E7 |
| Greywell Hants | | 30 | B2 |
| Griff Warwks | | 86 | D5 |
| Griffithstown Torfn | | 53 | L7 |
| Grimeford Village | | | |
| Lancs | | 121 | J7 |
| Grimesthorpe Sheff | | 115 | G4 |
| Grimethorpe Barns | | 124 | C8 |
| Grimister Shet | | 235 | d2 |
| Grimley Worcs | | 70 | E3 |
| Grimmet S Ayrs | | 163 | H7 |
| Grimoldby Lincs | | 118 | E4 |
| Grimpo Shrops | | 98 | A7 |
| Grimsargh Lancs | | 121 | H4 |
| Grimsby NE Lin | | 127 | G7 |
| Grimscote Nhants | | 73 | J4 |
| Grimscott Cnwll | | 9 | H4 |
| Grimshader W Isls | | 232 | f3 |
| Grimsthorpe Lincs | | 103 | H7 |
| Grimston Leics | | 102 | B7 |
| Grimston Norfk | | 105 | H7 |
| Grimstone Dorset | | 14 | C4 |
| Grimstone End Suffk | | 77 | L2 |
| Grindale E R Yk | | 135 | H5 |
| Grindleford Derbys | | 114 | E6 |
| Grindleton Lancs | | 121 | L2 |
| Grindley Brook | | | |
| Shrops | | 98 | D4 |
| Grindlow Derbys | | 114 | D6 |
| Grindon Staffs | | 100 | B2 |
| Gringley on the Hill | | | |
| Notts | | 116 | C4 |
| Grinsdale Cumb | | 148 | C4 |
| Grinshill Shrops | | 98 | D7 |
| Grinton N York | | 140 | D7 |
| Griomsiadar W Isls | | 232 | f3 |
| Grishipoll Ag & B | | 188 | F4 |
| Gristhorpe N York | | 135 | H3 |
| Griston Norfk | | 91 | L4 |
| Gritley Ork | | 234 | d6 |
| Grittenham Wilts | | 40 | B4 |
| Grittleton Wilts | | 39 | K4 |
| Grizebeck Cumb | | 128 | F3 |
| Grizedale Cumb | | 137 | K7 |
| Groby Leics | | 87 | G3 |
| Groes Conwy | | 110 | D8 |
| Groes-faen Rhondd | | 37 | G4 |
| Groeslon Gwynd | | 95 | H2 |
| Groes-Wen Caerph | | 37 | H3 |
| Grogarry W Isls | | 233 | b7 |
| Grogport Ag & B | | 161 | K1 |
| Groigearraidh W Isls | | 233 | b7 |
| Gronant Flints | | 110 | F5 |
| Groombridge E Susx | | 32 | F5 |
| Grosebay W Isls | | 232 | e4 |
| Grosmont Mons | | 54 | B3 |
| Grosmont N York | | 143 | H6 |
| Groton Suffk | | 77 | L6 |
| Grouville Jersey | | 236 | e7 |
| Grove Notts | | 116 | C5 |
| Grove Oxon | | 41 | H3 |
| Grove Green Kent | | 33 | K3 |
| Grove Park Gt Lon | | 45 | H5 |
| Grovesend Swans | | 51 | H5 |
| Gruinard Highld | | 219 | L4 |
| Gruinart Ag & B | | 170 | F5 |
| Grula Highld | | 208 | F8 |
| Gruline Ag & B | | 190 | B7 |
| Grundisburgh Suffk | | 78 | F4 |
| Gruting Shet | | 235 | c5 |
| Grutness Shet | | 235 | c8 |
| Gualachulain Highld | | 192 | B7 |
| Guardbridge Fife | | 187 | G4 |
| Guarlford Worcs | | 70 | E5 |
| Guay P & K | | 194 | F6 |
| Guernsey Guern | | 236 | c3 |
| *Guernsey Airport* | | | |
| Guern | | 236 | c3 |
| Guestling Green | | | |
| E Susx | | 21 | G3 |
| Guestling Thorn | | | |
| E Susx | | 21 | G3 |
| Guestwick Norfk | | 106 | C6 |
| Guide Bridge Tamesd | | 113 | L3 |
| Guilden Morden | | | |
| Cambs | | 75 | K5 |
| Guilden Sutton | | | |
| Ches W | | 112 | C7 |
| Guildford Surrey | | 31 | G2 |
| Guildtown P & K | | 186 | B2 |
| Guilsborough Nhants | | 87 | J8 |
| Guilsfield Powys | | 82 | E2 |
| Guiltreehill S Ayrs | | 163 | J7 |
| Guineaford Devon | | 23 | J4 |
| Guisborough R & Cl | | 142 | D4 |
| Guiseley Leeds | | 123 | J3 |
| Guist Norfk | | 106 | B7 |
| Guiting Power | | | |
| Gloucs | | 56 | C3 |
| Gullane E Loth | | 178 | B2 |
| Gulval Cnwll | | 2 | E5 |
| Gulworthy Devon | | 6 | C2 |
| Gumfreston Pembks | | 49 | J7 |
| Gumley Leics | | 87 | K5 |
| Gunby Lincs | | 102 | E7 |
| Gundleton Hants | | 29 | L5 |
| Gun Hill E Susx | | 20 | C3 |
| Gunn Devon | | 23 | K5 |
| Gunnerside N York | | 139 | L7 |
| Gunnerton Nthumb | | 158 | A7 |
| Gunness N Linc | | 125 | K7 |
| Gunnislake Cnwll | | 6 | C2 |
| Gunnista Shet | | 235 | d6 |
| Gunthorpe C Pete | | 89 | H3 |
| Gunthorpe N Linc | | 116 | D3 |
| Gunthorpe Norfk | | 106 | B5 |
| Gunthorpe Notts | | 102 | B4 |
| Gunwalloe Cnwll | | 3 | H6 |
| Gurnard IoW | | 16 | F4 |
| Gurney Slade Somset | | 26 | F2 |
| Gurnos Powys | | 52 | B6 |
| Gussage All Saints | | | |
| Dorset | | 15 | J1 |
| Gussage St Andrew | | | |
| Dorset | | 27 | L8 |
| Gussage St Michael | | | |
| Dorset | | 15 | J1 |

Guston Kent ...............35 J5
Gutcher Shet ..............235 d2
Guthrie Angus...........196 F6
Guyhirn Cambs..........90 B3
Guyzance Nthumb......158 F2
Gwaenysgor Flints ...110 F5
Gwalchmai IoA .........108 E6
Gwaun-Cae-
Gurwen Carmth.........51 K3
Gweek Cnwll ................3 J6
Gwenddwr Powys.......68 B6
Gwennap Cnwll ...........3 J4
Gwennap Mining
District Cnwll.............3 K3
Gwernaffield Flints ....111 H7
Gwernesney Mons.......54 B7
Gwernogle Carmth ....66 C7
Gwernymynydd
Flints.......................97 J1
Gwersyllt Wrexhm......97 L2
Gwespyr Flints...........110 F5
Gwinear Cnwll ..............3 G4
Gwithian Cnwll .............3 G3
Gwyddelwern
Denbgs....................97 G3
Gwyddgrug Carmth...66 B7
Gwytherin Conwy........96 D1

H

Habberley Shrops......83 H3
Habberley Worcs ........84 E7
Habergham Lancs ...122 B4
Habertoft Lincs .........119 G7
Habrough NE Lin.......126 E7
Hacconby Lincs........103 J7
Haceby Lincs ...........103 G5
Hacheston Suffk........79 G3
Hackbridge Gt Lon ....44 F6
Hackenthorpe Sheff ...115 H5
Hackford Norfk..........92 C3
Hackforth N York ......132 C2
Hackland Ork ...........234 c5
Hackleton Nhants ......74 B4
Hacklinge Kent..........35 J4
Hackness N York ......134 F2
Hackney Gt Lon .........45 G3
Hackthorn Lincs .......117 G5
Hackthorpe Cumb ...138 D3
Hadley Worcs ............70 F2
Hadley Wrekin............84 C2
Hadley End Staffs .....100 C7
Hadley Wood Gt Lon ...44 E1
Hadlow Kent...............33 H3
Hadlow Down E Susx..20 B2
Hadnall Shrops...........98 D7
Hadrian's Wall ..........150 B2
Hadstock Essex..........76 D5
Hadzor Worcs .............71 G3
Haggersta Shet.........235 c5
Haggerston Nthumb..168 F2
Haggs Falk................175 L3
Hagley Herefs ............69 L6
Hagley Worcs .............85 G7
Hagworthingham
Lincs......................118 D7
Haile Cumb...............136 E5
Hailey Oxon................57 G5
Hailsham E Susx.........20 C4
Hail Weston Cambs.....75 H3
Hainault Gt Lon ..........45 J2
Hainford Norfk..........106 F8
Hainton Lincs...........117 K5
Haisthorpe E R Yk.....135 H6
Hakin Pembks.............48 F6

Halam Notts ............102 B2
Halbeath Fife............176 F1
Halberton Devon........24 F8
Halcro Highld............231 J4
Hale Cumb...............129 K4
Hale Halton .............112 C5
Hale Hants.................28 D7
Hale Surrey................30 D2
Hale Traffd..............113 H4
Hale Barns Traffd....113 H4
Hales Norfk................93 H4
Hales Staffs ...............99 G5
Halesowen Dudley.....85 G6
Hales Place Kent........34 F3
Hale Street Kent........33 H4
Halesworth Suffk......93 H7
Halewood Knows ....112 C4
Halford Devon..............7 J2
Halford Warwks..........72 C5
Halfpenny Green
Staffs......................84 E5
Halfway House
Shrops....................83 G2
Halfway Houses Kent.....46 F5
Halifax Calder..........123 G5
Halket E Ayrs...........174 D7
Halkirk Highld...........231 G4
Halkyn Flints............111 H7
Hall E Rens..............174 D7
Halland E Susx...........20 A3
Hallaton Leics............87 L4
Hallatrow BaNES........38 F8
Hallbankgate Cumb..149 G3
Hall Dunnerdale
Cumb....................137 H7
Hallen S Glos.............38 D4
Hallgarth Dur...........151 H6
Hallglen Falk............176 B3
Hall Green Birm..........85 K7
Hallin Highld............208 D3
Halling Medway..........46 B7
Hallington Lincs........118 D4
Hallington Nthumb....158 C6
Halliwell Bolton.........121 K7
Halloughton Notts....102 B3
Hallow Worcs..............70 E3
Hall's Green Herts......59 L3
Hallyne Border..........166 B2
Halmore Gloucs..........55 G7
Halnaker W Susx........18 B4
Halsall Lancs............120 E7
Halse Nhants.............73 H6
Halse Somset.............25 H5
Halsetown Cnwll..........2 E4
Halsham E R Yk.......127 G5
Halstead Essex...........61 K2
Halstead Kent.............45 J7
Halstead Leics............87 L3
Halstock Dorset.........14 A2
Haltham Lincs...........118 C8
Halton Bucks.............58 E6
Halton Halton...........112 D5
Halton Lancs............129 K6
Halton Leeds............123 L4
Halton Nthumb.........150 C2
Halton Wrexhm..........97 L4
Halton East N York...131 K8
Halton Gill N York....131 G4
Halton Holegate
Lincs......................118 F7
Halton Lea Gate
Nthumb.................149 H4
Halton Shields
Nthumb.................150 C2
Halton West N York...130 F8
Haltwhistle Nthumb..149 J3
Halvergate Norfk........93 J3
Halwell Devon..............7 H5
Halwill Devon.............10 C5
Halwill Junction
Devon....................10 C5
Ham Devon...............13 G3
Ham Gloucs...............55 G7
Ham Gt Lon...............44 D5
Ham Kent...................35 J4
Ham Somset.............25 L6
Ham Wilts.................41 G7
Hambleden Bucks.......42 C3

Hambledon Hants......29 M7
Hambledon Surrey......30 F4
Hamble-le-Rice
Hants.......................16 F2
Hambleton Lancs......120 E3
Hambleton N York....124 E4
Hambridge Somset.....26 B6
Hambrook W Susx......17 L2
Hameringham Lincs...118 D7
Hamerton Cambs........89 G7
Ham Green Worcs.......71 H2
Hamilton S Lans.......175 J7
Hamilton Services
(northbound)
S Lans...................175 J6
Hamlet Dorset............14 B2
Hammersmith Gt Lon....44 E4
Hammerwich Staffs...85 J3
Hammoon Dorset........27 J8
Hamnavoe Shet.......235 c6
Hampden Park
E Susx....................20 C5
Hampnett Gloucs........56 C5
Hampole Donc...........124 D7
Hampreston Dorset....15 K3
Hampstead Gt Lon.....44 E3
Hampstead Norreys
W Berk....................41 K5
Hampsthwaite N York.132 C7
Hampton C Pete.........89 H5
Hampton Gt Lon.........43 J6
Hampton Kent............47 K6
Hampton Shrops.........84 D6
Hampton Swindn........40 D3
Hampton Worcs..........71 H5
Hampton Bishop
Herefs......................69 L6
Hampton Court
Palace Gt Lon..........44 D6
Hampton Heath
Ches W....................98 D3
Hampton-in-Arden
Solhll.......................86 B7
Hampton Lovett
Worcs......................70 F2
Hampton Lucy
Warwks....................72 B3
Hampton Magna
Warwks....................72 C2
Hampton Park Wilts....28 D5
Hampton Poyle Oxon...57 J5
Hampton Wick
Gt Lon....................44 D6
Hamptworth Wilts......28 E7
Hamsey E Susx...........19 L3
Hamstall Ridware
Staffs....................100 C8
Hamstead Birm...........85 J5
Hamstead Marshall
W Berk....................41 H7
Hamsterley Dur........140 E2
Hamsterley Dur........150 E4
Hamstreet Kent..........34 D7
Hamworthy BCP.........15 J4
Hanbury Staffs.........100 D6
Hanbury Worcs...........71 G2
Hanchurch Staffs........99 J4
Handa Island Highld...228 A3
Hand and Pen Devon....12 D4
Handbridge Ches W...112 B7
Handcross W Susx.......31 L5
Handforth Ches E.......113 J5
Handley Ches W..........98 C2
Handley Derbys.........101 G1
Handsworth Birm.......85 J5
Handsworth Sheff.....115 H4
Hanford C Stke...........99 K4
Hanging Heaton Kirk..123 K6
Hanging Houghton
Nhants.....................87 L8
Hanging Langford
Wilts.......................28 B4
Hangleton Br & H.......19 H4
Hanham S Glos...........38 F6
Hankelow Ches E.........98 F4
Hankerton Wilts..........39 L3
Hanley C Stke.............99 K3

Hanley Castle Worcs....70 E6
Hanley Child Worcs......70 B2
Hanley Swan Worcs.....70 E6
Hanley William
Worcs......................70 C2
Hanlith N York..........131 G7
Hanmer Wrexhm.........98 C4
Hannaford Devon........23 J5
Hannington Hants.......29 K1
Hannington Nhants....74 B1
Hannington Swindn....40 D2
Hannington Wick
Swindn....................40 D2
Hanslope M Keyn.......74 B5
Hanthorpe Lincs.......103 H7
Hanwell Gt Lon..........44 D4
Hanwell Oxon.............72 E5
Hanwood Shrops........83 J1
Hanworth Gt Lon........43 J6
Hanworth Norfk........106 C5
Happendon S Lans....165 G3
Happendon
Services S Lans.....165 G3
Happisburgh Norfk..107 H6
Happisburgh
Common Norfk......107 H6
Hapsford Ches W......112 C6
Hapton Lancs...........122 B4
Hapton Norfk............92 E4
Harberton Devon..........7 H4
Harbertonford Devon...7 H5
Harbledown Kent........34 F3
Harborne Birm...........85 H6
Harborough Magna
Warwks....................86 F7
Harbottle Nthumb....158 B2
Harbourneford
Devon......................7 G4
Harburn W Loth.......176 E6
Harbury Warwks.........72 D3
Harby Leics..............102 C6
Harby Notts..............116 E7
Harcombe Devon........11 K8
Harcombe Devon........12 F4
Harcombe Bottom
Devon......................13 J4
Harden C Brad.........123 G4
Harden Wsall.............85 H4
Hardenhuish Wilts......39 K5
Hardgate Abers........206 E5
Hardgate D & G.......146 E2
Hardgate W Duns.....174 F4
Hardham W Susx........18 E3
Hardingham Norfk......92 C3
Hardingstone Nhants..73 L3
Hardington Somset.....27 H2
Hardington
Mandeville
Somset....................13 M1
Hardington Marsh
Somset....................13 M1
Hardington Moor
Somset....................26 D8
Hardisworthy Devon...22 C7
Hardley Hants............16 E2
Hardley Street Norfk...93 H4
Hardraw N York.......131 G2
Hardstoft Derbys......115 H8
Hardway Hants..........17 H3
Hardway Somset........27 G5
Hardwick Bucks.........58 D4
Hardwick Cambs........75 L3
Hardwick Nhants........74 B1
Hardwick Norfk..........92 F5
Hardwick Oxon..........57 G6
Hardwick Oxon..........57 L3
Hardwick Wsall..........85 J4
Hardwicke Gloucs......55 H5
Hardwicke Gloucs......55 K3
Hardwick Hall
Derbys...................115 J8
Hardy's Green Essex...61 M4
Hare Croft C Brad....123 G4
Harefield Gt Lon........43 H3
Hare Green Essex.......62 D3
Hare Hatch Wokham...42 D5
Harehill Derbys.........100 D5
Harehills Leeds.........123 L4

| | | |
|---|---|---|
| Harelaw Border | 167 | H5 |
| Harelaw D & G | 156 | D6 |
| Harescombe Gloucs | 55 | J6 |
| Haresfield Gloucs | 55 | J6 |
| Harestock Hants | 29 | J5 |
| Hare Street Essex | 60 | C6 |
| Hare Street Herts | 60 | C3 |
| Harewood Leeds | 123 | L2 |
| Harewood End | | |
| Herefs | 54 | D3 |
| Harford Devon | 6 | F4 |
| Hargrave Ches W | 98 | C1 |
| Hargrave Nhants | 74 | F1 |
| Hargrave Suffk | 77 | H3 |
| Harkstead Suffk | 78 | E7 |
| Harlaston Staffs | 86 | B2 |
| Harlaxton Lincs | 102 | E6 |
| Harlech Gwynd | 95 | K6 |
| Harlech Castle | | |
| Gwynd | 95 | K6 |
| Harlescott Shrops | 83 | K1 |
| Harlesden Gt Lon | 44 | E4 |
| Harlesthorpe Derbys | 115 | J6 |
| Harleston Devon | 7 | J6 |
| Harleston Norfk | 92 | F6 |
| Harleston Suffk | 78 | B3 |
| Harlestone Nhants | 73 | K2 |
| Harle Syke Lancs | 122 | C4 |
| Harley Rothm | 115 | G2 |
| Harley Shrops | 83 | L3 |
| Harlington C Beds | 59 | G2 |
| Harlington Donc | 115 | J2 |
| Harlington Gt Lon | 43 | H5 |
| Harlosh Highld | 208 | D6 |
| Harlow Essex | 60 | D6 |
| Harlow Carr RHS | | |
| N York | 132 | D8 |
| Harlow Hill Nthumb | 150 | D2 |
| Harlthorpe E R Yk | 125 | H3 |
| Harlton Cambs | 75 | L4 |
| Harlyn Cnwll | 4 | D2 |
| Harman's Cross | | |
| Dorset | 15 | J6 |
| Harmby N York | 131 | L2 |
| Harmer Green Herts | 59 | L5 |
| Harmer Hill Shrops | 98 | C7 |
| Harmston Lincs | 116 | F8 |
| Harnage Shrops | 83 | L3 |
| Harnhill Gloucs | 56 | B7 |
| Harold Hill Gt Lon | 45 | K2 |
| Haroldston West | | |
| Pembks | 48 | E4 |
| Haroldswick Shet | 235 | e1 |
| Harold Wood Gt Lon | 45 | K3 |
| Harome N York | 133 | K3 |
| Harpenden Herts | 59 | J5 |
| Harpford Devon | 12 | E4 |
| Harpham E R Yk | 135 | H7 |
| Harpley Norfk | 105 | J7 |
| Harpley Worcs | 70 | C3 |
| Harpole Nhants | 73 | K3 |
| Harpsdale Highld | 231 | G4 |
| Harpswell Lincs | 116 | F4 |
| Harpurhey Manch | 113 | K2 |
| Harraby Cumb | 148 | D4 |
| Harracott Devon | 23 | J6 |
| Harrapool Highld | 199 | K2 |
| Harras Cumb | 136 | D4 |
| Harrietfield P & K | 185 | K2 |
| Harrietsham Kent | 33 | L3 |
| Harringay Gt Lon | 44 | F3 |
| Harrington Cumb | 136 | D3 |
| Harrington Lincs | 118 | E6 |
| Harrington Nhants | 87 | L2 |
| Harringworth Nhants | 88 | D4 |
| Harris W Isls | 232 | d4 |
| Harrogate N York | 132 | D7 |
| Harrold Bed | 74 | D3 |
| Harrow Gt Lon | 44 | D3 |
| Harrowbarrow Cnwll | 6 | B2 |
| Harrowgate Village | | |
| Darltn | 141 | H4 |
| Harrow Green Suffk | 77 | J4 |
| Harrow on the Hill | | |
| Gt Lon | 44 | D3 |
| Harrow Weald Gt Lon | 44 | D2 |
| Harston Cambs | 76 | B4 |
| Harston Leics | 102 | D6 |
| Harswell E R Yk | 125 | J3 |
| Hart Hartpl | 151 | L7 |
| Hartburn Nthumb | 158 | D5 |
| Hartburn S on T | 141 | K4 |
| Hartest Suffk | 77 | J4 |
| Hartfield E Susx | 32 | E6 |
| Hartford Cambs | 89 | J8 |
| Hartford Ches W | 112 | F6 |
| Hartfordbridge | | |
| Hants | 42 | C8 |
| Hartford End Essex | 61 | G4 |
| Harthill N York | 140 | F6 |
| Hartgrove Dorset | 27 | J7 |
| Harthill Ches W | 98 | D2 |
| Harthill N Lans | 176 | B5 |
| Harthill Rothm | 115 | J5 |
| Harthope D & G | 165 | K6 |
| Hartington Derbys | 100 | C1 |
| Hartland Devon | 22 | D6 |
| Hartland Quay Devon | 22 | C6 |
| Hartlebury Worcs | 70 | E1 |
| Hartlepool Hartpl | 151 | L7 |
| Hartley Cumb | 139 | H5 |
| Hartley Kent | 33 | K6 |
| Hartley Kent | 45 | L6 |
| Hartley Wespall | | |
| Hants | 42 | B8 |
| Hartley Wintney | | |
| Hants | 30 | C1 |
| Hartlip Kent | 46 | D7 |
| Harton N York | 133 | L6 |
| Harton S Tyne | 151 | J2 |
| Hartpury Gloucs | 55 | J3 |
| Hartshead Kirk | 123 | J6 |
| Hartshead Moor | | |
| Services Calder | 123 | H5 |
| Hartshill C Stke | 99 | K4 |
| Hartshill Warwks | 86 | D5 |
| Hartshorne Derbys | 100 | F7 |
| Hartwell Nhants | 73 | L4 |
| Hartwith N York | 132 | C6 |
| Hartwood N Lans | 175 | L6 |
| Hartwoodmyres | | |
| Border | 166 | F4 |
| Harvel Kent | 46 | A7 |
| Harvington Worcs | 71 | J5 |
| Harvington Worcs | 84 | F8 |
| Harwell Notts | 116 | B3 |
| Harwell Oxon | 41 | J3 |
| Harwich Essex | 62 | F2 |
| Harwood Dale | | |
| N York | 143 | K7 |
| Harworth Notts | 115 | L3 |
| Hasbury Dudley | 85 | G6 |
| Hascombe Surrey | 31 | G4 |
| Haselbech Nhants | 87 | K7 |
| Haselbury Plucknett | | |
| Somset | 13 | L1 |
| Haseley Warwks | 72 | B2 |
| Haselor Warwks | 71 | K3 |
| Hasfield Gloucs | 55 | J3 |
| Haskayne Lancs | 120 | E8 |
| Hasketon Suffk | 78 | F4 |
| Haslemere Surrey | 30 | E5 |
| Haslingden Lancs | 122 | B6 |
| Haslingfield Cambs | 76 | B4 |
| Haslington Ches E | 99 | G2 |
| Hassingham Norfk | 93 | H3 |
| Hassocks W Susx | 19 | J3 |
| Hassop Derbys | 114 | E6 |
| Haster Highld | 231 | K5 |
| Hastingleigh Kent | 34 | E5 |
| Hastings E Susx | 21 | G4 |
| Hastingwood Essex | 60 | D6 |
| Hastoe Herts | 58 | F6 |
| Haswell Dur | 151 | J6 |
| Haswell Plough Dur | 151 | J6 |
| Hatch Beauchamp | | |
| Somset | 25 | L7 |
| Hatch End Gt Lon | 43 | J3 |
| Hatchmere Ches W | 112 | D6 |
| Hatch Warren Hants | 29 | L2 |
| Hatcliffe NE Lin | 117 | K2 |
| Hatfield Donc | 125 | G8 |
| Hatfield Herefs | 69 | L3 |
| Hatfield Herts | 59 | L6 |
| Hatfield Broad Oak | | |
| Essex | 60 | E5 |
| Hatfield Heath Essex | 60 | E5 |
| Hatfield Peverel | | |
| Essex | 61 | J5 |
| Hatfield Woodhouse | | |
| Donc | 125 | G8 |
| Hatford Oxon | 41 | G2 |
| Hatherden Hants | 29 | G2 |
| Hatherleigh Devon | 10 | D4 |
| Hathern Leics | 101 | J7 |
| Hatherop Gloucs | 56 | D6 |
| Hathersage Derbys | 114 | E5 |
| Hathersage Booths | | |
| Derbys | 114 | E5 |
| Hatherton Ches E | 99 | G3 |
| Hatherton Staffs | 85 | G2 |
| Hatley St George | | |
| Cambs | 75 | K4 |
| Hatt Cnwll | 6 | B4 |
| Hattersley Tamesd | 113 | M3 |
| Hatton Abers | 217 | K6 |
| Hatton Angus | 196 | D7 |
| Hatton Derbys | 100 | E6 |
| Hatton Gt Lon | 43 | J5 |
| Hatton Lincs | 117 | K6 |
| Hatton Shrops | 83 | J5 |
| Hatton Warrtn | 112 | E5 |
| Hatton Warwks | 72 | B2 |
| Hatton of Fintray | | |
| Abers | 206 | F3 |
| Haugh E Ayrs | 163 | L4 |
| Haugham Lincs | 118 | D5 |
| Haughhead E Duns | 175 | G3 |
| Haughley Suffk | 78 | B3 |
| Haughley Green | | |
| Suffk | 78 | B2 |
| Haugh of Glass | | |
| Moray | 215 | J6 |
| Haugh of Urr D & G | 146 | E2 |
| Haughs of Kinnaird | | |
| Angus | 197 | G5 |
| Haughton Ches E | 98 | E2 |
| Haughton Shrops | 98 | B6 |
| Haughton Staffs | 99 | K7 |
| Haughton le Skerne | | |
| Darltn | 141 | H4 |
| Haultwick Herts | 60 | B4 |
| Haunton Staffs | 86 | B2 |
| Hautes Croix Jersey | 236 | c6 |
| Hauxton Cambs | 76 | B4 |
| Havant Hants | 17 | K2 |
| Havenstreet IoW | 17 | G4 |
| Havercroft Wakefd | 124 | B7 |
| Haverfordwest | | |
| Pembks | 48 | F4 |
| Haverhill Suffk | 76 | F5 |
| Haverigg Cumb | 128 | E4 |
| Havering-atte- | | |
| Bower Gt Lon | 45 | K2 |
| Haversham M Keyn | 74 | B6 |
| Haverthwaite Cumb | 129 | H3 |
| Havyatt N Som | 38 | C7 |
| Hawarden Flints | 111 | J7 |
| Hawbush Green | | |
| Essex | 61 | J4 |
| Hawen Cerdgn | 65 | K5 |
| Hawes N York | 131 | G2 |
| Hawe's Green Norfk | 92 | F4 |
| Hawford Worcs | 70 | E3 |
| Hawick Border | 167 | G6 |
| Hawkchurch Devon | 13 | J3 |
| Hawkedon Suffk | 77 | H4 |
| Hawkeridge Wilts | 27 | K2 |
| Hawkesbury S Glos | 39 | H3 |
| Hawkesbury Upton | | |
| S Glos | 39 | H3 |
| Hawkhurst Kent | 33 | K6 |
| Hawkinge Kent | 35 | G6 |
| Hawkley Hants | 30 | C5 |
| Hawkridge Somset | 24 | D5 |
| Hawkshead Cumb | 137 | K7 |
| Hawkshead Hill | | |
| Cumb | 137 | K7 |
| Hawksland S Lans | 165 | G2 |
| Hawkstone Shrops | 98 | E6 |
| Hawkswick N York | 131 | H5 |
| Hawksworth Leeds | 123 | H3 |
| Hawksworth Notts | 102 | C4 |
| Hawkwell Essex | 46 | E2 |
| Hawley Hants | 42 | E8 |
| Hawling Gloucs | 56 | B4 |
| Hawnby N York | 133 | H2 |
| Haworth C Brad | 122 | F3 |
| Hawstead Suffk | 77 | J3 |
| Hawthorn Dur | 151 | K5 |
| Hawthorn Hill Lincs | 103 | K2 |
| Hawton Notts | 102 | C3 |
| Haxby C York | 133 | J7 |
| Haxey N Linc | 116 | C2 |
| Haydock St Hel | 112 | E3 |
| Haydon Bridge | | |
| Nthumb | 149 | L3 |
| Haydon Wick Swindn | 40 | C3 |
| Hayes Gt Lon | 43 | J4 |
| Hayes Gt Lon | 45 | H6 |
| Hayes End Gt Lon | 43 | H4 |
| Hayfield Ag & B | 182 | F3 |
| Hayfield Derbys | 114 | B4 |
| Hayhillock Angus | 196 | E7 |
| Hayle Cnwll | 2 | F4 |
| Hayle Port Cnwll | 2 | F4 |
| Hayley Green Dudley | 85 | G6 |
| Hayling Island Hants | 17 | K3 |
| Hayne Devon | 11 | H7 |
| Haynes C Beds | 75 | G6 |
| Haynes Church End | | |
| C Beds | 74 | F6 |
| Haynes West End | | |
| C Beds | 74 | F6 |
| Hay-on-Wye Powys | 68 | E6 |
| Hayscastle Pembks | 48 | F3 |
| Hayscastle Cross | | |
| Pembks | 48 | F3 |
| Hay Street Herts | 60 | C3 |
| Hayton Cumb | 147 | K6 |
| Hayton Cumb | 148 | E4 |
| Hayton E R Yk | 125 | J2 |
| Hayton Notts | 116 | B5 |
| Haytor Vale Devon | 7 | H1 |
| Haytown Devon | 9 | K3 |
| Haywards Heath | | |
| W Susx | 19 | J2 |
| Haywood Donc | 124 | E7 |
| Hazelbank S Lans | 165 | G1 |
| Hazelbury Bryan | | |
| Dorset | 14 | E2 |
| Hazeleigh Essex | 61 | K7 |
| Hazel Grove Stockp | 113 | L4 |
| Hazelton Walls Fife | 186 | E3 |
| Hazelwood Derbys | 101 | G4 |
| Hazlemere Bucks | 42 | E2 |
| Hazlerigg N u Ty | 159 | G7 |
| Hazleton Gloucs | 56 | B4 |
| Heacham Norfk | 105 | G5 |
| Headbourne Worthy | | |
| Hants | 29 | J5 |
| Headcorn Kent | 33 | L4 |
| Headingley Leeds | 123 | K4 |
| Headington Oxon | 57 | K6 |
| Headlam Dur | 140 | F4 |
| Headlesscross | | |
| N Lans | 176 | B6 |
| Headless Cross | | |
| Worcs | 71 | J2 |
| Headley Hants | 30 | D4 |
| Headley Hants | 41 | K7 |
| Headley Surrey | 31 | K1 |
| Headley Down Hants | 30 | D4 |
| Headon Notts | 116 | C6 |
| Heads Nook Cumb | 148 | E4 |
| Heage Derbys | 101 | G3 |
| Healaugh N York | 124 | D2 |
| Healaugh N York | 140 | C7 |
| Heald Green Stockp | 113 | J4 |
| Heale Somset | 25 | K7 |
| Heale Somset | 26 | B6 |
| Healey N York | 132 | B4 |
| Healeyfield Dur | 150 | D5 |
| Healing NE Lin | 126 | F7 |
| Heamoor Cnwll | 2 | E5 |
| Heanor Derbys | 101 | H3 |
| Heanton Punchardon | | |
| Devon | 23 | H4 |
| Heapham Lincs | 116 | E4 |
| Heart of Scotland | | |
| Services N Lans | 176 | B5 |

Heasley Mill Devon ........24 B5
Heaste Highld................199 K2
Heath Derbys ................115 H7
Heath Wakefd.................123 L6
**Heath and Reach**
  C Beds..........................58 F3
Heathcote Derbys........100 D1
Heather Leics..................86 E2
Heathfield E Susx ...........20 C2
Heathfield Somset.........25 J6
Heath Green Worcs........71 J1
Heath Hall D & G ..........155 H6
**Heath Hayes &**
  **Wimblebury**
  Staffs............................85 H2
Heath Hill Shrops ..........84 D2
*Heathrow Airport*
  *Gt Lon*..........................43 H5
Heathton Shrops ............84 E5
Heath Town Wolves ......85 G4
Heatley Warrtn .............113 G4
Heaton C Brad ..............123 H4
Heaton N u Ty ...............151 G2
Heaton Staffs...............113 L8
**Heaton Chapel**
  Stockp..........................113 K3
**Heaton Mersey**
  Stockp..........................113 K4
Heaton Norris Stockp..113 K4
**Heaton's Bridge**
  Lancs............................120 E7
Heaverham Kent............33 G2
Heavitree Devon ............12 B4
Hebburn S Tyne............151 H3
Hebden N York..............131 J6
**Hebden Bridge**
  Calder...........................122 E5
Hebing End Herts...........60 A4
Hebron Carmth...............49 K3
Hebron Nthumb............158 F4
Heckfield Hants ..............42 B7
**Heckfield Green**
  Suffk..............................92 E7
**Heckfordbridge**
  Essex.............................61 M4
Heckington Lincs..........103 J4
Heckmondwike Kirk....123 J5
Heddington Wilts..........39 M6
**Heddon-on-the-**
  **Wall** Nthumb............150 E2
Hedenham Norfk ............93 G5
Hedge End Hants ...........29 J8
Hedgerley Bucks.............42 F3
Hedging Somset..............25 L5
**Hedley on the Hill**
  Nthumb........................150 D3
Hednesford Staffs...........85 H2
Hedsor Bucks..................42 E3
Heeley Sheff..................115 G5
Heglibister Shet ...........235 c5
Heighington Darltn .....141 G3
Heighington Lincs........117 G7
Heightington Worcs.......70 D1
Heiton Border ...............167 L4
Hele Devon .....................12 C2
Hele Devon .....................23 H3
Helensburgh Ag & B ....174 B2
Helenton S Ayrs ...........163 K3
Helford Cnwll ....................3 K6
**Helford Passage**
  Cnwll................................3 K6
Helhoughton Norfk.....105 K7
**Helions Bumpstead**
  Essex.............................76 F6
Helland Cnwll ...................5 G2
Hellescott Cnwll...............9 H6
Hellesdon Norfk.............92 E2
Hellidon Nhants.............73 G3
Hellifield N York ...........131 G7
Hellingly E Susx .............20 C4
Helmdon Nhants ...........73 H5
Helme Kirk ....................123 G7
Helmingham Suffk..........78 E3
Helmsdale Highld .........227 H5
Helmshore Lancs..........122 B6
Helmsley N York...........133 J3
Helperby N York...........133 G5

Helperthorpe N York....134 E5
Helpringham Lincs........103 J4
Helpston C Pete..............89 G3
Helsby Ches W...............112 C6
Helston Cnwll....................3 H5
Helstone Cnwll .................8 E8
Helton Cumb .................138 D3
**Hemel Hempstead**
  Herts..............................59 H6
Hemerdon Devon..............6 E4
**Hemingbrough**
  N York..........................125 G4
Hemingby Lincs.............118 C6
**Hemingford Abbots**
  Cambs............................75 K1
**Hemingford Grey**
  Cambs............................75 K1
Hemingstone Suffk........78 D4
Hemington Leics...........101 J6
Hemington Nhants.........88 F6
Hemington Somset.........27 G2
Hemley Suffk...................79 G6
Hemlington Middsb.....142 B4
Hempnall Norfk..............92 F5
**Hempnall Green**
  Norfk.............................92 F5
Hempriggs Moray.........214 D2
Hempstead Essex...........76 F6
Hempstead Medway......46 C6
Hempstead Norfk.........106 D5
Hempstead Norfk.........107 J6
Hempton Norfk.............105 L6
Hempton Oxon................57 H2
Hemsby Norfk...............107 K8
Hemswell Lincs.............116 F4
Hemswell Cliff Lincs ...116 F4
Hemsworth Wakefd.....124 C7
Hemyock Devon..............25 H8
Henbury Bristl.................38 E5
Hendon Gt Lon...............44 E3
Hendon Sundld .............151 K4
Hendy Carmth.................51 H5
Henfield W Susx ............19 G3
Hengoed Caerph.............37 J2
Hengoed Powys...............68 E4
Hengrave Suffk...............77 J2
Henham Essex.................60 E3
Heniarth Powys...............82 C2
Henlade Somset..............25 L6
Henley Dorset..................14 D2
Henley Somset................26 B5
Henley Suffk....................78 E4
Henley W Susx ...............30 E6
Henley Green Covtry......86 D6
**Henley-in-Arden**
  Warwks..........................71 L2
**Henley-on-Thames**
  Oxon..............................42 C4
**Henley's Down**
  E Susx.............................20 E3
Henllan Cerdgn...............65 K6
Henllan Denbgs.............110 E7
Henllys Torfn..................37 K3
Henlow C Beds................75 H6
Henlow Camp C Beds....75 H7
Hennock Devon................11 J8
Henny Street Essex........77 K6
Henryd Conwy...............109 L6
**Henry's Moat**
  **(Castell Hendre)**
  Pembks..........................49 H3
Hensall N York ..............124 F5
Henshaw Nthumb.........149 J3
Hensingham Cumb.......136 D4
Henstead Suffk...............93 K6
Hensting Hants...............29 J6
Henstridge Somset.........27 G7
**Henstridge Ash**
  Somset...........................27 G7
Henton Oxon...................58 C7
Henton Somset...............26 C3
Henwick Worcs...............70 E4
Henwood Cnwll................5 L2
Heol-y-Cyw Brdgnd.......36 E4
Hepple Nthumb..............158 C2
Hepscott Nthumb.........158 F5
Heptonstall Calder.......122 E5
Hepworth Kirk..............114 D1

Hepworth Suffk..............92 B8
**Herbrandston**
  Pembks..........................48 E6
Hereford Herefs..............69 K6
Hereson Kent...................35 K2
Heribusta Highld...........218 B7
Heriot Border .................177 L7
Hermiston C Edin..........177 G4
Hermitage Border .........156 E3
Hermitage Dorset...........14 C2
Hermitage W Berk...........41 J5
Hermon Carmth..............65 K7
Hermon Pembks..............49 L2
Herne Kent......................47 K6
Herne Bay Kent...............47 K6
Herne Hill Gt Lon............44 F5
Herne Pound Kent..........33 H3
Hernhill Kent...................34 E3
Herodsfoot Cnwll.............5 K4
Heronsford S Ayrs .......152 D5
Herriard Hants................30 A3
Herringfleet Suffk...........93 K4
Herringswell Suffk.........77 G1
**Herringthorpe**
  Rothm..........................115 J3
Herrington Sundld .......151 J4
Hersden Kent..................35 G3
Hersham Surrey...............43 J7
**Herstmonceux**
  E Susx.............................20 D3
Herston Dorset................15 J6
Herston Ork...................234 c7
Hertford Herts................60 B5
Hertford Heath Herts....60 B5
**Hertingfordbury**
  Herts..............................60 A5
Hesketh Bank Lancs.....120 F5
Hesketh Lane Lancs......121 J3
**Hesket Newmarket**
  Cumb............................148 C2
Hesleden Dur.................151 K7
Heslington C York.........124 F1
Hessay C York ...............133 H8
Hessenford Cnwll.............5 L4
Hessett Suffk...................77 L3
Hessle E R Yk................126 C5
Hessle Wakefd...............124 C6
Hest Bank Lancs............129 K6
Heston Gt Lon.................43 J5
**Heston Services**
  *Gt Lon*..........................43 J5
Hestwall Ork.................234 b5
Heswall Wirral...............111 J5
Hethe Oxon.....................57 L3
Hethersett Norfk.............92 D3
Hethersgill Cumb.........148 E2
Hett Dur........................151 G7
Hetton N York...............131 H7
**Hetton-le-Hole**
  Sundld..........................151 J5
Heugh Nthumb.............158 D7
Heughhead Abers.........205 J3
Heugh Head Border.....179 H6
Heveningham Suffk........93 G8
Hever Kent......................32 E4
Heversham Cumb.........129 K3
Hevingham Norfk.........106 E7
Hewas Water Cnwll..........4 F6
Hewelsfield Gloucs.........54 E7
Hewish Somset...............13 K2
Hewood Dorset...............13 J2
Hexham Nthumb...........150 B3
Hextable Kent.................45 K6
Hexthorpe Donc...........115 K2
Hexton Herts...................59 J2
Hexworthy Cnwll.............9 K8
Hexworthy Devon............6 F2
Heybridge Essex.............61 G7
Heybridge Essex.............61 K6
Heybrook Bay Devon......6 D6
Heydon Cambs................76 B6
Heydon Norfk................106 D6
Heydour Lincs................103 G5
Heylipoll Ag & B ...........188 C7
Heylor Shet....................235 c3
Heysham Lancs..............129 J7
Heyshott W Susx ...........18 B3
Heytesbury Wilts............27 L3

Heythrop Oxon................57 G3
Heywood Rochdl...........122 C7
Heywood Wilts................27 K2
Hibaldstow N Linc.........116 F2
Hickleton Donc..............115 J1
Hickling Norfk...............107 J7
Hickling Notts...............102 B6
Hickling Green Norfk...107 J7
Hickstead W Susx...........31 L7
**Hidcote Bartrim**
  Gloucs...........................71 L6
**Hidcote Boyce**
  Gloucs...........................71 L6
**High Ackworth**
  Wakefd.........................124 C6
Higham Barns...............114 F1
Higham Derbys..............101 H2
Higham Kent...................33 G4
Higham Kent...................46 B5
Higham Lancs................122 B3
Higham Suffk..................77 H2
Higham Suffk..................78 B7
**Higham Ferrers**
  Nhants..........................74 D2
**Higham Gobion**
  C Beds............................59 J2
Higham Hill Gt Lon.........45 G3
**Higham on the Hill**
  Leics..............................86 E4
Highampton Devon........10 C4
Highams Park Gt Lon....45 H2
High Ardwell D & G ....144 C6
High Auldgirth D & G..154 F5
High Bankhill Cumb.....148 F6
High Beach Essex............60 C7
High Bentham N York..130 C5
**High Bickington**
  Devon............................23 J7
High Biggins Cumb ......130 B4
High Blantyre S Lans ...175 J6
**High Bonnybridge**
  Falk..............................175 L3
High Bray Devon............23 L5
Highbridge Somset........25 L3
Highbrook W Susx..........32 C7
High Brooms Kent..........33 G5
Highburton Kirk...........123 J7
Highbury Gt Lon.............44 F3
Highbury Somset............27 G2
High Catton E R Yk.......133 L8
Highclere Hants..............41 H8
Highcliffe BCP.................16 B4
**High Coniscliffe**
  Darltn...........................141 G4
High Crosby Cumb .......148 E3
High Cross E Ayrs ........163 K1
High Cross Hants............30 B6
High Cross Herts.............60 B4
High Cross Warwks........71 L2
**High Drummore**
  D & G............................144 D7
High Easter Essex...........60 F5
High Ellington N York..132 B3
Higher Ansty Dorset......14 E2
Higher Bartle Lancs......121 G4
**Higher**
  **Bockhampton**
  Dorset...........................14 D4
**Higher Brixham**
  Torbay..............................7 L5
High Ercall Wrekin.........98 E8
**Higher Chillington**
  Somset...........................13 K1
Higher Folds Wigan.....113 G2
**Higher Gabwell**
  Devon..............................7 L3
**Higher Heysham**
  Lancs............................129 J7
Higher Irlam Salfd.......113 G3
**Higher Kinnerton**
  Flints..............................97 L1
**Higher Muddiford**
  Devon............................23 J4
**Higher Penwortham**
  Lancs............................121 G5
**Higher Prestacott**
  Devon..............................9 K5
Higher Town Cnwll..........4 C6

**Higher Town** Cnwll .......... 4 F4
**Higher Town** IoS............. 2 b1
**Higher Walton** Lancs... 121 H5
**Higher Walton**
 Warrtn................... 112 E4
**Higher Wambrook**
 Somset.....................13 H2
**Higher Waterston**
 Dorset......................14 D4
**Higher Wheelton**
 Lancs.....................121 J6
**Higher Whitley**
 Ches W....................112 F5
**Higher Wincham**
 Ches W....................113 G6
**Higher Wraxhall**
 Dorset......................14 B3
**Higher Wych** Ches W.....98 C4
**High Etherley** Dur......140 F2
**Highfield** Gatesd..........150 E3
**Highfield** N Ayrs.........174 C7
**Highfields**
 Caldecote Cambs......75 L3
**High Garrett** Essex........61 J3
**Highgate** Gt Lon...........44 F3
**Highgate** Kent.............33 K6
**High Grantley** N York...132 C5
**High Green** Norfk...........92 D3
**High Green** Norfk...........92 E5
**High Green** Sheff.........115 G3
**High Halden** Kent..........34 B7
**High Halstow**
 Medway....................46 C5
**High Ham** Somset..........26 B5
**High Harrington**
 Cumb.....................136 D3
**High Harrogate**
 N York....................132 D7
**High Hatton** Shrops.......98 E2
**High Hauxley** Nthumb..159 G2
**High Hawsker** N York...134 J5
**High Hesket** Cumb......148 E6
**High Hoyland** Barns....123 K8
**High Hurstwood**
 E Susx.....................32 E7
**High Hutton** N York......134 B5
**High Ireby** Cumb........147 M7
**High Kilburn** N York....133 H4
**High Lands** Dur...........140 E3
**Highlane** Derbys.........115 H5
**High Lane** Stockp.......113 L4
**High Lanes** Cnwll..........3 G4
**Highleadon** Gloucs........55 H4
**High Legh** Ches E........113 G5
**Highleigh** W Susx..........18 A6
**High Leven** S on T......141 K5
**Highley** Shrops............84 D6
**High Littleton** BaNES....38 F8
**High Lorton** Cumb......137 G3
**High Marnham** Notts....116 D7
**High Melton** Donc.......115 K2
**High Mickley**
 Nthumb..................150 D3
**Highmoor** Oxon...........42 B4
**Highmoor Cross**
 Oxon......................42 B4
**Highnam** Gloucs..........55 H4
**High Newport** Sundld..151 J4
**High Newton** Cumb.....129 J3
**High Newton-by-**
 **the-Sea** Nthumb...169 J4
**High Nibthwaite**
 Cumb.....................129 G2
**High Offley** Staffs..........99 H7
**High Ongar** Essex.........60 E7
**High Onn** Staffs.............84 E1
**High Park Corner**
 Essex......................62 C4
**High Pennyvenie**
 E Ayrs....................163 L7
**High Pittington** Dur....151 H6
**High Roding** Essex........60 F4
**High Salvington**
 W Susx....................18 H4
**Highsted** Kent..............34 B3
**High Street** Cnwll...........4 F5
**Highstreet** Kent............34 E3

**Highstreet Green**
 Surrey....................31 G4
**Hightae** D & G..........155 J6
**Highter's Heath** Birm....85 J7
**Hightown** Sefton.........111 J2
**Hightown Green**
 Suffk.....................77 L4
**High Toynton** Lincs.....118 C7
**High Valleyfield** Fife....176 D2
**Highweek** Devon............7 J2
**Highwood** Essex...........61 G7
**Highwood Hill** Gt Lon....44 E2
**Highworth** Swindn........40 D2
**High Wray** Cumb.........137 K7
**High Wych** Herts..........60 D5
**High Wycombe**
 Bucks.....................42 E2
**Hilborough** Norfk..........91 J4
**Hilcott** Wilts...............40 C8
**Hildenborough** Kent.......32 F4
**Hilden Park** Kent..........33 G4
**Hildersham** Cambs.........76 D5
**Hilderstone** Staffs..........99 L5
**Hilderthorpe** E R Yk....135 J6
**Hilgay** Norfk................90 K4
**Hill** S Glos...................38 F2
**Hill** Warwks.................72 F2
**Hillam** N York............124 D5
**Hill Brow** Hants...........30 C6
**Hillbutts** Dorset............15 J3
**Hill Chorlton** Staffs.......99 H5
**Hillclifflane** Derbys.....100 F3
**Hill Common** Somset.....25 H6
**Hilldyke** Lincs............104 B3
**Hillend** Fife................176 F2
**Hill End** Fife..............185 L7
**Hill End** Gloucs.............70 F6
**Hillend** Mdloth...........177 H5
**Hillend** N Lans...........175 L5
**Hillesden** Bucks...........58 B3
**Hillesley** Gloucs............39 H3
**Hillfarrance** Somset......25 J6
**Hill Green** Kent............46 D7
**Hillhead** Abers...........216 B7
**Hill Head** Hants............17 G2
**Hillhead** S Lans...........165 J2
**Hillhead of Cocklaw**
 Abers....................217 K5
**Hilliclay** Highld..........231 H3
**Hillingdon** Gt Lon..........43 H4
**Hillington** C Glas..........174 F5
**Hillington** Norfk..........105 H7
**Hillmorton** Warwks........87 G8
**Hill of Beath** Fife.........176 F1
**Hill of Fearn** Highld.....223 H5
**Hillowton** D & G..........146 D3
**Hill Ridware** Staffs......100 B8
**Hillside** Abers.............207 H5
**Hillside** Angus............197 H4
**Hill Side** Kirk.............123 H6
**Hills Town** Derbys......115 J7
**Hillstreet** Hants............29 G7
**Hillswick** Shet............235 c3
**Hill Top** Sandw............85 H5
**Hill Top** Wakefd.........123 L7
**Hillwell** Shet.............235 c8
**Hilmarton** Wilts...........40 A5
**Hilperton** Wilts............39 K8
**Hilsea** C Port...............17 J2
**Hilston** E R Yk...........127 G4
**Hilton** Border.............179 H7
**Hilton** Cambs...............75 K2
**Hilton** Cumb..............139 G3
**Hilton** Derbys............100 E6
**Hilton** Dorset..............14 E2
**Hilton** Dur.................140 F3
**Hilton** S on T.............141 K5
**Hilton** Shrops.............84 D4
**Hilton of Cadboll**
 Highld...................223 J6
**Hilton Park**
 Services Staffs.......85 G3
**Himbleton** Worcs..........71 J3
**Himley** Staffs...............84 F5
**Hincaster** Cumb..........129 L3
**Hinchley Wood**
 Surrey....................44 D6
**Hinckley** Leics.............86 E5

**Hinderclay** Suffk...........92 B7
**Hinderwell** N York........143 G4
**Hindhead** Surrey..........30 E4
**Hindhead Tunnel**
 Surrey....................30 E4
**Hindley** Wigan.............112 F1
**Hindlip** Worcs..............70 F3
**Hindolveston** Norfk......106 C6
**Hindon** Wilts................27 K5
**Hindringham** Norfk......106 B5
**Hingham** Norfk.............92 B3
**Hinstock** Shrops............99 G7
**Hintlesham** Suffk..........78 C5
**Hinton** Herefs..............69 G6
**Hinton** Nhants..............73 G4
**Hinton** S Glos...............39 G5
**Hinton** Shrops..............83 H2
**Hinton Ampner**
 Hants.....................29 L6
**Hinton Blewett**
 BaNES.....................26 E1
**Hinton**
 **Charterhouse**
 BaNES.....................39 H8
**Hinton-in-the-**
 **Hedges** Nhants........73 H6
**Hinton Martell**
 Dorset......................15 J2
**Hinton on the**
 **Green** Worcs............71 H6
**Hinton Parva** Swindn....40 E4
**Hinton St George**
 Somset.....................26 B8
**Hinton St Mary**
 Dorset......................27 H7
**Hinton Waldrist**
 Oxon......................57 G7
**Hints** Staffs..................85 L3
**Hinwick** Bed.................74 D3
**Hinxhill** Kent................34 D6
**Hinxton** Cambs.............76 C5
**Hinxworth** Herts...........75 J6
**Hipperholme** Calder....123 H5
**Hipswell** N York..........140 F7
**Hirn** Abers.................206 D5
**Hirnant** Powys.............97 G7
**Hirst** Nthumb..............159 G5
**Hirst Courtney**
 N York....................124 F5
**Hirwaun** Rhondd..........52 E6
**Hiscott** Devon...............23 J6
**Histon** Cambs...............76 B2
**Hitcham** Suffk...............78 B4
**Hitcham Causeway**
 Suffk.....................78 B4
**Hitcham Street** Suffk.....78 B4
**Hitchin** Herts................59 K3
**Hither Green** Gt Lon......45 H5
**Hittisleigh** Devon..........11 H5
**Hive** E R Yk.................125 J4
**Hixon** Staffs.................100 A7
**Hoaden** Kent................35 H3
**Hoar Cross** Staffs.......100 C7
**Hoarwithy** Herefs..........54 D3
**Hoath** Kent...................47 K7
**Hobarris** Shrops............82 F7
**Hobkirk** Border...........167 J7
**Hobson** Dur................150 F4
**Hoby** Leics.................102 A8
**Hockering** Norfk............92 C2
**Hockerton** Notts..........102 B2
**Hockley** Essex...............46 D2
**Hockley Heath** Solhll.....85 L8
**Hockliffe** C Beds...........58 F3
**Hockwold cum**
 **Wilton** Norfk............91 G6
**Hockworthy** Devon........25 G7
**Hoddesdon** Herts..........60 B6
**Hoddlesden** Bl w D......121 L6
**Hoddom Cross**
 D & G....................155 L7
**Hoddom Mains**
 D & G....................155 K7
**Hodgeston** Pembks........49 H7
**Hodnet** Shrops..............98 E6
**Hodsock** Notts.............115 L4
**Hodsoll Street** Kent.......45 M7
**Hodson** Swindn............40 D4

**Hodthorpe** Derbys.......115 K6
**Hoe** Norfk....................92 B1
**Hogben's Hill** Kent........34 D4
**Hoggeston** Bucks...........58 D3
**Hoggrill's End**
 Warwks....................86 B5
**Hoghton** Lancs.............121 J5
**Hognaston** Derbys.......100 E3
**Hogsthorpe** Lincs.........119 H6
**Holbeach** Lincs............104 B7
**Holbeach Bank**
 Lincs.....................104 B6
**Holbeach Clough**
 Lincs.....................104 B6
**Holbeach Drove**
 Lincs.......................89 K2
**Holbeach Hurn** Lincs....104 C6
**Holbeach St Johns**
 Lincs.....................104 B8
**Holbeach St Mark's**
 Lincs.....................104 B6
**Holbeach St**
 **Matthew** Lincs.......104 C6
**Holbeck** Notts............115 K6
**Holberrow Green**
 Worcs......................71 H3
**Holbeton** Devon.............6 F5
**Holborn** Gt Lon.............44 F4
**Holbrook** Derbys.........101 G4
**Holbrook** Suffk.............78 E6
**Holbrooks** Covtry.........86 D6
**Holbury** Hants..............16 E2
**Holcombe** Devon..........12 B7
**Holcombe** Somset.........26 F2
**Holcombe Rogus**
 Devon......................25 G7
**Holcot** Nhants...............73 L1
**Holden** Lancs..............122 B1
**Holdenby** Nhants...........73 K2
**Holder's Green** Essex.....61 G3
**Holdgate** Shrops............83 L5
**Holdingham** Lincs.......103 H3
**Holditch** Dorset.............13 J2
**Holemoor** Devon...........10 B4
**Holford** Somset.............25 J3
**Holgate** C York............124 E1
**Holker** Cumb..............129 H4
**Holkham** Norfk............105 L4
**Hollacombe** Devon.........9 K4
**Holland Fen** Lincs........103 L3
**Holland-on-Sea**
 Essex......................62 E5
**Hollandstoun** Ork.......234 e3
**Hollee** D & G..............148 A2
**Hollesley** Suffk.............79 H5
**Hollicombe** Torbay.........7 K4
**Hollingbourne** Kent........33 L3
**Hollingbury** Br & H........19 J4
**Hollingdon** Bucks..........58 E3
**Hollington** Derbys........100 E5
**Hollington** Staffs.........100 B5
**Hollingworth** Tamesd...114 A3
**Hollinsclough** Staffs.....114 B7
**Hollins End** Sheff........115 G5
**Hollins Green** Warrtn...113 G4
**Hollinswood** Wrekin......84 C2
**Hollocombe** Devon........10 F4
**Holloway** Derbys.........100 F2
**Holloway** Gt Lon...........44 F3
**Hollowell** Nhants...........73 K1
**Hollowmoor Heath**
 Ches W...................112 C7
**Hollows** D & G............156 C6
**Hollybush** Caerph.........53 J7
**Hollybush** E Ayrs.........163 K6
**Hollybush** Herefs..........70 D6
**Hollym** E R Yk............127 H5
**Holmbridge** Kirk.........114 C1
**Holmbury St Mary**
 Surrey....................31 J3
**Holmbush** Cnwll............5 G5
**Holmcroft** Staffs............99 K7
**Holme** Cambs...............89 H6
**Holme** Cumb...............129 L4
**Holme** Kirk.................114 C1
**Holme** N York.............132 E3
**Holme** Notts...............102 D2
**Holme Chapel** Lancs...122 C5

Holme Hale Norfk....91 K3
Holme Lacy Herefs....69 L7
Holme Marsh Herefs....69 G4
Holme next the Sea
  Norfk....105 H4
Holme on the Wolds
  E R Yk....126 B2
Holme Pierrepont
  Notts....101 L5
Holmer Herefs....69 K6
Holmer Green Bucks....42 E2
Holme St Cuthbert
  Cumb....147 J5
Holmes Chapel
  Ches E....113 H7
Holmesfield Derbys....114 F6
Holmeswood Lancs....120 F6
Holmethorpe Surrey....32 B3
Holme upon
  Spalding Moor
  E R Yk....125 J3
Holmewood Derbys....115 H7
Holmfirth Kirk....123 H8
Holmhead E Ayrs....164 B5
Holmpton E R Yk....127 J5
Holmrook Cumb....136 E7
Holmside Dur....150 F5
Holne Devon....7 G3
Holnicote Somset....24 E3
Holsworthy Devon....9 J4
Holsworthy Beacon
  Devon....9 K3
Holt Dorset....15 J2
Holt Norfk....106 C5
Holt Wilts....39 K7
Holt Worcs....70 E3
Holt Wrexhm....98 B2
Holtby C York....133 K8
Holt End Worcs....71 J1
Holt Heath Worcs....70 E2
Holton Oxon....57 L6
Holton Somset....27 G6
Holton Suffk....93 J7
Holton cum
  Beckering Lincs....117 J5
Holton le Clay Lincs....118 C2
Holton le Moor Lincs....117 H3
Holton St Mary Suffk....78 C6
Holwell Dorset....14 D1
Holwell Herts....59 K2
Holwell Leics....102 B7
Holwell Oxon....56 E6
Holwick Dur....139 K2
Holybourne Hants....30 B4
Holyhead IoA....108 C5
Holy Island IoA....108 C5
Holy Island Nthumb....169 H2
Holy Island Nthumb....169 H2
Holymoorside
  Derbys....115 G7
Holyport W & M....42 E5
Holystone Nthumb....158 B2
Holytown N Lans....175 K6
Holywell C Beds....59 G5
Holywell Cambs....75 L1
Holywell Cnwll....4 B4
Holywell Dorset....14 B2
Holywell Flints....111 G6
Holywell Green
  Calder....123 G6
Holywell Lake
  Somset....25 H7
Holywell Row Suffk....91 G7
Holywood D & G....155 G6
Holywood Village
  D & G....155 G6
Homer Shrops....84 B3
Homersfield Suffk....93 G6
Homington Wilts....28 C6
Honeybourne Worcs....71 K5
Honeychurch Devon....10 F4
Honeystreet Wilts....40 C7
Honey Tye Suffk....77 L7
Honiley Warwks....86 B8
Honing Norfk....107 G6
Honingham Norfk....92 D2
Honington Lincs....102 F4
Honington Suffk....91 K8

Honington Warwks....72 C6
Honiton Devon....12 F3
Honley Kirk....123 H7
Hooe C Plym....6 D5
Hooe E Susx....20 E4
Hoo Green Ches E....113 G5
Hoohill Bpool....120 D3
Hook E R Yk....125 H5
Hook Gt Lon....44 D7
Hook Hants....30 B1
Hook Pembks....49 G5
Hook Wilts....40 B4
Hooke Dorset....14 A3
Hook Green Kent....33 H6
Hook Norton Oxon....57 G2
Hookway Devon....11 K5
Hooley Surrey....32 B3
Hoo St Werburgh
  Medway....46 C5
Hooton Levitt Rothm....115 K3
Hooton Pagnell
  Donc....124 D8
Hooton Roberts
  Rothm....115 J3
Hope Derbys....114 D5
Hope Devon....7 G7
Hope Flints....97 L2
Hope Staffs....100 C2
Hope Bagot Shrops....83 L8
Hope Bowdler
  Shrops....83 J5
Hopehouse Border....166 D6
Hopeman Moray....214 E1
Hope Mansell Herefs....54 F4
Hopesay Shrops....83 H6
Hope under
  Dinmore Herefs....69 K4
Hopgrove C York....133 K8
Hopperton N York....132 F7
Hopstone Shrops....84 D5
Hopton Derbys....100 E2
Hopton Staffs....99 L7
Hopton Suffk....92 B7
Hopton Cangeford
  Shrops....83 K7
Hopton Castle
  Shrops....83 G7
Hoptonheath Shrops....83 H7
Hopton on Sea Norfk....93 L4
Hopton Wafers
  Shrops....84 B7
Hopwas Staffs....85 L3
Hopwood Worcs....85 J7
Hopwood Park
  Services Worcs....85 J8
Horam E Susx....20 C3
Horbling Lincs....103 J5
Horbury Wakefd....123 K6
Horden Dur....151 K6
Hordle Hants....16 C4
Hordley Shrops....98 B6
Horfield Bristl....38 E5
Horham Suffk....92 E8
Horkesley Heath
  Essex....62 B3
Horkstow N Linc....126 B6
Horley Oxon....72 E5
Horley Surrey....32 B5
Hornblotton Green
  Somset....26 E5
Hornby Lancs....130 B5
Hornby N York....132 C2
Hornby N York....141 J6
Horncastle Lincs....118 C7
Hornchurch Gt Lon....45 K3
Horncliffe Nthumb....179 J7
Horndean Border....179 J8
Horndean Hants....30 B8
Horndon Devon....10 D8
Horndon on the Hill
  Thurr....46 A4
Horne Surrey....32 C4
Horner Somset....24 D3
Horning Norfk....107 H8
Horninghold Leics....88 B4
Horninglow Staffs....100 E7
Horningsea Cambs....76 C3
Horningsham Wilts....27 J3

Horningtoft Norfk....105 M7
Horns Cross Devon....22 F6
Hornsea E R Yk....126 F2
Hornsey Gt Lon....44 F3
Hornton Oxon....72 E5
Horrabridge Devon....6 D2
Horringer Suffk....77 J3
Horrocksford Lancs....121 L2
Horsebridge Devon....6 B2
Horsebridge E Susx....20 C4
Horsebridge Hants....29 G5
Horsehay Wrekin....84 C3
Horseheath Cambs....76 E5
Horsehouse N York....131 K4
Horsell Surrey....43 G8
Horseman's Green
  Wrexhm....98 C4
Horsey Norfk....107 K7
Horsey Somset....25 L4
Horsford Norfk....92 E1
Horsforth Leeds....123 J3
Horsham W Susx....31 K5
Horsham Worcs....70 D3
Horsham St Faith
  Norfk....92 E1
Horsington Lincs....117 K7
Horsington Somset....27 G6
Horsley Derbys....101 G4
Horsley Gloucs....39 J2
Horsley Nthumb....150 D2
Horsley Nthumb....157 L3
Horsleycross Street
  Essex....62 D3
Horsleyhill Border....167 H5
Horsley Woodhouse
  Derbys....101 H4
Horsmonden Kent....33 J5
Horspath Oxon....57 L6
Horstead Norfk....106 F8
Horsted Keynes
  W Susx....32 C7
Horton Bucks....58 F4
Horton Dorset....15 J2
Horton Lancs....122 C1
Horton Nhants....74 B4
Horton S Glos....39 H4
Horton Somset....25 L7
Horton Staffs....99 L2
Horton Swans....50 F7
Horton W & M....43 G5
Horton Wilts....40 B7
Horton Wrekin....84 C1
Horton-cum-
  Studley Oxon....57 L5
Horton Green
  Ches W....98 C3
Horton-in-
  Ribblesdale
  N York....130 F5
Horton Kirby Kent....45 K6
Horwich Bolton....121 J7
Horwood Devon....23 H6
Hoscote Border....166 F6
Hose Leics....102 B6
Hosh P & K....185 H3
Hoswick Shet....235 c7
Hotham E R Yk....125 L4
Hothfield Kent....34 C5
Hoton Leics....101 L7
Hough Ches E....99 G3
Hougham Lincs....102 E4
Hough Green Halton....112 C4
Hough-on-the-Hill
  Lincs....102 F3
Houghton Cambs....75 K1
Houghton Hants....29 G5
Houghton Pembks....49 G6
Houghton W Susx....18 D4
Houghton Conquest
  C Beds....74 F6
Houghton Green
  E Susx....21 H2
Houghton-le-
  Spring Sundld....151 H5
Houghton on the
  Hill Leics....87 J3
Houghton Regis
  C Beds....59 G4

Houghton St Giles
  Norfk....105 L5
Hound Green Hants....42 B8
Houndslow Border....178 D8
Houndwood Border....179 H5
Hounslow Gt Lon....43 J5
Househill Highld....213 L4
Houses Hill Kirk....123 J6
Housieside Abers....207 G1
Houston Rens....174 D5
Houstry Highld....227 K2
Houton Ork....234 b6
Hove Br & H....19 J5
Hoveringham Notts....102 B3
Hoveton Norfk....107 G8
Hovingham N York....133 K4
How Caple Herefs....54 E3
Howden E R Yk....125 H5
Howden-le-Wear
  Dur....150 E7
Howe Highld....231 K3
Howe N York....132 E4
Howe Norfk....92 F4
Howe Green Essex....61 J7
Howegreen Essex....61 K7
Howell Lincs....103 J4
Howe of Teuchar
  Abers....216 E5
Howes D & G....147 L2
Howe Street Essex....61 H5
Howe Street Essex....77 G2
Howey Powys....68 B3
Howgate Cumb....136 D3
Howgate Mdloth....177 H6
Howick Nthumb....169 K5
Howlett End Essex....76 E7
Howley Somset....13 H1
How Mill Cumb....148 E4
Howmore W Isls....233 b7
Hownam Border....168 B5
Howsham N Linc....117 H2
Howsham N York....133 L6
Howtel Nthumb....168 D3
How Wood Herts....59 J7
Howwood Rens....174 D6
Hoxa Ork....234 c7
Hoxne Suffk....92 E7
Hoy Ork....234 b7
Hoylake Wirral....111 H4
Hoyland Barns....115 G2
Hoylandswaine
  Barns....114 E1
Hubberston
  Pembks....48 E6
Huby N York....123 K2
Huby N York....133 J6
Hucclecote Gloucs....55 K4
Hucking Kent....33 L2
Hucknall Notts....101 K3
Huddersfield Kirk....123 H7
Huddington Worcs....71 G3
Hudswell N York....140 E7
Huggate E R Yk....134 D7
Hughenden Valley
  Bucks....42 E2
Hughley Shrops....83 L4
Hugh Town IoS....2 b2
Huish Devon....10 D3
Huish Wilts....40 C7
Huish Champflower
  Somset....25 G5
Huish Episcopi
  Somset....26 B6
Hùisinis W Isls....232 d3
Huisinish W Isls....232 d3
Hulcott Bucks....58 D5
Hulham Devon....12 C5
Hulland Derbys....100 E3
Hulland Ward
  Derbys....100 E3
Hullavington Wilts....39 K4
Hullbridge Essex....46 D2
Hull, Kingston upon
  C KuH....126 D5
Hulme Manch....113 J3
Hulme Staffs....99 L4
Hulme Warrtn....112 E4
Hulme End Staffs....100 C2

**Hulme Walfield**
Ches E .................. 113 J7
**Hulton Lane Ends**
Bolton.................. 113 G1
**Hulverstone** IoW....... 16 E5
**Hulver Street** Suffk .... 93 K6
**Humber Bridge**
N Linc .................. 126 C5
*Humberside Airport*
N Linc .................. 126 D7
**Humberston** NE Lin.... 118 D1
**Humberstone** C Leic ... 87 J3
**Humbie** E Loth .......... 178 B5
**Humbleton** E R Yk..... 126 F4
**Humby** Lincs ............ 103 G6
**Hume** Border.......... 167 L2
**Humshaugh** Nthumb ... 158 A7
**Huna** Highld............ 231 L2
**Huncote** Leics.......... 87 G4
**Hundalee** Border ...... 167 K5
**Hunderthwaite** Dur ... 140 C3
**Hundleby** Lincs ........ 118 E7
**Hundleton** Pembks ..... 49 G7
**Hundon** Suffk............ 77 G5
**Hundred House**
Powys.................. 68 C4
**Hungarton** Leics ........ 87 K3
**Hungerford** Somset..... 25 G4
**Hungerford** W Berk..... 41 G6
**Hungerford**
Newtown W Berk..... 41 G6
**Hungerstone** Herefs.... 69 J7
**Hunmanby** N York...... 135 H4
**Hunningham** Warwks ... 72 D2
**Hunsbury Hill** Nhants ...73 K3
**Hunsdon** Herts.......... 60 C5
**Hunsingore** N York .... 132 F8
**Hunslet** Leeds .......... 123 L4
**Hunsonby** Cumb........ 149 G7
**Hunstanton** Norfk....... 105 G4
**Hunstanworth** Dur..... 150 B5
**Hunsterson** Ches E...... 99 G4
**Hunston** Suffk........... 77 L2
**Hunston** W Susx ........ 18 B5
**Hunstrete** BaNES........ 38 F7
**Hunsworth** Kirk........ 123 J5
**Hunter's Quay** Ag & B.. 173 K3
**Huntham** Somset........ 25 M6
**Hunthill Lodge**
Angus .................. 196 D3
**Huntingdon** Cambs......89 J8
**Huntingfield** Suffk.......93 G8
**Huntington** C York..... 133 J7
**Huntington** Ches W..... 112 B8
**Huntington** E Loth ..... 178 B4
**Huntington** Herefs...... 68 E4
**Huntington** Staffs.......85 H2
**Huntingtowerfield**
P & K .................. 185 M3
**Huntley** Gloucs.......... 55 G4
**Huntly** Abers ........... 215 L6
**Hunton** Kent ............. 33 J4
**Hunton** N York ......... 132 B2
**Huntscott** Somset...... 24 E3
**Huntsham** Devon........ 24 F7
**Huntshaw** Devon........ 23 H6
**Huntspill** Somset........ 25 L3
**Huntstile** Somset........ 25 K5
**Huntworth** Somset...... 25 L4
**Hunwick** Dur ........... 140 F2
**Hunworth** Norfk........ 106 C5
**Hurdcott** Wilts.......... 28 D5
**Hurdsfield** Ches E....... 113 L6
**Hurley** W & M........... 42 D4
**Hurley** Warwks........... 86 B4
**Hurley Common**
Warwks................86 B4
**Hurlford** E Ayrs ........ 163 L3
**Hurn** BCP ................ 15 L3
**Hursley** Hants ........... 29 H6
**Hurst** Wokham.......... 42 C5
**Hurstbourne Priors**
Hants..................29 H3
**Hurstbourne Tarrant**
Hants..................29 G2
**Hurst Green** E Susx .... 33 J7
**Hurst Green** Essex...... 62 C5
**Hurst Green** Lancs ..... 121 K3

**Hurst Green** Surrey........ 32 D3
**Hurst Hill** Dudley............ 85 G5
**Hurstpierpoint**
W Susx..................19 J3
**Hurstwood** Lancs......... 122 C4
**Hurtiso** Ork ................ 234 c6
**Hurworth-on-Tees**
Darltn ................. 141 H5
**Hurworth Place**
Darltn ................. 141 H5
**Husbands Bosworth**
Leics ....................87 J6
**Husborne Crawley**
C Beds..................74 D7
**Husthwaite** N York...... 133 H4
**Huthwaite** Notts ........ 101 J2
**Huttoft** Lincs ............ 119 G6
**Hutton** Border............ 179 J7
**Hutton** E R Yk............ 134 F8
**Hutton** Essex............. 45 M2
**Hutton** Lancs............. 121 G5
**Hutton** N Som ............ 37 M8
**Hutton Buscel**
N York ................. 134 F3
**Hutton Conyers**
N York ................. 132 E5
**Hutton Cranswick**
E R Yk.................. 126 C1
**Hutton End** Cumb ...... 148 D7
**Hutton Henry** Dur ...... 151 K7
**Hutton-le-Hole**
N York ................. 133 L2
**Hutton Lowcross**
R & Cl ................. 142 D4
**Hutton Magna** Dur ...... 140 E5
**Hutton Roof** Cumb ...... 130 B4
**Hutton Roof** Cumb ...... 148 C7
**Hutton Rudby** N York... 141 K6
**Hutton Sessay** N York.. 133 G4
**Hutton Wandesley**
N York ................. 124 D1
**Huxham** Devon ........... 12 B3
**Huxley** Ches W............ 98 D1
**Huyton** Knows........... 112 C4
**Hycemoor** Cumb ........ 128 D2
**Hyde** Tamesd............. 113 L3
**Hyde Heath** Bucks........ 58 F7
**Hyde Lea** Staffs........... 99 K8
**Hylands House &**
Park Essex.............. 61 G7
**Hyndford Bridge**
S Lans ................. 165 H2
**Hynish** Ag & B............ 188 C8
**Hyssington** Powys........82 F5
**Hythe** Hants............... 16 E2
**Hythe** Kent................ 34 F7
**Hythe End** W & M........ 43 G6

**I**

**Ibberton** Dorset............ 14 E2
**Ible** Derbys................ 100 E2
**Ibsley** Hants............... 15 L1
**Ibstock** Leics.............. 86 E2
**Ibstone** Bucks............. 42 C2
**Ibthorpe** Hants........... 29 G2
**Iburndale** N York........ 143 H5
**Ibworth** Hants............ 29 K1
**Ichrachan** Ag & B........ 182 E2
**Ickburgh** Norfk........... 91 J4
**Ickenham** Gt Lon......... 43 H3
**Ickford** Bucks............. 57 M6
**Ickham** Kent.............. 35 G3
**Ickleford** Herts........... 59 K2
**Icklesham** E Susx........ 21 H3
**Ickleton** Cambs........... 76 C5
**Icklingham** Suffk......... 91 H8
**Ickornshaw** N York...... 122 E2
**Ickwell Green** C Beds.... 75 G5
**Icomb** Gloucs............. 56 E4
**Idbury** Oxon.............. 56 E4
**Iddesleigh** Devon......... 10 E3
**Ide** Devon ................. 11 K6
**Ideford** Devon.............. 7 K1
**Ide Hill** Kent.............. 32 E3

**Iden** E Susx ................. 21 H2
**Iden Green** Kent ........... 33 J5
**Iden Green** Kent ........... 33 K6
**Idle** C Brad ................ 123 H3
**Idless** Cnwll ................. 4 C6
**Idlicote** Warwks............ 72 C5
**Idmiston** Wilts............. 28 D4
**Idole** Carmth................ 50 E3
**Idridgehay** Derbys........ 100 F3
**Idrigill** Highld.............. 208 F2
**Idstone** Oxon............... 40 E4
**Iffley** Oxon.................. 57 K7
**Ifield** W Susx............... 31 L4
**Ifold** W Susx ................ 31 G5
**Iford** BCP.................... 15 L4
**Iford** E Susx ................ 19 L4
**Ifton** Mons ................. 38 C3
**Ightfield** Shrops............ 98 E5
**Ightham** Kent............... 33 G2
**Ilam** Staffs ................ 100 C3
**Ilchester** Somset........... 26 D6
**Ilderton** Nthumb ......... 168 F5
**Ilford** Gt Lon............... 45 H3
**Ilford** Somset.............. 26 A7
**Ilfracombe** Devon......... 23 H2
**Ilkeston** Derbys........... 101 J4
**Ilketshall St Andrew**
Suffk...................93 H6
**Ilketshall St**
Margaret Suffk.......93 H6
**Ilkley** C Brad .............. 123 G2
**Illand** Cnwll.................. 5 L1
**Illey** Dudley................ 85 H7
**Illogan** Cnwll ................ 3 H3
**Illston on the Hill**
Leics ....................87 K4
**Ilmer** Bucks................ 58 C6
**Ilmington** Warwks......... 72 B5
**Ilminster** Somset.......... 26 A8
**Ilsington** Devon............. 7 H2
**Ilston** Swans................ 51 H7
**Ilton** N York............... 132 B4
**Ilton** Somset............... 25 M7
**Imachar** N Ayrs........... 161 L2
**Immingham** NE Lin...... 126 F7
**Immingham Dock**
NE Lin................. 126 F7
**Impington** Cambs......... 76 C2
**Ince** Ches W................ 112 C6
**Ince Blundell** Sefton.... 111 K2
**Ince-in-Makerfield**
Wigan................. 112 E1
**Inchbae Lodge**
Hotel Highld......... 221 K7
**Inchbare** Angus........... 196 F4
**Inchberry** Moray.......... 215 G4
**Incheril** Highld............ 211 G3
**Inchinnan** Rens........... 174 E5
**Inchlaggan** Highld........ 201 J5
**Inchmichael** P & K....... 186 D3
**Inchmore** Highld.......... 212 E5
**Inchnadamph** Highld.... 224 F4
**Inchture** P & K............ 186 D2
**Inchyra** P & K............. 186 C4
**Indian Queens** Cnwll...... 4 E4
**Ingatestone** Essex......... 61 G7
**Ingbirchworth** Barns.... 114 E1
**Ingestre** Staffs............. 99 L7
**Ingham** Lincs.............. 116 F5
**Ingham** Norfk............. 107 H7
**Ingham** Suffk............... 77 J1
**Ingham Corner**
Norfk.................. 107 H6
**Ingleby** Derbys........... 101 G6
**Ingleby Arncliffe**
N York ................. 141 K6
**Ingleby Barwick**
S on T ................. 141 K4
**Ingleby Greenhow**
N York ................. 142 C6
**Ingleigh Green**
Devon.................. 10 E4
**Inglesbatch** BaNES........ 39 G7
**Inglesham** Swindn........ 56 D7
**Ingleston** D & G.......... 147 G2
**Ingleton** Dur.............. 140 F3
**Ingleton** N York.......... 130 D5
**Inglewhite** Lancs ........ 121 H3

**Ingoe** Nthumb............ 158 C7
**Ingol** Lancs............... 121 G4
**Ingoldisthorpe** Norfk... 105 G6
**Ingoldmells** Lincs ....... 119 H7
**Ingoldsby** Lincs .......... 103 G6
**Ingram** Nthumb.......... 168 F6
**Ingrave** Essex............. 45 M2
**Ingrow** C Brad............ 122 F3
**Ings** Cumb ................ 138 C7
**Ingst** S Glos................ 38 E3
**Ingthorpe** RutInd.......... 88 E2
**Ingworth** Norfk.......... 106 E6
**Inkberrow** Worcs......... 71 H3
**Inkersall Green**
Derbys................. 115 H6
**Inkhorn** Abers........... 217 H6
**Inkpen** W Berk............ 41 G7
**Inkstack** Highld.......... 231 J2
**Innellan** Ag & B.......... 173 K4
**Innerleithen** Border .... 166 E3
**Innerleven** Fife .......... 186 F7
**Innermessan** D & G..... 144 C3
**Innerwick** E Loth........ 178 F4
**Innesmill** Moray.......... 215 G2
**Insch** Abers............... 216 C8
**Insh** Highld............... 203 J5
**Inshes** Highld............. 213 G5
**Inskip** Lancs.............. 120 F3
**Instow** Devon............. 23 G5
**Intake** Sheff............... 115 H5
**Inver** Abers............... 204 F6
**Inver** Highld.............. 223 J5
**Inver** P & K............... 194 F7
**Inverailort** Highld....... 190 F1
**Inveralligin** Highld...... 210 C3
**Inverallochy** Abers...... 217 K2
**Inveran** Highld........... 222 D2
**Inveraray** Ag & B........ 182 F5
**Inverarish** Highld........ 209 J7
**Inverarity** Angus......... 196 D7
**Inverarnan** Stirlg........ 183 K4
**Inverasdale** Highld...... 219 J4
**Inverbeg** Ag & B......... 183 K7
**Inverbervie** Abers....... 197 K2
**Inverboyndie** Abers..... 216 C2
**Invercreran Lodge**
Ag & B................. 191 K6
**Inverdruie** Highld....... 203 L3
**Inveresk** E Loth.......... 177 K4
**Inveresragan** Ag & B.... 182 E1
**Inverey** Abers............ 204 D7
**Inverfarigaig** Highld.... 202 D2
**Inverfolla** Highld........ 191 J7
**Invergarry** Highld....... 201 L5
**Invergeldie** P & K....... 184 F2
**Invergloy** Highld........ 201 K7
**Invergordon** Highld..... 222 F7
**Invergowrie** P & K...... 186 F2
**Inverguseran** Highld.... 200 B4
**Inverhadden** P & K...... 193 L5
**Inverie** Highld............ 200 B5
**Inverinan** Ag & B........ 182 L4
**Inverinate** Highld....... 200 E2
**Inverkeilor** Angus....... 197 G6
**Inverkeithing** Fife ...... 176 F2
**Inverkeithny** Abers..... 216 C5
**Inverkip** Inver............ 173 L4
**Inverkirkaig** Highld..... 224 C4
**Inverlael** Highld......... 220 F4
**Inverlair** Highld.......... 192 E1
**Inverliever Lodge**
Ag & B................. 182 C6
**Inverlochy** Ag & B....... 183 H2
**Invermark** Angus........ 196 D1
**Invermoriston** Highld... 202 C3
**Invernaver** Highld....... 229 L4
**Inverneill** Ag & B........ 172 E3
**Inverness** Highld......... 213 G5
*Inverness Airport*
Highld.................. 213 J4
**Invernettie** Abers....... 217 L5
**Invernoaden** Ag & B.... 183 G7
**Inveroran Hotel**
Ag & B................. 192 D7
**Inverquharity** Angus.... 196 C5
**Inverquhomery**
Abers.................. 217 J5
**Inverroy** Highld.......... 201 K8

**Inversanda** Highld........ **191** J4
**Invershiel** Highld .......... **200** E2
**Invershin** Highld .......... **222** D3
**Invershore** Highld .......... **231** J8
**Inversnaid Hotel**
Stirlg .................... **183** K5
**Inverugie** Abers ............ **217** L5
**Inveruglas** Ag & B........ **183** K5
**Inveruglass** Highld........ **203** J5
**Inverurie** Abers ............ **206** E2
**Inwardleigh** Devon........ **10** E5
**Inworth** Essex............... **61** L4
**Iochdar** W Isls ............. **233** b7
**Iona** Ag & B .................. **180** D3
**Iping** W Susx................. **30** D6
**iPort Logistics Park**
Donc...................... **115** L2
**Ipplepen** Devon ............ **7** J3
**Ipsden** Oxon ................ **41** M4
**Ipstones** Staffs ............ **100** A3
**Ipswich** Suffk ............... **78** E5
**Irby** Wirral ................... **111** J5
**Irby in the Marsh**
Lincs ..................... **118** F8
**Irby upon Humber**
NE Lin ................... **117** K1
**Irchester** Nhants ......... **74** D2
**Ireby** Cumb ................. **147** M7
**Ireby** Lancs ................ **130** C4
**Ireleth** Cumb .............. **128** F4
**Ireshopeburn** Dur ....... **149** L7
**Irlam** Salfd ................. **113** G3
**Irnham** Lincs .............. **103** G7
**Iron Acton** S Glos......... **39** G4
**Ironbridge** Wrekin........ **84** C3
**Ironbridge Gorge**
Wrekin................... **84** C3
**Ironmacannie** D & G.... **154** B6
**Ironville** Derbys .......... **101** H3
**Irstead** Norfk.............. **107** H7
**Irthington** Cumb.......... **148** E3
**Irthlingborough**
Nhants.................... **74** D1
**Irton** N York ............... **134** F3
**Irvine** N Ayrs ............. **163** H2
**Isauld** Highld ............. **230** E3
**Isbister** Shet.............. **235** c2
**Isbister** Shet.............. **235** d4
**Isfield** E Susx ............. **19** L3
**Isham** Nhants ............. **88** C8
**Isington** Hants............ **30** C3
**Islay** Ag & B ............... **171** G6
*Islay Airport* Ag & B..... **170** F7
**Isle Abbotts** Somset..... **26** A7
**Isle Brewers** Somset..... **26** A7
**Isleham** Cambs ........... **90** F8
**Isle of Dogs** Gt Lon...... **45** G4
**Isle of Grain** Medway... **46** E5
**Isle of Lewis** W Isls .... **232** f2
**Isle of Man** IoM ......... **237** c4
*Isle of Man
Ronaldsway
Airport* IoM ............ **237** b7
**Isle of Mull** Ag & B ..... **181** J1
**Isle of Purbeck**
Dorset ................... **15** J5
**Isle of Sheppey** Kent... **46** F6
**Isle of Skye** Highld ..... **208** F6
**Isle of Thanet** Kent..... **35** J2
**Isle of Walney** Cumb... **128** E6
**Isle of Whithorn**
D & G..................... **145** K7
**Isle of Wight** IoW....... **17** G5
**Isleornsay** Highld ....... **199** L3
*Isles of Scilly* IoS......... **2** b1
*Isles of Scilly St
Mary's Airport*
IoS.......................... **2** b2
**Islesteps** D & G ......... **155** G7
**Islet Village** Guern..... **236** d2
**Isleworth** Gt Lon........ **44** D5
**Isley Walton** Leics ..... **101** H7
**Islibhig** W Isls........... **232** d3
**Islington** Gt Lon........ **44** F3
**Islip** Nhants.............. **88** E7
**Islip** Oxon ................ **57** K5
**Islivig** W Isls............. **232** d3
**Isombridge** Wrekin..... **83** L2

**Istead Rise** Kent.......... **45** M6
**Itchen Abbas** Hants.... **29** K5
**Itchen Stoke** Hants .... **29** K5
**Itchingfield** W Susx..... **31** J3
**Itteringham** Norfk ..... **106** D6
**Itton** Mons ................. **38** C2
**Itton Common** Mons... **38** C2
**Ivegill** Cumb .............. **148** D6
**Iver** Bucks ................. **43** G4
**Iver Heath** Bucks........ **43** G4
**Iveston** Dur ............... **150** E5
**Ivinghoe** Bucks........... **58** F5
**Ivinghoe Aston**
Bucks..................... **58** F4
**Ivington** Herefs ......... **69** J3
**Ivybridge** Devon ........ **6** F5
**Ivychurch** Kent........... **21** K1
**Ivy Hatch** Kent........... **33** G3
**Iwade** Kent................. **46** E6
**Iwerne Courtney**
Dorset ................... **27** K8
**Iwerne Minster**
Dorset ................... **27** K8
**Ixworth** Suffk ............ **77** L1
**Ixworth Thorpe** Suffk.. **91** K8

## J

**Jack-in-the-Green**
Devon..................... **12** C4
**Jackton** S Lans ........... **175** G7
**Jacobstow** Cnwll......... **9** G5
**Jacobstowe** Devon...... **10** E4
**Jameston** Pembks ....... **49** H7
**Jamestown** Highld...... **212** D3
**Jamestown** W Duns.... **174** D3
**Janetstown** Highld ..... **227** L3
**Janetstown** Highld ..... **231** L5
**Jardine Hall** D & G ..... **155** J5
**Jarrow** S Tyne ........... **151** H3
**Jasper's Green** Essex.... **61** H3
**Jawcraig** Falk ............ **175** L4
**Jaywick** Essex ........... **62** D5
**Jedburgh** Border ....... **167** K5
**Jeffreyston** Pembks..... **49** J6
**Jemimaville** Highld .... **213** H2
**Jerbourg** Guern......... **236** d4
**Jersey** Jersey............. **236** c6
*Jersey Airport* Jersey.. **236** b7
**Jesmond** N u Ty......... **151** G2
**Jevington** E Susx ....... **20** B5
**Jockey End** Herts ...... **59** H5
**Jodrell Bank** Ches E.... **113** H7
**Johnby** Cumb............ **148** D7
*John Lennon
Airport* Lpool ........ **112** B5
**John o' Groats** Highld.. **231** L2
**Johnshaven** Abers ..... **197** J3
**Johnston** Pembks....... **48** F5
**Johnstone** D & G ....... **155** M3
**Johnstone** Rens......... **174** D5
**Johnstonebridge**
D & G..................... **155** J4
**Johnstown** Carmth..... **50** E2
**Johnstown** Wrexhm.... **97** L4
**Joppa** C Edin ............. **177** J4
**Joppa** Cerdgn............ **66** D2
**Joppa** S Ayrs ............ **163** K5
**Jordanston** Pembks.... **64** C7
**Joyden's Wood** Kent... **45** K5
**Juniper** Nthumb........ **150** B3
**Juniper Green**
C Edin .................... **177** G5
**Jura** Ag & B ............... **171** J2
**Jurassic Coast** Devon.. **13** H4
**Jurby** IoM ................. **237** c2

## K

**Kaber** Cumb............... **139** H5
**Kaimend** S Lans ........ **165** J1
**Kames** Ag & B ........... **173** G4
**Kames** E Ayrs ............ **164** D4
**Kea** Cnwll ................. **4** C7

**Keadby** N Linc .......... **125** K7
**Keal Cotes** Lincs ....... **104** B1
**Kearsley** Bolton ........ **113** H1
**Kearsney** Kent........... **35** H6
**Kearstwick** Cumb....... **130** B4
**Kedington** Suffk......... **77** G5
**Kedleston** Derbys ..... **100** F4
**Keelby** Lincs ............. **126** E8
**Keele** Staffs .............. **99** J4
*Keele Services* Staffs .. **99** J4
**Keelham** C Brad ........ **123** G4
**Keeston** Pembks........ **48** F4
**Keevil** Wilts............... **39** L8
**Kegworth** Leics ........ **101** J7
**Kehelland** Cnwll......... **3** G3
**Keig** Abers ................ **206** B2
**Keighley** C Brad......... **122** F3
**Keilarsbrae** Clacks..... **185** J8
**Keillour** P & K ........... **185** K3
**Keiloch** Abers ........... **204** E6
**Keils** Ag & B .............. **171** K5
**Keinton Mandeville**
Somset.................. **26** D5
**Keir Mill** D & G.......... **154** E4
**Keisley** Cumb............ **139** G3
**Keiss** Highld.............. **231** L4
**Keith** Moray ............. **215** J4
**Keithick** P & K........... **195** K8
**Keithock** Angus ........ **196** F4
**Keithtown** Highld ...... **212** E3
**Kelbrook** Lancs.......... **122** D2
**Kelby** Lincs............... **103** G4
**Keld** N York .............. **139** K6
**Kelfield** N York.......... **124** F3
**Kelham** Notts............ **102** C2
**Kelhead** D & G .......... **147** K2
**Kellamergh** Lancs...... **120** E5
**Kellas** Angus............. **187** G1
**Kellas** Moray ............ **214** E4
**Kellaton** Devon ......... **7** J7
**Kelling** Norfk............. **106** C4
**Kellington** N York...... **124** E5
**Kelloe** Dur ............... **151** J7
**Kelloholm** D & G........ **164** E6
**Kells** Cumb ............... **136** D4
**Kelly** Devon .............. **9** K8
**Kelmarsh** Nhants....... **87** K7
**Kelmscott** Oxon......... **56** E7
**Kelsale** Suffk ............ **79** H2
**Kelsall** Ches W .......... **112** D7
**Kelshall** Herts........... **75** K7
**Kelsick** Cumb ........... **147** L5
**Kelso** Border ............ **167** L3
**Kelstedge** Derbys...... **115** G8
**Kelstern** Lincs........... **118** C4
**Kelston** BaNES.......... **39** G6
**Keltneyburn** P & K..... **194** B6
**Kelton** D & G ............ **155** H7
**Kelty** Fife ................. **186** B8
**Kelvedon** Essex......... **61** K4
**Kelvedon Hatch**
Essex..................... **60** F7
**Kelynack** Cnwll.......... **2** C5
**Kemback** Fife ............ **187** G4
**Kemberton** Shrops..... **84** D3
**Kemble** Gloucs.......... **39** M2
**Kemerton** Worcs........ **71** G6
**Kemeys
Commander**
Mons..................... **53** M6
**Kemnay** Abers .......... **206** E3
**Kempley** Gloucs......... **54** F3
**Kempley Green**
Gloucs.................... **55** G3
**Kempsey** Worcs......... **70** F5
**Kempsford** Gloucs...... **40** D2
**Kempshott** Hants....... **29** L2
**Kempston** Bed........... **74** F5
**Kempton** Shrops........ **83** G6
*Kemp Town* Br & H ..... **19** L3
**Kemsing** Kent............ **32** F2
**Kenardington** Kent..... **34** C7
**Kenchester** Herefs .... **69** J6
**Kencot** Oxon............. **56** E6
**Kendal** Cumb ............ **129** L2
**Kenfig** Brdgnd........... **36** C4
**Kenfig Hill** Brdgnd..... **36** C4
**Kenilworth** Warwks... **72** C1

**Kenley** Gt Lon ........... **32** B2
**Kenley** Shrops........... **83** L4
**Kenmore** Highld ....... **210** B3
**Kenmore** P & K .......... **194** B7
**Kenn** Devon .............. **11** L7
**Kenn** N Som.............. **38** B6
**Kennacraig** Ag & B .... **172** D5
*Kennall Vale* Cnwll...... **3** J4
**Kennerleigh** Devon .... **11** J4
**Kennet** Clacks .......... **176** C1
**Kennethmont** Abers .. **215** L8
**Kennett** Cambs.......... **77** G2
**Kenninghall** Norfk..... **92** C6
**Kennington** Kent ....... **34** D5
**Kennington** Oxon....... **57** K7
**Kennoway** Fife ......... **186** F6
**Kenny** Somset .......... **25** L7
**Kenny Hill** Suffk........ **90** F7
**Kennythorpe** N York.. **134** C6
**Kenovay** Ag & B ........ **188** C6
**Kensaleyre** Highld..... **208** F4
**Kensington** Gt Lon..... **44** E4
**Kensington Palace**
Gt Lon.................... **44** E4
**Kensworth Common**
C Beds.................... **59** G4
**Kentallen** Highld ...... **191** K5
**Kentchurch** Herefs.... **54** B3
**Kentford** Suffk .......... **77** G2
**Kentisbeare** Devon..... **12** D2
**Kentisbury** Devon ..... **23** K3
**Kentish Town** Gt Lon.. **44** F3
**Kentmere** Cumb ....... **138** C6
**Kenton** Devon ........... **12** B5
**Kenton** Gt Lon .......... **44** D3
**Kenton** N u Ty .......... **150** F2
**Kenton** Suffk ............ **78** E2
**Kenton Bankfoot**
N u Ty.................... **150** F2
**Kentra** Highld ........... **190** D3
**Kent's Green** Gloucs... **55** H4
**Kent's Oak** Hants ...... **28** F6
**Kenwyn** Cnwll........... **4** C6
**Keoldale** Highld ........ **228** F3
**Keppoch** Highld ........ **200** D1
**Kepwick** N York ........ **133** G2
**Keresley** Covtry ........ **86** D6
**Kerrera** Ag & B .......... **182** B2
**Kerry** Powys .............. **82** D5
**Kerrycroy** Ag & B ...... **173** J6
**Kersall** Notts ............ **116** B8
**Kersbrook** Devon ...... **12** D5
**Kersey** Suffk ............. **78** B5
**Kershader** W Isls ....... **232** f3
**Kerswell** Devon ........ **12** D2
**Kerswell Green**
Worcs..................... **70** F5
**Kesgrave** Suffk ......... **78** F5
**Kessingland** Suffk ..... **93** L6
**Kestle** Cnwll.............. **4** F6
**Kestle Mill** Cnwll....... **4** D4
**Keston** Gt Lon........... **45** H7
**Keswick** Cumb .......... **137** J3
**Keswick** Norfk........... **92** E3
**Kettering** Nhants....... **88** C7
**Ketteringham** Norfk... **92** E3
**Kettins** P & K............. **195** K8
**Kettlebaston** Suffk..... **77** L4
**Kettlebridge** Fife ...... **186** F6
**Kettlebrook** Staffs...... **86** B3
**Kettleburgh** Suffk ...... **78** F3
**Kettleholm** D & G ...... **155** K6
**Kettleshulme** Ches E.. **113** M5
**Kettlesing** N York....... **132** C7
**Kettlesing Bottom**
N York .................... **132** C7
**Kettlestone** Norfk...... **106** A6
**Kettlethorpe** Lincs..... **116** D6
**Kettletoft** Ork............ **234** d4
**Kettlewell** N York ...... **131** H5
**Ketton** Rutlnd............ **88** E3
**Kew** Gt Lon................ **44** D5
**Kew Royal Botanic
Gardens** Gt Lon...... **44** D5
**Kewstoke** N Som ...... **37** M7
**Kexby** C York............. **125** G1

Kexby Lincs...... 116 E4
Key Green Ches E .... 113 K8
Keyham Leics......87 J3
Keyhaven Hants ....16 C4
Keyingham E R Yk... 127 G5
Keymer W Susx....19 J3
Keynsham BaNES....38 F6
Keysoe Bed......74 F3
Keysoe Row Bed......74 F3
Keyston Cambs....88 F7
Keyworth Notts.... 101 L6
Kibblesworth Dur.. 151 G4
Kibworth
  Beauchamp Leics..87 K5
Kibworth Harcourt
  Leics......87 K5
Kidbrooke Gt Lon....45 H5
Kidderminster Worcs..84 E7
Kidlington Oxon....57 J5
Kidmore End Oxon....42 B5
Kidsdale D & G .... 145 J7
Kidsgrove Staffs....99 J2
Kidwelly Carmth......50 E4
Kiel Crofts Ag & B.. 191 H8
Kielder Nthumb..... 157 G4
Kielder Forest.... 157 G5
Kiells Ag & B..... 171 H5
Kilbarchan Rens .... 174 D5
Kilbeg Highld..... 199 K4
Kilberry Ag & B.... 172 C5
Kilbirnie N Ayrs.... 174 C7
Kilbride Ag & B.... 172 C3
Kilbride Ag & B.... 173 H5
Kilconquhar Fife.... 187 H6
Kilcot Gloucs......55 G3
Kilcoy Highld..... 212 E4
Kilcreggan Ag & B.. 173 L3
Kildale N York .... 142 D5
Kildalloig Ag & B.... 161 J5
Kildary Highld..... 223 G6
Kildavaig Ag & B.... 173 G5
Kildavanan Ag & B.. 173 H5
Kildonan Highld..... 227 G4
Kildonan N Ayrs.... 162 D5
Kildonan Lodge
  Highld..... 226 F4
Kildonnan Highld.... 199 G7
Kildrochet House
  D & G..... 144 C4
Kildrummy Abers.... 205 K2
Kildwick N York.... 122 F2
Kilfinan Ag & B.... 172 F3
Kilfinnan Highld.... 201 K6
Kilgetty Pembks.....49 J6
Kilgrammie S Ayrs.. 152 F2
Kilgwrrwg Common
  Mons......38 C2
Kilham E R Yk..... 135 G6
Kilkenneth Ag & B.. 188 B7
Kilkenzie Ag & B.... 161 H4
Kilkerran Ag & B.... 161 J5
Kilkhampton Cnwll......9 H3
Killamarsh Derbys.. 115 J5
Killay Swans......51 H6
Killearn Stirlg.... 174 F2
Killen Highld..... 213 G3
Killerby Darltn .... 140 F3
Killerton Devon......12 C3
Killichonan Highld.. 193 J5
Killiechonate Highld.. 192 D1
Killiechronan Ag & B.. 190 B7
Killiecrankie P & K... 194 E4
Killilan Highld..... 210 E7
Killimster Highld.... 231 K4
Killin Stirlg..... 184 C2
Killinghall N York.. 132 D7

Killington Cumb .... 130 C2
Killington Lake
  Services Cumb ...... 130 B2
Killingworth N Tyne .... 159 G7
Killochyett Border .... 167 G1
Kilmacolm Inver.... 174 C4
Kilmahog Highld..... 184 D5
Kilmahumaig Ag & B.. 182 A8
Kilmaluag Highld..... 218 C6
Kilmany Fife..... 186 F3
Kilmarnock E Ayrs.. 163 K2
Kilmartin Ag & B.... 182 B7
Kilmaurs E Ayrs.... 163 K2
Kilmelford Ag & B... 182 B5
Kilmersdon Somset......27 G2
Kilmeston Hants......29 L6
Kilmichael Ag & B... 161 H5
Kilmichael Glassary
  Ag & B..... 182 B8
Kilmichael of
  Inverlussa Ag & B.. 172 D2
Kilmington Devon......13 H3
Kilmington Wilts......27 H4
Kilmington
  Common Wilts......27 H4
Kilmington Street
  Wilts......27 H4
Kilmorack Highld..... 212 D5
Kilmore Ag & B.... 182 C3
Kilmore Highld..... 199 K4
Kilmory Ag & B.... 172 C4
Kilmory Highld..... 190 B3
Kilmory N Ayrs.... 162 B5
Kilmuir Highld..... 208 D5
Kilmuir Highld..... 213 G4
Kilmuir Highld..... 218 B7
Kilmuir Highld..... 223 G6
Kilmun Ag & B.... 173 K3
Kilnave Ag & B.... 170 F4
Kilncadzow S Lans.. 176 B8
Kilndown Kent......33 J6
Kilninver Ag & B.... 182 B3
Kilnsea E R Yk..... 127 J7
Kilnsey N York .... 131 H6
Kilnwick E R Yk..... 126 C1
Kiloran Ag & B.... 180 E7
Kilpatrick N Ayrs.. 162 A4
Kilpeck Herefs......54 C3
Kilpin E R Yk..... 125 J5
Kilrenny Fife..... 187 J6
Kilsby Nhants......73 H1
Kilspindie P & K.... 186 C3
Kilstay D & G..... 144 D7
Kilsyth N Lans..... 175 J3
Kiltarlity Highld..... 212 D6
Kilton R & Cl..... 142 E4
Kilton Thorpe R & Cl.. 142 E4
Kilvaxter Highld..... 218 B7
Kilve Somset......25 H3
Kilvington Notts.... 102 D4
Kilwinning N Ayrs.. 163 H2
Kimberley Norfk......92 C3
Kimberley Notts.... 101 J4
Kimberworth Rothm.. 115 H3
Kimblesworth Dur.. 151 G5
Kimbolton Cambs....75 G2
Kimbolton Herefs....69 K3
Kimcote Leics......87 H6
Kimmeridge Dorset....15 H6
Kimpton Hants......28 F3
Kimpton Herts......59 K4
Kinbrace Highld..... 226 F3
Kinbuck Stirlg..... 185 G6
Kincaple Fife..... 187 G4
Kincardine Fife.... 176 C2
Kincardine Highld.. 222 E4
Kincardine Bridge
  Fife..... 176 C2
Kincardine O'Neil
  Abers..... 206 B5
Kinclaven P & K .... 195 J8
Kincorth C Aber.... 207 H5
Kincorth House
  Moray..... 214 C3
Kincraig Highld..... 203 K4
Kincraigie P & K.... 194 F6
Kindallachan P & K.. 194 F6
Kinerarach Ag & B.. 172 B7

Kineton Gloucs......56 C3
Kineton Warwks.....72 D4
Kinfauns P & K..... 186 C3
Kingarth Ag & B.... 173 J6
Kingcausie Abers.... 207 G5
Kingcoed Mons......54 B6
Kingerby Lincs..... 117 H3
Kingham Oxon......56 E3
Kingholm Quay
  D & G..... 155 G7
Kinghorn Fife..... 177 H2
Kinglassie Fife.... 186 D7
Kingoodie P & K.... 186 E2
Kingsand Cnwll......6 C5
Kingsbarns Fife.... 187 K5
Kingsbridge Devon......7 H6
Kingsbridge Somset....24 F4
King's Bromley Staffs..85 K1
Kingsburgh Highld.... 208 F4
Kingsbury Gt Lon......44 D3
Kingsbury Warwks......86 B4
Kingsbury Episcopi
  Somset......26 B7
King's Caple Herefs....54 E3
Kingsclere Hants.... 41 K8
King's Cliffe Nhants....88 E4
Kings Clipstone
  Notts..... 115 L8
Kingscote Gloucs......39 J2
Kingscott Devon......23 H7
King's Coughton
  Warwks......71 J3
Kingscross N Ayrs.. 162 D4
Kingsdon Somset......26 D6
Kingsdown Kent......35 K5
Kingsdown Swindn....40 D3
Kingsdown Wilts......39 J6
Kingseat Abers.... 207 G2
Kingseat Fife..... 176 F1
Kingsey Bucks......58 C6
Kingsfold W Susx......31 K4
Kingsford C Aber.... 206 F4
Kingsford E Ayrs.... 174 E8
Kingsgate Kent......35 K1
Kingshall Street
  Suffk......77 K3
King's Heath Birm......85 J7
Kings Hill Kent......33 H3
King's Hill Wsall......85 H4
Kings House Hotel
  Highld..... 192 D5
Kingshurst Solhll......85 L6
Kingskerswell Devon......7 K3
Kingskettle Fife.... 186 E5
Kingsland Herefs....69 J3
Kingsland IoA..... 108 C5
Kings Langley Herts....59 H7
Kingsley Ches W .... 112 D6
Kingsley Hants......30 C4
Kingsley Staffs.... 100 A3
Kingsley Green
  W Susx......30 E5
Kingsley Park Nhants..73 L3
King's Lynn Norfk.... 104 F8
Kings Meaburn
  Cumb..... 138 E3
King's Mills Guern.... 236 c3
Kingsmuir Angus.... 196 D6
Kings Muir Border.. 166 C2
Kingsmuir Fife..... 187 J5
Kingsnorth Kent......34 D6
King's Norton Birm......85 J7
King's Norton Leics......87 K4
Kings Nympton
  Devon......23 L7
King's Pyon Herefs....69 J4
Kings Ripton Cambs....89 J7
King's Somborne
  Hants......29 G5
King's Stag Dorset.....14 D1
King's Stanley Gloucs....55 J7
King's Sutton Nhants....72 F7
Kingstanding Birm......85 J4
Kingsteignton Devon......7 K2
Kingsteps Highld.... 213 L3
Kingsthorne Herefs......54 E3
Kingsthorpe Nhants....73 L2
Kingston Cambs......75 L4

Kingston Cnwll......6 A2
Kingston Devon......6 F6
Kingston Dorset......14 E1
Kingston Dorset......15 H6
Kingston E Loth.... 178 C3
Kingston IoW......16 F6
Kingston Kent......35 G4
Kingston Bagpuize
  Oxon......57 H7
Kingston Blount
  Oxon......58 C7
Kingston by Sea
  W Susx......19 H4
Kingston Deverill
  Wilts......27 J4
Kingstone Herefs....69 H7
Kingstone Somset....26 B8
Kingstone Staffs.... 100 B6
Kingston Lacy
  House &
  Gardens Dorset....15 J3
Kingston Lisle Oxon....40 F3
Kingston near
  Lewes E Susx......19 K4
Kingston on Soar
  Notts..... 101 J6
Kingston on Spey
  Moray..... 215 H2
Kingston Russell
  Dorset......14 B4
Kingston St Mary
  Somset......25 K5
Kingston Seymour
  N Som......38 B6
Kingston upon Hull
  C KuH..... 126 D5
Kingston upon
  Thames Gt Lon......44 D6
King's Walden Herts....59 K4
Kingswear Devon......7 K5
Kingswells C Aber.. 207 G4
Kings Weston Bristl....38 D5
Kingswinford Dudley....84 F5
Kingswood Bucks......58 B4
Kingswood Gloucs......39 H3
Kingswood S Glos.....38 F5
Kingswood Somset....25 H4
Kingswood Surrey......31 L1
Kingswood Warwks......71 L1
Kingswood
  Common Staffs....84 E3
Kings Worthy Hants....29 J5
Kingthorpe Lincs.... 117 J6
Kington Herefs......68 F3
Kington S Glos......38 F3
Kington Worcs......71 H4
Kington Langley
  Wilts......39 L5
Kington Magna
  Dorset......27 H6
Kington St Michael
  Wilts......39 K5
Kingussie Highld.... 203 H5
Kingweston Somset....26 D5
Kinharrachie Abers.. 217 H7
Kinharvie D & G .... 147 G2
Kinkell Bridge P & K.. 185 J4
Kinknockie Abers.... 217 J6
Kinleith C Edin .... 177 G5
Kinlet Shrops......84 C7
Kinloch Highld..... 198 F5
Kinloch Highld..... 225 H2
Kinloch Highld..... 229 H5
Kinloch P & K..... 195 J7
Kinlochard Stirlg.... 184 B6
Kinlochbervie Highld.. 228 C4
Kinlocheil Highld.... 191 J1
Kinlochewe Highld.. 210 F3
Kinloch Hourn Highld.. 200 E4
Kinlochlaggan Highld.. 202 E7
Kinlochleven Highld.. 192 C4
Kinlochmoidart
  Highld..... 190 E2
Kinlochnanuagh
  Highld..... 200 B8
Kinloch Rannoch
  P & K..... 193 L5
Kinloss Moray..... 214 C3

Kinmel Bay Conwy........ 110 D5
Kinmuck Abers........ 206 F2
Kinmundy Abers........ 207 G2
Kinnabus Ag & B........ 160 B2
Kinnadie Abers........ 217 H5
Kinnaird P & K........ 194 F5
Kinneff Abers........ 197 K2
Kinnelhead D & G........ 155 H2
Kinnell Angus........ 196 F6
Kinnerley Shrops........ 97 M7
Kinnersley Herefs........ 69 G5
Kinnersley Worcs........ 70 F5
Kinnerton Powys........ 68 E2
Kinnesswood P & K........ 186 C6
Kinnordy Angus........ 196 B5
Kinoulton Notts........ 102 B6
Kinross P & K........ 186 B6
Kinrossie P & K........ 186 C2
Kinross Services
    P & K........ 186 B6
Kinsham Herefs........ 69 G2
Kinsham Worcs........ 71 G7
Kinsley Wakefd........ 124 C7
Kinson BCP........ 15 K3
Kintail Highld........ 200 F2
Kintbury W Berk........ 41 L6
Kintessack Moray........ 214 B3
Kintillo P & K........ 186 B4
Kinton Herefs........ 83 H8
Kinton Shrops........ 98 A8
Kintore Abers........ 206 E3
Kintour Ag & B........ 171 H7
Kintra Ag & B........ 170 F8
Kintra Ag & B........ 180 D3
Kintraw Ag & B........ 182 B6
Kintyre Ag & B........ 161 J2
Kinveachy Highld........ 203 L2
Kinver Staffs........ 84 E6
Kippax Leeds........ 124 C4
Kippen Stirlg........ 184 E7
Kippford D & G........ 146 E4
Kipping's Cross Kent........ 33 H5
Kirbister Ork........ 234 b6
Kirby Bedon Norfk........ 93 G3
Kirby Bellars Leics........ 102 B8
Kirby Cane Norfk........ 93 H5
Kirby Cross Essex........ 62 E4
Kirby Grindalythe
    N York........ 134 D6
Kirby Hill N York........ 132 F5
Kirby Hill N York........ 140 E6
Kirby Knowle N York........ 133 G3
Kirby-le-Soken
    Essex........ 62 F4
Kirby Misperton
    N York........ 134 B4
Kirby Muxloe Leics........ 87 G3
Kirby Underdale
    E R Yk........ 134 C7
Kirby Wiske N York........ 132 E3
Kirdford W Susx........ 31 G6
Kirk Highld........ 231 K4
Kirkabister Shet........ 235 d6
Kirkandrews D & G........ 146 A5
Kirkandrews upon
    Eden Cumb........ 148 C4
Kirkbampton Cumb........ 148 B4
Kirkbean D & G........ 147 G3
Kirk Bramwith Donc........ 124 F7
Kirkbride Cumb........ 147 M4
Kirkbuddo Angus........ 196 E7
Kirkburn Border........ 166 D2
Kirkburn E R Yk........ 134 F7
Kirkburton Kirk........ 123 J7
Kirkby Knows........ 111 L2
Kirkby N York........ 142 C6
Kirkby Fleetham
    N York........ 141 G7
Kirkby Green Lincs........ 103 H2
Kirkby-in-Ashfield
    Notts........ 101 J2
Kirkby-in-Furness
    Cumb........ 128 F2
Kirkby la Thorpe
    Lincs........ 103 J4
Kirkby Lonsdale
    Cumb........ 130 B4

Kirkby Malham
    N York........ 131 G7
Kirkby Mallory Leics........ 86 F4
Kirkby Malzeard
    N York........ 132 C5
Kirkbymoorside
    N York........ 133 L3
Kirkby on Bain Lincs........ 118 C8
Kirkby Overblow
    N York........ 123 L2
Kirkby Stephen
    Cumb........ 139 H5
Kirkby Thore Cumb........ 138 F3
Kirkby Underwood
    Lincs........ 103 H6
Kirkby Wharf N York........ 124 D3
Kirkcaldy Fife........ 186 D8
Kirkcambeck Cumb........ 148 F2
Kirkchrist D & G........ 146 B5
Kirkcolm D & G........ 144 B2
Kirkconnel D & G........ 154 E6
Kirkconnell D & G........ 147 G2
Kirkcowan D & G........ 145 G3
Kirkcudbright D & G........ 146 B5
Kirkdale Lpool........ 111 K3
Kirk Deighton N York........ 124 B1
Kirk Ella E R Yk........ 126 C5
Kirkfieldbank S Lans........ 165 G2
Kirkgunzeon D & G........ 146 F2
Kirk Hallam Derbys........ 101 J4
Kirkham Lancs........ 120 F4
Kirkham N York........ 134 B6
Kirkhamgate Wakefd........ 123 K6
Kirk Hammerton
    N York........ 133 G7
Kirkhaugh Nthumb........ 149 H5
Kirkheaton Kirk........ 123 H6
Kirkheaton Nthumb........ 158 C6
Kirkhill Highld........ 212 E5
Kirkhope S Lans........ 165 J7
Kirkibost Highld........ 199 H2
Kirkinch P & K........ 195 L7
Kirkinner D & G........ 145 J5
Kirkintilloch E Duns........ 175 H4
Kirk Ireton Derbys........ 100 E3
Kirkland Cumb........ 136 E4
Kirkland D & G........ 154 E4
Kirkland D & G........ 155 H4
Kirkland D & G........ 155 H4
Kirk Langley Derbys........ 100 F5
Kirkleatham R & Cl........ 142 D3
Kirklevington S on T........ 141 K5
Kirkley Suffk........ 93 L5
Kirklington N York........ 132 D4
Kirklington Notts........ 102 B2
Kirklinton Cumb........ 148 D2
Kirkliston C Edin........ 176 F4
Kirkmabreck D & G........ 145 K4
Kirkmaiden D & G........ 144 D7
Kirk Merrington Dur........ 141 G2
Kirk Michael IoM........ 237 c4
Kirkmichael P & K........ 195 H4
Kirkmichael S Ayrs........ 163 J7
Kirkmuirhill S Lans........ 164 F2
Kirknewton Nthumb........ 168 D4
Kirknewton W Loth........ 176 F5
Kirkney Abers........ 215 L7
Kirk of Shotts
    N Lans........ 175 L5
Kirkoswald Cumb........ 148 F6
Kirkoswald S Ayrs........ 163 G5
Kirkpatrick D & G........ 154 F4
Kirkpatrick Durham
    D & G........ 154 D7
Kirkpatrick-
    Fleming D & G........ 156 B7
Kirk Sandall Donc........ 124 F8
Kirksanton Cumb........ 128 D4
Kirk Smeaton N York........ 124 D7
Kirkstall Leeds........ 123 K4
Kirkstead Lincs........ 103 K1
Kirkstile Abers........ 215 L7
Kirkstile D & G........ 156 C4
Kirkstyle Highld........ 231 L2
Kirkthorpe Wakefd........ 124 B6
Kirkton Abers........ 206 C1
Kirkton D & G........ 155 G6
Kirkton Fife........ 186 F3

Kirkton Highld........ 210 C8
Kirkton Highld........ 210 D6
Kirkton P & K........ 185 K4
Kirkton Manor
    Border........ 166 C2
Kirkton of Airlie
    Angus........ 195 L6
Kirkton of
    Auchterhouse
    Angus........ 196 B8
Kirkton of Barevan
    Highld........ 213 K5
Kirkton of Collace
    P & K........ 186 C2
Kirkton of Durris
    Abers........ 206 E6
Kirkton of
    Glenbuchat
    Abers........ 205 J3
Kirkton of Glenisla
    Angus........ 195 K4
Kirkton of
    Kingoldrum
    Angus........ 196 B5
Kirkton of Lethendy
    P & K........ 195 H7
Kirkton of Logie
    Buchan Abers........ 217 J7
Kirkton of
    Maryculter Abers........ 207 G5
Kirkton of Menmuir
    Angus........ 196 E4
Kirkton of Monikie
    Angus........ 196 E8
Kirkton of Rayne
    Abers........ 216 D7
Kirkton of Skene
    Abers........ 206 F4
Kirkton of Tealing
    Angus........ 196 C8
Kirkton of Tough
    Abers........ 206 C3
Kirktown Abers........ 217 J2
Kirktown Abers........ 217 K4
Kirktown of Alvah
    Abers........ 216 D3
Kirktown of Bourtie
    Abers........ 206 F1
Kirktown of
    Deskford Moray........ 215 L3
Kirktown of
    Fetteresso Abers........ 206 F7
Kirktown of
    Mortlach Moray........ 215 H6
Kirktown of Slains
    Abers........ 217 K8
Kirkurd Border........ 165 M1
Kirkwall Ork........ 234 c6
Kirkwall Airport Ork........ 234 c6
Kirkwhelpington
    Nthumb........ 158 C5
Kirk Yetholm Border........ 168 C4
Kirmington N Linc........ 126 D7
Kirmond le Mire
    Lincs........ 117 K3
Kirn Ag & B........ 173 K3
Kirriemuir Angus........ 196 C5
Kirstead Green Norfk........ 93 G4
Kirtlebridge D & G........ 155 M7
Kirtling Cambs........ 77 G3
Kirtling Green Cambs........ 76 F4
Kirtlington Oxon........ 57 J4
Kirtomy Highld........ 229 M3
Kirton Lincs........ 104 A5
Kirton Notts........ 116 B7
Kirton Suffk........ 78 F6
Kirtonhill W Duns........ 174 D4
Kirton in Lindsey
    N Linc........ 116 F2
Kirwaugh D & G........ 145 J4
Kishorn Highld........ 210 C6
Kislingbury Nhants........ 73 K3
Kittisford Somset........ 25 G6
Kitt's Green Birm........ 85 L6
Kittybrewster C Aber........ 207 H4
Kivernoll Herefs........ 54 C2
Kiveton Park Rothm........ 115 J5
Knaith Lincs........ 116 D5

Knap Corner Dorset........ 27 J6
Knaphill Surrey........ 42 F8
Knapp Somset........ 25 L6
Knapton C York........ 124 E1
Knapton N York........ 134 D4
Knapton Norfk........ 107 G5
Knapwell Cambs........ 75 K2
Knaresborough
    N York........ 132 E7
Knarsdale Nthumb........ 149 H4
Knaven Abers........ 217 G5
Knayton N York........ 132 F2
Knebworth Herts........ 59 L4
Knedlington E R Yk........ 125 H5
Kneesall Notts........ 116 B8
Kneeton Notts........ 102 B4
Knelston Swans........ 50 F7
Knenhall Staffs........ 99 L5
Knightcote Warwks........ 72 E4
Knightley Staffs........ 99 J7
Knighton C Leic........ 87 H4
Knighton Dorset........ 14 C1
Knighton Powys........ 68 F1
Knighton Somset........ 25 J3
Knighton Staffs........ 99 G4
Knighton Staffs........ 99 H6
Knighton on Teme
    Worcs........ 70 B1
Knightwick Worcs........ 70 D4
Knill Herefs........ 68 F3
Knipoch Ag & B........ 182 B3
Knipton Leics........ 102 D6
Kniveton Derbys........ 100 E3
Knock Cumb........ 138 F2
Knock Highld........ 199 K4
Knock Moray........ 215 L4
Knock W Isls........ 232 g2
Knockally Highld........ 227 K3
Knockan Highld........ 224 F6
Knockando Moray........ 214 F6
Knockbain Highld........ 212 E5
Knockbain Highld........ 212 F3
Knock Castle N Ayrs........ 173 L5
Knockdee Highld........ 231 H4
Knockdow Ag & B........ 173 J4
Knockdown Wilts........ 39 J3
Knockeen S Ayrs........ 153 G3
Knockenkelly N Ayrs........ 162 D4
Knockentiber E Ayrs........ 163 K2
Knockholt Kent........ 32 E2
Knockholt Pound
    Kent........ 32 E2
Knockin Shrops........ 97 M7
Knockinlaw E Ayrs........ 163 K2
Knocknain D & G........ 144 B3
Knockrome Ag & B........ 171 K4
Knocksharry IoM........ 237 b4
Knocksheen D & G........ 153 M5
Knockvennie
    Smithy D & G........ 154 D7
Knodishall Suffk........ 79 J3
Knodishall Common
    Suffk........ 79 J3
Knole Somset........ 26 C6
Knolls Green Ches E........ 113 J5
Knolton Wrexhm........ 98 B5
Knook Wilts........ 27 L3
Knossington Leics........ 88 B2
Knott End-on-Sea
    Lancs........ 120 E2
Knotting Bed........ 74 E2
Knotting Green Bed........ 74 E3
Knottingley Wakefd........ 124 D5
Knotty Ash Lpool........ 112 B3
Knowbury Shrops........ 83 L7
Knowe D & G........ 153 G7
Knowehead D & G........ 154 A4
Knoweside S Ayrs........ 163 G6
Knowes of Elrick
    Abers........ 216 B4
Knowle Bristl........ 38 F6
Knowle Devon........ 11 H5
Knowle Devon........ 12 C2
Knowle Devon........ 12 D6
Knowle Devon........ 12 E7
Knowle Shrops........ 83 L8
Knowle Solhll........ 85 L7
Knowle Somset........ 24 E3

Knowlefield Cumb....... 148 D4
Knowle Green Lancs ... 121 J3
Knowle St Giles
  Somset.....................13 J1
Knowl Hill W & M.......42 D4
Knowsley Knows.........112 C3
Knowsley Safari
  Park Knows..............112 C3
Knowstone Devon.......24 C6
Knox Bridge Kent.......33 K5
Knoydart Highld.........200 C6
Knucklas Powys..........82 F8
Knuston Nhants...........74 D2
Knutsford Ches E.......113 H5
Knutsford Services
  Ches E.....................113 G6
Krumlin Calder...........122 F6
Kuggar Cnwll................3 J7
Kyleakin Highld...........200 B1
Kyle of Lochalsh
  Highld.....................210 B8
Kylerhea Highld...........200 B2
Kylesku Highld............224 F2
Kylesmorar Highld.......200 C6
Kyles Scalpay W Isls ...232 e4
Kylestrome Highld.......224 F2
Kynnersley Wrekin.......84 C1
Kyrewood Worcs............69 L2

**L**

La Bellieuse Guern.......236 d3
Lacasaigh W Isls..........232 f3
Lacasdal W Isls............232 f2
Laceby NE Lin..............117 K1
Lacey Green Bucks.......58 D7
Lach Dennis Ches W....113 G6
Lackford Suffk..............77 H1
Lackford Green Suffk....77 H1
Lacock Wilts.................39 K6
Ladbroke Warwks........72 E3
Laddingford Kent.........33 J4
Ladock Cnwll.................4 D5
Lady Ork....................234 d4
Ladybank Fife.............186 E5
Ladygill S Lans...........165 H4
Lady Hall Cumb...........128 E3
Ladykirk Border..........179 J8
Ladywood Birm............85 J6
Ladywood Worcs..........70 F3
La Fontenelle Guern....236 e1
La Fosse Guern...........236 d4
Lag D & G..................154 F5
Laga Highld................190 D4
Lagavulin Ag & B.......160 C1
Lagg N Ayrs...............162 B5
Laggan Highld............201 L6
Laggan Highld............202 F6
Lagganlia Highld.........203 K5
La Greve Guern..........236 d2
La Grève de Lecq
  Jersey.....................236 b5
La Hougue Bie
  Jersey.....................236 d7
La Houguette Guern...236 b3
Laid Highld................228 F4
Laide Highld...............219 L3
Laig Highld.................199 G7
Laigh Clunch E Ayrs...174 E8
Laigh Fenwick E Ayrs..163 L2
Laigh Glenmuir
  E Ayrs.....................164 C5
Laighstonehall
  S Lans.....................175 J7
Laindon Essex.............46 B3
Lairg Highld...............225 M7
Laisterdyke C Brad.....123 J4
Lake IoW.....................17 H5
Lake Wilts....................28 C4
Lake District Cumb....137 H5
**Lake District
  National Park**
  Cumb......................137 H5
Lakenheath Suffk........91 G6
Lakes End Norfk..........90 D4
Laleston Brdgnd..........36 D4

Lamarsh Essex.............77 K7
Lamas Norfk...............106 F7
Lambden Border.........167 L2
Lamberhurst Kent.......33 H6
Lamberhurst Down
  Kent.........................33 H6
Lamberton Border.......179 K6
Lambeth Gt Lon...........44 F4
Lambfair Green Suffk...77 G4
Lambley Notts............101 M4
Lambley Nthumb.........149 H4
Lambourn W Berk.........40 F5
Lambourne End
  Essex.......................45 J2
Lambs Green W Susx...31 L4
Lamerton Devon............6 C1
Lamesley Gatesd.........151 G4
Lamington S Lans.......165 J3
Lamlash N Ayrs..........162 C3
Lamonby Cumb...........148 D7
Lamorna Cnwll..............2 E6
Lamorran Cnwll.............4 D7
Lampeter Cerdgn.........66 D5
Lampeter Velfrey
  Pembks....................49 K5
Lamphey Pembks.........49 H7
Lamplugh Cumb..........136 F3
Lamport Nhants...........87 L8
Lamyatt Somset...........26 F4
Lanark S Lans............165 G2
Lancaster Lancs..........129 K7
Lancaster Services
  Lancs.......................121 G1
Lanchester Dur...........150 F5
Lancing W Susx............19 G5
L'Ancresse Guern........236 d1
Landbeach Cambs........76 C2
Landcross Devon..........23 G6
Landerberry Abers......206 E4
Landford Wilts..............28 E7
Land-hallow Highld......227 L2
Landimore Swans.........50 F6
Landkey Devon............23 J5
Landore Swans............51 J6
Landrake Cnwll..............6 B4
**Land's End Airport**
  Cnwll........................2 C5
Landulph Cnwll.............6 C4
Lane Cnwll....................4 C4
Laneast Cnwll...............9 G7
Lane End Bucks............42 D3
Lane End Kent.............45 L5
Lane End Wilts.............27 J3
Lane Ends Derbys.......100 E5
Laneham Notts...........116 D6
Lane Head Dur...........140 E5
Lanehead Dur.............149 L6
Lane Head Wsall...........85 H4
Lane Side Lancs.........122 B6
Langal Highld.............190 E3
Langaller Somset..........25 K6
Langar Notts..............102 B5
Langbank Rens..........174 D4
Langbar N York..........123 G1
Langcliffe N York........130 F6
Langdale End N York...134 E2
Langdon Hills Essex.....46 B3
Langdown Hants..........16 E2
Langdyke Fife............186 E6
Langenhoe Essex.........62 B4
Langford C Beds..........75 H6
Langford Devon...........12 D2
Langford Essex.............61 K6
Langford Notts...........102 D2
Langford Oxon.............56 E7
Langford Budville
  Somset......................25 H6
Langham Essex............62 B2
Langham Norfk...........106 B4
Langham Rutlnd...........88 B2
Langham Suffk.............77 L1
Langho Lancs..............121 K4
Langholm D & G.........156 C5
Langland Swans...........51 H7
Langlee Border...........167 H3
Langley Hants..............16 F3
Langley Herts..............59 K4
Langley Kent................33 K3

Langley Nthumb.........149 L3
Langley Slough............43 G5
Langley Somset............25 G5
Langley W Susx............30 D5
Langley Warwks..........71 L3
Langley Burrell Wilts...39 L5
Langley Green Essex...61 L4
**Langley Marsh**
  Somset......................25 G5
Langley Mill Derbys...101 H3
Langley Park Dur.......150 F6
Langley Street Norfk...93 H3
**Langley Upper
  Green** Essex............76 C7
Langney E Susx...........20 D5
Langold Notts.............115 L4
Langore Cnwll...............9 J7
Langport Somset..........26 B6
Langrick Lincs............103 L3
Langridge BaNES.........39 H6
Langrigg Cumb...........147 K5
Langrish Hants.............30 B6
Langsett Barns...........114 E2
Langside P & K...........185 G5
Langstone Hants..........17 K2
Langthorne N York......132 C2
Langthorpe N York......132 F6
Langthwaite N York....140 C6
Langtoft E R Yk..........134 F6
Langtoft Lincs..............89 G2
Langton Dur...............140 F4
Langton Lincs.............118 C7
Langton Lincs.............118 E7
Langton N York..........134 C6
Langton by Wragby
  Lincs.......................117 J6
Langton Green Kent.....32 F5
**Langton Herring**
  Dorset.......................14 C6
**Langton Matravers**
  Dorset.......................15 J6
Langtree Devon............10 C2
Langwathby Cumb.......148 F7
Langwell Highld..........224 E7
**Langwell House**
  Highld.....................227 K4
Langwith Derbys.........115 K7
Langwith Junction
  Derbys.....................115 K7
Langworth Lincs.........117 H6
**Lanhydrock House
  & Gardens** Cnwll......5 H3
Lanivet Cnwll................5 G3
Lanlivery Cnwll.............5 G4
Lanner Cnwll.................3 J4
Lanreath Cnwll..............5 J4
Lansallos Cnwll.............5 J5
Lanteglos Cnwll............5 J4
Lanteglos Highway
  Cnwll........................5 J5
Lanton Border............167 J5
Lanton Nthumb..........168 D3
La Passee Guern.........236 d2
Lapford Devon.............11 H3
Laphroaig Ag & B.......160 C1
Lapley Staffs...............84 F2
Lapworth Warwks........71 L1
Larachbeg Highld........190 E6
Larbert Falk...............176 B3
Largie Abers...............216 B7
Largiemore Ag & B.....172 F2
Largoward Fife...........187 H5
Largs N Ayrs...............173 L6
Largybeg N Ayrs........162 D5
Largymore N Ayrs.......162 D4
Larkfield Inver............173 L4
Larkfield Kent..............33 J2
Larkhall S Lans...........175 K7
Larkhill Wilts...............28 C3
Larling Norfk................92 B5
La Rocque Jersey......236 e8
**La Rousaillerie**
  Guern.....................236 d2
Lartington Dur...........140 C4
Lasham Hants..............30 A3
Lasswade Mdloth.......177 J5
Lastingham N York.....133 L2

Latchford Warrtn........112 F4
Latchingdon Essex.......61 L7
Latchley Cnwll..............6 B2
Lathbury M Keyn..........74 C5
Latheron Highld..........227 L2
Latheronwheel
  Highld.....................227 L3
Lathones Fife.............187 H5
Latimer Bucks.............59 G7
Latteridge S Glos.........38 F4
Lattiford Somset..........27 G6
Latton Wilts.................40 C2
Lauder Border............178 C8
Laugharne Carmth........50 C4
Laughterton Lincs.......116 D6
Laughton E Susx..........20 A3
Laughton Leics............87 J5
Laughton Lincs...........103 H6
Laughton Lincs...........118 D3
**Laughton Common**
  Rothm......................115 K4
Laughton-en-le-
  Morthen Rothm.......115 K4
Launceston Cnwll..........9 J7
Launton Oxon..............57 L4
Laurencekirk Abers....197 H3
Laurieston D & G.......146 B3
Laurieston Falk..........176 B3
La Villette Guern.......236 d4
Lavendon M Keyn........74 D4
Lavenham Suffk...........77 K5
Lavernock V Glam........37 J6
Laversdale Cumb.........148 E3
Laverstock Wilts...........28 D5
Laverstoke Hants.........29 J2
Laverton Gloucs...........71 J7
Laverton N York.........132 C5
Laverton Somset..........27 H2
La Villette Guern.......236 d4
Lawers P & K..............193 L7
Lawford Essex..............62 C2
Lawford Somset...........25 H4
Law Hill S Lans...........175 L7
Lawhitton Cnwll............9 J7
Lawkland N York.........130 E6
Lawley Wrekin..............84 C2
**Lawrence Weston**
  Bristl........................38 D5
Lawrenny Pembks........49 H6
Lawshall Suffk..............77 K4
Laxay W Isls...............232 f3
Laxdale W Isls............232 f2
Laxey IoM...................237 d4
Laxfield Suffk..............93 G8
**Laxford Bridge**
  Highld.....................228 C6
Laxo Shet..................235 d4
Laxton E R Yk.............125 J5
Laxton Nhants.............88 D4
Laxton Notts..............116 B7
Laycock C Brad..........122 F3
Layer Breton Essex.....61 M4
Layer-de-la-Haye
  Essex.......................62 A4
Layer Marney Essex.....61 L4
Laymore Dorset...........13 K2
Laytham E R Yk..........125 H3
Lazonby Cumb............148 F6
Lea Derbys................101 G2
Lea Herefs..................54 F4
Lea Lincs...................116 D4
Lea Shrops..................83 G5
Lea Wilts.....................39 L3
Leachkin Highld.........212 F5
Leadburn Border........177 H7
Leadenham Lincs........102 F3
Leaden Roding Essex...60 F5
Leadgate Dur.............150 E5
Leadhills S Lans..........165 G6
Leafield Oxon...............56 F5
Leagrave Luton............59 H4
**Leake Common
  Side** Lincs...............104 C3
Lealholm N York.........142 F5
Lealt Highld................209 H3
Lea Marston Warwks...86 B5

Leamington
  Hastings Warwks .......**72** F2
Leamington Spa
  Warwks .........................**72** D2
Leap Cross E Susx ...........**20** C4
Learney Abers ...............**206** C5
Leasgill Cumb ................**129** K3
Leasingham Lincs .........**103** H3
Leasingthorne Dur ......**141** G2
Leatherhead Surrey .......**31** K1
Leathley N York ...........**123** J2
Leaton Shrops ................**98** C8
Leaveland Kent ..............**34** D4
Leavenheath Suffk .........**77** L6
Leavening N York .........**134** C6
Leaves Green Gt Lon ......**45** H7
Lebberston N York .......**135** G3
Le Bigard Guern ...........**236** c4
Le Bourg Guern ...........**236** c4
Le Bourg Jersey ...........**236** e8
Lechlade on
  Thames Gloucs ...........**56** E7
Lecht Gruinart
  Ag & B .........................**170** E5
Leck Lancs ....................**130** C4
Leckbuie P & K .............**193** L7
Leckford Hants ...............**29** G4
Leckhampstead
  Bucks ............................**73** K6
Leckhampstead
  W Berk ..........................**41** H5
Leckhampstead
  Thicket W Berk ...........**41** H5
Leckhampton Gloucs .....**55** L4
Leckmelm Highld .........**220** F4
Leconfield E R Yk .........**126** C2
Ledaig Ag & B ...............**191** H8
Ledburn Bucks ...............**58** E4
Ledbury Herefs ..............**70** C6
Ledgemoor Herefs .........**69** H4
Ledmore Highld ...........**224** F6
Ledsham Leeds .............**124** C4
Ledston Leeds ..............**124** C5
Ledwell Oxon .................**57** H3
Lee Devon ......................**23** H3
Lee Gt Lon ......................**45** H5
Leebotwood Shrops .......**83** J4
Lee Brockhurst
  Shrops ..........................**98** D6
Leece Cumb ..................**128** F5
Lee Chapel Essex ..........**46** B3
Lee Clump Bucks ............**58** E6
Leeds Kent ......................**33** L3
Leeds Leeds ..................**123** K4
Leeds Bradford
  Airport Leeds .............**123** J3
Leeds Castle Kent ..........**33** L3
Leeds Skelton Lake
  Services Leeds ...........**123** L4
Leedstown Cnwll ..............**3** G4
Leek Staffs .....................**99** M2
Leek Wootton
  Warwks ........................**72** C2
Lee Mill Devon .................**6** E5
Leeming N York ............**132** D2
Leeming Bar N York .....**132** D2
Leeming Bar Rest
  Area N York ...............**132** D2
Lee-on-the-Solent
  Hants ............................**17** G3
Lees Derbys ..................**100** E5
Lees Oldham .................**113** L2
Lees Green Derbys .......**100** E5
Leesthorpe Leics ...........**87** L2
Leeswood Flints .............**97** K1
Leetown P & K ..............**186** C3
Leftwich Ches W ...........**112** F6
Legbourne Lincs ...........**118** E5
Legerwood Border .......**167** J2
Legoland W & M .............**42** F5
Le Gron Guern ..............**236** c3
Legsby Lincs .................**117** J4
Le Haguais Jersey ........**236** d8
Le Hocq Jersey .............**236** d8
Leicester C Leic ..............**87** H3
Leicester Forest
  East Services
  Leics .............................**87** G3

Leigh Dorset ...................**14** C2
Leigh Gloucs ...................**55** K3
Leigh Kent ......................**32** F4
Leigh Surrey ...................**31** L3
Leigh Wigan ..................**112** F2
Leigh Wilts ......................**40** B3
Leigh Worcs ....................**70** D4
Leigh Beck Essex ...........**46** D4
Leigh Delamere
  Wilts .............................**39** K5
Leigh Delamere
  Services Wilts ............**39** K5
Leigh Green Kent ...........**34** B7
Leigh Knoweglass
  S Lans .........................**175** H7
Leigh-on-Sea Sthend .....**46** D3
Leigh Park Dorset ...........**15** J3
Leigh Park Hants ............**17** K2
Leigh Sinton Worcs ........**70** D4
Leighswood Wsall ..........**85** J3
Leighterton Gloucs .........**39** J3
Leighton Powys ..............**82** E3
Leighton Shrops .............**84** B3
Leighton
  Bromswold
  Cambs ..........................**89** G7
Leighton Buzzard
  C Beds ..........................**58** F3
Leigh upon Mendip
  Somset .........................**27** G3
Leigh Woods N Som .......**38** E6
Leinthall Earls
  Herefs ...........................**69** J2
Leinthall Starkes
  Herefs ...........................**69** J1
Leintwardine Herefs .....**83** H8
Leire Leics ......................**87** G5
Leiston Suffk ...................**79** J3
Leith C Edin ...................**177** H3
Leitholm Border ...........**168** B1
Lelant Cnwll ......................**2** F4
Lelley E R Yk ..................**126** F4
Lempitlaw Border .........**168** B3
Lemreway W Isls ..........**232** f3
Lemsford Herts ..............**59** L5
Lenchwick Worcs ...........**71** J5
Lendalfoot S Ayrs .........**152** D4
Lendrick Stirlg ...............**184** C6
Lendrum Terrace
  Abers ...........................**217** L6
Lenham Kent ..................**34** B4
Lenham Heath Kent .......**34** B5
Lenie Highld .................**202** D1
Lennel Border ...............**168** C2
Lennox Plunton
  D & G ..........................**146** A5
Lennoxtown E Duns .....**175** H3
Lent Bucks ......................**42** F4
Lenton C Nott ...............**101** K5
Lenton Lincs ..................**103** G6
Lenwade Norfk .............**106** D8
Lenzie E Duns ...............**175** H4
Leochel-Cushnie
  Abers ...........................**205** L4
Leominster Herefs .........**69** K3
Leonard Stanley
  Gloucs ...........................**55** J7
Leoville Jersey ..............**236** b6
Lephin Highld ...............**208** B4
Leppington N York .......**134** B7
Lepton Kirk ...................**123** J7
Lerags Ag & B ...............**182** B3
L'Erée Guern .................**236** b3
Lerryn Cnwll .....................**5** J4
Lerwick Shet .................**235** d6
Les Arquêts Guern .......**236** b3
Lesbury Nthumb ..........**169** J6
Les Hubits Guern .........**236** d3
Leslie Abers ..................**206** B1
Leslie Fife .....................**186** D6
Les Lohiers Guern ........**236** c3
Lesmahagow S Lans .....**164** F2
Les Murchez Guern ......**236** c4
Lesnewth Cnwll ...............**8** F6
Les Nicolles Guern .......**236** c4
Les Quartiers Guern ....**236** d2
Les Quennevais
  Jersey .........................**236** b7

Les Sages Guern ...........**236** b3
Lessingham Norfk .......**107** H6
Lessonhall Cumb ..........**147** L5
Les Villets Guern ..........**236** c4
Leswalt D & G ...............**144** B3
L'Etacq Jersey ..............**236** a6
Letchmore Heath
  Herts .............................**43** J2
Letchworth Garden
  City Herts .....................**59** L2
Letcombe Bassett
  Oxon .............................**41** G4
Letcombe Regis
  Oxon .............................**41** G3
Letham Angus ..............**196** E6
Letham Border ..............**167** K7
Letham Falk ..................**176** B2
Letham Fife ...................**186** E4
Letham Grange
  Angus ..........................**197** G7
Lethenty Abers ............**206** B2
Lethenty Abers ............**216** F6
Letheringham Suffk .......**78** F3
Letheringsett Norfk .....**106** C5
Letterewe Highld .........**219** L7
Letterfearn Highld .......**200** D2
Letterfinlay Lodge
  Hotel Highld ..............**201** K6
Letters Highld ...............**220** F4
Lettershaw S Lans ........**165** H5
Letterston Pembks .........**48** F2
Lettoch Highld .............**204** C2
Lettoch Highld .............**214** D7
Letton Herefs .................**69** G5
Letty Green Herts ..........**59** M5
Letwell Rothm ..............**115** K4
Leuchars Fife ................**187** G3
Leumrabhagh W Isls ...**232** f3
Leurbost W Isls ............**232** f3
Levan Inver ...................**173** L3
Levedale Staffs ...............**84** F1
Leven E R Yk ..................**126** D2
Leven Fife .....................**186** F7
Levens Cumb .................**129** K3
Levens Green Herts ........**60** B4
Levenshulme Manch .....**113** K3
Levenwick Shet ............**235** c7
Leverburgh W Isls .......**232** d5
Leverington Cambs ........**90** C2
Leverstock Green
  Herts .............................**59** H6
Leverton Lincs ..............**104** C3
Le Villocq Guern ..........**236** c2
Levington Suffk ..............**78** F6
Levisham N York ..........**134** C2
Lew Oxon ........................**56** F6
Lewannick Cnwll ..............**9** H8
Lewdown Devon .............**10** C7
Lewes E Susx ..................**19** L4
Leweston Pembks ..........**48** F3
Lewisham Gt Lon ...........**45** G5
Lewiston Highld ...........**212** D8
Lewistown Brdgnd .........**36** E3
Lewknor Oxon ................**42** B2
Lewson Street Kent .......**34** C3
Lewtrenchard Devon .....**10** C7
Lexden Essex ..................**62** A3
Lexworthy Somset .........**25** K4
Leybourne Kent .............**33** H2
Leyburn N York .............**131** L2
Leygreen Herts ..............**59** K3
Ley Hill Bucks .................**59** G7
Leyland Lancs ...............**121** H6
Leylodge Abers .............**206** E3
Leys Abers ....................**217** J4
Leys P & K .....................**195** K8
Leysdown-on-Sea
  Kent ..............................**47** G6
Leysmill Angus .............**196** F6
Leys of Cossans
  Angus ..........................**196** C6
Leysters Herefs ..............**69** L2
Leyton Gt Lon .................**45** G3
Leytonstone Gt Lon .......**45** H3
Lezant Cnwll .....................**5** M1
Lhanbryde Moray .........**215** G3
Libanus Powys ...............**52** F3
Libberton S Lans ..........**165** J2

Liberton C Edin .............**177** J4
Lichfield Staffs ...............**85** K2
Lickey Worcs ...................**85** H7
Lickey End Worcs ...........**85** H8
Lickfold W Susx ..............**30** F6
Liddesdale Highld .........**190** F4
Liddington Swindn .........**40** E4
Lidgate Suffk ..................**77** G3
Lidlington C Beds ...........**74** E6
Liff Angus .....................**186** E2
Lifford Birm ....................**85** J7
Lifton Devon .....................**9** K7
Liftondown Devon ...........**9** K7
Lighthorne Warwks ........**72** D4
Lighthorne Heath
  Warwks ........................**72** D4
Lightwater Surrey ..........**42** F7
Lightwater Valley
  Theme Park
  N York .........................**132** D4
Lightwood C Stke ...........**99** L4
Lilbourne Nhants ...........**87** H7
Lilleshall Wrekin ............**84** D1
Lilley Herts .....................**59** J3
Lilliesleaf Border ..........**167** H4
Lillingstone Dayrell
  Bucks ............................**73** K6
Lillingstone Lovell
  Bucks ............................**73** K6
Lillington Dorset ............**26** F8
Lilliput BCP ....................**15** K4
Lilstock Somset ..............**25** J3
Limbury Luton ................**59** H3
Limekilnburn S Lans ....**175** J7
Limekilns Fife ...............**176** E2
Limerigg Falk ...............**176** B4
Limerstone IoW ..............**16** E6
Lime Street Worcs ..........**55** J2
Limington Somset ..........**26** D6
Limmerhaugh E Ayrs ...**164** C4
Limpenhoe Norfk ...........**93** H3
Limpley Stoke Wilts ......**39** H7
Limpsfield Surrey ...........**32** D3
Limpsfield Chart
  Surrey ...........................**32** D3
Linby Notts ...................**101** K3
Linchmere W Susx ..........**30** E5
Lincluden D & G ...........**155** G6
Lincoln Lincs .................**116** F7
Lincomb Worcs ...............**70** E2
Lindale Cumb ................**129** J4
Lindal in Furness
  Cumb ...........................**128** F4
Lindfield W Susx .............**32** C7
Lindford Hants ................**30** D4
Lindley Kirk ...................**123** G6
Lindores Fife ................**186** D4
Lindridge Worcs .............**70** C2
Lindsell Essex ..................**61** G3
Lindsey Suffk ..................**77** L5
Lindsey Tye Suffk ...........**78** B5
Lingdale R & Cl .............**142** E4
Lingen Herefs .................**69** G2
Lingfield Surrey ..............**32** C4
Lingfield Common
  Surrey ...........................**32** C4
Lingwood Norfk ..............**93** H2
Liniclate W Isls ............**233** b7
Linicro Highld ...............**218** B7
Linkend Worcs ................**55** J2
Linkenholt Hants ............**41** G8
Linkinhorne Cnwll ............**5** L2
Linktown Fife ................**177** J1
Linkwood Moray ..........**214** F3
Linley Shrops ..................**83** G5
Linley Green Herefs .......**70** C4
Linlithgow W Loth ........**176** D3
Linsidemore Highld .....**222** D2
Linslade C Beds ..............**58** E3
Linstead Parva Suffk .....**93** G7
Linstock Cumb ..............**148** D4
Linthurst Worcs ..............**85** H8
Linthwaite Kirk .............**123** G7
Lintlaw Border ..............**179** H6
Lintmill Moray ..............**215** L2
Linton Border ...............**168** B4
Linton Cambs ..................**76** E5
Linton Derbys .................**86** C1

**Linton** Herefs......54 F3
**Linton** Kent......33 K3
**Linton** Leeds......124 B2
**Linton** N York......131 J6
**Linton Hill** Herefs......54 F3
**Linton-on-Ouse**
N York......133 G7
**Linwood** Lincs......117 J4
**Linwood** Rens......174 E5
**Lionacleit** W Isls......233 b7
**Lional** W Isls......232 g1
**Liphook** Hants......30 D5
**Liscard** Wirral......111 J3
**Liscombe** Somset......24 D5
**Liskeard** Cnwll......5 K3
**Lismore** Ag & B......191 G7
**Liss** Hants......30 C5
**Lissett** E R Yk......135 H7
**Lissington** Lincs......117 J5
**Lisvane** Cardif......37 J4
**Liswerry** Newpt......37 M3
**Litcham** Norfk......105 L8
**Litchborough** Nhants......73 J4
**Litchfield** Hants......29 J2
**Litherland** Sefton......111 K2
**Litlington** Cambs......75 K6
**Litlington** E Susx......20 B5
**Little Abington**
Cambs......76 D5
**Little Addington**
Nhants......88 D8
**Little Airies** D & G......145 J5
**Little Alne** Warwks......71 K3
**Little Altcar** Sefton......111 J1
**Little Amwell** Herts......60 B5
**Little Aston** Staffs......85 K4
**Little Ayton** N York......142 C5
**Little Baddow** Essex......61 J6
**Little Badminton**
S Glos......39 J4
**Little Bampton** Cumb......148 A4
**Little Bardfield** Essex......61 G2
**Little Barford** Bed......75 H3
**Little Barningham**
Norfk......106 D5
**Little Barrington**
Gloucs......56 D5
**Little Barrow** Ches W......112 C7
**Little Bavington**
Nthumb......158 C6
**Little Bedwyn** Wilts......40 F7
**Little Bentley** Essex......62 D3
**Little Berkhamsted**
Herts......59 M6
**Little Billing** Nhants......74 B3
**Little Billington**
C Beds......58 F4
**Little Birch** Herefs......54 D2
**Little Blakenham**
Suffk......78 D5
**Little Blencow** Cumb......148 E7
**Little Bloxwich** Wsall......85 H3
**Little Bognor** W Susx......31 G7
**Little Bollington**
Ches E......113 G4
**Little Bookham**
Surrey......31 J1
**Littleborough** Notts......116 D5
**Littleborough** Rochdl......122 D7
**Littlebourne** Kent......35 G3
**Little Bourton** Oxon......72 F5
**Little Braxted** Essex......61 K5
**Little Brechin** Angus......196 F4
**Littlebredy** Dorset......14 B5
**Little Brickhill**
M Keyn......58 E2
**Little Brington**
Nhants......73 J2
**Little Bromley** Essex......62 C3
**Little Budworth**
Ches W......112 E7
**Littleburn** Highld......212 F4
**Little Burstead** Essex......46 A2
**Littlebury** Essex......76 D6
**Littlebury Green**
Essex......76 C6
**Little Bytham** Lincs......103 G8
**Little Carlton** Lincs......118 E4

**Little Casterton**
Rutlnd......88 E2
**Little Cawthorpe**
Lincs......118 E5
**Little Chalfont** Bucks......43 G2
**Little Chart** Kent......34 C5
**Little Chesterford**
Essex......76 D6
**Little Cheverell** Wilts......27 M2
**Little Chishill** Cambs......76 B6
**Little Clacton** Essex......62 E4
**Little Clifton** Cumb......136 E2
**Little Coates** NE Lin......127 G8
**Little Comberton**
Worcs......71 G5
**Little Common**
E Susx......20 E4
**Little Compton**
Warwks......56 E3
**Little Cornard** Suffk......77 K6
**Little Cowarne**
Herefs......69 L4
**Little Coxwell** Oxon......40 F2
**Little Crakehall**
N York......132 C2
**Little Cressingham**
Norfk......91 K4
**Little Crosby** Sefton......111 K2
**Little Cubley** Derbys......100 D5
**Little Dalby** Leics......87 L2
**Littledean** Gloucs......54 F5
**Little Dewchurch**
Herefs......54 D2
**Little Ditton** Cambs......76 F3
**Little Downham**
Cambs......90 D6
**Little Driffield** E R Yk......134 F7
**Little Dunham** Norfk......91 K2
**Little Dunkeld** P & K......195 G7
**Little Dunmow** Essex......61 G4
**Little Durnford** Wilts......28 C5
**Little Easton** Essex......60 F3
**Little Eaton** Derbys......101 G4
**Little Ellingham**
Norfk......92 B4
**Little Everdon** Nhants......73 H3
**Little Eversden**
Cambs......75 L4
**Little Faringdon**
Oxon......56 E7
**Little Fencote** N York......132 D2
**Little Fenton** N York......124 D4
**Littleferry** Highld......223 H3
**Little Fransham**
Norfk......91 K2
**Little Gaddesden**
Herts......59 G5
**Little Glemham** Suffk......79 H3
**Little Gorsley** Herefs......55 G3
**Little Gransden**
Cambs......75 J4
**Little Green** Somset......27 G2
**Little Hadham** Herts......60 C4
**Little Hale** Lincs......103 J4
**Little Hallam** Derbys......101 J4
**Little Hallingbury**
Essex......60 D4
**Littleham** Devon......12 D6
**Littleham** Devon......23 G6
**Littlehampton**
W Susx......18 D5
**Little Harrowden**
Nhants......74 C1
**Little Haseley** Oxon......57 M7
**Little Haven** Pembks......48 E5
**Littlehaven** W Susx......31 K5
**Little Hay** Staffs......85 K3
**Little Haywood** Staffs......100 A7
**Littlehempston**
Devon......7 J4
**Little Hereford**
Herefs......69 K2
**Little Horkesley**
Essex......62 A2
**Little Hormead** Herts......60 C3
**Little Horsted** E Susx......19 M3
**Little Horton** C Brad......123 H4
**Little Horwood** Bucks......58 C2

**Little Houghton**
Barns......115 H1
**Little Houghton**
Nhants......74 B3
**Little Hucklow**
Derbys......114 D5
**Little Hutton** N York......133 G4
**Little Irchester**
Nhants......74 C2
**Little Keyford** Somset......27 H3
**Little Kimble** Bucks......58 D6
**Little Kineton**
Warwks......72 D4
**Little Kingshill** Bucks......58 E7
**Little Knox** D & G......146 E3
**Little Langdale** Cumb......137 J6
**Little Langford** Wilts......28 B4
**Little Leigh** Ches W......112 F6
**Little Leighs** Essex......61 H5
**Little Lever** Bolton......121 L8
**Little Linford** M Keyn......74 B5
**Little Load** Somset......26 C6
**Little London** Cambs......90 B4
**Little London** E Susx......20 C2
**Little London** Hants......29 G2
**Little London** Hants......41 L8
**Little Longstone**
Derbys......114 D6
**Little Maplestead**
Essex......77 J7
**Little Marcle** Herefs......70 C2
**Little Marlow** Bucks......42 E3
**Little Massingham**
Norfk......105 J7
**Little Melton** Norfk......92 E3
**Littlemill** Abers......205 H6
**Littlemill** Highld......213 L4
**Little Mill** Mons......53 L7
**Little Milton** Oxon......57 L7
**Little Missenden**
Bucks......58 F7
**Littlemore** Oxon......57 K7
**Little Musgrave**
Cumb......139 H5
**Little Ness** Shrops......98 B8
**Little Newcastle**
Pembks......49 G2
**Little Newsham** Dur......140 E4
**Little Norton** Somset......26 C7
**Little Oakley** Essex......62 F3
**Little Oakley** Nhants......88 C6
**Little Orton** Cumb......148 C4
**Littleover** C Derb......101 G5
**Little Packington**
Warwks......86 B6
**Little Paxton** Cambs......75 H3
**Little Petherick**
Cnwll......4 E2
**Little Plumstead**
Norfk......93 G2
**Little Ponton** Lincs......102 F6
**Littleport** Cambs......90 E6
**Little Preston** Nhants......73 H4
**Littler** Ches W......112 F7
**Little Raveley** Cambs......89 J7
**Little Reedness**
E R Yk......125 J6
**Little Ribston** N York......132 F8
**Little Rissington**
Gloucs......56 D4
**Little Rollright** Oxon......56 F3
**Little Ryburgh** Norfk......106 A6
**Little Salkeld** Cumb......148 F7
**Little Sampford**
Essex......76 F7
**Little Saughall**
Ches W......111 K7
**Little Saxham** Suffk......77 H2
**Little Scatwell** Highld......212 B3
**Little Shelford**
Cambs......76 C4
**Little Singleton**
Lancs......120 E3
**Little Skipwith**
N York......125 G3
**Little Smeaton**
N York......124 D6
**Little Snoring** Norfk......106 A6

**Little Sodbury** S Glos......39 H4
**Little Somborne**
Hants......29 G5
**Little Somerford**
Wilts......39 L4
**Little Soudley** Shrops......99 G6
**Little Stainton**
Darltn......141 J3
**Little Stanney**
Ches W......112 B6
**Little Staughton** Bed......75 G3
**Little Steeping** Lincs......118 F8
**Little Stoke** Staffs......99 K6
**Littlestone-on-Sea**
Kent......21 L2
**Little Stonham** Suffk......78 D3
**Little Stretton** Leics......87 J4
**Little Stretton** Shrops......83 J5
**Little Strickland**
Cumb......138 E4
**Little Stukeley**
Cambs......89 H7
**Little Sugnall** Staffs......99 J6
**Little Swinburne**
Nthumb......158 B6
**Little Sypland** D & G......146 C4
**Little Tew** Oxon......57 G3
**Little Tey** Essex......61 L4
**Little Thetford** Cambs......90 D7
**Little Thorpe** Dur......151 K6
**Littlethorpe** Leics......87 G4
**Littlethorpe** N York......132 E5
**Little Thurlow** Suffk......76 F4
**Little Thurrock** Thurr......45 L4
**Littleton** Ches W......112 C7
**Littleton** D & G......146 B4
**Littleton** Hants......29 J5
**Littleton** Somset......26 C5
**Littleton** Surrey......43 H6
**Littleton Drew** Wilts......39 J4
**Littleton of Airlie**
Angus......196 B6
**Littleton-on-Severn**
S Glos......38 E3
**Littleton Panell** Wilts......27 M1
**Little Torrington**
Devon......10 D2
**Littletown** Dur......151 H6
**Little Town** Lancs......121 K4
**Little Urswick** Cumb......128 F5
**Little Wakering**
Essex......46 F3
**Little Walden** Essex......76 D6
**Little Waldingfield**
Suffk......77 K5
**Little Walsingham**
Norfk......105 M5
**Little Waltham** Essex......61 H5
**Little Weighton**
E R Yk......126 B4
**Little Wenlock**
Wrekin......84 B3
**Little Weston** Somset......26 H4
**Little Whitefield** IoW......17 H4
**Littlewick Green**
W & M......42 D4
**Little Wilbraham**
Cambs......76 D3
**Little Witcombe**
Gloucs......55 K5
**Little Witley** Worcs......70 D2
**Little Wittenham**
Oxon......41 K2
**Little Wolford**
Warwks......72 C7
**Little Woodcote**
Gt Lon......44 F7
**Littleworth** Oxon......40 F2
**Littleworth** Staffs......99 L7
**Littleworth** Worcs......70 F4
**Little Wymington**
Bed......74 D2
**Little Wymondley**
Herts......59 K3
**Little Wyrley** Staffs......85 H3
**Little Yeldham** Essex......77 H6
**Littley Green** Essex......61 H4
**Litton** Derbys......114 D6

Litton N York .................. 131 G5
Litton Somset .................. 26 E1
Litton Cheney Dorset ..... 14 A4
Liurbost W Isls .............. 232 f3
Liverpool Lpool .............. 111 K4
Liverpool Maritime
  Mercantile City
  Lpool ........................ 111 K4
Liversedge Kirk .............. 123 J5
Liverton Devon .................. 7 J2
Liverton R & Cl .............. 142 F4
Livingston W Loth .......... 176 E5
Livingston Village
  W Loth ...................... 176 E5
Lixwm Flints ................ 111 G7
Lizard Cnwll ...................... 3 J8
Llanaelhaearn Gwynd ....95 G4
Llanafan Cerdgn .......... 80 F8
Llanafan-Fawr
  Powys ........................ 67 L4
Llanallgo IoA .............. 109 G4
Llanarmon Dyffryn
  Ceiriog Wrexhm .....97 J6
Llanarmon-yn-Ial
  Denbgs ....................97 J2
Llanarth Cerdgn ......... 65 L3
Llanarth Mons ............. 54 B5
Llanarthne Carmth ...... 51 G2
Llanasa Flints ............. 110 F5
Llanbadarn Fawr
  Cerdgn ...................... 80 E7
Llanbadarn Fynydd
  Powys ........................ 82 C7
Llanbadoc Mons ........... 54 B7
Llanbeder Newpt .......... 38 B3
Llanbedr Gwynd .......... 95 K6
Llanbedr Powys ........... 53 K4
Llanbedr-Dyffryn-
  Clwyd Denbgs .....97 H2
Llanbedrgoch IoA ...... 109 G5
Llanbedrog Gwynd ....... 94 F6
Llanbedr-y-Cennin
  Conwy .................... 109 L7
Llanberis Gwynd ......... 95 K1
Llanbethêry V Glam .....37 G6
Llanbister Powys ......... 82 C8
Llanblethian V Glam .... 36 F5
Llanboidy Carmth ........ 49 L3
Llanbradach Caerph .....37 J3
Llanbrynmair Powys .....81 J3
Llancadle V Glam ......... 37 G6
Llancarfan V Glam ....... 37 G6
Llancloudy Herefs ....... 54 D4
Llandaff Cardif ............ 37 J3
Llandanwg Gwynd ....... 95 K6
Llanddaniel Fab IoA ... 109 G7
Llanddarog Carmth ...... 51 G3
Llanddeiniol Cerdgn ....66 D1
Llanddeiniolen
  Gwynd ................... 109 H7
Llandd: ferfel Gwynd ..... 96 F5
Llanddeusant IoA ...... 108 D4
Llanddew Powys ......... 53 G2
Llanddewi Swans ........ 50 F7
Llanddewi Brefi
  Cerdgn ...................... 66 F4
Llanddewi
  Rhydderch Mons ....53 M5
Llanddewi Velfrey
  Pembks ...................... 49 K4
Llanddewi
  Ystradenni Powys ...68 C2
Llanddoged Conwy ... 109 M8
Llanddona IoA ........... 109 H5
Llanddowror Carmth .... 50 B3
Llanddulas Conwy ...... 110 C6
Llanddwywe Gwynd ....95 K7
Llanddyfnan IoA ........ 109 G5
Llandefaelog-Tre'r-
  Graig Powys ...........53 H3
Llandefalle Powys ....... 68 C7
Llandegfan IoA .......... 109 H6
Llandegla Denbgs ........ 97 J3
Llandegley Powys ........ 68 D2
Llandegveth Mons ........37 M2
Llandeilo Carmth ......... 51 J2
Llandeilo Graban
  Powys ........................ 68 C5

Llandeloy Pembks .........48 E3
Llandenny Mons ...........54 B7
Llandevaud Newpt .......38 B3
Llandevenny Mons .......38 B3
Llandinam Powys ......... 82 B5
Llandissilio Pembks .....49 J3
Llandogo Mons ............54 D7
Llandough V Glam .......36 F6
Llandough V Glam .......37 J5
Llandovery Carmth ......67 G7
Llandow V Glam ..........36 E5
Llandre Carmth ............66 F6
Llandre Cerdgn .............80 E6
Llandre Isaf Pembks .....49 J2
Llandrillo Denbgs .........97 G5
Llandrillo-yn-Rhos
  Conwy .................... 110 B5
Llandrindod Wells
  Powys ........................ 68 B3
Llandrinio Powys ......... 97 L8
Llandudno Conwy ...... 109 L5
Llandudno Junction
  Conwy .................... 109 M6
Llandulas Powys .......... 67 J6
Llandwrog Gwynd .......95 H2
Llandybie Carmth ......... 51 J3
Llandyfaelog Carmth .... 50 E3
Llandyfriog Cerdgn ...... 65 K6
Llandygai Gwynd ...... 109 H7
Llandygwydd
  Cerdgn ...................... 65 H5
Llandyrnog Denbgs ... 110 F8
Llandyssil Powys .......... 82 E4
Llandysul Cerdgn ......... 65 L6
Llanedeyrn Cardif ........37 K4
Llaneglwys Powys ........68 B6
Llanegryn Gwynd ........80 D3
Llanegwad Carmth ....... 51 G2
Llaneilian IoA ............ 108 F3
Llanelian-yn-Rhôs
  Conwy .................... 110 B6
Llanelidan Denbgs ........97 H3
Llanelieu Powys ...........68 D7
Llanellen Mons ............ 53 L5
Llanelli Carmth ............ 51 G5
Llanelltyd Gwynd ........ 96 A8
Llanelwedd Powys ........68 B4
Llanenddwyn Gwynd ....95 K7
Llanengan Gwynd .........94 E6
Llanerchymedd IoA .... 108 E5
Llanerfyl Powys ............82 B2
Llanfachraeth IoA ...... 108 D5
Llanfachreth Gwynd .....96 B7
Llanfaelog IoA ........... 108 D6
Llanfaelrhys Gwynd .....94 D6
Llanfaethlu IoA .......... 108 D4
Llanfair Gwynd ............95 K6
Llanfair Caereinion
  Powys ........................ 82 C3
Llanfair Clydogau
  Cerdgn ...................... 66 E4
Llanfair Dyffryn
  Clwyd Denbgs ......97 H2
Llanfairfechan
  Conwy .................... 109 K6
Llanfairpwllgwyngyll
  IoA ......................... 109 G6
Llanfair Talhaiarn
  Conwy .................... 110 C7
Llanfair Waterdine
  Shrops ....................... 82 E7
Llanfairynghornwy
  IoA ......................... 108 D4
Llanfair-yn-
  Neubwll IoA ....... 108 C6
Llanfallteg Carmth .......49 K4
Llanfallteg West
  Carmth ...................... 49 K4
Llanfarian Cerdgn ........80 D7
Llanfechain Powys ........97 J7
Llanfechell IoA ........... 108 E3
Llanferres Denbgs ........97 J1
Llan Ffestiniog
  Gwynd ...................... 96 A4
Llanfihangel-ar-
  arth Carmth ...........66 B6
Llanfihangel Glyn
  Myfyr Conwy ........96 F3

Llanfihangel Nant
  Bran Powys ...........67 K7
Llanfihangel
  Rhydithon Powys ...68 D2
Llanfihangel Rogiet
  Mons ........................ 38 C3
Llanfihangel-y-
  Creuddyn Cerdgn ...80 F7
Llanfihangel-yng-
  Ngwynfa Powys .....82 C1
Llanfihangel yn
  Nhowyn IoA ........ 108 D6
Llanfilo Powys ............. 53 H2
Llanfoist Mons ............. 53 L5
Llanfor Gwynd .............. 96 E5
Llanfrechfa Torfn ......... 37 L2
Llanfrynach Powys ....... 53 G3
Llanfwrog Denbgs .........97 H2
Llanfwrog IoA ........... 108 C5
Llanfyllin Powys ...........97 H8
Llanfynydd Carmth ...... 66 D8
Llanfynydd Flints ......... 97 L2
Llanfyrnach Pembks .....49 L2
Llangadfan Powys ........81 L2
Llangadog Carmth ....... 66 F8
Llangadwaladr IoA ..... 108 E7
Llangaffo IoA ............. 108 F7
Llangammarch
  Wells Powys ...........67 K5
Llangan V Glam ...........36 E5
Llangarron Herefs ........54 D4
Llangathen Carmth ...... 51 H2
Llangattock Powys ....... 53 K4
Llangattock
  Lingoed Mons .......54 A4
Llangedwyn Powys .......97 J7
Llangefni IoA ............. 108 F6
Llangeinor Brdgnd........36 E3
Llangeitho Cerdgn ....... 66 E3
Llangeler Carmth ......... 65 L6
Llangelynin Gwynd .....80 D3
Llangennech Carmth .... 51 H5
Llangennith Swans ...... 50 E7
Llangernyw Conwy .... 110 B7
Llangian Gwynd ...........94 E6
Llangloffan Pembks ..... 64 C7
Llanglydwen Carmth ....49 K3
Llangoed IoA ............. 109 J5
Llangollen Denbgs ........97 K4
Llangolman Pembks .....49 J3
Llangors Powys ............ 53 H3
Llangower Gwynd ........ 96 D6
Llangrannog Cerdgn .... 65 K4
Llangristiolus IoA ...... 108 F6
Llangrove Herefs .......... 54 D4
Llangunllo Powys ......... 68 E1
Llangunnor Carmth ...... 50 E2
Llangurig Powys ...........81 K7
Llangwm Conwy ...........96 F4
Llangwm Mons ............54 B7
Llangwm Pembks .........49 G5
Llangwnnadl Gwynd ....94 D6
Llangwyryfon Cerdgn ...66 D1
Llangybi Cerdgn ...........66 E4
Llangybi Gwynd ...........95 G4
Llangybi Mons .............38 A2
Llangyndeyrn Carmth ...50 F3
Llangynhafal Denbgs .. 110 F8
Llangynidr Powys ........ 53 J4
Llangynin Carmth .........50 B2
Llangynog Carmth ........50 D3
Llangynog Powys ..........97 G7
Llangynwyd Brdgnd......36 D3
Llanhamlach Powys ......53 H3
Llanharan Rhondd ........36 F4
Llanharry Rhondd .........36 F4
Llanhennock Mons .......38 A2
Llanhilleth Blae G .........53 K7
Llanidloes Powys ..........81 K6
Llaniestyn Gwynd ........94 E5
Llanigon Powys ............68 E6
Llanilar Cerdgn ............80 E8
Llanilid Rhondd ...........36 F4
Llanina Cerdgn ............ 65 L3
Llanishen Cardif ...........37 J4
Llanishen Mons ............54 C7
Llanllechid Gwynd ...... 109 J7
Llanllowell Mons ..........54 B7

Llanllugan Powys ..........82 B3
Llanllwch Carmth .........50 E2
Llanllwchaiarn
  Powys ........................ 82 C5
Llanllwni Carmth ..........66 C6
Llanllyfni Gwynd ..........95 H3
Llanmadoc Swans ........50 F6
Llanmaes V Glam ........36 F6
Llanmartin Newpt .........38 B3
Llanmiloe Carmth ........ 50 B4
Llannefydd Conwy ...... 110 D7
Llannon Carmth ............ 51 G4
Llannor Gwynd .............94 F5
Llanon Cerdgn ............. 66 C2
Llanover Mons .............. 53 L6
Llanpumsaint Carmth ... 65 L8
Llanrhaeadr-ym-
  Mochnant Powys ...97 H7
Llanrhian Pembks .........48 D2
Llanrhidian Swans ....... 50 F6
Llanrhychwyn Conwy ...96 B1
Llanrhyddlad IoA ....... 108 D4
Llanrhystud Cerdgn ......66 C1
Llanrug Gwynd ........... 109 G8
Llanrumney Cardif .......37 K4
Llanrwst Conwy ...........96 C1
Llansadurnen Carmth ...50 C4
Llansadwrn Carmth ......66 F7
Llansadwrn IoA ......... 109 H6
Llansaint Carmth ..........50 E4
Llansamlet Swans ........ 51 K6
Llansanffraid Glan
  Conwy Conwy ..... 110 A6
Llansannan Conwy .... 110 C7
Llansantffraed
  Powys ........................ 53 H4
Llansantffraed-
  Cwmdeuddwr
  Powys ........................ 67 L2
Llansantffraed-in-
  Elvel Powys ...........68 C4
Llansantffraid
  Cerdgn ...................... 66 C2
Llansantffraid-ym-
  Mechain Powys .....97 K7
Llansawel Carmth .........66 E7
Llansilin Powys ............ 97 K6
Llansoy Mons ...............54 C7
Llanspyddid Powys .......52 F3
Llanstadwell Pembks ....48 F6
Llansteffan Carmth ....... 50 D4
Llantarnam Torfn .........37 L2
Llanteg Pembks ............ 49 K5
Llanthewy Skirrid
  Mons ........................ 53 M5
Llanthony Mons ........... 53 L3
Llantilio-Crossenny
  Mons ........................ 54 B5
Llantilio Pertholey
  Mons ........................ 53 L5
Llantrisant Mons ..........38 B2
Llantrisant Rhondd .......37 G4
Llantrithyd V Glam .......37 G6
Llantwit Fardre
  Rhondd ...................... 37 G4
Llantwit Major
  V Glam ...................... 36 F6
Llanuwchllyn Gwynd ....96 D6
Llanvaches Newpt .........38 B3
Llanvair Discoed
  Mons ........................ 38 C3
Llanvapley Mons ..........54 A5
Llanvetherine Mons ......54 A5
Llanvihangel
  Crucorney Mons .....53 L4
Llanwddyn Powys .........96 F8
Llanwenog Cerdgn ....... 66 C5
Llanwern Newpt ...........38 A3
Llanwinio Carmth .........50 C1
Llanwnda Gwynd .........95 H2
Llanwnda Pembks ........ 64 C6
Llanwnnen Cerdgn .......66 C5
Llanwnog Powys ..........82 B5
Llanwrda Carmth ..........66 F7
Llanwrin Powys ...........81 H3
Llanwrthwl Powys ........67 L2
Llanwrtyd Wells
  Powys ........................ 67 J5

Llanwyddelan Powys......82 C4
Llanyblodwel Shrops......97 K7
Llanybri Carmth..............50 D3
Llanybydder Carmth......66 C5
Llanycefn Pembks..........49 J3
Llanychaer Pembks........64 D7
Llanymawddwy
  Gwynd..........................96 D8
Llanymynech Powys......97 K7
Llanynghenedl IoA......108 D5
Llanynys Denbgs..........110 F8
Llanyre Powys..............68 B3
Llanystumdwy Gwynd....95 H5
Llanywern Powys...........53 H3
Llawhaden Pembks........49 H4
Llawryglyn Powys..........81 K5
Llay Wrexhm................97 M2
Llechrhyd Caerph..........53 H6
Llechryd Cerdgn............65 H5
Lledrod Cerdgn..............66 E1
Lleyn Peninsula
  Gwynd..........................94 E5
Llithfaen Gwynd............94 F4
Lloc Flints....................111 G6
Llowes Powys...............68 D6
Llwydcoed Rhondd........52 F6
Llwydiarth Powys...........82 B1
Llwyncelyn Cerdgn........66 B3
Llwyndafydd Cerdgn......65 K4
Llwyngwril Gwynd..........80 D2
Llwynmawr Wrexhm......97 K5
Llwynypia Rhondd..........36 F2
Llynclys Shrops.............97 L7
Llynfaes IoA................108 E5
Llysfaen Conwy...........110 B6
Llyswen Powys..............68 C6
Llysworney V Glam........36 E5
Llys-y-frân Pembks.......49 H3
Llywel Powys.................52 D3
Loan Falk....................176 C3
Loanhead Mdloth..........177 J5
Loaningfoot D & G........147 G4
Loans S Ayrs...............163 J3
Lobhillcross Devon........10 C7
Lochailort Highld..........200 B8
Lochaline Highld..........190 D7
Lochans D & G.............144 C4
Locharbriggs D & G......155 H6
Lochavich Ag & B.........182 D4
Lochawe Ag & B..........183 G2
Loch Baghasdail
  W Isls........................233 c8
Lochboisdale W Isls......233 c8
Lochbuie Ag & B..........181 J3
Lochcarron Highld........210 D6
Lochdon Ag & B............181 L2
Lochdonhead Ag & B.....181 L2
Lochead Ag & B............172 D3
Lochearnhead Stirlg......184 D3
Lochee C Dund.............186 F2
Loch Eil Highld.............191 L2
Locheilside Station
  Highld.........................191 K1
Lochend Highld.............212 F6
Locheport W Isls..........233 c6
Loch Euphoirt W Isls.....233 c6
Lochfoot D & G.............154 F7
Lochgair Ag & B............172 F1
Lochgelly Fife...............186 C8
Lochgilphead Ag & B.....172 E2
Lochgoilhead Ag & B.....183 H6
Lochieheads Fife...........186 D5
Lochill Moray...............215 G2
Lochindorb Lodge
  Highld.........................214 B7
Lochinver Highld..........224 D4
Loch Lomond and
  The Trossachs
  National Park Ag & B...184 A5
Loch Loyal Lodge
  Highld.........................229 J6
Lochluichart Highld.......211 L2
Lochmaben D & G.........155 J5
Lochmaddy W Isls........233 c6
Loch nam Madadh
  W Isls........................233 c6
Loch Ness Highld.........202 E1
Lochore Fife.................186 C7

Loch Portain W Isls......233 c6
Lochportain W Isls........233 c6
Lochranza N Ayrs..........172 F7
Loch Sgioport W Isls....233 c7
Lochside Abers.............197 H4
Lochside D & G.............155 G6
Lochside Highld............213 J4
Lochskipport W Isls......233 c7
Lochslin Highld.............223 J5
Lochton S Ayrs.............152 F6
Lochty Angus...............196 E4
Lochty Fife..................187 H5
Lochuisge Highld..........190 F5
Lochwinnoch Rens........174 C6
Lochwood D & G...........155 J3
Lockengate Cnwll............5 G4
Lockerbie D & G...........155 K5
Lockeridge Wilts............40 C6
Lockerley Hants............28 F6
Locking N Som..............38 A8
Locking Stumps
  Warrtn.......................112 F3
Lockington E R Yk.........126 B2
Lockleywood Shrops......99 G6
Locksbottom Gt Lon......45 H6
Locks Heath Hants.........17 G2
Lockton N York.............134 C2
Loddington Leics............87 L3
Loddington Nhants.........88 B7
Loddiswell Devon............7 G6
Loddon Norfk.................93 H4
Lode Cambs...................76 D3
Lode Heath Solhll...........85 L7
Loders Dorset................13 L4
Lodsworth W Susx.........30 F6
Lofthouse Leeds...........123 L5
Lofthouse N York..........131 L5
Lofthouse Gate
  Wakefd......................123 L5
Loftus R & Cl...............142 F4
Logan E Ayrs................164 C5
Loganlea W Loth..........176 C6
Loggerheads Staffs........99 G5
Logie Angus.................197 H4
Logie Fife....................186 F4
Logie Moray.................214 C4
Logie Coldstone
  Abers.........................205 K4
Logie Newton Abers......216 C6
Logie Pert Angus..........197 G4
Logierait P & K............194 F6
Logierieve Abers...........217 H8
Login Carmth.................49 K3
Lolworth Cambs.............75 L2
Lonbain Highld.............209 L4
Londesborough
  E R Yk.......................125 K2
London Gt Lon..............45 G4
London Apprentice
  Cnwll.............................4 F6
London City Airport
  Gt Lon.........................45 H4
London Colney Herts......59 K7
Londonderry N York......132 D2
London Gateway
  Services Gt Lon............44 D2
London Gatwick
  Airport W Susx............32 B5
London Heathrow
  Airport Gt Lon..............43 H5
London Luton
  Airport Luton...............59 J4
London Oxford
  Airport Oxon................57 J5
London Southend
  Airport Essex...............46 E3
London Stansted
  Airport Essex...............60 E4
Londonthorpe Lincs......102 F5
London Zoo ZSL
  Gt Lon.........................44 F4
Londubh Highld.............219 K5
Lonemore Highld..........219 J6
Long Ashton N Som........38 D6
Long Bank Worcs...........84 D8
Long Bennington
  Lincs..........................102 D4
Longbenton N Tyne......151 G2

Longborough Gloucs......56 D3
Long Bredy Dorset.........14 B4
Longbridge Birm............85 H7
Longbridge Deverill
  Wilts............................27 K4
Long Buckby Nhants.......73 J2
Longburton Dorset.........26 F8
Long Clawson Leics......102 B6
Longcliffe Derbys..........100 E2
Longcombe Devon...........7 J4
Long Compton Staffs......99 J7
Long Compton
  Warwks.......................56 F2
Longcot Oxon.................40 F3
Long Crendon Bucks......58 B6
Long Crichel Dorset.......15 J1
Longden Shrops.............83 J3
Long Ditton Surrey.........44 D6
Longdon Staffs..............85 J2
Longdon Worcs..............70 E7
Longdon Green
  Staffs..........................85 J2
Longdon upon Tern
  Wrekin.........................84 B1
Longdown Devon............11 K6
Longdowns Cnwll.............3 J4
Long Duckmanton
  Derbys.......................115 H7
Long Eaton Derbys.......101 J5
Longfield Kent...............45 L6
Longford Covtry.............86 D6
Longford Derbys...........100 E5
Longford Gloucs.............55 J4
Longford Shrops.............98 F5
Longford Wrekin.............99 G8
Longforgan P & K.........186 E2
Longformacus
  Border.......................178 E6
Longframlington
  Nthumb......................158 E3
Long Green Ches W......112 C7
Longham Dorset.............15 K3
Longham Norfk..............91 L1
Long Hanborough
  Oxon............................57 H5
Longhaven Abers..........217 L6
Longhirst Nthumb.........158 F4
Longhope Gloucs...........55 G4
Longhope Ork...............234 b7
Longhorsley Nthumb.....158 E4
Longhoughton
  Nthumb......................169 J6
Long Itchington
  Warwks........................72 E2
Longlane Derbys...........100 E5
Long Lawford
  Warwks........................86 F7
Longleat Safari &
  Adventure Park
  Wilts............................27 J3
Longlevens Gloucs.........55 J4
Longleys P & K............195 L7
Long Load Somset.........26 C6
Longmanhill Abers........216 E2
Long Marston Herts........58 E5
Long Marston N York.....124 D1
Long Marston
  Warwks........................71 L5
Long Marton Cumb.......138 F3
Long Melford Suffk........77 J5
Longmoor Camp
  Hants..........................30 C5
Longmorn Moray..........214 F3
Longmoss Ches E.........113 K6
Long Newton
  Gloucs.........................39 K3
Longnewton Border......178 B7
Long Newton E Loth......178 B5
Longnewton S on T.......141 J4
Longney Gloucs..............55 H5
Longniddry E Loth.........177 L3
Longnor Shrops.............83 J4
Longnor Staffs..............114 C8
Longparish Hants...........29 H3
Long Preston N York.....130 F7
Longridge Lancs...........121 J3
Longridge W Loth.........176 C5
Longriggend N Lans......175 L4

Long Riston E R Yk.......126 E3
Longrock Cnwll................2 E5
Longsdon Staffs.............99 L2
Longside Abers.............217 K5
Longstanton Cambs........76 B2
Longstock Hants.............29 G4
Longstowe Cambs..........75 K4
Long Stratton Norfk........92 E5
Long Street M Keyn.......74 B5
Longstreet Wilts.............28 C2
Long Sutton Hants..........30 C3
Long Sutton Lincs.........104 C7
Long Sutton Somset.......26 C6
Longthorpe C Pete.........89 H4
Long Thurlow Suffk........78 B2
Longthwaite Cumb........138 B3
Longton Lancs..............121 G5
Longtown Cumb............148 C2
Longtown Herefs............53 L3
Longueville Jersey.......236 d7
Longville in the
  Dale Shrops.................83 K5
Long Waste Wrekin........84 B1
Long Whatton Leics......101 J7
Longwick Bucks.............58 C6
Long Wittenham
  Oxon............................41 K2
Longwitton Nthumb......158 D4
Longwood D & G..........146 C3
Longworth Oxon............57 G7
Longyester E Loth.........178 C5
Lonmay Abers..............217 J3
Lonmore Highld............208 D5
Looe Cnwll......................5 K5
Loose Kent....................33 K3
Loosley Row Bucks........58 D7
Lootcherbrae Abers......216 C4
Lopen Somset................26 B8
Loppington Shrops.........98 C6
Lordshill C Sotn.............29 H7
Lords Wood Medway.....46 C7
Lornty P & K................195 J6
Loscoe Derbys..............101 H3
Losgaintir W Isls...........232 d4
Lossiemouth Moray......214 F1
Lostock Gralam
  Ches W......................113 G6
Lostock Green
  Ches W......................113 G6
Lostwithiel Cnwll.............5 H4
Lothbeg Highld.............227 G6
Lothersdale N York.......122 E2
Lothmore Highld..........227 G6
Loudwater Bucks...........42 E3
Loughborough Leics.....101 K8
Loughor Swans..............51 H6
Loughton Essex.............45 H2
Loughton M Keyn...........74 B6
Lound Lincs.................103 H8
Lound Notts.................116 B4
Lound Suffk...................93 K4
Lount Leics..................101 G8
Louth Lincs..................118 D4
Lover Wilts....................28 E7
Loversall Donc.............115 L2
Loveston Pembks...........49 J5
Lovington Somset..........26 E5
Low Ackworth
  Wakefd......................124 C6
Low Barbeth D & G.......144 B2
Low Bentham N York.....130 C5
Low Biggins Cumb........130 B4
Low Borrowbridge
  Cumb.........................138 E6
Low Bradfield Sheff......114 E3
Low Bradley N York......122 F2
Low Burnham N Linc....116 C2
Lowca Cumb.................136 D3
Low Catton E R Yk........133 L8
Low Crosby Cumb........148 D3
Lowdham Notts............102 A3
Low Dinsdale Darltn.....141 J5
Lower Aisholt
  Somset........................25 J4
Lower Ansty Dorset.......14 E2
Lower Apperley
  Gloucs.........................55 J3
Lower Arboll Highld......223 J5

**Lower Ashton** Devon ......11 J7
**Lower Assendon**
  Oxon......................**42** C4
**Lower Badcall**
  Highld....................**228** B6
**Lower Bartle** Lancs.....**121** G4
**Lower Basildon**
  W Berk...................**41** L5
**Lower Beeding**
  W Susx...................**31** L6
**Lower Benefield**
  Nhants...................**88** E5
**Lower Bentley** Worcs ....**71** H2
**Lower Boddington**
  Nhants...................**72** F4
**Lower Bourne** Surrey ....**30** D3
**Lower Brailes**
  Warwks..................**72** C6
**Lower Breakish**
  Highld....................**199** L2
**Lower Broadheath**
  Worcs....................**70** E3
**Lower Broxwood**
  Herefs...................**69** G4
**Lower Bullingham**
  Herefs...................**69** K6
**Lower Burgate** Hants ....**28** D7
**Lower Caldecote**
  C Beds...................**75** H5
**Lower Chapel** Powys...**68** B7
**Lower Chicksgrove**
  Wilts.....................**27** L5
**Lower Chute** Wilts .......**28** F2
**Lower Clapton**
  Gt Lon...................**45** G3
**Lower Clent** Worcs.....**85** G7
**Lower**
  **Cumberworth**
  Kirk......................**123** J8
**Lower Darwen**
  Bl w D..................**121** K5
**Lower Dean** Bed.......**74** F2
**Lower Diabaig**
  Highld...................**210** C3
**Lower Dicker** E Susx....**20** B4
**Lower Down** Shrops....**83** G6
**Lower Dunsforth**
  N York..................**133** G6
**Lower Egleton**
  Herefs...................**70** B5
**Lower End** M Keyn.......**74** D6
**Lower Eythorne** Kent....**35** H5
**Lower Failand** N Som...**38** D5
**Lower Farringdon**
  Hants....................**30** B4
**Lower Feltham**
  Gt Lon...................**43** H6
**Lower Froyle** Hants .....**30** C3
**Lower Gabwell**
  Devon...................**7** L2
**Lower Gledfield**
  Highld....................**222** D4
**Lower Godney**
  Somset..................**26** C3
**Lower Gornal** Dudley.....**85** G5
**Lower Gravenhurst**
  C Beds...................**75** G7
**Lower Green** Kent.......**32** F5
**Lower Green** Kent.......**33** G5
**Lower Halstow** Kent.....**46** E6
**Lower Hamworthy**
  BCP......................**15** J4
**Lower Hardres** Kent.....**34** F4
**Lower Hartwell**
  Bucks....................**58** C5
**Lower Hergest**
  Herefs...................**68** F4
**Lower Heyford** Oxon....**57** J3
**Lower Heysham**
  Lancs....................**129** J7
**Lower Houses** Kirk .....**123** H7
**Lower Irlam** Salfd........**113** G3
**Lower Killeyan**
  Ag & B..................**160** A2
**Lower Langford**
  N Som...................**38** C7
**Lower Largo** Fife........**187** G6
**Lower Leigh** Staffs......**100** A5

**Lower Loxhore**
  Devon...................**23** K4
**Lower Lydbrook**
  Gloucs...................**54** E5
**Lower Lye** Herefs.......**69** H2
**Lower Machen**
  Newpt...................**37** K3
**Lower Merridge**
  Somset..................**25** J4
**Lower Middleton**
  **Cheney** Nhants.....**73** G6
**Lower Moor** Worcs.......**71** H5
**Lower Morton** S Glos....**38** F3
**Lower Nazeing** Essex....**60** C6
**Lower Oddington**
  Gloucs...................**56** E3
**Lower Penarth**
  V Glam...................**37** J6
**Lower Penn** Staffs.......**84** F4
**Lower Peover** Ches E....**113** H6
**Lower Place** Rochdl .....**122** D7
**Lower Quinton**
  Warwks..................**71** L5
**Lower Raydon** Suffk.....**78** C6
**Lower Roadwater**
  Somset..................**25** G4
**Lower Seagry** Wilts......**39** L4
**Lower Shelton**
  C Beds...................**74** E6
**Lower Shiplake** Oxon....**42** C4
**Lower Shuckburgh**
  Warwks..................**72** F3
**Lower Slaughter**
  Gloucs...................**56** D4
**Lower Standen** Kent .....**35** H6
**Lower Stanton St**
  **Quintin** Wilts........**39** L4
**Lower Stoke** Medway ....**46** D5
**Lower Stondon**
  C Beds...................**75** H7
**Lower Stone** Gloucs......**38** F2
**Lower Stow Bedon**
  Norfk....................**91** L5
**Lower Street** Norfk ......**106** F5
**Lower Street** Suffk.......**78** D4
**Lower Swanwick**
  Hants....................**16** F1
**Lower Swell** Gloucs ......**56** D3
**Lower Tasburgh**
  Norfk....................**92** E4
**Lower Tean** Staffs........**100** A5
**Lower Town** Devon .......**7** G2
**Lower Town** Pembks .....**64** D6
**Lower Upham** Hants.......**29** K7
**Lower Weare** Somset.....**26** B2
**Lower Welson** Herefs.....**68** F4
**Lower Westmancote**
  Worcs....................**71** G6
**Lower Whatley**
  Somset..................**27** H3
**Lower Whitley**
  Ches W..................**112** E5
**Lower Wield** Hants ......**29** M4
**Lower Willingdon**
  E Susx...................**20** C5
**Lower Withington**
  Ches E..................**113** J7
**Lower Woodford**
  Wilts.....................**28** C4
**Lower Wraxhall**
  Dorset...................**14** B3
**Lowesby** Leics..........**87** K3
**Lowestoft** Suffk.........**93** L5
**Loweswater** Cumb........**137** G3
**Low Fell** Gatesd.........**151** G3
**Lowfield Heath**
  W Susx..................**31** L4
**Low Gartachorrans**
  Stirlg....................**174** E2
**Low Grantley** N York....**132** C5
**Low Ham** Somset.........**26** B5
**Low Harrogate**
  N York..................**132** D7
**Low Hesket** Cumb........**148** E5
**Low Hutton** N York.......**134** B6
**Lowick** Nhants...........**88** E7
**Lowick** Nthumb..........**168** F2
**Lowick Green** Cumb .....**129** G3

**Low Lorton** Cumb.........**137** G3
**Low Marnham** Notts......**116** D7
**Low Mill** N York...........**142** E7
**Low Moorsley** Sundld ..**151** H5
**Low Moresby** Cumb......**136** D3
**Low Newton** Cumb.......**129** J3
**Low Row** Cumb...........**149** G3
**Low Row** N York.........**140** B7
**Low Salchrie** D & G......**144** B2
**Low Santon** N Linc......**125** L7
**Lowsonford** Warwks......**71** L2
**Low Tharston** Norfk......**92** E4
**Lowther** Cumb............**138** D3
**Lowthorpe** E R Yk........**135** G7
**Lowton** Somset...........**25** J7
**Lowton Common**
  Wigan...................**112** F3
**Low Torry** Fife...........**176** D2
**Low Worsall** N York......**141** J5
**Low Wray** Cumb..........**137** K6
**Loxbeare** Devon..........**11** L2
**Loxhill** Surrey.............**31** G4
**Loxhore** Devon............**23** K4
**Loxley** Warwks............**72** C4
**Loxton** N Som............**26** A1
**Loxwood** W Susx.........**31** H5
**Lubenham** Leics..........**87** K6
**Luccombe** Somset........**24** E3
**Luccombe Village**
  IoW......................**17** H6
**Lucker** Nthumb...........**169** H4
**Luckett** Cnwll.............**6** B2
**Lucking Street** Essex ....**77** J7
**Luckington** Wilts..........**39** J4
**Lucklawhill** Fife..........**187** G3
**Luckwell Bridge**
  Somset..................**24** E4
**Lucton** Herefs............**69** J2
**Ludag** W Isls.............**233** b9
**Ludborough** Lincs........**118** D3
**Ludbrook** Devon..........**6** F5
**Ludchurch** Pembks.......**49** K5
**Luddenden** Calder........**122** F5
**Luddenden Foot**
  Calder...................**122** F5
**Luddesdown** Kent........**46** A6
**Luddington** N Linc........**125** J7
**Luddington** Warwks......**71** L4
**Luddington in the**
  **Brook** Nhants........**89** G6
**Ludford** Lincs............**117** K4
**Ludford** Shrops..........**83** K8
**Ludgershall** Bucks........**58** A4
**Ludgershall** Wilts........**28** E2
**Ludgvan** Cnwll............**2** E5
**Ludham** Norfk.............**107** H8
**Ludlow** Shrops...........**83** K7
**Ludney** Somset...........**26** B8
**Ludwell** Wilts.............**27** K6
**Ludworth** Dur.............**151** J6
**Luffness** E Loth...........**178** B3
**Lugar** E Ayrs.............**164** C5
**Luggate Burn** E Loth....**178** D4
**Luggiebank** N Lans.......**175** K4
**Lugton** E Ayrs............**174** D7
**Lugwardine** Herefs.......**69** K6
**Luib** Highld.................**209** J8
**Luing** Ag & B.............**181** L5
**Lulham** Herefs............**69** H6
**Lullington** Derbys........**86** B2
**Lullington** Somset........**27** H2
**Lulsgate Bottom**
  N Som...................**38** D7
**Lulsley** Worcs............**70** D4
**Lumb** Calder..............**122** F6
**Lumby** N York............**124** D4
**Lumphanan** Abers........**206** B4
**Lumphinnans** Fife.........**186** C8
**Lumsden** Abers...........**205** K2
**Lunan** Angus.............**197** H6
**Lunanhead** Angus........**196** D6
**Luncarty** P & K...........**186** A2
**Lund** E R Yk.............**126** B2
**Lund** N York..............**125** G4
**Lundie** Angus............**186** E1
**Lundin Links** Fife.........**187** G6
**Lundin Mill** Fife...........**187** G6
**Lundy** Devon..............**22** B3

**Lunga** Ag & B.............**181** L5
**Lunna** Shet...............**235** d4
**Lunsford** Kent............**33** J2
**Lunsford's Cross**
  E Susx..................**20** E4
**Lunt** Sefton...............**111** K2
**Luppitt** Devon............**12** F2
**Lupset** Wakefd...........**123** L6
**Lupton** Cumb.............**129** L4
**Lurgashall** W Susx.......**30** F6
**Lurley** Devon.............**11** L2
**Luscombe** Devon..........**7** J4
**Luskentyre** W Isls.........**232** d4
**Luss** Ag & B..............**183** L8
**Lussagiven** Ag & B.......**171** L2
**Lusta** Highld..............**208** D3
**Lustleigh** Devon..........**11** H8
**Luston** Herefs............**69** J2
**Luthermuir** Abers........**197** G3
**Luthrie** Fife...............**186** E4
**Luton** Devon..............**7** K1
**Luton** Devon..............**12** D2
**Luton** Luton..............**59** H4
**Luton** Medway...........**46** C6
_Luton Airport_ Luton .....**59** J4
**Lutterworth** Leics........**87** G6
**Lutton** Devon.............**6** E4
**Lutton** Devon.............**7** G4
**Lutton** Lincs.............**104** C7
**Lutton** Nhants...........**89** G6
**Luxborough** Somset......**24** F4
**Luxulyan** Cnwll............**5** G4
_Luxulyan Valley_ Cnwll.....**5** G4
**Lybster** Highld............**231** J7
**Lydbury North**
  Shrops..................**83** G6
_Lydd Airport_ Kent.........**21** L2
**Lydden** Kent..............**35** H5
**Lydden** Kent..............**35** K2
**Lyddington** Rutlnd........**88** C4
**Lydeard St**
  **Lawrence** Somset....**25** H5
**Lydford** Devon............**10** D7
**Lydford on Fosse**
  Somset..................**26** E5
**Lydgate** Calder...........**122** D5
**Lydham** Shrops...........**83** G6
**Lydiard Millicent**
  Wilts.....................**40** C3
**Lydiard Tregoze**
  Swindn..................**40** C4
**Lydiate** Sefton...........**111** K2
**Lydiate Ash** Worcs.......**85** H7
**Lydlinch** Dorset..........**27** H8
**Lydney** Gloucs............**54** F7
**Lydstep** Pembks..........**49** J7
**Lye** Dudley...............**85** G6
**Lye Green** E Susx........**32** F6
**Lye Green** Warwks.......**71** L2
**Lye's Green** Wilts........**27** J3
**Lyford** Oxon..............**41** H2
**Lymbridge Green**
  Kent.....................**34** F6
**Lyme Regis** Dorset.......**13** J4
**Lyminge** Kent.............**34** F6
**Lymington** Hants..........**16** C4
**Lyminster** W Susx........**18** D5
**Lymm** Warrtn.............**113** G4
_Lymm Services_
  Warrtn...................**112** F4
**Lympne** Kent..............**34** F7
**Lympsham** Somset........**25** M1
**Lympstone** Devon.........**12** C5
**Lynchat** Highld............**203** J5
**Lynch Green** Norfk.......**92** D3
**Lyndhurst** Hants..........**16** C2
**Lyndon** Rutlnd............**88** C3
**Lyndon Green** Birm......**85** K6
**Lyne** Border..............**166** B2
**Lyne** Surrey..............**43** G7
**Lyneal** Shrops............**98** C6
**Lyneham** Oxon............**56** F4
**Lyneham** Wilts............**40** A5
**Lynemouth** Nthumb.......**159** H4
**Lyne of Skene** Abers....**206** E4
**Lyness** Ork...............**234** b7
**Lyng** Norfk...............**106** C8

**Lyng** Somset ...................... 25 M5
**Lynmouth** Devon ............... 23 L2
**Lynsted** Kent ..................... 34 C3
**Lynton** Devon .................... 23 L2
**Lyon's Gate** Dorset ........... 14 C2
**Lyonshall** Herefs ............... 69 G4
**Lytchett Matravers**
  Dorset ............................. 15 H4
**Lytchett Minster**
  Dorset ............................. 15 H4
**Lyth** Highld ...................... 231 K3
**Lytham** Lancs ................... 120 E5
**Lytham St Annes**
  Lancs .............................. 120 D5
**Lythe** N York ..................... 143 H5
**Lythmore** Highld .............. 230 F3

**M**

**Maaruig** W Isls ................. 232 e4
**Mabe Burnthouse**
  Cnwll ................................... 3 K4
**Mablethorpe** Lincs .......... 119 G4
**Macclesfield** Ches E........ 113 K6
**Macduff** Abers ................. 216 D2
**Macharioch** Ag & B........ 161 J7
**Machen** Caerph ................. 37 K3
**Machrie** N Ayrs ............... 162 A3
**Machrihanish** Ag & B...... 161 G5
**Machrins** Ag & B.............. 180 E8
**Machroes** Gwynd ............... 94 F7
**Machynlleth** Powys........... 81 G4
**Machynys** Carmth .............. 51 G5
**Mackworth** Derbys .......... 100 F5
**Macmerry** E Loth ............. 177 L4
**Madderty** P & K................ 185 K3
**Maddiston** Falk ............... 176 C3
**Madeley** Staffs ................... 99 H4
**Madeley** Wrekin ................. 84 C3
**Madingley** Cambs .............. 76 B3
**Madley** Herefs ................... 69 H6
**Madresfield** Worcs ............ 70 E6
**Madron** Cnwll ...................... 2 E5
**Maenclochog**
  Pembks ............................. 49 J3
**Maendy** V Glam ................. 36 F5
**Maentwrog** Gwynd ............. 95 L4
**Maen-y-groes**
  Cerdgn ............................. 65 L3
**Maer** Staffs ........................ 99 H5
**Maerdy** Conwy ................... 96 F4
**Maerdy** Rhondd ................. 36 F2
**Maesbrook** Shrops ............ 97 L7
**Maesbury** Shrops .............. 97 L7
**Maesbury Marsh**
  Shrops .............................. 97 L7
**Maesllyn** Cerdgn .............. 65 K5
**Maesteg** Brdgnd ................ 36 D3
**Maesybont** Carmth ............ 51 H3
**Maesycwmmer**
  Caerph ............................. 37 J2
**Maggieknockater**
  Moray ............................. 215 H5
**Magham Down**
  E Susx ............................. 20 C4
**Maghull** Sefton ............... 111 K2
**Magna Park** Leics............ 87 G6
**Magor** Mons ....................... 38 B3
**Magor Services**
  Mons .............................. 38 B3
**Maidenbower** W Susx...... 32 B6
**Maiden Bradley** Wilts....... 27 J4
**Maidencombe** Torbay....... 7 L3
**Maidenhayne** Devon........ 13 H4
**Maiden Head** N Som....... 38 E6
**Maidenhead** W & M........ 42 E4
**Maiden Newton**
  Dorset .............................. 14 B3
**Maidens** S Ayrs ............... 163 G7
**Maiden's Green**
  Br For .............................. 42 E5
**Maiden Wells**
  Pembks ............................. 49 G7
**Maidford** Nhants ............... 73 H4
**Maids Moreton**
  Bucks ............................... 73 K7

**Maidstone** Kent ............... 33 K3
**Maidstone Services**
  Kent ................................. 33 L3
**Maidwell** Nhants ............... 87 L7
**Mail** Shet ........................ 235 d6
**Maindee** Newpt ................. 37 L3
**Mainland** Ork .................. 234 c6
**Mainland** Shet ................ 235 c5
**Mainsforth** Dur ............... 141 H2
**Mains of Balhall**
  Angus ............................. 196 E4
**Mains of**
  **Balnakettle** Abers .. 197 G2
**Mains of Dalvey**
  Highld ............................ 214 D7
**Mains of Haulkerton**
  Abers .............................. 197 H2
**Mains of Lesmoir**
  Abers .............................. 215 K8
**Mains of Melgunds**
  Angus ............................. 196 E5
**Mainsriddle** D & G......... 147 G4
**Mainstone** Shrops ............ 82 F6
**Maisemore** Gloucs ........... 55 J4
**Major's Green** Worcs...... 85 K7
**Malborough** Devon ............. 7 K7
**Maldon** Essex .................... 61 K6
**Malham** N York ............... 131 G6
**Maligar** Highld ................ 209 G2
**Mallaig** Highld ................ 199 L6
**Mallaigvaig** Highld ......... 199 L5
**Malleny Mills** C Edin .... 177 G5
**Malltraeth** IoA ................ 108 E7
**Mallwyd** Gwynd ................ 81 J2
**Malmesbury** Wilts ............ 39 L3
**Malmsmead** Devon ........... 24 C2
**Malpas** Ches W .................. 98 C3
**Malpas** Cnwll ...................... 4 D7
**Malpas** Newpt ................... 37 L3
**Maltby** Rothm .................. 115 K3
**Maltby** S on T ................. 141 L4
**Maltby le Marsh**
  Lincs .............................. 118 F5
**Maltman's Hill** Kent........ 34 B6
**Malton** N York ................. 134 C5
**Malvern** Worcs ................... 70 D5
**Malvern Hills** ................... 70 D5
**Malvern Link** Worcs......... 70 E5
**Malvern Wells** Worcs....... 70 D6
**Mamble** Worcs ................... 70 C1
**Mamhilad** Mons ................ 53 L7
**Manaccan** Cnwll ................. 3 K6
**Manafon** Powys ................. 82 C3
**Mànais** W Isls ................ 232 d5
**Manaton** Devon ................ 11 H8
**Manby** Lincs .................... 118 E4
**Mancetter** Warwks .......... 86 D4
**Manchester** Manch ........ 113 J3
**Manchester Airport**
  Manch .............................. 113 J5
**Mancot** Flints .................. 111 K7
**Mandally** Highld ............. 201 L5
**Manea** Cambs .................... 90 C5
**Maney** Birm ...................... 85 K4
**Manfield** N York .............. 140 F4
**Mangersta** W Isls ........... 232 d2
**Mangotsfield** S Glos ....... 38 F5
**Mangurstadh** W Isls ..... 232 d2
**Manish** W Isls ................ 232 d5
**Manley** Ches W ................ 112 D7
**Manmoel** Caerph .............. 53 J7
**Mannal** Ag & B................ 188 C7
**Manningford**
  **Bohune** Wilts............... 40 C8
**Manningford Bruce**
  Wilts ................................ 40 C8
**Manningham** C Brad...... 123 H4
**Mannings Heath**
  W Susx ............................. 31 K5
**Mannington** Dorset ......... 15 K2
**Manningtree** Essex ......... 62 D2
**Mannofield** C Aber ....... 207 H4
**Manorbier** Pembks ........... 49 H7
**Manorbier Newton**
  Pembks ............................. 49 H7
**Manordeilo** Carmth ......... 51 J2
**Manorhill** Border ........... 167 K3
**Manorowen** Pembks .......... 64 C7
**Manor Park** Gt Lon ......... 45 H3

**Mansell Gamage**
  Herefs .............................. 69 H5
**Mansell Lacy** Herefs....... 69 H5
**Mansfield** E Ayrs ............ 164 C6
**Mansfield** Notts ............. 101 K1
**Mansfield**
  **Woodhouse** Notts... 115 K8
**Manston** Dorset ................ 27 J7
**Manston** Kent .................... 35 J2
**Manston** Leeds ................ 124 B4
**Manswood** Dorset ............ 15 J2
**Manthorpe** Lincs ............... 88 F1
**Manton** N Linc ................ 116 F2
**Manton** Rutlnd ................. 88 C3
**Manton** Wilts .................... 40 D6
**Manuden** Essex ................. 60 D3
**Maperton** Somset ............. 26 F6
**Maplebeck** Notts ............ 102 B1
**Mapledurham** Oxon......... 42 A5
**Mapledurwell** Hants ........ 30 B2
**Maplehurst** W Susx .......... 31 K6
**Maplescombe** Kent........... 45 K7
**Mapleton** Derbys ............ 100 D3
**Mapperley** Derbys .......... 101 H4
**Mapperley Park**
  C Nott ............................ 101 L4
**Mapperton** Dorset ............ 13 L3
**Mappleborough**
  **Green** Warwks ............ 71 J2
**Mappleton** E R Yk ........ 126 F2
**Mapplewell** Barns ......... 123 L7
**Mappowder** Dorset ......... 14 E2
**Màraig** W Isls ................ 232 e4
**Marazion** Cnwll .................. 2 F5
**Marbhig** W Isls ............. 232 f3
**Marbury** Ches E................ 98 E4
**March** Cambs ..................... 90 B4
**March** S Lans .................. 165 J6
**Marcham** Oxon ................. 41 J2
**Marchamley** Shrops ......... 98 E6
**Marchington** Staffs ....... 100 C6
**Marchwiel** Wrexhm .......... 98 A3
**Marchwood** Hants ............ 16 D1
**Marcross** V Glam .............. 36 E6
**Marden** Herefs .................. 69 K5
**Marden** Kent ..................... 33 J4
**Marden** Wilts .................... 40 C8
**Marden Thorn** Kent.......... 33 K5
**Mardy** Mons ..................... 53 L5
**Mareham le Fen**
  Lincs .............................. 103 L1
**Mareham on the**
  **Hill** Lincs .................. 118 C7
**Marehill** W Susx ............... 18 E3
**Maresfield** E Susx ............ 19 M2
**Marfleet** C KuH .............. 126 E5
**Marford** Wrexhm .............. 98 A2
**Margam** Neath .................. 36 B3
**Margaret Marsh**
  Dorset .............................. 27 J7
**Margaretting** Essex .......... 61 G7
**Margaretting Tye**
  Essex ............................... 61 G7
**Margate** Kent .................... 35 K1
**Margnaheglish**
  N Ayrs ............................ 162 D3
**Margrie** D & G.................. 145 M5
**Margrove Park**
  R & Cl ............................. 142 E4
**Marham** Norfk ................. 91 G2
**Marhamchurch** Cnwll....... 9 G4
**Marholm** C Pete ............... 89 G3
**Mariansleigh** Devon......... 24 B6
**Marine Town** Kent............ 46 F5
**Marionburgh** Abers ....... 206 D4
**Marishader** Highld......... 209 H2
**Maristow** Devon ................. 6 C3
**Marjoriebanks** D & G... 155 J5
**Mark** Somset ..................... 26 B2
**Markbeech** Kent ............... 32 E5
**Markby** Lincs .................. 119 G5
**Mark Cross** E Susx........... 33 G6
**Market Bosworth**
  Leics ................................ 86 E3
**Market Deeping**
  Lincs ................................ 89 G2
**Market Drayton**
  Shrops .............................. 98 F5

**Market Harborough**
  Leics ................................ 87 K6
**Market Lavington**
  Wilts ................................ 28 A1
**Market Overton**
  Rutlnd .............................. 88 C1
**Market Rasen** Lincs ...... 117 J4
**Market Stainton**
  Lincs .............................. 118 B5
**Market Warsop** Notts... 115 K7
**Market Weighton**
  E R Yk ............................ 125 K3
**Market Weston** Suffk...... 92 B7
**Markfield** Leics ................. 86 F2
**Markham** Caerph .............. 53 J7
**Markham Moor**
  Notts .............................. 116 B6
**Markinch** Fife ................. 186 E6
**Markington** N York ....... 132 D6
**Markle** E Loth ................ 178 C3
**Marksbury** BaNES............ 38 F7
**Marks Tey** Essex .............. 61 L4
**Markyate** Herts ................ 59 H5
**Marlborough** Wilts........... 40 D6
**Marlcliff** Warwks .............. 71 K4
**Marldon** Devon ................... 7 L3
**Marlesford** Suffk .............. 79 G3
**Marlingford** Norfk ........... 92 D2
**Marloes** Pembks ............... 48 D5
**Marlow** Bucks ................... 42 D3
**Marlow Bottom**
  Bucks ............................... 42 D3
**Marlpit Hill** Kent.............. 32 D4
**Marnhull** Dorset ............... 27 H7
**Marple** Stockp ................ 113 L4
**Marr** Donc ...................... 115 K1
**Marrick** N York ............... 140 D7
**Marsden** Kirk .................. 122 F7
**Marsden** S Tyne ............. 151 J3
**Marshalswick** Herts ........ 59 K6
**Marsham** Norfk .............. 106 E7
**Marsh Baldon** Oxon....... 57 K7
**Marshborough** Kent ........ 35 J3
**Marshbrook** Shrops ......... 83 J5
**Marshchapel** Lincs ........ 118 E2
**Marsh Farm** Luton........... 59 H3
**Marshfield** Newpt ............ 37 K4
**Marshfield** S Glos ............ 39 H5
**Marshgate** Cnwll ............... 8 F6
**Marsh Gibbon** Bucks....... 57 M4
**Marsh Green** Devon ....... 12 D4
**Marsh Green** Kent........... 32 D4
**Marshland St**
  **James** Norfk ............... 90 D2
**Marsh Lane** Derbys ...... 115 H5
**Marsh Street** Somset...... 24 F3
**Marshwood** Dorset .......... 13 J3
**Marske** N York ............... 140 D6
**Marske-by-the-Sea**
  R & Cl ............................. 142 D3
**Marston** Herefs ................. 69 G3
**Marston** Lincs ................. 102 E4
**Marston** Oxon ................... 57 K6
**Marston** Staffs .................. 99 L6
**Marston** Wilts .................... 27 L1
**Marston Green** Solhll...... 85 L6
**Marston Magna**
  Somset ............................. 26 E6
**Marston Meysey**
  Wilts ................................ 40 C2
**Marston**
  **Montgomery**
  Derbys ........................... 100 C5
**Marston Moretaine**
  C Beds .............................. 74 E6
**Marston on Dove**
  Derbys ............................ 100 E6
**Marston St**
  **Lawrence** Nhants........ 73 G6
**Marston Trussell**
  Nhants .............................. 87 K6
**Marstow** Herefs ................ 54 D4
**Marsworth** Bucks.............. 58 F5
**Marten** Wilts ..................... 40 F7
**Martham** Norfk ............... 107 J8
**Martin** Hants .................... 28 B7
**Martin** Kent ...................... 35 J5
**Martin** Lincs .................... 103 J1

Martinhoe Devon.............23 L2
Martin Hussingtree
  Worcs.........................70 F3
Martinstown Dorset.......14 C5
Martlesham Suffk..........78 F5
Martlesham Heath
  Suffk..........................78 F5
Martletwy Pembks.........49 H5
Martley Worcs................70 D3
Martock Somset............26 C7
Marton Ches E .............113 J7
Marton E R Yk..............126 F3
Marton Lincs ...............116 D5
Marton Middsb .............142 B4
Marton N York..............132 F6
Marton N York..............134 B3
Marton Shrops................82 F3
Marton Warwks..............72 E2
Marton-le-Moor
  N York .....................132 E5
Martyr Worthy Hants....29 K5
Marvig W Isls...............232 f3
Marwell Wildlife
  Hants.........................29 J6
Marwick Ork................234 b5
Marwood Devon.............23 H4
Marybank Highld.........212 D4
Maryburgh Highld........212 E3
Marygold Border...........179 G6
Maryhill C Glas............175 G4
Marykirk Abers.............197 H3
Marylebone Gt Lon........44 F4
Marylebone Wigan........121 H8
Marypark Moray...........214 F6
Maryport Cumb.............147 H7
Maryport D & G............144 D7
Marystow Devon............10 C7
Mary Tavy Devon............6 D1
Maryton Angus.............197 H5
Marywell Abers.............206 B6
Marywell Abers.............207 H5
Marywell Angus............197 G7
Masham N York.............132 C4
Masongill N York..........130 C4
Mastin Moor Derbys....115 J6
Matching Green
  Essex.........................60 E5
Matching Tye Essex.......60 E5
Matfen Nthumb............158 C7
Matfield Kent.................33 H5
Mathern Mons................38 D3
Mathon Herefs................70 D5
Mathry Pembks...............48 E2
Matlask Norfk...............106 D5
Matlock Derbys.............100 F1
Matlock Bath
  Derbys.....................100 F2
Matson Gloucs................55 J5
Mattersey Notts............116 B4
Mattingley Hants............42 B8
Mattishall Norfk.............92 C2
Mattishall Burgh
  Norfk.........................92 C2
Mauchline E Ayrs..........163 L4
Maud Abers...................217 H5
Maufant Jersey.............236 d6
Maugersbury Gloucs.......56 D3
Maughold IoM...............237 e3
Mauld Highld................212 C6
Maulden C Beds..............74 F6
Maulds Meaburn
  Cumb.......................138 F4
Maunby N York.............132 E3
Maundown Somset..........25 G5
Mautby Norfk..................93 K2
Mavesyn Ridware
  Staffs..........................85 J1
Mavis Enderby Lincs ...118 E7
Mawbray Cumb............147 J5
Mawdesley Lancs..........121 G7
Mawdlam Brdgnd...........36 C4
Mawgan Cnwll..................3 J6
Mawgan Porth Cnwll......4 D3
Mawla Cnwll....................3 J3
Mawnan Cnwll.................3 K5
Mawnan Smith Cnwll......3 K5
Mawsley Nhants.............88 B7
Maxey C Pete..................89 G2

Maxstoke Warwks..........86 B6
Maxton Border...............167 J4
Maxton Kent...................35 J6
Maxwelltown D & G .....155 G6
Maxworthy Cnwll.............9 H6
May Bank Staffs.............99 J3
Maybole S Ayrs.............163 H7
Maybury Surrey..............43 G8
Mayfield E Susx.............33 G7
Mayfield Mdloth...........177 K5
Mayfield Staffs.............100 D4
Mayford Surrey...............31 G1
May Hill Gloucs...............55 G4
Mayland Essex................61 L7
Maylandsea Essex..........61 L7
Maynard's Green
  E Susx.......................20 C3
Maypole Birm................85 J7
Maypole Green Norfk.....93 J4
Maypole Green Suffk.....77 K3
Meadgate BaNES...........39 G8
Meadle Bucks.................58 D6
Meadowfield Dur..........151 G6
Meadwell Devon...............9 K8
Mealabost W Isls..........232 g2
Mealsgate Cumb.............147 J7
Meanwood Leeds...........123 K3
Meare Somset.................26 C3
Meare Green Somset.....25 L6
Meare Green Somset.....25 M6
Mearns E Rens..............174 F7
Mears Ashby Nhants......74 B2
Measham Leics...............86 D2
Meath Green Surrey.......32 B4
Meathop Cumb..............129 J4
Meavaig W Isls.............232 d2
Meavy Devon....................6 D3
Medbourne Leics............88 B5
Meddon Devon..................9 H2
Meden Vale Notts..........115 L7
Medmenham Bucks.........42 D4
Medomsley Dur............150 E4
Medstead Hants..............30 A4
Medway Services
  Medway ...................46 D7
Meerbrook Staffs............99 M1
Meesden Herts................60 C2
Meeth Devon..................10 E3
Meeting House Hill
  Norfk.......................107 G6
Meidrim Carmth.............50 C2
Meifod Powys.................82 D2
Meigle P & K................195 L7
Meikle Carco D & G......164 F6
Meikle Earnock
  S Lans.....................175 J7
Meikle Ferry Highld.....223 G4
Meikle Kilmory
  Ag & B.....................173 H6
Meikle Obney P & K....195 G8
Meikleour P & K...........195 J7
Meikle Wartle Abers ...216 D7
Meinciau Carmth............50 F4
Meir C Stke....................99 L4
Melbost W Isls.............232 g2
Melbourn Cambs............75 L5
Melbourne Derbys.........101 G7
Melbourne E R Yk.........125 H2
Melbury Abbas
  Dorset.......................27 K7
Melbury Bubb Dorset.....14 B2
Melbury Osmond
  Dorset.......................14 B2
Melchbourne Bed...........74 E2
Melcombe Bingham
  Dorset.......................14 E2
Meldon Devon.................10 E6
Meldon Nthumb............158 E6
Meldreth Cambs.............75 L5
Meldrum Stirlg.............184 F7
Melfort Ag & B.............182 B5
Meliden Denbgs............110 E5
Melin-y-wig Denbgs........97 G3
Melkinthorpe Cumb.....138 D3
Melkridge Nthumb........149 J3
Melksham Wilts.............39 K7
Melling Lancs................130 B5
Melling Sefton..............111 L2
Mellis Suffk....................92 C8

Mellon Charles
  Highld......................219 K3
Mellon Udrigle
  Highld......................219 K3
Mellor Lancs ...............121 J4
Mellor Stockp...............113 M4
Mellor Brook Lancs ....121 J4
Mells Somset..................27 G2
Melmerby Cumb............149 G7
Melmerby N York..........131 K3
Melmerby N York..........132 E4
Melness Highld.............229 J3
Melplash Dorset.............13 L3
Melrose Border.............167 H3
Melsetter Ork...............234 b7
Melsonby N York...........140 F5
Meltham Kirk................123 G7
Melton E R Yk...............126 B5
Melton Suffk...................79 G4
Melton Constable
  Norfk.......................106 C6
Melton Mowbray
  Leics.......................102 C8
Melton Ross N Linc.....126 D7
Melvaig Highld.............219 H4
Melverley Shrops............83 G1
Melvich Highld.............230 C3
Membury Devon.............13 H2
Membury Services
  W Berk......................40 F5
Memsie Abers...............217 H2
Memus Angus................196 C5
Menai Bridge IoA.........109 H6
Mendham Suffk..............92 F6
Mendip Hills.................26 D2
Mendlesham Suffk..........78 D2
Mendlesham Green
  Suffk.........................78 D2
Menheniot Cnwll.............5 L4
Mennock D & G.............164 F7
Menston C Brad............123 H2
Menstrie Clacks............185 H7
Mentmore Bucks............58 E4
Meoble Highld..............200 C7
Meole Brace Shrops.......83 J2
Meonstoke Hants............29 L7
Meopham Kent................45 M6
Mepal Cambs..................90 B7
Meppershall C Beds.......75 G7
Mere Ches E ................113 G5
Mere Wilts.....................27 J5
Mere Brow Lancs.........120 F6
Mereclough Lancs.........122 C4
Mere Green Birm...........85 K4
Mereworth Kent..............33 H3
Meriden Solhll...............86 B6
Merkadale Highld.........208 F7
Merley BCP....................15 J3
Merrion Pembks..............48 F7
Merriott Somset.............26 C8
Merrow Surrey................31 G2
Merry Hill Herts.............43 J2
Merryhill Wolves............84 F4
Merrymeet Cnwll.............5 L3
Mersea Island Essex......62 B5
Mersey Crossing
  Halton.....................112 D5
Mersham Kent................34 E6
Merstham Surrey............32 B3
Merston W Susx.............18 B5
Merstone IoW................17 G5
Merthyr Cynog
  Powys.......................67 L6
Merthyr Mawr
  Brdgnd.....................36 D5
Merthyr Tydfil Myr Td...53 G6
Merthyr Vale Myr Td......53 G7
Merton Devon.................10 D3
Merton Gt Lon................44 E6
Merton Norfk..................91 K4
Merton Oxon...................57 L4
Meshaw Devon...............24 B7
Messing Essex.................61 L4
Messingham N Linc......116 E2
Metfield Suffk.................93 G7
Metherell Cnwll...............6 B3
Metheringham Lincs ....103 H1
Methil Fife...................186 F7

Methilhill Fife ..............186 F7
Methlick Abers..............217 G6
Methven P & K.............185 L3
Methwold Norfk.............91 G4
Methwold Hythe
  Norfk.........................91 G4
Mettingham Suffk .........93 H5
Metton Norfk................106 E5
Mevagissey Cnwll............4 F6
Mexborough Donc.......115 J2
Mey Highld...................231 K2
Meysey Hampton
  Gloucs.......................56 C7
Miabhaig W Isls............232 d2
Michaelchurch
  Herefs.......................54 D3
Michaelchurch
  Escley Herefs............69 G7
Michaelstone-y-
  Fedw Newpt...............37 K3
Michaelston-le-Pit
  V Glam......................37 J5
Michaelstow Cnwll..........5 G1
Michaelwood
  Services Gloucs........39 G2
Micheldever Hants..........29 K4
Micheldever Station
  Hants.........................29 K3
Michelmersh Hants........29 G6
Mickfield Suffk...............78 D3
Micklebring Donc.........115 K3
Mickleby N York...........143 G5
Micklefield Leeds..........124 C4
Mickleham Surrey..........31 K2
Mickleover C Derb.......100 F5
Mickleton Dur..............140 B3
Mickleton Gloucs...........71 L5
Mickletown Leeds.........124 B5
Mickle Trafford
  Ches W.....................112 C7
Mickley N York.............132 C4
Mickley Square
  Nthumb.....................150 D3
Mid Ardlaw Abers........217 H2
Midbea Ork..................234 c4
Mid Beltie Abers...........206 C5
Mid Calder W Loth......176 E5
Mid Clyth Highld..........231 K7
Mid Culbeuchly
  Abers.......................216 C3
Middle Aston Oxon........57 J3
Middle Barton Oxon......57 H3
Middlebie D & G...........155 L6
Middlebridge P & K......194 D3
Middle Chinnock
  Somset......................26 C8
Middle Claydon
  Bucks.......................58 B3
Middlecroft Derbys......115 H6
Middleham N York.........131 L3
Middle Handley
  Derbys.....................115 H6
Middlehill Wilts..............39 J6
Middlehope Shrops........83 K5
Middle Kames
  Ag & B.....................172 F1
Middle Littleton
  Worcs.......................71 J5
Middlemarsh Dorset......14 C2
Middle Mayfield
  Staffs.......................100 C4
Middle Rasen Lincs ....117 H4
Middle Rocombe
  Devon.........................7 K2
Middlesbrough
  Middsb.....................141 L4
Middleshaw Cumb........129 L2
Middlesmoor N York....131 K5
Middle Stoke
  Medway ...................46 D5
Middlestone Dur..........141 G2
Middlestown Wakefd....123 K6
Middlethird Border......167 K2
Middleton Ag & B.........188 B7
Middleton Derbys.........100 F2
Middleton Derbys.........114 D8
Middleton Essex.............77 K6
Middleton Hants............29 H3

Middleton Herefs ...........69 K1
Middleton Leeds ...........123 L5
Middleton N York ...........123 G2
Middleton N York ...........134 B3
Middleton Nhants ...........88 B5
Middleton Norfk ...........90 F1
Middleton Nthumb ...........158 D5
Middleton P & K ...........186 B6
Middleton Rochdl ...........113 K1
Middleton Shrops ...........83 K7
Middleton Suffk ...........79 J2
Middleton Swans ...........50 E7
Middleton Warwks ...........85 L4
Middleton Cheney
  Nhants ...........73 G6
Middleton-in-
  Teesdale Dur ...........139 L3
Middleton Moor
  Suffk ...........79 J2
Middleton One Row
  Darltn ...........141 J5
Middleton-on-Sea
  W Susx ...........18 C5
Middleton on the
  Hill Herefs ...........69 K2
Middleton on the
  Wolds E R Yk ...........125 L2
Middleton Park
  C Aber ...........207 H3
Middleton
  Quernhow N York ...........132 E4
Middleton St
  George Darltn ...........141 J5
Middleton Scriven
  Shrops ...........84 C6
Middleton Stoney
  Oxon ...........57 K4
Middleton Tyas
  N York ...........141 G6
Middle Town IoS ...........2 a2
Middletown Powys ...........82 F2
Middle Tysoe Warwks ...........72 D5
Middle Wallop Hants ...........28 F4
Middlewich Ches E ...........113 G7
Middle Winterslow
  Wilts ...........28 E5
Middlewood Cnwll ...........5 L2
Middle Woodford
  Wilts ...........28 C4
Middlewood Green
  Suffk ...........78 D3
Middlezoy Somset ...........26 B5
Midford BaNES ...........39 H7
Midgham W Berk ...........41 K6
Midgley Calder ...........122 F5
Midgley Wakefd ...........123 K7
Midhopestones Sheff ...........114 E2
Midhurst W Susx ...........30 E6
Mid Lavant W Susx ...........18 B4
Midlem Border ...........167 H4
Mid Mains Highld ...........212 C6
Midpark Ag & B ...........173 H6
Midsomer Norton
  BaNES ...........26 F1
Midtown Highld ...........229 J4
Mid Yell Shet ...........235 d3
Migdale Highld ...........222 E3
Migvie Abers ...........205 K4
Milborne Port
  Somset ...........26 F7
Milborne St Andrew
  Dorset ...........14 F3
Milborne Wick
  Somset ...........26 F7
Milbourne Nthumb ...........158 E6
Milbourne Wilts ...........39 L3
Milburn Cumb ...........138 F2
Milbury Heath S Glos ...........38 F3
Milby N York ...........132 F6
Milcombe Oxon ...........72 E7
Milden Suffk ...........77 L5
Mildenhall Suffk ...........91 G8
Mildenhall Wilts ...........40 E6
Mileham Norfk ...........105 L8
Mile Oak Br & H ...........19 H4
Milesmark Fife ...........176 E2
Miles Platting Manch ...........113 J2
Mile Town Kent ...........46 F5

Milfield Nthumb ...........168 D3
Milford Derbys ...........101 G4
Milford Devon ...........22 C6
Milford Staffs ...........99 L7
Milford Surrey ...........30 F3
Milford Haven
  Pembks ...........48 F6
Milford on Sea Hants ...........16 C4
Milkwall Gloucs ...........54 E6
Millais Jersey ...........236 a5
Milland W Susx ...........30 D5
Mill Bank Calder ...........122 F6
Millbreck Abers ...........217 J5
Millbridge Surrey ...........30 D3
Millbrook C Beds ...........74 E6
Millbrook C Sotn ...........29 G8
Millbrook Cnwll ...........6 B5
Millbrook Jersey ...........236 c7
Mill Brow Stockp ...........113 L4
Millbuie Abers ...........206 F4
Millbuie Highld ...........212 E4
Millcorner E Susx ...........21 G2
Millcraig Highld ...........222 E7
Milldale Staffs ...........100 C2
Mill End Bucks ...........42 C4
Mill End Herts ...........60 B2
Millerhill Mdloth ...........177 J4
Miller's Dale Derbys ...........114 C6
Millerston C Glas ...........175 H5
Mill Green Cambs ...........76 F5
Mill Green Essex ...........61 G7
Mill Green Lincs ...........103 L7
Mill Green Suffk ...........77 L6
Mill Green Suffk ...........78 B3
Mill Green Suffk ...........78 D3
Millhalf Herefs ...........68 F5
Millheugh S Lans ...........175 K7
Mill Hill Gt Lon ...........44 E2
Millhouse Ag & B ...........173 G4
Millhousebridge
  D & G ...........155 K5
Millhouse Green
  Barns ...........114 E2
Millhouses Sheff ...........115 G5
Milliken Park Rens ...........174 D6
Millington E R Yk ...........125 J1
Millmeece Staffs ...........99 J5
Mill of Drummond
  P & K ...........185 H4
Mill of Haldane
  W Duns ...........174 D2
Millom Cumb ...........128 E4
Millport N Ayrs ...........173 K7
Mill Street Suffk ...........78 C1
Millthrop Cumb ...........130 C2
Milltimber C Aber ...........207 G5
Milltown Abers ...........205 G4
Milltown Abers ...........205 K3
Milltown D & G ...........156 C6
Milltown Devon ...........23 J4
Milltown Highld ...........209 L5
Milltown of
  Auchindoun
  Moray ...........215 H6
Milltown of
  Campfield Abers ...........206 C5
Milltown of
  Edinvillie Moray ...........215 G6
Milltown of
  Rothiemay Moray ...........215 L5
Milnathort P & K ...........186 B6
Milngavie E Duns ...........175 G4
Milnrow Rochdl ...........122 D7
Milnthorpe Cumb ...........129 K3
Milovaig Highld ...........208 B4
Milson Shrops ...........84 B8
Milstead Kent ...........34 B3
Milston Wilts ...........28 D3
Milthorpe Nhants ...........73 H5
Milton C Stke ...........99 K3
Milton Cambs ...........76 C2
Milton Cumb ...........148 F3
Milton D & G ...........144 F4
Milton D & G ...........154 E7
Milton Derbys ...........100 F7
Milton Highld ...........212 D7
Milton Highld ...........212 E4
Milton Highld ...........223 G6

Milton Highld ...........231 L5
Milton Inver ...........174 C5
Milton Kent ...........46 A5
Milton Moray ...........204 E2
Milton Moray ...........215 L2
Milton N Som ...........37 M7
Milton Notts ...........116 B6
Milton Oxon ...........41 J3
Milton Oxon ...........72 F7
Milton P & K ...........195 G4
Milton Pembks ...........49 H6
Milton Somset ...........26 C6
Milton Stirlg ...........184 B6
Milton W Duns ...........174 D4
Milton Abbas Dorset ...........14 F3
Milton Abbot Devon ...........9 K8
Milton Bridge Mdloth ...........177 H5
Milton Bryan C Beds ...........58 F3
Milton Clevedon
  Somset ...........26 F4
Milton Combe Devon ...........6 D3
Milton Damerel
  Devon ...........9 K3
Milton Ernest Bed ...........74 E4
Milton Green Ches W ...........98 C2
Milton Hill Oxon ...........41 J3
Milton Keynes
  M Keyn ...........74 C6
Milton Lilbourne
  Wilts ...........40 D7
Milton Malsor
  Nhants ...........73 K4
Milton Morenish
  P & K ...........184 D1
Milton of
  Auchinhove
  Abers ...........206 B5
Milton of Balgonie
  Fife ...........186 E7
Milton of Buchanan
  Stirlg ...........174 E1
Milton of Campsie
  E Duns ...........175 H3
Milton of Finavon
  Angus ...........196 D5
Milton of Leys
  Highld ...........213 G6
Milton of Murtle
  C Aber ...........207 G5
Milton on Stour
  Dorset ...........27 J5
Milton Regis Kent ...........46 E6
Milton-under-
  Wychwood Oxon ...........56 E4
Milverton Somset ...........25 H6
Milverton Warwks ...........72 C2
Milwich Staffs ...........99 L6
Minard Ag & B ...........182 D7
Minchinhampton
  Gloucs ...........55 K7
Minehead Somset ...........24 F3
Minera Wrexhm ...........97 L3
Minety Wilts ...........40 A3
Minffordd Gwynd ...........95 K5
Mingarrypark
  Highld ...........190 D3
Miningsby Lincs ...........118 D8
Minions Cnwll ...........5 L2
Minishant S Ayrs ...........163 J6
Minllyn Gwynd ...........81 J2
Minnigaff D & G ...........145 J2
Minnonie Abers ...........216 E3
Minskip N York ...........132 F6
Minstead Hants ...........16 C1
Minsted W Susx ...........30 D7
Minster Kent ...........35 J2
Minsterley Shrops ...........83 G3
Minster Lovell Oxon ...........56 F5
Minster-on-Sea
  Kent ...........46 F5
Minsterworth Gloucs ...........55 H5
Minterne Magna
  Dorset ...........14 C2
Minting Lincs ...........117 K6
Mintlaw Abers ...........217 J5
Minto Border ...........167 H5
Minton Shrops ...........83 H5
Mirehouse Cumb ...........136 D4

Mireland Highld ...........231 K4
Mirfield Kirk ...........123 J6
Miserden Gloucs ...........55 L6
Miskin Rhondd ...........37 G4
Misson Notts ...........116 B3
Misterton Notts ...........116 C3
Misterton Somset ...........13 L2
Mistley Essex ...........62 D2
Mitcham Gt Lon ...........44 F6
Mitcheldean Gloucs ...........54 F4
Mitchell Cnwll ...........4 D5
Mitchellslacks D & G ...........155 G3
Mitchel Troy Mons ...........54 C6
Mitford Nthumb ...........158 F5
Mithian Cnwll ...........3 J2
Mixbury Oxon ...........73 H7
Mobberley Ches E ...........113 H5
Mobberley Staffs ...........100 A4
Mochdre Powys ...........82 B5
Mochrum D & G ...........145 H5
Mockbeggar Kent ...........33 J4
Mockerkin Cumb ...........136 F3
Modbury Devon ...........6 F5
Moddershall Staffs ...........99 L5
Moelfre IoA ...........109 G4
Moelfre Powys ...........97 J6
Moffat D & G ...........155 J2
Moggerhanger
  C Beds ...........75 G5
Moira Leics ...........86 C1
Molash Kent ...........34 D4
Mol-chlach Highld ...........199 G3
Mold Flints ...........111 H8
Moldgreen Kirk ...........123 H7
Molehill Green Essex ...........60 E3
Molescroft E R Yk ...........126 C3
Molesworth Cambs ...........88 F7
Moll Highld ...........209 J7
Molland Devon ...........24 C5
Mollington Ches W ...........111 L7
Mollington Oxon ...........72 F5
Mollinsburn N Lans ...........175 J4
Mondynes Abers ...........197 J1
Monewden Suffk ...........78 F3
Moneydie P & K ...........185 M2
Moniaive D & G ...........154 D4
Monifieth Angus ...........187 H2
Monikie Angus ...........196 E8
Monimail Fife ...........186 E5
Monken Hadley
  Gt Lon ...........44 E1
Monk Fryston N York ...........124 D5
Monkhide Herefs ...........70 B5
Monkhill Cumb ...........148 C3
Monkhopton Shrops ...........84 B5
Monkland Herefs ...........69 J3
Monkleigh Devon ...........23 G7
Monknash V Glam ...........36 E6
Monkokehampton
  Devon ...........10 E4
Monkseaton N Tyne ...........159 H1
Monks Eleigh Suffk ...........77 L5
Monk's Gate W Susx ...........31 K6
Monks Heath Ches E ...........113 J6
Monk Sherborne
  Hants ...........29 L1
Monksilver Somset ...........25 G4
Monks Kirby Warwks ...........86 F6
Monk Soham Suffk ...........78 E2
Monks Risborough
  Bucks ...........58 D6
Monksthorpe Lincs ...........118 F7
Monk Street Essex ...........60 F3
Monkswood Mons ...........53 M7
Monkton Devon ...........12 F2
Monkton Kent ...........47 M6
Monkton S Ayrs ...........163 J4
Monkton S Tyne ...........151 H3
Monkton Combe
  BaNES ...........39 H7
Monkton Deverill
  Wilts ...........27 J4
Monkton Farleigh
  Wilts ...........39 J7
Monkton Heathfield
  Somset ...........25 K6
Monkton Wyld
  Dorset ...........13 J3

**Monkwearmouth**
Sundld .................... 151 J4
**Monkwood** Hants ........ 30 A5
**Monmore Green**
Wolves .................. 85 G4
**Monmouth** Mons ......... 54 D5
**Monnington on Wye**
Herefs ................... 69 G5
**Monreith** D & G ........ 145 H6
**Montacute** Somset ........ 26 D7
**Montford** Shrops .......... 83 H1
**Montford Bridge**
Shrops ................... 83 H1
**Montgarrie** Abers ...... 206 B2
**Montgomery** Powys ...... 82 E4
**Montrose** Angus ........ 197 H5
**Mont Saint** Guern ...... 236 b3
**Monxton** Hants .......... 28 F3
**Monyash** Derbys ........ 114 D7
**Monymusk** Abers ...... 206 D3
**Monzie** P & K .......... 185 H3
**Moodiesburn**
N Lans .................. 175 J4
**Moonzie** Fife .......... 186 E4
**Moor Allerton** Leeds .. 123 L3
**Moorby** Lincs .......... 118 D8
**Moor Crichel** Dorset ... 15 J2
**Moordown** BCP .......... 15 K4
**Moore** Halton ......... 112 E5
**Moor End** Calder ...... 122 F5
**Moorends** Donc ........ 125 G7
**Moorhead** C Brad ...... 123 H3
**Moorhouse** Cumb ...... 148 B4
**Moorhouse** Notts ...... 116 C7
**Moorhouse Bank**
Surrey ................... 32 D3
**Moorlinch** Somset ....... 26 B4
**Moor Monkton**
N York .................. 133 H7
**Moorsholm** R & Cl .... 142 E4
**Moorside** Dorset ........ 27 H7
**Moorswater** Cnwll ........ 5 K3
**Moorthorpe** Wakefd .. 124 C7
**Moortown** Leeds ...... 123 K3
**Moortown** Lincs ...... 117 H2
**Morangie** Highld ...... 223 G5
**Morar** Highld .......... 199 L6
**Morborne** Cambs ....... 89 G5
**Morchard Bishop**
Devon .................... 11 H4
**Morcombelake**
Dorset ................... 13 K4
**Morcott** Rutlnd ......... 88 D4
**Morda** Shrops ........... 97 L6
**Morden** Dorset .......... 15 H4
**Morden** Gt Lon ......... 44 E6
**Mordiford** Herefs ....... 69 L6
**Mordon** Dur .......... 141 H2
**More** Shrops ............ 83 G5
**Morebath** Devon ........ 24 E6
**Morebattle** Border ..... 168 B4
**Morecambe** Lancs ...... 129 J6
**Moredon** Swindn ........ 40 C3
**Morefield** Highld ...... 220 E3
**Morehall** Kent .......... 35 G7
**Moreleigh** Devon ......... 7 H5
**Morenish** P & K ....... 184 D1
**Morestead** Hants ........ 29 K6
**Moreton** Dorset ......... 14 F4
**Moreton** Essex ......... 60 E6
**Moreton** Herefs ......... 69 K2
**Moreton** Oxon .......... 58 B6
**Moreton** Wirral ....... 111 J4
**Moreton Corbet**
Shrops ................... 98 E7
**Moretonhampstead**
Devon .................... 11 H7
**Moreton-in-Marsh**
Gloucs ................... 56 D2
**Moreton Jeffries**
Herefs ................... 69 L5
**Moreton Morrell**
Warwks .................. 72 C4
**Moreton on Lugg**
Herefs ................... 69 K5
**Moreton Pinkney**
Nhants ................... 73 H5
**Moreton Say** Shrops .... 98 F5

**Moreton Valence**
Gloucs ................... 55 H6
**Morfa Nefyn** Gwynd ..... 94 E4
**Morham** E Loth ........ 178 C4
**Morland** Cumb ......... 138 E3
**Morley** Ches E ......... 113 J5
**Morley** Derbys ........ 101 H4
**Morley** Leeds ......... 123 K5
**Morley Green** Ches E ... 113 J5
**Morley St Botolph**
Norfk .................... 92 C4
**Morningside** C Edin ... 177 H4
**Morningside** N Lans ... 175 L7
**Morningthorpe** Norfk ... 92 F5
**Morpeth** Nthumb ...... 158 F5
**Morphie** Abers ........ 197 H4
**Morrey** Staffs ........ 100 C8
**Morriston** Swans ....... 51 J6
**Morston** Norfk ........ 106 B4
**Mortehoe** Devon ........ 23 G3
**Morthen** Rothm ....... 115 J4
**Mortimer** W Berk ....... 41 M7
**Mortimer West End**
Hants .................... 41 M7
**Mortlake** Gt Lon ....... 44 E5
**Morton** Cumb ......... 148 C4
**Morton** Derbys ........ 101 H1
**Morton** Lincs ......... 103 H7
**Morton** Lincs ......... 116 D3
**Morton** Notts ......... 102 B3
**Morton** Shrops ......... 97 L7
**Morton-on-Swale**
N York .................. 132 E2
**Morton on the Hill**
Norfk .................... 92 D1
**Morvah** Cnwll ........... 2 D4
**Morvich** Highld ....... 200 E2
**Morville** Shrops ........ 84 C5
**Morwenstow** Cnwll ....... 9 G2
**Mosborough** Sheff ..... 115 H5
**Moscow** E Ayrs ....... 163 L2
**Moseley** Birm ......... 85 J4
**Moseley** Wolves ........ 85 G4
**Moseley** Worcs ......... 70 E3
**Moss** Ag & B ......... 188 B7
**Moss** Donc ........... 124 F7
**Mossat** Abers ......... 205 K2
**Mossbank** Shet ........ 235 d4
**Moss Bank** St Hel ..... 112 D3
**Mossbay** Cumb ......... 136 D2
**Mossblown** S Ayrs ..... 163 K4
**Mossburnford**
Border ................. 167 K6
**Mossdale** D & G ...... 154 B7
**Mossdale** E Ayrs ...... 153 K2
**Moss Edge** Lancs ...... 120 F2
**Mossend** N Lans ...... 175 K6
**Mossley** Tamesd ...... 113 L2
**Mosspaul Hotel**
Border ................. 156 D3
**Moss-side** Highld ..... 213 K4
**Mosstodloch** Moray ... 215 H3
**Mossyard** D & G ...... 145 L5
**Mossy Lea** Lancs ...... 121 H7
**Mosterton** Dorset ....... 13 L2
**Moston** Manch ....... 113 K2
**Mostyn** Flints ......... 111 G5
**Motcombe** Dorset ....... 27 J6
**Mothecombe** Devon ....... 6 F6
**Motherby** Cumb ....... 138 B2
**Motherwell** N Lans .... 175 K6
**Motspur Park** Gt Lon ... 44 E6
**Mottingham** Gt Lon ..... 45 H5
**Mottisfont** Hants ........ 28 F6
**Mottisfont** Hants ........ 28 F6
**Mottistone** IoW ......... 16 E5
**Mottram in Longdendale**
Tamesd ................. 113 M3
**Mottram St Andrew**
Ches E .................. 113 K5
**Mouilpied** Guern ...... 236 c3
**Mouldsworth**
Ches W .................. 112 D7
**Moulin** P & K .......... 194 E4
**Moulscoomb** Br & H ..... 19 J4
**Moulsford** Oxon ........ 41 L4
**Moulsoe** M Keyn ........ 74 C6

**Moultavie** Highld ..... 222 E7
**Moulton** Ches W ...... 112 F7
**Moulton** Lincs ........ 104 A7
**Moulton** N York ...... 141 G6
**Moulton** Nhants ........ 73 L2
**Moulton** Suffk ......... 77 G2
**Moulton** V Glam ....... 37 G6
**Moulton Chapel**
Lincs ................... 103 M8
**Moulton St Mary**
Norfk .................... 93 H3
**Moulton Seas End**
Lincs ................... 104 A6
**Mount** Cnwll ............ 5 J3
**Mountain** C Brad ...... 123 G4
**Mountain Ash**
Rhondd .................. 53 G7
**Mountain Cross**
Border ................. 176 F8
**Mount Ambrose**
Cnwll ..................... 3 J3
**Mount Bures** Essex ..... 61 L2
**Mountfield** E Susx ...... 20 E2
**Mountgerald** Highld ... 212 E3
**Mount Hawke** Cnwll ...... 3 J2
**Mountjoy** Cnwll ......... 4 D4
**Mount Lothian**
Mdloth .................. 177 H6
**Mountnessing** Essex ... 60 F8
**Mounton** Mons ......... 38 D2
**Mount Pleasant**
Derbys .................. 101 G3
**Mount Pleasant**
Suffk .................... 77 G5
**Mountsorrel** Leics ...... 87 H2
**Mount Tabor** Calder ... 122 F5
**Mousehole** Cnwll ......... 2 E6
**Mouswald** D & G ...... 155 J7
**Mow Cop** Ches E ....... 99 J2
**Mowhaugh** Border .... 168 B5
**Mowmacre Hill**
C Leic ................... 87 H3
**Mowsley** Leics ......... 87 J5
**Moy** Highld ........... 202 C8
**Moy** Highld ........... 213 J7
**Moyle** Highld ......... 200 D2
**Moylegrove** Pembks ..... 64 F5
**Muasdale** Ag & B ...... 161 H2
**Muchalls** Abers ....... 207 G6
**Much Birch** Herefs ...... 54 D3
**Much Cowarne**
Herefs ................... 70 B5
**Much Dewchurch**
Herefs ................... 54 C2
**Muchelney** Somset ....... 26 B6
**Muchelney Ham**
Somset ................... 26 C6
**Much Hadham** Herts ..... 60 C4
**Much Hoole** Lancs .... 120 F6
**Muchlarnick** Cnwll ....... 5 K5
**Much Marcle** Herefs .... 54 F2
**Much Wenlock**
Shrops ................... 84 B4
**Muck** Highld .......... 189 K1
**Muckleburgh**
Collection Norfk ..... 106 D4
**Mucklestone** Staffs ..... 99 G5
**Muckton** Lincs ........ 118 E5
**Muddiford** Devon ........ 23 J4
**Muddles Green**
E Susx ................... 20 B3
**Mudeford** BCP .......... 16 A4
**Mudford** Somset ........ 26 E7
**Mudford Sock**
Somset ................... 26 E7
**Mugdock** Stirlg ....... 175 G3
**Mugeary** Highld ...... 209 G6
**Mugginton** Derbys .... 100 F4
**Muirden** Abers ....... 216 D4
**Muirdrum** Angus ...... 196 F8
**Muiresk** Abers ....... 216 D5
**Muirhead** Angus ...... 186 E1
**Muirhead** Fife ....... 186 E6
**Muirhead** N Lans ..... 175 J4
**Muirhouses** Falk ..... 176 D3
**Muirkirk** E Ayrs ..... 164 D4
**Muirmill** Stirlg ...... 175 J2
**Muir of Fowlis** Abers .. 206 B3

**Muir of Miltonduff**
Moray .................. 214 E3
**Muir of Ord** Highld ... 212 E4
**Muirshearlich** Highld .. 192 B1
**Muirtack** Abers ....... 217 J6
**Muirton** P & K ....... 185 J5
**Muirton Mains**
Highld .................. 212 C4
**Muirton of Ardblair**
P & K ................... 195 J7
**Muker** N York ........ 139 K7
**Mulbarton** Norfk ....... 92 E4
**Mulben** Moray ....... 215 H4
**Mull** Ag & B .......... 181 J1
**Mullardoch** Highld ... 211 K7
**Mullion** Cnwll ........... 3 H7
**Mullion Cove** Cnwll ..... 3 H7
**Mumby** Lincs ......... 119 G6
**Munderfield Row**
Herefs ................... 70 B4
**Munderfield Stocks**
Herefs ................... 70 B4
**Mundesley** Norfk ..... 107 G5
**Mundford** Norfk ....... 91 H5
**Mundham** Norfk ....... 93 G4
**Mundon Hill** Essex ..... 61 K7
**Mungrisdale** Cumb .... 137 K2
**Munlochy** Highld ..... 213 G4
**Munnoch** N Ayrs ..... 174 B8
**Munsley** Herefs ........ 70 B6
**Munslow** Shrops ....... 83 K6
**Murchington** Devon .... 11 G7
**Murcott** Oxon ......... 57 L5
**Murkle** Highld ....... 231 H2
**Murlaggan** Highld .... 200 F6
**Murroes** Angus ....... 187 G1
**Murrow** Cambs ........ 89 L3
**Mursley** Bucks ........ 58 D3
**Murston** Kent ......... 46 F7
**Murthill** Angus ...... 196 D5
**Murthly** P & K ....... 195 H8
**Murton** C York ....... 133 K8
**Murton** Cumb ........ 139 G3
**Murton** Dur .......... 151 J5
**Murton** Nthumb ...... 179 K8
**Musbury** Devon ........ 13 H4
**Musselburgh** E Loth .. 177 K4
**Muston** Leics ......... 102 D5
**Muston** N York ....... 135 H4
**Muswell Hill** Gt Lon ... 44 F3
**Mutehill** D & G ...... 146 C5
**Mutford** Suffk ......... 93 K6
**Muthill** P & K ....... 185 H4
**Mybster** Highld ...... 231 H5
**Myddfai** Carmth ....... 52 B3
**Myddle** Shrops ........ 98 C7
**Mydroilyn** Cerdgn ..... 66 B4
**Mylor** Cnwll ............ 4 C8
**Mylor Bridge** Cnwll ..... 4 C8
**Mynachlog ddu**
Pembks .................. 49 K2
**Mynydd-bach** Mons .... 38 C2
**Mynydd-Bach** Swans ... 51 J4
**Mynyddgarreg**
Carmth .................. 50 E4
**Mynydd Isa** Flints .... 111 J8
**Myrebird** Abers ...... 206 E5
**Myredykes** Border .... 157 G3
**Mytchett** Surrey ....... 30 E1
**Mytholm** Calder ...... 122 E5
**Mytholmroyd** Calder .. 122 F5
**Myton-on-Swale**
N York .................. 132 F2

**N**

**Naast** Highld ......... 219 J5
**Na Buirgh** W Isls ..... 232 d4
**Naburn** C York ....... 124 F2
**Nackington** Kent ....... 34 F4
**Nacton** Suffk .......... 78 F6
**Nafferton** E R Yk ..... 135 G7
**Nailsbourne** Somset .... 25 K5
**Nailsea** N Som ......... 38 C6
**Nailstone** Leics ........ 86 E3
**Nailsworth** Gloucs ..... 55 J7

Nairn Highld .................. 213 K3
Nannerch Flints............ 111 G7
Nanpantan Leics....... 101 K8
Nanpean Cnwll................... 4 F5
Nanstallon Cnwll.............. 5 G3
Nanternis Cerdgn.......... 65 L3
Nantgaredig Carmth .....50 F2
Nantglyn Denbgs......... 96 F1
Nantmel Powys.......... 68 B2
Nantmor Gwynd............ 95 K4
Nant Peris Gwynd...... 95 K2
Nantwich Ches E........ 98 F3
Nantyglo Blae G ........ 53 J6
Nant-y-moel Brdgnd....36 E2
Naphill Bucks................ 42 D2
Napton on the Hill
  Warwks.......................72 F3
Narberth Pembks.......49 J4
Narborough Leics......87 G4
Narborough Norfk......91 H2
Nasareth Gwynd......... 95 H3
Naseby Nhants..........87 K7
Nash Bucks..................73 L7
Nash Newpt................37 M4
Nash Shrops............... 69 L1
Nassington Nhants.....88 F4
Nateby Cumb.............139 H6
Nateby Lancs............120 F2
National Memorial
  Arboretum Staffs.....85 L1
National Motor
  Museum
  (Beaulieu) Hants...16 E2
National Space
  Centre C Leic......... 87 H3
Natland Cumb............129 L2
Naughton Suffk...........78 B5
Naunton Gloucs.........56 C4
Naunton Worcs.........70 F6
Naunton
  Beauchamp
  Worcs.....................71 G4
Navenby Lincs..........103 G2
Navestock Essex.......45 K1
Navestock Side
  Essex.......................60 E8
Navidale Highld.........227 J5
Navity Highld.............213 J2
Nawton N York..........133 K3
Nayland Suffk.............77 L7
Nazeing Essex...........60 C6
Neap Shet...................235 d5
Near Cotton Staffs...100 B4
Near Sawrey Cumb...137 K7
Neasden Gt Lon..........44 E3
Neasham Darltn........141 H5
Neath Neath.................51 L6
Neatham Hants.........30 C4
Neatishead Norfk......107 H7
Nebo Cerdgn...............66 D2
Nebo Conwy................96 C2
Nebo Gwynd................95 H3
Nebo IoA...................108 F4
Necton Norfk..............91 K2
Nedd Highld..............224 D3
Nedging Suffk.............78 B5
Nedging Tye Suffk ....78 B4
Needham Norfk..........92 F6
Needham Market
  Suffk........................78 C4
Needingworth Cambs..75 L1
Neen Savage Shrops..84 C7
Neen Sollars Shrops..84 B8
Neenton Shrops.........84 B6
Nefyn Gwynd..............94 E4
Neilston E Rens........174 E6
Nelson Caerph............37 H2
Nelson Lancs.............122 C3
Nemphlar S Lans......165 G1
Nempnett Thrubwell
  BaNES......................38 D7
Nenthead Cumb.......149 K6
Nenthorn Border......167 K2
Nerabus Ag & B........170 E7
Nercwys Flints............97 K1
Nerston S Lans.........175 H6
Nesbit Nthumb.........168 E3
Nesfield N York........123 G1

Nesscliffe Shrops............98 B8
Neston Ches W............ 111 J6
Neston Wilts.....................39 K6
Netchwood Shrops...........84 B5
Nether Abington
  S Lans.........................165 H5
Nether Alderley
  Ches E.......................... 113 J6
Netheravon Wilts............28 D2
Nether Blainslie
  Border........................167 H2
Netherbrae Abers.......216 F3
Nether Broughton
  Leics.............................102 B7
Netherburn S Lans......175 L8
Netherbury Dorset......... 13 L3
Netherby N York..........123 L2
Nether Cerne Dorset....14 C3
Nethercleuch D & G....155 K5
Nether Compton
  Dorset...........................26 E7
Nether Crimond
  Abers...........................206 F2
Nether Dallachy
  Moray...........................215 H2
Netherend Gloucs...........54 E7
Netherfield E Susx..........20 E2
Netherfield Notts...........101 L4
Nether Fingland
  S Lans..........................165 H7
Netherhampton
  Wilts..............................28 C5
Nether Handwick
  Angus...........................196 B7
Nether Haugh Rothm...115 H3
Netherhay Dorset........... 13 K2
Nether Headon Notts...116 C6
Nether Heage Derbys...101 G3
Nether Heyford
  Nhants...........................73 J3
Nether Kellet Lancs....129 K6
Nether Kinmundy
  Abers...........................217 K5
Nether Langwith
  Notts............................115 K7
Netherley Abers...........207 G6
Nethermill D & G.........155 H5
Nethermuir Abers.......217 G5
Netherne-on-the-
  Hill Surrey....................32 B3
Netheroyd Hill Kirk....123 H6
Nether Padley
  Derbys.......................... 114 E6
Nether Poppleton
  C York..........................133 J8
Netherseal Derbys........86 C2
Nether Silton N York...133 G2
Nether Stowey
  Somset...........................25 J4
Netherthong Kirk.........123 H8
Netherton Angus..........196 E5
Netherton Devon............. 7 K2
Netherton Dudley..........85 G6
Netherton Kirk.............123 H7
Netherton N Lans........175 K7
Netherton Nthumb.......168 E7
Netherton P & K..........195 J6
Netherton Sefton.........111 K2
Netherton Stirlg..........175 G3
Netherton Wakefd......123 K6
Nethertown Cumb.......136 D5
Nethertown Highld......231 L1
Nethertown Staffs......100 C8
Netherurd Border.........165 L1
Nether Wallop Hants....28 F4
Nether Wasdale
  Cumb..........................136 F6
Nether Westcote
  Gloucs............................56 E4
Nether Whitacre
  Warwks...........................86 B5
Nether Whitecleuch
  S Lans..........................165 G5
Nether Winchendon
  Bucks..............................58 B5
Netherwitton Nthumb..158 D4
Nethy Bridge Highld...204 B2
Netley Hants...................16 F2

Netley Marsh Hants.......29 G8
Nettlebed Oxon.............42 B3
Nettlebridge Somset....26 F2
Nettlecombe Dorset.....13 M4
Nettleden Herts............59 G6
Nettleham Lincs..........117 G6
Nettlestead Kent.........33 H3
Nettlestead Green
  Kent..............................33 H3
Nettlestone IoW...........17 H4
Nettlesworth Dur.........151 G5
Nettleton Lincs............117 J2
Nettleton Wilts.............39 J5
Netton Wilts.................28 C4
Nevern Pembks.............64 F6
Nevill Holt Leics..........88 B5
New Abbey D & G.......147 G2
New Aberdour
  Abers...........................217 G2
New Addington
  Gt Lon..........................45 G7
Newall Leeds...............123 J2
New Alresford Hants....29 L5
New Alyth P & K..........195 K6
Newark C Pete.............89 H4
Newark Ork.................234 e4
Newark-on-Trent
  Notts............................102 D2
New Arley Warwks........86 C5
Newarthill N Lans........175 K6
New Ash Green Kent....45 L6
New Balderton
  Notts............................102 D3
New Barn Kent..............45 L6
New Barnet Gt Lon.......44 F2
Newbattle Mdloth.......177 J4
New Bewick Nthumb...169 G5
Newbie D & G..............147 L3
Newbiggin Cumb.........138 C2
Newbiggin Cumb.........138 F2
Newbiggin Cumb.........148 F5
Newbiggin Dur............139 K2
Newbiggin N York.......131 J3
Newbiggin-by-the-
  Sea Nthumb...............159 H5
Newbigging Angus......187 H1
Newbigging Angus......195 L7
Newbigging Angus......196 C8
Newbigging S Lans....165 K1
Newbiggin-on-
  Lune Cumb.................139 G6
New Bilton Warwks.......86 F7
Newbold Derbys.........115 G6
Newbold on Avon
  Warwks...........................86 F7
Newbold on Stour
  Warwks...........................72 B5
Newbold Pacey
  Warwks...........................72 C3
Newbold Verdon
  Leics..............................86 F3
New Bolingbroke
  Lincs............................104 A2
Newborough C Pete.....89 H3
Newborough IoA..........108 E7
Newborough Staffs.....100 C7
New Boultham Lincs...116 F7
Newbourne Suffk..........78 F6
New Bradwell
  M Keyn...........................74 B6
New Brampton
  Derbys.........................115 G7
New Brancepeth Dur...151 G6
Newbridge C Edin........176 F4
Newbridge Caerph.......37 K2
Newbridge Cnwll............ 2 D5
Newbridge D & G.........155 G6
Newbridge Hants...........28 F7
Newbridge IoW.............16 E5
Newbridge Green
  Worcs............................70 E6
Newbridge-on-Wye
  Powys............................67 L3
New Brighton Wirral...111 J3
Newbrough Nthumb....149 L2
New Buckenham
  Norfk..............................92 C5
Newbuildings Devon.....11 J4

Newburgh Abers..........207 J1
Newburgh Abers..........217 H3
Newburgh Fife.............186 D4
Newburgh Lancs..........121 G7
Newburn N u Ty...........150 F2
Newbury Somset...........27 G2
Newbury W Berk............41 J4
Newbury Park Gt Lon....45 J3
Newby Cumb................138 E3
Newby Lancs................122 B2
Newby N York..............130 D5
Newby N York..............134 F2
Newby N York..............142 B5
Newby Bridge Cumb...129 H3
Newby East Cumb.......148 E4
New Byth Abers...........216 F4
Newby West Cumb......148 C4
Newcastle Mons...........54 C5
Newcastle Shrops.........82 E6
Newcastle Airport
  Nthumb.......................158 F7
Newcastle Emlyn
  Carmth...........................65 J6
Newcastleton Border...156 E5
Newcastle-under-
  Lyme Staffs..................99 J3
Newcastle upon
  Tyne N u Ty................151 G3
Newchapel Pembks......65 H6
Newchapel Surrey.......32 C5
Newchurch IoW............17 G5
Newchurch Kent..........34 E7
Newchurch Mons.........38 C2
Newchurch Powys........68 E4
Newchurch Staffs.......100 D7
New Costessey Norfk...92 E2
Newcraighall C Edin...177 J4
New Crofton Wakefd...124 B6
New Cross Gt Lon.........45 G5
New Cross Somset.......26 B7
New Cumnock E Ayrs..164 C6
New Deer Abers...........217 G5
New Denham Bucks......43 H4
Newdigate Surrey.........31 K3
New Duston Nhants.......73 K3
New Earswick C York...133 J7
New Edlington Donc...115 K2
New Elgin Moray.........214 F3
New Ellerby E R Yk......126 E3
Newell Green Br For.....42 E6
New Eltham Gt Lon.......45 H5
New End Worcs.............71 J3
Newenden Kent............33 L7
New England C Pete.....89 H4
Newent Gloucs..............55 G3
New Ferry Wirral.........111 K4
Newfield Dur...............150 F7
Newfield Highld..........223 H6
New Fletton C Pete.......89 H4
New Forest
  National Park............16 C2
Newgale Pembks...........48 E3
New Galloway D & G....154 B6
Newgate Street
  Herts..............................59 M6
New Gilston Fife..........187 G5
New Grimsby IoS............. 2 a1
Newhall Ches E.............98 E4
New Hartley Nthumb...159 H6
Newhaven C Edin........177 H3
Newhaven E Susx..........19 L5
New Haw Surrey...........43 H7
New Hedges Pembks....49 J6
New Holland N Linc....126 D5
Newholm N York.........143 H5
New Houghton
  Derbys.........................115 J7
New Houghton Norfk...105 J6
Newhouse N Lans........175 L6
New Hutton Cumb.......130 B2
Newick E Susx...............19 L2
Newingreen Kent..........35 G6
Newington Kent............46 E6
Newington Oxon..........41 L2
New Inn Carmth...........66 B6
New Inn Torfn..............53 L7
New Invention
  Shrops...........................82 F7

**New Lakenham**
Norfk............................92 F3
**New Lanark** S Lans......165 G2
New Lanark Village
S Lans...........................165 G2
**Newland** C KuH............126 D4
**Newland** Gloucs............54 D6
**Newland** N York............125 G5
**Newland** Somset............24 C4
**Newland** Worcs............70 E5
**Newlandrig** Mdloth......177 K6
**Newlands** Border..........156 E4
**Newlands** Nthumb........150 D4
**Newlands of**
Dundurcas Moray... 215 G4
**New Langholm**
D & G............................156 C5
**New Leake** Lincs..........104 C2
**New Leeds** Abers..........217 J4
**New Lodge** Barns..........123 L8
**New Longton** Lancs......121 G5
**New Luce** D & G............144 E3
**Newlyn** Cnwll..................2 E5
**Newmachar** Abers........207 G2
**Newmains** N Lans........175 L6
**New Malden** Gt Lon......44 E6
**Newman's Green**
Suffk...............................77 K5
**Newmarket** Suffk..........76 F2
**Newmarket** W Isls........232 f2
**New Marske** R & Cl......142 D3
**New Marston** Oxon........57 K6
**New Mill** Abers..............206 E8
**New Mill** Cnwll................2 E4
**New Mill** Border............167 G7
**New Mill** Kirk................123 H8
**Newmill** Moray............215 K4
**Newmillerdam**
Wakefd.........................123 L7
**Newmill of**
Inshewan Angus.....196 C4
**Newmills** C Edin..........177 G5
**New Mills** Derbys........113 M4
**Newmills** Fife..............176 D2
**Newmills** Mons............54 D6
**New Mills** Powys..........82 C4
**Newmilln** P & K............186 B2
**Newmilns** E Ayrs........164 B2
**New Milton** Hants..........16 B4
**New Mistley** Essex........62 D2
**New Moat** Pembks........49 H3
**Newney Green** Essex....61 G6
**Newnham** Hants............30 B2
**Newnham** Herts............75 J6
**Newnham** Kent............34 C3
**Newnham** Nhants..........73 H3
**Newnham Bridge**
Worcs.............................70 B2
**Newnham on**
Severn Gloucs..........55 G5
**New Ollerton** Notts......116 A7
**New Oscott** Birm............85 K5
**New Pitsligo** Abers......217 G3
**Newport** Cnwll.................9 J7
**Newport** E R Yk............125 K4
**Newport** Essex..............76 D7
**Newport** Gloucs............39 G2
**Newport** Highld............227 K4
**Newport** IoW..................16 F5
**Newport** Newpt..............37 L3
**Newport** Pembks............64 E6
**Newport** Wrekin............99 H8
**Newport-on-Tay**
Fife...............................187 G2
**Newport Pagnell**
M Keyn..........................74 C5
Newport Pagnell
Services M Keyn..........74 C5
**New Prestwick**
S Ayrs...........................163 J4
**New Quay** Cerdgn........65 L3
**Newquay** Cnwll................4 C4
Newquay Zoo Cnwll........4 C4
**New Rackheath**
Norfk.............................93 G2
**New Radnor** Powys........68 E3
**New Ridley** Nthumb......150 D3
**New Romney** Kent..........21 L2

**New Rossington**
Donc.............................115 L2
**New Sauchie** Clacks......185 J7
**Newseat** Abers..............216 D7
**Newsham** Lancs............121 G4
**Newsham** N York..........132 E3
**Newsham** N York..........140 E5
**Newsham** Nthumb........159 H6
**New Sharlston**
Wakefd.........................124 B6
**Newsholme** E R Yk........125 H5
**New Silksworth**
Sundld.........................151 J4
**Newsome** Kirk..............123 H7
**New Somerby** Lincs......102 F5
**Newstead** Border..........167 H3
**Newstead** Notts............101 K3
**Newstead** Nthumb........169 H4
**New Stevenston**
N Lans.........................175 K6
**New Swanage** Dorset....15 J6
**Newthorpe** Notts..........101 J4
**New Thundersley**
Essex.............................46 C3
**Newton** Ag & B............182 F7
**Newton** Border..............167 J5
**Newton** Brdgnd............36 C5
**Newton** C Beds..............75 J5
**Newton** Cambs..............76 B5
**Newton** Cambs..............90 B1
**Newton** Ches W............98 D1
**Newton** Ches W............112 B7
**Newton** Cumb..............128 F5
**Newton** Derbys............101 H2
**Newton** Herefs..............53 M2
**Newton** Herefs..............69 K4
**Newton** Highld............212 F4
**Newton** Highld............213 H5
**Newton** Highld............213 J2
**Newton** Highld............231 L5
**Newton** Lincs..............103 H5
**Newton** Mdloth............177 J4
**Newton** Moray............214 E2
**Newton** Moray............215 H2
**Newton** Nhants............88 C6
**Newton** Norfk................91 J1
**Newton** Notts..............102 B4
**Newton** Nthumb..........150 C3
**Newton** S Lans............165 H3
**Newton** S Lans............175 H6
**Newton** Sandw..............85 J5
**Newton** Staffs............100 B7
**Newton** Suffk................77 K6
**Newton** W Loth............176 E3
**Newton** Warwks............87 G7
**Newton Abbot** Devon....7 K2
**Newton Arlosh**
Cumb...........................147 L4
**Newton Aycliffe** Dur....141 G3
**Newton Bewley**
Hartpl...........................141 K2
**Newton**
Blossomville
M Keyn...........................74 D4
**Newton Bromswold**
Nhants...........................74 E2
**Newton Burgoland**
Leics...............................86 D2
**Newton by Toft** Lincs... 117 H4
**Newton Ferrers**
Devon...............................6 E6
**Newton Ferry** W Isls... 232 c5
**Newton Flotman**
Norfk.............................92 E4
**Newtongrange**
Mdloth.........................177 J5
**Newton Green** Mons....38 D3
**Newton Harcourt**
Leics...............................87 J4
**Newton Heath** Manch...113 K2
**Newtonhill** Abers........207 G6
**Newton-in-**
Bowland Lancs........121 K1
**Newton Kyme** N York...124 C2
**Newton-le-Willows**
N York...........................132 C2
**Newton-le-Willows**
St Hel...........................112 E3

**Newtonloan** Mdloth......177 J5
**Newton Longville**
Bucks.............................58 D2
**Newton Mearns**
E Rens...........................174 F7
**Newtonmill** Angus......196 F4
**Newtonmore** Highld....203 H5
**Newton Morrell**
N York...........................141 G5
**Newton of**
Balcanquhal
P & K............................186 B5
**Newton of**
Balcormo Fife............187 H6
**Newton of Belltrees**
Rens.............................174 D6
**Newton-on-Ouse**
N York...........................133 H7
**Newton-on-**
Rawcliffe N York....134 C2
**Newton-on-the-**
Moor Nthumb............158 F2
**Newton on Trent**
Lincs.............................116 D6
**Newton Poppleford**
Devon.............................12 E4
**Newton Purcell** Oxon....57 L3
**Newton Regis**
Warwks...........................86 C3
**Newton Reigny**
Cumb...........................138 C2
**Newton St Cyres**
Devon.............................11 K5
**Newton St Faith**
Norfk.............................92 F1
**Newton St Loe**
BaNES.............................39 G7
**Newton St Petrock**
Devon...............................9 K3
**Newton Solney**
Derbys.........................100 F7
**Newton Stacey** Hants...29 H4
**Newton Stewart**
D & G............................145 J3
**Newton Tony** Wilts......28 E4
**Newton Tracey** Devon...23 H6
**Newton under**
Roseberry R & Cl...142 C5
**Newton upon**
Derwent E R Yk......125 H2
**Newton Valence**
Hants.............................30 B5
**Newton Wamphray**
D & G............................155 K3
**Newton with Scales**
Lancs...........................120 F4
**Newtown** BCP..............15 K4
**Newtown** Cumb............147 J5
**Newtown** Cumb............148 E3
**Newtown** D & G............164 F7
**Newtown** Devon............12 D3
**Newtown** Devon............24 B6
**New Town** E Susx..........19 M2
**Newtown** Gloucs............54 F7
**Newtown** Hants............29 L8
**Newtown** Herefs............70 B5
**Newtown** Highld..........202 B4
**Newtown** IoW................16 E4
**Newtown** Nthumb........168 F4
**Newtown** Powys............82 C5
**Newtown** Shrops............98 C6
**Newtown** Somset............25 L8
**Newtown** Staffs............99 K1
**Newtown** Wigan..........112 E1
**Newtown** Worcs............70 F4
**Newtown Linford**
Leics...............................87 G2
**Newtown St**
Boswells Border......167 J3
**New Tredegar** Caerph...53 H7
**New Trows** S Lans........164 F2
**Newtyle** Angus............195 L7
**New Walsoken**
Cambs.............................90 C2
**New Waltham** NE Lin...118 C1
**New Winton** E Loth......177 L4
**Newyork** Ag & B..........182 D5
**New York** Lincs............103 L2

**New York** N Tyne..........159 H7
**Neyland** Pembks............49 G6
**Nicholashayne** Devon...25 H7
**Nicholaston** Swans........51 G7
**Nidd** N York..................132 D7
**Nigg** C Aber..................207 H5
**Nigg** Highld..................223 H6
**Nigg Ferry** Highld........223 H7
**Ninebanks** Nthumb......149 K4
**Nine Elms** Swindn........40 C3
**Ninfield** E Susx..............20 E3
**Ningwood** IoW................16 E5
**Nisbet** Border................167 K4
**Nisbet Hill** Border........179 G7
**Niton** IoW......................17 F6
**Nitshill** C Glas..............174 F6
**Nocton** Lincs................117 H8
**Noke** Oxon......................57 K5
**Nolton** Pembks..............48 E4
**Nolton Haven**
Pembks...........................48 E4
**No Man's Heath**
Ches W...........................98 D3
**No Man's Heath**
Warwks...........................86 C2
**Nomansland** Devon......11 J3
**Nomansland** Wilts........28 E7
**Noneley** Shrops..............98 C6
**Nonington** Kent............35 H4
**Nook** Cumb..................129 L3
**Norbiton** Gt Lon............44 D6
**Norbury** Ches E..............98 E3
**Norbury** Derbys............100 C4
**Norbury** Gt Lon............44 F6
**Norbury** Shrops..............83 G5
**Norbury** Staffs..............99 H7
**Norchard** Worcs............70 F2
**Nordelph** Norfk..............90 D4
**Nordley** Shrops..............84 C4
Norfolk Broads Norfk... 93 K2
**Norham** Nthumb..........179 J8
**Norley** Ches W..............112 E6
**Norleywood** Hants........16 D3
**Normanby** Lincs............117 G4
**Normanby** N Linc..........125 K7
**Normanby** N York........134 B3
**Normanby** R & Cl........142 C4
**Normanby le Wold**
Lincs.............................117 J3
**Normandy** Surrey..........30 F2
**Norman's Green**
Devon.............................12 D2
**Normanton** C Derb......101 G5
**Normanton** Leics........102 D4
**Normanton** Notts........102 B2
**Normanton** Wakefd......124 B6
**Normanton le**
Heath Leics................86 D2
**Normanton on**
Cliffe Lincs..............102 F4
**Normanton on Soar**
Notts...........................101 K7
**Normanton on the**
Wolds Notts..............101 L6
**Normanton on Trent**
Notts...........................116 C7
**Norris Green** Lpool......111 L3
**Norris Hill** Leics............86 D1
**Norristhorpe** Kirk........123 J6
**Northall** Bucks..............58 F4
**Northallerton** N York...141 J7
**Northam** C Sotn............29 H8
**Northam** Devon..............23 G5
**Northampton** Nhants....73 L3
**Northampton** Worcs......70 E2
Northampton
Services Nhants......73 K3
**North Anston** Rothm....115 K5
**North Ascot** Br For........42 E6
**North Aston** Oxon........57 J3
**Northaw** Herts..............59 L2
**Northay** Somset............13 H1
**North Baddesley**
Hants.............................29 H7
**North Ballachulish**
Highld.........................191 L4
**North Barrow** Somset...26 E5
**North Barsham** Norfk...105 L5

Northbay W Isls ............ 233 b9
North Benfleet Essex.... 46 C3
North Berwick E Loth... 178 C2
North Boarhunt
Hants.....................17 H1
Northborough C Pete...89 H3
Northbourne Kent.......35 J4
North Bovey Devon .... 11 H7
North Bradley Wilts....27 J1
North Brentor Devon....10 C8
North Brewham
Somset....................27 G4
Northbrook Hants ......29 K4
North Buckland
Devon.....................23 G4
North Burlingham
Norfk......................93 H2
North Cadbury
Somset....................26 F6
North Carlton Lincs .. 116 F6
North Carlton Notts... 115 L4
North Cave E R Yk .... 125 K4
North Cerney Gloucs ...56 A6
North Chailey E Susx...19 K2
Northchapel W Susx....30 F5
North Charford
Hants.....................28 D7
North Charlton
Nthumb ................. 169 H5
North Cheam Gt Lon....44 E6
North Cheriton
Somset....................27 G6
North Chideock
Dorset....................13 K4
Northchurch Herts.....58 F6
North Cliffe E R Yk.... 125 K3
North Clifton Notts.... 116 D6
North Cockerington
Lincs.................... 118 E4
North Connel Ag & B... 182 C1
North Cornelly
Brdgnd....................36 C4
North Cotes Lincs....... 118 E2
Northcott Devon ......... 9 J6
Northcourt Oxon...........57 J7
North Cove Suffk.........93 K5
North Cowton
N York................... 141 G6
North Crawley
M Keyn....................74 D5
North Creake Norfk ... 105 K5
North Curry Somset.....25 L6
North Dalton E R Yk... 125 L1
North Deighton
N York................... 124 B1
Northdown Kent.........35 K2
North Downs..............34 B4
North Duffield
N York................... 125 G3
North Elmham Norfk.. 106 B7
North Elmsall Wakefd.. 124 D7
North End C Port........17 J3
North End Essex..........61 G4
North End Hants..........28 C7
North End Nhants........74 D2
North End W Susx.......18 D5
Northend Warwks.......72 E4
Northenden Manch .... 113 J4
North Erradale
Highld................... 219 H5
North Evington
C Leic......................87 J3
North Fambridge
Essex......................61 K7
North Ferriby E R Yk... 126 B5
Northfield Birm...........85 H7
Northfield C Aber...... 207 G4
Northfield E R Yk...... 126 C5
Northfields Lincs.........88 E2
Northfleet Kent...........45 M5
North Frodingham
E R Yk................... 135 H8
North Gorley Hants....15 M1
North Green Suffk.......79 G3
North Greetwell
Lincs.................... 117 G6
North Grimston
N York................... 134 C6

North Hayling Hants....17 K2
North Hill Cnwll ......... 5 L1
North Hillingdon
Gt Lon....................43 H4
North Hinksey
Village Oxon............57 J6
North Holmwood
Surrey....................31 K3
North Huish Devon....... 7 G5
North Hykeham
Lincs.................... 116 F7
Northiam E Susx..........21 G2
Northill C Beds...........75 G5
Northington Hants......29 K4
North Kelsey Lincs.... 117 H2
North Kessock
Highld................... 213 G5
North Killingholme
N Linc................... 126 E6
North Kilvington
N York................... 132 F3
North Kilworth Leics...87 H6
North Kyme Lincs..... 103 J3
North Landing
E R Yk................... 135 K5
Northlands Lincs....... 104 B2
Northleach Gloucs......56 C5
North Lee Bucks.........58 D6
Northleigh Devon.......12 F3
North Leigh Oxon........57 H5
North Leverton with
Habblesthorpe
Notts.................... 116 C5
Northlew Devon..........10 D5
North Littleton
Worcs.....................71 J5
North Lopham Norfk...92 C6
North Luffenham
Rutlnd....................88 D3
North Marden
W Susx....................30 D7
North Marston Bucks...58 C4
North Middleton
Mdloth.................. 177 K6
North Millbrex Abers.. 216 F5
North Milmain D & G.. 144 C4
North Molton Devon....24 B5
Northmoor Oxon.........57 H7
North Moreton Oxon....41 K3
Northmuir Angus..... 196 C5
North Mundham
W Susx....................18 B5
North Muskham
Notts.................... 102 D2
North Newbald
E R Yk................... 125 L3
North Newington
Oxon......................72 E6
North Newnton Wilts..40 C8
North Newton
Somset....................25 L5
Northney Hants..........17 K2
North Nibley Gloucs....39 H2
Northolt Gt Lon..........43 J4
Northolt Airport
Gt Lon....................43 H4
Northop Flints ........ 111 H7
Northop Hall Flints .. 111 J7
North Ormesby
Middsb.................. 142 B4
North Ormsby Lincs.. 118 C3
Northorpe Kirk......... 123 J6
Northorpe Lincs....... 103 K5
Northorpe Lincs....... 116 E3
North Otterington
N York................... 132 E2
North Owersby Lincs.. 117 H3
Northowram Calder.. 123 G5
North Perrott Somset..13 L1
North Petherton
Somset....................25 L5
North Petherwin
Cnwll....................... 9 H6
North Pickenham
Norfk......................91 J3
North Piddle Worcs....71 G4
North Poorton
Dorset....................13 M3

Northport Dorset........15 H5
North Queensferry
Fife...................... 176 F3
North Rauceby Lincs.. 103 G3
Northrepps Norfk..... 106 F5
North Reston Lincs... 118 E5
North Rigton N York.. 123 K1
North Rode Ches E.... 113 K7
North Roe Shet........ 235 c3
North Ronaldsay Ork.. 234 e3
North Ronaldsay
Airport Ork.......... 234 e3
North Runcton Norfk..90 F1
North Scarle Lincs.... 116 D7
North Shian Ag & B... 191 H7
North Shields N Tyne.. 151 J2
North Shoebury
Sthend....................46 F3
North Shore Bpool ... 120 D3
North Side C Pete......89 K4
North Somercotes
Lincs.................... 118 F3
North Stainley N York.. 132 D4
North Stifford Thurr....45 L4
North Stoke BaNES....39 G6
North Stoke Oxon.......41 L3
North Stoke W Susx....18 D4
North Street Kent......34 D3
North Street W Berk....41 M6
North Sunderland
Nthumb ................. 169 J3
North Tamerton
Cnwll....................... 9 J5
North Tawton Devon....10 F4
North Third Stirlg .... 175 K1
North Thoresby Lincs.. 118 D2
North Tolsta W Isls... 232 g2
Northton W Isls....... 232 d5
North Town Devon......10 D3
North Town Somset.....26 E3
North Town W & M.....42 E4
North Tuddenham
Norfk......................92 C2
North Uist W Isls..... 233 b6
Northumberland
National Park
Nthumb ................. 157 K5
North Walsham
Norfk.................... 107 G6
North Waltham
Hants.....................29 K3
North Warnborough
Hants.....................30 B2
North Weald
Bassett Essex........60 D7
North Wheatley
Notts.................... 116 C4
Northwich Ches W.... 112 F6
Northwick Worcs.......70 E3
North Widcombe
BaNES.....................38 E8
North Willingham
Lincs.................... 117 K4
North Wingfield
Derbys.................. 115 H8
North Witham Lincs.. 102 F7
Northwold Norfk.......91 H4
Northwood Gt Lon.....43 H3
Northwood IoW..........16 F4
Northwood Shrops.....98 C6
Northwood Green
Gloucs....................55 G5
North Wootton
Dorset....................26 F8
North Wootton
Norfk.................... 105 G7
North Wootton
Somset....................26 E3
North Wraxall Wilts....39 J5
North York Moors
National Park....... 142 F6
Norton Donc........... 124 E7
Norton E Susx...........19 M5
Norton Gloucs...........55 J3
Norton Halton........ 112 D5
Norton Nhants...........73 H2
Norton Notts........... 115 L6

Norton Powys............68 F2
Norton S on T.......... 141 K3
Norton Sheff........... 115 G5
Norton Shrops..........84 D4
Norton Suffk.............77 L2
Norton Swans...........51 H7
Norton W Susx..........18 C4
Norton Wilts.............39 K4
Norton Worcs...........70 F4
Norton Worcs...........71 J5
Norton Bavant Wilts....27 K3
Norton Canes Staffs...85 H2
Norton Canes
Services Staffs...........85 H3
Norton Canon Herefs...69 H5
Norton Disney Lincs.. 102 E2
Norton Fitzwarren
Somset....................25 J6
Norton Green IoW.......16 D5
Norton Hawkfield
BaNES.....................38 E7
Norton Heath Essex....60 F6
Norton in Hales
Shrops....................99 G5
Norton-Juxta-
Twycross Leics.......86 D3
Norton-le-Clay
N York................... 132 F5
Norton-le-Moors
C Stke.....................99 K3
Norton Lindsey
Warwks...................72 B2
Norton Little Green
Suffk......................77 L2
Norton Malreward
BaNES.....................38 E7
Norton-on-Derwent
N York................... 134 C5
Norton St Philip
Somset....................27 H1
Norton Subcourse
Norfk......................93 J4
Norton sub Hamdon
Somset....................26 C7
Norwell Notts.......... 102 C1
Norwell Woodhouse
Notts.................... 116 B8
Norwich Norfk...........92 F2
Norwich Airport
Norfk......................92 E2
Norwick Shet.......... 235 e1
Norwood Clacks...... 185 J8
Norwood Green
Gt Lon....................43 J5
Norwood Hill Surrey...31 L3
Norwoodside Cambs...90 B4
Noss Mayo Devon........ 6 E6
Nosterfield N York.... 132 D4
Nostie Highld.......... 210 D8
Notgrove Gloucs........56 C4
Nottage Brdgnd..........36 C5
Nottingham C Nott... 101 L5
Notton Wakefd........ 123 L7
Notton Wilts.............39 K6
Noutard's Green
Worcs.....................70 E2
Nuffield Oxon...........42 A3
Nunburnholme
E R Yk................... 125 K2
Nuneaton Warwks.....86 D5
Nunhead Gt Lon.........45 G5
Nun Monkton N York.. 133 H7
Nunney Somset..........27 G3
Nunnington N York... 133 K4
Nunsthorpe NE Lin... 127 G8
Nunthorpe C York.... 124 F1
Nunthorpe Middsb... 142 C4
Nunthorpe Village
Middsb.................. 142 C5
Nunton Wilts............28 D6
Nunwick N York....... 132 E5
Nursling Hants..........29 G7
Nutbourne W Susx.....17 L2
Nutbourne W Susx.....18 E3
Nutfield Surrey..........32 B3
Nuthall Notts.......... 101 K4
Nuthampstead Herts..76 B7
Nuthurst W Susx........31 K6

Nutley E Susx ...... 32 D7
Nuttall Bury .......... 122 B7
Nybster Highld ...... 231 L3
Nyetimber W Susx ...... 18 B6
Nyewood W Susx ...... 30 D6
Nymans W Susx ...... 31 L5
Nymet Rowland
   Devon .......... 11 G4
Nymet Tracey Devon ...... 11 G5
Nympsfield Gloucs ...... 55 J7
Nynehead Somset ...... 25 H6
Nyton W Susx ...... 18 C5

## O

Oadby Leics .......... 87 J4
Oad Street Kent ...... 34 B3
Oakamoor Staffs ...... 100 B4
Oakbank W Loth ...... 176 E5
Oak Cross Devon ...... 10 D5
Oakdale Caerph ...... 37 J2
Oake Somset .......... 25 J6
Oaken Staffs .......... 84 F3
Oakenclough Lancs ...... 121 H2
Oakengates Wrekin ...... 84 C2
Oakenshaw Dur ...... 150 F7
Oakenshaw Kirk ...... 123 H5
Oakford Cerdgn ...... 66 B3
Oakford Devon ...... 24 E6
Oakham RutInd ...... 88 C2
Oakhanger Hants ...... 30 C4
Oakhill Somset ...... 26 F3
Oakington Cambs ...... 76 B2
Oaklands Herts ...... 59 L4
Oakle Street Gloucs ...... 55 H4
Oakley Bed .......... 74 E4
Oakley Bucks .......... 57 M5
Oakley Fife .......... 176 D1
Oakley Hants .......... 29 K2
Oakley Suffk .......... 92 E7
Oakridge Lynch
   Gloucs .......... 55 K7
Oaksey Wilts .......... 39 M2
Oakthorpe Leics ...... 86 D2
Oakwood C Derb ...... 101 G5
Oakworth C Brad ...... 122 F3
Oare Kent .......... 34 D3
Oare Somset .......... 24 C3
Oare Wilts .......... 40 D7
Oasby Lincs .......... 103 G5
Oath Somset .......... 26 B6
Oathlaw Angus ...... 196 D5
Oatlands Park Surrey ...... 43 H7
Oban Ag & B .......... 182 B2
Oban Airport Ag & B ...... 182 C1
Obley Shrops .......... 83 G7
Obney P & K .......... 195 G8
Oborne Dorset .......... 26 F7
Occold Suffk .......... 78 D1
Occumster Highld ...... 231 J7
Ockbrook Derbys ...... 101 H5
Ocker Hill Sandw ...... 85 H5
Ockham Surrey .......... 31 H1
Ockle Highld .......... 190 B3
Ockley Surrey .......... 31 J4
Ocle Pychard Herefs ...... 69 L5
Odcombe Somset ...... 26 D7
Odd Down BaNES ...... 39 H7
Oddingley Worcs ...... 71 G3
Oddington Oxon ...... 57 K5
Odell Bed .......... 74 D3
Odiham Hants .......... 30 C2
Odsal C Brad .......... 123 H5
Odsey Cambs .......... 75 K6
Odstock Wilts .......... 28 D6
Odstone Leics .......... 86 E3
Offchurch Warwks ...... 72 D2
Offenham Worcs ...... 71 J5
Offerton Stockp ...... 113 K4
Offham E Susx ...... 19 L3
Offham Kent .......... 33 H2
Offham W Susx ...... 18 D4
Offord Cluny Cambs ...... 75 J2
Offord D'Arcy Cambs ...... 75 J2
Offton Suffk .......... 78 C5

Offwell Devon .......... 12 F3
Ogbourne Maizey
   Wilts .......... 40 D6
Ogbourne St
   Andrew Wilts ...... 40 D6
Ogbourne St
   George Wilts ...... 40 D5
Ogle Nthumb .......... 158 E6
Oglet L'pool .......... 112 C5
Ogmore V Glam ...... 36 D5
Ogmore-by-Sea
   V Glam. .......... 36 D5
Ogmore Vale Brdgnd ...... 36 E3
Okeford Fitzpaine
   Dorset .......... 14 F1
Okehampton Devon ...... 10 E5
Oker Side Derbys ...... 100 F1
Okewood Hill Surrey ...... 31 J4
Old Nhants .......... 87 L8
Old Aberdeen C Aber ...... 207 H4
Old Alresford Hants ...... 29 L5
Oldany Highld .......... 224 D2
Old Arley Warwks ...... 86 C5
Old Auchenbrack
   D & G .......... 154 D3
Old Basford C Nott ...... 101 K4
Old Basing Hants ...... 30 A2
Old Beetley Norfk ...... 106 A8
Oldberrow Warwks ...... 71 K2
Old Bewick Nthumb ...... 169 G5
Old Bolingbroke
   Lincs .......... 118 E8
Old Bramhope Leeds ...... 123 J2
Old Brampton
   Derbys .......... 115 G6
Old Bridge of Urr
   D & G .......... 146 D2
Old Buckenham
   Norfk .......... 92 C5
Old Burghclere
   Hants .......... 41 J8
Oldbury Sandw ...... 85 H5
Oldbury Shrops ...... 84 C5
Oldbury Warwks ...... 86 C5
Oldbury-on-Severn
   S Glos .......... 38 E2
Oldbury on the Hill
   Gloucs .......... 39 J3
Old Byland N York ...... 133 H3
Old Cantley Donc ...... 115 L2
Oldcastle Mons ...... 53 L3
Old Catton Norfk ...... 92 F2
Old Clee NE Lin ...... 127 G8
Old Cleeve Somset ...... 25 G3
Old Colwyn Conwy ...... 110 B6
Oldcotes Notts ...... 115 L4
Old Dailly S Ayrs ...... 152 F3
Old Dalby Leics ...... 102 A7
Old Deer Abers ...... 217 J5
Old Edlington Donc ...... 115 K3
Old Ellerby E R Yk ...... 126 E3
Old Felixstowe Suffk ...... 79 G7
Oldfield Worcs ...... 70 E2
Old Fletton C Pete ...... 89 H4
Oldford Somset ...... 27 H2
Old Forge Herefs ...... 54 E4
Old Grimsby IoS ...... 2 a1
Old Hall Green Herts ...... 60 B4
Oldham Oldham ...... 113 L1
Oldhamstocks E Loth ...... 178 F4
Old Harlow Essex ...... 60 D5
Old Hunstanton
   Norfk .......... 105 G4
Old Hurst Cambs ...... 89 K7
Old Hutton Cumb ...... 130 B2
Old Inns Services
   N Lans .......... 175 K3
Old Kilpatrick
   W Duns .......... 174 E4
Old Knebworth Herts ...... 59 L4
Old Lakenham Norfk ...... 92 F3
Oldland S Glos ...... 38 F6
Old Langho Lancs ...... 121 K4
Old Leake Lincs ...... 104 C3
Old Malton N York ...... 134 C4
Oldmeldrum Abers ...... 216 F8
Oldmill Cnwll .......... 6 B2

Old Milverton
   Warwks .......... 72 C2
Oldmixon N Som ...... 37 M8
Old Newton Suffk ...... 78 C3
Old Portlethen Abers. ...... 207 H6
Old Radford C Nott ...... 101 K4
Old Radnor Powys ...... 68 E3
Old Rayne Abers ...... 216 D8
Old Romney Kent ...... 21 K2
Old Shoreham
   W Susx .......... 19 G4
Oldshoremore Highld. ...... 228 C4
Old Sodbury S Glos ...... 39 H4
Old Somerby Lincs ...... 102 F5
Oldstead N York ...... 133 H4
Old Stratford Nhants ...... 73 L6
Old Struan P & K ...... 194 C4
Old Swinford Dudley ...... 84 F6
Old Thirsk N York ...... 132 F3
Old Town Cumb. ...... 130 B3
Old Town E Susx ...... 20 C5
Old Town IoS .......... 2 b2
Old Trafford Traffd ...... 113 J3
Oldwall Cumb .......... 148 E3
Oldwalls Swans ...... 50 F6
Old Warden C Beds ...... 75 G5
Old Weston Cambs ...... 89 G7
Old Wick Highld ...... 231 L5
Old Windsor W & M ...... 43 G5
Old Wives Lees Kent ...... 34 E4
Old Woking Surrey ...... 43 G8
Olgrinmore Highld ...... 231 G5
Olive Green Staffs ...... 100 C8
Oliver's Battery
   Hants .......... 29 J6
Ollaberry Shet ...... 235 c3
Ollach Highld .......... 209 H6
Ollerton Ches E ...... 113 H6
Ollerton Notts. ...... 116 A7
Ollerton Shrops ...... 98 F7
Olney M Keyn ...... 74 C4
Olrig House Highld. ...... 231 H3
Olton Solhll .......... 85 K6
Olveston S Glos ...... 38 E3
Ombersley Worcs ...... 70 E2
Ompton Notts ...... 116 B7
Onchan IoM .......... 237 d5
Onecote Staffs ...... 100 B2
Onibury Shrops ...... 83 J7
Onich Highld .......... 191 K4
Onllwyn Neath ...... 52 C6
Onneley Staffs ...... 99 H4
Onslow Green Essex ...... 61 G4
Onslow Village
   Surrey .......... 31 G2
Onston Ches W ...... 112 E6
Opinan Highld .......... 219 H6
Orbliston Moray ...... 215 G3
Orbost Highld .......... 208 D5
Orby Lincs .......... 119 G7
Orchard Portman
   Somset .......... 25 K6
Orcheston Wilts ...... 28 B3
Orcop Herefs .......... 54 C3
Orcop Hill Herefs ...... 54 C3
Ord Abers .......... 216 C3
Ordhead Abers ...... 206 C3
Ordie Abers .......... 205 K5
Ordiequish Moray ...... 215 H3
Ordsall Notts .......... 116 B5
Ore E Susx .......... 21 G4
Orford Suffk .......... 79 J4
Orford Warrtn ...... 112 E4
Organford Dorset ...... 15 H4
Orkney Islands Ork ...... 234 c6
Orkney Neolithic
   Ork .......... 234 b6
Orlestone Kent ...... 34 D7
Orleton Herefs ...... 69 J2
Orleton Worcs ...... 70 C2
Orlingbury Nhants ...... 74 C1
Ormesby R & Cl ...... 142 C4
Ormesby St
   Margaret Norfk ...... 93 K1
Ormesby St Michael
   Norfk .......... 93 K1
Ormiscaig Highld ...... 219 K4
Ormiston E Loth ...... 177 L4

Ormsaigmore Highld ...... 189 L4
Ormsary Ag & B ...... 172 C4
Ormskirk Lancs ...... 120 F8
Oronsay Ag & B ...... 171 G2
Orphir Ork .......... 234 b6
Orpington Gt Lon ...... 45 J6
Orrell Sefton .......... 111 K3
Orrell Wigan .......... 112 D2
Orroland D & G ...... 146 D5
Orsett Thurr .......... 45 M4
Orslow Staffs .......... 84 E1
Orston Notts .......... 102 C4
Orton Cumb .......... 138 F5
Orton Nhants .......... 88 B7
Orton Staffs .......... 84 F4
Orton Longueville
   C Pete .......... 89 H4
Orton-on-the-Hill
   Leics .......... 86 C3
Orton Waterville
   C Pete .......... 89 H4
Orwell Cambs .......... 75 L4
Osbaldeston Lancs ...... 121 J4
Osbaldwick C York. ...... 124 F1
Osbaston Leics ...... 86 E3
Osbaston Shrops ...... 97 L7
Osborne House IoW ...... 17 G4
Osbournby Lincs ...... 103 H5
Oscroft Ches W ...... 112 D7
Ose Highld. .......... 208 E6
Osgathorpe Leics ...... 101 H8
Osgodby Lincs ...... 117 H3
Osgodby N York ...... 124 F4
Osgodby N York ...... 135 G3
Oskaig Highld. .......... 209 H6
Oskamull Ag & B ...... 189 L7
Osmaston Derbys ...... 100 D4
Osmington Dorset ...... 14 D5
Osmington Mills
   Dorset .......... 14 E6
Osmondthorpe
   Leeds .......... 123 L4
Osmotherley N York ...... 141 K7
Osney Oxon .......... 57 J6
Ospringe Kent ...... 34 D3
Ossett Wakefd ...... 123 K6
Ossington Notts ...... 116 C8
Osterley Gt Lon ...... 44 D5
Oswaldkirk N York ...... 133 K4
Oswaldtwistle Lancs ...... 121 L5
Oswestry Shrops ...... 97 L6
Otairnis W Isls ...... 232 c5
Otford Kent .......... 32 F2
Otham Kent .......... 33 K3
Othery Somset ...... 26 B5
Otley Leeds .......... 123 J2
Otley Suffk .......... 78 E4
Otterbourne Hants ...... 29 J6
Otterburn N York. ...... 131 G7
Otterburn Nthumb ...... 157 M4
Otter Ferry Ag & B ...... 172 C2
Otterham Cnwll ...... 8 F6
Otterhampton
   Somset .......... 25 K3
Otternish W Isls ...... 232 c5
Ottershaw Surrey ...... 43 G7
Otterswick Shet ...... 235 d3
Otterton Devon ...... 12 E5
Ottery St Mary Devon ...... 12 E4
Ottinge Kent .......... 34 F6
Ottringham E R Yk. ...... 127 G5
Oughterside Cumb ...... 147 K6
Oughtibridge Sheff ...... 114 F3
Oughtrington Warrtn ...... 113 G4
Oulston N York. ...... 133 H5
Oulton Cumb .......... 147 M5
Oulton Norfk .......... 106 C6
Oulton Staffs .......... 99 K5
Oulton Suffk .......... 93 L5
Oulton Broad Suffk ...... 93 L5
Oulton Street Norfk ...... 106 D6
Oundle Nhants ...... 88 F6
Ounsdale Staffs ...... 84 F5
Our Dynamic Earth
   C Edin .......... 177 H4
Ousby Cumb .......... 149 G2
Ousden Suffk .......... 77 G3
Ousefleet E R Yk. ...... 125 K6

Ouston Dur......151 G4
Outgate Cumb......137 K7
Outhgill Cumb......139 H6
Outhill Warwks......71 K2
Outlane Kirk......123 G6
Out Rawcliffe Lancs. 120 E3
Out Skerries Shet...235 e4
Outwell Norfk......90 D3
Outwood Surrey......32 B4
Outwoods Staffs......99 H8
Ouzlewell Green
  Leeds......123 L5
Ovenden Calder...123 G5
Over Cambs......75 L1
Over Ches W......112 F7
Overbury Worcs......71 G6
Overcombe Dorset...14 D6
Over Compton
  Dorset......26 E7
Over Haddon Derbys...114 D7
Over Hulton Bolton...113 G1
Over Kellet Lancs...129 L5
Over Kiddington
  Oxon......57 H4
Overleigh Somset......26 C4
Over Norton Oxon......56 F3
Over Peover Ches E...113 H6
Overpool Ches W......111 L6
Overscaig Highld......225 J4
Overseal Derbys......86 C1
Over Silton N York...133 G2
Oversland Kent......34 E3
Overstone Nhants......74 B2
Over Stowey Somset...25 J4
Overstrand Norfk......106 F4
Over Stratton Somset...26 B7
Overthorpe Nhants......72 F6
Overton C Aber......207 G3
Overton Hants......29 K2
Overton Lancs......129 J7
Overton N York......133 H7
Overton Shrops......69 K1
Overton Swans......50 F7
Overton Wakefd......123 K7
Overtown N Lans......175 L7
Over Wallop Hants......28 F4
Over Whitacre
  Warwks......86 B5
Over Worton Oxon......57 H3
Oving Bucks......58 C4
Oving W Susx......18 B5
Ovingdean Br & H......19 K5
Ovingham Nthumb...150 D3
Ovington Dur......140 E4
Ovington Essex......77 H6
Ovington Hants......29 K5
Ovington Norfk......91 K3
Ovington Nthumb...150 D3
Ower Hants......28 F7
Owermoigne Dorset...14 E5
Owlerton Sheff......115 G4
Owlsmoor Br For......42 D7
Owlswick Bucks......58 C6
Owmby Lincs......117 G4
Owmby Lincs......117 H1
Owslebury Hants......29 K6
Owston Donc......124 E7
Owston Leics......87 L3
Owston Ferry N Linc...116 D2
Owstwick E R Yk......127 G4
Owthorne E R Yk......127 H5
Owthorpe Notts......102 A5
Owton Manor Hartpl...141 L2
Oxborough Norfk......91 G3
Oxcombe Lincs......118 D6
Oxenholme Cumb...129 L2
Oxenhope C Brad...122 F4
Oxen Park Cumb......129 G3
Oxenpill Somset......26 C3
Oxenton Gloucs......55 L2
Oxenwood Wilts......40 F8
Oxford Oxon......57 K6
Oxford Airport Oxon...57 J5
Oxford Services
  Oxon......57 L6
Oxgangs C Edin......177 H4
Oxhey Herts......43 J2

Oxhill Dur......150 F4
Oxhill Warwks......72 C5
Oxley Wolves......84 F3
Oxley Green Essex...61 L5
Oxlode Cambs......90 C6
Oxnam Border......167 L5
Oxnead Norfk......106 F7
Oxshott Surrey......43 J7
Oxspring Barns......114 F2
Oxted Surrey......32 D3
Oxton Border......178 B7
Oxton N York......124 D2
Oxton Notts......101 M3
Oxton Wirral......111 J4
Oxwich Swans......51 G7
Oxwich Green Swans...50 F7
Oykel Bridge Highld...221 K2
Oyne Abers......206 D1
Oystermouth Swans...51 H7

P

Pabail W Isls......232 g2
Packington Leics......86 D1
Packmoor C Stke......99 K2
Padanaram Angus...196 C6
Padbury Bucks......58 B2
Paddington Gt Lon......44 F4
Paddlesworth Kent...35 G6
Paddlesworth Kent......46 B7
Paddock Wood Kent...33 H4
Padiham Lancs......122 B4
Padside N York......132 B7
Padstow Cnwll......4 E2
Padworth W Berk......41 L7
Pagham W Susx......18 B6
Paglesham Essex......46 F2
Paignton Torbay......7 K4
Pailton Warwks......86 F6
Painscastle Powys......68 D5
Painshawfield
  Nthumb......150 D3
Painsthorpe E R Yk...134 C7
Painswick Gloucs......55 K6
Painter's Forstal
  Kent......34 D3
Paisley Rens......174 E5
Pakefield Suffk......93 L5
Pakenham Suffk......77 L2
Paley Street W & M...42 E5
Palfrey Wsall......85 H4
Palgrave Suffk......92 D7
Pallington Dorset......14 E4
Palmarsh Kent......34 F7
Palmerston E Ayrs...163 L5
Palnackie D & G......146 E4
Palnure D & G......145 J3
Palterton Derbys......115 J7
Pamber End Hants......41 L8
Pamber Green Hants...41 L8
Pamber Heath Hants...41 L7
Pamington Gloucs......55 L2
Pamphill Dorset......15 J3
Pampisford Cambs...76 C5
Panbride Angus......187 J1
Pancrasweek Devon......9 H4
Pandy Mons......53 M4
Pandy Tudur Conwy...110 B8
Panfield Essex......61 H3
Pangbourne W Berk...41 M5
Pangdean W Susx......19 J4
Pannal N York......123 L1
Pannal Ash N York...132 D8
Pant Shrops......97 L7
Pantasaph Flints......111 G6
Pant-ffrwyth Brdgnd...36 E4
Pant Glas Gwynd......95 H3
Pantglas Powys......81 G4
Panton Lincs......117 K5
Pantside Caerph......37 K2
Pant-y-dwr Powys......81 L8
Pantymwyn Flints......111 H8
Panxworth Norfk......93 H2
Papa Stour Shet......235 b5
Papa Stour Airport
  Shet......235 b5

Papa Westray Ork...234 c3
Papa Westray
  Airport Ork......234 c3
Papcastle Cumb......136 F2
Papigoe Highld......231 L5
Papple E Loth......178 D4
Papplewick Notts......101 K3
Papworth Everard
  Cambs......75 K3
Papworth St Agnes
  Cambs......75 J2
Par Cnwll......5 G5
Parbold Lancs......121 G7
Parbrook Somset......26 E4
Parc Gwynd......96 D5
Parc Seymour Newpt...38 B3
Pardshaw Cumb......136 F3
Parham Suffk......79 G3
Park D & G......154 F4
Park Nthumb......149 H3
Park Corner Oxon......42 B3
Parkend Gloucs......54 E6
Parker's Green Kent...33 G4
Park Farm Kent......34 D6
Parkgate Ches W......111 J6
Parkgate D & G......155 H4
Park Gate Hants......17 G2
Park Gate Leeds......123 J3
Parkgate Surrey......31 K3
Parkhall W Duns......174 E4
Parkham Devon......22 F6
Parkmill Swans......51 G7
Park Royal Gt Lon......44 D4
Parkside Dur......151 K5
Parkside N Lans......175 L6
Parkstone BCP......15 J4
Park Street Herts......59 J6
Parracombe Devon......23 L3
Parson Drove Cambs...89 L2
Parson's Heath Essex...62 B3
Partick C Glas......174 F5
Partington Traffd...113 G3
Partney Lincs......118 F7
Parton Cumb......136 D3
Partridge Green
  W Susx......19 G2
Parwich Derbys......100 D2
Passenham Nhants...73 L6
Paston C Pete......89 H3
Paston Norfk......107 G5
Patcham Br & H......19 J4
Patching W Susx......18 E4
Patchway S Glos......38 E4
Pateley Bridge
  N York......132 B6
Pathhead Fife......186 E8
Pathhead Mdloth...177 K5
Path of Condie
  P & K......185 M5
Patna E Ayrs......163 K7
Patney Wilts......40 B8
Patrick IoM......237 b5
Patrick Brompton
  N York......132 C2
Patricroft Salfd......113 H2
Patrington E R Yk...127 H6
Patrington Haven
  E R Yk......127 H6
Patrixbourne Kent...35 G4
Patterdale Cumb......137 L4
Pattingham Staffs......84 E4
Pattishall Nhants......73 J4
Pattiswick Green
  Essex......61 K3
Paul Cnwll......2 E5
Paulerspury Nhants...73 K5
Paull E R Yk......126 E5
Paulton BaNES......26 F1
Paultons Park Hants...28 F4
Pauperhaugh
  Nthumb......158 D3
Pavenham Bed......74 E4
Pawlett Somset......25 L3
Paxford Gloucs......71 L6
Paxton Border......179 J7
Payhembury Devon...12 E3
Paythorne Lancs......122 C1
Peacehaven E Susx...19 L5

Peak District
  National Park......114 D3
Peak Forest Derbys...114 C5
Peakirk C Pete......89 H3
Peasedown St John
  BaNES......39 G8
Peasemore W Berk......41 J5
Peasenhall Suffk......79 H2
Pease Pottage
  W Susx......31 L5
Pease Pottage
  Services W Susx...31 L5
Peaslake Surrey......31 H3
Peasley Cross St Hel...112 D3
Peasmarsh E Susx......21 H2
Peathill Abers......217 H2
Peat Inn Fife......187 G5
Peatling Magna
  Leics......87 H5
Peatling Parva Leics...87 H6
Pebmarsh Essex......77 J7
Pebsham E Susx......20 F4
Pebworth Worcs......71 K5
Pecket Well Calder...122 E5
Peckforton Ches E......98 D2
Peckham Gt Lon......45 G5
Peckleton Leics......86 F4
Pedlinge Kent......34 F7
Pedmore Dudley......85 G6
Pedwell Somset......26 B4
Peebles Border......166 C2
Peel IoM......237 b4
Peene Kent......35 G6
Pegsdon C Beds......59 J2
Pegswood Nthumb...159 G5
Pegwell Kent......35 K2
Peinchorran Highld...209 H7
Peinlich Highld......208 F3
Peldon Essex......62 B5
Pelsall Wsall......85 H3
Pelton Dur......151 G4
Pelynt Cnwll......5 K5
Pemberton Carmth...51 G5
Pemberton Wigan...112 D2
Pembrey Carmth......50 E5
Pembridge Herefs......69 H3
Pembroke Pembks......49 G7
Pembroke Dock
  Pembks......49 G6
Pembrokeshire
  Coast National
  Park Pembks......48 E4
Pembury Kent......33 G5
Pen-allt Herefs......54 E3
Penallt Mons......54 D6
Penally Pembks......49 J7
Penarth V Glam......37 J6
Pen-bont
  Rhydybeddau
  Cerdgn......80 F6
Penbryn Cerdgn......65 J4
Pencader Carmth......66 B7
Pencaitland E Loth...177 L5
Pencarnisiog IoA......108 D6
Pencarreg Carmth......66 C5
Pencelli Powys......53 H3
Penclawdd Swans......51 G6
Pencoed Brdgnd......36 E4
Pencombe Herefs......69 L4
Pencraig Herefs......54 E4
Pencraig Powys......97 G6
Pendeen Cnwll......2 C4
Penderyn Rhondd......52 E6
Pendine Carmth......50 B4
Pendlebury Salfd......113 H2
Pendleton Lancs......121 L3
Pendock Worcs......55 H2
Pendoggett Cnwll......8 D8
Pendomer Somset......13 M1
Pendoylan V Glam......37 G5
Penegoes Powys......81 G4
Pen-ffordd Pembks...49 J3
Pengam Caerph......37 J2
Pengam Cardif......37 K5
Penge Gt Lon......45 G6
Pengelly Cnwll......8 E7
Penhallow Cnwll......3 J4
Penhalvean Cnwll......3 J4

Penhill Swindn..............40 D3
Penhow Newpt.............38 B3
Penicuik Mdloth.........177 H6
Penifiler Highld.........209 G6
Peninver Ag & B........161 J4
Penistone Barns........114 E2
Penkill S Ayrs...........152 F3
Penkridge Staffs.........85 G2
Penley Wrexhm............98 B4
Penllyn V Glam............36 F5
Penmachno Conwy......96 C3
Penmaen Caerph.........37 J2
Penmaen Swans...........51 G7
Penmaenmawr
    Conwy...................109 K6
Penmaenpool Gwynd...95 M8
Penmark V Glam...........37 G6
Penmynydd IoA..........109 G6
Pennal Gwynd...............80 F4
Pennan Abers............216 F2
Pennant Powys.............81 J4
Pennar Pembks............49 G6
Pennerley Shrops.........83 G4
Pennines..................122 E4
Pennington Cumb.......128 F4
Pennorth Powys...........53 H3
Penn Street Bucks........42 F2
Penny Bridge Cumb....129 G3
Pennycross Ag & B.....181 G3
Pennyghael Ag & B.....181 H3
Pennyglen S Ayrs........163 H7
Pennymoor Devon........11 K3
Pennywell Sundld.......151 J4
Penparc Cerdgn...........65 H5
Penperlleni Mons.........53 L6
Penpoll Cnwll...............5 J5
Penponds Cnwll............3 H4
Penpont D & G...........154 E4
Pen-rhiw Pembks.........65 H6
Penrhiwceiber
    Rhondd..................37 G2
Pen Rhiwfawr Neath....51 L4
Penrhiwllan Cerdgn......65 K6
Penrhiwpal Cerdgn......65 K5
Penrhos Gwynd............94 F5
Penrhos Mons..............54 B5
Penrhyn Bay Conwy...110 A5
Penrhyn-coch
    Cerdgn...................80 E6
Penrhyndeudraeth
    Gwynd....................95 K5
Penrice Swans..............50 F7
Penrioch N Ayrs..........161 L1
Penrith Cumb.............138 D2
Penrose Cnwll...............4 D2
Penruddock Cumb......138 B2
Penryn Cnwll................3 K4
Pensarn Conwy..........110 C5
Pensax Worcs..............70 C2
Penselwood Somset.....27 H5
Pensford BaNES...........38 F7
Pensham Worcs...........71 G5
Penshaw Sundld.........151 H4
Penshurst Kent............32 F4
Pensilva Cnwll..............5 L2
Pensnett Dudley...........85 G5
Pentewan Cnwll.............4 F6
Pentir Gwynd.............109 H7
Pentire Cnwll................4 C4
Pentlow Essex..............77 J5
Pentney Norfk..............91 G2
Pentonbridge Cumb...156 D6
Penton Mewsey
    Hants.....................29 G3
Pentraeth IoA.............109 G5
Pentre Mons................54 B7
Pentre Rhondd............36 F2
Pentre Shrops..............98 A8
Pentrebach Myr Td......53 G7
Pentre-bach Powys.......52 E2
Pentrecelyn Denbgs......97 J2
Pentre-celyn Powys......81 J3
Pentre-chwyth
    Swans....................51 J6
Pentre-cwrt Carmth.....65 L6
Pentredwr Denbgs........97 J3
Pentrefelin Gwynd........95 J5

Pentrefoelas Conwy......96 D3
Pentregat Cerdgn.........65 K4
Pentre-Gwenlais
    Carmth...................51 H3
Pentre Hodrey
    Shrops....................83 G7
Pentre Llanrhaeadr
    Denbgs..................110 F8
Pentre Meyrick
    V Glam....................36 E5
Pentre-tafarn-y-
    fedw Conwy.............96 C1
Pentrich Derbys..........101 G3
Pentridge Dorset..........28 B7
Pentwyn Cardif............37 J4
Pen-twyn Mons............54 D6
Pentwynmaur Caerph....37 J2
Pentyrch Cardif............37 H4
Penwithick Cnwll............5 G5
Penybanc Carmth..........51 H2
Penybont Powys............68 C2
Pen-y-bont Powys.........97 K7
Penybontfawr Powys.....97 G7
Pen-y-bryn Pembks......65 G6
Penycae Wrexhm..........97 L4
Pen-y-clawdd Mons......54 C6
Pen-y-coedcae
    Rhondd...................37 G3
Penycwm Pembks.........48 E3
Pen-y-felin Flints.........111 G7
Penyffordd Flints..........97 L1
Pen-y-Garnedd
    Powys.....................97 H7
Pen-y-graig Gwynd.......94 D5
Penygraig Rhondd........36 F3
Penygroes Carmth.........51 H3
Penygroes Gwynd.........95 H2
Pen-y-Mynydd
    Carmth...................50 F5
Penymynydd Flints.......97 L1
Penysarn IoA..............108 F4
Pen-y-stryt Denbgs......97 J3
Penywaun Rhondd........52 F6
Penzance Cnwll.............2 E5
Peopleton Worcs..........71 G4
Peplow Shrops..............98 F7
Perceton N Ayrs..........163 J2
Percyhorner Abers.......217 H2
Perelle Guern..............236 b3
Perham Down Wilts......28 E2
Periton Somset............24 E3
Perivale Gt Lon............44 D4
Perkins Village
    Devon.....................12 D4
Perlethorpe Notts.......115 M7
Perranarworthal
    Cnwll......................3 K4
Perranporth Cnwll.........3 K1
Perranuthnoe Cnwll.......2 F5
Perranwell Cnwll............3 K4
Perranzabuloe Cnwll......3 K2
Perry Birm.................85 J5
Perry Cambs................75 G2
Perry Barr Birm............85 J5
Perry Green Wilts.........39 L3
Pershall Staffs..............99 J6
Pershore Worcs............71 G5
Pertenhall Bed.............74 F2
Perth P & K...............186 B3
Perthy Shrops..............98 A5
Perton Herefs...............69 L6
Perton Staffs................84 F4
Peterborough C Pete......89 H4
Peterborough
    Services Cambs........89 G5
Peterchurch Herefs......69 G6
Peterculter C Aber.......206 F5
Peterhead Abers.........217 L5
Peterlee Dur...............151 K6
Petersfield Hants..........30 C6
Peter's Green Herts......59 J4
Petersham Gt Lon.........44 D5
Peters Marland
    Devon.....................10 C3
Peterstone
    Wentlooge Newpt....37 K4
Peterston-super-
    Ely V Glam..............37 G5

Peterstow Herefs..........54 E3
Peter Tavy Devon...........6 D1
Petham Kent...............34 F4
Petherwin Gate
    Cnwll.......................9 H6
Petrockstow Devon......10 D3
Pett E Susx................21 H3
Pettaugh Suffk.............78 E3
Petterden Angus.........196 C7
Pettinain S Lans..........165 J2
Pettistree Suffk............79 G4
Petton Devon................24 F6
Petts Wood Gt Lon........45 J6
Pettycur Fife...............177 H2
Pettymuk Abers..........207 G1
Petworth W Susx..........31 G6
Pevensey E Susx..........20 D5
Pevensey Bay E Susx....20 D5
Pewsey Wilts................40 D7
Pewsham Wilts.............39 L6
Phepson Worcs............71 G3
Philham Devon.............22 D6
Philiphaugh Border......166 F4
Phillack Cnwll................2 F4
Philleigh Cnwll..............4 D7
Philpstoun W Loth.......176 E3
Phoenix Green Hants....30 C1
Pibsbury Somset...........26 C6
Pickburn Donc............115 K1
Pickering N York.........134 C3
Pickford Covtry............86 C6
Pickhill N York.............132 E3
Picklescott Shrops.........83 J4
Pickmere Ches E.........113 G4
Pickney Somset............25 J5
Pickwell Leics...............87 L2
Pickworth Lincs..........103 H5
Pickworth Rutlnd..........88 E2
Picton Ches W.............112 B7
Picton N York..............141 K5
Piddinghoe E Susx........19 L5
Piddington Nhants........74 B4
Piddington Oxon..........57 M5
Piddlehinton Dorset......14 D3
Piddletrenthide
    Dorset....................14 D3
Pidley Cambs...............89 K7
Piercebridge Darltn.....140 F4
Pierowall Ork..............234 C3
Pilgrims Hatch Essex....45 L2
Pilham Lincs...............116 E3
Pillaton Cnwll................6 A3
Pillerton Hersey
    Warwks...................72 C5
Pillerton Priors
    Warwks...................72 C5
Pilley Barns................115 G2
Pilley Hants................16 D3
Pillgwenlly Newpt.........37 L3
Pilling Lancs...............120 E2
Pilning S Glos...............38 D4
Pilsbury Derbys..........114 C8
Pilsdon Dorset.............13 K3
Pilsley Derbys.............101 H1
Pilsley Derbys.............114 E7
Pilson Green Norfk.......93 H2
Piltdown E Susx...........19 L2
Pilton Devon................23 J5
Pilton Nhants................88 E6
Pilton Rutlnd................88 D3
Pilton Somset..............26 E3
Pimlico Herts...............59 H6
Pimperne Dorset..........15 G1
Pinchbeck Lincs..........103 L7
Pin Green Herts............59 L3
Pinhoe Devon..............12 C4
Pinley Green Warwks....72 B2
Pinminnoch S Ayrs.....152 E4
Pinmore S Ayrs..........152 E4
Pinn Devon..................12 E5
Pinner Gt Lon...............43 J3
Pinner Green Gt Lon......43 J3
Pinvin Worcs...............71 G5
Pinwherry S Ayrs........152 E5
Pinxton Derbys...........101 J2
Pipe and Lyde Herefs....69 K5
Pipe Aston Herefs.........69 J1
Pipe Gate Shrops.........99 G4

Piperdam Angus..........186 E1
Piperhill Highld...........213 K4
Pipewell Nhants...........88 B6
Pirbright Surrey...........30 F1
Pirnie Border..............167 K4
Pirnmill N Ayrs...........161 L1
Pirton Herts.................59 J2
Pishill Oxon.................42 B3
Pistyll Gwynd................94 F4
Pitblae Abers..............217 J2
Pitcairngreen P & K.....185 M3
Pitcalnie Highld..........223 H6
Pitcaple Abers............206 D1
Pitcarity Angus...........196 B4
Pitchcombe Gloucs.......55 J6
Pitchcott Bucks............58 C4
Pitchford Shrops...........83 K3
Pitch Green Bucks........58 C7
Pitchroy Moray...........214 E6
Pitcombe Somset..........26 F4
Pitcox E Loth..............178 E4
Pitfichie Abers............206 D3
Pitglassie Abers..........216 D5
Pitgrudy Highld...........223 H3
Pitlessie Fife...............186 E5
Pitlochry P & K..........194 E5
Pitmachie Abers..........216 C8
Pitmain Highld............203 H5
Pitmedden Abers.........217 G8
Pitmedden Garden
    Abers.....................217 G8
Pitminster Somset........25 K7
Pitmuies Angus...........196 F6
Pitmunie Abers............206 C3
Pitney Somset..............26 C5
Pitroddie P & K..........186 C3
Pitscottie Fife.............187 G5
Pitsea Essex.................46 C3
Pitsford Nhants.............73 L2
Pitstone Bucks.............58 F5
Pittarrow Abers..........197 H2
Pittenweem Fife..........187 J6
Pitteuchar Fife............186 D7
Pittodrie House
    Hotel Abers............206 D1
Pitton Wilts.................28 E5
Pittulie Abers.............217 H2
Pity Me Dur...............151 G5
Pixham Surrey.............31 K2
Plains N Lans.............175 L5
Plaish Shrops...............83 K4
Plaistow Gt Lon............45 H4
Plaistow W Susx...........31 G5
Plaitford Hants.............28 F7
Plawsworth Dur..........151 G5
Plaxtol Kent.................33 G3
Playden E Susx............21 H1
Playford Suffk..............78 F5
Play Hatch Oxon..........42 C5
Playing Place Cnwll........4 C7
Playley Green Gloucs....55 H2
Plealey Shrops..............83 H3
Plean Stirlg................175 L2
Pleasance Fife............186 D5
Pleasington Bl w D......121 J5
Pleasley Derbys..........115 J8
Pleasurewood Hills
    Suffk......................93 L4
Pleinheaume Guern.....236 d2
Plemont Jersey...........236 a5
Plemstall Ches W.........112 C7
Pleshey Essex..............61 G5
Plockton Highld..........210 D2
Plowden Shrops............83 H6
Pluckley Kent................34 B5
Pluckley Thorne Kent....34 B5
Plumbland Cumb........147 K6
Plumley Ches E...........113 G6
Plumpton Cumb..........148 E7
Plumpton E Susx..........19 K3
Plumpton Nhants..........73 H5
Plumpton Green
    E Susx....................19 K3
Plumstead Gt Lon.........45 J4
Plumstead Norfk.........106 D5
Plumtree Notts...........101 L6
Plungar Leics.............102 C5
Plurenden Kent............34 C7

**Plush** Dorset..............14 D3
**Plwmp** Cerdgn ..............65 K4
**Plymouth** C Plym..............6 C5
**Plympton** C Plym..............6 D5
**Plymstock** C Plym..............6 D5
**Plymtree** Devon..............12 D2
**Pockley** N York..............133 K3
**Pocklington** E R Yk......125 J2
**Podimore** Somset..............26 D6
**Podington** Bed..............74 D3
**Podmore** Staffs..............99 H5
**Pointon** Lincs..............103 J6
**Pokesdown** BCP..............15 L4
**Polbain** Highld..............224 B6
**Polbathic** Cnwll..............6 A4
**Polbeth** W Loth..............176 D5
**Poldark Mine** Cnwll ..........3 H5
**Polebrook** Nhants..............88 F6
**Polegate** E Susx..............20 C5
**Polesden Lacey**
  Surrey ..............31 J2
**Polesworth** Warwks..............86 C3
**Polglass** Highld..............224 C6
**Polgooth** Cnwll..............4 F5
**Polgown** D & G..............154 C2
**Poling** W Susx..............18 E5
**Poling Corner**
  W Susx..............18 E5
**Polkerris** Cnwll..............5 H5
**Pollington** E R Yk..............124 F6
**Polloch** Highld..............190 F3
**Pollokshaws** C Glas..............175 G6
**Pollokshields** C Glas....175 G5
**Polmassick** Cnwll..............4 F6
**Polmont** Falk..............176 C3
**Polnish** Highld..............200 B8
**Polperro** Cnwll..............5 K5
**Polruan** Cnwll..............5 H5
**Polstead** Suffk..............78 B6
**Poltalloch** Ag & B..............182 B7
**Poltimore** Devon..............12 C3
**Polton** Mdloth..............177 J5
**Polwarth** Border ..............178 F7
**Polyphant** Cnwll..............9 H7
**Polzeath** Cnwll..............4 E1
**Pomathorn** Mdloth..............177 H6
**Pondersbridge**
  Cambs..............89 J5
**Ponders End** Gt Lon......45 G2
**Ponsanooth** Cnwll..............3 K4
**Ponsworthy** Devon..............7 G2
**Pont Abraham**
  Services Carmth ......51 H4
**Pontac** Jersey..............236 e8
**Pontantwn** Carmth..............50 F3
**Pontardawe** Neath..............51 K5
**Pontarddulais** Swans .....51 H5
**Pont-ar-gothi**
  Carmth..............51 G2
**Pontarsais** Carmth..............66 B8
**Pontblyddyn** Flints..........97 L1
**Pontcysyllte**
  Aqueduct Wrexhm....97 L4
**Pontefract** Wakefd......124 C6
**Ponteland** Nthumb......158 F7
**Ponterwyd** Cerdgn..............81 G7
**Pontesbury** Shrops..............83 H3
**Pontesford** Shrops..............83 H3
**Pontfadog** Wrexhm......97 K5
**Pontfaen** Pembks..............64 E7
**Pont-faen** Powys..............67 L7
**Pontgarreg** Cerdgn..............65 K4
**Ponthenri** Carmth..............50 F4
**Ponthir** Torfn..............37 M2
**Ponthirwaun** Cerdgn ....65 J5
**Pontllanfraith**
  Caerph..............37 J2
**Pontlliw** Swans..............51 H5
**Pontllyfni** Gwynd..............95 G3
**Pontlottyn** Caerph ..........53 H6
**Pontnêddfechan**
  Neath..............52 D6
**Pontnewydd** Torfn......37 L2
**Pontrhydfendigaid**
  Cerdgn..............67 G2
**Pontrhydyfen** Neath ....36 C2
**Pont-rhyd-y-groes**
  Cerdgn..............81 G8

**Pontrilas** Herefs..............54 B3
**Pont Robert** Powys......82 C2
**Pontshaen** Cerdgn..............66 B5
**Pontsticill** Myr Td..............53 G5
**Pontwelly** Carmth..............65 L6
**Pontyates** Carmth..............50 F4
**Pontyberem** Carmth....51 G4
**Pontybodkin** Flints..............97 L2
**Pontyclun** Rhondd..............37 G4
**Pontycymer** Brdgnd......36 D3
**Pontymister** Caerph......37 K3
**Pont-y-pant** Conwy......96 B2
**Pontypool** Torfn..............53 L7
**Pontypridd** Rhondd ..........37 G3
**Pontywaun** Caerph......37 K2
**Pool** Cnwll..............3 H3
**Poole** BCP..............15 J4
**Poole Keynes** Gloucs......39 M2
**Poolewe** Highld..............219 K5
**Pooley Bridge** Cumb....138 C3
**Poolfold** Staffs..............99 K1
**Poolhill** Gloucs..............55 G3
**Pool in Wharfedale**
  Leeds..............123 J2
**Pool of Muckhart**
  Clacks..............185 L7
**Pool Street** Essex..............77 H6
**Poplar** Gt Lon..............45 G4
**Porchfield** IoW..............16 F4
**Poringland** Norfk..............92 F3
**Porkellis** Cnwll..............3 J5
**Porlock** Somset..............24 D3
**Porlock Weir** Somset....24 D2
**Portachoillan** Ag & B....172 C6
**Port-an-Eorna**
  Highld..............210 B7
**Port Appin** Ag & B..............191 H7
**Port Askaig** Ag & B......171 H5
**Portavadie** Ag & B..............172 F4
**Port Bannatyne**
  Ag & B..............173 J5
**Portbury** N Som..............38 D5
**Port Carlisle** Cumb......147 M3
**Port Charlotte**
  Ag & B..............170 E6
**Portchester** Hants..............17 H2
**Port Driseach** Ag & B..173 G4
**Port Ellen** Ag & B..............160 C1
**Port Elphinstone**
  Abers..............206 E2
**Portencalzie** D & G......152 B7
**Portencross** N Ayrs......173 K8
**Port Erin** IoM..............237 a6
**Portesham** Dorset..............14 B5
**Portessie** Moray..............215 K2
**Port Eynon** Swans..............50 F7
**Portfield Gate**
  Pembks..............48 F4
**Portgate** Devon..............10 B7
**Port Gaverne** Cnwll..............8 D8
**Port Glasgow** Inver .....174 C4
**Portgordon** Moray......215 J2
**Portgower** Highld......227 H5
**Porth** Cnwll..............4 C4
**Porth** Rhondd..............36 F3
**Porthallow** Cnwll..............3 K6
**Porthallow** Cnwll..............5 K5
**Porthcawl** Brdgnd......36 C5
**Porthcothan** Cnwll..............4 D2
**Porthcurno** Cnwll..............2 C6
**Port Henderson**
  Highld..............219 H6
**Porthgain** Pembks......64 A7
**Porthgwarra** Cnwll..............2 C6
**Porthill** Staffs..............99 J3
**Porthkerry** V Glam......37 G6
**Porthleven** Cnwll..............3 H6
**Porthmadog** Gwynd......95 K5
**Porth Navas** Cnwll..............3 K5
**Porthoustock** Cnwll..............3 K6
**Porthpean** Cnwll..............5 G5
**Porthtowan** Cnwll..............3 J2
**Porthyrhyd** Carmth......51 G3
**Portincaple** Ag & B......183 J8
**Portinfer** Jersey..............236 a5
**Portington** E R Yk......125 J4
**Portinnisherrich**
  Ag & B..............182 D5

**Portinscale** Cumb......137 H3
**Port Isaac** Cnwll..............8 D8
**Portishead** N Som..............38 C5
**Portknockie** Moray......215 K2
**Portland** Dorset..............14 D7
**Portlethen** Abers..............207 H6
**Portling** D & G..............146 F4
**Portloe** Cnwll..............4 E7
**Port Logan** D & G..............144 D6
**Portmahomack**
  Highld..............223 K5
**Port Mary** D & G..............146 D6
**Portmeirion** Gwynd......95 K5
**Portmellon** Cnwll..............4 F6
**Port Mòr** Highld..............189 K1
**Portnacroish** Ag & B....191 H6
**Portnaguran** W Isls ....232 g2
**Portnahaven** Ag & B....170 D7
**Portnalong** Highld......208 E7
**Portnancon** Highld......228 F4
**Port nan Giùran**
  W Isls..............232 g2
**Port nan Long**
  W Isls..............232 c5
**Port Nis** W Isls..............232 g1
**Portobello** C Edin..............177 J4
**Portobello** Wolves..............85 G4
**Port of Menteith**
  Stirlg..............184 D6
**Port of Ness** W Isls....232 g1
**Porton** Wilts..............28 D4
**Portpatrick** D & G..............144 B4
**Port Quin** Cnwll..............8 C8
**Port Ramsay** Ag & B....191 H7
**Portreath** Cnwll..............3 H3
**Portreath Harbour**
  Cnwll..............3 H3
**Portree** Highld..............209 G5
**Port Righ** Ag & B..............161 K2
**Port St Mary** IoM..............237 b7
**Portscatho** Cnwll..............4 D8
**Portsea** C Port..............17 J3
**Portskerra** Highld......230 C3
**Portskewett** Mons..............38 D3
**Portslade** Br & H..............19 H4
**Portslade-by-Sea**
  Br & H..............19 H5
**Portslogan** D & G..............144 B3
**Portsmouth** C Port..............17 J3
**Portsmouth** Calder......122 D5
**Portsmouth**
  Dockyard C Port......17 J3
**Port Soderick** IoM......237 c6
**Portsonachan Hotel**
  Ag & B..............182 F3
**Portsoy** Abers..............216 B2
**Port Sunlight** Wirral....111 K5
**Portswood** C Sotn..............29 H8
**Port Talbot** Neath..............36 B3
**Port Tennant** Swans......51 K6
**Portuairk** Highld..............189 K3
**Portway** Sandw..............85 H6
**Portway** Worcs..............85 J8
**Port Wemyss** Ag & B....170 D7
**Port William** D & G......145 H6
**Portwrinkle** Cnwll..............6 A5
**Portyerrock** D & G......145 K7
**Poslingford** Suffk..............77 H5
**Posso** Border..............166 B3
**Postbridge** Devon..............10 F8
**Postcombe** Oxon..............58 B7
**Postling** Kent..............34 F6
**Postwick** Norfk..............93 G2
**Potarch** Abers..............206 B6
**Potten End** Herts..............59 G6
**Potter Brompton**
  N York..............134 F4
**Potterhanworth**
  Lincs..............117 H7
**Potterhanworth**
  Booths Lincs..............117 H7
**Potter Heigham**
  Norfk..............107 J8
**Potterne** Wilts..............39 M8
**Potterne Wick** Wilts......39 M8
**Potters Bar** Herts..............59 L7
**Potters Corner** Kent......34 D5
**Potters Crouch** Herts....59 J6

**Potters Green** Covtry......86 D6
**Potters Marston**
  Leics..............87 G4
**Potterspury** Nhants......73 L6
**Potter Street** Essex......60 D6
**Potterton** Abers..............207 H3
**Potto** N York..............141 L6
**Potton** C Beds..............75 J5
**Pott Shrigley** Ches E....113 L5
**Poughill** Cnwll..............9 G4
**Poughill** Devon..............11 K3
**Poulner** Hants..............15 M2
**Poulshot** Wilts..............39 L7
**Poulton** Gloucs..............56 C7
**Poulton** Wirral..............111 J4
**Poulton-le-Fylde**
  Lancs..............120 D3
**Poundbury** Dorset..............14 D4
**Poundffald** Swans..............51 H6
**Pound Green** E Susx......20 B2
**Pound Green** Suffk......77 G4
**Pound Hill** W Susx..............32 B5
**Poundon** Bucks..............57 M3
**Poundsgate** Devon..............7 G2
**Poundstock** Cnwll..............9 G5
**Pouton** D & G..............145 K5
**Povey Cross** Surrey......31 L3
**Powburn** Nthumb......168 F6
**Powderham** Devon..............12 C5
**Powerstock** Dorset......13 M3
**Powfoot** D & G..............147 K2
**Powick** Worcs..............70 E4
**Powmill** P & K..............185 L7
**Poxwell** Dorset..............14 E5
**Poyle** Slough..............43 G5
**Poynings** W Susx..............19 H4
**Poyntington** Dorset......26 F7
**Poynton** Ches E..............113 L5
**Poynton Green**
  Wrekin..............98 E8
**Praa Sands** Cnwll..............3 G5
**Praze-an-Beeble**
  Cnwll..............3 H4
**Prees** Shrops..............98 D5
**Preesall** Lancs..............120 E2
**Prees Green** Shrops......98 E6
**Prees Heath** Shrops......98 D5
**Prees Higher Heath**
  Shrops..............98 E5
**Pren-gwyn** Cerdgn......65 L5
**Prenteg** Gwynd..............95 K4
**Prescot** Knows..............112 C3
**Prescott** Devon..............25 H8
**Presnerb** Angus..............195 J3
**Prestatyn** Denbgs......110 E5
**Prestbury** Ches E..............113 K6
**Prestbury** Gloucs..............55 L4
**Presteigne** Powys..............69 G2
**Prestleigh** Somset..............26 F4
**Preston** Border..............179 G6
**Preston** Br & H..............19 J4
**Preston** Devon..............7 K2
**Preston** Dorset..............14 D5
**Preston** E R Yk..............126 F4
**Preston** Gloucs..............56 B7
**Preston** Herts..............59 K3
**Preston** Kent..............34 D3
**Preston** Kent..............35 H3
**Preston** Lancs..............121 H4
**Preston** Nthumb..............169 H4
**Preston** Rutlnd..............88 C3
**Preston** Somset..............25 H4
**Preston** Torbay..............7 K4
**Preston** Wilts..............40 B5
**Preston Bagot**
  Warwks..............71 L2
**Preston Bissett**
  Bucks..............58 A3
**Preston Bowyer**
  Somset..............25 H6
**Preston Brockhurst**
  Shrops..............98 D7
**Preston Brook**
  Halton..............112 E5
**Preston Candover**
  Hants..............29 L3
**Preston Capes**
  Nhants..............73 H4

**Preston Green**
Warwks .....................**71** L2
**Preston Gubbals**
Shrops........................**98** C8
**Preston on Stour**
Warwks .....................**72** B4
**Preston on the Hill**
Halton .....................**112** E5
**Preston on Wye**
Herefs ........................**69** H6
**Prestonpans** E Loth.....**177** K4
**Preston Patrick**
Cumb .......................**129** L3
**Preston Plucknett**
Somset........................**26** D7
**Preston St Mary**
Suffk...........................**77** L4
**Preston-under-**
**Scar** N York...............**131** K2
**Preston upon the**
**Weald Moors**
Wrekin .......................**84** C1
**Preston Wynne**
Herefs ........................**69** L5
**Prestwich** Bury ..........**113** J1
**Prestwick** S Ayrs ........**163** J4
*Prestwick Airport*
*S Ayrs.........................163 J4*
**Prestwood** Bucks..........**58** E7
**Prickwillow** Cambs .......**90** E6
**Priddy** Somset...............**26** D2
**Priest Hutton** Lancs ....**129** L5
**Priestland** E Ayrs .......**164** B2
**Priest Weston** Shrops....**82** F4
**Primrosehill** Border ...**179** G6
**Primrose Hill** Dudley ...**85** G6
**Primsidemill** Border ...**168** B4
**Prince of Wales**
**Bridge** Mons ..............**38** D3
**Princes Risborough**
Bucks ........................**58** D7
**Princethorpe** Warwks....**72** E1
**Princetown** Devon......... **6** E2
**Priors Hardwick**
Warwks .....................**72** F4
**Priorslee** Wrekin.........**84** C2
**Priors Marston**
Warwks .....................**72** F3
**Priors Norton** Gloucs....**55** K3
**Priors Park** Gloucs .....**55** K2
**Priston** BaNES.............**39** G7
**Prittlewell** Sthend.........**46** E3
**Privett** Hants................**30** B6
**Prixford** Devon.............**23** J4
**Probus** Cnwll................. **4** E6
**Prora** E Loth...............**178** C3
**Prospect** Cumb ..........**147** K6
**Prospidnick** Cnwll ......... **3** H5
**Protstonhill** Abers......**216** F2
**Prudhoe** Nthumb........**150** D3
**Pubil** P & K ................**193** G7
**Publow** BaNES...............**38** F7
**Puckeridge** Herts..........**60** C4
**Puckington** Somset........**26** B7
**Pucklechurch** S Glos....**39** G5
**Puddington** Ches W.....**111** K6
**Puddington** Devon........**11** J3
**Puddletown** Dorset........**14** E4
**Pudsey** Leeds ..............**123** J4
**Pulborough** W Susx........**18** E3
**Pulford** Ches W.............**98** A2
**Pulham** Dorset..............**14** D2
**Pulham Market**
Norfk...........................**92** E6
**Pulham St Mary**
Norfk...........................**92** E6
**Pulloxhill** C Beds..........**74** F7
**Pulverbatch** Shrops.......**83** H3
**Pumpherston** W Loth....**176** E4
**Pumsaint** Carmth..........**66** E6
**Puncheston** Pembks ......**49** G2
**Puncknowle** Dorset ......**14** A5
**Punnett's Town**
E Susx........................**20** C2
**Purbrook** Hants.............**17** J2
**Purfleet-on-**
**Thames** Thurr.........**45** K4
**Puriton** Somset.............**25** L3

**Purleigh** Essex ..............**61** K7
**Purley** Gt Lon.................**44** F7
**Purley on Thames**
W Berk .......................**42** A5
**Purse Caundle**
Dorset.........................**27** G2
**Purtington** Somset........**13** K2
**Purton** Gloucs ..............**54** F6
**Purton** Gloucs ..............**55** G7
**Purton** Wilts.................**40** C3
**Purton Stoke** Wilts........**40** C3
**Pury End** Nhants...........**73** K5
**Pusey** Oxon...................**41** G2
**Putley** Herefs................**70** B6
**Putley Green** Herefs.....**70** B6
**Putney** Gt Lon...............**44** E5
**Puttenham** Surrey.........**30** F2
**Puxley** Nhants...............**73** L6
**Puxton** N Som...............**38** B7
**Pwll** Carmth..................**50** F5
**Pwll-glâs** Denbgs.........**97** H2
**Pwllgloyw** Powys..........**68** B7
**Pwllheli** Gwynd.............**94** F5
**Pwllmeyric** Mons...........**38** D2
**Pwll-trap** Carmth..........**50** C3
**Pwll-y-glaw** Neath........**36** C2
**Pye Bridge** Derbys ......**101** H3
**Pyecombe** W Susx..........**19** J3
**Pyle** Brdgnd..................**36** C4
**Pyleigh** Somset.............**25** H5
**Pylle** Somset.................**26** E4
**Pymoor** Cambs..............**90** C6
**Pymore** Dorset...............**13** L4
**Pyrford** Surrey...............**43** H8
**Pyrton** Oxon..................**42** B2
**Pytchley** Nhants............**88** C8
**Pyworthy** Devon............. **9** J4

## Q

**Quadring** Lincs ...........**103** L6
**Quadring Eaudike**
Lincs .........................**103** L5
**Quainton** Bucks............**58** C4
**Quantock Hills**
Somset........................**25** J4
**Quarff** Shet.................**235** c6
**Quarley** Hants...............**28** F3
**Quarndon** Derbys ........**101** G4
**Quarrier's Village**
Inver .........................**174** C5
**Quarrington** Lincs .......**103** H4
**Quarrington Hill** Dur....**151** H7
**Quarry Bank** Dudley......**85** G6
**Quarrywood** Moray......**214** C2
**Quarter** N Ayrs ...........**173** L6
**Quarter** S Lans.............**175** J7
**Quatford** Shrops............**84** D5
**Quatt** Shrops.................**84** D6
**Quebec** Dur.................**150** F6
**Quedgeley** Gloucs.........**55** J5
**Queen Adelaide**
Cambs.........................**90** E7
**Queenborough** Kent......**46** E5
**Queen Camel** Somset....**26** E6
**Queen Charlton**
BaNES.........................**38** F6
**Queen Elizabeth**
**Forest Park** Stirlg...**184** B6
**Queen Elizabeth II**
**Bridge** Thurr............**45** L5
**Queenhill** Worcs...........**70** F6
**Queen Oak** Dorset.........**27** H5
**Queen's Bower** IoW......**17** H5
**Queensbury** C Brad......**123** G4
**Queensferry** Flints.......**111** K7
**Queensferry**
**Crossing** Fife.........**176** F3
**Queenslie** C Glas.........**175** H5
**Queen's Park** Bed.........**74** F4
**Queen's Park** Essex......**46** A2
**Queen's Park** Nhants....**73** L3
**Queenzieburn**
N Lans.......................**175** J3
**Quendon** Essex ............**60** E3
**Queniborough** Leics......**87** J2

**Quenington** Gloucs .......**56** C7
**Queslett** Birm...............**85** J4
**Quethiock** Cnwll ............. **5** L3
**Quidenham** Norfk..........**92** B6
**Quidhampton** Wilts........**28** C5
**Quinton** Nhants .............**73** L4
**Quintrell Downs**
Cnwll .......................... **4** D4
**Quixwood** Border ........**179** G5
**Quoig** P & K ................**185** H3
**Quorn** Leics ..................**87** H1
**Quothquan** S Lans .......**165** J2
**Quoyburray** Ork ..........**234** c6
**Quoyloo** Ork................**234** b5

## R

**Raasay** Highld .............**209** J5
**Rachan Mill** Border .....**165** L3
**Rachub** Gwynd.............**109** J7
**Rackenford** Devon.........**24** D7
**Rackham** W Susx............**18** E3
**Rackheath** Norfk............**93** G1
**Racks** D & G ................**155** H7
**Rackwick** Ork..............**234** a7
**Radbourne** Derbys .......**100** F5
**Radcliffe** Bury ............**113** H1
**Radcliffe on Trent**
Notts.........................**101** M5
**Radclive** Bucks...............**73** J7
**Raddery** Highld ...........**213** H3
**Radernie** Fife...............**187** G5
**Radford** Covtry ............**86** D7
**Radford Semele**
Warwks .....................**72** D2
**Radlett** Herts................**59** K7
**Radley** Oxon..................**57** K7
**Radley Green** Essex......**60** F6
**Radnage** Bucks..............**42** C2
**Radstock** BaNES............**27** G1
**Radstone** Nhants............**73** H6
**Radway** Warwks.............**72** D5
**Radwell** Bed.................**74** E3
**Radwell** Herts................**75** J7
**Radwinter** Essex............**76** E6
**Radyr** Cardif.................**37** H4
**Rafford** Moray.............**214** C3
**RAF Museum**
**Cosford** Shrops.........**84** E3
**RAF Museum**
**Hendon** Gt Lon .........**44** E3
**Ragdale** Leics .............**102** A8
**Raglan** Mons .................**54** B6
**Ragnall** Notts...............**116** D6
**Raigbeg** Highld ...........**213** J8
**Rainbow Hill** Worcs......**70** F4
**Rainford** St Hel............**112** C2
**Rainham** Gt Lon.............**45** K4
**Rainham** Medway..........**46** D6
**Rainhill** St Hel.............**112** C4
**Rainhill Stoops**
St Hel.......................**112** D4
**Rainow** Ches E.............**113** L6
**Rainton** N York.............**132** E4
**Rainworth** Notts...........**101** L2
**Rait** P & K....................**186** D3
**Raithby** Lincs...............**118** D5
**Raithby** Lincs...............**118** E7
**Rake** Hants....................**30** D5
**Ralia** Highld ................**203** H5
**Ramasaig** Highld .........**208** B5
**Rame** Cnwll..................... **3** J4
**Rame** Cnwll..................... **6** B6
**Rampisham** Dorset ........**14** B3
**Rampside** Cumb...........**128** F6
**Rampton** Cambs.............**76** B2
**Rampton** Notts.............**116** D5
**Ramsbottom** Bury........**122** B6
**Ramsbury** Wilts.............**40** F6
**Ramscraigs** Highld......**227** K3
**Ramsdean** Hants............**30** B6
**Ramsdell** Hants..............**41** L8
**Ramsden** Oxon...............**57** G5
**Ramsden Bellhouse**
Essex.........................**46** B2
**Ramsey** Cambs...............**89** K6

**Ramsey** Essex ...............**62** E2
**Ramsey** IoM.................**237** e3
**Ramsey Forty Foot**
Cambs.........................**89** K6
**Ramsey Heights**
Cambs.........................**89** J6
**Ramsey Island** Essex....**61** M6
**Ramsey Island**
Pembks .......................**48** B3
**Ramsey Mereside**
Cambs.........................**89** K5
**Ramsey St Mary's**
Cambs.........................**89** J6
**Ramsgate** Kent..............**35** K2
**Ramsgill** N York...........**131** L5
**Ramshope** Nthumb.......**157** J2
**Ramshorn** Staffs..........**100** B4
**Ramsnest Common**
Surrey.........................**30** F5
**Ranby** Lincs .................**118** B5
**Ranby** Notts.................**116** A5
**Rand** Lincs ...................**117** J5
**Randwick** Gloucs ..........**55** J6
**Ranfurly** Rens..............**174** D5
**Rangemore** Staffs........**100** D7
**Rangeworthy** S Glos .....**39** G3
**Rankinston** E Ayrs .......**163** L6
**Rannoch Station**
P & K .......................**193** G5
**Ranscombe** Somset........**24** E3
**Ranskill** Notts..............**116** A4
**Ranton** Staffs.................**99** J7
**Ranton Green** Staffs......**99** J7
**Ranworth** Norfk.............**93** H1
**Raploch** Stirlg..............**185** G7
**Rapness** Ork................**234** c4
**Rascarrel** D & G ..........**146** D5
**Rashfield** Ag & B .........**173** K2
**Rashwood** Worcs...........**71** G2
**Raskelf** N York.............**133** G5
**Rastrick** Calder............**123** H6
**Ratagan** Highld ...........**200** E2
**Ratby** Leics ...................**87** G3
**Ratcliffe Culey** Leics....**86** D4
**Ratcliffe on Soar**
Notts.........................**101** J4
**Ratcliffe on the**
**Wreake** Leics............**87** J1
**Rathen** Abers...............**217** J3
**Rathillet** Fife...............**186** F3
**Rathmell** N York...........**130** F7
**Ratho** C Edin...............**176** F4
**Ratho Station** C Edin....**176** F4
**Rathven** Moray............**215** K2
**Ratley** Warwks...............**72** E5
**Ratling** Kent..................**35** H4
**Ratlinghope** Shrops.......**83** H4
**Rattar** Highld...............**231** J2
**Rattery** Devon ............... **7** H4
**Rattlesden** Suffk............**77** L3
**Ratton Village** E Susx....**20** C5
**Rattray** P & K ..............**195** J7
**Raunds** Nhants..............**88** E8
**Ravenfield** Rothm........**115** J3
**Ravenglass** Cumb .......**136** F7
**Raveningham** Norfk.......**93** H4
**Ravenscar** N York.........**143** K6
**Ravenscraig** N Lans ....**175** K6
**Ravensden** Bed.............**74** F4
**Ravenshead** Notts........**101** K2
**Ravensthorpe** Kirk........**123** J6
**Ravensthorpe** Nhants....**73** J1
**Ravenstone** Leics..........**86** E2
**Ravenstone** M Keyn.......**74** B4
**Ravenstonedale**
Cumb .......................**139** G6
**Ravenstruther**
S Lans.......................**165** H1
**Ravensworth** N York....**140** E5
**Rawcliffe** C York..........**133** J8
**Rawcliffe** E R Yk..........**125** G6
**Rawdon** Leeds .............**123** J3
**Rawling Street** Kent......**34** B3
**Rawmarsh** Rothm........**115** H3
**Rawreth** Essex...............**46** C2
**Rawridge** Devon............**12** F2
**Rawtenstall** Lancs ......**122** B6
**Raydon** Suffk.................**78** C6

Rayleigh Essex .............. 46 D2
Rayne Essex ................. 61 H4
Raynes Park Gt Lon ..... 44 E6
Reach Cambs ................ 76 E2
Read Lancs ................. 122 B4
Reading Readg .............. 42 B5
Reading Services
  W Berk ...................... 42 A6
Reading Street Kent .... 34 B8
Reading Street Kent .... 35 K2
Reagill Cumb. .............. 138 E4
Rearquhar Highld ........ 223 G3
Rearsby Leics. .............. 87 J2
Reawla Cnwll .................. 3 G4
Reay Highld ................. 230 D3
Reculver Kent ............... 47 L6
Red Ball Devon ............. 25 H7
Redberth Pembks .......... 49 J6
Redbourn Herts ............ 59 J5
Redbourne N Linc ....... 116 F2
Redbrook Gloucs .......... 54 D6
Redbrook Wrexhm ....... 98 D4
Redbrook Street
  Kent ........................ 34 C7
Redburn Highld .......... 213 L5
Redcar R & Cl. ............ 142 D3
Redcastle D & G. ........ 146 E2
Redcastle Highld ........ 212 F4
Redding Falk. .............. 176 C3
Reddingmuirhead
  Falk ....................... 176 C3
Reddish Stockp. .......... 113 K3
Redditch Worcs ............ 71 J2
Rede Suffk ................... 77 J4
Redenhall Norfk ........... 92 F6
Redesmouth Nthumb ... 157 L5
Redford Abers ............. 197 J3
Redford Angus ........... 196 F7
Redford W Susx ............ 30 E6
Redfordgreen
  Border ................... 166 E6
Redgate Rhondd .......... 36 F3
Redgorton P & K. ....... 186 A2
Redgrave Suffk ............ 92 C7
Redhill Abers .............. 206 E4
Red Hill BCP ................ 15 K4
Redhill Herts ............... 59 M2
Redhill N Som .............. 38 D7
Redhill Surrey .............. 32 B3
Redisham Suffk ............ 93 J6
Redland Bristl. ............. 38 E5
Redland Ork. .............. 234 b5
Redlingfield Suffk ........ 78 E1
Redlingfield Green
  Suffk ....................... 78 E1
Red Lodge Suffk ........... 77 G1
Redlynch Somset ......... 27 G5
Redlynch Wilts .............. 28 D7
Redmarley Worcs ......... 70 D2
Redmarley D'Abitot
  Gloucs ..................... 55 H2
Redmarshall S on T .... 141 J3
Redmile Leics. ............. 102 D5
Redmire N York ........... 131 K2
Redmyre Abers ........... 197 J2
Rednal Shrops .............. 98 A6
Redpath Border .......... 167 J3
Red Point Highld ......... 219 H7
Red Roses Carmth ........ 49 L5
Red Row Nthumb ........ 159 G3
Redruth Cnwll ................ 3 J3
Redstone P & K. ......... 186 C1
Red Street Staffs ......... 99 J3
Red Wharf Bay IoA .... 109 G5
Redwick Newpt ............ 38 B4
Redwick S Glos. ........... 38 D3
Redworth Darltn ......... 141 G3
Reed Herts ................... 75 L7
Reedham Norfk ............ 93 J3
Reedness E R Yk. ........ 125 J6
Reeds Holme Lancs ..... 122 B5
Reepham Lincs. .......... 117 H6
Reepham Norfk .......... 106 D7
Reeth N York .............. 140 C7
Reeves Green Solhll ..... 86 C7
Regil N Som .................. 38 D7
Reiff Highld ................ 224 B5
Reigate Surrey .............. 31 L2

Reighton N York ......... 135 H4
Reinigeadal W Isls ..... 232 e4
Reisque Abers ............ 207 G2
Reiss Highld ............... 231 L5
Relubbus Cnwll .............. 2 F5
Relugas Moray. ........... 214 B5
Remenham Wokham ..... 42 C4
Remenham Hill
  Wokham ................... 42 C4
Rempstone Notts ........ 101 L7
Rendcomb Gloucs ........ 56 A6
Rendham Suffk ............ 79 H2
Rendlesham Suffk ........ 79 G4
Renfrew Rens ............. 174 F5
Renhold Bed. ............... 74 F4
Renishaw Derbys ........ 115 J6
Rennington Nthumb ... 169 J5
Renton W Duns .......... 174 D3
Renwick Cumb. .......... 149 G6
Repps Norfk ................. 93 J1
Repton Derbys ........... 100 F6
Reraig Highld ............. 210 C8
Resaurie Highld ......... 213 H5
Rescorla
  Highld .................... 190 E4
Reskadinnick Cnwll ....... 3 H3
Resolis Highld ............ 213 G2
Resolven Neath ........... 52 C7
Rest and be
  thankful Ag & B. ..... 183 J6
Reston Border ............ 179 H6
Reswallie Angus. ....... 196 E6
Retford Notts ............. 116 B5
Rettendon Essex .......... 61 J7
Revesby Lincs ............ 103 M1
Rewe Devon .................. 12 B3
Rew Street IoW ............ 16 F4
Reymerston Norfk ........ 92 B3
Reynalton Pembks ....... 49 J5
Reynoldston Swans ...... 50 F7
Rezare Cnwll .................. 6 A1
Rhandirmwyn
  Carmth .................... 67 H5
Rhayader Powys .......... 67 L2
Rheindown Highld ..... 212 D5
Rhenigidale W Isls ..... 232 e4
Rhes-y-cae Flints ....... 111 G7
Rhewl Denbgs .............. 97 H1
Rhewl Denbgs .............. 97 J4
Rhicarn Highld ........... 224 D4
Rhiconich Highld ....... 228 C5
Rhicullen Highld ........ 222 F6
Rhigos Rhondd ............. 52 E6
Rhives Highld ............. 223 H2
Rhiwbina Cardif ........... 37 J4
Rhiwderyn Newpt ........ 37 K3
Rhiwlas Gwynd .......... 109 H7
Rhoden Green Kent ..... 33 H4
Rhodes Minnis Kent .... 34 F6
Rhodiad-y-brenin
  Pembks .................... 48 C3
Rhonehouse D & G. ... 146 C3
Rhoose V Glam ............ 37 G6
Rhos Carmth ............... 65 L7
Rhos Neath ................. 51 L5
Rhoscolyn IoA ........... 108 C6
Rhoscrowther
  Pembks .................... 48 F6
Rhosesmor Flints ....... 111 H7
Rhosgoch Powys ......... 68 D5
Rhoshill Pembks .......... 65 H6
Rhoshirwaun Gwynd .... 94 D6
Rhoslefain Gwynd ....... 80 D3
Rhosllanerchrugog
  Wrexhm ................... 97 L3
Rhosmeirch IoA ......... 108 F6
Rhosneigr IoA ........... 108 D6
Rhosnesni Wrexhm ...... 97 M3
Rhôs-on-Sea Conwy ... 110 B5
Rhossili Swans ............. 50 E7
Rhostryfan Gwynd ....... 95 H2
Rhostyllen Wrexhm ...... 97 L3
Rhosybol IoA ............. 108 F4
Rhos-y-gwaliau
  Gwynd ..................... 96 E5
Rhosymedre Wrexhm .... 97 L4
Rhu Ag & B. ............... 174 B2
Rhuallt Denbgs .......... 110 F6

Rhubodach Ag & B. .... 173 H4
Rhuddlan Denbgs ....... 110 E6
Rhue Highld .............. 220 E3
Rhunahaorine
  Ag & B. ................... 172 C8
Rhyd Gwynd ................ 95 L4
Rhydargaeau Carmth .... 50 F1
Rhydcymerau Carmth ... 66 D6
Rhyd-Ddu Gwynd. ........ 95 K3
Rhydlewis Cerdgn ........ 65 K5
Rhydowen Cerdgn ........ 66 B5
Rhyd-uchaf Gwynd ....... 96 D5
Rhyd-y-clafdy
  Gwynd ..................... 94 F5
Rhyd-y-foel Conwy ..... 110 C6
Rhydyfro Neath ........... 51 K4
Rhyd-y-groes Gwynd .. 109 H7
Rhyd-y-pennau
  Cerdgn ..................... 80 E6
Rhyl Denbgs .............. 110 D5
Rhymney Caerph ......... 53 H6
Rhynd P & K. .............. 186 B4
Rhynie Abers ............. 215 L8
Rhynie Highld ............ 223 J5
Ribbesford Worcs ........ 84 D8
Ribbleton Lancs ......... 121 H4
Ribchester Lancs ........ 121 J4
Riby Lincs. ................. 126 F8
Riccall N York ............ 124 F3
Riccarton Border ....... 156 F3
Riccarton E Ayrs ........ 163 K3
Richards Castle
  Herefs ..................... 69 J1
Richmond Gt Lon ....... 44 D5
Richmond N York ...... 140 F6
Richmond Sheff ........ 115 H4
Rickerscote Staffs ....... 99 L7
Rickford N Som ........... 38 C8
Rickham Devon ............. 7 H7
Rickinghall Suffk ......... 92 C7
Rickling Green Essex ... 60 E3
Rickmansworth
  Herts ....................... 43 H2
Riddell Border ........... 167 H4
Riddlecombe Devon .... 10 F3
Riddlesden C Brad. .... 123 G3
Ridge Dorset ............... 15 H5
Ridge Herts ................. 59 K7
Ridge Wilts ................. 27 L5
Ridge Lane Warwks ..... 86 C4
Ridgeway Derbys ....... 115 H5
Ridgewell Essex ........... 77 G6
Ridgewood E Susx ....... 19 M2
Ridgmont C Beds ......... 74 E7
Riding Mill Nthumb ... 150 C3
Ridlington Norfk ........ 107 H6
Ridlington Rutlnd ....... 88 B3
Ridsdale Nthumb ...... 158 A5
Rievaulx N York ......... 133 J3
Rigg D & G. ............... 148 B2
Riggend N Lans ......... 175 K4
Righoul Highld .......... 213 K4
Rigsby Lincs ............... 118 F6
Rigside S Lans ........... 165 G3
Riley Green Lancs ...... 121 J5
Rilla Mill Cnwll ............. 5 L2
Rillington N York ....... 134 D5
Rimington Lancs ....... 122 B2
Rimpton Somset ......... 26 E6
Rimswell E R Yk ........ 127 H5
Rinaston Pembks ......... 49 G3
Rindleford Shrops ....... 84 D4
Ringford D & G. ........ 146 C4
Ringland Norfk ........... 92 D2
Ringmer E Susx .......... 19 L3
Ringmore Devon ........... 6 F6
Ringmore Devon ........... 7 L2
Ringorm Moray ......... 215 G5
Ringsfield Suffk .......... 93 J5
Ringsfield Corner
  Suffk ....................... 93 J6
Ringshall Herts ........... 59 G5
Ringshall Suffk ........... 78 C4
Ringshall Stocks
  Suffk ....................... 78 C4
Ringstead Nhants ....... 88 E7
Ringstead Norfk ........ 105 H4
Ringwood Hants ......... 15 L2

Ringwould Kent .......... 35 K5
Rinmore Abers ........... 205 J3
Ripe E Susx .................. 20 B4
Ripley Derbys ............ 101 H3
Ripley Hants ................ 15 M3
Ripley N York ............ 132 D7
Ripley Surrey .............. 31 H1
Riplington Hants ......... 30 A6
Ripon N York ............. 132 D5
Rippingale Lincs ....... 103 H6
Ripple Kent ................. 35 J5
Ripple Worcs. .............. 70 F6
Ripponden Calder. .... 122 F6
Risabus Ag & B. ....... 160 B2
Risbury Herefs. ........... 69 K4
Risby Suffk ................. 77 H2
Risca Caerph ............... 37 K3
Rise E R Yk. ............... 126 E3
Risegate Lincs ........... 103 K6
Riseley Bed ................. 74 F3
Riseley Wokham .......... 42 B7
Rishangles Suffk ......... 78 E2
Rishton Lancs ............ 121 L4
Rishworth Calder. ...... 122 F6
Risley Derbys ............ 101 J5
Risley Warrtn. ............ 112 F3
Risplith N York .......... 132 C5
River Kent ................... 35 J6
River W Susx ............... 30 F6
Riverford Highld ........ 212 E4
Riverhead Kent ........... 32 F3
Rivington Lancs ........ 121 J7
Rivington Services
  Lancs ..................... 121 J7
Roade Nhants ............. 73 L4
Roadmeetings S Lans.. 176 B7
Roadside E Ayrs ........ 164 B5
Roadside Highld ........ 231 H4
Roadwater Somset ...... 25 G4
Roag Highld .............. 208 D5
Roan of Craigoch
  S Ayrs .................... 153 G2
Roath Cardif ............... 37 J5
Roberton Border ....... 166 F6
Roberton S Lans ........ 165 H4
Robertsbridge E Susx .. 20 E2
Robertstown Kirk ...... 123 J6
Robeston Wathen
  Pembks .................... 49 J4
Robgill Tower D & G... 155 M7
Robin Hood's Bay
  N York .................... 143 K6
Roborough Devon ......... 6 D4
Roborough Devon ....... 10 E2
Robroyston C Glas. .... 175 H5
Roby Knows. ............. 112 B4
Rocester Staffs. ......... 100 C5
Roch Pembks. .............. 48 E3
Rochdale Rochdl. ...... 122 D7
Roche Cnwll .................. 4 F4
Rochester Medway. .... 46 C6
Rochester Nthumb ..... 157 L3
Rochford Essex ........... 46 E3
Rochford Worcs .......... 70 B2
Rock Cnwll .................... 4 E2
Rock Nthumb ............. 169 J5
Rock Worcs. ................. 70 D1
Rockbeare Devon ........ 12 C4
Rockbourne Hants ...... 28 C7
Rockcliffe Cumb ....... 148 C3
Rockcliffe D & G ....... 146 E4
Rockend Torbay ............ 7 L4
Rock Ferry Wirral ...... 111 K4
Rockfield Highld ........ 223 K5
Rockfield Mons ........... 54 C5
Rockford Devon ........... 24 B2
Rockhampton S Glos... 38 F2
Rockhill Shrops ........... 82 F7
Rockingham Nhants .... 88 C5
Rockland All Saints
  Norfk ....................... 92 B4
Rockland St Mary
  Norfk ....................... 93 G3
Rockland St Peter
  Norfk ....................... 92 B4
Rockley Notts ............ 116 B6
Rockliffe Lancs .......... 122 C6
Rockville Ag & B. ...... 173 L1

Rockwell End Bucks .......42 D3
Rodborough Gloucs ......55 J6
Rodbourne Swindn.......40 C4
Rodbourne Wilts.........39 L4
Rodden Dorset .............14 B5
Rode Somset ................27 J2
Rode Heath Ches E .....99 J2
Rodel W Isls ...............232 d5
Roden Wrekin ..............83 L1
Rodhuish Somset..........24 F4
Rodington Wrekin........83 L1
Rodington Heath
  Wrekin ......................83 L1
Rodley Gloucs ..............55 H5
Rodley Leeds .............123 J3
Rodmarton Gloucs........39 L2
Rodmell E Susx............19 L4
Rodmersham Kent.........34 B3
Rodmersham Green
  Kent ..........................34 B3
Rodney Stoke
  Somset ......................26 C2
Rodsley Derbys .........100 D4
Roecliffe N York .......132 L6
Roe Green Herts..........59 K6
Roe Green Herts..........75 K7
Roehampton Gt Lon......44 E5
Roffey W Susx..............31 K5
Rogart Highld............226 C7
Rogate W Susx.............30 D6
Rogerstone Newpt........37 L3
Roghadal W Isls.........232 d5
Rogiet Mons.................38 C3
Roke Oxon....................41 L2
Roker Sundld .............151 J3
Rollesby Norfk..............93 J1
Rolleston Leics.............87 K4
Rolleston Notts .........102 C3
Rolleston on Dove
  Staffs .......................100 E6
Rolston E R Yk ...........126 F2
Rolvenden Kent ...........33 L6
Rolvenden Layne
  Kent ..........................33 L7
Romaldkirk Dur.........140 C3
Romanby N York........132 E2
Romanno Bridge
  Border ......................177 G8
Romansleigh Devon......24 B7
Romesdal Highld.......208 F4
Romford Dorset ...........15 K1
Romford Gt Lon ...........45 K3
Romiley Stockp .........113 L4
Romsey Cambs ............76 C3
Romsey Hants..............29 G6
Romsley Shrops............84 D6
Romsley Worcs.............85 G7
Rona Highld ...............209 K3
Ronachan Ag & B .......172 C7
Rookhope Dur............150 B6
Rookley IoW .................17 G5
Rooks Bridge Somset ...26 A2
Rooks Nest Somset ......25 H5
Rookwith N York .......132 C3
Roos E R Yk................127 G4
Roothams Green
  Bed ............................75 G3
Ropley Hants................29 M5
Ropley Dean Hants ......29 L5
Ropsley Lincs .............103 G5
Rora Abers .................217 K4
Rorrington Shrops.......82 F4
Rosarie Moray ...........215 J4
Rose Cnwll ....................3 K1
Rose Ash Devon............24 C6
Rosebank S Lans.........175 L7
Rosebush Pembks.........49 J2
Rosedale Abbey
  N York .....................142 F7
Rose Green Essex .......61 L3
Rose Green Suffk........77 L5
Rose Green Suffk.........77 L6
Rose Green W Susx......18 B5
Rosehall Highld..........225 K7
Rosehearty Abers .......217 H2
Rose Hill Lancs...........122 C4
Roseisle Moray ..........214 E2
Roselands E Susx.........20 C5

Rosemarket Pembks .....49 G5
Rosemarkie Highld.....213 H3
Rosemary Lane
  Devon .......................25 J7
Rosemount P & K .......195 J7
Rosenannon Cnwll........4 E3
Rosewell Mdloth ........177 J6
Roseworth S on T ......141 K3
Rosgill Cumb..............138 D4
Roskhill Highld .........208 D5
Rosley Cumb...............148 B6
Roslin Mdloth ...........177 H5
Rosliston Derbys..........86 B1
Rosneath Ag & B .......174 B2
Ross D & G .................146 B6
Rossett Wrexhm ..........98 A2
Rossett Green
  N York .....................132 D8
Rossington Donc .......115 L2
Ross-on-Wye Herefs ....54 E4
Roster Highld ............231 J7
Rostherne Ches E ......113 H5
Rosthwaite Cumb ......137 H4
Roston Derbys ...........100 C4
Rosyth Fife .................176 F2
Rothbury Nthumb......158 D2
Rotherby Leics .............87 J1
Rotherfield E Susx......32 F7
Rotherfield Greys
  Oxon ..........................42 B4
Rotherfield Peppard
  Oxon ..........................42 B4
Rotherham Rothm .....115 H3
Rothersthorpe
  Nhants .......................73 K3
Rotherwick Hants .......30 B1
Rothes Moray .............215 G4
Rothesay Ag & B .......173 J5
Rothiebrisbane
  Abers ........................216 E6
Rothiemurchus
  Lodge Highld...........204 B4
Rothienorman Abers..216 D7
Rothley Leics ..............87 H2
Rothmaise Abers .......216 D7
Rothwell Leeds...........123 L5
Rothwell Lincs ...........117 J2
Rothwell Nhants..........88 B7
Rottal Lodge Angus ..196 B3
Rottingdean Br & H.....19 L5
Rottington Cumb ......136 D5
Roucan D & G ............155 H6
Rougham Norfk..........105 K6
Rougham Suffk...........77 K3
Rough Common
  Kent ..........................34 F3
Roughpark Abers ......205 H3
Roughton Lincs .........118 C8
Roughton Norfk.........106 F5
Roughton Shrops.........84 D5
Roundbush Green
  Essex .........................60 F5
Round Green Luton.....59 J4
Roundham Somset.......13 K1
Roundhay Leeds.........123 L3
Rounds Green Sandw...85 H5
Roundswell Devon.......23 H5
Roundway Wilts..........40 A7
Roundyhill Angus ......196 C6
Rousay Ork.................234 c4
Rousdon Devon...........13 H4
Rousham Oxon.............57 J3
Rous Lench Worcs.......71 H4
Routenburn N Ayrs....173 L6
Routh E R Yk..............126 D3
Row Cumb..................129 K2
Rowanburn D & G......156 D6
Rowardennan Stirlg...183 L7
Rowarth Derbys.........114 A4
Rowberrow Somset......38 C8
Rowde Wilts................39 L7
Rowen Conwy ............109 L6
Rowfoot Nthumb .......149 H3
Rowhedge Essex..........62 B4
Rowington Warwks.....72 B2
Rowland Derbys.........114 E6
Rowland's Castle
  Hants .........................17 K1

Rowlands Gill
  Gatesd......................150 E4
Rowledge Surrey .........30 D3
Rowley Dur.................150 D5
Rowley Regis Sandw ....85 H6
Rowlstone Herefs........54 A3
Rowly Surrey................31 H4
Rowner Hants...............17 H3
Rowney Green Worcs...71 J1
Rownhams Hants .........29 G7
Rownhams Services
  Hants .........................29 H7
Rowrah Cumb ............136 E4
Rowsham Bucks...........58 D4
Rowsley Derbys..........114 E7
Rowston Lincs ...........103 H2
Rowton Ches W ..........112 C8
Rowton Wrekin ...........98 E8
Roxburgh Border .......167 L4
Roxby N Linc..............125 L6
Roxton Bed ..................75 G4
Roxwell Essex...............61 G6
Royal Leamington
  Spa Warwks...............72 D2
Royal Sutton
  Coldfield Birm...........85 K4
Royal Tunbridge
  Wells Kent .................33 G5
Royal Wootton
  Bassett Wilts............40 B4
Royal Yacht
  Britannia C Edin......177 H3
Roy Bridge Highld.....192 D1
Roydon Essex .............60 C6
Roydon Norfk..............92 D7
Roydon Norfk............105 H7
Roydon Hamlet
  Essex .........................60 C6
Royston Barns ...........124 B7
Royston Herts..............75 L6
Royton Oldham .........122 D8
Rozel Jersey ...............236 e6
Ruabon Wrexhm..........97 L4
Ruaig Ag & B .............188 D6
Ruan Lanihorne
  Cnwll ...........................4 D7
Ruan Major Cnwll........3 J7
Ruan Minor Cnwll........3 J7
Ruardean Gloucs.........54 F4
Ruardean Hill Gloucs..54 F5
Ruardean Woodside
  Gloucs ........................54 F5
Rubery Birm................85 H7
Rubha Ban W Isls......233 c9
Ruckhall Herefs...........69 J6
Ruckinge Kent.............34 D7
Ruckley Shrops...........83 K4
Rudby N York.............141 L6
Rudchester Nthumb...150 E2
Ruddington Notts......101 L6
Rudge Somset..............27 J2
Rudgeway S Glos........38 F3
Rudgwick W Susx .......31 H5
Rudheath Ches W ......112 F6
Rudley Green Essex....61 K7
Rudloe Wilts................39 J6
Rudry Caerph ..............37 J3
Rudston E R Yk..........135 H6
Rudyard Staffs............99 L2
Ruecastle Border ......167 J5
Rufford Lancs ...........120 F7
Rufford Abbey Notts..115 M8
Rufforth C York.........124 D1
Rugby Warwks...........87 G7
Rugby Services
  Warwks......................87 G7
Rugeley Staffs ...........100 B8
Ruigh'riabhach
  Highld......................220 D3
Ruisgarry W Isls.......232 c5
Ruishton Somset.........25 K6
Ruisigearraidh
  W Isls........................232 c5
Ruislip Gt Lon.............43 H3
Rùm Highld ...............198 F5
Rumbach Moray.........215 J4
Rumbling Bridge
  P & K ........................185 L7

Rumburgh Suffk..........93 H7
Rumford Cnwll..............4 D2
Rumford Falk............176 C3
Rumney Cardif............37 K5
Runcorn Halton .........112 D5
Runcton W Susx..........18 B5
Runcton Holme
  Norfk..........................90 E2
Runfold Surrey ...........30 E3
Runhall Norfk..............92 C3
Runham Norfk.............93 K2
Runnington Somset .....25 H6
Runswick N York .......143 G4
Runtaleave Angus......195 L3
Runwell Essex ............46 C2
Ruscombe Wokham ....42 D5
Rushall Herefs.............70 B7
Rushall Norfk..............92 E6
Rushall Wilts...............28 C1
Rushall Wsall...............85 H4
Rushbrooke Suffk........77 K3
Rushbury Shrops.........83 K5
Rushden Herts.............60 A2
Rushden Nhants..........74 D2
Rushenden Kent..........46 E5
Rushford Norfk............91 K7
Rush Green Essex........62 E5
Rush Green Gt Lon......45 K3
Rush Green Warrtn....113 G4
Rushlake Green
  E Susx ........................20 D3
Rushmere Suffk...........93 K6
Rushmoor Surrey.........30 E4
Rushock Worcs............70 F1
Rusholme Manch .......113 J3
Rushton Nhants...........88 B6
Rushton Spencer
  Staffs .......................113 L8
Rushwick Worcs.........70 E4
Rushyford Dur...........141 G2
Ruskie Stirlg..............184 D7
Ruskington Lincs ......103 H3
Rusland Cross Cumb..129 H2
Rusper W Susx.............31 K4
Ruspidge Gloucs.........54 F5
Russell's Water Oxon..42 B3
Russ Hill Surrey...........31 L4
Rusthall Kent...............32 F5
Rustington W Susx .....18 E5
Ruston N York ...........134 E3
Ruston Parva E R Yk..135 G6
Ruswarp N York.........143 H5
Rutherford Border.....167 K4
Rutherglen S Lans.....175 H6
Ruthernbridge Cnwll....4 F3
Ruthin Denbgs............97 H2
Ruthrieston C Aber ...207 H4
Ruthven Abers ..........215 L5
Ruthven Angus ..........195 L6
Ruthven Highld.........203 H5
Ruthven Highld.........213 J7
Ruthvoes Cnwll............4 E3
Ruthwell D & G .........147 J2
Ryton-XI-Towns
  Shrops ........................98 B7
Ryal Nthumb .............158 C7
Ryall Dorset................13 K4
Ryall Worcs.................70 F6
Ryarsh Kent................33 H2
Rydal Cumb...............137 K6
Ryde IoW.....................17 H4
Rye E Susx ..................21 H2
Rye Foreign E Susx ....21 H2
Rye Street Worcs.........70 D7
Ryhall Rutlnd...............88 F2
Ryhill Wakefd ...........124 B7
Ryhope Sundld ..........151 K4
Ryland Lincs ..............117 G5
Rylstone N York ........131 H7
Ryme Intrinseca
  Dorset .......................14 B1
Ryther N York ...........124 E3
Ryton Gatesd.............150 E3
Ryton Shrops...............84 D3
Ryton-on-
  Dunsmore
  Warwks......................86 E8

RZSS Edinburgh
Zoo C Edin ................ 177 G4

## S

Sabden Lancs ............ 122 B3
Sacombe Herts ..............60 B4
Sacriston Dur ............ 151 G5
Sadberge Darltn......... 141 H4
Saddell Ag & B........... 161 K3
Saddington Leics..........87 J5
Saddlebow Norfk..........90 E1
Saddlescombe
W Susx........................19 H4
Saffron Walden
Essex..........................76 D6
Sageston Pembks ......49 H6
Saham Hills Norfk.......91 K3
Saham Toney Norfk.....91 K3
Saighton Ches W ..........98 C1
St Abbs Border ......... 179 J5
St Agnes Border ........ 178 E5
St Agnes Cnwll..............3 J2
St Agnes IoS...................2 a2
St Agnes Mining
District Cnwll..............3 J2
St Albans Herts ...........59 J6
St Allen Cnwll ................4 C5
St Andrew Guern ...... 236 c3
St Andrews Fife ........ 187 H4
St Andrews Botanic
Garden Fife............. 187 H4
St Andrews Major
V Glam........................37 H6
St Andrews Well
Dorset........................13 L4
St Anne's Lancs ........ 120 D5
St Ann's D & G .......... 155 J4
St Ann's Chapel
Cnwll............................6 B2
St Ann's Chapel
Devon..........................6 F6
St Anthony-in-
Meneage Cnwll...........3 K6
St Anthony's Hill
E Susx........................20 D5
St Arvans Mons...........38 D2
St Asaph Denbgs...... 110 E6
St Athan V Glam..........36 F6
St Aubin Jersey ........ 236 b7
St Austell Cnwll .............4 F5
St Bees Cumb............ 136 D5
St Blazey Cnwll..............5 G5
St Boswells Border ... 167 J3
St Brelade Jersey ..... 236 b7
St Brelade's Bay
Jersey...................... 236 b7
St Breock Cnwll..............4 F2
St Breward Cnwll..........5 H1
St Briavels Gloucs......54 E6
St Brides Major
V Glam........................36 D5
St Brides-super-Ely
V Glam........................37 H5
St Brides
Wentlooge Newpt...37 L4
St Budeaux C Plym........6 C4
Saintbury Gloucs.........71 K4
St Buryan Cnwll .............2 D6
St Catherines Ag & B... 183 G6
St Chloe Gloucs...........55 J7
St Clears Carmth..........50 C3
St Cleer Cnwll ................5 K3
St Clement Cnwll............4 D6
St Clement Jersey .... 236 e8
St Clether Cnwll............9 G7
St Colmac Ag & B ..... 173 H5
St Columb Major
Cnwll............................4 E3
St Columb Minor
Cnwll............................4 D4
St Columb Road
Cnwll............................4 E4
St Combs Abers ........ 217 K2
St Cross South
Elmham Suffk..........93 G6

St Cyrus Abers............ 197 J4
St David's P & K......... 185 K4
St Davids Pembks .......48 C3
St Davids Cathedral
Pembks......................48 C3
St Day Cnwll ..................3 J3
St Dennis Cnwll..............4 E4
St Dogmaels Pembks...65 G5
St Dominick Cnwll..........6 B3
St Donats V Glam........36 E6
St Endellion Cnwll..........4 F1
St Enoder Cnwll.............4 D4
St Erme Cnwll.................4 D6
St Erney Cnwll ...............6 B4
St Erth Cnwll .................2 F4
St Erth Praze Cnwll.......3 G4
St Ervan Cnwll ..............4 D2
St Eval Cnwll .................4 D3
St Ewe Cnwll..................4 F6
St Fagans Cardif..........37 H5
St Fagans: National
History Museum
Cardif.........................37 H5
St Fergus Abers ........ 217 K4
St Fillans P & K .......... 184 F3
St Florence Pembks ....49 J7
St Gennys Cnwll............8 F5
St George Conwy...... 110 D6
St Georges N Som......38 B7
St George's V Glam.....37 H5
St Germans Cnwll..........6 A4
St Giles in the
Wood Devon..............23 H7
St Giles-on-the-
Heath Devon..............9 K6
St Harmon Powys.........81 L8
St Helen Auckland
Dur.......................... 140 F2
St Helen's E Susx.........21 G4
St Helens IoW..............17 J5
St Helens M Susx....... 112 D3
St Helier Gt Lon...........44 E6
St Helier Jersey ....... 236 d7
St Hilary Cnwll...............2 F5
St Hilary V Glam..........36 F5
St Ippolyts Herts..........59 K3
St Ishmael's Pembks ...48 E6
St Issey Cnwll ................4 E2
St Ive Cnwll....................5 L3
St Ives Cambs...............75 K1
St Ives Cnwll..................2 F3
St James's End
Nhants.......................73 L3
St James South
Elmham Suffk..........93 G7
St Jidgey Cnwll..............4 E3
St John Cnwll ................6 B5
St John Jersey .......... 236 c5
St John's E Susx..........32 E6
St John's IoM ............. 237 b5
St John's Kent .............32 F3
St Johns Surrey ..........43 G8
St Johns Worcs...........70 E4
St John's Chapel
Devon.........................23 H5
St John's Chapel
Dur.......................... 149 M7
St John's Fen End
Norfk..........................90 D2
St John's Kirk S Lans... 165 J3
St John's Town of
Dalry D & G ............. 154 B6
St John's Wood
Gt Lon........................44 F4
St Judes IoM ............. 237 d3
St Just Cnwll..................2 C5
St Just-in-Roseland
Cnwll............................4 D8
St Just Mining
District Cnwll..............2 D5
St Katherines Abers ... 216 E7
St Keverne Cnwll ..........3 K6
St Kew Cnwll...................5 G1
St Kew Highway
Cnwll............................5 G2
St Keyne Cnwll...............5 K4
St Lawrence Essex......62 A6
St Lawrence IoW..........17 G6

St Lawrence Jersey ... 236 c6
St Lawrence Kent.........35 K2
St Leonards Bucks......58 E6
St Leonards Dorset .....15 L2
St Leonards E Susx.....20 F4
St Levan Cnwll ..............2 C6
St Lythans V Glam........37 H6
St Mabyn Cnwll..............5 G2
St Madoes P & K........ 186 C3
St Margarets Herefs ...69 G7
St Margarets Herts......60 B5
St Margaret's at
Cliffe Kent..................35 K5
St Margaret's Hope
Ork.......................... 234 c7
St Margaret South
Elmham Suffk..........93 G6
St Marks IoM............. 237 c6
St Martin Cnwll ..............3 J6
St Martin Cnwll ..............5 K5
St Martin Guern ........ 236 d3
St Martin Jersey ....... 236 e6
St Martin's IoS...............2 b1
St Martin's P & K ....... 186 B2
St Martin's Shrops......97 L5
St Mary Jersey .......... 236 b6
St Mary Bourne
Hants.........................29 H2
St Marychurch
Torbay..........................7 L3
St Mary Church
V Glam........................36 F6
St Mary Cray Gt Lon...45 J6
St Mary in the
Marsh Kent................21 L1
St Mary's IoS.................2 b1
St Mary's Ork............ 234 c6
St Mary's Bay Kent......21 L1
St Mary's Hoo
Medway.....................46 D5
St Mary's Platt Kent....33 G2
St Maughans Green
Mons.........................54 C5
St Mawes Cnwll.............3 L5
St Mawgan Cnwll..........4 D3
St Mellion Cnwll ............6 B3
St Mellons Cardif........37 K4
St Merryn Cnwll ............4 D2
St Michael
Caerhays Cnwll..........4 F7
St Michael Church
Somset......................25 L5
St Michael Penkevil
Cnwll............................4 D7
St Michaels Kent..........34 B7
St Michaels Worcs......69 L2
St Michael's Mount
Cnwll............................2 F5
St Michael's on
Wyre Lancs.............. 120 F3
St Minver Cnwll..............4 F1
St Monans Fife .......... 187 H6
St Neot Cnwll..................5 J3
St Neots Cambs...........75 H3
St Newlyn East Cnwll ....4 C5
St Nicholas Pembks ....64 C7
St Nicholas V Glam......37 H5
St Nicholas-at-
Wade Kent.................47 L6
St Ninians Stirlg........ 185 G8
St Olaves Norfk............93 J4
St Osyth Essex............62 D5
St Ouen Jersey ......... 236 b6
St Owen's Cross
Herefs........................54 D3
St Paul's Cray Gt Lon...45 J6
St Paul's Walden
Herts..........................59 K4
St Peter Jersey ........ 236 b6
St Peter Port Guern ... 236 d3
St Peter's Guern....... 236 b3
St Peter's Kent............35 K2
St Peter's Hill Cambs...89 J8
St Pinnock Cnwll...........5 J3
St Quivox S Ayrs....... 163 J5
St Sampson Guern .... 236 d2
St Saviour Guern ...... 236 c3
St Saviour Jersey ..... 236 d7

St Stephen Cnwll............4 E5
St Stephens Cnwll..........6 B4
St Stephens Cnwll..........9 J7
St Teath Cnwll.................8 E8
St Thomas Devon........11 K6
St Tudy Cnwll..................5 G1
St Twynnells Pembks...48 F7
St Veep Cnwll.................5 J5
St Vigeans Angus ..... 197 G7
St Wenn Cnwll ...............4 F3
St Weonards Herefs....54 D3
Salcombe Devon............7 H7
Salcombe Regis
Devon.........................12 F5
Salcott-cum-Virley
Essex..........................61 M5
Sale Traffd................. 113 H3
Saleby Lincs.............. 118 F5
Sale Green Worcs........71 G3
Salehurst E Susx.........20 F2
Salem Cerdgn...............80 F6
Salen Ag & B.............. 190 C7
Salen Highld.............. 190 D4
Salford C Beds.............74 D4
Salford Oxon................56 F3
Salford Salfd.............. 113 J3
Salford Priors
Warwks......................71 J4
Salfords Surrey ..........32 B4
Salhouse Norfk............93 G1
Saline Fife................. 185 L8
Salisbury Wilts.............28 C5
Salisbury Plain Wilts....28 B3
Salkeld Dykes Cumb... 148 F7
Sallachy Highld.......... 225 L6
Salle Norfk................. 106 D7
Salmonby Lincs......... 118 D6
Salperton Gloucs........56 B4
Salsburgh N Lans...... 175 L5
Salt Staffs....................99 L6
Saltaire C Brad ......... 123 H3
Saltaire C Brad ......... 123 H3
Saltash Cnwll .................6 B4
Saltburn Highld......... 223 G7
Saltburn-by-the-
Sea R & Cl................ 142 E3
Saltby Leics............... 102 D7
Saltcoats N Ayrs....... 163 G2
Saltcotes Lancs......... 120 E5
Saltdean Br & H ...........19 K5
Salterbeck Cumb...... 136 D3
Salterforth Lancs....... 122 D2
Salterswall Ches W ... 112 F7
Salterton Wilts............28 C4
Saltfleet Lincs............ 118 F3
Saltfleetby All
Saints Lincs............. 118 F4
Saltfleetby St
Clement Lincs......... 118 F3
Saltfleetby St Peter
Lincs......................... 118 F4
Saltford BaNES...........39 G6
Salthouse Norfk......... 106 C4
Saltley Birm.................85 K6
Saltmarshe E R Yk..... 125 J5
Saltney Flints............ 111 L8
Salton N York............ 133 L4
Saltrens Devon............23 G6
Saltwood Kent.............34 F7
Salvington W Susx......18 F5
Salwarpe Worcs..........70 F3
Salway Ash Dorset......13 L3
Sambourne Warwks....71 J3
Sambrook Wrekin ........99 G7
Sampford Arundel
Somset......................25 H7
Sampford Brett
Somset......................25 H4
Sampford
Courtenay Devon......10 F5
Sampford Moor
Somset......................25 H7
Sampford Peverell
Devon.........................25 G8
Sampford Spiney
Devon...........................6 D2
Samsonlane Ork........ 234 d5
Samuelston E Loth.... 178 B4

Sanaigmore Ag & B.... **170** E4
Sancreed Cnwll........... **2** D5
Sancton E R Yk.......... **125** L3
Sandaig Highld........... **199** L5
Sandal Magna
  Wakefd................. **123** L6
Sanday Ork.............. **234** d4
Sanday Airport Ork.... **234** d4
Sandbach Ches E......... **99** H1
Sandbach Services
  Ches E................. **99** H1
Sandbank Ag & B....... **173** K3
Sandbanks BCP.......... **15** K5
Sandend Abers.......... **216** B2
Sanderstead Gt Lon..... **45** G7
Sandford Cumb......... **139** G4
Sandford Devon......... **11** J4
Sandford Dorset........ **15** H5
Sandford Hants......... **15** M3
Sandford IoW........... **17** G6
Sandford N Som........ **38** B8
Sandford S Lans....... **164** E2
Sandford-on-
  Thames Oxon........ **57** K7
Sandford Orcas
  Dorset................. **26** F7
Sandford St Martin
  Oxon.................. **57** H3
Sandgate Kent........... **35** G7
Sandhaven Abers...... **217** H2
Sandhead D & G....... **144** D5
Sand Hills Leeds....... **124** B3
Sandhills Oxon.......... **57** K6
Sandhills Surrey......... **30** F4
Sandhoe Nthumb...... **150** B2
Sandhole Ag & B...... **182** E7
Sand Hole E R Yk...... **125** J3
Sandholme E R Yk...... **125** J4
Sandhurst Br For........ **42** D7
Sandhurst Gloucs....... **55** J4
Sandhurst Kent.......... **33** K7
Sandhutton N York.... **132** F3
Sand Hutton N York... **133** L7
Sandiacre Derbys...... **101** J5
Sandilands Lincs...... **119** G5
Sandleheath Hants..... **28** C7
Sandleigh Oxon......... **57** J7
Sandley Dorset.......... **27** H6
Sandness Shet......... **235** b5
Sandon Essex........... **61** H6
Sandon Herts........... **75** K7
Sandon Staffs........... **99** L6
Sandon Bank Staffs.... **99** L6
Sandown IoW........... **17** H5
Sandplace Cnwll......... **5** K4
Sandridge Herts........ **59** K6
Sandringham Norfk... **105** H6
Sandsend N York...... **143** H5
Sandtoft N Linc....... **125** H8
Sandway Kent........... **34** B5
Sandwich Kent.......... **35** J3
Sandwick Shet......... **235** c7
Sandwick W Isls....... **232** g2
Sandwith Cumb........ **136** D4
Sandy C Beds........... **75** H5
Sandyford D & G...... **155** L4
Sandygate Devon....... **7** K2
Sandygate IoM........ **237** d3
Sandyhills D & G...... **146** F4
Sandylands Lancs..... **129** J6
Sandy Lane Wilts....... **39** L6
Sandy Park Devon...... **11** G6
Sangobeg Highld...... **228** F3
Sangomore Highld.... **228** F3
Sankyn's Green
  Worcs................. **70** E2
Sanna Highld.......... **189** K3
Sanndabhaig W Isls.. **232** g2
Sannox N Ayrs......... **162** C1
Sanquhar D & G....... **164** F7
Santon Bridge Cumb.. **136** F6
Santon Downham
  Suffk.................. **91** J6
Sapcote Leics........... **86** F5
Sapey Common
  Herefs................. **70** C2
Sapiston Suffk.......... **91** K7
Sapley Cambs.......... **89** J8

Sapperton Gloucs....... **55** L7
Sapperton Lincs...... **103** G5
Saracen's Head
  Lincs................. **104** B6
Sarclet Highld........ **231** L6
Sarisbury Hants........ **17** G2
Sarn Powys............. **82** E5
Sarnau Cerdgn......... **65** K4
Sarnau Powys.......... **82** E1
Sarn Mellteyrn
  Gwynd................ **94** D6
Sarn Park Services
  Brdgnd................. **36** D4
Saron Carmth.......... **51** H3
Saron Gwynd......... **109** G7
Sarratt Herts............ **59** H7
Sarre Kent.............. **47** L6
Sarsden Oxon........... **56** F4
Satley Dur.............. **150** E6
Satterleigh Devon....... **23** L6
Satterthwaite Cumb... **129** H2
Sauchen Abers........ **206** D3
Saucher P & K......... **186** C2
Sauchieburn Abers... **197** G3
Saul Gloucs............. **55** H6
Saundby Notts........ **116** C4
Saundersfoot
  Pembks................ **49** K6
Saunderton Bucks...... **58** C7
Saunton Devon......... **23** G4
Sausthorpe Lincs..... **118** E7
Savile Town Kirk..... **123** K6
Sawbridge Warwks..... **73** G2
Sawbridgeworth
  Herts.................. **60** D5
Sawdon N York....... **134** E3
Sawley Lancs.......... **122** B2
Sawley N York........ **132** C6
Sawston Cambs......... **76** C5
Sawtry Cambs.......... **89** H6
Saxby Leics........... **102** D8
Saxby Lincs........... **117** G4
Saxby All Saints
  N Linc................ **126** B7
Saxelbye Leics........ **102** B7
Saxham Street Suffk.... **78** C3
Saxilby Lincs.......... **116** E6
Saxlingham Norfk.... **106** B5
Saxlingham Green
  Norfk.................. **92** F4
Saxlingham
  Nethergate Norfk... **92** F4
Saxlingham Thorpe
  Norfk.................. **92** E4
Saxmundham Suffk.... **79** H2
Saxondale Notts...... **102** B4
Saxon Street Cambs.... **76** F3
Saxtead Suffk.......... **78** F2
Saxtead Green Suffk.... **78** F2
Saxtead Little Green
  Suffk.................. **78** F2
Saxthorpe Norfk...... **106** D6
Saxton N York........ **124** D3
Sayers Common
  W Susx................ **19** H3
Scackleton N York.... **133** K5
Scadabay W Isls...... **232** e4
Scadabhagh W Isls.. **232** e4
Scafell Pike Cumb... **137** H5
Scaftworth Notts..... **116** A3
Scagglethorpe
  N York............... **134** C5
Scalasaig Ag & B..... **180** E8
Scalby E R Yk......... **125** K5
Scalby N York........ **134** F2
Scaldwell Nhants...... **73** L1
Scaleby Cumb......... **148** D3
Scalebyhill Cumb..... **148** D3
Scales Cumb.......... **129** G5
Scales Cumb.......... **137** K2
Scalford Leics........ **102** C7
Scaling N York........ **142** F4
Scalloway Shet....... **235** c6
Scalpay Highld....... **209** J7
Scalpay W Isls....... **232** e4
Scamblesby Lincs.... **118** C5
Scamodale Highld... **191** G2
Scampston N York.... **134** D4

Scampton Lincs...... **116** F5
Scaniport Highld..... **212** F6
Scapegoat Hill Kirk... **123** G2
Scarba Ag & B........ **181** K6
Scarborough N York.. **135** G2
Scarcewater Cnwll...... **4** E5
Scarcliffe Derbys..... **115** J7
Scarcroft Leeds....... **124** B3
Scarfskerry Highld... **231** J2
Scarinish Ag & B..... **188** D7
Scarisbrick Lancs.... **120** E7
Scarning Norfk......... **91** L2
Scarrington Notts.... **102** B4
Scartho NE Lin....... **118** C1
Scatsta Airport Shet.. **235** c4
Scaur D & G........... **146** E4
Scawby N Linc........ **116** F1
Scawsby Donc........ **115** K1
Scawthorpe Donc.... **115** K1
Scawton N York...... **133** H3
Scayne's Hill W Susx... **19** K2
Scethrog Powys........ **53** H3
Scholar Green
  Ches E................. **99** J2
Scholes Kirk.......... **123** H8
Scholes Leeds........ **124** B3
Scholes Rothm....... **115** H3
Scholes Wigan....... **112** E1
Scissett Kirk......... **123** K7
Scleddau Pembks...... **64** C7
Scofton Notts........ **115** M5
Scole Norfk............. **92** D7
Scone P & K.......... **186** B3
Sconser Highld....... **209** H7
Scoonie Fife.......... **186** F6
Scopwick Lincs...... **103** H2
Scoraig Highld....... **220** C3
Scorborough E R Yk.. **126** C2
Scorrier Cnwll........... **3** J3
Scorton Lancs........ **121** G2
Scorton N York....... **141** G7
Scotby Cumb......... **148** D4
Scotch Corner
  N York............... **140** F6
Scotch Corner Rest
  Area N York......... **140** F6
Scotforth Lancs...... **129** K7
Scothern Lincs....... **117** G6
Scotlandwell P & K.. **186** C6
Scotscalder Station
  Highld................ **231** G4
Scot's Gap Nthumb.. **158** C5
Scotsmill Abers...... **206** B2
Scotstoun C Glas.... **174** F5
Scotswood N u Ty... **150** F3
Scotter Lincs......... **116** E2
Scotterthorpe Lincs.. **116** E2
Scottish Seabird
  Centre E Loth....... **178** C2
Scottish Wool
  Centre Stirlg........ **184** C7
Scotton Lincs........ **116** E2
Scotton N York....... **132** E7
Scotton N York....... **140** F7
Scoulton Norfk......... **92** B4
Scourie Highld....... **228** B6
Scourie More Highld.. **228** B6
Scousburgh Shet.... **235** c7
Scrabster Highld..... **231** G2
Scraesburgh Border.. **167** K5
Scrane End Lincs.... **104** C4
Scraptoft Leics........ **87** J3
Scratby Norfk.......... **93** K1
Scrayingham N York.. **133** L2
Scredington Lincs... **103** H4
Scremby Lincs....... **118** F7
Scremerston Nthumb. **179** L8
Screveton Notts..... **102** B4
Scriven N York....... **132** E7
Scrooby Notts....... **115** M4
Scropton Derbys..... **100** D6
Scrub Hill Lincs..... **103** L2
Scruton N York...... **132** D2
Scullomie Highld.... **229** J4
Sculthorpe Norfk.... **105** L6
Scunthorpe N Linc... **125** K7
Seaborough Dorset... **13** K2
Seabridge Staffs...... **99** J4

Seabrook Kent......... **35** G7
Seaburn Sundld...... **151** J3
Seacombe Wirral..... **111** K4
Seacroft Leeds....... **123** L4
Seafield W Loth..... **176** D5
Seaford E Susx........ **20** A6
Seaforth Sefton...... **111** K3
Seagrave Leics....... **101** L8
Seaham Dur.......... **151** K5
Seahouses Nthumb.. **169** J3
Seal Kent............... **32** F2
Sealand Flints........ **111** K7
Seale Surrey........... **30** E2
Seamer N York....... **134** F3
Seamer N York....... **142** B5
Seamill N Ayrs....... **173** L8
Sea Palling Norfk.... **107** J6
Searby Lincs.......... **117** H1
Seasalter Kent......... **47** H6
Seascale Cumb...... **136** E6
Seathwaite Cumb... **137** H7
Seatoller Cumb...... **137** H4
Seaton Cnwll............ **5** L5
Seaton Cumb........ **136** E2
Seaton Devon.......... **13** G4
Seaton E R Yk....... **126** E2
Seaton Kent........... **35** G3
Seaton Nthumb..... **159** H6
Seaton Rutlnd......... **88** C4
Seaton Carew Hartpl. **142** B2
Seaton Delaval
  Nthumb.............. **159** H6
Seaton Ross E R Yk.. **125** J3
Seaton Sluice
  Nthumb.............. **159** H6
Seatown Dorset....... **13** K4
Seatown Moray...... **214** F1
Seave Green N York.. **142** C7
Seaview IoW........... **17** J4
Seaville Cumb....... **147** K4
Seavington St Mary
  Somset................ **26** B7
Seavington St
  Michael Somset..... **26** B7
Sebastopol Torfn...... **37** L2
Sebergham Cumb.... **148** C6
Seckington Warwks... **86** C3
Second Severn
  Crossing Mons...... **38** D3
Sedbergh Cumb..... **130** C2
Sedbury Gloucs....... **38** D2
Sedbusk N York..... **131** G2
Sedgeberrow Worcs.. **71** H6
Sedgebrook Lincs... **102** D5
Sedgefield Dur...... **141** J2
Sedgeford Norfk..... **105** H5
Sedgehill Wilts........ **27** K5
Sedgemoor
  Services Somset..... **26** A2
Sedgley Dudley....... **85** G5
Sedgley Park Bury... **113** J2
Sedgwick Cumb..... **129** L3
Sedlescombe E Susx.. **20** F3
Sedrup Bucks.......... **58** D5
Seend Wilts............ **39** L7
Seend Cleeve Wilts... **39** L7
Seer Green Bucks...... **42** F3
Seething Norfk........ **93** G4
Sefton Sefton......... **111** K2
Seighford Staffs....... **99** K7
Seion Gwynd......... **109** H7
Seisdon Staffs......... **84** E4
Selattyn Shrops....... **97** K5
Selborne Hants........ **30** C5
Selby N York......... **124** F4
Selham W Susx........ **30** F7
Selhurst Gt Lon....... **45** G6
Selkirk Border....... **167** G4
Sellack Herefs......... **54** E3
Sellafield Station
  Cumb................ **136** E6
Sellafirth Shet....... **235** d2
Sellindge Kent......... **34** F6
Selling Kent........... **34** D4
Sells Green Wilts...... **39** L7
Selly Oak Birm........ **85** J6
Selmeston E Susx..... **20** B4
Selsdon Gt Lon....... **45** G7

Selsey W Susx ...... 18 B6
Selside N York ...... 130 E4
Selsley Gloucs ...... 55 J7
Selsted Kent ...... 35 G5
Selston Notts ...... 101 J4
Selworthy Somset ...... 24 E3
Semer Suffk ...... 78 B5
Semington Wilts ...... 39 K7
Semley Wilts ...... 27 K6
Send Surrey ...... 31 G1
Senghenydd Caerph ...... 37 H3
Sennen Cnwll ...... 2 C6
Sennen Cove Cnwll ...... 2 C6
Sennybridge Powys ...... 52 E3
Sessay N York ...... 133 G4
Setchey Norfk ...... 90 F2
Seton Mains E Loth ...... 177 L4
Settle N York ...... 130 F6
Settrington N York ...... 134 C5
Sevenhampton
  Gloucs ...... 56 B4
Sevenhampton
  Swindn ...... 40 E3
Seven Kings Gt Lon ...... 45 J3
Sevenoaks Kent ...... 32 F3
Sevenoaks Weald
  Kent ...... 32 F3
Seven Sisters Neath ...... 52 C6
Seven Star Green
  Essex ...... 61 M3
Severn Beach S Glos ...... 38 D4
Severn Bridge S Glos ...... 38 E4
Severn Stoke Worcs ...... 70 F5
Severn View
  Services S Glos ...... 38 E3
Sevington Kent ...... 34 D6
Sewards End Essex ...... 76 E6
Sewell C Beds ...... 59 G4
Sewerby E R Yk ...... 135 J5
Seworgan Cnwll ...... 3 J3
Sewstern Leics ...... 102 E7
Sgalpaigh W Isls ...... 232 e4
Sgiogarstaigh W Isls ...... 232 g1
Shabbington Bucks ...... 58 A6
Shackerstone Leics ...... 86 D3
Shackleford Surrey ...... 30 F3
Shader W Isls ...... 232 f1
Shadforth Dur ...... 151 H6
Shadingfield Suffk ...... 93 J6
Shadoxhurst Kent ...... 34 C6
Shadwell Leeds ...... 123 L3
Shadwell Norfk ...... 91 L6
Shaftenhoe End
  Herts ...... 76 B6
Shaftesbury Dorset ...... 27 K6
Shafton Barns ...... 124 B7
Shakerley Wigan ...... 113 G2
Shalbourne Wilts ...... 40 F7
Shalden Hants ...... 30 B3
Shaldon Devon ...... 7 L2
Shalfleet IoW ...... 16 E5
Shalford Essex ...... 61 H3
Shalford Surrey ...... 31 G3
Shalford Green
  Essex ...... 61 H3
Shalmsford Street
  Kent ...... 34 E4
Shalstone Bucks ...... 73 J7
Shamley Green
  Surrey ...... 31 G3
Shandford Angus ...... 196 D4
Shandon Ag & B ...... 174 B2
Shandwick Highld ...... 223 J6
Shangton Leics ...... 87 K4
Shanklin IoW ...... 17 H6
Shantron Ag & B ...... 174 C2
Shap Cumb ...... 138 E4
Shapinsay Ork ...... 234 c5
Shapwick Dorset ...... 15 H3
Shapwick Somset ...... 26 B4
Shard End Birm ...... 85 L5
Shardlow Derbys ...... 101 H6
Shareshill Staffs ...... 85 G3
Sharlston Wakefd ...... 124 B6
Sharmans Cross
  Solhll ...... 85 K7
Sharnbrook Bed ...... 74 E3
Sharnford Leics ...... 86 F5

Sharoe Green Lancs ...... 121 G4
Sharow N York ...... 132 E5
Sharpenhoe C Beds ...... 59 H2
Sharperton Nthumb ...... 158 B2
Sharpness Gloucs ...... 54 F7
Sharrington Norfk ...... 106 C5
Shatterford Worcs ...... 84 E7
Shaugh Prior Devon ...... 6 D3
Shavington Ches E ...... 99 G3
Shaw Oldham ...... 122 D8
Shaw Swindn ...... 40 C4
Shaw W Berk ...... 41 J6
Shaw Wilts ...... 39 K7
Shawbirch Wrekin ...... 84 B2
Shawbost W Isls ...... 232 e2
Shawbury Shrops ...... 98 E7
Shawell Leics ...... 87 G7
Shawford Hants ...... 29 J6
Shawhead D & G ...... 154 F6
Shaw Mills N York ...... 132 C6
Shawsburn S Lans ...... 175 K7
Shearington D & G ...... 147 H2
Shearsby Leics ...... 87 J5
Shearston Somset ...... 25 L5
Shebbear Devon ...... 10 C3
Shebdon Staffs ...... 99 H7
Shebster Highld ...... 230 E3
Shedfield Hants ...... 29 K8
Sheen Staffs ...... 100 C1
Sheepridge Kirk ...... 123 H6
Sheepscar Leeds ...... 123 L4
Sheepscombe Gloucs ...... 55 K6
Sheepstor Devon ...... 6 E3
Sheepwash Devon ...... 10 C4
Sheepy Magna Leics ...... 86 D3
Sheepy Parva Leics ...... 86 D3
Sheering Essex ...... 60 E5
Sheerness Kent ...... 46 F5
Sheerwater Surrey ...... 43 G7
Sheet Hants ...... 30 C6
Sheffield Sheff ...... 115 G4
Sheffield Park E Susx ...... 19 L2
Shefford C Beds ...... 75 G6
Sheigra Highld ...... 228 B4
Sheinton Shrops ...... 83 L3
Shelderton Shrops ...... 83 H7
Sheldon Birm ...... 85 L6
Sheldon Derbys ...... 114 D7
Sheldon Devon ...... 12 E2
Sheldwich Kent ...... 34 D4
Shelfanger Norfk ...... 92 D6
Shelford Notts ...... 102 A4
Shelley Kirk ...... 123 J7
Shelley Suffk ...... 78 B6
Shellingford Oxon ...... 40 F2
Shellow Bowells
  Essex ...... 60 F6
Shelsley
  Beauchamp
  Worcs ...... 70 D2
Shelsley Walsh
  Worcs ...... 70 C2
Shelton Bed ...... 74 F2
Shelton Norfk ...... 92 F5
Shelton Notts ...... 102 C4
Shelton Lock C Derb ...... 101 G6
Shelton Under
  Harley Staffs ...... 99 J5
Shelve Shrops ...... 83 G4
Shelwick Herefs ...... 69 K6
Shenfield Essex ...... 45 L2
Shenington Oxon ...... 72 D6
Shenley Herts ...... 59 K7
Shenley Brook End
  M Keyn ...... 74 B7
Shenley Church End
  M Keyn ...... 74 B7
Shenmore Herefs ...... 69 H6
Shennanton D & G ...... 145 H3
Shenstone Staffs ...... 85 K3
Shenstone Worcs ...... 84 F8
Shenton Leics ...... 86 E4
Shenval Moray ...... 214 F7
Shephall Herts ...... 59 L4
Shepherd's Bush
  Gt Lon ...... 44 E4
Shepherdswell Kent ...... 35 H5
Shepley Kirk ...... 123 J8

Shepperton Surrey ...... 43 H6
Shepreth Cambs ...... 76 B5
Shepshed Leics ...... 101 J8
Shepton
  Beauchamp
  Somset ...... 26 B7
Shepton Mallet
  Somset ...... 26 F3
Shepton Montague
  Somset ...... 27 G5
Shepway Kent ...... 33 K3
Sheraton Dur ...... 151 K7
Sherborne Dorset ...... 26 F7
Sherborne Gloucs ...... 56 D5
Sherborne Somset ...... 26 E1
Sherborne St John
  Hants ...... 29 L1
Sherbourne Warwks ...... 72 C3
Sherburn Dur ...... 151 H6
Sherburn N York ...... 134 E4
Sherburn Hill Dur ...... 151 H6
Sherburn in Elmet
  N York ...... 124 D4
Shere Surrey ...... 31 H2
Shereford Norfk ...... 105 L6
Sherfield English
  Hants ...... 28 F6
Sherfield on
  Loddon Hants ...... 42 B8
Sherford Devon ...... 7 H6
Sheriffhales Shrops ...... 84 D2
Sheriff Hutton N York ...... 133 K6
Sheringham Norfk ...... 106 E4
Sherington M Keyn ...... 74 C5
Shernborne Norfk ...... 105 H6
Sherrington Wilts ...... 27 L4
Sherston Wilts ...... 39 J3
Sherwood C Nott ...... 101 K4
Sherwood Forest
  Notts ...... 101 L1
Shetland Islands
  Shet ...... 235 c5
Shettleston C Glas ...... 175 H5
Shevington Wigan ...... 121 H8
Shevington Vale
  Wigan ...... 121 G8
Sheviock Cnwll ...... 6 B5
Shibden Head
  C Brad ...... 123 G5
Shide IoW ...... 16 F5
Shidlaw Nthumb ...... 168 B2
Shiel Bridge Highld ...... 200 E2
Shieldaig Highld ...... 210 C4
Shieldhill D & G ...... 155 H5
Shieldhill Falk ...... 176 B3
Shieldhill House
  Hotel S Lans ...... 165 J2
Shields N Lans ...... 175 K7
Shielfoot Highld ...... 190 D3
Shielhill Angus ...... 196 C5
Shielhill Inver ...... 173 L4
Shifnal Shrops ...... 84 D2
Shilbottle Nthumb ...... 169 J7
Shildon Dur ...... 141 G3
Shillford E Rens ...... 174 E6
Shillingford Devon ...... 24 F6
Shillingford Oxon ...... 41 L2
Shillingford Abbot
  Devon ...... 11 K6
Shillingford St
  George Devon ...... 11 K7
Shillingstone Dorset ...... 14 F1
Shillington C Beds ...... 75 G7
Shilton Oxon ...... 56 E6
Shilton Warwks ...... 86 E6
Shimpling Norfk ...... 92 D6
Shimpling Suffk ...... 77 J4
Shimpling Street
  Suffk ...... 77 K4
Shincliffe Dur ...... 151 H6
Shiney Row Sundld ...... 151 H4
Shinfield Wokham ...... 42 B6
Shinness Highld ...... 225 L5
Shipbourne Kent ...... 33 G3
Shipdham Norfk ...... 91 L3
Shipham Somset ...... 38 C8
Shiphay Torbay ...... 7 K3
Shiplake Oxon ...... 42 C5

Shipley C Brad ...... 123 H3
Shipley W Susx ...... 31 J6
Shipley Bridge
  Surrey ...... 32 B5
Shipmeadow Suffk ...... 93 H5
Shippon Oxon ...... 41 J2
Shipston-on-Stour
  Warwks ...... 72 B6
Shipton Gloucs ...... 56 B4
Shipton N York ...... 133 H7
Shipton Shrops ...... 83 L5
Shipton Bellinger
  Hants ...... 28 E3
Shipton Gorge
  Dorset ...... 13 L4
Shipton Green
  W Susx ...... 17 L3
Shipton Moyne
  Gloucs ...... 39 K3
Shipton-on-
  Cherwell Oxon ...... 57 J5
Shiptonthorpe
  E R Yk ...... 125 K2
Shipton-under-
  Wychwood Oxon ...... 56 F4
Shirburn Oxon ...... 42 B2
Shirdley Hill Lancs ...... 120 E7
Shirebrook Derbys ...... 115 K7
Shiregreen Sheff ...... 115 G3
Shirehampton Bristl ...... 38 D5
Shiremoor N Tyne ...... 159 H7
Shirenewton Mons ...... 38 C2
Shireoaks Notts ...... 115 K5
Shirland Derbys ...... 101 H2
Shirley C Sotn ...... 29 H8
Shirley Derbys ...... 100 E4
Shirley Gt Lon ...... 45 G6
Shirley Solhll ...... 85 K7
Shirrell Heath Hants ...... 29 L8
Shirwell Devon ...... 23 J4
Shiskine N Ayrs ...... 162 B4
Shobdon Herefs ...... 69 H3
Shobrooke Devon ...... 11 K5
Shoby Leics ...... 102 B7
Shocklach Ches W ...... 98 C3
Shoeburyness Sthend ...... 46 F3
Sholden Kent ...... 35 K4
Sholing C Sotn ...... 16 F1
Shop Cnwll ...... 9 G2
Shoreditch Gt Lon ...... 45 G4
Shoreditch Somset ...... 25 K6
Shoreham Kent ...... 45 K7
Shoreham-by-Sea
  W Susx ...... 19 H5
Shorley Hants ...... 29 L6
Shorne Kent ...... 46 B6
Shortgate E Susx ...... 20 A3
Short Heath Birm ...... 85 K5
Short Heath Wsall ...... 85 H4
Shortlanesend Cnwll ...... 4 C6
Shortlees E Ayrs ...... 163 K3
Shorwell IoW ...... 16 F5
Shoscombe BaNES ...... 27 G1
Shotesham Norfk ...... 92 F4
Shotgate Essex ...... 46 C2
Shotley Suffk ...... 78 F7
Shotley Bridge Dur ...... 150 D4
Shotley Gate Suffk ...... 78 F7
Shottenden Kent ...... 34 D4
Shottery Warwks ...... 71 L4
Shotteswell Warwks ...... 72 E5
Shottisham Suffk ...... 79 G5
Shottlegate Derbys ...... 100 F3
Shotton Dur ...... 151 K6
Shotton Flints ...... 111 J7
Shotton Colliery Dur ...... 151 J6
Shotts N Lans ...... 176 B6
Shotwick Ches W ...... 111 K6
Shougle Moray ...... 214 F4
Shouldham Norfk ...... 90 F2
Shouldham Thorpe
  Norfk ...... 90 F2
Shoulton Worcs ...... 70 E3
Shrawardine Shrops ...... 83 H1
Shrawley Worcs ...... 70 E2
Shrewley Warwks ...... 72 B2
Shrewsbury Shrops ...... 83 J2
Shrewton Wilts ...... 28 B3

Shripney W Susx ..............18 C5
Shrivenham Oxon ..............40 E3
Shropham Norfk ..............92 B5
Shroton Dorset ..............27 K8
Shucknall Herefs ..............69 L6
Shudy Camps Cambs ......76 E5
Shuna Ag & B ..............181 M5
Shurdington Gloucs ......55 L4
Shurlock Row W & M ......42 D5
Shurrery Highld ..........230 F4
Shurrery Lodge
  Highld ..................230 F4
Shurton Somset ..............25 J3
Shustoke Warwks ..........86 B5
Shute Devon ..............11 K5
Shute Devon ..............13 G3
Shutford Oxon ..............72 E6
Shut Heath Staffs ..........99 K7
Shuthonger Gloucs ......70 F7
Shutlanger Nhants ......73 K4
Shuttington Warwks......86 B3
Shuttlewood Derbys ....115 J6
Shuttleworth Bury ......122 B6
Siabost W Isls ..............232 e2
Siadar W Isls ..............232 f1
Sibbertoft Nhants ..........87 K6
Sibford Ferris Oxon ......72 D6
Sibford Gower Oxon ......72 D6
Sible Hedingham
  Essex ....................77 H7
Sibley's Green Essex ....60 F3
Sibsey Lincs ..............104 B3
Sibson Cambs ..............89 G4
Sibson Leics ..............86 D4
Sibster Highld ..........231 K5
Sibthorpe Notts ..........102 C4
Sibthorpe Notts ..........116 B6
Sibton Suffk ..............79 H1
Sicklesmere Suffk ........77 K3
Sicklinghall N York ....124 B2
Sidbury Devon ..............12 E4
Sidbury Shrops ..............84 C6
Sidcot N Som ..............38 B8
Sidcup Gt Lon ..............45 J3
Siddington Ches E ......113 J7
Siddington Gloucs ......56 B7
Sidestrand Norfk ......106 F4
Sidford Devon ..............12 E4
Sidlesham W Susx ..........18 B6
Sidley E Susx ..............20 E4
Sidmouth Devon ..............12 E5
Sigglesthorne E R Yk ..126 E2
Sigingstone V Glam ......36 F6
Silchester Hants ..........41 L7
Sileby Leics ..............87 H1
Silecroft Cumb ..........128 D3
Silfield Norfk ..............92 D4
Silkstone Barns ..........114 F1
Silkstone Common
  Barns ..................114 F1
Silk Willoughby
  Lincs ..................103 H4
Silloth Cumb ..............147 K4
Silpho N York ..............134 E2
Silsden C Brad ..........122 F2
Silsoe C Beds ..............74 F7
Silton Dorset ..............27 H5
Silverburn Mdloth ......177 G6
Silverdale Lancs ........129 K4
Silverdale Staffs ..........99 J3
Silver End Essex ..........61 K4
Silverford Abers ........216 E2
Silverstone Nhants ......73 J5
Silverton Devon ..............12 B2
Silvington Shrops ..........84 B7
Simonburn Nthumb ....157 L7
Simonsbath Somset ......24 B4
Simonstone Lancs ......122 B4
Simprim Border ..........168 C1
Simpson M Keyn ..........74 C7
Simpson Cross
  Pembks ..................48 F4
Sinclair's Hill Border ...179 G7
Sinclairston S Ayrs ....163 L6
Sinderby N York ..........132 E3
Sinderland Green
  Traffd ..................113 G4
Sindlesham Wokham......42 C6

Sinfin C Derb ..............101 G6
Singleton Kent ..............34 D6
Singleton Lancs ..........120 E3
Singleton W Susx ..........18 B3
Singlewell Kent ..............46 A6
Sinnahard Abers ........205 K3
Sinnington N York ......134 B3
Sinton Worcs ..............70 E3
Sinton Worcs ..............70 F2
Sinton Green Worcs......70 E3
Sissinghurst Kent..........33 K5
Siston S Glos ..............39 G5
Sithney Cnwll ..............3 H5
Sittingbourne Kent........34 B3
Six Ashes Shrops ..........84 E5
Sixhills Lincs ..............117 K4
Six Mile Bottom
  Cambs ..................76 E3
Sixpenny Handley
  Dorset ..................27 M7
Six Rues Jersey ..........236 c6
Skaill Ork ..................234 d6
Skara Brae Ork ..........234 b5
Skares E Ayrs ..............164 B6
Skateraw Abers ..........207 G6
Skateraw E Loth ..........178 F4
Skeabost Highld ........208 F5
Skeeby N York ..............140 F6
Skeffington Leics ..........87 L3
Skeffling E R Yk ..........127 J6
Skegby Notts ..............101 J1
Skegby Notts ..............116 C7
Skegness Lincs ..........119 H8
Skelbo Highld ..............223 H3
Skelbo Street Highld....223 H3
Skelbrooke Donc ........124 D7
Skeldyke Lincs ..........104 B5
Skellingthorpe Lincs ..116 F6
Skellow Donc ..............124 E7
Skelmanthorpe Kirk....123 J7
Skelmersdale Lancs....112 C1
Skelmorlie N Ayrs ......173 L5
Skelpick Highld ..........229 L4
Skelston D & G ..........154 E5
Skelton C York ..........133 J7
Skelton Cumb ..............148 D7
Skelton E R Yk ..........125 H5
Skelton R & Cl ..........142 E4
Skelton on Ure
  N York ..................132 E5
Skelwith Bridge
  Cumb ....................137 K6
Skendleby Lincs ..........118 F7
Skene House Abers ....206 E4
Skenfrith Mons ..............54 C4
Skerne E R Yk ..............135 G7
Skerray Highld ..........229 K3
Skerricha Highld ........228 C5
Skerton Lancs ..........129 K6
Sketchley Leics ..........86 E5
Sketty Swans ..............51 J6
Skewsby N York ..........133 K5
Skiall Highld ..............230 E3
Skidby E R Yk ............126 C4
Skigersta W Isls ........232 g1
Skilgate Somset ..........24 F6
Skillington Lincs ........102 E7
Skinburness Cumb ......147 K4
Skinflats Falk ............176 B2
Skinidin Highld ..........208 C5
Skipness Ag & B ........172 F6
Skipper's Bridge
  D & G. ..................156 C5
Skipsea E R Yk ..........135 J8
Skipton N York ..........122 E1
Skipton-on-Swale
  N York ..................132 E4
Skipwith N York ........125 G3
Skirlaugh E R Yk ........126 E3
Skirling Border ..........165 L2
Skirmett Bucks ..........42 C3
Skirpenbeck E R Yk....134 B7
Skirwith Cumb ..........149 G7
Skirza Highld ............231 L2
Skokholm Island
  Pembks ..................48 C6
Skomer Island
  Pembks ..................48 C5

Skulamus Highld ........199 K2
Skye Green Essex..........61 L4
Skye of Curr Highld....204 B1
Slack Calder ..............122 E5
Slackbuie Highld ........213 G6
Slacks of
  Cairnbanno
    Abers ................216 F5
Slad Gloucs ..............55 K6
Slade Devon ..............23 H3
Slade Green Gt Lon......45 K5
Slade Hooton Rothm ..115 K4
Slaggyford Nthumb....149 H4
Slaidburn Lancs ........130 D8
Slaithwaite Kirk ........123 G7
Slaley Nthumb ..........150 B4
Slamannan Falk ........176 B4
Slapton Bucks ..............58 F4
Slapton Devon ..............7 J6
Slapton Nhants ..........73 J5
Slaugham W Susx ........31 L5
Slaughterford Wilts ....39 J5
Slawston Leics ..........87 L5
Sleaford Hants ..........30 D4
Sleaford Lincs ..........103 H4
Sleagill Cumb ..........138 E4
Sleapford Wrekin ........84 B1
Sleasdairidh Highld....222 E3
Sledmere E R Yk ........134 E6
Sleetbeck Cumb ........156 E6
Sleights N York ..........143 H5
Slickly Highld ..........231 K3
Sliddery N Ayrs ........162 B5
Sligachan Highld ......209 G7
Sligrachan Ag & B ......173 K1
Slimbridge Gloucs ......55 H7
Slindon Staffs ..............99 J6
Slindon W Susx ..........18 C4
Slinfold W Susx ..........31 J5
Slingsby N York ........133 L4
Slip End C Beds ..........59 H4
Slip End Herts ..............75 K6
Slipton Nhants ..........88 D7
Slitting Mill Staffs ......100 B8
Slockavullin Ag & B ..182 B7
Sloncombe Devon ..........11 H7
Sloothby Lincs ..........119 G7
Slough Slough ..............43 G4
Slough Green
  Somset ..................25 L7
Slumbay Highld ..........210 D6
Slyfield Surrey ..............31 G2
Slyne Lancs ..............129 K6
Smailholm Border ......167 K3
Smallburgh Norfk ......107 G7
Smallburn E Ayrs ......164 D4
Small Dole W Susx ........19 G3
Smalley Derbys ..........101 H4
Smallfield Surrey ..........32 B5
Small Heath Birm ........85 K6
Small Hythe Kent ..........34 B8
Smallridge Devon ........13 H3
Smallthorne C Stke ......99 K3
Smallworth Norfk ........92 B7
Smannell Hants ..........29 G2
Smarden Kent ..............34 B6
Smarden Bell Kent........34 B6
Smart's Hill Kent ..........32 F5
Smeatharpe Devon ......12 F1
Smeeth Kent ..............34 E6
Smeeton Westerby
  Leics ....................87 K5
Smerral Highld ..........227 L2
Smestow Staffs ..........84 F5
Smethwick Sandw........85 H6
Smirisary Highld ........190 D2
Smisby Derbys ..........101 G8
Smithfield Cumb ........148 D3
Smith's Green Essex....76 F6
Smithstown Highld....219 J6
Smithton Highld ........213 H5
Smoo Highld ..............228 F3
Smythe's Green
  Essex....................61 L4
Snade D & G ............154 E5
Snailbeach Shrops ......83 G3
Snailwell Cambs ..........76 F2
Snainton N York ........134 E3

Snaith E R Yk ............124 F6
Snape N York ............132 D3
Snape Suffk ..............79 H3
Snape Street Suffk......79 H3
Snaresbrook Gt Lon......45 H3
Snarestone Leics ..........86 D2
Snarford Lincs ..........117 H5
Snargate Kent ............34 D8
Snave Kent ..............34 D8
Sneaton N York ..........143 J5
Snelland Lincs ..........117 H5
Snelston Derbys ........100 D4
Snetterton Norfk ..........92 B5
Snettisham Norfk ......105 G5
Snitter Nthumb ..........158 C2
Snitterby Lincs ..........117 G3
Snitterfield Warwks ....72 B3
Snitton Shrops ..........83 L1
Snodland Kent ..............46 B7
Snowdon Gwynd ..........95 K2
Snowdonia National
  Park ....................96 C6
Snow End Herts ..........60 C2
Snowshill Gloucs ..........71 K7
Soake Hants ..............17 J1
Soay Highld ..............199 G3
Soberton Hants ..........29 L7
Soberton Heath
  Hants ....................29 L8
Sockburn Darltn ......141 J6
Soham Cambs ..............90 E8
Solas W Isls ............232 c5
Soldridge Hants ..........29 M4
Sole Street Kent ..........34 E5
Sole Street Kent ..........46 A6
Solihull Solhll ..............85 L7
Sollas W Isls ............232 c5
Sollers Dilwyn
  Herefs ..................69 H4
Sollers Hope Herefs......54 E2
Solva Pembks ..............48 D3
Solwaybank D & G ......156 B6
Somerby Leics ............87 L2
Somerby Lincs ..........117 H1
Somercotes Derbys ....101 H2
Somerford BCP ............15 M4
Somerford Keynes
  Gloucs ..................40 A3
Somerley W Susx ..........17 M3
Somerleyton Suffk ......93 K4
Somersal Herbert
  Derbys ..................100 C5
Somersby Lincs ..........118 D6
Somersham Cambs ......89 L7
Somersham Suffk ........78 C5
Somerton Oxon ..........57 J3
Somerton Somset ........26 C5
Somerton Suffk ..........77 J4
Sompting W Susx ..........19 G5
Sonning Wokham ..........42 C5
Sonning Common
  Oxon ....................42 B4
Sopley Hants ..............15 M3
Sopwell Herts ..............59 J6
Sopworth Wilts ..........39 J3
Sorbie D & G ............145 J5
Sordale Highld ..........231 G3
Sorisdale Ag & B ......189 H4
Sorn E Ayrs ............164 B4
Sornhill E Ayrs ........163 M3
Sortat Highld ..........231 K5
Sotby Lincs ............117 K5
Sotterley Suffk ..........93 J4
Soughton Flints ........111 H7
Soulbury Bucks ..........58 E3
Soulby Cumb ............139 H5
Souldern Oxon ..........57 K2
Souldrop Bed ............74 E3
Sound Ches E ............98 F3
Sound Muir Moray ....215 H4
Soundwell S Glos ........38 F5
Sourton Devon ..........10 D6
Soutergate Cumb ......128 F3
South Acre Norfk ........91 J2
South Alkham Kent ....35 H6
Southall Gt Lon ..........43 J4
South Allington
  Devon ....................7 J7

South Alloa Falk............ 185 J8
Southam Gloucs ............... 55 L3
Southam Warwks............. 72 E3
South Ambersham
    W Susx...................... 30 E7
Southampton C Sotn ... 29 H8
Southampton
    Airport Hants ........... 29 J7
South Anston Rothm ... 115 K5
South Ashford Kent....... 34 D6
South Baddesley
    Hants........................ 16 D3
South Bank C York.... 124 F1
South Barrow
    Somset...................... 26 E5
South Beddington
    Gt Lon....................... 44 F7
South Benfleet Essex.. 46 C3
Southborough Gt Lon... 45 H6
Southborough Kent....... 33 G5
Southbourne BCP........... 15 L4
Southbourne W Susx.... 17 L2
South Bramwith
    Donc........................ 124 F7
South Brent Devon............ 7 G4
South Brewham
    Somset...................... 27 G4
South Broomhill
    Nthumb ................... 159 G3
Southburgh Norfk........ 92 B3
South Burlington
    Norfk........................ 93 H3
Southburn E R Yk....... 134 F8
South Cadbury
    Somset...................... 26 F6
South Carlton Lincs..... 116 F6
South Carlton Notts ... 115 L5
South Cave E R Yk..... 125 L4
South Cerney Gloucs... 40 B2
South Chailey E Susx.... 19 K3
South Charlton
    Nthumb ................... 169 H5
South Cheriton
    Somset...................... 27 G6
Southchurch Sthend.... 46 E3
South Cliffe E R Yk.... 125 K4
South Clifton Notts.... 116 D7
South Cockerington
    Lincs........................ 118 E4
South Cornelly
    Brdgnd ..................... 36 C4
Southcott Cnwll .............. 9 G5
Southcott Devon............ 11 H8
Southcourt Bucks......... 58 D5
South Cove Suffk........... 93 K7
South Creake Norfk.... 105 K5
South Croxton Leics.... 87 K2
South Dalton E R Yk... 126 B2
South Darenth Kent..... 45 K6
South Dell W Isls...... 232 g1
South Downs
    National Park .......... 19 K4
South Duffield
    N York....................... 125 G4
South Earlswood
    Surrey ...................... 32 B4
Southease E Susx......... 19 L5
South Elkington
    Lincs........................ 118 D4
South Elmsall
    Wakefd..................... 124 D7
Southend Ag & B....... 161 H7
Southend Airport
    Essex......................... 46 E3
Southend-on-Sea
    Sthend........................ 46 E3
Southerndown
    V Glam....................... 36 D5
Southerness D & G..... 147 G4
South Erradale
    Highld..................... 219 H7
Southerton Devon .......... 12 D4
Southery Norfk............ 90 E5
South Fambridge
    Essex......................... 46 E2
South Ferriby N Linc... 126 B6
South Field E R Yk...... 126 C5

Southfield Falk........... 175 L4
Southfleet Kent............. 45 L5
Southgate Gt Lon......... 44 F2
Southgate Swans.......... 51 G7
South Gorley Hants ... 15 M1
South Gosforth
    N u Ty..................... 151 G2
South Green Essex...... 46 B2
South Green Kent........ 33 L2
South Green Norfk...... 92 C2
South Gyle C Edin...... 177 G4
South Hanningfield
    Essex......................... 61 H8
South Harting
    W Susx...................... 30 C7
South Hayling Hants.... 17 K3
South Heath Bucks....... 58 E7
South Heighton
    E Susx....................... 19 L5
South Hetton Dur....... 151 J6
South Hiendley
    Wakefd..................... 124 B7
South Hill Cnwll ............. 5 M2
South Hinksey Oxon.... 57 K7
South Holmwood
    Surrey ...................... 31 K3
South Hornchurch
    Gt Lon....................... 45 K4
South Huish Devon........ 7 G7
South Hykeham
    Lincs........................ 116 F8
South Hylton Sundld... 151 J4
Southill C Beds............. 75 H6
Southington Hants..... 29 J2
South Kelsey Lincs..... 117 H2
South Kessock
    Highld..................... 213 G5
South Killingholme
    N Linc...................... 126 E7
South Kilvington
    N York....................... 132 F3
South Kilworth Leics... 87 H6
South Kirkby Wakefd... 124 C7
South Kyme Lincs....... 103 K3
Southleigh Devon......... 12 F4
South Leigh Oxon........ 57 H6
South Leverton
    Notts....................... 116 C5
South Littleton
    Worcs......................... 71 J5
South Lopham Norfk... 92 C7
South Luffenham
    Rutlnd........................ 88 D3
South Lynn Norfk...... 104 F8
South Malling E Susx.. 19 L4
South Marston
    Swindn....................... 40 D3
South Merstham
    Surrey ...................... 32 B3
South Milford N York.. 124 D4
South Milton Devon........ 7 G7
South Mimms Herts.... 59 L7
South Mimms
    Services Herts........... 59 L7
Southminster Essex..... 62 A7
South Molton Devon... 23 L6
South Moor Dur ......... 150 F5
Southmoor Oxon......... 41 H2
South Moreton Oxon... 41 K3
Southmuir Angus...... 196 C5
South Mundham
    W Susx...................... 18 B5
South Newbald
    E R Yk...................... 125 L4
South Newington
    Oxon......................... 57 H2
South Newton Wilts.... 28 C4
South Nitshill C Glas.. 174 F6
South Normanton
    Derbys..................... 101 H2
South Norwood
    Gt Lon....................... 45 G6
South Ockendon
    Thurr......................... 45 L4
Southoe Cambs............. 75 H2
Southolt Suffk............. 78 E2
South Ormsby Lincs.... 118 E6
Southorpe C Pete......... 88 F3

South Otterington
    N York....................... 132 E3
Southover Dorset......... 14 C4
South Owersby
    Lincs........................ 117 H3
Southowram Calder.... 123 G5
South Park Surrey....... 31 L2
South Perrott Dorset... 13 L2
South Petherton
    Somset...................... 26 B7
South Petherwin
    Cnwll .......................... 9 J8
South Pickenham
    Norfk......................... 91 J3
South Pill Cnwll .............. 6 B4
South Pool Devon............ 7 H7
South Poorton
    Dorset....................... 13 M3
Southport Lancs......... 120 D6
South Queensferry
    C Edin..................... 176 F3
South Rauceby Lincs.. 103 G4
South Raynham
    Norfk....................... 105 L7
South Reddish
    Stockp..................... 113 K3
Southrepps Norfk...... 106 F5
South Reston Lincs.... 118 E5
Southrey Lincs........... 117 J7
South Ronaldsay
    Ork.......................... 234 c7
Southrop Gloucs......... 56 D7
Southrope Hants......... 30 A3
South Runcton Norfk.. 90 F2
South Scarle Notts.... 116 D8
Southsea C Port.......... 17 J3
South Shian Ag & B... 191 H7
South Shields S Tyne.. 151 J2
South Shore Bpool.... 120 D4
Southside Dur............ 140 E2
South Stainley
    N York....................... 132 D6
South Stifford Thurr... 45 L4
South Stoke BaNES...... 39 H7
South Stoke Oxon........ 41 L4
South Stoke W Susx... 18 D4
South Street Kent........ 34 E3
South Street Kent........ 47 J6
South Tarbrax S Lans.. 176 D7
South Tawton Devon... 10 F6
South Tehidy Cnwll......... 3 H3
South Thoresby
    Lincs........................ 118 E6
Southtown Norfk......... 93 L3
South Uist W Isls...... 233 c8
Southwaite Cumb...... 148 D6
Southwaite
    Services Cumb ........ 148 D6
South Walsham
    Norfk......................... 93 H2
Southwark Gt Lon...... 44 F4
South Warnborough
    Hants........................ 30 B3
Southwater W Susx..... 31 J6
Southway C Plym........... 6 C4
South Weald Essex...... 45 L2
Southwell Notts........ 102 B2
South Weston Oxon..... 42 B2
South Wheatley
    Notts....................... 116 C4
Southwick Hants......... 17 J2
Southwick Nhants....... 88 E5
Southwick Sundld..... 151 J4
Southwick W Susx....... 19 H5
Southwick Wilts........... 27 J1
South Widcombe
    BaNES....................... 38 E8
South Wigston Leics... 87 H4
South Willingham
    Lincs........................ 117 K5
South Wingfield
    Derbys..................... 101 G2
South Witham Lincs.... 102 F8
Southwold Suffk........... 93 K7
South Woodham
    Ferrers Essex............ 61 J7
South Wootton Norfk. 105 G7
South Wraxall Wilts.... 39 J7

South Zeal Devon........... 10 F6
Sovereign Harbour
    E Susx....................... 20 D5
Sowerby Calder......... 122 F6
Sowerby N York........ 132 F4
Sowerby Bridge
    Calder..................... 122 F5
Sowood Calder.......... 123 G6
Sowton Devon................ 6 D3
Sowton Devon............... 12 C4
Soyland Town Calder.. 122 F6
Spain's End Essex....... 76 F6
Spalding Lincs........... 103 L7
Spaldington E R Yk.... 125 H4
Spaldwick Cambs....... 89 G8
Spalford Notts........... 116 D7
Spanby Lincs............. 103 H5
Sparham Norfk.......... 106 C8
Spark Bridge Cumb... 129 G3
Sparkford Somset....... 26 E6
Sparkhill Birm............ 85 K6
Sparkwell Devon............ 6 E4
Sparrowpit Derbys.... 114 C5
Sparrows Green
    E Susx....................... 33 H6
Sparsholt Hants......... 29 H5
Sparsholt Oxon........... 41 G3
Spaunton N York...... 133 L2
Spaxton Somset.......... 25 K4
Spean Bridge Highld.. 201 K8
Spearywell Hants........ 28 F6
Speen Bucks................ 58 D7
Speen W Berk.............. 41 J6
Speeton N York......... 135 K5
Speke Lpool............... 112 C5
Speldhurst Kent.......... 32 F5
Spellbrook Herts......... 60 D4
Spencers Wood
    Wokham..................... 42 B6
Spen Green Ches E..... 99 J1
Spennithorne N York.. 131 L2
Spennymoor Dur...... 151 G7
Spetchley Worcs.......... 70 F4
Spetisbury Dorset....... 15 G3
Spexhall Suffk............. 93 H7
Spey Bay Moray....... 215 H2
Speybridge Highld.... 204 C1
Speyview Moray....... 215 G6
Spilsby Lincs............. 118 E7
Spinkhill Derbys........ 115 J5
Spinningdale Highld.. 222 F4
Spital Wirral............ 111 K5
Spital Hill Donc........ 115 L3
Spittal E Loth............ 178 B3
Spittal Highld........... 231 H5
Spittal Nthumb.......... 179 L7
Spittal Pembks............ 49 G3
Spittalfield P & K...... 195 H7
Spital of
    Glenmuick Abers ... 205 G7
Spittal of Glenshee
    P & K...................... 195 H3
Spittal-on-Rule
    Border..................... 167 J5
Spixworth Norfk......... 92 F1
Splatt Devon................ 10 E4
Splayne's Green
    E Susx....................... 19 L2
Splott Cardif.............. 37 J5
Spofforth N York...... 124 B1
Spondon C Derb....... 101 H5
Spooner Row Norfk... 92 D4
Sporle Norfk............... 91 J2
Spott E Loth............. 178 E4
Spottiswoode Border.. 178 D7
Spratton Nhants......... 73 K1
Spreakley Surrey......... 30 D3
Spreyton Devon........... 11 G5
Spriddlestone Devon..... 6 D5
Spridlington Lincs...... 117 G5
Springburn C Glas.... 175 G5
Springfield D & G..... 148 B2
Springfield Essex....... 61 H6
Springfield Fife........ 186 E5
Springholm D & G..... 154 E7
Springside N Ayrs.... 163 J2
Springthorpe Lincs.... 116 E4
Springwell Sundld ... 151 H4

**Sproatley** E R Yk...... **126** F4
**Sproston Green**
Ches W........... **113** G7
**Sprotbrough** Donc ...... **115** K2
**Sproughton** Suffk......**78** D5
**Sprouston** Border ...... **168** A3
**Sprowston** Norfk.........**92** F2
**Sproxton** Leics.......... **102** D7
**Sproxton** N York ........ **133** J3
**Spurstow** Ches E..........**98** D2
**Spyway** Dorset.............**14** A4
**Stableford** Shrops......**84** D4
**Stacey Bank** Sheff ...... **114** H4
**Stackhouse** N York .... **130** F6
**Stackpole** Pembks ......**49** G7
**Stackpole Elidor**
Pembks .................**49** G7
**Staddiscombe**
C Plym...................... **6** D5
**Stadhampton** Oxon......**57** L7
**Stadhlaigearraidh**
W Isls....................... **233** b7
**Staffield** Cumb.......... **148** F6
**Staffin** Highld .......... **218** D7
**Stafford** Staffs............**99** L7
**Stafford Services
(northbound)**
Staffs.......................**99** K6
**Stafford Services
(southbound)**
Staffs.......................**99** K6
**Stagsden** Bed ............**74** E5
**Stainburn** Cumb ...... **136** E2
**Stainby** Lincs........... **102** E7
**Staincross** Barns ...... **123** L7
**Staindrop** Dur ......... **140** E3
**Staines-upon-
Thames** Surrey......**43** G6
**Stainforth** Donc........ **124** F7
**Stainforth** N York...... **130** F6
**Staining** Lancs .......... **120** D4
**Stainland** Calder ...... **123** G6
**Stainsacre** N York ...... **143** J5
**Stainton** Cumb.......... **129** L3
**Stainton** Cumb.......... **138** C2
**Stainton** Donc........... **115** K3
**Stainton** Dur ............ **140** D4
**Stainton** Middsb ...... **141** L4
**Stainton by
Langworth** Lincs.... **117** H6
**Staintondale** N York.... **143** K7
**Stainton le Vale** L
incs......................... **117** K3
**Stainton with
Adgarley** Cumb .... **128** F5
**Stair** E Ayrs ............. **163** K5
**Stairhaven** D & G...... **144** E4
**Staithes** N York......... **143** G4
**Stakes** Hants.............**17** K2
**Stalbridge** Dorset......**27** G7
**Stalbridge Weston**
Dorset.....................**27** G7
**Stalham** Norfk.......... **107** H7
**Stalisfield Green**
Kent.......................**34** C4
**Stallen** Dorset............**26** E7
**Stallingborough**
NE Lin..................... **126** F7
**Stalmine** Lancs......... **120** E2
**Stalybridge** Tamesd.... **113** L2
**Stambourne** Essex......**77** G6
**Stambourne Green**
Essex......................**77** G6
**Stamford** Lincs............**88** E3
**Stamford** Nthumb...... **169** J5
**Stamford Bridge**
Ches W.................... **112** C7
**Stamford Bridge**
E R Yk..................... **133** L7
**Stamfordham**
Nthumb................... **158** D7
**Stamford Hill** Gt Lon....**45** G3
**Stanbridge** C Beds......**58** F3
**Stanbury** C Brad........ **122** F3
**Stand** N Lans ............ **175** K5
**Standburn** Falk......... **176** C4
**Standeford** Staffs........**85** G3
**Standen** Kent.............**33** L1

**Standerwick** Somset......**27** J2
**Standford** Hants..........**30** D4
**Standingstone** Cumb.... **147** J7
**Standish** Wigan ........ **121** H7
**Standlake** Oxon..........**57** H7
**Standon** Hants............**29** H6
**Standon** Herts...........**60** C4
**Standon** Staffs............**99** J5
**Stane** N Lans ............ **176** B6
**Stanfield** Norfk......... **105** M7
**Stanford** C Beds..........**75** H6
**Stanford** Kent............**34** F6
**Stanford Bishop**
Herefs.....................**70** C4
**Stanford Bridge**
Worcs......................**70** C2
**Stanford Dingley**
W Berk.....................**41** L6
**Stanford in the Vale**
Oxon.......................**41** G2
**Stanford le Hope**
Thurr......................**46** B4
**Stanford on Avon**
Nhants.....................**87** H7
**Stanford on Soar**
Notts...................... **101** K7
**Stanford on Teme**
Worcs......................**70** C2
**Stanfree** Derbys........ **115** J6
**Stanghow** R & Cl....... **142** E4
**Stanground** C Pete......**89** H4
**Stanhoe** Norfk.......... **105** J5
**Stanhope** Border ...... **165** L4
**Stanhope** Dur .......... **150** C6
**Stanhope** Kent ..........**34** D6
**Stanion** Nhants..........**88** D6
**Stanley** Derbys......... **101** H4
**Stanley** Dur ............. **150** F4
**Stanley** P & K ........... **186** B2
**Stanley** Staffs.............**99** L3
**Stanley Crook** Dur .... **150** E7
**Stanley Pontlarge**
Gloucs.....................**55** M3
**Stanmer** Br & H..........**19** K4
**Stanmore** Gt Lon........**44** D2
**Stanmore** Hants..........**29** J5
**Stannersburn**
Nthumb................... **157** J5
**Stanningfield** Suffk......**77** K3
**Stannington** Nthumb.... **158** F6
**Stannington** Sheff...... **114** F4
**Stannington Station**
Nthumb................... **158** F5
**Stansbatch** Herefs......**69** G3
**Stansfield** Suffk..........**77** H4
**Stanstead** Suffk..........**77** K5
**Stanstead Abbotts**
Herts......................**60** C5
**Stansted** Kent............**45** L7
**Stansted Airport**
Essex......................**60** E4
**Stansted
Mountfitchet**
Essex......................**60** E3
**Stanton** Gloucs..........**71** J7
**Stanton** Nthumb........ **158** E4
**Stanton** Staffs.......... **100** C4
**Stanton** Suffk............**91** L8
**Stanton by Bridge**
Derbys.................... **101** G6
**Stanton by Dale**
Derbys.................... **101** J5
**Stanton Drew** BaNES....**38** E7
**Stanton Fitzwarren**
Swindn....................**40** D3
**Stanton Harcourt**
Oxon.......................**57** H6
**Stanton in Peak**
Derbys.................... **114** E8
**Stanton Lacy** Shrops....**83** K7
**Stanton Lees**
Derbys.................... **114** E8
**Stanton Long** Shrops....**83** L5
**Stanton-on-the-
Wolds** Notts.......... **101** M6
**Stanton Prior** BaNES....**39** G7
**Stanton St Bernard**
Wilts......................**40** C7

**Stanton St John**
Oxon.......................**57** L6
**Stanton St Quintin**
Wilts......................**39** K4
**Stanton Street** Suffk......**77** L2
**Stanton under
Bardon** Leics..........**86** F2
**Stanton upon Hine
Heath** Shrops.........**98** E7
**Stanton Wick** BaNES....**38** E7
**Stanway** Essex............**61** M3
**Stanway** Gloucs..........**56** B2
**Stanwell** Surrey..........**43** H5
**Stanwick** Nhants........**74** E1
**Stanwix** Cumb........... **148** D4
**Staoinebrig** W Isls...... **233** b8
**Stape** N York............. **143** G7
**Stapeley** Ches E..........**99** G3
**Stapenhill** Staffs........ **100** E7
**Staple** Kent...............**35** H4
**Staple Cross** Devon......**25** G7
**Staplecross** E Susx......**20** F2
**Staplefield** W Susx......**32** B7
**Staple Fitzpaine**
Somset.....................**25** K7
**Stapleford** Cambs........**76** C4
**Stapleford** Herts........**60** A5
**Stapleford** Leics........ **102** D8
**Stapleford** Lincs........ **102** E2
**Stapleford** Notts........ **101** J5
**Stapleford** Wilts..........**28** B4
**Stapleford Abbotts**
Essex......................**45** K2
**Staplegrove** Somset......**25** K4
**Staplehay** Somset........**25** K6
**Staplehurst** Kent..........**33** K5
**Staplers** IoW...............**17** G4
**Staplestreet** Kent..........**34** E3
**Stapleton** Herefs........**69** G2
**Stapleton** Leics..........**86** E4
**Stapleton** N York....... **141** G5
**Stapleton** Shrops........**83** J3
**Stapleton** Somset........**26** C7
**Stapley** Somset...........**25** J8
**Staploe** Bed ..............**75** G3
**Staplow** Herefs..........**70** C6
**Star** Fife.................. **186** E6
**Star** Pembks..............**65** H7
**Star** Somset...............**38** C8
**Starbeck** N York........ **132** E7
**Starbotton** N York...... **131** H5
**Starcross** Devon..........**12** C6
**Stareton** Warwks........**72** D1
**Starlings Green**
Essex......................**60** D2
**Starston** Norfk............**92** F6
**Startforth** Dur .......... **140** D4
**Startley** Wilts.............**39** L4
**Statenborough** Kent......**35** J4
**Statham** Warrtn......... **112** F4
**Stathe** Somset............**26** A5
**Stathern** Leics.......... **102** C6
**Staunton** Gloucs..........**54** D5
**Staunton** Gloucs..........**55** H3
**Staunton on Arrow**
Herefs.....................**69** G3
**Staunton on Wye**
Herefs.....................**69** G5
**Staveley** Cumb.......... **138** C7
**Staveley** Derbys......... **115** H6
**Staveley** N York......... **132** E6
**Staveley-in-
Cartmel** Cumb....... **129** H3
**Staverton** Devon.......... **7** J3
**Staverton** Gloucs.........**55** K4
**Staverton** Nhants........**73** G3
**Staverton** Wilts..........**39** J7
**Stawell** Somset...........**26** A4
**Stawley** Somset...........**25** G6
**Staxigoe** Highld ........ **231** L5
**Staxton** N York......... **134** F4
**Staynall** Lancs........... **120** E2
**Stean** N York............. **131** K5
**Stearsby** N York......... **133** J5
**Steart** Somset.............**25** L3
**Stebbing** Essex...........**61** G3
**Stechford** Birm...........**85** K6
**Stedham** W Susx..........**30** E6

**Steelend** Fife............ **185** L8
**Steele Road** Border...... **156** F4
**Steen's Bridge**
Herefs.....................**69** K3
**Steep** Hants...............**30** C6
**Steep Lane** Calder...... **122** F5
**Steeple** Essex............**61** M7
**Steeple Ashton** Wilts....**27** K1
**Steeple Aston** Oxon......**57** J3
**Steeple Bumpstead**
Essex......................**76** F6
**Steeple Claydon**
Bucks......................**58** B3
**Steeple Gidding**
Cambs.....................**89** G7
**Steeple Langford**
Wilts......................**28** B4
**Steeple Morden**
Cambs.....................**75** K6
**Steeton** C Brad......... **122** F2
**Stein** Highld ............ **208** D3
**Stelling Minnis** Kent....**34** F5
**Stembridge** Somset......**26** B7
**Stenalees** Cnwll.......... **4** F4
**Stenhouse** D & G....... **154** D4
**Stenhousemuir**
Falk.......................**176** B2
**Stenscholl** Highld ...... **218** D7
**Stenson Fields**
Derbys.................... **101** G6
**Stenton** E Loth......... **178** D4
**Steornabhagh**
W Isls..................... **232** f2
**Stepaside** Pembks......**49** K6
**Stepford** D & G......... **154** E5
**Stepney** Gt Lon..........**45** G4
**Steppingley** C Beds......**74** E7
**Stepps** N Lans .......... **175** H5
**Sternfield** Suffk..........**79** H3
**Stert** Wilts.................**40** B8
**Stetchworth** Cambs......**76** F3
**Stevenage** Herts........**59** L3
**Stevenston** N Ayrs...... **163** H2
**Steventon** Hants..........**29** K2
**Steventon** Oxon..........**41** J3
**Steventon End** Essex....**76** E6
**Stevington** Bed ..........**74** E4
**Stewartby** Bed ..........**74** E4
**Stewartfield** S Lans..... **175** H7
**Stewarton** Ag & B...... **161** H5
**Stewarton** E Ayrs...... **163** K1
**Stewkley** Bucks..........**58** D3
**Stewley** Somset...........**25** L7
**Steyning** W Susx..........**19** G4
**Steynton** Pembks........**48** F5
**Stibb** Cnwll................. **9** G3
**Stibbard** Norfk.......... **106** B6
**Stibb Cross** Devon......**10** C2
**Stibb Green** Wilts........**40** E7
**Stibbington** Cambs......**88** F4
**Stichill** Border .......... **167** L2
**Sticker** Cnwll.............. **4** F5
**Stickford** Lincs.......... **104** B1
**Sticklepath** Devon......**10** F6
**Stickney** Lincs.......... **104** B2
**Stiffkey** Norfk.......... **106** A4
**Stifford Clays** Thurr......**45** L4
**Stilligarry** W Isls....... **233** b7
**Stillingfleet** N York.... **124** F3
**Stillington** N York..... **133** J3
**Stillington** S on T...... **141** J3
**Stilton** Cambs............**89** H5
**Stinchcombe** Gloucs....**55** G7
**Stinsford** Dorset..........**14** D4
**Stiperstones** Shrops.....**83** G4
**Stirchley** Wrekin..........**84** C3
**Stirling** Abers .......... **217** L6
**Stirling** Stirlg .......... **185** G8
**Stirling Castle**
Stirlg......................185 G8
**Stirling Services**
Stirlg......................175 L2
**Stirtloe** Cambs...........**75** H2
**Stirton** N York.......... **131** H8
**Stisted** Essex.............**61** J3
**Stithians** Cnwll........... **3** J4
**Stivichall** Covtry..........**86** D7
**Stixwould** Lincs......... **117** K7

St Michaels Fife .......... 187 G3
Stoak Ches W ................. 112 B6
Stobo Border ................. 166 B2
Stoborough Dorset ........ 15 H5
Stobs Castle Border ...... 167 H7
Stobswood Nthumb. ...... 158 F3
Stock Essex .................... 61 H7
Stockbridge Hants......... 29 G4
Stockbridge W Susx...... 18 B5
Stockbriggs S Lans ...... 164 F3
Stockbury Kent ............. 46 D7
Stockcross W Berk ........ 41 H6
Stockerston Leics.......... 88 B4
Stock Green Worcs ....... 71 H3
Stocking Herefs ............ 54 F2
Stockingford
   Warwks....................... 86 D5
Stocking Pelham
   Herts ........................... 60 D3
Stockland Devon........... 13 G2
Stockland Bristol
   Somset ........................ 25 K3
Stockleigh English
   Devon .......................... 11 K4
Stockleigh Pomeroy
   Devon .......................... 11 K4
Stockley Wilts................ 39 M6
Stocklinch Somset........ 26 B7
Stockport Stockp ....... 113 K4
Stocksbridge Sheff .... 114 E2
Stocksfield Nthumb..... 150 D3
Stockton Herefs ........... 69 K3
Stockton Norfk.............. 93 H5
Stockton Shrops............ 84 C4
Stockton Warwks.......... 72 E2
Stockton Wilts............... 27 M4
Stockton Wrekin........... 84 D1
Stockton Brook
   Staffs........................... 99 K3
Stockton Heath
   Warrtn ....................... 112 E4
Stockton-on-Tees
   S on T ......................... 141 K4
Stockton on Teme
   Worcs.......................... 70 C2
Stockton on the
   Forest C York ............ 133 K7
Stockwell End
   Wolves......................... 84 F4
Stockwood Bristl........... 38 F6
Stockwood Dorset......... 14 B2
Stock Wood Worcs......... 71 H3
Stodmarsh Kent............ 35 G3
Stody Norfk ................. 106 C5
Stoer Highld ............... 224 C3
Stoford Somset............. 26 E8
Stoford Wilts................. 28 B4
Stogumber Somset....... 25 H4
Stogursey Somset.......... 25 J3
Stoke Covtry ................. 86 D7
Stoke Devon .................. 22 C6
Stoke Hants .................. 17 K3
Stoke Hants .................. 29 H2
Stoke Medway............... 46 D5
Stoke Abbott Dorset..... 13 L3
Stoke Albany Nhants ... 88 B5
Stoke Ash Suffk............. 78 D1
Stoke Bardolph
   Notts ......................... 101 M4
Stoke Bliss Worcs......... 70 B2
Stoke Bruerne
   Nhants........................ 73 L4
Stoke-by-Clare Suffk...77 G5
Stoke-by-Nayland
   Suffk........................... 78 B7
Stoke Canon Devon...... 12 B3
Stoke Charity Hants...... 29 J4
Stoke Climsland
   Cnwll............................. 6 A2
Stoke Cross Herefs...... 70 B4
Stoke D'Abernon
   Surrey ......................... 43 J8
Stoke Doyle Nhants...... 88 E6
Stoke Dry Rutlnd........... 88 C4
Stoke Edith Herefs........ 69 L6
Stoke Farthing Wilts .... 28 B6
Stoke Ferry Norfk........... 91 G4

Stoke Fleming Devon ...... 7 K6
Stokeford Dorset ........... 15 G5
Stoke Gabriel Devon....... 7 J4
Stoke Gifford S Glos ...... 38 F4
Stoke Golding Leics....... 86 E4
Stoke Goldington
   M Keyn ........................ 74 B5
Stokeham Notts .......... 116 C6
Stoke Hammond
   Bucks ........................... 58 E3
Stoke Holy Cross
   Norfk........................... 92 F3
Stokeinteignhead
   Devon ............................ 7 L2
Stoke Lacy Herefs......... 70 B5
Stoke Lyne Oxon........... 57 K3
Stoke Mandeville
   Bucks .......................... 58 D6
Stokenchurch Bucks... 42 C2
Stoke Newington
   Gt Lon.......................... 45 G3
Stokenham Devon .......... 7 J7
Stoke-on-Trent
   C Stke.......................... 99 K3
Stoke Orchard
   Gloucs ......................... 55 K3
Stoke Poges Bucks ...... 42 F4
Stoke Prior Herefs........ 69 K3
Stoke Prior Worcs........ 71 G2
Stoke Rivers Devon...... 23 K4
Stoke Rochford
   Lincs......................... 102 F6
Stoke Row Devon.......... 42 B4
Stoke St Gregory
   Somset ....................... 25 M6
Stoke St Mary
   Somset ........................ 25 K6
Stoke St Michael
   Somset ........................ 26 F3
Stoke St
   Milborough
   Shrops......................... 83 L6
Stokesby Norfk............. 93 J2
Stokesley N York ........ 142 B5
Stoke sub Hamdon
   Somset ........................ 26 C7
Stoke Talmage Oxon.... 58 B7
Stoke Trister Somset.... 27 H5
Stoke upon Tern
   Shrops......................... 98 F6
Stolford Somset............ 25 K3
Stondon Massey
   Essex........................... 60 F7
Stone Bucks ................. 58 C5
Stone Gloucs ............... 39 G2
Stone Rothm............... 115 K4
Stone Staffs.................. 99 K5
Stone Worcs.................. 84 F7
Stone Allerton
   Somset ........................ 26 B2
Ston Easton Somset..... 26 F2
Stonebridge N Som..... 38 B7
Stonebridge Warwks .... 86 B6
Stonebroom Derbys... 101 H2
Stone Cross Kent.......... 35 J4
Stonecrouch Kent........ 33 J6
Stoneferry C KuH....... 126 D4
Stonefield Castle
   Hotel Ag & B........... 172 E4
Stonegate E Susx.......... 33 H7
Stonegrave N York .... 133 K4
Stonehenge Wilts......... 28 C3
Stonehouse C Plym ....... 6 C5
Stonehouse Gloucs ...... 55 J6
Stonehouse S Lans..... 175 K8
Stone in Oxney Kent .... 21 J1
Stoneleigh Warwks...... 86 D8
Stonesby Leics........... 102 D7
Stonesfield Oxon.......... 57 H4
Stones Green Essex...... 62 E3
Stone Street Kent......... 33 G3
Stone Street Suffk....... 93 H6
Stonewells Moray...... 215 G2
Stoneybridge W Isls... 233 b8
Stoneyburn W Loth... 176 D5
Stoneygate C Leic........ 87 H3
Stoneykirk D & G ...... 144 C4

Stoney Middleton
   Derbys....................... 114 E6
Stoney Stanton Leics... 86 F4
Stoney Stoke Somset.... 27 G5
Stoney Stratton
   Somset ........................ 26 F4
Stoneywood C Aber.... 207 G3
Stoneywood Falk........ 175 L2
Stonham Aspal
   Suffk........................... 78 D3
Stonnall Staffs.............. 85 J3
Stonor Oxon.................. 42 B3
Stonton Wyville
   Leics........................... 87 K4
Stonybreck Shet......... 235 e7
Stony Houghton
   Derbys....................... 115 J7
Stony Stratford
   M Keyn ........................ 73 L6
Stoodleigh Devon......... 23 K5
Stoodleigh Devon......... 24 E7
Stop 24 Services
   Kent............................ 34 F7
Stopham W Susx........... 18 D2
Stopsley Luton.............. 59 J3
Stornoway W Isls ...... 232 f2
Stornoway Airport
   W Isls........................ 232 g2
Storrington W Susx...... 18 E3
Storth Cumb................ 129 K4
Storwood E R Yk ........ 125 H2
Stotfield Moray.......... 214 F1
Stotfold C Beds............ 75 J7
Stottesdon Shrops....... 84 C6
Stoughton Leics........... 87 J3
Stoughton Surrey......... 31 G2
Stoughton W Susx........ 17 L1
Stoulton Worcs............. 70 F4
Stourbridge Dudley..... 84 F6
Stourhead Wilts............ 27 H5
Stourpaine Dorset........ 15 G1
Stourport-on-
   Severn Worcs............. 70 E1
Stour Provost Dorset.... 27 H6
Stour Row Dorset......... 27 J7
Stourton Staffs............. 84 F6
Stourton Warwks.......... 72 C6
Stourton Wilts............... 27 H5
Stourton Caundle
   Dorset ......................... 27 G7
Stove Shet .................. 235 c7
Stoven Suffk.................. 93 J6
Stow Border ............... 167 G1
Stow Lincs ................. 116 E5
Stow Bardolph
   Norfk........................... 90 F3
Stow Bedon Norfk........ 91 L4
Stowbridge Norfk......... 90 E3
Stow-cum-Quy
   Cambs ........................ 76 D3
Stowe Shrops............... 82 F8
Stowe-by-Chartley
   Staffs......................... 100 A6
Stowell Somset............. 27 G6
Stowey BaNES.............. 38 E7
Stowford Devon............ 10 C7
Stowford Devon............ 12 E4
Stowlangtoft Suffk........ 77 L2
Stow Longa Cambs ...... 75 G1
Stow Maries Essex........ 61 K7
Stowmarket Suffk......... 78 C3
Stow-on-the-Wold
   Gloucs ......................... 56 D3
Stowting Kent............... 34 F6
Stowupland Suffk......... 78 C3
Straad Ag & B............. 173 H6
Straanruie Highld ...... 204 B3
Strachan Abers .......... 206 D6
Strachur Ag & B ........ 182 F6
Stradbroke Suffk.......... 92 F8
Stradishall Suffk........... 77 H4
Stradsett Norfk............. 90 F3
Stragglethorpe
   Lincs......................... 102 E3
Straiton Mdloth.......... 177 H5
Straiton S Ayrs.......... 153 H2
Straloch Abers .......... 207 G2
Straloch P & K............ 195 G4

Stramshall Staffs.......... 100 B5
Strang IoM ................. 237 c5
Strangeways Salfd .... 113 J2
Strangford Herefs ........ 54 E3
Stranraer D & G ........ 144 C3
Stratfield Mortimer
   W Berk ........................ 42 A7
Stratfield Saye Hants... 42 B7
Stratfield Turgis
   Hants........................... 42 B7
Stratford Gt Lon........... 45 H3
Stratford St Andrew
   Suffk........................... 79 H3
Stratford St Mary
   Suffk........................... 78 C7
Stratford sub Castle
   Wilts............................ 28 C5
Stratford Tony Wilts...... 28 C6
Stratford-upon-
   Avon Warwks............. 72 B4
Strath Highld .............. 219 J5
Strathan Highld .......... 224 D4
Strathan Highld .......... 229 J3
Strathaven S Lans...... 164 D1
Strathblane Stirlg....... 175 G3
Strathcanaird
   Highld........................ 220 F2
Strathcarron
   Highld........................ 210 E6
Strathcoil Ag & B ...... 181 K2
Strathdon Abers ........ 205 H3
Strathkinness Fife ...... 187 G4
Strathloanhead
   W Loth....................... 176 C4
Strathmashie House
   Highld........................ 202 F6
Strathmiglo Fife ......... 186 C5
Strathpeffer Highld.... 212 D3
Strathtay P & K........... 194 E5
Strathwhillan
   N Ayrs........................ 162 D3
Strathy Highld ............ 230 B3
Strathy Inn Highld ..... 230 B3
Strathyre Stirlg.......... 184 C4
Stratton Cnwll................. 9 G4
Stratton Dorset............. 14 C4
Stratton Gloucs ............ 56 A7
Stratton Audley Oxon... 57 L3
Stratton-on-the-
   Fosse Somset............. 26 F2
Stratton St
   Margaret Swindn..... 40 D3
Stratton St Michael
   Norfk........................... 92 D5
Stratton Strawless
   Norfk......................... 106 F7
Streat E Susx ............... 19 K3
Streatham Gt Lon......... 44 F5
Streatley C Beds........... 59 H3
Streatley W Berk........... 41 L4
Street Devon ................ 12 F5
Street Somset............... 26 C4
Street Ashton
   Warwks....................... 86 F6
Street Dinas Shrops...... 97 M5
Street End Kent............. 34 F4
Street End W Susx........ 18 A5
Streethay Staffs............ 85 K2
Streetlam N York........ 141 H7
Streetly End Cambs...... 76 E5
Street on the Fosse
   Somset ........................ 26 F4
Strelitz P & K.............. 186 C1
Strelley Notts............. 101 J4
Strensall C York......... 133 K7
Strensham Services
   (northbound)
   Worcs.......................... 70 F6
Strensham Services
   (southbound)
   Worcs.......................... 70 F6
Stretcholt Somset......... 25 L3
Strete Devon .................. 7 J6
Stretford Traffd.......... 113 H3
Strethall Essex.............. 76 C6
Stretham Cambs........... 90 D8
Strettington W Susx..... 18 B4
Stretton Derbys........... 101 H1

Stretton Rutlnd..........88 D1
Stretton Staffs..........84 F2
Stretton Staffs..........100 E7
Stretton Warrtn..........112 F5
Stretton Grandison
  Herefs..........70 B5
Stretton-on-
Dunsmore
  Warwks..........86 E8
Stretton on Fosse
  Warwks..........72 B6
Stretton Sugwas
  Herefs..........69 J6
Stretton under
  Fosse Warwks..........86 F7
Stretton Westwood
  Shrops..........83 L4
Strichen Abers..........217 H4
Stringston Somset..........25 J3
Strixton Nhants..........74 C3
Stroat Gloucs..........38 E2
Strollamus Highld..........209 J8
Stroma Highld..........231 L1
Stromeferry Highld..........210 D7
Stromness Ork..........234 b6
Stronaba Highld..........201 J8
Stronachlachar
  Stirlg..........183 L5
Stronafian Ag & B..........173 H3
Stronchrubie Highld..........224 F5
Strone Ag & B..........173 L3
Strone Highld..........192 B1
Strone Highld..........212 E8
Stronmilchan
  Ag & B..........183 G2
Stronsay Ork..........234 d5
Stronsay Airport
  Ork..........234 d5
Strontian Highld..........191 G4
Strood Medway..........46 B6
Strood Gloucs..........55 J6
Stroud Hants..........30 B6
Stroud Green Gloucs....55 J6
Stroxton Lincs..........102 E6
Struan Highld..........208 E6
Struan P & K..........194 C4
Strumpshaw Norfk..........93 H3
Strutherhill S Lans..........175 K7
Struthers Fife..........186 F5
Struy Highld..........212 B6
Stuartfield Abers..........217 H5
Stubbington Hants..........17 G2
Stubbins Lancs..........122 B6
Stubton Lincs..........102 E3
Stuckton Hants..........28 D8
Studham C Beds..........59 G5
Studland Dorset..........15 J6
Studley Warwks..........71 J2
Studley Wilts..........39 L6
Studley Common
  Warwks..........71 J2
Studley Roger
  N York..........132 D5
Studley Royal
  N York..........132 D5
Studley Royal Park
  & Fountains
  Abbey N York....132 D5
Stuntney Cambs..........90 D7
Sturmer Essex..........77 G5
Sturminster
  Common Dorset..........27 H8
Sturminster
  Marshall Dorset..........15 H3
Sturminster Newton
  Dorset..........27 H8
Sturry Kent..........35 G3
Sturton N Linc..........116 F2
Sturton by Stow
  Lincs..........116 E5
Sturton le Steeple
  Notts..........116 C5
Stuston Suffk..........92 D7
Stutton N York..........124 D3
Stutton Suffk..........78 D7
Styal Ches E..........113 J5
Stynie Moray..........215 H3
Styrrup Notts..........115 L4

Succoth Ag & B..........183 K6
Suckley Worcs..........70 C4
Sudborough Nhants....88 D6
Sudbourne Suffk..........79 J4
Sudbrook Lincs..........102 F4
Sudbrook Mons..........38 D3
Sudbrooke Lincs..........117 G6
Sudbury Derbys..........100 D6
Sudbury Gt Lon..........44 D3
Sudbury Suffk..........77 K6
Suffield N York..........134 F2
Suffield Norfk..........106 F6
Sugnall Staffs..........99 H6
Sugwas Pool Herefs....69 J6
Suisnish Highld..........199 J3
Sulby IoM..........237 d3
Sulgrave Nhants..........73 G5
Sulham W Berk..........41 M5
Sulhamstead W Berk....41 M6
Sullom Shet..........235 c4
Sullom Voe Shet..........235 c4
Sully V Glam..........37 J6
Sumburgh Airport
  Shet..........235 c8
Summerbridge
  N York..........132 C6
Summercourt Cnwll........4 D5
Summerfield Norfk....105 J5
Summerhill Pembks....49 K6
Summerhouse
  Darltn..........140 F4
Summersdale
  W Susx..........18 B4
Summerseat Bury....122 B7
Summertown Oxon....57 K6
Sunbury-on-
Thames Surrey..........43 J6
Sundaywell D & G....154 E5
Sunderland Ag & B....170 E5
Sunderland Cumb....147 L2
Sunderland Lancs....129 J7
Sunderland Sundld....151 J4
Sunderland Bridge
  Dur..........151 G7
Sundhope Border....166 E4
Sundon Park Luton....59 H3
Sundridge Kent..........32 E3
Sunningdale W & M....42 F6
Sunninghill W & M....42 F6
Sunningwell Oxon....57 J7
Sunniside Dur..........150 E7
Sunniside Gatesd....150 F3
Sunnyhill C Derb....101 G6
Sunnyhurst Bl w D....121 K6
Sunnylaw Stirlg..........185 G7
Sunnymead Oxon....57 J6
Surbiton Gt Lon..........44 D6
Surfleet Lincs..........103 L6
Surlingham Norfk....93 G3
Surrex Essex..........61 L4
Sustead Norfk..........106 E5
Susworth Lincs..........116 D2
Sutcombe Devon..........9 J3
Sutcombemill
  Devon..........9 J3
Sutterby Lincs..........118 E6
Sutterton Lincs..........103 M5
Sutton C Beds..........75 J5
Sutton C Pete..........89 G4
Sutton Cambs..........90 C7
Sutton Devon..........7 G7
Sutton E Susx..........20 A5
Sutton Gt Lon..........44 E7
Sutton Kent..........35 J5
Sutton N York..........124 D5
Sutton Norfk..........107 H7
Sutton Notts..........102 C5
Sutton Oxon..........57 H6
Sutton Shrops..........83 K2
Sutton Shrops..........84 D6
Sutton Staffs..........99 H7
Sutton Suffk..........79 G5
Sutton W Susx..........18 D3
Sutton-at-Hone
  Kent..........45 K6
Sutton Bassett
  Nhants..........87 L5
Sutton Benger Wilts....39 L5

Sutton Bonington
  Notts..........101 J7
Sutton Bridge Lincs....104 D7
Sutton Cheney Leics....86 E4
Sutton Coldfield
  Birm..........85 K4
Sutton Courtenay
  Oxon..........41 J2
Sutton cum Lound
  Notts..........116 B5
Sutton Green Surrey....31 G1
Sutton Heath Suffk....79 G5
Sutton Howgrave
  N York..........132 D4
Sutton-in-Ashfield
  Notts..........101 J1
Sutton-in-Craven
  N York..........122 F2
Sutton Maddock
  Shrops..........84 C3
Sutton Mallet Somset....26 A4
Sutton Mandeville
  Wilts..........27 M5
Sutton Montis
  Somset..........26 F6
Sutton-on-Hull
  C KuH..........126 E4
Sutton on Sea Lincs....119 G5
Sutton-on-the-
Forest N York..........133 J6
Sutton on the Hill
  Derbys..........100 E5
Sutton on Trent
  Notts..........116 D7
Sutton St Edmund
  Lincs..........89 L2
Sutton St James
  Lincs..........104 C8
Sutton St Nicholas
  Herefs..........69 K5
Sutton Scotney
  Hants..........29 J4
Sutton-under-
Brailes Warwks..........72 C6
Sutton-under-
Whitestonecliffe
  N York..........133 G3
Sutton upon
  Derwent E R Yk....125 G2
Sutton Valence Kent....33 L4
Sutton Veny Wilts....27 K3
Sutton Waldron
  Dorset..........27 K7
Sutton Weaver
  Ches W..........112 D5
Sutton Wick BaNES....38 E8
Sutton Wick Oxon....41 J2
Swaby Lincs..........118 E6
Swadlincote Derbys....100 F8
Swaffham Norfk..........91 J2
Swaffham Bulbeck
  Cambs..........76 D3
Swaffham Prior
  Cambs..........76 E2
Swafield Norfk..........107 G6
Swainby N York..........141 L6
Swainsthorpe Norfk....92 F4
Swainswick BaNES....39 H6
Swalcliffe Oxon..........72 E6
Swalecliffe Kent..........47 J6
Swallow Lincs..........117 K2
Swallow Beck Lincs....116 F7
Swallowcliffe Wilts....27 L6
Swallowfield
  Wokham..........42 B7
Swanage Dorset..........15 J6
Swanbourne Bucks....58 D3
Swan Green
  Ches W..........113 G6
Swanland E R Yk....126 B5
Swanley Kent..........45 K6
Swanley Village Kent....45 K6
Swanmore Hants..........29 L7
Swannington Leics....86 E1
Swannington Norfk....106 D8
Swanpool Lincs..........116 F7
Swanscombe Kent....45 L5
Swansea Swans..........51 J6

Swansea Airport
  Swans..........51 H7
Swansea West
  Services Swans....51 J5
Swanton Abbot
  Norfk..........106 F7
Swanton Morley
  Norfk..........92 B1
Swanton Novers
  Norfk..........106 B6
Swan Village Sandw....85 H5
Swanwick Derbys....101 H2
Swanwick Hants..........17 G1
Swarby Lincs..........103 H4
Swardeston Norfk....92 E3
Swarkestone Derbys....101 G6
Swarland Nthumb....158 F2
Swarraton Hants..........29 K4
Swarthmoor Cumb....129 G4
Swaton Lincs..........103 J5
Swavesey Cambs..........75 L2
Sway Hants..........16 C3
Swayfield Lincs..........103 G7
Swaythling C Sotn....29 H7
Sweetham Devon..........11 K5
Sweethaws E Susx....32 E7
Sweets Cnwll..........8 F5
Sweetshouse Cnwll......5 H4
Swefling Suffk..........79 H2
Swepstone Leics..........86 D2
Swerford Oxon..........57 G2
Swettenham Ches E....113 J7
Swilland Suffk..........78 E4
Swillington Leeds....124 B4
Swimbridge Devon....23 K5
Swimbridge
  Newland Devon....23 J5
Swinbrook Oxon..........56 F5
Swincliffe N York....132 C7
Swinderby Lincs..........116 E8
Swindon Gloucs..........55 L3
Swindon Staffs..........84 F5
Swindon Swindn..........40 D4
Swine E R Yk..........126 E4
Swinefleet E R Yk....125 H6
Swineshead Bed....74 F2
Swineshead Lincs....103 L4
Swiney Highld..........227 M2
Swinford Leics..........87 H7
Swingfield Minnis
  Kent..........35 G6
Swingfield Street
  Kent..........35 H6
Swingleton Green
  Suffk..........77 L5
Swinhoe Nthumb....169 J4
Swinithwaite N York....131 K2
Swinside Cumb..........137 H3
Swinstead Lincs..........103 G7
Swinton Border....179 H8
Swinton N York..........132 C4
Swinton N York..........134 B5
Swinton Rothm..........115 J2
Swinton Salfd..........113 H2
Swiss Valley Carmth....51 G5
Swithland Leics..........87 G2
Swordale Highld..........212 E2
Swordland Highld....200 B6
Swordly Highld..........229 L3
Swynnerton Staffs....99 J5
Swyre Dorset..........13 M5
Sychtyn Powys..........81 L3
Syde Gloucs..........55 L5
Sydenham Gt Lon....45 G5
Sydenham Oxon..........58 B7
Sydenham Damerel
  Devon..........6 B2
Syderstone Norfk....105 K6
Sydling St Nicholas
  Dorset..........14 C3
Sydmonton Hants....41 J8
Syerston Notts..........102 C3
Sykehouse Donc....124 F6
Symbister Shet..........235 d4
Symington S Ayrs....163 J3
Symington S Lans....165 J3
Symondsbury
  Dorset..........13 K4

**Symonds Yat (West)**
Herefs..................54 E5
Syre Highld..................229 L6
Syreford Gloucs..........56 B4
Syresham Nhants........73 J6
Syston Leics..............87 J2
Syston Lincs............102 F4
Sytchampton Worcs....70 E2
Sywell Nhants............74 B2

## T

Tackley Oxon................57 J4
Tacolneston Norfk........92 D4
Tadcaster N York........124 D2
Taddington Derbys....114 C7
Tadley Hants..............41 L7
Tadlow Cambs............75 K5
Tadmarton Oxon..........72 E6
Tadpole Swindn..........40 C3
Tadworth Surrey........44 E8
Taff's Well Rhondd......37 H4
Taibach Neath............36 B3
Tain Highld..............223 G5
Tain Highld..............231 J3
Takeley Essex............60 F4
Takeley Street Essex...60 F4
Talaton Devon............12 D3
Talbenny Pembks........48 E5
Talbot Village BCP......15 K4
Taleford Devon..........12 E3
Talerddig Powys..........81 K4
Talgarreg Cerdgn........65 L4
Talgarth Powys............68 D7
Talisker Highld..........208 E7
Talke Staffs..............99 J2
Talke Pits Staffs........99 J3
Talkin Cumb..............148 F4
Talladale Highld........219 L7
Talla Linnfoots
  Border..................165 M5
Tallaminnock
  S Ayrs..................153 J3
Tallarn Green
  Wrexhm..................98 C4
Tallentire Cumb........147 K7
Talley Carmth............66 E7
Tallington Lincs........88 F2
Talmine Highld..........229 J3
Talog Carmth............50 D1
Talsarn Cerdgn..........66 D4
Talsarnau Gwynd........95 K5
Talskiddy Cnwll..........4 E3
Talwrn IoA..............109 G6
Tal-y-bont Cerdgn......80 E5
Tal-y-Bont Conwy......109 L7
Talybont Gwynd..........95 K7
Tal-y-bont Gwynd......109 J7
Talybont-on-Usk
  Powys..................53 H4
Tal-y-Cafn Conwy......109 M7
Tal-y-coed Mons........54 B5
Talysarn Gwynd..........95 H2
Tamar Valley Mining
  District Devon........6 C3
Tamerton Foliot
  C Plym..................6 C4
Tamworth Staffs........86 B3
Tamworth Services
  Warwks..................86 B4
Tandridge Surrey........32 C3
Tanfield Dur............150 F4
Tanfield Lea Dur........150 F4
Tangasdale W Isls......233 b9
Tangley Hants............28 F2
Tangmere W Susx........18 B4
Tankerness Ork..........234 c6
Tankersley Barns......115 G2
Tankerton Kent..........47 J6
Tannach Highld..........231 K6
Tannachie Abers........206 E8
Tannadice Angus......196 D5
Tanner's Green
  Worcs..................85 J8
Tannington Suffk........78 F2
Tannochside N Lans....175 J6

Tansley Derbys..........100 F1
Tansor Nhants............88 F5
Tantobie Dur............150 F4
Tanworth in Arden
  Warwks..................71 K1
Tan-y-groes Cerdgn......65 J5
Taobh Tuath W Isls....232 d5
Taplow Bucks............42 E4
Tarbert Ag & B..........172 B7
Tarbert Ag & B..........172 E5
Tarbert W Isls..........232 e4
Tarbet Ag & B..........183 K6
Tarbet Highld..........200 B6
Tarbet Highld..........228 B5
Tarbolton S Ayrs......163 K4
Tarbrax S Lans..........176 D7
Tardebigge Worcs........71 H2
Tarfside Angus..........196 D1
Tarland Abers..........205 K4
Tarleton Lancs..........120 F6
Tarlton Gloucs..........55 L7
Tarnock Somset..........26 B2
Tarporley Ches W......112 D8
Tarrant Crawford
  Dorset..................15 H2
Tarrant Gunville
  Dorset..................27 L8
Tarrant Hinton
  Dorset..................15 H1
Tarrant Keyneston
  Dorset..................15 H2
Tarrant Launceston
  Dorset..................15 H1
Tarrant Monkton
  Dorset..................15 H2
Tarrant Rawston
  Dorset..................15 H2
Tarrant Rushton
  Dorset..................15 H2
Tarring Neville
  E Susx..................19 L5
Tarrington Herefs......70 B6
Tarskavaig Highld......199 J4
Tarves Abers............217 G7
Tarvin Ches W..........112 C7
Tasburgh Norfk..........92 E4
Tatenhill Staffs......100 D7
Tathwell Lincs..........118 D5
Tatsfield Surrey........32 D2
Tattenhall Ches W......98 C2
Tatterford Norfk......105 K6
Tattersett Norfk......105 K6
Tattershall Lincs......103 K2
Tattershall Thorpe
  Lincs..................103 L1
Tattingstone Suffk......78 D6
Tattingstone White
  Horse Suffk............78 D6
Tatton Park Ches E....113 H5
Tatworth Somset........13 J2
Tauchers Moray........215 J4
Taunton Somset..........25 K6
Taunton Deane
  Services Somset......25 J7
Taverham Norfk..........92 E2
Tavernspite Pembks....49 K5
Tavistock Devon..........6 C2
Tavistock Devon..........6 C2
Taw Green Devon........10 F5
Tawstock Devon..........23 J5
Taxal Derbys............114 A5
Tay Bridge C Dund....187 G2
Taychreggan Hotel
  Ag & B..................182 F3
Tay Forest Park
  P & K..................194 C4
Tayinloan Ag & B......161 H1
Taynton Gloucs..........55 G4
Taynton Oxon............56 E5
Taynuilt Ag & B........182 E2
Tayport Fife............187 G2
Tayvallich Ag & B......172 C2
Tealby Lincs............117 J4
Tealing Angus..........196 C8
Team Valley Gatesd....151 G3
Teangue Highld........199 K4
Teanord Highld........212 F2
Tebay Cumb............138 E6

Tebay Services
  Cumb..................138 E6
Tebworth C Beds........59 G3
Tedburn St Mary
  Devon..................11 J6
Teddington Gloucs......55 L2
Teddington Gt Lon......44 D6
Tedstone Delamere
  Herefs..................70 C3
Tedstone Wafer
  Herefs..................70 C3
Teeton Nhants............73 K1
Teffont Evias Wilts....27 M5
Teffont Magna Wilts....27 M5
Tegryn Pembks............65 H7
Teigh Rutlnd..............88 C1
Teigngrace Devon..........7 K2
Teignmouth Devon........12 B7
Teindside Border......166 F7
Telford Wrekin..........84 C2
Telford Services
  Shrops..................84 D2
Tellisford Somset........27 J1
Telscombe E Susx........19 L5
Tempar P & K..........193 L5
Templand D & G........155 J5
Temple Cnwll..............5 J2
Temple Mdloth..........177 J6
Temple Bar Cerdgn......66 C4
Temple Cloud BaNES....38 F8
Templecombe
  Somset..................27 G6
Temple Grafton
  Warwks..................71 K4
Temple Guiting
  Gloucs..................56 C3
Temple Hirst N York..124 F5
Temple Normanton
  Derbys..................115 H7
Temple of Fiddes
  Abers..................206 F8
Temple Sowerby
  Cumb..................138 E2
Templeton Devon........11 K3
Templeton Pembks......49 J5
Templetown Dur........150 E5
Tempsford C Beds........75 H4
Tenbury Wells Worcs....69 L2
Tenby Pembks............49 J7
Tendring Essex..........62 D3
Tendring Green
  Essex..................62 D3
Tendring Heath
  Essex..................62 D3
Ten Mile Bank Norfk....90 E4
Tenterden Kent..........34 B7
Terling Essex............61 J5
Ternhill Shrops..........98 F6
Terregles D & G........155 G6
Terrington N York......133 K5
Terrington St
  Clement Norfk........104 E7
Terrington St John
  Norfk..................90 D2
Teston Kent..............33 J3
Testwood Hants..........29 G8
Tetbury Gloucs..........39 K2
Tetchill Shrops..........98 B6
Tetcott Devon............9 J5
Tetford Lincs............118 D6
Tetney Lincs............118 D2
Tetsworth Oxon..........58 B7
Tettenhall Wolves......84 F4
Tettenhall Wood
  Wolves..................84 F4
Teversal Notts..........101 J1
Teversham Cambs........76 C3
Teviothead Border......156 D2
Tewin Herts..............59 L5
Tewkesbury Gloucs......55 K2
Teynham Kent............34 C3
Thackley C Brad........123 H3
Thainstone Abers......206 E2
Thakeham W Susx........18 F3
Thame Oxon..............58 B6
Thames Ditton
  Surrey..................44 D6
Thamesmead Gt Lon....45 J4

Thamesport Medway......46 E5
Thanington Kent..........34 F4
Thankerton S Lans......165 J2
Tharston Norfk..........92 E5
Thatcham W Berk........41 K6
Thaxted Essex............60 F2
Theakston N York......132 D3
Thealby N Linc..........125 K6
Theale Somset............26 C3
Theale W Berk............41 M6
Thearne E R Yk..........126 D3
The Beeches Gloucs......56 B7
Theberton Suffk..........79 J2
The Braes Highld......209 H7
The Bridge Kent..........45 K5
*The Broads*............93 K2
The Brunt E Loth......178 E4
The Bungalow IoM......237 d4
The City Bucks..........42 C2
The Common Wilts........28 E5
Theddingworth Leics....87 J6
Theddlethorpe All
  Saints Lincs..........118 F4
Theddlethorpe St
  Helen Lincs............119 G4
The Deep C KuH........126 D5
The Den N Ayrs........174 C7
The Forstal Kent........34 D6
The Green Cumb........128 E3
The Green Essex........61 J4
The Green N York......143 G6
The Green Wilts..........27 K5
The Headland Hartpl..151 M7
The Hill Cumb..........128 E3
The Lee Bucks............58 E6
The Lhen IoM..........237 d2
Thelnetham Suffk........92 B7
The Lochs Moray......215 G2
Thelveton Norfk..........92 E7
Thelwall Warrtn........112 F4
Themelthorpe Norfk....106 C7
The Middles Dur........150 F5
The Moor Kent............33 K7
The Mumbles Swans......51 J7
The Murray S Lans....175 H7
The Neuk Abers........206 D5
Thenford Nhants..........73 G6
The Reddings Gloucs....55 K4
Therfield Herts..........75 L6
The Ross P & K........185 G3
The Spring Warwks......86 C8
The Stocks Kent..........21 H1
The Strand Wilts........39 L8
Thetford Norfk............91 K6
Thetford Forest
  Park..................91 J5
Theydon Bois Essex......60 D7
Thickwood Wilts..........39 J5
Thimbleby Lincs........118 C7
Thimbleby N York......141 K7
Thingwall Wirral......111 J5
Thirkleby N York......133 G4
Thirlby N York..........133 G3
Thirlestane Border....178 C8
Thirn N York............132 C3
Thirsk N York..........132 F3
Thistleton Lancs......120 E3
Thistleton Rutlnd......102 E8
Thistley Green Suffk....90 F7
Thixendale N York......134 C7
Thockrington
  Nthumb..................158 B6
Tholomas Drove
  Cambs..................90 B3
Tholthorpe N York......133 G6
Thomastown Abers......216 B6
Thompson Norfk..........91 K4
Thomshill Moray........214 F3
Thongsbridge Kirk....123 H8
Thoralby N York........131 J3
Thoresway Lincs........117 K3
Thorganby Lincs........117 K3
Thorganby N York......125 G3
Thorgill N York........142 E7
Thorington Suffk........93 J8
Thorington Street
  Suffk..................78 B7

Thorlby N York.............131 H8
Thorley Herts.............60 D4
Thorley Street IoW .......16 D5
Thormanby N York..........133 G5
Thornaby-on-Tees
  S on T..................141 K4
Thornage Norfk............106 C5
Thornborough Bucks......73 L7
Thornborough
  N York..................132 D4
Thornbury C Brad.........123 J4
Thornbury Devon...........9 K3
Thornbury Herefs..........70 B3
Thornbury S Glos.........38 F3
Thornby Nhants............87 J7
Thorncliff Staffs........100 A2
Thorncombe Dorset.......13 J2
Thorndon Suffk............78 D1
Thorndon Cross
  Devon...................10 D6
Thorne Donc..............125 G7
Thorner Leeds............124 B3
Thorne St Margaret
  Somset..................25 H7
Thorney C Pete...........89 K3
Thorney Notts............116 E6
Thorney Somset............26 B6
Thorney Hill Hants........16 A3
Thorney Island
  W Susx..................17 L2
Thornfalcon Somset........25 L6
Thornford Dorset..........26 E8
Thorngrafton
  Nthumb..................149 K2
Thorngumbald
  E R Yk..................126 F5
Thornham Norfk...........105 H4
Thornham Magna
  Suffk...................78 D1
Thornham Parva
  Suffk...................92 D8
Thornhaugh C Pete........88 F4
Thornhill C Sotn.........29 J8
Thornhill Cumb...........136 D5
Thornhill D & G..........154 F3
Thornhill Derbys.........114 D5
Thornhill Kirk...........123 K6
Thornhill Stirlg.........184 E7
Thornholme E R Yk........135 H6
Thornicombe Dorset........15 G2
Thornington Nthumb......168 D3
Thornley Dur.............150 E7
Thornley Dur.............151 J6
Thornliebank E Rens ....174 F6
Thorns Suffk.............77 G4
Thornsett Derbys.........114 A4
Thornthwaite Cumb........137 H3
Thornthwaite N York .....132 B7
Thornton Angus...........196 C6
Thornton Bucks............73 L7
Thornton C Brad.........123 G4
Thornton E R Yk..........125 H2
Thornton Fife............186 E7
Thornton Lancs...........120 D3
Thornton Leics............86 F3
Thornton Middsb..........141 L4
Thornton Nthumb..........179 K8
Thornton Curtis
  N Linc..................126 D6
Thorntonhall S Lans .....175 G7
Thornton Heath
  Gt Lon...................44 F6
Thornton Hough
  Wirral..................111 J5
Thornton-in-
  Craven N York..........122 D2
Thornton in
  Lonsdale N York........130 D5
Thornton-le-Beans
  N York..................132 F2
Thornton-le-Clay
  N York..................133 L6
Thornton-le-Dale
  N York..................134 C3
Thornton le Moor
  Lincs...................117 H3
Thornton-le-Moor
  N York..................132 F2

Thornton-le-Moors
  Ches W..................112 C6
Thornton-le-Street
  N York..................132 F3
Thorntonloch E Loth.....178 F4
Thornton Rust
  N York..................131 H2
Thornton Steward
  N York..................132 B3
Thornton Watlass
  N York..................132 C3
Thornydykes Border ....178 D8
Thornythwaite Cumb......137 L3
Thoroton Notts...........102 C4
Thorp Arch Leeds.........124 C2
Thorpe Derbys............100 D3
Thorpe E R Yk............126 B2
Thorpe N York............131 J6
Thorpe Notts.............102 C3
Thorpe Surrey.............43 G6
Thorpe Abbotts
  Norfk....................92 E7
Thorpe Arnold Leics.....102 C7
Thorpe Audlin
  Wakefd..................124 D7
Thorpe Bassett
  N York..................134 D5
Thorpe Bay Sthend........46 E3
Thorpe by Water
  Rutlnd...................88 C4
Thorpe Constantine
  Staffs...................86 C2
Thorpe End Norfk..........93 G2
Thorpe Green Essex.......62 E4
Thorpe Green Suffk........77 L4
Thorpe Hesley Rothm.. 115 G3
Thorpe in Balne
  Donc....................124 F7
Thorpe Langton
  Leics....................87 L5
Thorpe Lea Surrey........43 G6
Thorpe-le-Soken
  Essex....................62 E4
Thorpe le Street
  E R Yk..................125 K2
Thorpe Malsor
  Nhants...................88 B7
Thorpe Mandeville
  Nhants...................73 G5
Thorpe Market
  Norfk...................106 F5
Thorpe Marriot
  Norfk....................92 E1
Thorpe Morieux
  Suffk....................77 L4
Thorpeness Suffk..........79 K3
Thorpe on the Hill
  Lincs...................116 E7
Thorpe Park Surrey.......43 G6
Thorpe St Andrew
  Norfk....................92 F2
Thorpe St Peter
  Lincs...................104 D1
Thorpe Salvin Rothm.. 115 K5
Thorpe Satchville
  Leics....................87 K2
Thorpe Thewles
  S on T..................141 J3
Thorpe Tilney Lincs......103 J2
Thorpe Underwood
  N York..................133 G7
Thorpe Waterville
  Nhants...................88 E7
Thorpe Willoughby
  N York..................124 E4
Thorrington Essex........62 C4
Thorverton Devon.........11 L4
Thrandeston Suffk........92 D7
Thrapston Nhants.........88 E7
Threapwood Ches W........98 C4
Threapwood Staffs......100 B4
Threave S Ayrs..........163 J7
Three Bridges
  W Susx...................32 B5
Three Chimneys
  Kent.....................33 L5
Three Cocks Powys........68 D6
Three Crosses Swans.....51 H6

Three Cups Corner
  E Susx...................20 D2
Threekingham Lincs......103 H5
Three Leg Cross
  E Susx...................33 H6
Three Legged Cross
  Dorset...................15 K2
Three Mile Cross
  Wokham...................42 B6
Threemilestone
  Cnwll.....................3 K3
Threemiletown
  W Loth..................176 E3
Three Oaks E Susx........21 G3
Threlkeld Cumb...........137 J3
Threshers Bush
  Essex....................60 D6
Threshfield N York.......131 J6
Thrigby Norfk.............93 K2
Thrintoft N York.........132 D2
Thriplow Cambs............76 B5
Throcking Herts...........60 B3
Throckley N u Ty.........150 E2
Throckmorton
  Worcs....................71 H4
Throop BCP................15 L4
Thropton Nthumb.........158 C2
Throsk Stirlg............176 B1
Throughgate D & G.......154 F5
Throwleigh Devon.........11 G6
Throwley Forstal
  Kent.....................34 C4
Thrumpton Notts..........101 J6
Thrumster Highld........231 L6
Thrunscoe NE Lin.........127 H8
Thrupp Gloucs.............55 K7
Thrussington Leics.......87 J1
Thruxton Hants............28 F3
Thruxton Herefs..........69 J7
Thrybergh Rothm.........115 J3
Thulston Derbys..........101 H6
Thundersley Essex........46 C3
Thurcaston Leics.........87 H2
Thurcroft Rothm.........115 J4
Thurgarton Norfk........106 E5
Thurgarton Notts........102 B3
Thurgoland Barns........114 F2
Thurlaston Leics.........87 G4
Thurlaston Warwks........72 F1
Thurlbear Somset.........25 K7
Thurlby Lincs............89 G1
Thurlby Lincs............102 E1
Thurlby Lincs............119 G6
Thurleigh Bed............74 F3
Thurlestone Devon.........7 G7
Thurloxton Somset........25 L5
Thurlstone Barns........114 E2
Thurlton Norfk...........93 J4
Thurmaston Leics.........87 H2
Thurnby Leics............87 J3
Thurne Norfk.............93 J1
Thurnham Kent............33 K2
Thurning Nhants..........88 F6
Thurning Norfk..........106 C6
Thurnscoe Barns.........115 J1
Thursby Cumb............148 B5
Thursford Norfk.........106 B5
Thursley Surrey..........30 E4
Thurso Highld...........231 G2
Thurstaston Wirral......111 H5
Thurston Suffk...........77 K2
Thurstonfield Cumb.....148 B4
Thurstonland Kirk......123 H7
Thurton Norfk............93 G4
Thurvaston Derbys.......100 E5
Thuxton Norfk............92 B3
Thwaite N York..........139 K7
Thwaite Suffk............78 D2
Thwaite Head Cumb......129 H2
Thwaite St Mary
  Norfk....................93 G4
Thwing E R Yk...........135 G5

Tibberton Wrekin.........99 G7
Tibenham Norfk...........92 D5
Tibshelf Derbys.........101 H1
Tibshelf Services
  Derbys..................101 H1
Tibthorpe E R Yk........134 E7
Ticehurst E Susx.........33 H7
Tichborne Hants..........29 L5
Tickencote Rutlnd........88 E2
Tickenham N Som..........38 C6
Tickhill Donc...........115 L3
Ticklerton Shrops........83 J5
Ticknall Derbys.........101 G7
Tickton E R Yk..........126 D3
Tidcombe Wilts...........40 F8
Tiddington Oxon..........57 M6
Tiddington Warwks........72 B4
Tidebrook E Susx.........33 G7
Tideford Cnwll............6 A4
Tidenham Gloucs..........38 E2
Tideswell Derbys........114 D6
Tidmarsh W Berk..........41 M5
Tidmington Warwks........72 C6
Tidworth Wilts...........28 E2
Tiers Cross Pembks.......48 F5
Tiffield Nhants..........73 K4
Tigerton Angus..........196 E4
Tigh a' Ghearraidh
  W Isls..................233 b6
Tigharry W Isls.........233 b6
Tighnabruaich
  Ag & B..................173 G4
Tigley Devon..............7 H4
Tilbrook Cambs...........74 F2
Tilbury Thurr............45 M5
Tile Cross Birm..........85 L6
Tile Hill Covtry.........86 C2
Tilehurst Readg..........42 A5
Tilford Surrey...........30 E3
Tilgate W Susx...........31 L4
Tilham Street
  Somset...................26 E4
Tillicoultry Clacks.....185 J7
Tillietudlem S Lans ....164 F1
Tillingham Essex.........62 B7
Tillington Herefs........69 J5
Tillington W Susx........30 F6
Tillington Common
  Herefs...................69 J5
Tillybirloch Abers......206 D4
Tillyfourie Abers.......206 C3
Tillygreig Abers........207 G2
Tillyrie P & K..........186 B6
Tilmanstone Kent.........35 J4
Tilney All Saints
  Norfk...................104 F8
Tilney High End
  Norfk...................104 E8
Tilney St Lawrence
  Norfk....................90 D2
Tilshead Wilts...........28 B2
Tilstock Shrops..........98 D5
Tilston Ches W...........98 C3
Tilstone Fearnall
  Ches W...................98 E1
Tilsworth C Beds.........59 G3
Tilton on the Hill
  Leics....................87 L3
Tiltups End Gloucs.......39 J2
Timberland Lincs........103 J2
Timbersbrook
  Ches E..................113 K8
Timberscombe
  Somset...................24 E3
Timble N York...........132 B8
Timpanheck D & G........156 B7
Timperley Traffd........113 H4
Timsbury BaNES...........38 F8
Timsbury Hants...........29 G6
Timsgarry W Isls........232 d2
Timsgarraidh
  W Isls..................232 d2
Timworth Suffk...........77 J2
Timworth Green
  Suffk....................77 J2
Tincleton Dorset.........14 E4
Tindale Cumb............149 G3
Tingewick Bucks..........58 A2

Tingrith C Beds.................59 G2
*Tingwall Airport*
    Shet...........................235 c6
Tingwell Ork....................234 c5
Tinhay Devon........................9 K7
Tinsley Sheff..................115 H4
Tinsley Green W Susx....32 B5
Tintagel Cnwll......................8 E7
Tintern Mons.....................54 D7
Tintinhull Somset ...........26 D7
Tintwistle Derbys.........114 A3
Tinwald D & G .................155 H5
Tinwell Rutlnd..................88 E3
Tipton Sandw.....................85 G5
Tipton Green Sandw....85 G5
Tipton St John
    Devon.............................12 E4
Tiptree Essex.....................61 L5
Tiptree Heath Essex ...61 L5
Tirabad Powys...................67 J6
Tiree Ag & B .....................188 D7
*Tiree Airport*
    Ag & B ...........................188 C7
Tiretigan Ag & B............172 C6
Tirley Gloucs.....................55 J3
Tiroran Ag & B ...............181 G2
Tirphil Caerph...................53 H7
Tirril Cumb.......................138 D2
Tisbury Wilts......................27 L5
Tissington Derbys.........100 D3
Titchberry Devon..............22 C6
Titchfield Hants...............17 G2
Titchmarsh Nhants........88 E7
Titchwell Norfk..............105 J4
Tithby Notts.....................102 B5
Titley Herefs......................69 G3
Titsey Surrey......................32 D3
Titson Cnwll........................9 H5
Tittensor Staffs...............99 K5
Tittleshall Norfk............105 L7
Titton Worcs......................70 E1
Tiverton Ches W..............98 D1
Tiverton Devon.................24 E8
Tivetshall St
    Margaret Norfk........92 E6
Tivetshall St Mary
    Norfk.............................92 E6
Tixall Staffs.......................99 L7
Tixover Rutlnd..................88 E4
Toab Shet..........................235 c8
Tobermory Ag & B.........189 L5
Toberonochy Ag & B....181 L5
Tobha Mòr W Isls........233 b7
Tocher Abers..................216 D7
Tochieneal Moray.........215 L2
Tockenham Wilts.............40 B4
Tockholes Bl w D..........121 K6
Tockington S Glos..........38 E3
Tockwith N York...........133 G8
Todber Dorset...................27 J7
Toddington C Beds........59 G3
Toddington Gloucs........56 B2
*Toddington*
    *Services* C Beds..........59 G3
Todenham Gloucs...........72 B7
Todhills Angus................196 C8
*Todhills Rest Area*
    Cumb............................148 C3
Todmorden Calder........122 D5
Todwick Rothm..............115 J5
Toft Cambs.........................75 L4
Toft Lincs...........................88 F1
Toft Shet............................235 c3
Toft Hill Dur.....................140 E2
Toft Monks Norfk............93 J4
Toft next Newton
    Lincs............................117 H4
Toftrees Norfk................105 L6
Togston Nthumb.............159 G2
Tokavaig Highld..............199 J3
Tokers Green Oxon .......42 B5
Tolastadh bho
    Thuath W Isls..........232 g2
Tolland Somset.................25 H5
Tollard Royal Wilts.......27 L7
Toll Bar Donc...................124 E8
Toller Fratrum
    Dorset...........................14 B3

Toller Porcorum
    Dorset...........................14 B3
Tollerton N York............133 H6
Tollerton Notts...............101 L5
Tollesbury Essex.............62 A6
Tolleshunt D'Arcy
    Essex.............................61 L5
Tolleshunt Knights
    Essex.............................61 L5
Tolleshunt Major
    Essex.............................61 L5
Toll of Birness
    Abers...........................217 J7
Tolpuddle Dorset ...........14 E4
Tolworth Gt Lon..............44 D6
Tomatin Highld...............213 J8
Tomchrasky Highld.......201 K3
Tomdoun Highld............201 H5
Tomich Highld................211 L8
Tomich Highld................212 E5
Tomich Highld................222 F7
Tomich Highld................226 A7
Tomintoul Moray...........204 E2
Tomnacross Highld.......212 D6
Tomnavoulin Moray......204 F1
Tonbridge Kent................33 G4
Tondu Brdgnd....................36 D4
Tonedale Somset .............25 H6
Tong C Brad.....................123 J4
Tong Kent...........................34 C4
Tong Shrops.......................84 E3
Tong W Isls.......................232 g2
Tonge Leics......................101 H7
Tongham Surrey................30 E2
Tongland D & G..............146 C4
Tong Norton Shrops.......84 E2
Tongue Highld.................229 J4
Tongwynlais Cardif ........37 H4
Tonmawr Neath................36 C2
Tonna Neath......................52 B7
Tonwell Herts...................60 B5
Tonypandy Rhondd.........36 F3
Tonyrefail Rhondd...........36 F3
Toot Baldon Oxon...........57 K7
Toot Hill Essex.................60 E7
Toothill Swindn................40 C4
Tooting Gt Lon.................44 F5
Tooting Bec Gt Lon.........44 F5
Topcliffe N York............132 F4
Topcroft Norfk..................92 F5
Topcroft Street Norfk....92 F5
Toppesfield Essex............77 G6
Topsham Devon................12 C5
Torbeg N Ayrs................162 A4
Torboll Highld................223 G2
Torbreck Highld.............213 G6
Torbryan Devon..................7 J3
Torcastle Highld.............192 B2
Torcross Devon...................7 J7
Tore Highld.....................212 F4
Torinturk Ag & B............172 D5
Torksey Lincs..................116 D5
Torlundy Highld.............192 B2
Tormarton S Glos.............39 H5
Tormore N Ayrs..............161 M3
Tornagrain Highld..........213 J4
Tornaveen Abers............206 C4
Torness Highld................212 E8
Toronto Dur.....................140 F2
Torpenhow Cumb...........147 L6
Torphichen W Loth........176 C4
Torphins Abers................206 C5
Torpoint Cnwll...................6 C5
Torquay Torbay..................7 L3
Torquhan Border............177 L8
Torran Highld..................209 J5
Torrance E Duns.............175 H4
Torranyard N Ayrs.........163 J1
Torridon Highld..............210 D3
Torridon House
    Highld...........................210 D3
Torrin Highld...................199 J2
Torrisdale Ag & B..........161 K3
Torrisdale Highld...........229 K3
Torrish Highld.................227 G5
Torrisholme Lancs.........129 K6
Torrobull Highld.............226 A7

Torry C Aber....................207 H4
Torryburn Fife................176 D2
Torteval Guern................236 b4
Torthorwald D & G.........155 H6
Tortington W Susx..........18 D5
Torton Worcs....................84 E8
Tortworth S Glos.............39 G2
Torvaig Highld................209 H5
Torver Cumb...................137 J7
Torwood Falk..................175 L2
Torwoodlee Border.......167 G2
Torworth Notts...............116 A4
Toscaig Highld................209 L6
Toseland Cambs................75 J3
Tosside Lancs..................130 E7
Tostock Suffk....................77 L2
Totaig Highld...................208 C4
Tote Highld......................208 F5
Tote Highld......................209 H3
Totland IoW......................16 D5
Totley Sheff.....................114 F5
Totley Brook Sheff........114 F5
Totnes Devon......................7 J4
Toton Notts.....................101 J5
Totronald Ag & B..........188 F5
Totscore Highld..............208 F2
Tottenham Gt Lon...........45 G3
Tottenhill Norfk...............90 F2
Totteridge Gt Lon............44 E2
Totternhoe C Beds..........59 G4
Tottington Bury..............122 B7
Totton Hants....................29 G8
Toulston Somset...............25 J5
Toulvaddie Highld.........223 J5
Tovil Kent...........................33 K3
Toward Ag & B...............173 K5
Toward Quay Ag & B....173 J5
Towcester Nhants...........73 K5
Towednack Cnwll..............2 E4
*Tower of London*
    Gt Lon...........................45 G4
Towersey Oxon.................58 B6
Towie Abers.....................205 K3
Tow Law Dur...................150 E6
Town End Cambs..............90 B4
Townend W Duns...........174 D3
Townhead Barns............114 D2
Townhead D & G...........155 H4
Townhead of
    Greenlaw D & G.....146 C3
Townhill Fife...................176 F1
Town Littleworth
    E Susx..........................19 L3
Townshend Cnwll..............3 G5
Town Street Suffk............91 H6
Town Yetholm Border..168 B4
Towthorpe C York.........133 K7
Towton N York...............124 D3
Towyn Conwy..................110 D5
Toxteth Lpool.................111 K4
Toynton All Saints
    Lincs............................118 E8
Toy's Hill Kent.................32 E3
Trabboch E Ayrs.............163 K5
Trabbochburn E Ayrs...163 L5
Tradespark Highld.........213 K3
Trafford Park Traffd....113 H3
Trallong Powys.................52 E3
Tranent E Loth................177 L4
Tranmere Wirral............111 J4
Trantelbeg Highld..........230 C5
Trantlemore Highld.......230 C5
Trap Carmth......................51 J2
Traprain E Loth..............178 D4
Traquair Border..............166 E3
Trawden Lancs................122 D3
Trawsfynydd Gwynd......96 A5
Trealaw Rhondd...............36 F3
Treales Lancs..................120 F4
Trearddur Bay IoA........108 C5
Trebetherick Cnwll...........4 E1
Treborough Somset.........24 F4
Trebullett Cnwll.................5 M1
Treburley Cnwll..................5 M1
Trecastle Powys................52 D3
Trecwn Pembks................64 D7
Trecynon Rhondd............52 F7
Tredegar Blae G...............53 H6

Tredington Gloucs...........55 K3
Tredington Warwks.......72 C5
Tredunnock Mons...........38 B2
Treen Cnwll.........................2 D6
Treeton Rothm...............115 H4
Trefasser Pembks...........64 C6
Trefecca Powys.................53 H2
Trefechan Myr Td............53 G6
Trefeglwys Powys............81 L5
Treffgarne Pembks..........49 G3
Treffgarne Owen
    Pembks.........................48 E3
Trefilan Cerdgn................66 D3
Trefin Pembks.................64 B7
Trefnant Denbgs............110 E7
Trefonen Shrops...............97 K6
Trefor Gwynd...................94 F4
Treforest Rhondd............37 G3
Trefriw Conwy...............109 L8
Tregadillett Cnwll.............9 H7
Tregare Mons...................54 B6
Tregaron Cerdgn..............66 F3
Tregarth Gwynd.............109 H7
Tregeare Cnwll...................9 H7
Tregeiriog Wrexhm........97 J5
Tregele IoA......................108 D3
Treglemais Pembks.........48 D2
Tregonetha Cnwll..............4 E3
Tregonning &
    Gwinear Mining
    District Cnwll...............3 G5
Tregony Cnwll.....................4 E6
Tregorrick Cnwll...............4 F5
Tregoyd Powys..................68 E6
Tre-groes Cerdgn.............65 L5
Tregynon Powys................82 C4
Tre-gynwr Carmth...........50 E2
Trehafod Rhondd.............37 G3
Trehan Cnwll.......................6 B4
Treharris Myr Td..............37 H2
Treherbert Rhondd..........52 E7
Trekenner Cnwll................6 A1
Treknow Cnwll...................8 D7
Trelawnyd Flints............110 F5
Trelech Carmth.................65 J7
Treleddyd-fawr
    Pembks.........................48 C2
Trelewis Myr Td...............37 H2
Trelights Cnwll...................8 C8
Trelill Cnwll........................5 G1
Trellech Mons...................54 D6
Trelogan Flints...............110 F5
Tremadog Gwynd............95 K4
Tremail Cnwll......................8 F7
Tremain Cerdgn................65 H5
Tremaine Cnwll..................9 G6
Tremar Cnwll......................5 K3
Trematon Cnwll..................6 B4
Tremeirchion
    Denbgs........................110 F6
Trenance Cnwll..................4 D3
Trenance Cnwll..................4 E2
Trench Wrekin...................84 C2
Trenear Cnwll.....................3 H5
Treneglos Cnwll.................9 G7
Trent Dorset.....................26 E7
Trentham C Stke..............99 K4
Trentishoe Devon............23 K2
Trent Vale C Stke.............99 K4
Treoes V Glam..................36 E5
Treorchy Rhondd.............36 E2
Trequite Cnwll....................5 G1
Trerhyngyll V Glam.........36 F5
Trerulefoot Cnwll..............5 M4
Tresaith Cerdgn................65 J4
Tresco IoS...........................2 a1
Trescowe Cnwll..................3 G5
Tresean Cnwll.....................4 C4
Tresham Gloucs................39 H3
*Treshnish Isles*
    Ag & B ........................189 G7
Tresillian Cnwll..................4 D6
*Treskinnick Cross*
    Cnwll..............................9 G5
Tresmeer Cnwll..................9 G7
Tresparrett Cnwll..............8 F6
Tressait P & K.................194 C4
Tresta Shet......................235 c5

Tresta Shet .................. 235 e3
Treswall Notts ............. 116 C5
Tre Taliesin Cerdgn ....... 80 E5
Trethevey Cnwll ............... 8 E6
Trethewey Cnwll ............... 2 C6
Trethurgy Cnwll ............... 5 G5
Tretire Herefs ............... 54 D4
Tretower Powys ............. 53 J4
Treuddyn Flints .......... 97 K2
Trevalga Cnwll ................ 8 E6
Trevalyn Wrexhm .......... 98 B2
Trevarrian Cnwll ............. 4 D3
Treveal Cnwll .................. 4 C4
Treveighan Cnwll ............ 8 E8
Trevellas Downs
   Cnwll ....................... 3 J2
Trevelmond Cnwll .......... 5 K3
Treverva Cnwll ................ 3 K5
Trevescan Cnwll ............. 2 A5
Treviscoe Cnwll .............. 4 E5
Trevone Cnwll ................ 4 D2
Trevor Wrexhm ............ 97 L4
Trewalder Cnwll .............. 8 E7
Trewarmett Cnwll ........... 8 E7
Trewavas Mining
   District Cnwll .......... 3 G6
Trewen Cnwll ................. 9 H7
Trewint Cnwll ................. 9 G8
Trewithian Cnwll ............. 4 D7
Trewoon Cnwll ................ 4 F5
Treyford W Susx ........... 30 D7
Trimdon Dur ............. 151 J7
Trimdon Colliery
   Dur ...................... 151 J7
Trimdon Grange Dur ... 151 J7
Trimingham Norfk ....... 107 G5
Trimley St Martin
   Suffk ......................78 F6
Trimley St Mary
   Suffk ......................79 G7
Trimsaran Carmth .......... 50 F5
Trimstone Devon ........... 23 H3
Trinafour P & K ........... 194 B4
Tring Herts .................. 58 F5
Trinity Angus .............. 196 F4
Trinity Jersey ............. 236 d6
Trinity Gask P & K ..... 185 K4
Triscombe Somset ......... 25 J4
Trislaig Highld ........... 191 L2
Trispen Cnwll ................ 4 D5
Tritlington Nthumb ..... 158 F4
Trochry P & K ............ 194 F7
Troedyraur Cerdgn ........ 65 K5
Troedyrhiw Myr Td ....... 53 G7
Trois Bois Jersey ........ 236 c6
Troon Cnwll .................. 3 H4
Troon S Ayrs .............. 163 H3
Tropical World
   Roundhay Park
   Leeds ................. 123 L3
Trossachs Stirlg ......... 184 B5
Trossachs Pier Stirlg .. 184 B6
Troston Suffk ............... 91 K8
Trotshill Worcs ............ 70 F4
Trottiscliffe Kent .......... 33 H2
Trotton W Susx ........... 30 D6
Troutbeck Cumb ......... 137 L6
Troutbeck Bridge
   Cumb ................... 137 L7
Troway Derbys ............ 115 H5
Trowbridge Wilts .......... 39 J8
Trowell Notts ............. 101 J4
Trowell Services
   Notts ................... 101 J4
Trowle Common
   Wilts ...................... 39 J8
Trowse Newton
   Norfk ..................... 92 F3
Trudoxhill Somset ......... 27 H3
Trull Somset ................ 25 K6
Trumpan Highld .......... 208 C3
Trumpet Herefs ............ 70 B6
Trumpington Cambs ...... 76 C4
Trunch Norfk .............. 107 G5
Truro Cnwll ................... 4 C6
Trusham Devon ............ 11 K7
Trusley Derbys ........... 100 E5
Trusthorpe Lincs ........ 119 G5

Trysull Staffs ............... 84 F5
Tubney Oxon ................ 57 H7
Tuckenhay Devon ........... 7 J5
Tuckhill Shrops ............. 84 E6
Tuckingmill Cnwll ............ 3 H3
Tuckingmill Wilts .......... 27 L5
Tuckton BCP ............... 15 L4
Tuddenham Suffk ......... 77 G1
Tuddenham Suffk ......... 78 E5
Tudeley Kent ............... 33 G4
Tudhoe Dur ............... 151 G7
Tudweiliog Gwynd ........ 94 D5
Tuffley Gloucs ............. 55 J5
Tufton Hants ............... 29 J3
Tufton Pembks ............. 49 H2
Tugby Leics ................. 87 L4
Tugford Shrops ............ 83 L6
Tughall Nthumb .......... 169 J4
Tullibody Clacks ......... 185 H7
Tullich Abers ............. 205 J6
Tullich Highld ............ 212 F8
Tullich Highld ............ 223 J6
Tulliemet P & K .......... 194 F5
Tulloch Abers ............ 216 F7
Tullochgorm Ag & B .... 182 D7
Tulloch Station
   Highld .................. 192 F1
Tullymurdoch P & K .... 195 J5
Tullynessle Abers ....... 206 B2
Tulse Hill Gt Lon .......... 44 F5
Tumble Carmth ............ 51 G3
Tumby Lincs .............. 103 L1
Tumby Woodside
   Lincs .................... 103 L2
Tummel Bridge
   P & K .................... 194 B5
Tunbridge Wells
   Kent ...................... 33 G5
Tundergarth D & G ...... 155 L6
Tunga W Isls ............. 232 g2
Tunley BaNES .............. 39 G8
Tunstall E R Yk ........... 127 H4
Tunstall Kent ............... 34 B3
Tunstall Lancs ............ 130 B5
Tunstall N York .......... 140 F7
Tunstall Norfk ............. 93 J2
Tunstall Staffs ............. 99 H6
Tunstall Suffk ............. 79 H4
Tunstall Sundld .......... 151 J4
Tunstead Derbys ......... 114 C6
Tunstead Norfk .......... 107 G7
Tunstead Milton
   Derbys ................. 114 B5
Tupsley Herefs ............ 69 K6
Turgis Green Hants ...... 42 B8
Turkdean Gloucs .......... 56 C4
Tur Langton Leics ........ 87 K5
Turleigh Wilts ............. 39 J7
Turnastone Herefs ....... 69 G7
Turnberry S Ayrs ....... 152 E2
Turnditch Derbys ....... 100 F3
Turners Hill W Susx ...... 32 C6
Turnhouse C Edin ....... 177 G4
Turnworth Dorset ........ 14 F2
Turriff Abers ............. 216 D4
Turton Bottoms
   Bl w D .................. 121 L7
Turves Cambs .............. 89 L4
Turvey Bed ................. 74 D4
Turville Bucks .............. 42 C3
Turweston Bucks .......... 73 H6
Tushielaw Inn Border .. 166 D5
Tutbury Staffs ............ 100 E6
Tutshill Gloucs ............. 38 D2
Tuttington Norfk ........ 106 F6
Tuxford Notts ............ 116 C7
Twatt Ork ................. 234 b5
Twatt Shet ................. 235 c5
Twechar E Duns .......... 175 J3
Tweedbank Border ...... 167 H3
Tweedmouth
   Nthumb ................. 179 K7
Tweedsmuir Border ..... 165 L4
Twelveheads Cnwll ........ 3 K3
Twemlow Green
   Ches E ................. 113 H7
Twenty Lincs .............. 103 J7
Twerton BaNES ............ 39 G7

Twickenham Gt Lon ...... 44 D5
Twigworth Gloucs ......... 55 J4
Twineham W Susx ........ 19 H2
Twinstead Essex ........... 77 J6
Twitchen Devon ............ 24 C5
Two Dales Derbys ....... 114 F8
Two Gates Staffs .......... 86 B4
Two Waters Herts ......... 59 H6
Twycross Leics ............ 86 D3
Twycross Zoo Leics ...... 86 C3
Twyford Bucks ............. 58 A3
Twyford Hants ............. 29 J6
Twyford Leics .............. 87 K2
Twyford Norfk ........... 106 B7
Twyford Wokham ......... 42 C5
Twynholm D & G ........ 146 B4
Twyning Green
   Gloucs ................... 70 F6
Twynllanan Carmth ....... 51 L2
Twywell Nhants ............ 88 D7
Tyberton Herefs ........... 69 H6
Tyburn Birm ................ 85 K5
Tycroes Carmth ........... 51 H4
Tycrwyn Powys ............ 97 H8
Tydd Gote Lincs ......... 104 D8
Tydd St Giles Cambs ..... 90 B1
Tydd St Mary Lincs ..... 104 C8
Tye Green Essex .......... 76 F2
Tyldesley Wigan ......... 113 G2
Tyler Hill Kent ............. 34 F3
Tylorstown Rhondd ....... 36 F2
Ty-nant Conwy ............ 96 F4
Tyndrum Stirlg ........... 183 K2
Ty'n-dwr Denbgs ......... 97 K4
Tynemouth N Tyne ..... 151 J2
Tyne Tunnel S Tyne .... 151 H2
Tyningham E Loth ....... 178 D3
Tynron D & G ............ 154 E4
Tynygraig Cerdgn ......... 66 F1
Ty'n-y-Groes Conwy ... 109 L7
Tyrie Abers ............... 217 H2
Tyringham M Keyn ....... 74 C5
Tyseley Birm ............... 85 K6
Tythegston Brdgnd ....... 36 D5
Tytherington Ches E .... 113 K6
Tytherington S Glos ...... 38 F3
Tytherington Wilts ........ 27 K3
Tytherleigh Devon ........ 13 H2
Tytherton Lucas
   Wilts ...................... 39 L5
Tywardreath Cnwll ......... 5 H5
Tywyn Gwynd .............. 80 D4

## U

Ubbeston Green
   Suffk ...................... 79 G1
Ubley BaNES ............... 38 D8
Uckfield E Susx ........... 19 M2
Uckinghall Worcs ......... 70 F6
Uckington Gloucs ......... 55 K3
Uddington S Lans ....... 175 J6
Uddington S Lans ....... 165 G3
Udimore E Susx ........... 21 G2
Udny Green Abers ...... 207 G1
Udny Station Abers .... 207 G1
Uffculme Devon ........... 25 G8
Uffington Lincs ............ 88 F3
Uffington Oxon ............ 40 F3
Uffington Shrops .......... 83 K2
Ufford C Pete ............. 89 G3
Ufford Suffk ............... 79 G4
Ufton Warwks .............. 72 E3
Ufton Nervet W Berk .... 41 M6
Ugadale Ag & B .......... 161 K4
Ugborough Devon .......... 7 G5
Uggeshall Suffk ........... 93 J7
Ugglebarnby N York .... 143 H5
Ughill Sheff ............... 114 E4
Ugley Essex ............... 60 E3
Ugley Green Essex ....... 60 E3
Ugthorpe N York ........ 143 G5
Uibhist A Deas
   W Isls ................... 233 c8
Uibhist A Tuath
   W Isls ................... 233 b6

Uig Ag & B ............... 188 F5
Uig Highld ................ 208 C4
Uig Highld ................ 208 F2
Uig W Isls ................ 232 d2
Uigshader Highld ....... 209 G5
Uisken Ag & B .......... 180 E4
Ulbster Highld ........... 231 K7
Ulceby Lincs ............. 118 F6
Ulceby N Linc ........... 126 D7
Ulceby Skitter N Linc .. 126 E7
Ulcombe Kent ............. 33 L4
Uldale Cumb ............. 147 M7
Uley Gloucs ................ 55 H7
Ulgham Nthumb ........ 159 G4
Ullapool Highld ......... 220 E3
Ullenhall Warwks ......... 71 K2
Ulleskelf N York ......... 124 D3
Ullesthorpe Leics ........ 87 G6
Ulley Rothm .............. 115 J4
Ullingswick Herefs ....... 69 L4
Ullinish Lodge
   Hotel Highld .......... 208 E6
Ullock Cumb ............. 136 E3
Ullswater Cumb ......... 138 B3
Ullswater Steamers
   Cumb ................... 137 L4
Ulpha Cumb ............. 128 E2
Ulrome E R Yk .......... 135 J7
Ulsta Shet ................ 235 d3
Ulva Ag & B .............. 189 K7
Ulverley Green Solhll .... 85 K6
Ulverston Cumb ........ 129 G4
Ulwell Dorset ............. 15 J6
Ulzieside D & G ......... 164 F7
Umberleigh Devon ........ 23 K6
Unapool Highld ......... 224 F2
Underbarrow Cumb .... 129 K2
Under Burnmouth
   Border ................. 156 E5
Undercliffe C Brad. .... 123 J4
Underdale Shrops ........ 83 K2
Underriver Kent .......... 32 F3
Underwood Notts ...... 101 J3
Undy Mons ................ 38 C3
Union Mills IoM. ........ 237 c5
Unst Shet ................. 235 d1
Unstone Derbys ........ 115 G6
Upavon Wilts .............. 28 C1
Upchurch Kent ............ 46 D6
Upcott Devon ............. 24 B5
Up Exe Devon ............ 12 B2
Upgate Norfk ............ 106 D8
Uphall Dorset ............. 14 B2
Uphall W Loth ........... 176 E4
Upham Devon ............. 11 K3
Upham Hants ............. 29 K7
Uphampton Herefs ....... 69 H2
Uphampton Worcs ........ 70 E2
Uphill N Som .............. 37 L8
Up Holland Lancs ....... 112 D1
Uplawmoor E Rens ..... 174 E2
Upleadon Gloucs .......... 55 H3
Upleatham R & Cl ...... 142 D4
Uploders Dorset .......... 13 L4
Uplowman Devon ......... 24 F7
Uplyme Devon ............. 13 H4
Up Marden W Susx ...... 30 D8
Upminster Gt Lon ........ 45 K3
Up Mudford Somset ...... 26 E7
Up Nately Hants .......... 30 B2
Upottery Devon ........... 12 F2
Upper Affcot Shrops ..... 83 J6
Upper Arley Worcs ....... 84 D7
Upper Badcall
   Highld .................. 228 B7
Upper Basildon
   W Berk .................. 41 L5
Upper Beeding
   W Susx ................... 19 G4
Upper Benefield
   Nhants .................. 88 E5
Upper Bentley Worcs .... 71 J2
Upper Bighouse
   Highld .................. 230 C4
Upper Boddington
   Nhants .................. 72 F4
Upper Brailes
   Warwks .................. 72 C6

**Upper Broadheath**
Worcs............70 E4
**Upper Broughton**
Notts............102 B7
**Upper Bucklebury**
W Berk............41 K6
**Upper Burgate** Hants......28 D7
**Upperby** Cumb............148 D4
**Upper Caldecote**
C Beds............75 H5
**Upper Chapel** Powys......67 L6
**Upper Chicksgrove**
Wilts............27 L5
**Upper Chute** Wilts............28 F2
**Upper Clapton**
Gt Lon............45 G3
**Upper Clatford** Hants......29 G3
**Upper Cound** Shrops......83 K3
**Upper Cumberworth**
Kirk............123 J8
**Upper Dallachy**
Moray............215 H2
**Upper Deal** Kent............35 K4
**Upper Dean** Bed............74 F2
**Upper Denby** Kirk............114 E1
**Upper Dicker** E Susx......20 B4
**Upper Dounreay**
Highld............230 E3
**Upper Dovercourt**
Essex............62 F2
**Upper Drumbane**
Stirlg............184 E6
**Upper Dunsforth**
N York............133 G6
**Upper Eashing**
Surrey............30 F3
**Upper Eathie** Highld......213 J2
**Upper Egleton**
Herefs............70 B5
**Upper Elkstone**
Staffs............100 B2
**Upper Ellastone**
Staffs............100 C4
**Upper Farringdon**
Hants............30 B4
**Upper Framilode**
Gloucs............55 H6
**Upper Froyle** Hants......30 C3
**Upperglen** Highld......208 E4
**Upper Godney**
Somset............26 C6
**Upper Gravenhurst**
C Beds............75 G7
**Upper Green** W Berk......41 G7
**Upper Grove Common** Herefs......54 E3
**Upper Hale** Surrey......30 D2
**Upper Halliford**
Surrey............43 H6
**Upper Hambleton**
Rutlnd............88 C3
**Upper Harbledown**
Kent............34 F3
**Upper Hartfield**
E Susx............32 E6
**Upper Hatherley**
Gloucs............55 L4
**Upper Heaton** Kirk......123 H6
**Upper Helmsley**
N York............133 L7
**Upper Hergest**
Herefs............68 F4
**Upper Heyford**
Nhants............73 J3
**Upper Heyford** Oxon......57 J3
**Upper Hill** Herefs......69 J4
**Upper Hopton** Kirk......123 J6
**Upper Hulme** Staffs......100 A1
**Upper Inglesham**
Swindn............40 D2
**Upper Killay** Swans......51 H6
**Upper Kinchrackine**
Ag & B............183 G2
**Upper Knockando**
Moray............214 E5
**Upper Lambourn**
W Berk............40 F4

**Upper Landywood**
Staffs............85 H3
**Upper Langford**
N Som............38 C7
**Upper Langwith**
Derbys............115 K7
**Upper Largo** Fife......187 G6
**Upper Leigh** Staffs......100 A5
**Upper Lochton**
Abers............206 D6
**Upper Longdon**
Staffs............85 J2
**Upper Lybster**
Highld............231 J7
**Upper Lydbrook**
Gloucs............54 E5
**Upper Lye** Herefs......69 H2
**Uppermill** Oldham......113 M1
**Upper Milton** Worcs......84 E8
**Upper Minety** Wilts......40 A3
**Upper Mulben**
Moray............215 H4
**Upper Netchwood**
Shrops............83 L5
**Upper Nobut** Staffs......100 B5
**Upper Norwood**
W Susx............18 C3
**Upper Oddington**
Gloucs............56 E3
**Upper Poppleton**
C York............133 H8
**Upper Ratley** Hants......28 F6
**Upper Rissington**
Gloucs............56 D4
**Upper Rochford**
Worcs............70 B2
**Upper Ruscoe** D & G......145 L3
**Upper Sapey** Herefs......70 C2
**Upper Seagry** Wilts......39 L4
**Upper Shelton**
C Beds............74 E5
**Upper Sheringham**
Norfk............106 D4
**Upper Skelmorlie**
N Ayrs............173 L5
**Upper Slaughter**
Gloucs............56 D4
**Upper Soudley**
Gloucs............54 F6
**Upper Standen** Kent......35 H6
**Upper Stoke** Norfk......92 F3
**Upper Stondon**
C Beds............75 G7
**Upper Stowe** Nhants......73 J3
**Upper Street** Hants......28 D7
**Upper Street** Norfk......93 H1
**Upper Street** Norfk......107 G8
**Upper Street** Suffk......77 H4
**Upper Street** Suffk......78 D4
**Upper Sundon**
C Beds............59 H3
**Upper Swell** Gloucs......56 D3
**Upper Tean** Staffs......100 A5
**Upperthong** Kirk......123 H8
**Upperton** W Susx......30 F6
**Upper Town** Herefs......69 L5
**Uppertown** Highld......231 L1
**Upper Town** N Som......38 D7
**Upper Town** Suffk......77 K2
**Upper Tumble**
Carmth............51 G3
**Upper Tysoe** Warwks......72 D5
**Upper Victoria** Angus..187 J1
**Upper Wardington**
Oxon............72 F5
**Upper Welland**
Worcs............70 D6
**Upper Wellingham**
E Susx............19 L3
**Upper Weybread**
Suffk............92 F7
**Upper Wield** Hants......29 L4
**Upper Winchendon**
Bucks............58 C5
**Upper Woodford**
Wilts............28 C4
**Upper Wraxall** Wilts......39 J5
**Uppingham** Rutlnd......88 C4

**Uppington** Shrops......83 L2
**Upsall** N York............133 G3
**Upsettlington**
Border............168 C1
**Upshire** Essex............60 C7
**Up Somborne** Hants......29 H5
**Upstreet** Kent............35 G3
**Upton** Bucks............58 C5
**Upton** C Pete............89 G4
**Upton** Cambs............89 H7
**Upton** Ches W............112 B7
**Upton** Cnwll............5 L2
**Upton** Devon............7 G2
**Upton** Devon............12 E2
**Upton** Dorset............14 E5
**Upton** Dorset............15 J4
**Upton** Halton............112 C4
**Upton** Hants............29 G1
**Upton** Hants............29 G7
**Upton** Leics............86 D4
**Upton** Lincs............116 E4
**Upton** Norfk............93 H2
**Upton** Notts............102 B2
**Upton** Notts............116 C6
**Upton** Oxon............41 K3
**Upton** Slough............43 G5
**Upton** Somset............24 F5
**Upton** Somset............26 C6
**Upton** Wakefd............124 D7
**Upton** Wirral............111 J4
**Upton Bishop** Herefs......54 F3
**Upton Cheyney**
S Glos............39 G6
**Upton Cressett**
Shrops............84 B5
**Upton Grey** Hants......30 B2
**Upton Hellions**
Devon............11 J4
**Upton Lovell** Wilts......27 L4
**Upton Magna** Shrops......83 K2
**Upton Noble** Somset......27 G4
**Upton Pyne** Devon......11 L5
**Upton St Leonards**
Gloucs............55 K5
**Upton Scudamore**
Wilts............27 K2
**Upton Snodsbury**
Worcs............71 G4
**Upton-upon-Severn**
Worcs............70 F6
**Upton Warren** Worcs......71 G2
**Upwaltham** W Susx......18 C3
**Upwell** Norfk............90 C3
**Upwood** Cambs............89 J6
**Urchfont** Wilts............40 B8
**Urmston** Traffd......113 H3
**Urquhart** Moray......215 G2
**Urquhart Castle**
Highld............212 E8
**Urra** N York............142 C6
**Urray** Highld............212 D4
**Uryside** Abers......206 E2
**Usan** Angus............197 H5
**Ushaw Moor** Dur......151 G6
**Usk** Mons............54 B7
**Usselby** Lincs............117 H3
**Usworth** Sundld......151 H4
**Utkinton** Ches W......112 D7
**Utley** C Brad............122 F3
**Uton** Devon............11 J5
**Utterby** Lincs............118 D3
**Uttoxeter** Staffs......100 C5
**Uxbridge** Gt Lon......43 H4
**Uyeasound** Shet......235 d2
**Uzmaston** Pembks......49 G5

**V**

**Vale** Guern............236 d2
**Valley** IoA............108 C5
**Valtos** Highld............209 H2
**Valtos** W Isls............232 d2
**Vange** Essex............46 B3
**Vatsetter** Shet............235 d3
**Vatten** Highld............208 D5
**Vaynor** Myr Td......53 G6

**Vazon Bay** Guern......236 b3
**Veensgarth** Shet......235 c6
**Velindre** Powys......68 D7
**Venngreen** Devon......9 K3
**Venn Ottery** Devon......12 D4
**Ventnor** IoW............17 G6
**Venton** Devon............6 E4
**Vernham Dean** Hants......29 G1
**Vernham Street**
Hants............41 G8
**Verwood** Dorset......15 K2
**Veryan** Cnwll............4 E7
**Vickerstown** Cumb......128 E5
**Victoria** Cnwll............4 F4
**Vidlin** Shet............235 d4
**Viewfield** Moray......215 G2
**Viewpark** N Lans......175 J6
**Vigo** Kent............45 M7
**Village de Putron**
Guern............236 d3
**Ville la Bas** Jersey......236 a5
**Villiaze** Guern......236 d3
**Vines Cross** E Susx......20 C3
**Virginia Water**
Surrey............43 G6
**Virginstow** Devon......9 K6
**Vobster** Somset......27 G2
**Voe** Shet............235 c4
**Vowchurch** Herefs......69 G7

**W**

**Waberthwaite** Cumb......128 D2
**Wackerfield** Dur......140 E3
**Wacton** Norfk............92 E5
**Wadborough** Worcs......70 F5
**Waddesdon** Bucks......58 C5
**Waddesdon Manor**
Bucks............58 B5
**Waddeton** Devon......7 K4
**Waddingham** Lincs......117 G3
**Waddington** Lancs......121 L2
**Waddington** Lincs......116 F8
**Waddon** Gt Lon......44 F7
**Wadebridge** Cnwll......4 F2
**Wadeford** Somset......13 H1
**Wadenhoe** Nhants......88 E6
**Wadesmill** Herts......60 B4
**Wadhurst** E Susx......33 H6
**Wadshelf** Derbys......114 F7
**Wadworth** Donc......115 K3
**Wainfleet All Saints**
Lincs............104 D2
**Wainfleet St Mary**
Lincs............104 D2
**Wainhouse Corner**
Cnwll............9 G5
**Wainscott** Medway......46 C6
**Wainstalls** Calder......122 F5
**Waitby** Cumb......139 H5
**Waithe** Lincs......118 C2
**Wakefield** Wakefd......123 L6
**Wake Green** Birm......85 K6
**Wakehurst Place**
W Susx............32 C6
**Wakerley** Nhants......88 D4
**Wakes Colne** Essex......61 L3
**Walberswick** Suffk......93 K8
**Walberton** W Susx......18 C4
**Walbutt** D & G......146 D2
**Walcombe** Somset......26 D3
**Walcot** Lincs............103 H5
**Walcot** Shrops......83 L2
**Walcot** Swindn......40 D4
**Walcote** Leics......87 H6
**Walcot Green** Norfk......92 D7
**Walcott** Lincs......103 J2
**Walcott** Norfk......107 H6
**Walden Stubbs**
N York............124 E6
**Walderslade** Medway......46 C7
**Walderton** W Susx......17 L1
**Walditch** Dorset......13 L4
**Waldridge** Dur......151 G3
**Waldringfield** Suffk......79 G5
**Waldron** E Susx......20 B2

Wales Rothm ...... 115 J5
Wales Somset ...... 26 E6
Walesby Lincs ...... 117 J3
Walesby Notts ...... 116 B7
Walford Herefs ...... 54 E4
Walford Herefs ...... 83 H8
Walford Heath
  Shrops ...... 98 C8
Walgherton Ches E ...... 99 G3
Walgrave Nhants ...... 74 B1
Walkden Salfd ...... 113 G2
Walker N u Ty ...... 151 H3
Walkerburn Border ...... 166 E3
Walkeringham Notts ...... 116 C3
Walkerith Lincs ...... 116 C3
Walkern Herts ...... 59 M3
Walker's Heath Birm ...... 85 J7
Walkerton Fife ...... 186 D6
Walkford BCP ...... 16 B4
Walkhampton Devon ...... 6 D2
Walkington E R Yk ...... 126 B3
Walkley Sheff ...... 115 G4
Walk Mill Lancs ...... 122 C5
Walkwood Worcs ...... 71 J2
Wall Nthumb ...... 150 A2
Wall Staffs ...... 85 K3
Wallacetown S Ayrs ...... 153 G2
Wallacetown S Ayrs ...... 163 J5
Wallands Park E Susx ...... 19 L4
Wallasey Wirral ...... 111 J3
Wallasey
  (Kingsway)
  Tunnel Wirral ...... 111 K4
Wall Heath Dudley ...... 84 F5
Wallingford Oxon ...... 41 L3
Wallington Gt Lon ...... 44 F6
Wallington Hants ...... 17 H2
Wallington Herts ...... 75 K7
Wallington Heath
  Wsall ...... 85 H3
Wallisdown BCP ...... 15 K4
Walliswood Surrey ...... 31 J4
Walls Shet ...... 235 b5
Wallsend N Tyne ...... 151 H2
Wallyford E Loth ...... 177 K4
Walmer Kent ...... 35 K5
Walmer Bridge
  Lancs ...... 121 G5
Walmley Birm ...... 85 K5
Walmley Ash Birm ...... 85 K5
Walpole Suffk ...... 93 H8
Walpole Cross Keys
  Norfk ...... 104 E8
Walpole Highway
  Norfk ...... 90 D2
Walpole St Andrew
  Norfk ...... 104 D8
Walpole St Peter
  Norfk ...... 90 C1
Walsall Wsall ...... 85 H4
Walsden Calder ...... 122 D6
Walsgrave on Sowe
  Covtry ...... 86 E7
Walsham le Willows
  Suffk ...... 78 B1
Walshford N York ...... 132 F8
Walsoken Norfk ...... 90 C2
Walston S Lans ...... 165 K1
Walsworth Herts ...... 59 K3
Walter's Ash Bucks ...... 42 D2
Waltham Kent ...... 34 E5
Waltham NE Lin ...... 118 C2
Waltham Abbey
  Essex ...... 60 C7
Waltham Chase
  Hants ...... 29 K7
Waltham Cross Herts ...... 60 B7
Waltham on the
  Wolds Leics ...... 102 D7
Waltham St
  Lawrence W & M ...... 42 D5
Walthamstow Gt Lon ...... 45 G3
Walton C Pete ...... 89 H3
Walton Cumb ...... 148 F3
Walton Derbys ...... 115 G7
Walton Leeds ...... 124 C2
Walton Leics ...... 87 H6
Walton M Keyn ...... 74 C7

Walton Powys ...... 68 F3
Walton Somset ...... 26 C4
Walton Suffk ...... 79 G2
Walton W Susx ...... 17 M2
Walton Wakefd ...... 123 L6
Walton Wrekin ...... 98 E8
Walton Cardiff
  Gloucs ...... 55 K2
Walton East Pembks ...... 49 H3
Walton Highway
  Norfk ...... 90 C2
Walton-in-Gordano
  N Som ...... 38 B5
Walton-le-Dale
  Lancs ...... 121 H5
Walton-on-Thames
  Surrey ...... 43 J6
Walton-on-the-Hill
  Staffs ...... 99 L7
Walton-on-the-Hill
  Surrey ...... 31 L1
Walton-on-the-
  Naze Essex ...... 62 F4
Walton on the
  Wolds Leics ...... 101 L8
Walton-on-Trent
  Derbys ...... 100 E8
Walton Park N Som ...... 38 B6
Walton West Pembks ...... 48 E5
Walworth Darltn ...... 141 G4
Walworth Gt Lon ...... 45 G4
Walwyn's Castle
  Pembks ...... 48 E5
Wambrook Somset ...... 13 H2
Wanborough Surrey ...... 30 F2
Wanborough Swindn ...... 40 E4
Wandsworth Gt Lon ...... 44 E5
Wangford Suffk ...... 93 K7
Wanlip Leics ...... 87 H2
Wanlockhead D & G ...... 165 G6
Wannock E Susx ...... 20 C5
Wansford C Pete ...... 88 F4
Wansford E R Yk ...... 135 G7
Wanshurst Green
  Kent ...... 33 K4
Wanstead Gt Lon ...... 45 H3
Wanstrow Somset ...... 27 G3
Wanswell Gloucs ...... 55 G7
Wantage Oxon ...... 41 H3
Wappenbury Warwks ...... 72 E2
Wappenham Nhants ...... 73 J5
Warbleton E Susx ...... 20 C3
Warborough Oxon ...... 41 L2
Warboys Cambs ...... 89 K7
Warbreck Bpool ...... 120 D3
Warbstow Cnwll ...... 9 G6
Warburton Traffd ...... 113 G4
Warcop Cumb ...... 139 H4
Warden Nthumb ...... 150 A2
Ward End Birm ...... 85 K5
Wardington Oxon ...... 72 F5
Wardle Ches E ...... 98 E2
Wardle Rochdl ...... 122 D6
Wardley Gatesd ...... 151 H3
Wardley Rutlnd ...... 88 B4
Wardlow Derbys ...... 114 D6
Wardy Hill Cambs ...... 90 C7
Ware Herts ...... 60 B5
Wareham Dorset ...... 15 H5
Warehorne Kent ...... 34 D7
Warenford Nthumb ...... 169 H4
Wareside Herts ...... 60 C5
Waresley Cambs ...... 75 J4
Warfield Br For ...... 42 E6
Warfleet Devon ...... 7 K6
Wargrave Wokham ...... 42 C5
Warham Norfk ...... 105 M4
Wark Nthumb ...... 157 L6
Wark Nthumb ...... 168 C2
Warkleigh Devon ...... 23 K6
Warkton Nhants ...... 88 C7
Warkworth Nhants ...... 72 F6
Warkworth Nthumb ...... 159 G2
Warlaby N York ...... 132 E2
Warleggan Cnwll ...... 5 J3
Warley Town Calder ...... 122 F5
Warlingham Surrey ...... 32 C2
Warmfield Wakefd ...... 124 B6

Warmingham Ches E ...... 99 G1
Warmington Nhants ...... 88 F5
Warmington Warwks ...... 72 E5
Warminster Wilts ...... 27 K3
Warmley S Glos ...... 38 F5
Warmsworth Donc ...... 115 K2
Warmwell Dorset ...... 14 E5
Warner Bros. Studio
  Tour Herts ...... 59 H7
Warnford Hants ...... 29 L6
Warnham W Susx ...... 31 J5
Warningcamp
  W Susx ...... 18 D4
Warninglid W Susx ...... 31 L6
Warren Ches E ...... 113 K7
Warren Pembks ...... 48 F7
Warrenhill S Lans ...... 165 J2
Warren Row W & M ...... 42 D4
Warren Street Kent ...... 34 C4
Warrington M Keyn ...... 74 C4
Warrington Warrtn ...... 112 E4
Warriston C Edin ...... 177 H4
Warsash Hants ...... 16 F2
Warslow Staffs ...... 100 C2
Warter E R Yk ...... 125 K1
Warthermaske
  N York ...... 132 C4
Warthill N York ...... 133 K7
Wartling E Susx ...... 20 D4
Wartnaby Leics ...... 102 B7
Warton Lancs ...... 120 E5
Warton Lancs ...... 129 K5
Warton Warwks ...... 86 C3
Warwick Warwks ...... 72 C2
Warwick Bridge
  Cumb ...... 148 E4
Warwick Castle
  Warwks ...... 72 C2
Warwick Services
  Warwks ...... 72 D3
Wasbister Ork ...... 234 c4
Wasdale Head Cumb ...... 137 G5
Washaway Cnwll ...... 5 G2
Washbourne Devon ...... 7 J5
Washbrook Suffk ...... 78 D6
Washfield Devon ...... 11 L2
Washford Somset ...... 25 G3
Washford Pyne
  Devon ...... 11 J3
Washingborough
  Lincs ...... 117 G7
Washington Sundld ...... 151 H4
Washington W Susx ...... 18 F3
Washington
  Services Gatesd ...... 151 G4
Washwood Heath
  Birm ...... 85 K5
Wasperton Warwks ...... 72 C3
Wass N York ...... 133 H4
Wast Water Cumb ...... 137 G6
Watchet Somset ...... 25 G3
Watchfield Oxon ...... 40 E3
Watchgate Cumb ...... 138 D7
Water Devon ...... 11 H8
Waterbeach Cambs ...... 76 C2
Waterbeach W Susx ...... 18 B4
Waterbeck D & G ...... 155 M6
Water End E R Yk ...... 125 J3
Waterfall Staffs ...... 100 B3
Waterfoot Ag & B ...... 161 K3
Waterfoot E Rens ...... 175 G7
Waterfoot Lancs ...... 122 C6
Waterford Herts ...... 60 A5
Waterheads Border ...... 177 H7
Waterhouses Staffs ...... 100 B3
Wateringbury Kent ...... 33 H3
Waterloo Highld ...... 199 K2
Waterloo N Lans ...... 175 L7
Waterloo P & K ...... 195 G8
Waterloo Pembks ...... 49 G6
Waterloo Sefton ...... 111 K2
Waterlooville Hants ...... 17 J1
Watermead Bucks ...... 58 D5
Watermillock Cumb ...... 138 C3
Water Newton
  Cambs ...... 89 G4
Water Orton Warwks ...... 85 L5
Waterperry Oxon ...... 57 L6

Waterrow Somset ...... 25 G6
Watersfield W Susx ...... 18 D3
Waterside Bl w D ...... 121 K5
Waterside E Ayrs ...... 163 K7
Waterside E Ayrs ...... 163 L2
Waterside E Duns ...... 175 J4
Waterstein Highld ...... 208 B3
Waterstock Oxon ...... 57 M6
Waterston Pembks ...... 48 F6
Water Stratford
  Bucks ...... 73 J7
Waters Upton Wrekin ...... 98 F8
Watford Herts ...... 43 J2
Watford Nhants ...... 73 H2
Watford Gap
  Services Nhants ...... 73 H2
Wath N York ...... 132 B6
Wath N York ...... 132 K5
Wath upon Dearne
  Rothm ...... 115 H2
Watlington Norfk ...... 90 E2
Watlington Oxon ...... 42 B2
Watten Highld ...... 231 J5
Wattisfield Suffk ...... 92 B8
Wattisham Suffk ...... 78 B4
Watton Dorset ...... 13 L4
Watton E R Yk ...... 126 C1
Watton Norfk ...... 91 K4
Watton-at-Stone
  Herts ...... 60 A4
Wattston N Lans ...... 175 K4
Wattsville Caerph ...... 37 J3
Waulkmill Abers ...... 206 C6
Waunarlwydd Swans ...... 51 H6
Waunfawr Cerdgn ...... 80 E6
Waunfawr Gwynd ...... 95 J2
Wavendon M Keyn ...... 74 C6
Waverbridge Cumb ...... 147 L5
Waverton Ches W ...... 112 C8
Waverton Cumb ...... 147 L5
Wawne E R Yk ...... 126 D3
Waxham Norfk ...... 107 J7
Wayford Somset ...... 13 K2
Waytown Dorset ...... 13 L3
Way Village Devon ...... 11 J3
Weacombe Somset ...... 25 H4
Weald Oxon ...... 56 F7
Wealdstone Gt Lon ...... 44 D3
Weardley Leeds ...... 123 K2
Weare Somset ...... 26 B2
Weare Giffard Devon ...... 23 G6
Wearhead Dur ...... 149 L6
Wearne Somset ...... 26 B5
Weasenham All
  Saints Norfk ...... 105 K7
Weasenham St
  Peter Norfk ...... 105 K7
Weaste Salfd ...... 113 J2
Weaverham Ches W ...... 112 E6
Weaverthorpe
  N York ...... 134 E5
Webheath Worcs ...... 71 H2
Wedderlairs Abers ...... 216 F7
Weddington Warwks ...... 86 D5
Wedhampton Wilts ...... 40 B8
Wedmore Somset ...... 26 C2
Wednesbury Sandw ...... 85 H4
Wednesfield Wolves ...... 85 G4
Weedon Bucks ...... 58 D4
Weedon Bec Nhants ...... 73 J3
Weedon Lois Nhants ...... 73 H5
Weeford Staffs ...... 85 K3
Weeke Hants ...... 29 J5
Weekley Nhants ...... 88 C7
Week St Mary Cnwll ...... 9 H5
Weel E R Yk ...... 126 D3
Weeley Essex ...... 62 D4
Weeley Heath Essex ...... 62 D4
Weem P & K ...... 194 D6
Weethley Warwks ...... 71 J4
Weeting Norfk ...... 91 H5
Weeton E R Yk ...... 127 H6
Weeton Lancs ...... 120 E4
Weeton N York ...... 123 K2
Weetwood Leeds ...... 123 K3
Weir Lancs ...... 122 C5
Weir Quay Devon ...... 6 C3
Weisdale Shet ...... 235 c5

**Welborne** Norfk............92 C2
**Welbourn** Lincs............102 F2
**Welburn** N York............133 L6
**Welbury** N York............141 J6
**Welby** Lincs............102 F5
**Welcombe** Devon............22 C7
**Weldon** Nhants............88 D5
**Welford** Nhants............87 J7
**Welford** W Berk............41 H5
**Welford-on-Avon**
 Warwks............71 K4
**Welham** Leics............87 L5
**Welham** Notts............116 B5
**Welham Green** Herts............59 L6
**Well** Hants............30 C3
**Well** Lincs............118 F6
**Well** N York............132 D3
**Welland** Worcs............70 E6
**Wellbank** Angus............196 D8
**Wellesbourne**
 Warwks............72 C4
**Well Head** Herts............59 K3
**Welling** Gt Lon............45 J5
**Wellingborough**
 Nhants............74 C2
**Wellingham** Norfk............105 L7
**Wellingore** Lincs............103 G2
**Wellington** Cumb............136 F6
**Wellington** Herefs............69 K5
**Wellington** Somset............25 H7
**Wellington** Wrekin............84 B2
**Wellington Heath**
 Herefs............70 C6
**Wellow** BaNES............39 H8
**Wellow** IoW............16 E5
**Wellow** Notts............116 A7
**Wells** Somset............26 D3
**Wells-next-the-Sea**
 Norfk............105 L4
**Wellstye Green** Essex............61 G4
**Welltree** P & K............185 K3
**Wellwood** Fife............176 E2
**Welney** Norfk............90 D5
**Welshampton** Shrops............98 C5
**Welsh Frankton**
 Shrops............98 A6
**Welsh Newton**
 Herefs............54 D4
**Welshpool** Powys............82 E3
**Welsh St Donats**
 V Glam............36 F5
**Welton** Cumb............148 C6
**Welton** E R Yk............126 B5
**Welton** Lincs............117 G5
**Welton** Nhants............73 H2
**Welton le Marsh**
 Lincs............119 G7
**Welton le Wold** Lincs............118 C4
**Welwick** E R Yk............127 H6
**Welwyn** Herts............59 L5
**Welwyn Garden City**
 Herts............59 L5
**Wem** Shrops............98 D6
**Wembdon** Somset............25 L4
**Wembley** Gt Lon............44 D3
**Wembury** Devon............6 D6
**Wemworthy** Devon............10 F3
**Wemyss Bay** Inver............173 L4
**Wendens Ambo**
 Essex............76 D7
**Wendlebury** Oxon............57 K4
**Wendling** Norfk............91 L2
**Wendover** Bucks............58 E6
**Wendron** Cnwll............3 H5
**Wendron Mining**
 **District** Cnwll............3 J5
**Wendy** Cambs............75 K5
**Wenhaston** Suffk............93 J7
**Wennington** Cambs............89 J7
**Wennington** Gt Lon............45 K4
**Wennington** Lancs............130 C5
**Wensley** Derbys............100 E1
**Wensley** N York............131 K2
**Wentbridge** Wakefd............124 D6
**Wentnor** Shrops............83 H5
**Wentworth** Cambs............90 C7
**Wentworth** Rothm............115 G2
**Wenvoe** V Glam............37 H6

**Weobley** Herefs............69 H4
**Wepham** W Susx............18 E4
**Wereham** Norfk............90 F3
**Werrington** C Pete............89 H3
**Werrington** Cnwll............9 J7
**Wervin** Ches W............112 B6
**Wesham** Lancs............120 F4
**Wessington** Derbys............101 G2
**West Acre** Norfk............91 H1
**West Alvington**
 Devon............7 G6
**West Anstey** Devon............24 D6
**West Ashby** Lincs............118 C6
**West Ashling** W Susx............17 M2
**West Ashton** Wilts............27 K1
**West Auckland** Dur............140 F3
**West Ayton** N York............134 F3
**West Bagborough**
 Somset............25 J5
**West Bank** Halton............112 D5
**West Barkwith** Lincs............117 K5
**West Barnby** N York............143 G5
**West Barns** E Loth............178 E3
**West Barsham** Norfk............105 L5
**West Bay** Dorset............13 L4
**West Beckham**
 Norfk............106 D5
**West Bedfont** Surrey............43 H5
**Westbere** Kent............35 G3
**West Bergholt** Essex............62 A3
**West Bexington**
 Dorset............13 M5
**West Bilney** Norfk............91 G1
**West Blatchington**
 Br & H............19 J4
**West Boldon** S Tyne............151 J3
**Westborough** Lincs............102 D4
**Westbourne** BCP............15 K4
**Westbourne** W Susx............17 L2
**West Bowling** C Brad............123 H4
**West Bradenham**
 Norfk............91 K2
**West Bradford** Lancs............121 L2
**West Bradley** Somset............26 E4
**West Bretton** Wakefd............123 K7
**West Bridgford** Notts............101 L5
**West Bromwich**
 Sandw............85 H5
**Westbrook** Kent............35 J2
**Westbrook** W Berk............41 H6
**West Buckland**
 Devon............23 K5
**West Buckland**
 Somset............25 J7
**West Burrafirth** Shet............235 b5
**West Burton** N York............131 J3
**Westbury** Bucks............73 J7
**Westbury** Shrops............83 G2
**Westbury** Wilts............27 K2
**Westbury Leigh** Wilts............27 K2
**Westbury-on-**
 **Severn** Gloucs............55 G5
**Westbury-on-Trym**
 Bristl............38 E5
**Westbury-sub-**
 **Mendip** Somset............26 D2
**West Butterwick**
 N Linc............116 D1
**Westby** Lancs............120 E4
**West Byfleet** Surrey............43 H7
**West Cairngaan**
 D & G............144 D8
**West Caister** Norfk............93 K2
**West Calder** W Loth............176 D5
**West Camel** Somset............26 E6
**West Chaldon** Dorset............14 E5
**West Challow** Oxon............41 G3
**West Charleton**
 Devon............7 H7
**West Chiltington**
 W Susx............18 E3
**West Chinnock**
 Somset............26 C8
**West Clandon** Surrey............31 H2
**West Cliffe** Kent............35 J5
**Westcliff-on-Sea**
 Sthend............46 E3
**West Coker** Somset............26 D8

**Westcombe** Somset............27 G4
**West Compton**
 Somset............26 E3
**West Compton**
 **Abbas** Dorset............14 B4
**Westcote** Gloucs............56 E4
**Westcote Barton**
 Oxon............57 H3
**Westcott** Bucks............58 B5
**Westcott** Devon............12 C2
**Westcott** Surrey............31 J2
**West Cottingwith**
 N York............125 G3
**Westcourt** Wilts............40 E7
**West Cowick** E R Yk............124 F6
**West Cross** Swans............51 H7
**West Curthwaite**
 Cumb............148 B5
**Westdean** E Susx............20 B5
**West Dean** W Susx............18 B3
**West Dean** Wilts............28 E6
**West Deeping** Lincs............89 G2
**West Derby** Lpool............111 L3
**West Dereham** Norfk............90 F4
**West Down** Devon............23 H3
**Westdowns** Cnwll............8 E7
**West Drayton** Gt Lon............43 H4
**West Drayton** Notts............116 B6
**West Dunnet** Highld............231 J2
**West Ella** E R Yk............126 C5
**West End** Bed............74 E4
**West End** Hants............29 J8
**West End** N Som............38 C6
**West End** Norfk............93 K2
**West End** Surrey............42 F7
**West End** Surrey............43 J7
**West End** Wilts............27 M6
**West End Green**
 Hants............42 A7
**Wester Aberchalder**
 Highld............202 E2
**Westerdale** Highld............231 G5
**Westerdale** N York............142 E6
**Westerfield** Suffk............78 E5
**Westergate** W Susx............18 C5
**Westerham** Kent............32 D3
**Westerhope** N u Ty............150 F2
**Westerland** Devon............7 K4
**Westerleigh** S Glos............39 G4
**Western Isles** W Isls............232 d5
**Wester Ochiltree**
 W Loth............176 D4
**Wester Pitkierie** Fife............187 J6
**Wester Ross** Highld............220 C5
**Westerton of Rossie**
 Angus............197 G5
**Westerwick** Shet............235 c6
**West Farleigh** Kent............33 J3
**West Farndon** Nhants............73 G4
**West Felton** Shrops............97 M7
**Westfield** BaNES............26 F2
**Westfield** Cumb............136 D2
**Westfield** E Susx............21 G3
**Westfield** Highld............230 F3
**Westfield** N Lans............175 J4
**Westfield** Norfk............92 B2
**Westfield** Surrey............31 G1
**Westfield** W Loth............176 C4
**Westfields** Herefs............69 K6
**Westfields of**
 **Rattray** P & K............195 J6
**Westgate** Dur............150 A7
**Westgate** N Linc............125 J8
**Westgate-on-Sea**
 Kent............35 J2
**West Grafton** Wilts............40 E7
**West Green** Hants............30 C1
**West Grimstead**
 Wilts............28 E6
**West Grinstead**
 W Susx............31 K6
**West Haddlesey**
 N York............124 E5
**West Haddon** Nhants............73 J1
**West Hagbourne**
 Oxon............41 K3
**West Hagley** Worcs............84 F7
**Westhall** Suffk............93 J7

**West Hallam** Derbys............101 H4
**West Halton** N Linc............125 L6
**Westham** Dorset............14 C6
**Westham** E Susx............20 D5
**West Ham** Gt Lon............45 H4
**Westham** Somset............26 B3
**Westhampnett**
 W Susx............18 B4
**West Handley**
 Derbys............115 H6
**West Hanney** Oxon............41 H2
**West Hanningfield**
 Essex............61 H7
**West Harnham** Wilts............28 C5
**West Harptree**
 BaNES............38 E8
**West Harting** W Susx............30 C5
**West Hatch** Somset............25 L7
**West Hatch** Wilts............27 L5
**West Haven** Angus............187 J1
**Westhay** Somset............26 C3
**West Heath** Birm............85 J7
**West Helmsdale**
 Highld............227 H5
**West Hendred** Oxon............41 H3
**West Heslerton**
 N York............134 E4
**West Hewish** N Som............38 B7
**Westhide** Herefs............69 L5
**Westhill** Abers............206 F4
**West Hill** Devon............12 D4
**Westhill** Highld............213 H5
**West Hoathly** W Susx............32 C6
**West Holme** Dorset............15 G5
**Westhope** Herefs............69 J4
**Westhope** Shrops............83 J6
**West Horndon** Essex............45 M3
**Westhorpe** Lincs............103 L6
**Westhorpe** Suffk............78 C2
**West Horrington**
 Somset............26 E3
**West Horsley** Surrey............31 H2
**West Hougham** Kent............35 H6
**Westhoughton**
 Bolton............112 F1
**Westhouse** N York............130 D5
**Westhouses** Derbys............101 H2
**West Howe** BCP............15 K4
**Westhumble** Surrey............31 K2
**West Huntingtower**
 P & K............185 M3
**West Huntspill**
 Somset............25 L3
**West Hythe** Kent............34 F7
**West Ilsley** W Berk............41 J4
**West Itchenor**
 W Susx............17 L3
**West Kennett** Wilts............40 C6
**West Kilbride** N Ayrs............173 L8
**West Kingsdown**
 Kent............45 L7
**West Kington** Wilts............39 J5
**West Kirby** Wirral............111 H4
**West Knapton**
 N York............134 D4
**West Knighton**
 Dorset............14 D5
**West Knoyle** Wilts............27 K5
**Westlake** Devon............6 F5
**West Lambrook**
 Somset............26 B7
**West Langdon** Kent............35 J5
**West Lavington**
 W Susx............30 E7
**West Lavington** Wilts............28 A2
**West Layton** N York............140 E5
**West Leake** Notts............101 K7
**Westleigh** Devon............23 G5
**Westleigh** Devon............25 G7
**West Leigh** Somset............25 H5
**Westleton** Suffk............79 J2
**West Lexham** Norfk............91 J1
**Westley** Suffk............77 J2
**Westley Waterless**
 Cambs............76 E3
**West Lilling** N York............133 K6
**Westlington** Bucks............58 C6
**West Linton** Border............176 F7

Westlinton Cumb ......... 148 D3
West Littleton S Glos...39 H5
West Lockinge Oxon ....41 H3
West Lulworth
  Dorset.....................14 F6
West Lutton N York ... 134 E5
West Lydford Somset...26 E5
West Lyng Somset ...... 25 L5
West Lynn Norfk ....... 104 F7
West Malling Kent ...... 33 H2
West Malvern Worcs...70 D5
West Marden W Susx...30 C8
West Markham
  Notts ...................... 116 B6
Westmarsh Kent ........ 35 H3
West Marsh NE Lin ... 127 G8
West Marton N York... 122 D1
West Melbury Dorset...27 K7
West Meon Hants ....... 29 M6
West Mersea Essex....62 B5
Westmeston E Susx.... 19 K3
West Midland Safari
  Park Worcs.............84 E7
Westmill Herts ........... 60 B3
West Milton Dorset...... 13 L3
Westminster Gt Lon ...44 F4
Westminster Abbey
  & Palace Gt Lon ......44 F4
West Molesey Surrey...43 J6
West Monkton
  Somset....................25 K5
West Moors Dorset.....15 K2
West Morden Dorset ...15 G4
West Morriston
  Border ................... 167 J2
West Mudford
  Somset....................26 E7
Westmuir Angus......... 196 B5
West Ness N York...... 133 L4
Westnewton Cumb .... 147 K6
West Newton E R Yk ... 126 F3
West Newton Norfk ... 105 H6
West Newton Somset...25 L5
West Norwood
  Gt Lon.....................44 F5
Westoe S Tyne ........... 151 J2
West Ogwell Devon..... 7 J2
Weston BaNES ...........39 G6
Weston Ches E ...........99 G3
Weston Devon.............12 E3
Weston Devon.............12 F5
Weston Hants .............30 B6
Weston Herts .............59 L3
Weston Lincs............. 103 M7
Weston N York .......... 123 H2
Weston Nhants ...........73 H5
Weston Notts .............116 C7
Weston Shrops...........83 L5
Weston Shrops...........97 L6
Weston Staffs .............99 L6
Weston W Berk ...........41 H5
Weston Beggard
  Herefs .....................69 L6
Westonbirt Gloucs.....39 J3
Weston by Welland
  Nhants.....................87 L5
Weston Colville
  Cambs.....................76 E4
Weston Corbett
  Hants.......................30 B3
Weston Coyney
  C Stke.....................99 L4
Weston Favell Nhants....73 L3
Weston Green Cambs...76 F4
Weston Heath Shrops...84 D2
Westoning C Beds .......59 G2
Weston-in-Gordano
  N Som......................38 C5
Weston Jones Staffs...99 H7
Weston Longville
  Norfk ......................92 D1
Weston Lullingfields
  Shrops.....................98 B7
Weston-on-the-
  Green Oxon..............57 K4
Weston Park Staffs......84 E2
Weston Patrick
  Hants.......................30 B3

Weston Rhyn Shrops ....97 L5
Weston-sub-Edge
  Gloucs.....................71 K6
Weston-super-
  Mare N Som ..........37 L7
Weston Turville
  Bucks......................58 D6
Weston-under-
  Lizard Staffs..........84 E2
Weston under
  Penyard Herefs.......54 F4
Weston-under-
  Redcastle Shrops...98 E6
Weston under
  Wetherley
  Warwks..................72 D1
Weston Underwood
  Derbys.................... 100 F4
Weston Underwood
  M Keyn....................74 C4
Weston-upon-Trent
  Derbys.................... 101 H6
Westonzoyland
  Somset....................25 M4
West Orchard Dorset...27 J7
West Overton Wilts......40 C6
Westow N York.......... 134 B6
West Park Abers ...... 206 E5
West Parley Dorset......15 K3
West Peckham Kent...33 H3
West Pelton Dur ........ 151 G4
West Pennard
  Somset....................26 D4
West Pentire Cnwll .....4 B4
West Porlock Somset...24 D3
Westport Somset........26 B7
West Putford Devon....9 K2
West Quantoxhead
  Somset....................25 H3
Westquarter Falk....... 176 B3
West Rainton Dur ..... 151 H5
West Rasen Lincs...... 117 H4
Westray Ork............. 234 c3
Westray Airport Ork... 234 c3
West Raynham
  Norfk ..................... 105 L7
Westrigg W Loth...... 176 B5
Westrop Swindn ......... 40 D2
West Rounton
  N York.................... 141 K6
West Row Suffk .........90 F7
West Rudham Norfk... 105 K6
West Runton Norfk... 106 E4
Westruther Border .... 178 D7
Westry Cambs ...........90 B4
West Saltoun E Loth... 178 B5
West Sandford Devon...11 J4
West Sandwick Shet...235 d3
West Scrafton N York... 131 K3
West Stafford Dorset...14 D4
West Stockwith
  Notts ......................116 C3
West Stoke W Susx....17 M2
West Stour Dorset......27 H6
West Stourmouth
  Kent........................35 H3
West Stow Suffk.........77 J1
West Stowell Wilts......40 C7
West Street Suffk .......78 B1
West Tanfield N York... 132 D4
West Taphouse Cnwll...5 J3
West Tarbert Ag & B....172 E5
West Tarring W Susx...18 F5
West Thirston
  Nthumb ..................158 F3
West Thorney W Susx...17 L3
West Thorpe Notts .... 101 L7
West Thurrock Thurr...45 L4
West Tilbury Thurr......46 A4
West Tisted Hants......29 M5
West Torrington
  Lincs ......................117 J5
West Town Hants .......17 K3
West Town N Som .......38 C6
West Tytherley Hants...28 F5
West Walton Norfk......90 C2
Westward Cumb ....... 148 B6
Westward Ho! Devon...23 G5

Westwell Kent ...........34 D5
Westwell Oxon...........56 E6
Westwell Leacon
  Kent........................34 C5
West Wellow Hants....28 F7
West Wembury
  Devon ..................... 6 D6
West Wemyss Fife.... 186 E7
Westwick Cambs.......76 B2
West Wickham
  Cambs.....................76 E5
West Wickham
  Gt Lon.....................45 G6
West Williamston
  Pembks...................49 H6
West Winch Norfk......90 F1
West Winterslow
  Wilts.......................28 E5
West Wittering
  W Susx.....................17 L3
West Witton N York... 131 K2
Westwood Devon........12 C3
Westwood Kent...........35 K2
Westwood Wilts.........39 J8
West Woodburn
  Nthumb .................. 157 M5
West Woodhay
  W Berk.....................41 H7
Westwoodside
  N Linc ..................... 116 C2
West Worldham
  Hants.......................30 C4
West Worthing
  W Susx.....................18 F5
West Wratting
  Cambs.....................76 E4
West Wylam Nthumb... 150 E3
Wetheral Cumb......... 148 E4
Wetherby Leeds ...... 124 B2
Wetherby Services
  N York.................... 124 C1
Wetherden Suffk.......78 B3
Wetheringsett Suffk...78 D2
Wethersfield Essex... 61 H2
Wetherup Street
  Suffk.......................78 D2
Wetley Rocks Staffs...99 L3
Wettenhall Ches E .....98 F1
Wetton Staffs...........100 C2
Wetwang E R Yk....... 134 E7
Wetwood Staffs.........99 H5
Wexcombe Wilts........40 F8
Weybourne Norfk.... 106 D4
Weybourne Surrey.....30 D2
Weybread Suffk.........92 F7
Weybread Street
  Suffk.......................92 F7
Weybridge Surrey......43 H7
Weycroft Devon.........13 H3
Weydale Highld........ 231 H3
Weyhill Hants............28 F3
Weymouth Dorset......14 D6
Whaddon Bucks.........74 B7
Whaddon Cambs.......75 L5
Whaddon Gloucs.......55 J5
Whaddon Wilts..........28 D6
Whaddon Wilts.........39 K7
Whaley Derbys.........115 K7
Whaley Bridge
  Derbys.................... 114 A5
Whaley Thorns
  Derbys.................... 115 K7
Whaligoe Highld...... 231 K7
Whalley Lancs.......... 121 L4
Whalsay Shet........... 235 d4
Whalton Nthumb...... 158 E6
Whaplode Lincs........ 104 A7
Whaplode Drove
  Lincs ......................89 K2
Wharf Warwks...........72 E4
Wharfe N York.......... 130 E5
Wharles Lancs.......... 120 F4
Wharley End C Beds...74 D5
Wharncliffe Side
  Sheff.......................114 F3
Wharram-le-Street
  N York.................... 134 D6
Wharton Ches W...... 112 F7

Wharton Herefs .........69 K4
Whashton N York ..... 140 E6
Whasset Cumb......... 129 L4
Whatcote Warwks......72 C5
Whateley Warwks......86 B4
Whatfield Suffk...........78 B5
Whatley Somset.........13 J3
Whatley Somset.........27 G3
Whatley's End S Glos...38 F4
Whatlington E Susx....20 F3
Whatton-in-the-
  Vale Notts...............102 C5
Whauphill D & G....... 145 J5
Wheal Peevor Cnwll...3 J3
Wheatacre Norfk.......93 K5
Wheathampstead
  Herts.......................59 K5
Wheatley Hants.........30 C4
Wheatley Oxon..........57 L6
Wheatley Hill Dur..... 151 K4
Wheatley Hills Donc... 115 L1
Wheaton Aston
  Staffs......................84 F2
Wheddon Cross
  Somset....................24 E4
Wheeler's Green
  Wokham ..................42 C6
Wheelock Ches E.......99 H2
Wheelton Lancs........ 121 J6
Wheeldrake C York... 125 G2
Whelford Gloucs.......56 D7
Whelpley Hill Bucks...59 G6
Whempstead Herts.....60 A4
Whenby N York........ 133 K5
Whepstead Suffk.......77 J3
Wherstead Suffk.......78 E6
Wherwell Hants.........29 H3
Wheston Derbys....... 114 C6
Whetsted Kent..........33 H4
Whetstone Gt Lon.....44 E2
Whetstone Leics.......87 G4
Whicham Cumb........ 128 D3
Whichford Warwks....72 C7
Whickham Gatesd.... 150 F3
Whiddon Down
  Devon ..................... 11 G6
Whigstreet Angus..... 196 C6
Whilton Nhants..........73 J2
Whimple Devon..........12 D3
Whimpwell Green
  Norfk ..................... 107 H6
Whinburgh Norfk.......92 B2
Whinnieliggate
  D & G ..................... 146 C4
Whinnyfold Abers.... 217 K7
Whippingham IoW.....17 G4
Whipsnade C Beds.....59 G4
Whipsnade Zoo ZSL
  C Beds.....................59 G4
Whipton Devon..........12 B4
Whisby Lincs.............116 E7
Whissendine Rutlnd...88 B2
Whissonsett Norfk... 105 L7
Whistlefield Ag & B... 183 J8
Whistlefield Inn
  Ag & B.....................183 G8
Whistley Green
  Wokham ..................42 C5
Whiston Knows ........ 112 C3
Whiston Nhants.........74 B3
Whiston Rothm........ 115 H4
Whiston Staffs...........84 F2
Whiston Staffs.......... 100 B3
Whitbeck Cumb........ 128 D3
Whitbourne Herefs....70 D3
Whitburn S Tyne ...... 151 J3
Whitburn W Loth..... 176 C5
Whitby N York.......... 143 J5
Whitchester Border... 178 F6
Whitchurch BaNES....38 F6
Whitchurch Bucks.....58 D4
Whitchurch Cardif.....37 J4
Whitchurch Devon..... 6 D2
Whitchurch Hants.....29 J2
Whitchurch Herefs....54 D4
Whitchurch Oxon......41 M5
Whitchurch Pembks...48 D3
Whitchurch Shrops ....98 D4

**Whitchurch**
**Canonicorum**
Dorset......................13 K4
**Whitchurch Hill**
Oxon........................41 M5
**Whitcot** Shrops..........83 H5
**Whitcombe** Dorset......14 D5
**White Ball** Somset......25 H7
**Whitebridge** Highld.....202 D3
**Whitebrook** Mons........54 D6
**Whitebushes** Surrey....32 B4
**Whitecairns** Abers.....207 H2
**Whitechapel** Gt Lon.....45 G4
**White Chapel** Lancs....121 H3
**White Colne** Essex......61 L3
**Whitecraig** E Loth......177 K4
**Whitecrook** D & G......144 E4
**White Cross** Cnwll.......3 H6
**Whitecross** Falk........176 C3
**Whiteface** Highld.......222 F4
**Whitefarland** N Ayrs...161 L2
**Whitefaulds** S Ayrs....163 H7
**Whitefield** Bury.........113 J1
**Whitefield** Somset......25 G5
**Whiteford** Abers........206 D1
**Whitegate** Ches W.......112 F7
**Whitehall** Ork...........234 d5
**Whitehaven** Cumb......136 D4
**Whitehill** Hants.........30 C5
**Whitehills** Abers.......216 C2
**Whitehouse** Abers......206 C3
**Whitehouse** Ag & B....172 D6
**Whitehouse**
**Common** Birm.........85 K4
**Whitekirk** E Loth.......178 D3
**White Lackington**
Dorset....................14 D3
**Whitelackington**
Somset...................26 B7
**White Ladies Aston**
Worcs.....................71 G4
**Whiteleaf** Bucks........58 D6
**Whiteley** Hants..........17 G1
**Whiteley Bank** IoW.....17 G6
**Whitemire** Moray.......214 B4
**Whitemoor** C Nott.....101 K4
**Whitemoor** Cnwll........4 F4
**Whiteness** Shet.........235 c6
**White Notley** Essex.....61 J4
**Whiteparish** Wilts.......28 E6
**White Pit** Lincs.........118 E6
**Whiterashes** Abers.....206 F2
**White Roding** Essex.....60 E5
**Whiterow** Highld.......231 L5
**Whiterow** Moray........214 C3
**Whiteshill** Gloucs........55 J6
**Whitesmith** E Susx......20 B3
**Whitestaunton**
Somset...................13 H1
**Whitestone** Warwks.....86 E5
**Whitestone Cross**
Devon......................11 K6
**White Waltham**
W & M.....................42 D5
**Whitewell** Lancs........121 K2
**Whitfield** C Dund......187 G2
**Whitfield** Kent..........35 J5
**Whitfield** Nhants........73 H6
**Whitfield** Nthumb......149 K4
**Whitfield** S Glos.........38 F3
**Whitford** Devon.........13 G4
**Whitford** Flints.........111 G5
**Whitgift** E R Yk........125 J6
**Whitgreave** Staffs.......99 K6
**Whithorn** D & G........145 J6
**Whiting Bay** N Ayrs....162 D4
**Whitkirk** Leeds.........124 B4
**Whitland** Carmth........49 L4
**Whitlaw** Border........167 G6
**Whitletts** S Ayrs........163 J5
**Whitley** N York.........124 E6
**Whitley** Readg...........42 B6
**Whitley** Sheff..........115 G3
**Whitley** Wilts...........39 K6

**Whitley Bay** N Tyne....159 J7
**Whitley Chapel**
Nthumb..................150 B4
**Whitley Lower** Kirk....123 J6
**Whitminster** Gloucs....55 H6
**Whitmore** Staffs.........99 J4
**Whitnage** Devon.........25 G7
**Whitnash** Warwks.......72 D2
**Whitney-on-Wye**
Herefs....................68 F5
**Whitsbury** Hants........28 C7
**Whitsome** Border......179 H7
**Whitson** Newpt..........38 B4
**Whitstable** Kent.........47 J6
**Whitstone** Cnwll..........9 H5
**Whittingham**
Nthumb..................168 F6
**Whittingslow**
Shrops....................83 H5
**Whittington** Derbys....115 G6
**Whittington** Gloucs.....56 A4
**Whittington** Lancs......130 B4
**Whittington** Norfk......91 G4
**Whittington** Shrops.....97 L6
**Whittington** Staffs......84 F6
**Whittington** Staffs......85 L2
**Whittington** Warwks....86 C4
**Whittington** Worcs......70 F4
**Whittlebury** Nhants.....73 K5
**Whittle-le-Woods**
Lancs....................121 H6
**Whittlesey** Cambs.......89 J4
**Whittlesford** Cambs.....76 C5
**Whitton** N Linc.........125 L5
**Whitton** Nthumb.......158 D3
**Whitton** Powys...........68 F2
**Whitton** S on T.........141 J3
**Whitton** Shrops..........83 L8
**Whittonstall** Nthumb...150 D4
**Whitway** Hants...........41 J8
**Whitwell** Derbys.......115 K6
**Whitwell** Herts..........59 K4
**Whitwell** IoW............17 G6
**Whitwell** N York........141 G7
**Whitwell** Rutlnd.........88 D2
**Whitwell-on-the-**
**Hill** N York............133 L6
**Whitwell Street**
Norfk....................106 D7
**Whitwick** Leics.........86 E1
**Whitworth** Lancs.......122 D6
**Whixall** Shrops..........98 D5
**Whixley** N York.........133 G7
**Whorlton** Dur..........140 E4
**Whyle** Herefs...........69 L3
**Whyteleafe** Surrey......32 C2
**Wibsey** C Brad.........123 H4
**Wibtoft** Warwks........86 F6
**Wichelstowe** Swindn....40 C4
**Wichenford** Worcs......70 D3
**Wichling** Kent...........34 B4
**Wick** BCP................15 L4
**Wick** Highld............231 L5
**Wick** S Glos.............39 G5
**Wick** V Glam............36 E6
**Wick** W Susx............18 D5
**Wick** Worcs.............71 G5
**Wicken** Cambs..........76 C1
**Wicken** Nhants..........73 L6
**Wicken Bonhunt**
Essex.....................60 D2
**Wickenby** Lincs.......117 H5
**Wicken Green**
**Village** Norfk........105 K6
**Wickersley** Rothm......115 J3
**Wicker Street Green**
Suffk.....................77 L6
**Wickford** Essex.........46 C2
**Wickham** Hants.........17 H1
**Wickham** W Berk........41 H6
**Wickham Bishops**
Essex.....................61 K5
**Wickhambreaux**
Kent......................35 G3
**Wickhambrook** Suffk....77 H4
**Wickhamford** Worcs....71 J6
**Wickham Green**
Suffk.....................78 D2

**Wickham Market**
Suffk......................79 G4
**Wickhampton** Norfk....93 J3
**Wickham St Paul**
Essex......................77 J7
**Wickham Skeith**
Suffk......................78 C2
**Wickham Street**
Suffk......................78 C1
*Wick John o' Groats*
*Airport* Highld........231 L5
**Wicklewood** Norfk......92 C3
**Wickmere** Norfk........106 E5
**Wick St Lawrence**
N Som.....................38 A7
*Wicksteed Park*
Nhants....................88 C7
**Wickwar** S Glos.........39 G3
**Widdington** Essex......60 E2
**Widdrington**
Nthumb..................159 G3
**Widdrington Station**
Nthumb..................159 G4
**Widecombe in the**
**Moor** Devon............7 G1
**Widegates** Cnwll.........5 L4
**Widemouth Bay**
Cnwll......................9 G4
**Wide Open** N Tyne....159 G7
**Widford** Essex...........61 H6
**Widford** Herts..........60 C5
**Widmer End** Bucks.....42 E2
**Widmerpool** Notts.....101 M6
**Widmore** Gt Lon........45 H6
**Widnes** Halton.........112 D4
**Widworthy** Devon.......13 G3
**Wigan** Wigan..........112 E1
**Wigborough** Somset....26 C2
**Wiggaton** Devon.........12 E4
**Wiggenhall St**
**Germans** Norfk........90 E2
**Wiggenhall St Mary**
**Magdalen** Norfk......90 E2
**Wiggenhall St Mary**
**the Virgin** Norfk......90 E2
**Wigginton** C York.....133 J7
**Wigginton** Herts.........58 F6
**Wigginton** Oxon.........57 H2
**Wigginton** Staffs........86 B3
**Wigglesworth** N York..130 F7
**Wiggonby** Cumb........148 B4
**Wighill** N York.........124 D2
**Wighton** Norfk.........105 M4
**Wightwick** Wolves......84 F4
**Wigley** Hants............29 G7
**Wigmore** Herefs.........69 H2
**Wigmore** Medway.......46 D6
**Wigsley** Notts..........116 E7
**Wigsthorpe** Nhants......88 F6
**Wigston** Leics...........87 H4
**Wigston Fields** Leics....87 H4
**Wigston Parva** Leics....86 F5
**Wigthorpe** Notts.......115 L5
**Wigtoft** Lincs..........103 L5
**Wigton** Cumb..........148 A5
**Wigtown** D & G........145 J4
**Wike** Leeds.............123 L3
**Wilbarston** Nhants......88 B5
**Wilberfoss** E R Yk......125 H1
**Wilburton** Cambs........90 C7
**Wilby** Nhants............74 C2
**Wilby** Norfk.............92 B5
**Wilby** Suffk.............78 F1
**Wilcot** Wilts.............40 C7
**Wilcott** Shrops..........98 B8
**Wildboarclough**
Ches E....................113 M7
**Wilden** Bed..............75 G4
**Wilden** Worcs...........84 E8
**Wildmanbridge**
S Lans....................175 L7
**Wildmill** Brdgnd........36 D4
**Wildmoor** Worcs........85 G7
**Wildsworth** Lincs......116 D3
**Wilford** C Nott.........101 K5
**Wilkesley** Ches E........98 F4
**Wilkhaven** Highld.....223 K4
**Wilkieston** W Loth.....176 F5

**Willand** Devon..........12 D1
**Willaston** Ches E........99 G3
**Willaston** Ches W......111 K6
**Willen** M Keyn...........74 C6
**Willenhall** Covtry........86 D7
**Willenhall** Wsall.........85 H4
**Willerby** E R Yk........126 E3
**Willerby** N York........134 F4
**Willersey** Gloucs........71 K4
**Willersley** Herefs........68 F5
**Willesborough** Kent.....34 D6
**Willesborough Lees**
Kent......................34 D6
**Willesden** Gt Lon.......44 E3
**Willesley** Wilts..........39 J3
**Willett** Somset..........25 H5
**Willey** Shrops...........84 C4
**Willey** Warwks..........86 F6
**Willey Green** Surrey....30 F2
**Williamscot** Oxon........72 F5
**Willian** Herts............59 L2
**Willingale** Essex.........60 F6
**Willingdon** E Susx.......20 C5
**Willingham** Cambs......76 B1
**Willingham by Stow**
Lincs....................116 E5
**Willingham St Mary**
Suffk......................93 J6
**Willington** Bed..........75 G4
**Willington** Derbys.....100 F6
**Willington** Dur........150 F7
**Willington** Kent.........33 K3
**Willington** N Tyne.....151 H2
**Willington** Warwks.....72 C6
**Willitoft** E R Yk.......125 H4
**Williton** Somset.........25 G3
**Willoughby** Lincs......119 G6
**Willoughby** Warwks.....73 G2
**Willoughby-on-**
**the-Wolds** Notts....101 M7
**Willoughby**
**Waterleys** Leics......87 H5
**Willoughton** Lincs......116 F3
**Willows Green** Essex....61 H4
**Willtown** Somset.........26 B6
**Wilmcote** Warwks.......71 L3
**Wilmington** Devon.......13 G3
**Wilmington** E Susx......20 B5
**Wilmington** Kent........45 K5
**Wilmslow** Ches E.......113 J5
**Wilpshire** Lancs........121 K4
**Wilsden** C Brad........123 G3
**Wilsford** Lincs.........103 G4
**Wilsford** Wilts..........28 C4
**Wilsford** Wilts..........40 C8
**Wilshaw** Kirk..........123 G8
**Wilsill** N York..........132 B6
**Wilson** Leics...........101 H7
**Wilsontown** S Lans.....176 C2
**Wilstead** Bed............74 F5
**Wilsthorpe** Lincs........88 F2
**Wilstone** Herts..........58 E5
**Wilton** Herefs...........54 E3
**Wilton** N York.........134 D3
**Wilton** R & Cl.........142 C4
**Wilton** Wilts............28 C5
**Wilton** Wilts............40 E7
**Wilton Dean** Border...167 G6
**Wimbish Green**
Essex......................76 E7
**Wimbledon** Gt Lon......44 E4
**Wimblington** Cambs.....90 B5
**Wimboldsley** Ches W...113 G8
**Wimborne Minster**
Dorset....................15 J3
**Wimborne St Giles**
Dorset....................28 B8
**Wimbotsham** Norfk......90 E3
**Wimpole** Cambs.........75 L4
**Wimpstone** Warwks.....72 B5
**Wincanton** Somset......27 G5
**Winchburgh** W Loth...176 E4
**Winchcombe** Gloucs....56 A3
**Winchelsea** E Susx......21 H3
**Winchester** Hants.......29 J5
**Winchester**
**Services** Hants........29 K4
**Winchet Hill** Kent.......33 J5

Winchfield Hants......30 C1
**Winchmore Hill**
  Bucks......42 F2
**Winchmore Hill**
  Gt Lon......44 F2
Wincle Ches E......113 L7
Wincobank Sheff......115 G3
Windermere Cumb......137 L7
*Windermere Jetty*
  *Cumb......137 L7*
Winderton Warwks......72 D6
Windhill Highld......212 E5
Windlesham Surrey......42 F7
Windmill Cnwll......4 D2
Windmill Hill E Susx......20 D4
Windmill Hill Somset......25 L7
Windrush Gloucs......56 D5
Windsole Abers......216 B3
Windsor W & M......42 F5
*Windsor Castle*
  *W & M......42 F5*
Windsoredge Gloucs......55 J7
Windsor Green Suffk......77 K4
Windygates Fife......186 E7
Wineham W Susx......31 L7
Winestead E R Yk......127 G5
Winfarthing Norfk......92 D6
Winford IoW......17 G5
Winford N Som......38 D7
Winforton Herefs......68 F5
**Winfrith Newburgh**
  Dorset......14 F5
Wing Bucks......58 E4
Wing Rutlnd......88 C3
Wingate Dur......151 J7
Wingerworth Derbys......115 G7
Wingfield C Beds......59 G3
Wingfield Suffk......92 F7
Wingfield Wilts......27 J1
Wingham Kent......35 H3
Wingrave Bucks......58 E4
Winkburn Notts......102 B2
Winkfield Br For......42 E6
Winkfield Row Br For......42 E6
Winkhill Staffs......100 B3
Winkleigh Devon......10 F4
Winksley N York......132 C5
Winlaton Gatesd......150 F3
Winless Highld......231 K5
Winmarleigh Lancs......120 F2
Winnall Hants......29 J5
Winnersh Wokham......42 C6
Winnington Ches W......112 F6
Winscombe N Som......38 B4
Winsford Ches W......112 F7
Winsford Somset......24 E4
Winsham Somset......13 J2
Winshill Staffs......100 F7
Winshwen Swans......51 K6
Winskill Cumb......149 G7
Winsley Wilts......39 J7
Winslow Bucks......58 C3
Winson Gloucs......56 C6
Winsor Hants......28 F8
Winster Cumb......129 J2
Winster Derbys......100 E1
Winston Dur......140 E4
Winston Suffk......78 E3
Winstone Gloucs......55 L6
Winswell Devon......10 D3
**Winterborne Came**
  Dorset......14 D5
**Winterborne**
  **Clenston** Dorset......14 F2
**Winterborne**
  **Houghton** Dorset......14 F2
**Winterborne**
  **Kingston** Dorset......15 G3
**Winterborne**
  **Monkton** Dorset......14 D5
**Winterborne**
  **Stickland** Dorset......14 F2
**Winterborne**
  **Whitchurch**
  Dorset......14 F3
**Winterborne**
  **Zelston** Dorset......15 G3
Winterbourne S Glos......38 F4

**Winterbourne**
  W Berk......41 J6
**Winterbourne**
  **Abbas** Dorset......14 C4
**Winterbourne**
  **Bassett** Wilts......40 C5
**Winterbourne**
  **Dauntsey** Wilts......28 D4
**Winterbourne Earls**
  Wilts......28 D5
**Winterbourne**
  **Gunner** Wilts......28 D4
**Winterbourne**
  **Monkton** Wilts......40 C6
**Winterbourne**
  **Steepleton** Dorset......14 C4
**Winterbourne Stoke**
  Wilts......28 B3
Winterburn N York......131 H7
**Winteringham**
  N Linc......125 L6
Winterley Ches E......99 H2
Winterslow Wilts......28 E5
Winterton N Linc......125 L6
**Winterton-on-Sea**
  Norfk......107 K8
Winthorpe Notts......102 D2
Winton BCP......15 K4
Winton Cumb......139 H5
Wintringham Cambs......75 H3
Wintringham N York......134 D5
Winwick Cambs......89 G7
Winwick Nhants......87 J8
Winwick Warrtn......112 E3
Wirksworth Derbys......100 F2
Wirral......111 J4
Wirswall Ches E......98 D4
Wisbech Cambs......90 C2
**Wisbech St Mary**
  Cambs......90 B2
**Wisborough Green**
  W Susx......31 H6
**Wiseman's Bridge**
  Pembks......49 K6
Wiseton Notts......116 B4
Wishaw N Lans......175 L7
Wishaw Warwks......85 L5
*Wisley Garden RHS*
  *Surrey......43 H8*
Wispington Lincs......117 K6
Wissett Suffk......93 H7
Wissington Suffk......62 A2
Wistanstow Shrops......83 H6
Wistanswick Shrops......98 F6
Wistaston Ches E......99 G2
**Wistaston Green**
  Ches E......99 G2
Wiston Pembks......49 H4
Wiston S Lans......165 J3
Wiston W Susx......18 F3
Wistow Cambs......89 K7
Wistow N York......124 F4
Wiswell Lancs......121 L3
Witcham Cambs......90 C7
Witchampton Dorset......15 J2
Witchford Cambs......90 C7
Witcombe Somset......26 C6
Witham Essex......61 K5
**Witham Friary**
  Somset......27 H3
**Witham on the Hill**
  Lincs......88 F1
**Witham St Hughs**
  Lincs......102 E1
Withcall Lincs......118 C5
Withdean Br & H......19 J4
**Witherenden Hill**
  E Susx......33 H7
Witheridge Devon......11 J3
Witherley Leics......86 D4
Withern Lincs......118 F5
Withernsea E R Yk......127 H5
Withernwick E R Yk......126 F3
**Withersdale Street**
  Suffk......92 F7
Withersfield Suffk......76 F5
Witherslack Cumb......129 J3
Withiel Cnwll......4 F3

**Withiel Florey**
  Somset......24 F5
Withington Gloucs......56 B5
Withington Herefs......69 L5
Withington Manch......113 J3
Withington Shrops......83 L2
Withington Staffs......100 B5
Withleigh Devon......11 K3
Withnell Lancs......121 J6
**Withybed Green**
  Worcs......85 H8
Withybrook Warwks......86 E6
Withycombe Somset......24 F3
Withyham E Susx......32 E6
Withypool Somset......24 D4
Withywood Bristl......38 E6
Witley Surrey......30 F4
Witnesham Suffk......78 E4
Witney Oxon......57 G6
Wittering C Pete......88 F3
Wittersham Kent......21 H1
Witton Birm......85 J5
Witton Norfk......93 G2
Witton Norfk......107 H6
Witton Gilbert Dur......151 G5
Witton le Wear Dur......140 E2
Witton Park Dur......140 F2
**Wiveliscombe**
  Somset......25 G5
Wivelrod Hants......30 A4
Wivelsfield E Susx......19 K2
**Wivelsfield Green**
  E Susx......19 K2
Wivenhoe Essex......62 C4
Wiveton Norfk......106 C4
Wix Essex......62 E3
Wixams Bed......74 F5
Wixford Warwks......71 K4
Wixoe Suffk......77 G6
Woburn C Beds......58 F2
*Woburn Safari Park*
  *C Beds......74 D7*
**Woburn Sands**
  M Keyn......74 D7
Woking Surrey......43 G8
Wokingham Wokham......42 D6
Woldingham Surrey......32 C3
Wold Newton E R Yk......135 G5
Wold Newton NE Lin......118 C3
Wolfclyde S Lans......165 K3
Wolferton Norfk......105 G6
Wolfhill P & K......186 B2
Wolf's Castle Pembks......49 G3
Wolfsdale Pembks......48 F3
Wollaston Dudley......84 F6
Wollaston Nhants......74 C2
Wollaston Shrops......83 G2
Wollaton C Nott......101 K4
**Wollaton Hall &**
  **Park** C Nott......101 K5
Wollerton Shrops......98 F6
Wollescote Dudley......85 G6
**Wolseley Bridge**
  Staffs......100 A7
Wolsingham Dur......150 D7
Wolstanton Staffs......99 J3
Wolston Warwks......86 E7
Wolvercote Oxon......57 J6
**Wolverhampton**
  Wolves......85 G4
*Wolverhampton*
  *Halfpenny Green*
  *Airport* Staffs......84 E5
Wolverley Worcs......84 E7
Wolverton Hants......41 K8
Wolverton M Keyn......74 B6
Wolverton Warwks......72 B3
Wolverton Wilts......27 H5
Wolvesnewton Mons......54 C7
Wolvey Warwks......86 E6
**Wolvey Heath**
  Warwks......86 E6
Wolviston S on T......141 K3
Wombleton N York......133 K3
Wombourne Staffs......84 F5
Wombwell Barns......115 H2
Womenswold Kent......35 G5
Womersley N York......124 E6

Wonersh Surrey......31 G3
Wonford Devon......12 B4
Wonston Dorset......14 E2
Wonston Hants......29 J4
Wooburn Bucks......42 E3
**Wooburn Green**
  Bucks......42 E3
Woodacott Devon......9 K4
Woodall Rothm......115 J5
*Woodall Services*
  *Rothm......115 J5*
Woodbastwick Norfk......93 G1
**Wood Bevington**
  Warwks......71 J4
Woodborough Notts......101 M3
Woodborough Wilts......40 C7
Woodbridge Suffk......78 F5
Woodbury Devon......12 C5
**Woodbury Salterton**
  Devon......12 C5
Woodchester Gloucs......55 J7
Woodchurch Kent......34 C7
Woodcombe Somset......24 E3
Woodcote Gt Lon......44 F7
Woodcote Oxon......41 M4
Woodcote Wrekin......84 D1
Woodcroft Gloucs......38 D2
Wood Dalling Norfk......106 C6
Woodditton Cambs......76 F3
Woodeaton Oxon......57 K5
Wood End Gt Lon......43 J4
Wood End Herts......60 B3
Woodend Highld......190 F4
Woodend Nhants......73 H5
Woodend W Loth......176 C4
Woodend W Susx......17 M2
Wood End Warwks......71 K1
Wood End Wolves......85 G4
Wood Enderby Lincs......118 C8
Woodfalls Wilts......28 D7
Woodford Cnwll......9 G3
Woodford Gloucs......39 G2
Woodford Gt Lon......45 H2
Woodford Nhants......88 D7
Woodford Stockp......113 K5
**Woodford Bridge**
  Gt Lon......45 H2
**Woodford Green**
  Gt Lon......45 H2
**Woodford Halse**
  Nhants......73 G4
**Woodford Wells**
  Gt Lon......45 H2
Woodgate Birm......85 H6
Woodgate Devon......25 H7
Woodgate W Susx......18 C5
Woodgate Worcs......71 H2
Wood Green Gt Lon......44 F2
Woodgreen Hants......28 D7
Woodhall N York......131 J2
Woodhall Spa Lincs......117 K8
Woodham Bucks......58 B4
Woodham Surrey......43 H7
**Woodham Ferrers**
  Essex......61 J7
**Woodham Mortimer**
  Essex......61 K6
**Woodham Walter**
  Essex......61 K6
Wood Hayes Wolves......85 G3
Woodhead Abers......216 E6
Woodhill Shrops......84 D6
Woodhill Somset......26 A6
Woodhorn Nthumb......159 H4
Woodhouse Leeds......123 K4
Woodhouse Leics......87 G1
Woodhouse Sheff......115 H4
Woodhouse Wakefd......124 B6
**Woodhouse Eaves**
  Leics......87 G2
**Woodhouselee**
  Mdloth......177 H5
**Woodhouselees**
  D & G......156 D6
**Woodhouses**
  Oldham......113 K2
Woodhouses Staffs......100 D8
Woodhurst Cambs......89 K7

Woodingdean Br & H .....19 K5
Woodkirk Leeds .......... 123 K5
Woodland Abers .......... 207 G2
Woodland Devon............. 6 F5
Woodland Devon............ 7 J3
Woodland Dur............ 140 D2
Woodland S Ayrs......... 152 E3
Woodlands Donc .......... 124 E8
Woodlands Dorset.......... 15 K2
Woodlands Hants .......... 16 C1
Woodlands N York ........ 132 E8
Woodlands of
  Durris Abers .......... 206 E6
Woodlands Park
  W & M .................... 42 E5
Woodland View
  Sheff........................ 114 F4
Woodleigh Devon ............ 7 H6
Woodley Wokham ........... 42 C5
Woodmancote
  Gloucs....................... 39 H2
Woodmancote
  Gloucs....................... 55 L3
Woodmancote
  Gloucs....................... 56 A6
Woodmancote
  W Susx....................... 17 L2
Woodmancote
  W Susx....................... 19 H3
Woodmancott Hants ......29 K3
Woodmansey E R Yk ..... 126 C3
Woodmansgreen
  W Susx....................... 30 E6
Woodmansterne
  Surrey........................ 32 B2
Woodmanton Devon ......12 C5
Woodnesborough
  Kent........................... 35 J4
Woodnewton Nhants.......88 F5
Wood Norton Norfk ...... 106 B6
Woodplumpton
  Lancs....................... 121 G4
Woodrising Norfk..........92 B3
Wood's Corner
  E Susx ....................... 20 D2
Woodseaves Staffs..........99 H7
Woodsetts Rothm ........ 115 K5
Woodsford Dorset .......... 14 E4
Wood's Green E Susx......33 H6
Woodside Br For .......... 42 F6
Woodside Fife ............. 187 G5
Woodside Gt Lon............45 G6
Woodside P & K .......... 195 K8
Woodstock Oxon ............57 H5
Woodston C Pete ..........89 H4
Wood Street Norfk ...... 107 H7
Wood Street Village
  Surrey........................ 30 F2
Woodton Norfk..............93 G5
Woodtown Devon ..........22 F6
Woodville Derbys.......... 100 F8
Wood Walton Cambs.......89 J7
Woofferton Shrops..........69 K2
Wookey Somset ............. 26 D3
Wookey Hole Somset......26 D2
Wool Dorset .................. 14 F5
Woolacombe Devon........23 G3
Woolage Green Kent.......35 H5
Woolaston Gloucs..........54 E7
Woolaston Common
  Gloucs....................... 54 E7
Woolavington
  Somset...................... 25 M3
Woolbeding W Susx........30 E6
Woolbrook Devon..........12 E5
Wooler Nthumb........... 168 E4
Woolfardisworthy
  Devon........................ 11 J3
Woolfardisworthy
  Devon........................ 22 E7
Woolfords S Lans ........ 176 D6
Woolhampton
  W Berk....................... 41 L6
Woolhope Herefs............69 L7
Woolland Dorset ............ 14 E2
Woolley BaNES..............39 H6
Woolley Cambs..............89 G8
Woolley Wakefd.......... 123 L7

Woolley Edge
  Services Wakefd ..... 123 K7
Woolmere Green
  Worcs........................ 71 G2
Woolmer Green
  Herts......................... 59 L4
Woolminstone
  Somset...................... 13 K2
Woolpit Suffk................ 77 L3
Woolstaston Shrops........83 J4
Woolsthorpe by
  Belvoir Lincs ......... 102 D5
Woolsthorpe-by-
  Colsterworth
  Lincs....................... 102 F7
Woolston C Soth ...........16 E1
Woolston Shrops............97 L7
Woolston Somset............25 H4
Woolston Somset............26 F5
Woolston Warrtn.......... 112 F4
Woolstone Gloucs..........55 L3
Woolstone M Keyn.........74 C6
Woolstone Oxon ........... 40 F3
Woolston Green
  Devon......................... 7 H3
Woolton Lpool ........... 112 B4
Woolton Hill Hants ........41 H7
Woolverstone Suffk........78 E6
Woolverton Somset........27 H2
Woolwich Gt Lon............45 H4
Woonton Herefs............69 G4
Woore Shrops................99 G4
Wootten Green
  Suffk......................... 92 F8
Wootton Bed ................ 74 E5
Wootton Kent............... 35 G5
Wootton N Linc .......... 126 D7
Wootton Nhants............73 L3
Wootton Oxon ..............57 H4
Wootton Oxon ..............57 J4
Wootton Staffs .......... 100 C4
Wootton Bassett
  Wilts......................... 40 B4
Wootton Bridge IoW ......17 G4
Wootton Courtenay
  Somset...................... 24 E3
Wootton Fitzpaine
  Dorset....................... 13 J4
Wootton Rivers
  Wilts......................... 40 D7
Wootton St
  Lawrence Hants .........29 L2
Wootton Wawen
  Warwks...................... 71 L2
Worcester Worcs............70 F4
Worcester Park
  Gt Lon....................... 44 E6
Wordsley Dudley ............84 F6
Worfield Shrops ............84 D4
Workington Cumb........ 136 D2
Worksop Notts ........... 115 L5
Worlaby N Linc .......... 126 C7
Worlds End Hants ..........29 M8
Worlds End W Susx ........19 J2
Worle N Som ................38 A7
Worleston Ches E ..........98 F2
Worlingham Suffk..........93 J5
Worlington Devon ..........11 H3
Worlington Suffk............91 G8
Worlingworth Suffk........78 F2
Wormbridge Herefs........54 B2
Wormegay Norfk ..........90 F2
Wormelow Tump
  Herefs....................... 54 C3
Wormhill Derbys......... 114 C6
Wormingford Essex........61 M2
Worminghall Bucks........57 M6
Wormington Gloucs........71 J7
Wormit Fife ................ 186 F3
Wormleighton
  Warwks...................... 72 F4
Wormley Herts .............60 B6
Wormley Surrey ............30 F4
Wormshill Kent.............34 B3
Wormsley Herefs............69 H5
Worplesdon Surrey.........30 F2
Worrall Sheff .............. 114 F3
Worsbrough Barns...... 115 G2

Worsbrough Bridge
  Barns...................... 115 G2
Worsbrough Dale
  Barns...................... 115 G2
Worsley Salfd.............. 113 H2
Worstead Norfk........... 107 G7
Worsthorne Lancs ....... 122 C4
Worston Devon .............. 6 E5
Worston Lancs ........... 122 B3
Worth Kent .................. 35 J4
Wortham Suffk..............92 C7
Worthen Shrops............83 G3
Worthenbury
  Wrexhm .................... 98 B4
Worthing Norfk........... 106 B8
Worthing W Susx .......... 18 F5
Worthington Leics ....... 101 H7
Worth Matravers
  Dorset....................... 15 H6
Wortley Barns............. 114 F2
Wortley Leeds ........... 123 K4
Worton N York ........... 131 H2
Worton Wilts................ 39 L8
Wortwell Norfk..............92 F6
Wotton-under-
  Edge Gloucs .............. 39 H2
Wotton Underwood
  Bucks........................ 58 B5
Woughton on the
  Green M Keyn............74 C6
Wouldham Kent............46 B7
Wrabness Essex............62 E2
Wrafton Devon ............23 H4
Wragby Lincs .............. 117 J6
Wragby Wakefd .......... 124 C6
Wrangaton Devon........... 7 G4
Wrangle Lincs............. 104 C3
Wrangway Somset.........25 H7
Wrantage Somset.........25 L6
Wrawby N Linc........... 126 C8
Wraxall N Som ............. 38 C6
Wraxall Somset............ 26 E4
Wray Lancs ................ 130 B6
Wraysbury W & M......... 43 G5
Wrayton Lancs ........... 130 C5
Wrea Green Lancs ....... 120 E4
Wreay Cumb .............. 148 D5
Wrecclesham Surrey......30 D3
Wrekenton Gatesd ...... 151 G3
Wrelton N York ........... 134 B3
Wrenbury Ches E ..........98 E3
Wreningham Norfk........92 E4
Wrentham Suffk............93 K6
Wrentnall Shrops..........83 H3
Wressle E R Yk ........... 125 G4
Wressle N Linc ........... 126 B8
Wrestlingworth
  C Beds....................... 75 J5
Wretton Norfk..............91 G4
Wrexham Wrexhm .........97 M3
Wrexham Industrial
  Estate Wrexhm..........98 B3
Wribbenhall Worcs........84 E7
Wrinehill Staffs..............99 H3
Wrington N Som............38 C7
Writhlington BaNES.......27 G1
Writtle Essex.................61 G6
Wrockwardine
  Wrekin....................... 84 B2
Wroot N Linc .............. 116 B2
Wrose C Brad ............. 123 H3
Wrotham Kent...............33 G2
Wroughton Swindn........40 C4
Wroxall IoW.................. 17 G6
Wroxall Warwks............ 72 B1
Wroxeter Shrops............83 L2
Wroxham Norfk........... 107 G8
Wroxton Oxon...............72 E6
Wyaston Derbys......... 100 D4
Wyberton Lincs .......... 104 A4
Wyboston Bed ..............75 H3
Wybunbury Ches E.........99 G3
Wychbold Worcs............71 G2
Wychnor Staffs..............85 L1
Wyck Rissington
  Gloucs....................... 56 D4
Wycliffe Dur............... 140 E4
Wycoller Lancs ........... 122 D3

Wycomb Leics ............ 102 C7
Wycombe Marsh
  Bucks........................ 42 E3
Wyddial Herts................60 B2
Wye Kent...................... 34 E5
Wyke C Brad .............. 123 H5
Wyke Dorset................. 27 H6
Wyke Champflower
  Somset...................... 26 F4
Wykeham N York ........ 134 E3
Wyken Covtry ..............86 D7
Wyken Shrops...............84 D4
Wyke Regis Dorset........14 C6
Wykey Shrops................98 B7
Wylam Nthumb........... 150 E3
Wylde Green Birm.........85 K5
Wylye Wilts.................. 28 A4
Wymeswold Leics........ 101 L7
Wymington Bed............74 D2
Wymondham Leics...... 102 D8
Wymondham Norfk........92 D3
Wynford Eagle
  Dorset....................... 14 B3
Wyre Piddle Worcs........71 G5
Wysall Notts .............. 101 L6
Wythall Worcs...............85 J7
Wytham Oxon ...............57 J6
Wythenshawe Manch .. 113 J4
Wyton Cambs................89 K8
Wyton E R Yk .............. 126 E4
Wyverstone Suffk..........78 C2
Wyverstone Street
  Suffk......................... 78 B2

## Y

Yaddlethorpe N Linc .... 116 E1
Yafforth N York ........... 141 H7
Yalberton Torbay ............ 7 K4
Yalding Kent.................. 33 J3
Yanwath Cumb............ 138 D2
Yanworth Gloucs...........56 B5
Yapham E R Yk ........... 125 J1
Yapton W Susx.............. 18 D5
Yarborough N Som ........38 B8
Yarburgh Lincs ........... 118 E3
Yarcombe Devon .......... 13 G2
Yard Devon................... 24 B6
Yardley Birm................. 85 K6
Yardley Gobion
  Nhants....................... 73 L5
Yardley Hastings
  Nhants....................... 74 C3
Yardley Wood Birm........85 K7
Yarkhill Herefs...............69 L6
Yarley Somset............... 26 D3
Yarlington Somset.........26 F5
Yarm S on T................ 141 K5
Yarmouth IoW.............. 16 D4
Yarnbrook Wilts.............27 K1
Yarnfield Staffs..............99 K6
Yarnscombe Devon........23 J6
Yarnton Oxon................57 J5
Yarpole Herefs...............69 J2
Yarrow Border............. 166 E4
Yarrow Feus Border..... 166 E4
Yarrowford Border....... 166 F4
Yarwell Nhants..............88 F4
Yate S Glos................... 39 G4
Yateley Hants................ 42 D7
Yatesbury Wilts..............40 B6
Yattendon W Berk..........41 K5
Yatton Herefs................69 H2
Yatton N Som................38 B7
Yatton Keynell Wilts......39 K5
Yaverland IoW............... 17 H5
Yaxham Norfk...............92 B2
Yaxley Cambs................89 H5
Yaxley Suffk.................. 92 D8
Yazor Herefs................. 69 H5
Yeading Gt Lon............. 43 J4
Yeadon Leeds ............ 123 J3
Yealand Conyers
  Lancs...................... 129 K5
Yealand Redmayne
  Lancs...................... 129 K4

| | | |
|---|---|---|
| Yealmpton Devon | 6 | E5 |
| Yearsley N York | 133 | J5 |
| Yeaton Shrops | 98 | B8 |
| Yeaveley Derbys | 100 | D4 |
| Yeavering Nthumb | 168 | D4 |
| Yedingham N York | 134 | D4 |
| Yelford Oxon | 57 | G6 |
| Yell Shet | 235 | d3 |
| Yelling Cambs | 75 | J3 |
| Yelvertoft Nhants | 87 | H7 |
| Yelverton Devon | 6 | D3 |
| Yelverton Norfk | 93 | G3 |
| Yenston Somset | 27 | G7 |
| Yeoford Devon | 11 | H5 |
| Yeolmbridge Cnwll | 9 | J7 |
| Yeovil Somset | 26 | D7 |
| Yeovil Marsh Somset | 26 | D7 |
| Yeovilton Somset | 26 | D6 |
| Yesnaby Ork | 234 | b5 |
| Yetminster Dorset | 14 | B1 |
| Yettington Devon | 12 | D5 |
| Yetts o'Muckhart |  |  |
| Clacks | 185 | L6 |
| Yew Tree Sandw | 85 | H4 |
| Y Felinheli Gwynd | 109 | G7 |
| Y Ferwig Cerdgn | 65 | G5 |

| | | |
|---|---|---|
| Y Ffôr Gwynd | 95 | G5 |
| Yielden Bed | 74 | E2 |
| Yieldshields S Lans | 176 | B7 |
| Yiewsley Gt Lon | 43 | H4 |
| Ynys Gwynd | 95 | K5 |
| Ynysboeth Rhondd | 37 | G2 |
| Ynysddu Caerph | 37 | J2 |
| Ynyshir Rhondd | 36 | F3 |
| Ynystawe Swans | 51 | K5 |
| Ynysybwl Rhondd | 37 | G2 |
| Yockleton Shrops | 83 | H2 |
| Yokefleet E R Yk | 125 | J5 |
| Yoker C Glas | 174 | F5 |
| York C York | 124 | F1 |
| Yorkletts Kent | 34 | E3 |
| Yorkley Gloucs | 54 | F6 |
| *Yorkshire Dales* |  |  |
| *National Park* | 131 | G4 |
| York Town Surrey | 42 | E7 |
| Youlgreave Derbys | 114 | E8 |
| Youlthorpe E R Yk | 134 | B7 |
| Youlton N York | 133 | G6 |
| Yoxall Staffs | 100 | C8 |
| Yoxford Suffk | 79 | H2 |
| Y Rhiw Gwynd | 94 | D6 |
| Ysbyty Ifan Conwy | 96 | C3 |

| | | |
|---|---|---|
| Ysbyty Ystwyth |  |  |
| Cerdgn | 67 | G1 |
| Ysceifiog Flints | 111 | G7 |
| Ystalyfera Neath | 52 | B6 |
| Ystrad Rhondd | 36 | F2 |
| Ystrad Aeron Cerdgn | 66 | C4 |
| Ystradfellte Powys | 52 | E5 |
| Ystradgynlais Powys | 52 | C6 |
| Ystrad Meurig |  |  |
| Cerdgn | 66 | F2 |
| Ystrad Mynach |  |  |
| Caerph | 37 | H2 |
| Ystradowen V Glam | 36 | F5 |
| Ythanbank Abers | 217 | G7 |
| Ythanwells Abers | 216 | C6 |
| Ythsie Abers | 217 | G7 |

# Z

| | | |
|---|---|---|
| Zeal Monachorum |  |  |
| Devon | 11 | G4 |
| Zeals Wilts | 27 | H5 |
| Zelah Cnwll | 4 | C5 |
| Zennor Cnwll | 2 | E4 |

| | | |
|---|---|---|
| Zouch Notts | 101 | J7 |
| ZSL London Zoo |  |  |
| Gt Lon | 44 | F4 |
| ZSL Whipsnade Zoo |  |  |
| C Beds | 59 | G4 |

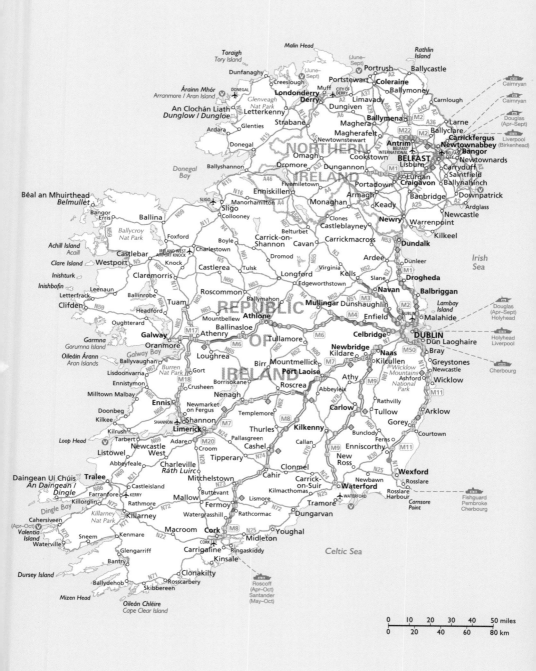

# Ireland

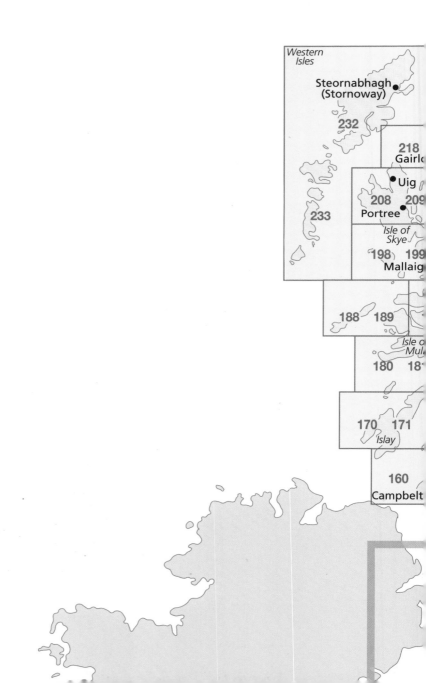

Western Isles

Steornabhagh (Stornoway)

232

218
Gairl

Uig

208    209

233    Portree

Isle of Skye

198    199
Mallaig

188    189

Isle o
Mul

180    18

170    171
Islay

160
Campbelt